D0304138

KEELE
UNIVERSITY   LIBRARY

A Stu... se return by the last date or time shown

1861–1911

5 193 218 3

THE MOBILE SCOT

A Study of Emigration and Migration 1861–1911

Jeanette M. Brock

JOHN DONALD PUBLISHERS LTD
EDINBURGH

© Jeanette M. Brock 1999

All rights reserved.
No part of this publication may be reproduced
in any form or by any means without
the prior permission of the publishers
John Donald Publishers Limited,
73 Logie Green Road, Edinburgh, EH7 5HF.

ISBN 0 85976 453 2

British Library Cataloguing in Publication Data.

A catalogue record for this book is available
from the British Library.

Typesetting and origination by Brinnoven, Livingston.
Printed and bound in Great Britain by Bell & Bain Ltd, Glasgow.

Contents

ACKNOWLEDGEMENTS

During the time that I have been working on this research. I have had considerable help from a large number of people. I would like to thank three people in particular. Firstly, I would like to acknowledge the tremendous help I have received from my supervisor Tom Devine, who has given me substantial encouragement, guidance, and prompt advice when it was needed. Secondly, I would like to recognise the enormous amount of support given to me by Stephen Tagg, who managed to convert me from a complete computer illiterate to a competent computer-user. Thirdly, I am very indebted to Dudley Baines who devised the original method of estimating emigration and whose interest in my work has been most reassuring. When I tried to name all the other people who had helped me the list just grew and grew. I now realise that virtually everybody I have met academically, and many other people as well, have had an imput in this book, I am very grateful to them all for their guidance. The errors that remain in this work are my own.

I am obliged to several libraries and archives for their help: University of Strathclyde; University of Glasgow (especially John Moore), the Mitchell Library, Glasgow; the National Library of Scotland, and particularly to the Reading room in the Registrar Generals Office, New Register House, Edinburgh without whose assistance this research would never have been possible. I would especially like acknowledge the help of Dr John Shaw, Miss Alison Horsburgh, Dr John Mackay, Mrs S. Mackenzie and the porters.

I am grateful to Her Majesty's Stationery Office for permitting me to cite material that is Crown copyright in my thesis and book. I would like to acknowledge the scholarship I received from the Scottish Education Department, which made this research possible. I want to thank John Donald Publishers Limited and in particular Russell Walker.

Finally I would like to thank my family for all their help and encouragement. To Jeremy for being very understanding, and also to Yvette and Gavin. To my family and my parents this book is dedicated.

LIST OF MAPS

LIST OF TABLES

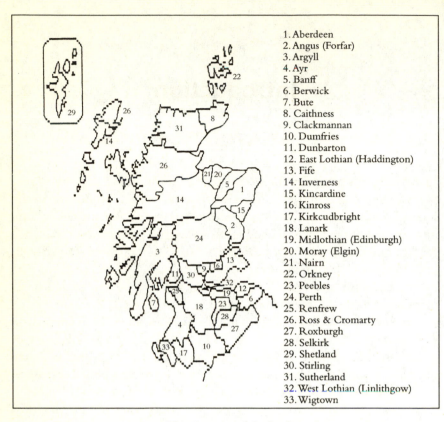

1. Aberdeen
2. Angus (Forfar)
3. Argyll
4. Ayr
5. Banff
6. Berwick
7. Bute
8. Caithness
9. Clackmannan
10. Dumfries
11. Dunbarton
12. East Lothian (Haddington)
13. Fife
14. Inverness
15. Kincardine
16. Kinross
17. Kirkcudbright
18. Lanark
19. Midlothian (Edinburgh)
20. Moray (Elgin)
21. Nairn
22. Orkney
23. Peebles
24. Perth
25. Renfrew
26. Ross & Cromarty
27. Roxburgh
28. Selkirk
29. Shetland
30. Stirling
31. Sutherland
32. West Lothian (Linlithgow)
33. Wigtown

The Counties of Scotland

Introduction

In entitling this book *The Mobile Scot* the author is indeed acknowledging the widespread assumption in literature that the Scottish population in the second half of the nineteenth century was especially prone to out-movement, both in terms of emigration and migration. However, evidence for this mobility is generally qualitative rather than quantitative and very little is known about the origins of the migratory population. The behaviour of the two sexes is usually considered to be similar and those moving are assumed to be young adults.

This study will quantify Scottish population movement, both emigration and migration, between 1861 and 1911. At present our knowledge of migration is confined to local or regional studies and research into occupational groups. Migration tends to be considered only in terms of rural–urban movement. Our understanding of emigration is rather greater, as we have national estimates of aggregate Scottish losses and also from the country of destination, and there are regional and local studies. There are however big gaps in our knowledge of both forms of mobility. We do not know at what age movement took place, whether both sexes behaved similarly, if there was a regional or county dimension to mobility or how migration and emigration interacted.

Population flows will be evaluated both regionally and by county-of-birth. The pattern of mobility in each sex will be analysed and the approximate age at which Scots first move will also be examined. Unfortunately any subsequent movement within Scotland cannot be recorded, due to limitations inherent in the method adopted. Indeed the methodology of necessity creates its own set of assumptions and these artificialities, together with possible errors in the original data, make precise quantification impossible. This study will quantify population flows and the discussion will concentrate on issues where the degree of error does not invalidate the results and conclusions. These estimates of national population movements will enable comparisons to be made at the county or regional level, between the types of mobility and over time, as well as distinguish gender specific trends.

1

This book is derived from the PhD thesis of the author.[1] However, it is now seven years since it was submitted and in that time research has progressed and ideas have developed or been modified. The book is not therefore a mere reprint of the thesis and indeed its eleven chapters have been reorganised and reduced to six, thus hopefully avoiding repetition. The huge number of appendices have also been simplified and halved in number, and finally some tables have been abandoned and new ones created. All the chapters have been substantially revised and in some cases rewritten. The appendices tabulate the entire findings on a topic, not just the aspects discussed in the text, so that researchers can find estimates on the region or county that interests them rather than just the specifics that I have chosen to highlight. Despite this work and researches of many others there remain huge gaps in our knowledge. Many of the findings even at the regional level cannot be accounted for, and by providing all the data it is hoped that this will encourage others to investigate and explain results. This book is therefore a beginning and not an end in itself.

Let us now consider the organisation this book. If it is to be argued that the Scots are an exceptionally mobile people one must review the evidence both for migration and emigration. Furthermore, the period under consideration must be shown to be part of a tradition or culture of leaving home and not to be exceptional. Chapter 1 will address these issues, and begin by considering evidence for a culture of out-migration from 1700 to 1914, considering literary evidence of migration and emigration separately and providing international comparisons if possible. The second part will consider the economic and social context of out-migration in this study in more detail and will include movement before the study period (1861–1911). Finally the discussion will end with an assessment of gaps in our knowledge.

The aim of the study is to establish approximately how many people emigrated from and migrated within Scotland by county during the period 1861 to 1911. Chapter 2 discusses the data sources and methodology. This will primarily interest specialists in demography, and the main points of the analysis in the rest of the book can be understood without reading this. The discussion will explain the methods and the assumptions behind the study as well as discussing the source material. The material used to estimate population movement in this study are mostly published, but it was not until a methodology was devised by Baines[2] that the potential value of these sources was appreciated. Even historians aware of Baines method considered that 'Government' statistics were inadequate for use in the Scottish context.[3] The present study has adapted Baines' approach for three reasons. Firstly the advent of computers made the processing of material much easier; secondly specifically Scottish problems needed to be accommodated, and finally to be able to make use of large samples of the migrant population. A discussion of the computer programming to calculate mobility is provided in Appendix 1. Despite its apparent brevity this was the entire programme and it still exists on disk.

Chapter 3 considers migration which is defined as crossing a county boundary. Migration can be divided into two types: lifetime, which includes all migrants regardless of the length of time they have lived outside their county-of-birth, and current, which consists of those migrants that have moved recently. The chapter begins by expanding information on migration from the census material, in order to provide an overview of life-time movement, but it will also show the drawbacks of this data source. (The limitations of the census as a source of information on migration are considered in Chapter 2). This section has been revised from the thesis. The second part of the chapter will analyse the computed estimates of current migration, providing first an overview, then a consideration of regional issues, and finally the age and gender of migrants. By looking first at the lifetime population, and then at current migration, it will show that the estimates for current migration are not just the product of the methodology used.

Chapter 4 analyses the computer estimations of emigrant losses, and a deliberate attempt has been made to keep the layout fairly similar to the latter part of Chapter 3 so that direct comparisons of the two forms of population movement can be made, but wider discussion of the two forms of movement will be reserved for Chapter 6.

If it is to be argued that the Scots are an exceptionally mobile people and indeed the evidence discussed so far will suggest that they are, then comparisons are necessary. Chapter 5 considers whether the period (1861–1911) was unequalled in terms of Scottish history. It is not a repeat of the literature survey in Chapter 1, but rather will reflect on whether there was a culture of out-movement within Scotland, that continued from generation to generation, reviewing first migration and then emigration, using evidence from the eighteenth century to the present. It will consider in what respects the Scots were more mobile than the English and Welsh, and whether the Scots justify their third ranking within Europe in terms of losses through emigration by country-of-birth.[4]

Thus far the discussion has examined Scottish current migration within and emigration separately. The final chapter brings them together. It can be argued that the two movements are similar insofar as people are deliberately leaving one area for another; whether this is through compulsion or out of choice, and that the connection between the two forms of mobility, is important. Chapter 6 examines this relationship using the work of Brindley Thomas,[5] who considers that rural migrants formed a mobile pool of people who migrated or emigrated depending on the trade cycle. This theory has been criticised with respect to movement within England and Wales, but is nevertheless a valid starting point for an analysis of mobility in general. This chapter also considers how total losses from both forms of mobility affected the population profile of individual counties or regions. Although the preceding chapters each have their own conclusion, this final one ends by bringing the main themes of the book together.

Notes

1. Brock, 'Scottish Migration and Emigration'.
2. Baines, *Migration in a Mature Economy*.
3. Flinn *et al*, *Scottish Population History*. p. 455.
4. Baines, *Emigration from Europe*. Table 3, p. 3.
5. Thomas, *Migration and Economic Growth*, ch. 6.

1

The Mobile Scot — A Culture of Out-Migration

If it is to be argued that the Scots are a particularly mobile people one must consider all forms of out-migration: migration and emigration. It must also be shown that the period under consideration is not one of exceptional out-movement but part of a trend, a tradition or culture of migration. This chapter will address these issues. It will begin by analysing evidence for a culture of out-migration (both emigration and migration) from 1700 to 1914. Migration and emigration will be considered separately and by century, beginning with the seventeenth, then the eighteenth century, with the last part reviewing what has been described as the 'long' nineteenth century, to include the period up to 1914. Throughout this discussion international comparisons will be introduced where known, looking first at migration and then emigration. The second part will consider the economic and social context of out-migration in more detail, beginning slightly before the study period. The final part of this section will end with an overview of gaps in our knowledge.

SCOTTISH OUT-MOVEMENT

Migration represents movement outside the immediately area of birth, but within one's own country. Emigration can best be defined as leaving ones country-of-birth. For Scots this therefore includes movement to England, Wales and Ireland as well as more long distance moves to Europe and beyond. Clearly this movement includes permanent emigration, but it also involves temporary movement such as military service which, if it results in a death whilst abroad can be considered permanent emigration. Likewise, migration can involve temporary as well as permanent moves. All these movements together, if large enough would imply a culture, or a tradition of mobility. Nevertheless, for this to be exceptional it also needs to be compared with that of other countries. This will prove more difficult, mainly because there are no standardised international statistics. However,

5

the seminal work by Baines[1] will enable direct comparisons to be made with movement from England and Wales.

There are relatively few studies that consider Scottish population movement in detail, but there are many other works that provide evidence of mobility and these will be included in the discussion. With regard to emigration, only literature from the perspective of the sending country, rather than the receiving one, will be considered, and the destinations of overseas emigrants will not be discussed unless it is of relevance to subsequent analysis.

MIGRATION

Early records of migration are rare and usually chronicle something quite exceptional. There are some early accounts of deliberate state encouragement of long distance migration. Thus in the fifteenth century, before Orkney and Shetland were even part of the Scottish Kingdom, the King of Norway deliberately encouraged Scots settlers in those islands. At the end of the sixteenth century James VI devised a scheme to settle communities of Lowlanders on 'Kintyre, Lochabir and the Lewis'.[2] However, by the sixteenth century and possibly earlier, Scottish rural society was beginning to change, capitalist forms of agriculture were being introduced and people were being cleared for sheep farming in the Borders, and already some areas had been depopulated as settlements were cleared.[3]

The Seventeenth and Eighteenth Centuries

In this period no overall information such as the census is available and therefore only such sources as have survived can be analysed, but they suggest a pattern of increasing mobility. Migration can conveniently be divided into two types: firstly movement within a rural environment and secondly movement into larger settlements and towns, which of course encouraged still further urban growth.

Rural Areas

The evidence suggests that there was a gradual expanding of migrants' horizons, so that throughout most of the seventeenth century the vast majority of migration was very localised within a radius of about ten miles or less, but by the mid-eighteenth century it had begun to expand. The discussion will look first at Lowland Scotland and then the Highlands, although it should be appreciated that in slightly different forms (and generally later in the Highlands) very similar processes were at work in both societies as agriculture became exposed to capitalist forces. In both societies many tenants and sub-tenants experienced dispossession, which as Devine has argued was in many respects very similar; there were indeed both Highland and Lowland Clearances.[4] However, despite the increasing commercialisation of farming, Scotland remained a poor country and famine and shortages occurred intermittently throughout the seventeenth century and particularly in the 1690s when destitution forced many to migrate in search of food. Greyfriar's church in Edinburgh erected a sort of refuge camp for beggars during the winter of 1697 and throughout 1698.[5]

In Lowland Scotland pressures on the rural population were increasing as landlords deliberately tried to increase the economic potential of their estates by encouraging commercial farming. In the seventeenth century multiple tenancy was replaced by single tenant farms and at the same time tenants holding their land at-will were finding this replaced by short-term written leases.[6] Although the paternalism of landowners meant many retained their farms, on the Panmure Estates in Angus (1660–1710) nearly 20% of tenants retained their lease for more than twenty years, but at the same time 37% disappeared from the rentals within five years. Some of this disappearance may have been through death, but it is likely that for others this must reflect loss of lease and migration. Of those traced as moving to another farm, over three-quarters had travelled less than five kilometres which shows how localised the migrations were.[7]

Farms were also being enlarged and improved so that higher rents could be charged. Farms were being combined into larger units and dispossessed tenants were unable to find alternative farms while at the same time the sub-division of farms between children was severely controlled. This meant that in every generation siblings were forced off the land. Sub-tenancies were also being phased out by the mid eighteenth century. In the south of Scotland this commercialisation of farming can be identified early as the 1660s in the counties of Kirkcudbright, Peebles, Roxburgh and Selkirk causing migration and depopulation and gradually the same effects were felt further north.[8] It was only in the northeast that new farms or crofts were being created on more marginal land.[9] Tenants sometimes had to migrate to find suitable farms. In the OSA (The Old Statistical Account of Scotland) it is recorded that in 1750, five farmers from the parish of Tortherwald near Dumfries 'emigrated' to the Isle of Bute; three later returned.[10]

Farm servants were employed on six month or one year contracts, and they rarely stayed at a farm very long, generally less than a year. Much of this localised movement was therefore amongst young adults and this pattern was likely to lead to considerable local mobility. Work however remained labour intensive and there is no evidence to suggest less workers were required. At busy seasons such as harvest, farmers relied on temporary migrants both from the Lowlands and the Highlands.

Capitalist farming involved clearing the land of surplus population. Many people were forced to leave rural areas because of a dearth of accommodation, and this was a deliberate part of estate policy. Unmarried farm servants lived on the farm, and only married ploughmen were provided with housing, but there was a particular shortage of provision for married people. Indeed it was often the changing circumstance of marriage that forced migration: firstly because farm service was no longer an employment option, secondly due to the lack of accommodation, and thirdly because although most people married somebody in their own or a nearby parish marriage, it could still result in localised migration.

Planned villages were often built to coincide with a reorganisation of the estate so that it could absorb some of the surplus farm labour and tradesmen, as well as being a profitable use of human resources for the landlord. As these villages were within the estate, it is not totally surprising that incomers to these villages were locals. Indeed research has shown that between 90% and 95% of the heads of households in these villages had moved less than twenty-five miles. It was the merchants and manufacturers who were the long distance migrants, and sometimes skilled craftsmen such as weavers had to be imported from major manufacturing centres.[11] Some form of industry was encouraged, but it was not always successful. Ormiston in East Lothian was founded in 1735, but by 1791 linen manufacture had failed, although there were two distilleries and a starch-works in the village.[12] Clearly tradesmen must have needed to be willing to migrate until they found a suitable village. At the same time industry was expanding and initially the need for water-power meant that much of it was rural-based and so movement to the nearest industrial centre was not necessarily very far. This enabled migrants to learn industrial and factory skills that would make the later transition to an urban environment less traumatic.

Fontaine has observed that throughout Western Europe regions of high or mountainous land had been marginalised areas, but with economic developments such as the expansion of towns, better transport facilities and greater prosperity, remote regions could fulfil the new demand for meat, wool and timber. The roots of this new role lay in the late Middle Ages, as the complementary economies of high and lowland areas emerged.[13] Thus the Highlands emerges in this period as a peasant society ripe for capitalist investment.

The notion of settled society in the Highlands prior to the clearances is dubious. Certainly the typical family could not boast 'continuous occupation of particular holdings over the period between 1500 and 1745'.[14] Estate rentals frequently record townships laying waste through desertion; this could have been the result of clan warfare or abandonment. Indeed a clan invasion could result in the eviction of all the tenants as happened in 1669 on the islands of Shuna, Luing, Seil and Torosay. For Rannoch lists exist of all men aged over fourteen years in the late seventeenth and early eighteenth century, and this includes all the main social groupings — tacksman, tenants, sub-tenants and cottars. From the lists a constant turnover in the occupants of particular townships can be identified. Thus despite the very few records, which may be extreme examples, the evidence suggests that we should not see Highland society as unchanging prior to the clearances.

The clearances began as early as the 1760s in some areas, and there was not one but four separate processes at work, each forcing at least localised migrations.[15] Firstly, in the south and eastern Highlands between 1780–1830, the existing structure was replaced by large farms, with wage labour and small-holders providing additional seasonal labour. The labour intensive farming meant that the dispossessed were generally absorbed. Secondly, in the northwest Highlands joint tenancies and communal farming were rejected in favour of smallholdings or crofts. It resulted in a considerable relocation of the population, generally near the coast. The third cause of migration was the introduction of large cattle farms after 1750 in Argyllshire, Dunbartonshire and Perthshire. Tenant farmers with small holdings lost them, but again it is argued that this caused relocation without upsetting the existing social structure. Fourthly, in the late eighteenth century commercial sheep farming began in the south and east and moved rapidly north and west. It was large scale and needed the peasants' land for wintering sheep. In this period (up to 1820) clearance resulted in resettlement on the coast or on marginal land, although some preferred to emigrate. Compulsory removal and even emigration were mid-nineteenth century phenomena; in the earlier period localised migration was still common, even if many chose to travel further.

Many Highlanders were first introduced to lowland life through seasonal migration to the Lowlands, which was mainly linked to peak seasons in agriculture such as harvest. By the late eighteenth century temporary migration already formed an important cash injection for the Highlands, but this is considered in more detail in the subsequent section on nineteenth century migration. In such a poor society it is not surprising that as well as temporary migration, and despite the local kin groups, the movement of Highland vagrants to the Lowlands is well recorded. With some vagrants turning up annually at the same time of year, this might reflect seasonal variations in the casual labour market.[16]

So we have a pattern of localised movement gradually increasing in distance, with the key factor influencing out-migration being the introduction of new farming methods, which resulted in the Lowlands in a lack of farm tenancies and therefore the need to find new land, work or accommodation. In the Highlands the deliberate dismantling of the old martial system, the breaking up of the joint tenancies and the introduction of the crofting system meant loss of land or status encouraged out-migration. Throughout the Scotland strong push factors were forcing many people from the land. The differences between town and country life were not that significant until later, and the pull factors such as attractions of urban life seem to occur more in the nineteenth century. Although not measured, the impression gained is that the majority of migrants were young adults

Urban Growth

In 1639 approximately six per cent of the Scottish population lived in towns of over 10,000 inhabitants, but by 1800 this had increased to sixteen percent, which means that the population in the largest urban centres increased by 161%. Scotland had risen from the eleventh to the fourth most urbanised country in Europe. However, urban growth began slowly but then increased speed steadily, so that it was much greater in the late eighteenth century than earlier. It is also apparent that the major cities of Edinburgh and Glasgow were growing much faster than the large towns and smaller royal burghs which experienced only modest growth.[17] The greatest growth was in the west, in particular the towns of Glasgow, Greenock and Paisley.

Large towns were notoriously unhealthy places. The 1640 plague hit towns far more seriously than the surrounding countryside, and it was only through constant in-migration that the populations of towns continued to increase. For example, in-migration enabled Edinburgh to double its population in the first half of the seventeenth century. Thus migration to urban centres performed two roles; firstly, it enabled the rural areas to shed surplus population and secondly it permitted the growth of towns.

We can identify two separate movements, temporary and permanent. Temporary migration implies that the migrant came to the city with a specific objective. An example would be to gain an apprenticeship, but only a quarter of Edinburgh apprentices became burgesses, so many of the rest must have returned home. Dingwall has shown that apprentices were highly mobile, with only relatively few completing their apprenticeships.[18] For rural dwellers attendance at university required migration. The Minister of Penpont in northwest Dumfriesshire noted with pride in the OSA in 1790 that ten students from the parish had attended university in the previous twenty years.[19] The key point is that the migrant intended to return thereafter, even if in reality he did not always come back. Permanent migration was deliberate out-migration, but it was not always out of choice. The early residents of the industrial village of New Lanark comprised in part the poorhouse residents of Glasgow and Edinburgh and also a group of Highland emigrants whose ship had stopped at Greenock.[20] The possibility of work was an obvious reason to migrate. In Prestonpans in 1793 salt panning, chemical manufacture, a pottery, and fisheries as well as agriculture appears to have provided a broad base to the economy, and 37% of the population were migrants in that they were born outside the parish.[21]

Evidence from Edinburgh suggests that in the late seventeenth century urban migration was gender specific, because there were 100 women for every 76 men,[22] and such a large gender imbalance was unlikely to occur naturally. The occupational structure of the town encouraged the imbalance in that the most numerically important job, domestic service, employed 100 females for every 33 males. The vast majority of these females were probably aged between 15 and 25 years. Many remained within the city, but others would have taken their experiences of city life back to their rural roots, providing a source of information for future potential migrants.

The Nineteenth Century 1800–1914

It has already been shown that Scottish urban growth was accelerating by the late eighteenth century, and this pattern continued so that by 1850 it was the second most urbanised country in Europe, exceeded only by England and Wales.[23] Furthermore, by 1851 mobility within Scotland can be quantified, and an estimate from the 1851 Census shows that a third of the population had crossed a county boundary or moved from a rural to an urban environment.[24]

It has already been argued that farming practices in lowland Scotland were forcing surplus labour to migrate. A slow, steady migration was unlikely to be recorded until its effects became critical; thus by 1870 farm labourers were in short supply in the Carse of Gowrie and much of the Northeast.[25] In Perth the dependence on unmarried farm labourers caused a drain from agriculture upon marriage.[26] In the Southwest it was the marginal hill country that lost its population first, people being replaced by sheep. Agricultural employment in Wigtown retained approximately the same proportion of the population throughout the period, but only because the total population fell sharply.[27]

In the Highlands the flow of out-migration was increasing. Famines had probably always occurred, there having been what Richards describes as a catastrophe in 1782–3 and times of exceptional hardship in 1806–7, 1811, 1816–7, 1836–7,[28] followed by the Highland Famine of 1846–55 which prompted the last major migration. In the face of destitution Highlanders were convinced of the need to seek work outside their homeland. Gray has compared Highland migration patterns in 1801 and 1851 using the census. He found that Highland-born migrants were mainly attracted to the West Central Lowlands, with almost half the migrant population going to Lanark and Renfrew.[29] They generally came from the farming regions of the Highlands (the fringe) rather than the far west, which were the really distressed rural areas.[30] However, the influence of the Lowlands was pervasive and as early as 1790–1 the Minister of Fortingall in northwest Perthshire noted that boys of 10–15 years tended sheep or cattle in order to learn a little English and then went south permanently into service or handicraft employment. Likewise crofters, cottars and day-labourers went to the 'great' towns to gain employment.[31]

Research on Highland in-migration to the towns of Greenock,[32] Dundee, Perth and Stirling[33] and to the police force in Glasgow[34] also shows that there was a pronounced regional dimension to Highland migration flows. Each urban centre had its own catchment area, although the out-movement was biased towards the west.[35] Thus the majority of movement into Greenock was initially from Argyll, but the Highland catchment area for Greenock became more distant over time.[36] Likewise highland Perth was the main exporter of population to Dundee in the early nineteenth century, but by the second half of the century Ross and Cromarty had exceeded Perth in importance.[37] Migrants did not necessarily travel directly to their final destination, but may have moved several times: indeed 334 Highland migrants took an average of 12 years to reach Glasgow.[38] Withers suggests that the evidence points towards the more distant parts of the Highlands experiencing an increased level of out-migration.[39] However, it is has already been argued that localised mobility had always existed, now that movement was over a greater distance.

Migrants remained an important component of urban growth. In Glasgow only 44% of the inhabitants of that city were natives in 1851, and almost as many (35%) came from other parts of Scotland, but improvements in health meant that by 1911 nearly 62% of Glasgewians were natives and only 26% came from other parts of Scotland.[40] Nevertheless, throughout the period over a quarter of the inhabitants of Glasgow, although Scots, were not natives. Moreover it should be noted that it was not just the Highlands that provided the migrants, as Campbell has calculated that 21%

of the Scots migrants to Lanarkshire in 1891 were born in southwest Scotland.[41]

There was a relatively low proportion of wholly Highland-born family groups moving south.[42] Withers found that the age structure of the migrant population was fairly constant over time. In both 1861 and 1891 approximately three quarters of the Highlanders in both Dundee and Perth were between the ages of 20–44 years.[43] However, in 1838 in Glasgow there appears to have been considerable family migration amongst Highlanders,[44] and almost a quarter of the Highland-born population were under 10 years.[45] It is difficult, as Withers notes, to be sure that only permanent and not temporary migration is being recorded, especially as the vast majority of the Highland population in the two towns moved as single men and women.[46] The position is further complicated by the fact that so many urban jobs were seasonal and this would have encouraged temporary migration. It has been estimated that in Glasgow between 20% to 23% of male jobs and 26% to 29% of female ones fell into this category of seasonal work.[47]

Female migrants consistently exceeded males in numbers in both Dundee and Perth.[48] This was generally also the situation in Greenock, but 'when a particular area first began sending migrants to Greenock, the initial contacts and first migrations were undertaken predominantly by men. After a short time, however the numbers of women from these districts came to equal and surpass the male migrants and thereafter they always remained in a majority among the migrants'.[49] At present it is not clear if Highland migrants generally were predominantly females, or whether it is a product of the places studied. If more industrial locations, or towns with fishing interests or ports such as Leith were explored, would Highland males be more in evidence?

Lowland rural populations could also have high local mobility, as research by Flinn *et al* has shown using the parish records of Greenlaw in Berwick (1839–42). This migration was related to the hiring practices in agriculture.[50] The Whitsun term records showed considerable family movement, and indeed child migrants were almost as numerous as adults.[51] However, can we presume that this level of mobility continued in the later nineteenth century?

Temporary migration had its roots in economic necessity. Its purpose was to maintain an existing lifestyle,[52] especially after 1815 when other bi-employments had failed. However, it also reflected the disparity between the Highlands and Lowlands both economically and demographically. There was greater economic growth in the Lowlands and labour shortages created opportunities for Highlanders.[53] Both Devine[54] and Macdonald[55] have studied this form of movement which existed in all the crofting areas of the Highlands. It was normally the young and single of both sexes that left, and if heads of household left, they were usually cottars.[56] In the Northeast the migration was often seasonal, to take advantage of the earlier harvests in Southeast Scotland before returning for their own.[57] Temporary migration could however last several years, and in times of exceptional hardship (such as the Highland famine), when cattle prices fell and potato blight hit crops, a very large proportion of the total population might leave.[58]

In more 'normal' years temporary migration was popular because it fitted in with the routine of the croft. Fewer mouths thus had to be fed in periods when shortages of food were most likely (May to September) and there was very little work, but it also introduced Highlanders to Lowland society. Initially, temporary migration was mainly to work in agriculture, but work was also found in military employment, urban centres and the herring fisheries.[59] It is generally argued that by the 1870s the east coast fishery was the single most important employer and agriculture and service in the regular army had diminished in significance. However, recent research has shown that service in the Militia and Royal Naval Reserves[60] was still a component of the interlocking pattern of several distinct temporary employments for crofters in the Western Isles.

This section has argued that despite a few notable long distance migrations, the vast majority of early moves were localised. It was not until the late eighteenth century that longer distance moves became more common and permitted the growth of urban centres, and at the same time allowed lowland rural areas to shed surplus population relatively painlessly. In Highland regions the compulsory evictions led to migration, but with a lack of alternative work in the nineteenth century Highlands, this led to depopulation in many areas. However, depopulation from one area meant growth elsewhere; with migration, people moving can be accounted for elsewhere in Scotland. Migration therefore does not represent total population loss, which is the consequence of emigration.

EMIGRATION

If we are to argue that emigration represents total population loss from Scotland, this movement must include more than just settler emigration abroad. It is for this reason that the discussion includes traders and even military service as emigration. These occupations represent temporary emigration if the person returns and emigration if the person concerned died abroad. Military service in particular represents a huge gender specific population loss for Scotland until at least 1860, and for that reason I have given it more prominence than is normally the case in discussions of emigration.

It is becoming increasingly clear that the Scots have always emigrated in significant numbers, this culture of emigration being established well before the seventeenth century. Scots are known to have been employed as mercenaries in Ireland by the Gaelic Irish Kings as early as the mid-thirteenth century and by 1474 the parliament in Dublin was complaining that there were 10,000 Scots in Ulster.[61] In the fifteenth century approximately 15,000 Scots, both Highlanders and Lowlanders, fought in France[62] and mercenaries were also in combat in Denmark, Prussia and Sweden.[63] Thus even before the seventeenth century large numbers of young males were leaving Scotland with very little chance of returning. Scots were also going abroad as tradesmen; they are recorded in Poland from the late fifteenth century[64] and in France in the subsequent century. They also went to England both as professionals and also as unskilled workers, and recent research has shown that as early as 1440, and despite severe restrictions on Scots in England, there were already between 7,000 and 11,000 Scots south of the border.[65] The patterns of emigration were therefore already in place both for mercenaries and traders by the seventeenth century.

The Seventeenth Century

In the seventeenth century Scottish population losses through emigration continued to be high. As Table 1.1 shows, estimates suggest that in the first half of the century the net outflow from Scotland was probably between 85,000 and 115,000 people, and in the second half somewhere between 78,000 and 127,000 left. This represents a loss of about 2,000 people a year from a Scottish population of only about one million. Indeed Smout has calculated that approximately 20% of young males must have left Scotland between 1600 and 1650 and observes that such losses within this group would have depressed the natural rate of population increase. Nevertheless,

Table 1.1. Estimates of Scots Emigrants by Destination in the Seventeenth Century[67]

| | 1600–1650 | | | 1650–1700 | |
	Minimum	Maximum		Minimum	Maximum
Ireland	20,000	30,000	Ireland	60,000	100,000
Poland	30,000	40,000	America	7,000	7,000
Scandinavia	25,000	30,000	Elsewhere	10,000	20,000
Elsewhere	10,000	15,000			
Total number lost	85,000	115,000	Total number lost	78,000	127,000

this high proportion of Scots leaving was not exceptional in European terms, as Switzerland is thought to have experienced similar losses, and those of Holland were even greater.[66]

The three main areas of attraction for Scots during the first half of the seventeenth century were Poland, Scandinavia and Ireland. All three were established emigrant destinations, Poland being the most popular country, which had been enticing increasing numbers of Scots since the latter part of the sixteenth century and emigration is thought to have peaked between 1610–19.[68] Scots emigrants could be found throughout the country and Municipal Records to show that Scots were resident in at least 420 different locations, although not all would have been first generation, but born abroad. Poland was attractive to pedlars and tradesmen such as weavers, cutlers and shoemakers who came with their families, and thousands of Scots were also employed as mercenaries. These could either be transported directly from Scotland, or recruited from the Scots already in Poland. Emigration to Poland showed a regional bias within Scotland, most people coming from the east and northeast.

Scots emigrants to Scandinavia also mainly became pedlars, tradesman or involved in commerce and Scots were prominent amongst merchants in Gothenburg and Bergen. Scots were clearly long established in some areas, and in 1518 2.6% of the taxable population in Malmo (Sweden) were Scots.[69] As in Poland the Scots emigrants offered new skills to these peripheral areas of Europe. This pattern was to be repeated in the nineteenth century, when Scots took their urban industrial skills to the New World. The emigrants in Bergen came mainly from Orkney and Shetland, but in general far less is known about the origins of emigrants to Scandinavia than those in Poland, although it seems likely that emigrants to both places came from the same regions of Scotland.

Scots emigrants to Scandinavia also served as mercenaries. Fallon has used estate records to investigate the method of recruitment between 1626 and 1632 and his study gives an impression of the numbers involved and their county of origin. He estimates that warrants were issued for a total of 58,880 men, and although some of these may never have been filled and others may have involved men re-enlisting, the numbers were nevertheless so great that approximately 5% of the male Scots population was affected.[70] The armies did not normally last long; a unit raised by Mackay lost 500 men (excluding officers) through death in six weeks and of the remaining 400, only a quarter were unscathed.[71] Indeed fighting in the Thirty Years War has been described by Smout as 'buying a one-way ticket to certain death'.[72] As well as death in action, illness was also a cause of military deaths and at least 10% of the strength of any regiment was normally lost through sickness. Losses like this, coupled with desertion and the lack of provision made for men when an army was disbanded meant that it is not surprising that only a very small proportion of men returned home to Scotland. Thus it can be seen that although military service has been classified as temporary emigration, for many it became in reality permanent emigration. Although some men did volunteer as mercenaries, recruitment was profitable for the Scottish landlord[73] and in many cases men were forced to sign up. Landlords would raise their armies from amongst their own tenantry and the impact in terms of loss of young men could be very significant in that its catchment was restricted to a single estate. Fallon has concluded that 'no part of Scotland escaped the recruiting net'. The counties of Argyll, Renfrew and Ayrshire do nevertheless appear to be less affected by army recruitment than the rest,[74] but McInnies has pointed out that these counties were popular areas for recruitment to the Navy. Thus throughout the first half of the seventeenth century there is evidence of a steady seepage of young males from Scotland due to military service.

Emigration to Ireland was not a new phenomenon, but the regions that were decanting population had changed by the seventeenth century. Whereas previously emigrants were mainly Gaels who became mercenaries, it was now farming people that left. These colonists were mainly small tenant farmers from Ayrshire and Galloway, but there were also settlers from Argyll and Fife.[75]

Emigrants clearly chose their destinations with some care and must have had information networks. Scots went to Europe as traders and soldiers whilst Ulster attracted farmers and servants. We therefore have two different types of out-movement, one of which would have involved entire families, and the other largely male emigration of mercenaries. By the mid-seventeenth century Scottish soldiers had become permanent settlers in Ireland, France, Denmark, Russia, Sweden and Poland.[76]

Table 1.1 shows that the destinations of emigrants changed after 1650. Total emigration losses remained high and the colonisation of Ireland continued, but with the exception of the Netherlands, Europe ceased to attract emigrants and there was a gradual rise in inter-continental emigration to America. One can therefore see that whereas mobility in the first half of the seventeenth century was a continuation of earlier emigration patterns, the latter part of the century represented the start of a steady change in direction.

In the first half of the seventeenth century, Scots preferred their traditional emigration routes and largely ignored America; indeed in 1648 there were only about 250 Scots in the New World. A further 2,000 Scots, often prisoners-of-war, went to the New World between 1640 and 1660,[77] and another 5,000 after 1660. Approximately half the settlers went to the Scottish colony in Darian which was a catastrophe and most died. The remainder went mainly to the West Indies, especially Barbados,[78] although some went to North America and about 600 settled in New Jersey. The majority Scots in America had arrived involuntarily,[79] but it does not alter the fact that some Scots were now considering emigrating further afield. Their numbers were not however, exceptional and indeed the movement of Irish servants to the West Indies exceeded the number of Scots.[80]

Within the British Isles Ireland continued to attract colonists but their numbers ebbed and flowed according to conditions both at home and in Ireland. Thus some returned to Scotland after 1641, but there was a sharp rise in emigration to Ireland in the Cromwellian period when about 40–50,000 Scots left, and again after the famines of the 1690s when a further 50,000 people are thought to have left.[81]

England must also have attracted emigrants during the seventeenth century, although very little research has been done on this. In the late sixteenth century, there were 2,500 Scots in Northumberland, but after 1660 there was a widening gap in the economies of Scotland and England and in particular the wage rates diverged making England increasingly attractive to emigrants.[82] The counties nearest Scotland were the most likely to attract Scots and therefore the presence of large numbers of Scots in Newcastle should not be seen as typical of England as a whole. Nevertheless, over 1,800 Scottish keelmen were recorded in Newcastle in 1637.[83] Some of this movement was temporary, but others emigrated with their wives and children. We can see this movement to England as a continuation of migration flows established much earlier. Galloway and Murray have shown that in the period 1400–1550 almost 40% of Scots emigrants, mainly the unskilled, lived in Northumberland. Those with skills such as craftsmen, professionals and clerical emigrants were mainly resident in the southeast, particularly London. This research also showed that the vast majority of Scots came from the east of Scotland and settled in the east of England. The authors speculated that England was more attractive to Eastern Scots, and Ireland to those living further west.[84] Finally, even before the Union of 1707 Scots joined the English army. John Short of Edinburgh is known to have enlisted in order to avoid the wrath of the Kirk Session over an accusation of immorality![85]

In conclusion the high levels of emigration in the seventeenth century should be seen in the context of the relatively small Scottish population, which was probably not much more than a million people. Scotland was a poor country, unable to feed itself reliably and other countries wanted Scottish skills or provided opportunities not available at home.

The Eighteenth Century

Whether the pattern of high levels of emigration seen in the seventeenth century continued into the early part of the eighteenth century is largely unknown. The famines of the 1690s and the massive emigration of the previous century may well have improved the opportunities for those remaining at home and thus reduced the need to emigrate.

Moreover, movement into England was probably substantial in both the sixteenth and seventeenth centuries. The Union of 1707 obviously created new opportunities for Scots; it certainly encouraged the nobility to move south and probably made England a generally more attractive emigrant destination. We know that those with qualifications, such as doctors, engineers, soldiers and other professional men went south,[86] although one must not ignore the movement of traders and even the unskilled. As Dr Johnson cynically observed in 1763 'the noblest prospect which a Scotchman ever sees, is the high road that leads him to England'.[87]

Some Scottish settlement in North America was already underway by the beginning of the eighteenth century. Commercial links created by the tobacco trade helped to create a transport infrastructure for large scale emigration from Scotland. Glasgow also had good transport connections with the Highlands, which thus developed the links with North America that made subsequent chain emigration possible. Indeed it has been argued that eighteenth century emigration was the 'beachhead for later movement'.[88] Bailyn had studied emigration to British North America between 1760 and 1776 and has shown that Scots were emigrating in proportionally larger numbers than the English. Although 52% of emigrants were single young adult males, Scots emigrants were far more likely to travel in family parties than the English, and because of this the

Table 1.2. Scots Leaving for North America by Region 1773–6[91]

	Male	Female	Unknown	% in families	% of all Scottish
Borders	274	192	4	73.2	12.1
East Lowlands	169	96	26	44.3	7.7
Far North	125	97	81	80.5	7.8
Highlands–Hebrides	577	503	19	54.1	28.4
Northeast	56	24	0	38.8	2.1
Perthshire	146	89	64	78.3	7.7
West Lowlands	314	129	34	43.3	12.3
Region Unknown	345	214	294	8.3	22.1
Scotland	2006	1344	522	47.9	100.0

gender balance was more favourable.[89] The majority of the emigrants were either farmers or weavers, and unlike the English there were very few merchants and there was a much narrower range of trades.[90] This suggests that in Scotland there were particular pressures on these two employment groups. Table 1.2 shows that although a thin sprinkling of emigrants left every region, there was nevertheless a strong regional bias with the under-populated Highlands–Hebrides being by far the most important, contributing over a third of the emigrants whose birthplace was known, despite comprising only 28% of the population of Scotland. Substantial numbers also left the West Lowlands, Borders, Perthshire and the Far North, while the East Lowlands and Northeast were under-represented.

Why were Scots leaving? One reason was that since agriculture had become more market-oriented in both the Highlands and Lowlands, many were losing access to the land. Landlord coercion could also be an important factor encouraging emigration. Thus it can be seen that it was both push factors at home and the pull factor of an opportunity to gain access to land in North America that tempted emigrants. Emigration was expensive in terms of both money and time, and many emigrants sold up stock before leaving so that they could afford to buy land and stock in America. As Gray points out, the emigrants were therefore not a 'poverty-stricken rabble',[92] but had made financial provision to meet the costs of emigration.

Table 1.3. Highland emigration, 1700–1815[95]

Period	Estimated Number of Highland Emigrants to North America
1700–60	>3,000
1760–75	c. 10,000
1775–1801	2–3,000
1801–3	c. 5,000
1803–15	c. 3,000

Emigration from the Highlands will now be considered in more detail. Table 1.3 shows that even in the first half of the eighteenth century Highland emigration to North America was already significant. Never-theless, it is clear that emigration from the Highlands really took off in the 1760s, which Devine ascribes to end of the Seven Years War. Highlanders had been mercenaries in this war and Devine suggests that the experience of overseas travel may have accustomed the society to greater mobility. However, it is also the case that Highlanders had a tradition of military employment and it has already been argued that many mercenaries were unlikely to return home. The lack of other employment opportunities once the war had finished and changing practices in estate management may have been additional push factors that encouraged soldiers to settle abroad. The decline in emigrants between 1775 and 1801 can be attributed partly to the American War of Independence, which made North America less attractive and to the increased demand for soldiers in the British army. In this war the British Government again encouraged landlords to raise armies, sometimes from a very limited area. Thus we have the Glengarry Fencibles raised in that area of Scotland and granted land in Canada where they had served, so they did not return to the Highlands. Indeed between 1745 and 1800 many other Highland regiments were raised by landlords, though they were disbanded fairly quickly, most lasting for less than ten years, in total fifty Highland regiments were raised between 1740 and 1800 and of these thirty four served in the European and American wars and in India.[93]. However, as discussed earlier it is not clear how many, if any, came back, as mortality rates were very high. The 78th Highlanders (Ross-shire Buffs) which had been raised by the Earl of Seaforth was sent to India in 1781 to fight in the Anglo-French War, but even before landing in India, two hundred and thirty men had died of scurvy on the voyage out.[94]

Emigration from the Highlands increased markedly between 1801 and 1803, after which this out-movement was almost halted by the Passenger Acts of 1803. These were introduced ostensibly as a humanitarian measure to improve conditions on emigrant shipping by reducing the numbers on board. However, the acts also increased the cost of a passage significantly, which may well account for the marked reduction in emigrants. This would have suited landlords who could not afford to lose their workforce.[96] Indeed in 1826 the Governor General for the Province of Nova Scotia asserted that before the Passenger Acts the cost of passage to Nova Scotia for adults 'never exceeded £3.10s or from that to £4. By the operation of these laws, the passage is raised to £10 a head'.[97] Yet at the same time as the Acts were passed the resumption of the Wars against France meant that there were increased opportunities for military service and the men may well have found this work preferable to emigration.

A situation thus existed where there were several push factors, in that changing estate management restricted access to the land and at the same time reduced the status of the tacksman class and broke up traditional society. Landlords were also keen to profit by creating armies from their tenants. Thus in 1798, a survey of the extensive parish of Gairloch reported that 'Recruiting Parties being so frequent among us for years past, have left us but few of our young men: so that our parish at this period chiefly consists of children, women and old men'.[98] We have therefore an overall pattern of fluctuating temporary and permanent emigration from the

Highlands, where sometimes only the males leave while at other times entire families depart.

Now let us consider the impact of military service on the Highlands. Some insight can be gained from the work of Henderson, who analysed the surviving Roll books of the 93rd Sutherland Highlanders.[99] These show that between 1799 and 1831 recruits came from the counties of Sutherland, Caithness, Ross, Inverness, Perth and Fife. Some recruits joined as young as 9 years, but most seem to have been in their late teens. Many signed on for life, although some only enlisted for nine years. Between the years 1823 to 1832 the regimental strength varied from 376 and 519 men (excluding officers) and in this period 220 deaths occurred, seven soldiers deserted and eight were dismissed. In order to maintain strength, the regiment recruited 1,263 men between 1799 and 1831. Military recruitment such as this removed young males from sparsely populated areas, and moved them overseas, if not forever, certainly for the most fertile period of their lives. Even if they finally returned home their optimum fertility within Scotland would be considerably reduced. Moreover, a pattern of extensive periods of overseas service was typical of all the Highland regiments between 1820–81, and as they were active fighting units[100] they would have experienced high levels of mortality.

The Royal Navy was an important employer in Shetland. It was said in 1774 that every year for the previous 20 years, 100 men had left to join the Navy or the merchant service. At the end of the Seven Years War 900 men were paid off and in the American War of 1776–83 two thousand Shetlanders were estimated as serving in the Royal Navy or merchant service.[101] In Shetland at this time there was very little settler emigration and the services appear to have creamed off surplus population to the extent that in the second half of the nineteenth century there were complaints of a labour shortage on the islands.

A second contribution to temporary emigration of increasing importance was colonial service. Henry Dundas' formidable powers of patronage enabled Scots to play a major role in the administration of India. Indeed it has been observed that such service provided 'a vast network of outdoor relief for Britain's upper classes'. The links created at this time proved durable over many generations and Scots still formed the core of the India Civil Service in the nineteenth century. By the late eighteenth century Scots were becoming so numerous in India that a letter written by a Scot in 1773 reported that it was no longer possible to enumerate his countrymen as he had in the past because they were too many.[102]

Thus the eighteenth century saw a remarkable expansion in world-wide emigration from Scotland, as well as a continuation of emigration to

England. The majority of emigrants continued to be male, although family parties were important especially in Highland emigration, and indeed it was probably the Highlanders who were most migration prone.

The Nineteenth Century (1800–1914)

Nineteenth century emigration splits neatly into two distinct periods, before after the Highland Famine. This is partly due to the Famine itself, in that the high levels of Highland emigration could not be maintained indefinitely. It is also an effect of the introduction of steamships, which meant that inter-continental emigration was feasible for the masses. Finally as a result of better recording including the census, the latter part of the period is easier to quantify than earlier. The discussion will be divided into three parts. The first section will consider permanent emigration up to and including the famine. The second period will deal with movement after 1860 and up to 1914, because patterns established in the later nineteenth century continue up to the First World War. The final part will discuss temporary emigration throughout the century both to other parts of Britain and overseas, as by now this was no longer restricted to military personnel and a few administrators and entrepreneurs.

In the first half of the nineteenth century Highland emigration remained high. In total 74,442 native Highlanders served in regiments of the Line, Fencibles, Militia and Volunteer forces between 1793 and 1811.[103] The Highlands had a population of 330,000 in 1811,[104] and so this level of participation is possibly an over-estimate, and some men may have served in more than one regiment and been counted twice. Nevertheless, it has prompted one historian to observe that it represents a per capita rate of military recruitment unequalled in any other part of Europe,[105] and how many came back is unknown. Expectations had also been raised by the economic boom during the war, but with peace troops were no longer required, kelping and cattle prices collapsed and the population, which had grown rapidly, was redundant. These factors all contributed to maintaining high levels of emigration after the war had ended. Bumstead has described it as an 'emigration of rising expectations'.[106] It was the middle ranks with capital who chose to leave, many of whom already had close connections overseas. The poor could only leave if they were subsidised or were prepared to become indentured servants and this was uncommon.[107] Thus it was a 'growth of population beyond the real productive capacity of agriculture that made emigration inevitable'.[108] Nevertheless, it is very difficult to quantify losses, although one finds intriguing clues to the volume of emigration in reports such as those from the Select Report on Emigration in 1826: in the years 1824 and 1825 'upon moderate calculation' at least 300 settlers come from the north of Scotland,[109] or that where once twenty five families lived there are now at least 1,500 families and almost all are from Scotland.[110] Both these references refer to Eastern Canada.

Even in an extreme situation like the Highland famine, there were two distinctive emigration flows from the Highlands which can be divided into unassisted (the better off) and assisted (the poor). The unassisted could leave first because they were not obliged to wait for help and are therefore more difficult, if not impossible, to quantify. These people were generally from the west mainland and southern islands. They had suffered less and left because of the failure of the potatoes and the falling cattle prices which resulted in a 'serious and rapidly increasing threat to their social and economic position'.[111] These people often had connections in the areas they chose. In contrast assisted emigrants came from the crofting parishes of the Northwest Highlands. The emigrant-attracting countries had different needs and the young and single tended to go to Australia and family parties to Canada. It was the poorest classes (the cottars) that were given assisted passages and who, if they had remained, would have been the greatest drain on estate relief. Thus between 1846 and 1857 at least 16,533 people are known to have been assisted to emigrate, and an unknown number were also helped by the Colonial Land and Emigration Commission.[112] Where assisted emigration was provided by the proprietors its effects were quite deliberately concentrated on their own estates, so the impact in different areas was therefore dependent on landlord attitudes.

The momentum of out-movement during the famine gradually increased, although the population loss was not all due to emigration, as some Highlanders migrated rather than emigrated. The crofting parishes lost an estimated 11.75% of their population between 1841–51 and 15.75% in the subsequent decade. The farming parishes of the Northwest experienced losses that were almost as dramatic with 8.0% in the earlier decade increasing to 15.6% in the latter.[113] Flinn has argued that the potato famine and subsequent emigration caused a permanent decline in the population in the Highlands.[114] However, this has been questioned by Devine who points to regional variations, as although Highland emigration had been a mass movement since the 1820s, its effects were mixed. Thus in Sutherland population losses peaked in the 1820s and 30s, well before the famine, whereas population evidence in Wester Ross, the Inner Hebrides and parts of Western Inverness-shire supports Flinn's analysis of permanent decline. In contrast the population of the Outer Hebrides recovered after the famine and experienced some growth, but Anderson has argued that the population had a very unbalanced age structure.[115] However, research suggests that temporary military service in the Militia was 'caught' by the late nineteenth century census enumerations and distorted the young adult male age-structure in the Outer Hebrides enough to account for much of the imbalance.[116]

Levitt and Smout[117] have analysed poor law data from 1840–42. This has made it possible to compare regional responses to emigration. There were marked differences in the rates of emigration, with the West Highlands providing two-fifths of the emigrants and the Highlands as a whole almost half.[118] Unfortunately coverage of population movement in the major urban centres was poor in the original material, though evidence does suggest that there was considerable emigration from these areas.[119] However, Gray has analysed movement in the lowlands from 1800 to 1851 using the census and shown that differences in the nature of economic development within a parish could also influence the type of population mobility. He concluded that parishes with no industrial development were more likely to have higher emigration than those with an industrial component.[120]

As has already been noted the Highland famine provides a watershed in nineteenth century emigration, and by 1860 different patterns were emerging for several reasons. Firstly, emigration flows began to vary enormously according to economic factors on both sides of the Atlantic.[121] Secondly, much faster steam ships, better conditions on board and cheaper fares encouraged mass emigration. More information was available on emigrant destinations through emigration societies, newspapers and letters, and emigrants intending to leave Scotland no longer faced a complete break with their homeland as for the first time it was feasible for emigrants who did not like their destination to return to Scotland. Indeed successful emigrants returned to Scotland for holidays or to retire.

Throughout the seventeenth century Ireland had been a very attractive emigrant destination for Scots. However, by the mid-nineteenth century, Ireland was no longer a magnet and only about ten percent of the Scots who emigrated to other parts of Britain went to Ireland. Moreover, it is probable that most of those who went to Ireland were in fact children born of Irish parents in Scotland. England and Wales thus becomes the main UK destination for Scots. However, there is very little information on Scottish movement south beyond estimates by Baines[122] and Flinn,[123] as the county-of-birth of Scottish emigrants was not stated in the English census until 1911[124] and the age of emigrants was not provided.

The number of Scots in England and Wales increased steadily throughout the period,[125] but when considered as a proportion of the total population they fell in the final census (1911),[126] which supports the evidence of Flinn that emigration declined in the decade 1901–11.[127] Anderson and Morse have found that the destination of those Scots moving south changed over time from being mainly to London, the Southeast and Lancashire; after 1870 more people went to areas of mining and heavy industry in England and Wales.[128] Certainly Shannon's findings suggest that the volume of Scottish emigration to London increased until 1891.[129] This change in the direction of the emigration flow implies that different occupational groups may have begun to emigrate south later in the century. Anderson and Morse consider that it was young, single, well educated or skilled males who moved south.[130] Evidence in the 1911 English and Welsh census does not support this conclusion, as the volume of Scots of both sexes was roughly equal, and if measured by county-of-birth then females exceeded males in over half the counties.[131] Clearly the evidence from 1911 does not necessarily present a true picture of the entire period, but it is also the case that the largest proportion of migrants from Scotland by county-of-birth came from the Borders.[132]

The total volume of overseas emigration from Scotland has been estimated by Carrier and Jeffery,[133] and varied significantly from year to year. However, they used shipping lists which Flinn has shown seriously under-estimate the numbers of emigrants prior to 1853 because they ignore Scots leaving English ports.[134] Net movement into England and Wales has been estimated by Baines.[135] The volume of emigrants in both estimates fluctuate markedly. It is however difficult to interpret the significance of the volume of emigrants, as although emigration was generally increasing over time (albeit with fluctuations), the total Scots population was also rising. There are no national studies of emigration from the perspective of the sending country, and therefore the county-of-birth of emigrants can only be gauged from regional research. Analysis of emigration overseas is inhibited by the fact that detailed passenger lists did not exist until 1912, and only after that date did the returns distinguish genuine emigrants from temporary departures.[136] This lack of information has meant that researchers are forced to use secondary sources and this biases research towards institutionally organised emigration. Thus regions such as the Highlands (which were recognised by contemporaries as having problems), are likely to have more information on movement than, for example, small relatively trouble-free towns.

The discussion on population movement has provided some information on regional emigration patterns, but it is impossible to estimate their relative importance nationally. In general emigration is referred to as a rural phenomenon.[137] This is not however born out by Stevenson's contemporary published record of experience of working class emigration to the United States. He travelled in 1879,[138] a year when emigration was increasing after a trough.[139] Stevenson noted the urban origins of the Scottish emigrants, and thought that many of the emigrants came from Glasgow,[140] and yet studies of urban emigration are rare. Erickson has emphasised the importance of this type of emigration using American passenger lists to study emigrants to the United States. She showed that in 1846–54, 58.9% of Scottish male emigrants were from industrial rather than agricultural counties and in 1885–8 this had increased to 79.9%.[141] Clearly the enlarged proportion of emigrants from the industrial counties reflected in part a national trend, but whereas in the 1850s the proportion of emigrants from the industrial counties was slightly below the national average, in the 1851 census and in the 1880s it was higher.[142] In the 1880s, unlike the earlier sample, there was a large emigration of urban labourers.[143] The marital status of emigrants also altered between the 1850s and 1880s. Whereas 'before 1854 single men outnumbered men travelling with families 2:1, in the 1880s the ratio was 8:1'.[144] Emigrants are generally portrayed as young, indeed Stevenson stresses that he had expected to find young emigrants but 'comparatively few men were below thirty; many were married and encumbered with families; not a few were already up in years'.[145] It has already been noted that volume of emigration varied dramatically and this may have been an atypical collection of passengers.

The motives of emigrants are of interest and Harper has considered emigration from north-east Scotland.[146] She has used the local press and emigrant letters to expand her information, and her study suggests that the emigrants were mainly rural-born farmers, who were emigrating to better themselves rather than out of poverty. Unfortunately the less prosperous farm workers and those who chose to migrate were probably less likely to write letters. Such people tend to be missing in this study. There are other studies in this region. Carter has considered farm service and has found evidence of emigration amongst crofters' children,[147] and Watson and Allan analysed clearances and found non-enforced emigration, (mostly later than the clearance) to be the main form of depopulation.[148]

We have some generalised information about the occupations of emigrants. Thomas has found that about 50% of Scottish male emigrants to the United States were skilled in the period 1875–1914. Scotland also provided the highest proportion of professional and entrepreneurial grades of the four UK countries.[149] Flinn's study of passenger lists in 1912–3 has shown that in those years only 29% of males were described as labourers, only 19% came from agriculture, and the occupational skills of male Scottish emigrants were important in deciding a destination. The majority of female emigrants had no stated occupation, but of those who worked, most described themselves as domestic servants. An occupation does not however imply that the females were travelling alone, many being sisters or daughters of other emigrants.[150]

Some worker's organisations encouraged emigration. Handloom weavers formed emigration societies to relieve distress in that trade.[151] Trades unions also encouraged emigration. Scots coal miners had been emigrating to North America since the 1830s, but in 1864 it became union policy to reduce surplus labour by encouraging emigration, with a fund to help miners and provide information.[152] However, there are no precise estimates of the numbers of emigrants helped in this way, and they were probably very low when compared with the volume emigrating nationally.

Stevenson stressed the poverty of some the steerage passengers, but it is hard to believe that 'many' had been long out of work,[153] as the fare for a family would have required considerable saving, unless the emigrant worked his passage.[154] The really poor could not emigrate without assistance. Campbell has argued that, regardless of their subsequent achievements abroad, many Scots often emigrated after relative failure at home.[155] Even the poorest emigrant was not necessarily going to a completely unknown destination. Scots had a long tradition of emigration. In Ireland the crisis emigration of the famine of 1845–8 has been shown not to have been an aimless movement, but emigration to confirmed links that had already been made with places overseas.[156] Devine has shown that this was also true of unassisted emigration during the Highland Famine.[157]

Initially it was possible to emigrate from many Scottish ports, but by the mid–nineteenth century the emigrant shipping trade was concentrated on Glasgow and Liverpool.[158] The development of steam shipping in the late 1860s altered attitudes to emigration by reducing the financial and emotional costs to emigrants. The steamship meant that emigrants wasted far less time travelling,[159] and therefore the costs in terms of lost income whilst travelling were far less, and for the first time returning was feasible, so workers could consider trans–Atlantic temporary emigration.[160]

Let us now consider temporary emigration. By the late nineteenth century there was undoubtedly a substantial temporary emigration by Scots to other parts of Britain, indeed the seasonal migration Scots to Cumberland was probably occurring in the fifteenth century[161] and was still in evidence in the early nineteenth century.[162] A study of the Great Yarmouth herring fishing industry in Eastern England shows the Scottish presence in Yarmouth increased rapidly to take advantage of the spectacular growth in the industry. By the peak year of 1913 about 38,000 Scots were employed in the industry of which nearly 13,000 were gutters.[163] Clearly the long journey was justified by the potential earnings, a female gutter earning an average of £25 after expenses. 'In the Helmsdale district the women workers had the unique experience of bringing more money home than the value of fish landed in that district during the whole year'.[164] It is probable that other industries were attracting temporary emigration to England.

Inter-continental temporary emigration only became practicable with the faster steam shipping. Erickson found evidence of temporary emigration amongst Scottish tradesmen to the United States in the 1880s.[165] Indeed 36% of all male emigrants in her samples were building workers and Erickson has argued that many were temporary emigrants.[166] The Scottish building workers included the granite masons which Harper has identified as temporary overseas emigrants from Aberdeen to both Canada[167] and the USA[168] This movement was encouraged by demand abroad, and indeed it was only in 1901 that the main motive for the emigration of granite workers was a bad slump and financial hardship in Scotland.[169] Temporary emigration was not restricted to the building trades; the coal miners were also very mobile,[170] and we should not ignore fishermen who had begun whaling off the Greenland by 1749[171] and by the early nineteenth century were also fishing for white fish in that area.[172]

Temporary emigration implies that return to Scotland was always planned in advance, but this was not always the case. Return emigration was not a new phenomenon, it having been recorded in 1816[173] and possibly even earlier.[174] However, the numbers of returning emigrants from the United States increased during the Civil War and during the Crimean War boom in Britain.[175] Shepperson has argued that prior to 1865, craftsmen and mechanics who recrossed the Atlantic did so because 'of real or imagined dissatisfaction with America and not because they were temporary labourers'.[176] Shepperson has studied nineteenth century return emigration from the United States. He shows that these emigrants were mature people often with families and who had taken time to investigate the possibilities in the United States before returning to Britain.[177] Nevertheless, those who returned were not necessarily people who had failed abroad, as real failures could not afford to return. The returnees were undoubtedly an important source of information or example for prospective emigrants. There is no known research on Scottish return emigrants, but Baines's estimate that about 30% of the English returned is probably realistic for Scotland as well.

In the seventeenth and eighteenth centuries military service abroad was a very important component of total losses through emigration. However, in the nineteenth century this pattern changed. It has already been observed the Highlanders were an important source of soldiers in the Napoleonic Wars. No evidence has been found of how many returned to Scotland, but one can assume a fairly high level of mortality. Indeed, it has been shown that British military recruits based in Britain, who had to pass a medical test on enlistment, nevertheless experienced a worse mortality rate than the comparable civilian cohorts.[178] Clearly active service abroad would have vastly increased mortality rates. Military service therefore continued in reality to represent permanent emigration or out-migration for many unfortunates until about 1856, when deliberate attempts were made to improve conditions. A major problem was that military service removed men from their communities for a considerable time. Short-term recruitment was not introduced until 1870, prior to which the vast majority of soldiers served for at least 12 years.[179] Military service was badly paid and in terms of the total population was attractive to mainly rural-born Scots.[180] Clearly the attraction of military service reflects a lack of alternative work in the rural areas. Even if some men finally returned belatedly to their county-of-birth the high mortality in military recruits could still account in part for declining rural populations.

In the early Victorian period Scots military participation was still above the British norm (Table 1.4). This period includes the Crimean War which

Table 1.4. The Proportion and number of Scots-born Non-Commissioned Officers and Men in the British Army[186]

Year*	Numbers of Scots	% of Scots in the British Army	Males resident in Scotland as a % of males in the British Isles in the nearest Census[187]
1830	13,800	13.6	9.5
1840	15,239	13.7	9.5
1870	16,163	9.6	10.5
1881	14,415	8.1	10.6
1891	16,409	8.2	10.6
1903	22,442	8.4	10.8
1911	18,581	7.8	10.5

*The years selected are those which correspond as closely as possible with the census years.

is known to have exacted horrendous casualties both in the conflict and also through sickness. Not everybody in a Scottish regiment was Scots-born,[181] but it is reasonable to assume that approximately 80% of men in Highland regiments and 50% of those in Lowland ones were Scots.[182] Let us consider the example of the Sutherland Highlanders (93rd), who suffered severe losses in the war and were an overwhelmingly Scottish regiment — only one person was not Scots-born in 1854.[183] A total of 1,408 officers and men were sent to the Crimea including reinforcements: of these 12% of the officers and 23% of the men were killed. Many were also invalided home so that in total 48% of officers and 41% of men were killed or invalided home.[184] The officers seem far more likely to be sent home than men, possibly because they had the right to ask for repatriation in case of illness.[185] If it is assumed that many of the injured died subsequently from their wounds, and the rest were severely incapacitated, casualty rates of this order would have had exactly the same effect on the Highland population as emigration and would have further depleted the young adult male population in a decade already ravaged by the Highland famine and the aftermath of economic depression.

However, by the late Victorian period Scotland ceased to be a major supplier of soldiers for the British army (as can be seen in Table 1.4) perhaps because better work opportunities for potential recruits were now available at home. Certainly by 1870 Scotland was providing less non-commissioned officers and men than the proportion of Scots in the British Isles. Indeed the nineteen Scots regiments had serious recruitment problems. By 1871 only three Scots regiments had more than 60% of their officers and men born in Scotland and five 'Scottish' regiments had less than 15% Scots-born.[188] It was the Highland regiments that continued to attract the most Scots, although many of the men recruited were not Highland-born.[189] Military service had declined in significance as a factor in emigration and indeed migration as well.

In conclusion it has been argued that over time out-migration changed in terms of area of origin, destination, and also distance travelled. In the seventeenth and early eighteenth centuries migration was a widespread but localised movement, but by the mid-nineteenth century horizons had widened and rural to urban movement in particular involved every county in Scotland. Emigration from Scotland has always been high, initially to Europe, but Scots were not slow to move further afield. For much of the period Scotland's most useful resource was her manpower and there does indeed appear to be evidence supporting a culture of emigration. Indeed it has been argued that in terms of the proportion of the population lost through emigration Scotland ranks third in Europe.[190]

THE ECONOMIC AND SOCIAL FACTORS INFLUENCING POPULATION MOVEMENT 1830–1911

Having analysed the evidence for a tradition of out-movement from Scotland, the discussion will now consider the economic and social factors influencing population movement in the period 1830–1911. This is the period immediately prior to and including the study period, so that the present study (1861–1911) can be placed in a wider perspective. The final part will consider the weaknesses in our knowledge.

This period of time has been described as 'making a nation within a nation'.[191] Scotland still retained her national distinctiveness, and this was apparent even in population movement.[192] During these years (1830–1914) the population of Scotland doubled, although this growth was not spread evenly throughout the regions, but concentrated in the Central Lowlands.[193] Scotland was part of a rapidly expanding world economy, having experienced a major social transformation in the period prior to 1830.[194] In 1830 however the assumptions, attitudes and experiences of a rural society still permeated much of Scotland, but by 1914 the entire population was more thoroughly urbanised.[195]

Macdonald's pioneering research on population movement identified three general causes or motives that encouraged out-migration: rural depopulation through changes in agricultural practices, the concentration of industrial development, mainly in the Central Lowlands, with a perceived better lifestyle, and finally poverty and poor-relief administration.[196] It is debatable whether these three causes are equally valid, but they do provide a framework for analysis.

Agriculture

By 1830 almost all the farmland in the Lowlands had been improved. This had considerably reduced the opportunities to acquire land, and increased the numbers dependent on wage labour. By the early twentieth century a diminishing proportion of the population lived in the rural areas, but as industrial development was confined to the densely populated but fairly narrow band of the Central Lowlands, most of Scotland was still essentially rural. In 1830 small scale domestic industry and agriculture were often practised together but this was to become increasingly threatened by greater specialisation in larger units. Handloom weaving for example began to decline in many areas by the 1850s.[197] Better transport facilities linked the Scottish regions, which improved the access to expanding markets but did not standardise agriculture. No single pattern of husbandry emerged; indeed areas of specialisation developed, with arable in the southeast, dairy farming in the southwest and livestock rearing in the northeast. Throughout central and southern Scotland the commercialisation of agriculture meant that labour was hired for six or twelve month periods and any surplus population was forced to migrate by the nature of the Scottish Poor Law and lack of housing other than that tied to the place of work. Additional labour needs were met by the employment of temporary migrants from the Highlands, Ireland, the larger towns and industrial villages.[198]

Throughout lowland Scotland there were increasing problems of attracting farm servants despite improving pay and conditions,[199] as workers preferred the attractions of urban life with less demanding work and more pay.[200] There had always been a marked shortage of accommodation for married farm servants, unless they were ploughmen in the Southeast and Fife, and so for the majority marriage meant leaving agricultural employment. The proportion of the national population employed in agriculture declined markedly over the period from 24.3% in 1841 to 10.6% in 1911.[201] This could have been due to the mechanisation of agriculture, but Devine cites contemporary opinion as being 'unanimous that most mechanical innovations were a consequence rather than a cause of labour shortage'.[202]

Much of the previous discussion also applies to the northeast, but here the enlarging of farms caused the displacement of small farmers from the 1840s, even though tilled land continued expanding until 1901 through the colonisation of uncultivated land. This did permit some small scale farming to continue,[203] and in this region crofters' children provided the majority of farm workers.

The Highlands cannot be considered as one unit, but rather as three regions and there was diversity even within these regions. Agriculture in the southern and eastern fringe resembled that further south, with family-size farms using wage labour, and consolidation was in progress.[204] Lobban's work on Greenock[205] shows that it was the increasing awareness of the benefits of town life, rather than eviction by landlords that caused out-migration from the southern fringe of the Highlands.[206] Further north and west large areas had been cleared for commercial sheep farms (Inverness alone had 700,000 sheep in 1880)[207] or, increasingly, for deer forests.[208]

On the western Highland seaboard the crofting system of farming was often unable to provide the bare necessities of life unless supplemented by temporary migration. Yet in 1831 the population in many crofting parishes was still rising[209] and social attitudes discouraged change. The climax came with the potato famine in the 1840s during which landlords encouraged and sometimes assisted the emigration of a redundant population.[210] Thereafter the removals were more subtle but still effective.[211] This pattern continued until the 1880s when, after considerable agitation, the Crofter Holdings (Scotland) Act of 1886 curbed the power of the landlords by giving crofters security of tenure. Nevertheless, the fundamental economic problems of the Highlands remained and may have been made worse by 'the freezing of the availability of land and so the structure of Highland society and economy'.[212]

Poverty And Poor-Relief Administration

Macdonald has argued that the lack of uniformity in the provisions of the poor law encouraged migration. There was a drift from unassessed parishes, which paid no poor relief, to assessed parishes who aided only 'the aged poor, impotent and decayed persons, who of necessity must live by alms'.[213] In rural areas 'poor-relief was meagre and unreliable or non-existent'.[214] However, Macdonald's analysis ended in 1851, when the New Poor Law of 1845 was only beginning to take effect. Thereafter the situation gradually improved,[215] as 'all parishes were compelled to raise money to relieve the poor'.[216] It was no longer necessary to migrate in order to obtain help, but it was still general practice to administer poor-relief on an out-door basis. For orphaned urban-born children, this could mean compulsory migration, as they were boarded with country families for a small fee.[217]

There were two famines in the Highlands where outside assistance was required. In the first, the mini-famine of 1836–7, the British Government recruitment policy for emigrants was specific; those subsidised had to be under 35 years and of good character.[218] A landlord might also provide free passages in order to secure clearances for sheep,[219] and 'philanthropy rode in tandem with landlord pressure to secure a vigorous exodus of the people'.[220]

In the major crisis of the period, the Highland famine, the state assumed responsibility for relief, but 'it allowed the detailed organisation of assistance to become the responsibility of the benevolent societies in the Lowlands, although the government officials still felt the need to influence the direction of their policies'. Emigration was assisted both by the landlords and the Highland and Island Emigration Society and almost 17,000 people left.[221]

Industrial Development

The proportion of the population in Scotland living in settlements of over 5,000 rose from 31.2% in 1831 to 58.6% in 1911.[222] This growth reflects the structural changes in the Scottish economy, which could only be achieved by considerable in-migration. There were new industries such as engineering, steelmaking and ship-building, and heavy industry thus replaced textiles as the leading sector.[223] The west of Scotland experienced the final decline of handloom weaving at the start of the period. In Ayrshire this deterioration provoked considerable emigration in the 1840s and 1850s,[224] but elsewhere weavers moved to new or expanding industries such as railways, iron and coal.[225] Industry grew, mechanised, but often remained essentially labour intensive.

Cities specialised in different industries; Glasgow had heavy industries, Dundee had textiles, while Edinburgh had a larger professional and service sector than the other major towns.[226] Thus the cities attracted different migrant populations, Dundee's textile mills attracting young females but relatively few males.[227] Potential migrants were aware of the comparative advantages of certain places, thus in 1911 the Census observes that the majority of male migrants from Lithlithgow (West Lothian), Perth and Sutherland went to Lanark, but most female migrants from Perth moved to Forfar (Angus) and from the other counties to Edinburgh (Midlothian).[228]

Industry did not develop at a steady pace with ever increasing growth but was subjected to troughs and booms. Treble has considered the construction industry, which employed approximately 7% of the occupied male labour force.[229] He found that between 1881–91, a poor decade for house building, the number of construction workers fell by 5.1%. In the subsequent decade, there was a vast increase in building work and employment increased by 43.4%. The following decade 1901–11 experienced another slump in building and the labour force contracted by 21.4%.[230] Clearly swings of this magnitude could not be accommodated easily by the labour force. In one decade the industry was attracting workers only to reject them subsequently. Some urban residents may have moved in and out of the trade, but the booms must have attracted vast numbers of in-migrants and the ensuing slumps probably encouraged out-migration and emigration.

ISSUES IN SCOTTISH POPULATION MOVEMENT 1830–1914

Throughout the period 1865–1910, the most popular destination for Scottish overseas emigrants was the United States.[231] Jerome first noted that the fluctuations in American immigration from Britain and Germany were linked to the American economic cycles, especially after 1870.[232] These fluctuations in the total number of emigrants from Scotland are apparent in the estimates by Flinn.[233] This distinctive pattern has been observed in several countries, and has been the source of considerable theoretical discussion.[234] However, it is the work of Thomas[235] that is of particular importance in this study because he has provided a theoretical framework linking the emigration and migration flows from Britain with America. He has argued that the British and American building cycles alternate. When the building cycle in America rose, it attracted capital from Britain and as employment improved emigrants were attracted to America. When however there was an industrial and building boom in Britain, potential emigrants migrate to British cities instead. This pattern is apparent in Scotland, in that the booms in the building cycle (which have already been considered) coincided with decades of low emigration and vice versa.

This study is mainly concerned with the question of how far Thomas's theory relates to Scottish population movement. Thomas has argued that rural areas were unable to absorb their natural increase, and therefore it was the rural–born population that was essentially mobile. In decades of industrial and building boom in Britain relatively few of these rural migrants emigrated, but in the decades of economic slump when investment was low, the same people were more likely to emigrate. Emigrants were therefore of rural origin.[236] There has been some regional research that supports the arguments on the rural origins of Scottish emigrants, for example that by Carter[237] and Harper[238] on out–movement from the northeast and the work by Devine on the Highland famine at the beginning of this period.[239] But the evidence of Stevenson and research by Erickson suggest that there was a large urban–born element amongst the emigrants. It is possible that as passenger lists recorded last address, some of the emigrants 'caught' by Erickson were rural-born, having migrated earlier.[240] Undoubtedly there is a need for more research on urban emigration. Thomas's theory is not without its critics, both from a theoretical perspective and from the results of Baines' research on England and Wales, which in fact showed that there was considerable urban–born emigration.[241]

Population movement is a broad term that includes both emigration and migration, and yet there is relatively little comparative work on emigration and migration. Thus Gray could fault Harper's work on 'the failure to discuss the relation between migration to other parts of Scotland and emigration'.[242] In most regions of Scotland it is simply not known whether out–movement was predominantly emigration or migration. Thus at present it impossible to provide a Scottish dimension to discussions of Thomas's theories on the mobility of the rural population.[243]

A comparative dimension is lacking in population movement, even where we already have some interesting research. For example, in temporary mobility, two distinctive types of movement have emerged. The first, within Britain, is the marginal, rural poor supplementing their income,[244] and the second, abroad, is skilled urban workers maximising their wages.

The research is restricted by its sources. We do not have adequate passenger lists and unlike Scandinavia, national registration did not exist. The relatively late introduction of registration of vital data in Scotland has also limited research. The registration of births, for example, does state the parish of parent's marriage, which could be a measure of population movement. The census has been used to measure total population loss, but the enumeration books, which provide a wealth of detail on movement (the birthplaces and occupations of all members of the family are stated) have only been used at the local level.[245] However, work on this source will remain very time consuming until the information in the books is computerised.

After 1861 the census provides a breakdown of the population of Scotland using a county-of-residence by county-of-birth. It does not supply a breakdown of ages other than above or below 20 years, but it does indicate where the residents of a county were born. Stage migration cannot be identified, as it does not record any intermediate moves. Information on stage migration could be gained at the parish level using the Census enumeration books to analyse the birthplaces of parents and siblings. Anderson and Morse have used census data to show which parishes were experiencing the greatest population gains or losses,[246] but it is still not known, even at the county level, which counties were losing mainly through migration and which through emigration. The census provides us with tabulations of the total migrant population, but it is impossible to tell whether these migrants were long time residents or newcomers. We cannot therefore identify a sudden increase in out-migration or an influx of newcomers.

It has already been emphasised that institutionally organised emigration tends to dominate research, because of the intractability and scarcity of other materials. Thus in the Highlands we know far more about the numbers involved in assisted rather than unassisted emigration.[247]

The census has provided estimates of aggregate net losses from Scotland in each decade, but we do not know which counties experienced the greatest proportional losses per head of population and whether this pattern changed over time. It is possible to estimate emigration from Scotland using Baines' method, if, instead of considering movement to other parts of Britain as out-migration (as Baines did), one regards it as emigration.

Erickson has found that the Lowland industrial counties were over-represented in Scottish emigration to the United States.[248] We do not know if this feature is restricted to the United States, occurred only in periods of exceptionally high emigration, or was actually a widespread phenomenon. Erickson has found several interesting differences between emigration patterns amongst Scots in the 1850s and those in the 1880s. Both studies were in periods of high emigration but the ratio of single to married male emigrants altered markedly between them. This clearly needs further investigation, as it is still not known if this was a national trait or a regional change, or whether the age at which people left was altering.

Relatively few studies really consider female emigrants at all, except as appendages to males or as children and many estimates of emigrants do not even disaggregate male and female movement.[249]. However Harper, in her study of emigration from the northeast, has recognised that despite their much smaller numbers female emigrants do justify separate consideration.[250]

In conclusion it has been argued that existing research shows that Scotland had developed a culture of emigration in particular, and to a lesser extent migration, prior to the period under review. There were a great many continuities in population movement as well as change, this should not surprise us, if somebody migrates or emigrates and are successful it is likely that others will emulate them. The period under consideration was one of rapid economic and social development which enabled Scotland to be described as a mature, urbanised, industrial society. Emigration in particular remained an important population movement, but we do not know the gender or age of emigrants and do not even know where they came from in Scotland. Far less is known about migrants, as there is not even quantitative evidence as to when people left, beyond information on the total life-time population.

Notes

1. Baines, *Migration in a Mature Economy*.
2. Dobson, *Scottish Emigration*, p10.
3. Devine, 'Social Responses to Agrarian Improvement' p. 149.
4. Ibid, pp. 148–68.
5. Flinn et al, *Scottish Population History*, pp. 162–71.
6. White, *Agriculture and Society*. pp. 152–60.
7. Whyte and Whyte, 'Continuity and Change' pp. 163–4.
8. Ibid. p. 150. For a more detailed explanation of the effects of the impact of changing farming practices on rural society see Devine, *The Transformation of Rural Scotland*. pp.110–64.
9. Devine, 'Social Responses to Agrarian 'Improvement' p. 153.
10. Sinclair, *OSA*. Vol. IV, Tortherwald, Dumfriesshire, p. 507
11. Lochart, 'The Planned Villages' pp. 257–9.
12. Sinclair, *OSA*. Vol. II, Ormiston, East Lothian, p. 542.
13. Fontaine, *History of Pedlars in Europe*, p. 8.
14. This paragraph is based on Dodgshon, 'Pretense of Blude' pp. 169–98.
15. This paragraph is based on Devine, 'The Highland Clearances'.
16. Whyte, 'Migration in early-modern Scotland' p. 98.

17. Whyte, 'Urbanization in early-modern Scotland' pp. 21–35. Much higher estimates can be found, (for example in Devine, 'Urbanisation' Table 1. p. 28). These estimates are.generally based on the work of De Vries which Whyte has questioned.

18. Dingwall, *Late Seventeenth Century Edinburgh,* pp. 186–96. Lovett, Whyte & White, 'Poisson Regression analysis' pp. 317–33. Whyte and Whyte, 'Patterns of Migration' have considered apprentices from Aberdeen and Inverness, pp. 80–92.

19. Sinclair, *OSA.* Vol. IV, Penpont, Dumfriesshire, p. 446.

20. Mitchison, *A History of Scotland*, pp. 358–9.

21. Sinclair, *OSA.* Vol. II, Prestonpans, East Lothian, p. 565–80.

22. Dingwall, *Late Seventeenth Century Edinburgh*, pp. 28–9.

23. Devine, 'Urbanisation' Table 1. p. 28.

24. It should be noted that this estimate included migrants that had not crossed a county boundary, a definition that is considerably broader than the one used in this study. Quoting 1851 Census Great Britain, Parliamentary Papers, 1852–3, LXXXV–LXXXVII, 'Birth Places of the People'. in Gray. 'Scottish Emigration' pp. 95–174.

25. Gray, 'Farm Workers' p. 21.

26. Gray, 'Scottish Emigration '. p. 165.

27. Campbell, 'Agricultural Labour' pp. 55–59.

28. Richards, *A History,* Vol. I, pp. 88–9.

29. Gray, *The Highland Economy* Table IXa, p. 255.

30. Devine, *The Great Highland Famine.* p. 197.

31. Sinclair, *OSA.* Vol. XII, Fortingal, Perthshire, p. 435

32. Lobban, 'The Migration of Highlanders'.

33. Withers, 'Highland Migration' pp. 395–418.

34. Withers, 'Highland-Lowland Migration, p. 79.

35. Withers, 'Highland Migration'. p. 399.

36. Lobban, 'The Migration of Highlanders'. p. 328.

37. Withers, 'Highland Migration' p. 401.

38. Whithers and Watson, 'Stepwise mobility' pp. 35–56.

39. Withers, 'Highland-Lowland Migration'. p. 79.

40. Withers, 'The Demographic History' Table 4.2 p. 149.

41. Campbell, 'Inter-county migration'. p. 59.

42. Withers, *Highland Communities* p. 36.

43. *Ibid.* pp. 16–8.

44. This year may have been exceptional, coming as it does immediately after the mini-famine in the Highlands in 1836–7.

45. Richards, *A History.* Vol. II. p. 237.

46. *Ibid.* p. 35.

47. Rodgers, 'The Labour force' p. 178.

48. Withers has estimated an age and sex structure for both 1851 and 1891. Withers, *Highland*. pp. 16–18.

49. Flinn, *Scottish Population* p. 478.

50. *Ibid*. pp. 467–72.

51. Table 6.3.5 recalculated measuring only movement at Whit term. All named individuals and spouses were considered adults, (Flinn notes that some farm servants classed as adults were very young). Total movement showed that 617 adults and 505 children migrated. *Ibid*. pp. 470–1.

52. Macdonald. *Scotland's Shifting Population*. p. 125.

53. Devine, 'Temporary Migration'. pp. 344–5.

54. Devine, *The Great Highland Famine*. pp. 146–70 and Devine. 'Temporary Migration'. pp. 344–59.

55. Macdonald, *Scotland's Shifting Population*. pp. 125–39.

56. Devine, *The Great Highland Famine*. p. 157.

57. Carter, *Farm Life*. p. 63.

58. Devine, *The Great Highland Famine*. pp. 156–65.

59. Devine, 'Temporary Migration'. pp. 344–54.

60. Brock, 'The Militia', pp. 135–51.

61. Lydon, 'The Scottish Soldier in Medieval Ireland' pp. 1–7.

62. Contamine, 'Scottish Soldiers in France' p. 26, fn.3.

63. Smout, Landsman & Devine, 'Scottish Emigration'. pp. 76–7.

64. Bieganska, 'A note on Scots in Poland' pp. 157–65.

65. Galloway & Murray, 'Scottish Migration to England' pp. 29–38.

66. Smout, Landsman & Devine, 'Scottish Emigration'. pp. 85–6.

67. Ibid. p. 85 and 90.

68. Almost 1,400 Scots arrived in Poland before 1600 and this number did not include any family they brought with them. Bieganska, 'A note on Scots in Poland' p. 162.

69. Riis, 'Scottish-Danish Relations' p. 89.

70. Fallon, 'Scottish Mercenaries'. p. 16.

71. Ibid. p. 233.

72. Smout, Landsman & Devine, 'Scottish Emigration' p. 84.

73. Although recruitment was generally profitable for landlords, this was not always the case see Alberg, 'Scottish Soldiers' p. 94.

74. Smout, Landsman & Devine, 'Scottish Emigration' p. 84 quoting Fallon 'Scottish Mercenaries'. p. 156.

75. Ibid. p. 79.

76. Simpson, 'Introduction' p. X.

77. Dobson, *Scottish Emigration*. pp. 31–4.

78. *Ibid*. pp. 66–80.

79. *Ibid.* p. 37.
80. Smout, Landsman & Devine, 'Scottish Emigration'. p. 87.
81. Cullen, 'Population Trends' p. 157.
82. Gibson & Smout, *Prices, Food and Wages,* pp. 164–7.
83. Scottish men and some of those from south of the border (Tynedale and Ribblesdale) seem to have been classified together. Fewster, 'The Keelmen', pp. 27–8.
84. Galloway & Murray, 'Scottish Migration to England' pp. 29–38.
85. Dingwall, *Late Seventeenth Century Edinburgh,* p. 251 citing New Kirk Session Minutes, 23 April 1706,
86. Lythe and Butt, *An Economic History of Scotland,* p. 97.
87. Boswell, *Life of Johnson,* p. 302.
88. Bumsted, *The People's Clearance.* p. 65.
89. For a detailed comparison with England and Wales see Bailyn. *Voyagers to the West.* p. 111.
90. Ferenczi and Wilcox, *International Migrations, Vol. 1.* p. 619–20.
91. Bailyn, *Voyagers to the West.* p. 111 & p. 140. Regions as defined in Scottish census and used in Flinn *Scottish Population History.* p. XXIII
92. Gray, *Scots on the Move,* p. 6.
93. McKay, 'The National Character' part 1, p. 9. For a list of Highland regiments created and disbanded between 1745 and 1800 see Barnes, *The Uniforms* p. 314–5.
94. Cain, *The Cornchest.* 13.
95. Devine, 'Landlordism'. p. 89.
96. Jones, 'Ulster Emigration, p. 58.
97. Evidence of R.J.Uniacke, the Governor General for the Province of Nova Scotia, in Report from the Select Committee on Emigration from the United Kingdom, p. 72.
98. Richards, *A History. Vol. I.* pp. 147–8.
99. Henderson, *Highland Soldier* pp. 53–82.
100. *Ibid.*
101. Smith, *Shetland Life,* p. 89.
102. Cain, *The Cornchest,* pp13–17.
103. McKay, 'The National Character' part 1, p. 9, based on McKerlie, 'An Account of the Scottish' p. 6
104. The regions classified by Flinn as 'Far North' and 'Highland Counties' have been considered as comprising the Highlands. They had a population of 314,608 in 1801, 330,299 in 1811 and 375,981 in 1821. While the higher figure for 1821 may reflect genuine population growth, it also includes men returned from the wars who were not included in the earlier censuses. Flinn, *Scottish Population History,* Table 5.1.2 pp. 304–5
105. Devine, *Clanship* p. 43.

106. Bumstead, *The People's Clearance.* p. 63.

107. Devine, 'Landlordism' pp. 89–90.

108. Richards, *A History. Vol. II.* p. 181.

109. Fn. 97.

110. Ibid. 567.

111. Devine, *The Great Highland Famine.* p. 200.

112. *Ibid.* pp. 200–1.

113. *Ibid.* p. 74.

114. Flinn, *Scottish Population History.* p. 438.

115. Anderson and Morse, 'The people' p. 22.

116. Brock, 'The militia', pp. 135–40.

117. Levitt & Smout, *The state of*

118. *Ibid.* pp. 238.

119. *Ibid.* pp. 236–7.

120. Gray, 'Scottish Emigration: the Social Impact' p. 97.

121. Brock, 'The Importance of Emigration'. pp. 104–34.

122. Baines, *Migration in a Mature Economy.* Table 4.5 p. 115.

123. Flinn, *Scottish Population History.* pp. 441–3.

124. *Census of England and Wales 1911,* Vol. IX. *Birthplaces of Persons enumerated in Administrative Counties, County Boroughs & c., and Ages and Occupations of Foreigners,* (London, HMSO 1913), [cd 7017], Table 6, Males and Females born in Scotland, Ireland, Islands in the British Seas, India and British Colonies and Dependencies and enumerated in England and Wales distinguishing those visiting from those resident in England and Wales in 1911. p. 242.

125. In 1851 there were 130,087 Scots in England and Wales but this had increased to 321,825 in 1911. *Ibid.* Table 8, Natives of several parts of the United Kingdom and elsewhere enumerated in England and Wales at each census 1851–1911, p. 243.

126. There were 726 Scots per 100,000 in England and Wales in 1851, this increased steadily to 974 in 1891–1901 and then fell in the final census (1911) to 892. *Ibid.* Table 9, Natives of several parts of the United Kingdom and elsewhere per 100,000 persons enumerated in England and Wales at each census 1851–1911, p. 243.

127. Flinn, *Scottish Population History.* Table 6.1.2 p. 442.

128. Anderson & Morse, 'The People'. p. 17.

129. Shannon, 'Migration', p. 83.

130. Anderson & Morse, 'The People'. p. 17.

131. *Census of England and Wales 1911,* Vol. IX. Table 6, p. 242. Females emigrants in England and Wales exceeded males from the following counties-of-birth: Aberdeen, Argyll, Banff, Bute, Caithness, Dumfries, Edinburgh (Midlothian), Elgin (Moray), Haddington (East Lothian), Inverness, Kincardine,

Kirkcudbright, Nairn, Orkney, Ross and Cromarty, Sutherland and Wigtown.

132. Mallet and Stevenson, 'Report', in *Census of England and Wales 1911,* Vol. IX. p. XIII.

133. Carrier and Jeffery, 'External Migration', p. 14.

134. Flinn *Scottish Population History,* p. 95.

135. Baines. *Migration in a Mature,* Table 4.5 p. 115.

136. Tranter, *Population and Society, p.* 29.

137. See for example Thomas, *Migration and Economic Growth* pp. 124–6.

138. Although Stevenson travelled to the United States in 1879, the book was not published until 1892 and so it is possible that the book is not entirely accurate. Certainly Raban who wrote the introduction considered it part fiction. However, Stevenson does stress that his purpose is to describe the type of people that emigrate. Stevenson, *The Amateur Emigrant. Part I,* pp. 5–6.

139. Flinn, *Scottish Population History.* Table 6.1.4, p. 447.

140. Stevenson, *The Amateur Emigrant.* p. 17.

141. See Table 11 for a list of counties classified as being industrial, defined as having less than 35% of the labour force employed in agriculture. Erickson 'Who were the English and Scots' Table 11, p. 377.

142. *Ibid.* Table 5, p. 362.

143. In a sample from 1828–54 male labourers were well represented but only 15% came from large towns. *Ibid.* pp. 364–8.

144. *Ibid.* p. 371.

145. Stevenson, *The Amateur Emigrant.* p. 14.

146. Harper, *Emigration* vol I and vol II.

147. Carter, *Farm Life.* p. 95.

148. Watson and Allan, 'Depopulation', pp. 31–46.

149. Thomas, *Migration and Economic Growt*h. p. 62.

150. Flinn, *Scottish Population History.* p. 453.

151. Murray, *The Scottish Hand Loom Weavers.* pp. 144–5.

152. Campbell, *The Lanarkshire Miners.* pp. 268–9.

153. Stevenson, *The Amateur Emigrant.* p. 17.

154. On the emigrant ship that Stevenson travelled two stowaways worked their passage. *Ibid.* pp. 51–64.

155. Campbell. 'Scotland', p. 2. using the evidence of Stevenson, *The Amateur Emigrant.* pp. 13–5.

156. Cousens, 'The Regional Pattern', pp. 119–34.

157. Devine, *The Great Highland Famine.* p. 200.

158. Harper, *Emigration Vol I.* p. 93.

159. Baines has pointed out that it took at least four or five weeks to cross the Atlantic by sail and steamships were a considerable improvement. However,

the contemporary evidence of Stevenson suggests that conditions in steerage class on the steamships was still very unpleasant, although the journey was much quicker. Baines, *Migration in a Mature Economy*, p. 33. Stevenson, *The Amateur Emigrant*. pp. 5–50.

160. This section is based on Baines, *Migration in a Mature Economy*, pp. 31–5.

161. Galloway & Murray, 'Scottish Migration to England' pp. 29–38.

162. Redford, *Labour Migration in England*.

163. Fewster, 'The Yarmouth Fishing Industry'. p. 101.

164. *Ibid*. p. 102.

165. Erickson, 'Who were'. pp. 347–81.

166. *Ibid*. pp. 366–7.

167. Harper, *Emigration*. Vol. II, pp. 161–6.

168. *Ibid*. Vol. I, pp. 254–9.

169. *Ibid*. p. 254.

170. Laslett, *Nature's Noblemen: The Fortunes of the Independent*. p. 35.

171. Jackson, *The British Whaling Trade*, p. 55.

172. Coull, *The Sea Fisheries*. p. 95.

173. *The Times,* August 24th. 1816, quoted in Shepperson, 'British Backtrailers'. p. 181.

174. Shepperson, *Emigration and Disenchantment,* p. 3.

175. Shepperson, 'British Backtrailers'. p. 183.

176. Shepperson, *Emigration and Disenchantment,* p. 78.

177. *Ibid*. pp. 186–7.

178. Skelly, *The Victorian Army*. pp. 22–7.

179. Ibid. 235–80.

180. Ibid. Table 6–7, p. 294.

181. The proportion of Scots in the British Army compared with those from other parts of Britain 1853–1859

	Average per million of the total population
England and Wales	8,421
Ireland	10,736
Scotland	11,614

McKerlie, *An Account of Scottish Regiments*, p. 40. I am very grateful to Mrs Edith Philip, the Librarian, Scottish United Services Museum, Edinburgh Castle, for drawing my attention to this paper and other relevant material.

182. I am very grateful to Thomas Mole, Honorary Secretary of the Scottish Military History for this information.

183. By 1856 several non-Scots had joined the regiment and the Scots-born fell to 91%. McKerlie, *An Account of Scottish Regiments*, pp. 27–8.

184. Cook, *Casualty Roll for the Crimea*, Appendix 1, no.13 p. 245.

185. Curtin, *Death by Migration*, p. 99.

186. Hanham, 'Religion and Nationality'. pp. 176–8.

187. Mitchell, *European Historical Statistics.* pp. 21–24.

188. Hanham, 'Religion and Nationality'. pp. 165–7.

189. Brock, 'Emigration by Default', pp. 17–19.

190. Baines, *Migration in a Mature Economy*, p. 10.

191. Morris, 'Introduction: Scotland, 1830–1914', pp. 1–7.

192. Baines, *Migration in a Mature Economy.* p. 45, fn.1.

193. Anderson & Morse, 'The People' p. 8.

194. Devine, 'Introduction'. pp. 1–8.

195. Campbell and Devine, 'The Rural Experience' p. 46.

196. Macdonald, *Scotland's Shifting Population.*

197. Gray, 'Scottish Emigration'. p. 154.

198. Devine, 'Temporary Migration' pp. 344–59.

199. Ploughmen, and those employed in the bothy and kitchen systems were all paid partly in kind. Campbell and Devine, 'The Rural Experience', pp. 51–7.

200. Devine, 'Woman Workers' pp. 98–123, and Devine, 'Scottish Farm Labour', pp. 243–255.

201. Campbell, 'Scotland'. Table 1.4, p. 14.

202. Devine, 'Scottish Farm Labour'. p. 251.

203. Carter, *Farm Life in Northeast Scotland.* pp. 53–7.

204. Devine, *The Great Highland Famine,* pp. 1–2.

205. Lobban, 'The Migration of Highlanders'.

206. Richards, *A History of the Highland Clearances.* pp. 181–2.

207. Devine, 'The Highland Clearances', p. 2.

208. Orr, *Deer Forests*, pp. 28–70 & 119–141.

209. Devine, *The Great Highland Famine.* Table 3.12 p. 73.

210. *Ibid.* pp. 192–225.

211. *Ibid.* pp. 212–43 and Orr, *Deer Forests,* pp. 119–41.

212. Campbell & Devine, 'The Rural Experience', p. 51.

213. In 1845 there were 650 unassessed and 230 assessed parishes. Macdonald, *Scotland's Shifting Population.* pp. 103–4.

214. *Ibid.* p. 105.

215. Patterson, 'The Poor Law in Nineteenth Century Scotland' pp. 171–193.

216. Crowther, 'Poverty, Health and Welfare', p. 268.

217. *Ibid.* p. 270.

218. Richards, *A History of the Highland Clearances.* Vol. II. p. 242.

219. This was the situation on the Mackenzie of Seaforth estates in 1838–41. *Ibid.* pp. 244–5.

220. *Ibid.* p. 245.

221. Devine, *The Great Highland Famine.* pp. 111–45.

222. Morris, 'Urbanisation and Scotland' Table 1, p. 74.

223. Campbell, 'Scotland'. p. 15

224. Murray, *The Scottish Hand Loom Weavers* p. 73.

225. Smout, *A History of the Scottish People* p. 402.

226. Morris, 'Urbanisation and Scotland', pp. 73–102.

227. Walker, *Juteopolis* pp. 1–31.

228. Census of Scotland 1911 Report on the Twelfth Decennial Census of Scotland, Vol. II [CD.6896] 1913, p. XCIII.

229. Treble, 'The Occupied Male Labour Force'. Appendix 1. pp. 195–6.

230. Ibid. p. 170.

231. Flinn, *Scottish Population History.* Table 6.1.7, p. 451.

232. Gould, 'European Inter-Continental Emigration' pp. 629–30. Jerome. *Migration and Business Cycles.*

233. Flinn, *Scottish Population History.* Table 6.1.4, pp. 446–7.

234. Gould, 'European Inter-Continental Emigration'. pp. 628–79.

235. Thomas, *Migration and Economic Growth.*

236. *Ibid.* pp. 124–6.

237. Carter, *Farmlife in North-East Scotland.* p. 95.

238. Harper, *Emigration from North-East Scotland.* vols. I & II.

239. Devine, *The Great Highland Famine.*

240. Erickson, 'Who were'. p. 355.

241. Baines, *Migration in a Mature Economy.* pp. 220–78.

242. Gray, 'Famine and Emigration'. p. 72.

243. Thomas, *Migration and Economic Growth.*

244. Devine, 'Temporary Migration'. pp. 344–59

245. See the work of Devine, *The Great Highland Famine.* and Withers on Aberdeen, Dundee, Perth and Stirling.

246. Anderson & Morse', The People'. pp. 21–2.

247. Devine, *The Great Highland Famine.* pp. 192–211.

248. Erickson, 'Who were'. p. 361.

249. See for example all the tables on emigration in Flinn, *Scottish Population History.* pp. 441–55.

250. Harper, *Emigration from North-East Scotland.* Vol. II, p. 231–87.

2

Sources and Methods

Discussions of data sources and methodology do not make exciting reading, and it is not essential to read this chapter in order to understand the main points of the analysis in the rest of the book. However this chapter aims to explain the methods and the assumptions behind the study as well as discussing the source material. The overall purpose of this research is to establish approximately how many people emigrated from and migrated within Scotland by county during the period 1861 to 1911. This type of study has never been attempted before on Scottish data, because the only available 'Government' statistics were considered inadequate for the task.[1] It was not until the publication of Baines' study of emigration in England and Wales, the product of twenty years research, that a proven method for the measurement of emigration became readily available.[2] The work of Baines was therefore the starting point for this study, although ultimately the methods used differed markedly in several respects. This will be considered subsequently. A discussion of the computer programming to calculate mobility will be confined to Appendix 1.

METHOD OF MEASURING POPULATION MOBILITY

Baines defined migration as being all population movement within the British Isles that crossed a county boundary and emigration as movement outwith Britain. The method of measuring migration and emigration appears superficially very simple. Firstly it is necessary to estimate how many people have left their county-of-birth between two consecutive censuses and then to establish how many have migrated to other counties. In theory the difference between the two estimates must represent the movement of people from that county abroad. However, additional information clearly has to be incorporated in the model, such as the number of births and deaths in the county under consideration and also the migrant deaths in all the receiving counties (all births in a county are, by definition, native). This procedure has to be applied to all the counties for the censuses under consideration. The estimation of the number of

47

emigrants from a county can therefore be described as the difference between the potential population of a county-of-birth (the native population including migrants from that county plus births minus deaths) and the actual native population at the subsequent census (including migrants from that county).

The methodology has three limitations, which are imposed by the data. Firstly, the census provides only a decennial 'snapshot' of all the migration flows that have occurred in the previous ten years. It therefore misses some population movements, because it ignores all the intervening moves a migrant might have made. Secondly, it is the sum total of population movement in a county and therefore the accurate measurement of both migration and emigration is masked by those people that return. Thirdly, there is no precise method of estimating the return flows despite the fact that they are an important phenomenon in this period.[3] These shortcomings have to be considered whenever analysis of the results is contemplated. Nevertheless, with regard to the accuracy of the arithmetic calculations, the main conclusions of the study do not depend on the estimates being exceptionally accurate.

A further weakness is due to the framework of measurement. The county is the smallest unit for which the census provides all the necessary data. The county is not however the ideal unit as it lacks consistency and uniformity, making comparisons between many counties impossible. In Scotland the counties vary enormously in population. In 1901 Kinross had the lowest population (6,981), whereas that of Lanark, the highest, was nearly 200 times greater with 1,339,327 people. The counties also vary considerably in area, Clackmannan being the smallest and Inverness the largest, some 80 times greater. Moreover, they are not homogeneous geographically, Perth, for example having a highland economy in the northwest but also forming part of the central industrial belt in the southeast. Rural counties with a major town such as Aberdeen or Ayr can have considerable rural-urban migration hidden within the county, whereas in counties such as Kinross or Sutherland the lack of any major town making rural-urban migration to another county more likely. Indeed even within entirely rural counties the direction of migration can vary. In the northwest Highland counties it has already been shown that the western crofting areas have a totally different pattern of migration to the inland farming communities. This variation cannot be distinguished using the county as the unit of measurement. Moreover, counties such as Kinross, which are small in area, tend to show an exaggerated degree of mobility simply because their ratio of boundary to area is greater than for larger counties. It is for this reason that the smaller counties will only be considered as part of a region for the purpose of drawing conclusions, even if many of the tables list the counties individually. This research is intended to establish migration trends and not absolute statistics, and the county can therefore be used as the unit for study despite its inadequacies. Finally, any estimates must be interpreted as an approximate figure for the county rather than the perfect answer.

This Scottish study cannot be a carbon copy of its southern counterpart, because although many of the problems inherent in Baines' data also exist in the Scottish context, other factors (to be considered hereafter) are peculiar to Scotland and require different solutions. Moreover, even the basic procedure could not be followed without modification of one of Baines' assumptions, which was that all population movement within Great Britain should be regarded as internal migration. Baines did not know the county-of-birth of out-migrants from England and Wales into Scotland. He distributed the total number of migrants as a percentage of every county, but allowed an increased proportion for those counties-of-birth near the Scottish border.[4] In Scotland a far greater proportion of a much smaller population migrated south, but again the county-of-birth was unknown, and numbers involved were too great a percentage to spread. Baines' assumption of an internal migration field embracing the entire British Isles had therefore to be abandoned, because it made the calculation of emigration impossible. A national 'Scottish' perspective has been adopted, which means that all population movement out of Scotland is considered to be emigration, even if it is only to England or Wales.

Other modifications had to be applied to the Scottish material in order to test its accuracy and standardise it will be considered subsequently. Finally, the use of a computer, which Baines did not have, has enabled the methodology and the data to be more rigorously tested.

THE SOURCE MATERIAL

The main sources of information for this research are: (I) the published 'Birth-Places of the People' and 'Ages of the People' tabulations in the decennial Censuses; (II) a manuscript source, the enumeration books; and (III) the tables of births and deaths in the published Detailed Annual Reports of the Registrar General. The census will be analysed first, and then enumeration books which are the primary source from which the census was derived. This discussion will end by considering the Detailed Annual Reports. It should be stressed that none of these sources was intended specifically for emigration research and caution must be exercised when using them for that purpose.

1. The Census

The 1861 Census was the first produced in Scotland, and followed the style of the earlier national censuses which were compiled in England, but included Scotland and used the county as the unit of measurement. In the Scottish census the thirty three Scots counties were arranged in geographical order, so that a zigzag line beginning at the north of Scotland and carried to the south passed successively through every county. 'In every series of tables therefore Shetland is No.1, Aberdeen No.10, Lanark No.23, Edinburgh No.25 and Dumfries No.31'.[5] This geographical system of numbering counties did not change until the 1911 Census, when they were reorganised alphabetically. The Census did not use the accepted name for some counties, for example Midlothian is referred to as Edinburgh.[6] The traditional county names will be used throughout this book including those in the alphabetically organised tables, although where feasible the alternative name will also be shown. Frequently the county name is the same as that of a major town within that county. Here the name alone will always refer to the county and the town or city will always have 'town' or 'city' written after it.

The Census used several county frameworks for its tabulations and these experienced boundary reorganisations in 1891. The two county units that concern this study are the civil and registration counties. The 'traditional' Scottish county was known as the civil county and was an area administered by Sheriffs and Justices of the Peace. To complicate matters still further, until 1891 thirteen civil counties 'possessed detached enclaves situated wholly within neighbouring counties'.[7] Nairn for example had five, and the civil county boundaries frequently crossed parish boundaries. A new arrangement of county boundaries was devised in Scotland for the purposes of recording vital data and census material, giving rise to the registration county.[8] These registration boundaries were more likely to follow the older parish boundaries, and so did not necessarily coincide with the 'traditional' civil counties; at its most extreme, in both Lanark and Renfrew the civil and registration counties contain quite dissimilar sized populations, the differences being significant enough to produce very different percentage rates of growth. In Renfrew, for example, between 1871 and 1881 the registration county growth rates are $+22.3\%$ for males and $+20.6\%$ for females, whereas in the civil county growth appears less remarkable (16.7% and 14.4% respectively). Amendments were made to the registration districts throughout the period up to 1891 and these account for the majority of the boundary changes. A more major adjustment of boundaries occurred in the 1891 census and thereafter many civil and registration boundaries were common. Although henceforth the birthplace tabulation was listed in civil county units, it was not until the 1911 Census that all county statistics in the census used this system.

The system for classifying residents was very similar in both the English and Welsh and the Scottish censuses, which simplifies the collation or comparison of statistics. In the Scottish county-of-birth tables, only people born in Scotland were enumerated by county. People from the rest of Britain only had their country of birth defined as England, Wales, Ireland or the Islands of Man, Guernsey and Jersey. Those born abroad were defined in a series of categories which changed and expanded with each census.

It has already been noted that the 1861 Census was the first produced in Scotland. With regard to the birthplace tabulations, it considerably improved upon the 1851 Census by increasing the number of categories of information for each county from two to four (male, female, above and below 20 years), and this does provide a finer breakdown of the population than was for example available in the comparable data for England and Wales. Starting this research in 1861 has enabled the study to take advantage of all the censuses containing these four classifications of age and gender up to the First World War.

The county-of-birth of Scots migrants was not normally provided in the English and Welsh and the Irish censuses. There is, however, one exception; the 1911 Census for England and Wales. This enumerates the county-of-birth and gender of and it also differentiates between residents and visitors.[9] However, these data may not be of value for much of the study period, as it has been shown that in England and Wales the counties exporting most population were not consistent over a long period of time.[10] It would therefore be unwise to extrapolate too far back in time from the 1911 material without further evidence. For the majority of the period under consideration, the lack of county-of-birth data in the rest of the British Isles has meant that inter-county migration cannot be measured with any degree of accuracy across the countries of the British Isles. The English and Welsh and the Irish censuses do, however, provide data on numbers of resident Scots and analysis of where they stay using the county unit for measurement. Approximately 7% of all Scots in the United Kingdom lived outside Scotland between 1861 and 1911.

The age-structure of the Scottish counties was also published in the Census.[11] The titles of the tables show that the tabulations were not necessarily intended primarily for information on age-structure, but for discussion on marital status or educational needs. The data provided therefore vary substantially between censuses. The 1861 and 1911 censuses record a category of 'age not stated',[12] so presumably in the remaining tabulations such individuals were spread proportionally throughout the age-bands, or ages simply guessed. Some censuses provided more detail than others, but it was possible to establish from every census an age profile for both sexes with children under five years split into age-bands of one year, and five year thereafter.

2. The Enumeration Returns

The hundred years rule means that the enumeration returns books up to and including 1891 are available and without these books the reconstruction of the 1891 pre-revision census would have been impossible. Each registration district was subdivided for enumeration purposes. In a rural area several enumeration books comprise a registration district, but as already noted, in a city the registration district may be sub-divided so that there are numerous enumeration books. 'When the Registration Act came into operation in 1855, the whole of the registration districts into which Scotland was then divided received a number, so that the districts were consecutively numbered 1–901 (in the same geographical arrangement as the counties, each county having a consecutive group of numbers for the districts). For the sake of reference these numbers have been considered permanent and fixed, so that when additional districts were added they were distinguished as a, b or c; for instance Eckford Rd. 789a; Edgerston Rd. 789b, or if a district were divided, such as Edinburgh or Glasgow, the divisions were numbered 1 to 5 or 1 to 10, as the case might be, retaining the original number for the complete district'.[13] This system was retained throughout the study period with only minor modifications although amendments were made to boundaries of the registration districts.

During the period for which enumeration books are available, the householder was given a schedule, which he was expected to complete, aided if necessary by the Enumerator. The Enumerator then copied particulars from the schedules into the enumeration book, checking them and totalling the number of males, females and households on each page. The county Registrar then checked the books for errors in classification, arithmetic problems and also for duplication or omission of households. The books were then sent to Edinburgh. It is these books and not the original schedules that have been preserved.[14] A copy of the householder's schedule is printed in all the censuses with the exception of those of 1861 and 1911. Typical of the early instructions on how to fill in county-of-birth questions is that on the Householders schedule for 1881 which states 'Where born. Opposite the names of those born in Scotland write the county and town or parish...'[15] The problem with this seemingly straightforward instruction is that it does not define whether the unit of enumeration is the civil or the registration county. This is a potential source of error, as it is liable to create spurious migration in areas where the two county boundaries differ. This form of migration can be defined as migration artificially created by the lack of consistency in the definition of county boundaries, rather than by the actual movement of people, so that a person who has never moved is nevertheless recorded as a migrant.

The enumeration books were very important in this study in six ways. Firstly, they were used to check whether natives were recording their birthplace in civil or registration counties. [16] The second use was to make a complete recount of the county of Nairn and thus use it as a test case in order to discover how the counties were being tallied. They were also consulted wherever registration and civil county boundaries differed; fortunately the enumeration books were available for the entire period when this problem occurred (1861–91). Fourthly, they were used to standardise the county boundaries when there was a boundary change prior to 1891. Fifthly, the books were referred to in order to create an 1891 pre-boundary reform set of county units.[17] This meant that two sets of county-of-birth data for 1891 became available, one using the old and the other the revised county units. Finally, the books were sampled to establish a migrant age-structure.

There were no collation or correction marks on the 1861 and 1871 enumerator's returns with regard to birthplace information, although arithmetic corrections of numbers of males, females and households were fairly common. This is a problem as it makes it impossible to check how a tally clerk might have transcribed a county-of-birth query. Thereafter red and blue pencils were used to distinguish natives of the county from outsiders (sometimes to the point of obliterating information). It was very rare for county-of-birth information to be amended; if only the parish or village was provided the county generally was not added to the enumeration book, and when a person was born abroad it was often not clear whether they were a British Subject or not.

3. The Detailed Annual Reports

When civil registration began in 1855, the returns show that it was 'very accurate from the start'. Abstracts were published, but these offer 'little more than tabulation of abstracts of returns'.[18] It is the processed data, which were presented in the Detailed Annual Reports and which were published later, that provide the material used in this study.[19] The births and deaths layout was consistent throughout the period 1861 to 1910, but in 1911 the approach was changed and data for that, the final year of this study, were unusable.[20] The information on births and deaths was published on a pre-revision registration county framework until 1892. Thereafter (1893)[21] it was tabulated in post-revision registration county units and indeed the revised registration county boundaries had their populations estimated for the 1881 census. Births and deaths were tabulated by sex and county, and the age at death was provided in impressive detail.[22] Babies were classified at three months, six month and one year. Children, aged between one and five years, had their deaths collated annually, and thereafter deaths were tallied in quinquennial age-bands up to a hundred years and above.

THE STANDARDISATION OF SOURCE MATERIAL

The quality of the source material is always important in research, but 'a residual method of estimating migration (the only possible way of estimating migration from the census) is totally dependent on the quality of the data',[23] as any under-recording will lead to an under-estimation of emigration and vice versa. This section will consider potential errors in the source material and how these problems have been minimised. It is almost inevitable that in any census some people are missed and others who are perhaps travelling are recorded in different locations as both resident and visitor. It is unrealistic to assume complete accuracy in the initial enumeration, and although some errors may cancel themselves out, other errors in tallying have probably crept in.

The Birthplace Information

The starting point for testing the data was the census because it was important to establish that the tabulations of birthplace information were accurate. There were several possible sources of error. First, were people recording their county-of-birth correctly? Secondly, was the tallying in this enumeration accurate? Finally how, could the differing county frameworks be reconciled?

In the Scottish Census prior to 1891, the birthplace tables used the registration county as the base unit. It was therefore important to establish whether natives were recording their birthplace on a registration or civil county framework. To test this, the recorded county-of-birth was examined in four enumeration districts with a wide geographical spread and which were known to lie across the boundary between two civil counties.[24] It is clear that people were recording their place-of-birth in civil counties, despite the fact that the birthplace data was enumerated in a registration county unit. In the most extreme example, in 1861 only 4.4% of the residents of Reay considered themselves to be Caithness-born and the overwhelming majority (91.7%) identified themselves as Sutherlanders by birth, despite the fact that they were residents in and were being recorded in Caithness registration county. This problem will be considered in more detail subsequently.

With regards to birthplace information, it can be concluded that, like that of occupation data, was probably not counted locally, because there is no evidence of such calculations in the enumeration books. (Although the later books 1881 and 1891 have coloured markings to differentiate information, and occasionally a county name is added, there are still no birthplace tallies on the books). Neither are there any instructions to Officers to complete the task.[25] Moreover, in the 1901 Preliminary Report, the Registrar refers to the 'summaries' prepared locally before being sent to Edinburgh. These 'summaries' were collated centrally and were published in the first volume of the report.[26] The county-of-birth information is included in the second volume and this seems to imply later tallying of this data. The centralised count of the data would ensure that a uniform approach was adopted with regard to the county boundary problem.

As it is assumed that the collation of birthplace data was centralised it follows that if one county were tallied manually it would probably be a fair test of how the other counties had been enumerated. The county of Nairn was therefore chosen to check whether the civil county unit that the native-born residents identified themselves with and recorded as their county-of-birth was being converted at a later stage to a registration county framework. Nairn was chosen because it was one of the smaller counties and there was a considerable discrepancy between the boundaries and the size of the population in the civil and registration counties, and would thus be a satisfactory test of whether or not it was feasible to convert the data to a civil county unit. It was hoped that this would make the identification of problems easier.

Using the 1861 enumeration returns for all the registration districts in the registration county of Nairn the total population was counted. The results indicated that civil county birthplace information do appear to have been calculated on a registration county base. This exercise was only possible because the enumeration books were available. Parts of adjoining registration counties were therefore added to Nairn where they fell within the civil county and other areas within the registration county were deducted because they were not in the civil county. By converting the data to the civil county it was hoped to show how much spurious migration was being created by errors in the original data. The registration county did indeed underestimate migration from Inverness by 8.5% and exaggerate that from Elgin (Moray) by 9.5%. Clearly the county could have been converted arithmetically to the civil county base, but if there was a strong bias caused by distortion in the direction of the differing boundaries, it would not be revealed by an arithmetic calculation of the boundary changes.

In retrospect it appears that Nairn was probably not an ideal choice to use as a 'guinea-pig', as it had an exceptionally mobile population. The 1861 statistics show that Nairn was the only county north of Dunbarton with less than 60% of residents native-born. The risk of spurious migration was even more significant in a less mobile population. Eightly-seven percent of the population of the registration county of Caithness were natives of that county, there were relatively few migrants and yet spurious migration meant that migrants were over-estimated by 17% and for those migrants from Sutherland the error was even greater, the over-estimation being 63%.[27] This inaccuracy was due to the registration district of Reay (civil county of Sutherland and registration county of Caithness), where an incredible 91.7% of the total population were spurious migrants. Moreover, the risk of spurious migration varied according to age and sex. In the example of Sutherland migrants to Caithness (Table 2.1), spurious migration is much greater for persons less than 20 years (63.8% for males and 65.5% for females) than in the older age-group (29.1% for males and 34.5% for females). This was because children and young adults were more likely to be resident in their county-of-birth than older people, but it implies a marked and quite erroneous migration eastward out of Sutherland.

Table 2.1. A Comparison of the Age and Gender of Sutherland-Born Migrants in the Civil and Registration Counties of Caithness in 1871 Showing Spurious Migration.

	MALES		FEMALES	
	<20years	>20years	<20years	>20years
Registration county	309	766	282	946
Civil county	112	543	100	620
Difference between registration and civil county	63.8%	29.1%	65.5%	34.5%

Civil county Data taken from the *1871 Census Vol. II* pp. 176–184. The registration county information was reconstructed using the enumeration books for 1871.

Obviously it was important to create a dataset that was as free from spurious migration as possible. It was therefore decided to reconstruct the county-of-birth enumeration on the civil county unit, which would provide data that would not create spurious migration. Moreover, enumeration books were available for the entire period when this problem was likely to occur, that is up to and including 1891. The amendments could therefore be made by direct reference to the books. There were two areas with distinctive problems, which could not be standardised in the normal way. These places will now be considered.

The civil county of Nairn had an unforeseen and unique problem in the anachronistic detached portion of Urquhart and Logie-Wester buried in the Black Isle, which while legally part of Nairn the residents considered themselves to all intents and purposes as part of Ross and Cromarty. For this reason all estimates and tables in the present study up to 1891[28] will assume Urquhart and Logie-Wester is included in Ross and Cromarty.

Another procedure has had to be adopted for Lanark and Renfrew, whose common boundary ran through the city of Glasgow. Here, as has already been shown, the difference in population between the civil and registration counties was very significant. Moreover, many people recorded their birthplace as Glasgow without defining the county. It has therefore been decided to combine the two counties for analysis purposes. The calculations for Lanark and Renfrew are carried out using modified registration counties and not on civil counties, and conversions of data between the two counties have not been attempted.[29]

The Reorganisation of the County Boundaries in 1891

In 1891 both the civil and registration counties were reorganised and Flinn is incorrect in his assertion that the revised county framework was not used in the census until the 1901.[30] In fact although the first volume of the 1891 Census published data using the old pre-revision county units, the second volume used the revised civil counties and the latter included the birthplace enumeration. It was therefore necessary to establish exactly how the enumeration had been organised in 1891 and the county of Nairn was tallied again. This examination showed that the 1891 enumeration books used the pre-revision boundaries and letters in the unedited letterbooks confirm that this was the planned arrangement. It was also stipulated that any proposed boundary amendments should be annotated.

The examination of the enumeration books for the county of Nairn contained a considerable number of notes on boundary changes. Nevertheless, the count revealed that despite minor discrepancies there had been no attempt to adjust the birthplace data to the revised counties, because if such an attempt had been made the discrepancy would have been much greater. The enumeration books were marked to distinguish natives and outsiders, but the system remained the same, even if a revised county boundary meant a change of county in the middle of the book, at that point the colour marking system ought to have been reversed or amended. This supports the earlier conclusion that there was no attempt to adjust the birthplace information despite the boundary changes. Indeed, in view of the scale of the task it is difficult to see how the Census Officers could have revised the entire country's data with any accuracy. It was decided that as there did not appear to have been any amendments to the 1891 enumeration books, the post-revision data had been calculated using pre-revision units for place-of-birth information.

Standardising the Birthplace Tabulations to One Year

The 1851 census was rejected for research purposes because it had a different and less satisfactory classification of persons, while the incredible carnage of men in the First World War meant that it was quite impossible to use the residual method of calculating emigration after the 1911 census. There was however, a further problem in that the data for the period 1861 to 1911 was not compatible because of the major boundary changes in 1891. This created two short compatible county-of-birth datasets (1861– 1881 and 1891–1911) but neither was long enough to be a satisfactory data source, an alternative solution was sought. The county of Elgin (Moray) was chosen to test whether it was possible to standardise enumerated data for the entire period (1861 to 1911). Elgin had an unusually large number of boundary adjustments between the civil and registration counties (ten separate districts were involved) and conversion to a standard unit was likely to be complicated. Furthermore, the population was not too large (43,431 in 1891).

It was found to be quite easy to standardise the data from 1861 up to 1891 and again it was possible to adjust the data back from 1911 to 1891; however no satisfactory method could be found to adjust all the data to either the pre- or the post-revision boundaries. Thus it was decided to produce two birthplace enumerations for 1891, one before and the other after the county boundary revision of that census (to be known hereafter as the 1891 pre-revision or post-revision enumerations).[31] All the pre- and post-revision enumerations were standardised to the two 1891 county bases.

The checking of birthplace tallying after 1891 cannot be aided by the enumeration books, which are still protected by the 'One Hundred Years Rule'. Yet census enumeration continued to be taken in registration districts, even though not all counties shared common civil and registration county boundaries. It was impossible to discover if an arithmetic or manual conversion of birthplace data from registration to the civil counties was applied. As has already been argued an arithmetic conversion would have an increased risk of spurious migration. The present study had no alternate but to assume that the conversation of data was satisfactory.

A second difficulty with migration data in this period arises because many migrants would probably continue to record their birthplace in the pre-revision civil county units. However, this is likely to become a decreasing problem, firstly because an increasing number of people will be born in the revised civil counties while the proportion born in the pre-revision counties will decline, and secondly because although there were massive amendments to the county boundaries the majority of the population was not affected by them. The two 1891 enumerations do reveal a different percentage of native-born inhabitants in many counties and almost all show a decline except Stirling and Nairn.[32] Clearly there is an increased risk of spurious migration in this post-boundary revision census enumeration as shown by Clackmannan (Table 2.2).

Table 2.2. The Significance of the 1891 Revision of County Boundaries and the Effect of these Changes thereafter in the County of Clackmannan.

County-of-Birth	1891 Pre-revision civil county*	1891 Post-revision civil county*	1891 Percentage change from pre- to post-revision county	1901	1911
Clackmannan	58.42	52.38	*-10.34*	63.70	63.35
Perth	7.26	6.96	*-4.13*	4.72	3.45
Stirling	7.21	15.48	*+114.70*	5.46	5.39

* percentage of the total population of the civil county of Clackmannan

After the 1891 boundary revision Clackmannan native-born residents decline by 10.3%, but the migrants resident in that county vary in their experience. Residents from Perth decline by only 4.1%, rather less than the native-born and those recorded from Stirling increase significantly by 114.7%. This, it must be stressed, is entirely the result of boundary amendments creating spurious migration; the calculations of civil counties are based on the same census enumeration books. The problem of spurious migration created by this 1891 boundary revision remains a possible source of error throughout the remaining study period, but all births hereafter are recorded in the revised counties and the death of older residents and migrants means the error is one of declining importance. Indeed Table 2.2 also suggests that by the 1901 Census the birthplace enumeration in Clackmannan had reverted to the 'normal' pattern, native-born residents having increased from 52.4% to 63.7% and Stirling-born migrants declined from 15.5% to 5.5%. Clearly the effects of the 1891 revision were soon dissipated.

The Lack of Clear Definition of Age in Birthplace Tabulations

It was decided to take advantage of the fact that the Scottish county-of-birth enumeration categorises persons by age, as well as gender. This additional breakdown of data by age is a considerable advantage to the research. The measurement of the age distribution of migrants is an important factor in the calculation of migrant death rates and any information that can aid that research is of immense value. However, it is important to assess the accuracy of the information on age. Birthplace information was split into two age categories 'under 20 years' and 'above 20 years', and this left the categorisation of 20-year olds very vague. The 1851 Census which included Scotland, but was produced in England, defined the age groups more precisely as 'under 20 years' and '20 years and upwards'.[33] In Scotland the age groups in birthplace data were not defined more clearly until 1901 when the descriptions 'under 20 years' and '20 years and upwards' were introduced.[34] It has been assumed that as both the 1851 and 1901 definitions of age are the same, it was also used in the intermediate censuses, despite the sloppy definition. Moreover, in the more detailed information on county age-structure, the population was classified in quinquennial age-bands, and the population under 20 years equalled that in the birthplace estimates.[35] Thus 'under 20 years' and '20 years and upwards' will be assumed throughout this study.

The registration of births had only begun in 1855 (much later than in England) and it seemed possible that people might have only a vague idea of their age. Certainly the number of persons enumerated in the censuses with ages between 95 and 105 years declines as the study period progresses, a feature tabulated in the 1911 Census.[36] There is a gradual decrease in the percentage of persons under 20 years and an increase in those between 20 and 69. Both sexes remain fairly constant in the over 70 years age-band. The decrease in the percentage of males under 20 years begins after the 1881 Census and by then the oldest people to have their births registered were 26 years. This decline cannot therefore be interpreted as a consequence of registration. Clearly Scots had a fairly accurate idea of their age, even if the very old may have been prone to exaggeration.

Checks by Computer on the Source Material

In this study all the data in its original form were entered on computer except the birthplace tabulations, which had been corrected manually first. Two checks were applied to the data once it was on the computer. The first was to check the original tallying and the correct transcription of data. The data was aggregated in both the x and y directions and compared automatically with the totals provided. This cross-tabulation meant errors were easily identified and amended. The second check was similar to one used by Baines. His procedure is based on the assumption that 'current migration makes a relatively unimportant contribution to the size of the lifetime migrant population compared to previous migration and the effects of mortality'. He searched for enumeration errors by fitting a trend 'to the most important migrant populations within each county'. He compared the population of native-born and migrants in counties from one census to the next and where there appeared 'a large deviation from trend the equivalent native…or migrant…population of adjoining counties were checked to see if they exhibited a comparable deviation from the trend'.[37] If a comparable deviation did occur in an adjoining county he presumed an enumeration error.

The procedure for investigating enumeration errors in Scotland was simplified by having all the relevant data on a computer. The number of residents from every county within a county was shown as a percentage of the total for that county. The data were reorganised so that for every county, census years were shown consecutively. The data thus organised were very easy to check visually on a print-out. Table 2.3 has been constructed from the print-out to show the percentage of native-born residents enumerated in the counties between 1861 and 1911. It can be seen that generally there is a steady relationship between consecutive years, be it a decline or (less commonly) a rise. Where there is a pronounced deviation, other than the inevitable one between the two censuses in 1891, it has been investigated by referring back to the original data as well as to trends in adjoining counties. In 1871 for example, the proportion of native-born in the population of Kirkcudbright rose markedly from 71.98% in 1861 to 79.41% in 1871 and then returned to 68.86% in 1881. The migrant populations were compared and in all the significant populations, including the English and Irish, a marked decline was found. As this was very unlikely to be an enumeration error, different reasons had to be sought. Around that time there was a serious slump in the textile industry of Gatehouse-of-Fleet, the only significant industry in Kirkcudbright, so it seems likely that the more mobile immigrant and migrant populations moved elsewhere. There is no comparable drop in the native population, hence the significant increase in the percentage of native-born. In contrast, a marked decline in the proportion of native-born of Selkirk in the same census year (1871) is probably the result of the rapid growth of industry in Galashiels attracting in-migrants. In no case where a deviation from the normal was observed could it be concluded that enumeration errors were responsible.

*Table 2.3. The Percentage of Native-Born Residents
Enumerated in Civil Counties 1861–1911*

CIVIL COUNTY	CENSUS YEAR						
	1861	1871	1881	1891	1891 pre-revision	1901 post-revision	1911
Aberdeen	85.33	85.39	85.09	85.24	84.89	84.42	83.24
Argyll	83.44	80.90	76.10	74.77	74.91	72.76	68.74★
Ayr	75.66	77.29	77.28	77.27	77.25	75.30	75.15
Banff	77.30	78.15	77.44	76.70	77.12	76.53	75.86
Berwick	72.23	72.79	71.77	71.90	71.98	68.60	66.55
Bute	59.39	55.26	53.15	51.53	51.53	49.94	48.98
Caithness	89.44	90.71	89.83	90.54	90.54	89.85	89.84
Clackmannan	61.53	60.23	59.94	58.42	52.38	63.70	63.35
Dumfries	80.98	81.48	76.28	74.04	74.03	71.47	68.67
Dunbarton	49.53	48.94	46.17	45.12	43.64	48.35	48.06
Edinburgh (Midlothian)	60.72	57.63	56.78	59.61	59.60	59.37	62.59
Elgin (Moray)	71.82	71.36	71.85	72.13	71.22	68.98	68.48
Fife	84.00	83.80	81.20	77.67	76.56	73.52	67.50★
Forfar (Angus)	72.92	71.76	72.07	73.93	73.93	75.93	76.54
Haddington (East Lothian)	70.62	70.25	68.32	66.93	67.06	61.82	57.65
Inverness	84.34	82.80	79.83	79.00	78.38	75.11	74.40
Kincardine	75.07	73.40	70.73	69.25	69.35	58.39	55.69
Kinross	63.76	60.86	56.86	51.31	47.88	46.77	43.22
Kirkcudbright	71.98	79.41	68.86	69.99	69.99	65.75	62.86
Lanark ★★	57.31	57.74	59.69	61.68	61.68	63.52	68.05
Linlithgow (West Lothian)	55.57	57.96	56.97	55.28	55.28	54.68	55.22★
Nairn ★★★	57.36	58.50	56.20	57.62	57.23	54.13	50.84
Orkney	91.94	93.55	92.67	92.67	92.67	90.06	92.39
Peebles	55.72	52.22	48.96	48.10	47.93	46.94	46.20
Perth	79.10	76.47	72.42	69.69	70.11	67.10	64.44
Renfrew ★★	58.22	56.62	56.80	60.88	60.89	60.53	58.89
Ross and Cromarty ★★★	90.03	89.50	88.45	87.54	87.47	86.21	80.85★
Roxburgh	67.17	70.54	68.48	68.86	68.77	68.30	65.83
Selkirk	53.68	38.98	46.90	43.31	42.76	56.28	54.35
Shetland	97.66	97.58	94.74	94.39	94.39	93.15	90.79
Stirling	64.13	63.87	62.49	61.27	61.47	60.22	60.48
Sutherland	87.60	86.57	83.87	84.28	84.28	81.54	79.18
Wigtown	74.59	77.57	78.17	79.82	79.82	79.24	78.00

★   Members of the Royal Navy have been included in the count (*1911 Census*, Vol. II p. 43).

★★   Lanark and Renfrew were not converted to civil counties but remained Modified registration counties until the 1891 revision of boundaries.

★★★   Data adjusted so that the detached portion of Nairn (Urquhart and Logie-Wester) is included in Ross and Cromarty between 1861–91 pre-revision censuses.

The lack of enumeration errors in the data suggests that the census enumeration was well executed. Moreover, the most critical counties for enumeration errors in Scotland (Lanark and Renfrew) were never converted to the civil county framework in the period up to 1891 but remained as modified registration counties, and no attempt was made to adjust data when the correction would have involved the boundary between these two counties in Glasgow.[38] Thus by not amending Lanark and Renfrew, the introduction of errors arising from such a correction may well have been avoided. Elsewhere for the period up to and including 1891 data had already been 'double checked' manually by the author in the process of converting from the registration to the civil county. It can therefore be argued that the lack of enumeration errors discovered at this stage is not altogether surprising. However, the data produced as a result of checking for deviant trends has provided a useful analytical tool.

The standardisation of Scottish data has meant that the standardised data covers a longer period than the comparable English study and has a finer breakdown of the age of residents. The procedure for investigating enumeration errors in Scotland was simplified by having all the relevant data on a computer.

Differences Between the Original Method Devised for England and Wales and the Present Study of Scotland

The method of establishing the volume of population movement in Scotland uses similar published data sources to those of Baines, that is the census tabulations and the annual records of births and deaths, but the way in which these data were used differs fundamentally from the original study. Baines used the same age ratios for current migrants of both sexes in every county and in every census.[39] These were fixed variables and the total number of current migrants was only influenced by age-specific mortality, calculated per 1,000 of the population, which itself was modified by what Baines described as the 'nurture assumption'. This was based on the argument that migrants were likely to be healthier than the indigenous population and were therefore given a lower age-specific death rate than the native population, for which the death rate was correspondingly increased.

The Scottish study has made considerable use of two large samples which attempt to establish the age-structure of the migrant population. This has resulted in the counties-of-residence being divided into four categories with different migrant age-structure ratios for each sex. During computation the number of migrants in each county remained unaltered, but the age-bands were expanded from two to sixteen. This has been achieved by applying one of the four migrant age-structure ratios, devised on a basis of population growth or decline and computed for each census year. Current migrants were therefore established as a result of the difference between the migrant age-structure with deaths applied in one census and the migrant age-structure ten years later. The migrant age-structure was categorised according to population growth or decline and was therefore probably more precise than Baines' work, as some variation in migrant age-structures doubtless occurred in England too. Moreover, in Scotland it was found that the age-structure of the migrant population varied over time and this was also allowed for by calculating the necessary values for every census.

The Scottish research used the estimated migrant age-structure ratios as the fixed variable and, with the number of deaths deducted, it predicted the current migrant age-structure. In contrast, in the English study the current migrant age-structure was critical and errors in its calculation were cumulative. In the Scottish study it is the accuracy of the migrant age-structure that is important, but the fact that it is calculated by using four different migrant age-structures for each sex is likely to make it more accurate, and as data are only estimated from census to census, any errors are not cumulative, which is a substantial advantage. The Scottish migrant age-structures have been calculated from samples derived from a manuscript source. The validity of the samples is therefore important and this will discussed in more detail subsequently. However, the migrant age-structure ratios are tightly held by the data[40] and minor errors in the age-structures do not affect the final conclusions.[41]

The deaths applied are the actual number of deaths for the county spread evenly throughout the age-band in question. The 'nurture' assumption that Baines made has been abandoned, except for migrants less than three months old, to be considered subsequently. The concept behind the 'nurture' assumption is that migrants are likely to have better health than the native population and therefore have a preferential death rate applied for migrants.[42] The evidence in Scotland indicates that this assumption is doubtful. Flinn has argued that differences between urban and rural crude death rates fell markedly between 1861 and 1891, and therefore for much of the period 1861–1911, urban migrants were not necessarily experiencing a considerably increased mortality risk.[43] Moreover, as will be shown subsequently, a considerable proportion of in-migrants were in fact urban-born. Finally, research on London,[44] admittedly for an earlier period (1675–1825), suggests that natives and migrants had similar mortality rates, and female convict data suggests that rural women may have experienced deteriorating living standards.[45] Moreover, research has shown that rural incomers who had previously not built up resistance may have been more susceptible to urban infections.[46]

Nevertheless, in order to make computation feasible, both the present method and that of Baines create a degree of artificiality which appears to be unavoidable, since although demography is dynamic in nature it inevitably has to be measured in a static situation. Although, this study is still adopting the original concept of measuring emigration by using the decennial census and vital data, it is no longer following Baines' method. This is because the 'nurture assumption' may not be valid in the Scottish context and the migrant samples have provided more precise migrant age-structures. In the Scottish study there is no need to estimate the current migrant age-structure although this is fairly critical to Baines' method. Computational problems have meant that all movement outside Scotland has to be considered emigration, less English movement into the rest of the British Isles meant that this did not create a similar problem further south and such movement could be more easily distinguished. However, differences in the method of estimating emigration will not prevent interesting comparisons of the results being made.

THE MIGRANT AGE-STRUCTURE SAMPLES

The published census has the advantage of aggregating vast quantities of information, but the value of the county-of-residence by county-of-birth tabulations to migration research is limited by its broad age-bands (above and below twenty years). The age-structure of the population tabulations is organised by county-of-residence, but does not distinguish native-born from outsiders. No nation-wide study of the age-structure of the Scottish migrant population exists, so in order to check whether the assumptions made by Baines were valid in a Scottish context, it was necessary to sample a manuscript source, the enumeration books, and establish a migrant age-structure. Furthermore this analysis of population movement in Scotland embraced a fifty year period from 1861 to 1911, so it seemed quite feasible that the age and sex ratios of migrants may have altered over time. Finally, during the conversion of registration counties to the civil county framework, it became apparent that Scottish migrants did not appear as concentrated into the young adult age-bands as had been suggested, indicating that further investigation by means of samples would be justified.

The original intention was to make two independent, large samples of the age-structure of the migrant population one in 1861 and the other in 1891. However, in the subsequent computation, it became apparent that there was considerable variation in migrant age-structures and both the initial samples required considerable expansion in certain areas to meet new criteria. The criteria on which the migrant sampling were now based was that of the expansion or decline of the county-of-residence population over the 50 years from 1861 to 1911. The counties were therefore divided into four population categories: the 'Central Lowlands', the 'Periphery and Northeast', the 'Highlands' and finally the 'Borders'. The four categories, listed in Table 2.4, were merely groups of counties linked only by similar percentage increase or decline in population and not homogeneous clusters. Moreover, although the population categories are counties classified according to population growth or decline, they do not necessarily reflect any other demographic characteristics of the county-of-residence. For example, Edinburgh and Lanark plus Renfrew have by far the greatest density of population in Scotland and both are within the 'Central Lowlands' category classification, yet that category also includes Selkirk, which has a much lower density of population.[47] It should be noted that the counties defined within the population categories are counties-of-residence and not of-birth for the migrants within them. It is therefore argued that the attracting county has a different migrant age-structure according to whether or not it is expanding.

In each of the migrant population categories, the migrant samples had to comprise at least 2% of the migrant population of both sexes in both 1861 and 1891, and the samples had to correspond as closely as possible to the category's migrant average for above and below 20 years, calculated from the census in both years. The population categories therefore have external validation. Thus this remains a judgmental sample, but one held by a known age-structure. The more detailed migrant age structures were finally computed from information from the two very large sets of migrant samples. The 78 samples taken from the 1891 enumeration books contained 40,313 migrants which represents 4.3% of the total Scottish migrant population in that census. A further 52 samples were taken from the 1861 enumeration, comprising a further 19,247 migrants, that is 3.1% of the Scottish migrant population.

THE FOUR SAMPLE POPULATION CATEGORIES

The population 'categories' are described thus because they cannot be called regions, and not all of them are geographical entities. The 'Highlands' category embraces more than just the Highland counties as it includes Kinross, while Bute is omitted. It also contains Caithness, Orkney and Shetland. All the counties that border either England or the coast of the Solway Firth are within the 'Borders', but the counties of Peebles and

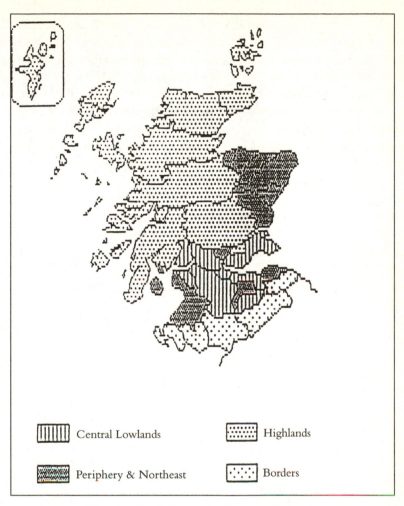

Central Lowlands

Highlands

Periphery & Northeast

Borders

Map 2.1. The Migrant Age-Structure Categories

Table 2.4. The Distribution of Counties into Migrant Population Category*
According to Population Growth or Decline 1861–1911

MIGRANT CATEGORY	CIVIL COUNTY	PERCENTAGE POPULATION GROWTH OR DECLINE
Central Lowlands		
	Dunbarton	+168.73
	Edinburgh (Midlothian)	+82.28
	Fife	+72.99
	Lanark & Renfrew	+117.71
	Linlithgow (West Lothian)	+107.41
	Selkirk	+147.31
	Stirling	+75.13
Periphery and the Northeast		
	Aberdeen	+40.89
	Ayr	+34.86
	Banff	+3.69
	Bute	+11.36
	Clackmannan	+45.09
	Elgin (Moray)	+1.71
	Forfar (Angus)	+37.66
	Haddington (East Lothian)	+14.93
	Kincardine	+18.98
	Nairn ⋆⋆	+2.68
	Peebles	+33.75
Highlands		
	Argyll	-11.07
	Caithness	-22.14
	Inverness	-1.82
	Kinross	-5.64
	Orkney	-20.06
	Perth	-6.86
	Ross and Cromarty ⋆⋆	-6.11
	Shetland	-11.87
	Sutherland	-20.07
Borders		
	Berwick	-19.48
	Dumfries	-4.02
	Kirkcudbright	-9.71
	Roxburgh	-10.35
	Wigtown	-23.99

⋆ Population category, not homogeneous clusters but counties with similar population growth patterns.

⋆⋆ Calculation based on modified civil county

Selkirk are not. The 'Periphery and Northeast' is the most disparate. The counties which normally comprise the Northeast are all included, but so also are six other widely dispersed counties (Ayr, Bute, Clackmannan, Forfar (Angus), Haddington (East Lothian) and Peebles), which form a peripheral band around the Central Lowlands. The 'Central Lowland' counties constitute the majority of those in the Central Lowland Belt of Scotland, but the counties of Ayr, Clackmannan, Haddington (East Lothian) and Kinross are not included, whereas Selkirk is considered within the 'Central Lowlands' because of its high levels of population growth. It should be noted that these population categories are the places migrants are attracted to, it being assumed that the final destination dictates the gender and age structure of the population. Thus for computational purposes they are not their categories-of-birth, but categories-of-residence. This is an important distinction, and Table 2.5 tabulates the different proportions in the two types of category. In the 'Central Lowlands' the rapidly growing population means that the proportion of the total population in the category-of-residence always exceeds that in the category-of-birth, whereas in the remaining categories the reverse is true.

Table 2.5. The Proportion of the Scottish Population in each Population Category of-Residence and of-Birth

Census Year		Population Category				Total Population*
		High-lands	Borders	Periphery & N. east	Central Lowlands	
1861	Category of residence	17.1	8.2	28.0	46.7	3,062,294
	Category of birth	*21.0*	*8.8*	*29.7*	*40.5*	*2,785,800*
1871	Category of residence	15.1	7.2	27.5	50.2	3,360,018
	Category of birth	*19.1*	*8.3*	*29.8*	*42.8*	*3,061,531*
1881	Category of residence	13.5	6.6	26.7	53.2	3,735,573
	Category of birth	*17.1*	*7.6*	*29.6*	*45.7*	*3,397,759*
1891	Category of residence	12.2	5.9	25.8	56.1	4,025,647
	Category of birth	*15.5*	*7.0*	*28.8*	*48.7*	*3,688,700*
1901	Category of residence	10.8	5.0	24.7	59.5	4,472,103
	Category of birth	*13.8*	*6.2*	*28.1*	*51.9*	*4,085,755*
1911	Category of residence	10.0	4.6	23.6	61.8	4,760,904
	Category of birth	*12.3*	*5.6*	*26.8*	*55.3*	*4,365,855*

* The total population in the population category-of-residence is higher than that in the category-of-birth. This is because the former includes immigrants and the latter does not.

The 'Central Lowlands'

All the counties in this category had rapid population growth in excess of 70% over the fifty year period (Table 2.4); indeed in Selkirk, the small population more than doubled due to the rapid growth of Galashiels. All the counties in the 'Central Lowlands' except Selkirk had fairly high densities of population. Moreover, in Table 2.5 it can be seen that the proportion of the total population resident in the 'Central Lowlands' increased from almost 47% in 1861 to nearly 62% in 1911. Indeed the population of this category first exceeded 50% of the total population in 1871. Thus this category contained the majority of the Scottish migrant population and indeed as Table 2.6 shows, over the study period the volume of migrants into this category more than doubled. The highest proportion of migrants was in 1871 for males and 1881 for females and not in 1911 as might be expected; indeed the proportion was lower in 1911 than in 1861. Nevertheless, these 'Central Lowlands' counties' share of the total Scottish migrant population increased from 58.2% in 1861 to 65.9% in 1911. This was the only category whose share of the total Scottish migrant population rose between the 1861 and 1911, indicating that migrants were increasingly attracted to this region as the study period progressed. This is the reason why in Table 2.5 there appears to be a far higher proportion of the total population in the 'Central Lowlands' category-of-residence than that of-birth.

The 'Periphery and Northeast'

Some counties in this category may have experienced periods of population decline, but overall the population of these counties increased between 1861 and 1911, albeit by less than 50%. However, the proportion of the total population living in this category declined from 28% in 1861 to nearly 24% in 1911. The counties had a very varied population density; at one extreme Clackmannan was as populous as many 'Central Lowlands' category counties, while Nairn and Peebles had very low densities.[48] The 'Periphery' had the second largest migrant population, which continued to increase throughout the period, both in volume and as a proportion of the Scottish population in that category.

The 'Borders' and 'Highlands'

Having considered the two population categories with varying amounts of population growth, the discussion will now move to consider those with declining populations. The 'Borders' and 'Highlands' both experienced a decline in population size and in the percentage of Scottish migrants

Table 2.6. The Volume and Percentage of Migrants in Each Population Category

CATEGORY/ YEAR		MALE			FEMALE	
	Nos.	% of Scots population*	% migrants <20yrs	Nos.	% of Scots population*	% migrants <20yrs
Highlands						
1861	32,398	13.55	33.52	33,685	12.36	30.22
1871	34,154	14.65	33.47	36,252	13.71	30.46
1881	41,377	17.63	33.70	42,125	16.26	31.35
1891a	42,279	18.59	31.14	44,376	17.52	29.14
1891b	41,987	18.59	31.32	44,020	17.50	29.37
1901	46,750	20.92	28.63	49,037	19.98	26.93
1911	47,711	22.16	29.13	51,524	21.69	26.46
Borders						
1861	20,282	18.84	33.27	22,635	18.57	29.19
1871	18,417	17.45	31.01	21,574	17.95	27.06
1881	21,932	20.50	33.06	25,710	21.44	28.87
1891a	21,543	20.87	32.70	26,030	22.37	27.13
1891b	21,530	20.88	32.77	25,991	22.37	27.15
1901	23,018	23.49	31.18	27,423	24.79	25.06
1911	24,419	25.41	29.02	29,055	27.09	23.50
Periphery and Northeast						
1861	72,035	19.05	30.83	81,200	18.99	26.80
1871	78,598	19.21	31.28	92,200	19.93	27.09
1881	87,117	19.48	32.06	103,011	20.66	27.67
1891a	90,936	19.51	31.57	108,373	20.75	26.80
1891b	93,096	19.89	32.40	110,939	21.15	27.59
1901	100,202	20.21	30.41	119,521	21.50	25.61
1911	104,823	20.82	29.49	126,479	22.22	25.23
Central Lowlands						
1861	169,886	29.06	30.02	195,918	29.94	26.09
1871	214,777	30.66	29.78	240,156	31.36	26.92
1881	249,812	30.13	29.13	281,394	31.44	26.17
1891a	289,284	29.97	28.77	317,897	30.87	26.58
1891b	290,843	30.14	29.00	319,568	31.05	26.78
1901	334,059	29.24	25.47	362,937	30.02	23.44
1911	353,340	27.66	23.89	389,609	28.73	21.82

* This proportion, which has been calculated for every population category, is the volume of Scottish migrants outside their county-of-birth, but including those from other counties within the category as a percentage of the total Scottish population in all the counties.

a b There are two estimates for 1891, the first (1891a) refers to the pre-revision civil county boundary and the second (1891b) to that post-revision.

attracted to these counties over the period 1861–1911. Clearly they could have been combined as one category, but it was thought to be unwise because as Table 2.6 shows the southern counties (the Borders), despite their falling total populations were still attracting proportionally more migrants than the 'Highlands'. The latter was also distinctive in that it was the only category that was consistently attracting proportionally more male than female migrants. Furthermore, the 'Borders' were more likely to be affected by the proximity of England than their northern counterparts. Finally, the two categories were fairly neat geographic units with very different historical backgrounds, which supported their being separated.

The population densities of the two categories were also different. In the 'Highlands' the counties were generally very large (with the exception of Kinross, Orkney and Shetland) and all were very thinly inhabited, particularly Sutherland. Orkney had the highest density in the northern category although even this was relatively low.[49] In contrast the 'Borders' counties were much smaller in area and whilst the population densities were still rather low they were nevertheless markedly higher than in the 'Highlands'.[50] The 'Borders' contained by far the smallest total population of the four population categories. Both the categories were rural areas, albeit with some towns, and although their share of the total migrant population fell, the volume and proportion of migrants in each category increased over time and this was despite the fact that their populations were decreasing.

It can be seen from this brief analysis of the population categories that their demographic and migrant experience differed markedly, but there were also aspects where they were similar. All the categories experienced an increasing volume of Scottish migrants over time, as is shown in Table 2.6. The lowest proportions of migrants were in the 'Highlands', but even there the proportion of migrants increased from one person in eight in 1861 to one in five by 1911. All the categories showed a decrease over time in the proportion of children and young people under 20 years in the migrant population, although this was least pronounced in the 'Periphery and Northeast'.

THE AGE-STRUCTURE OF THE MIGRANT
POPULATION CATEGORY SAMPLES

The population categories have been collated in aggregated age-bands in Table 2.7. The number of females exceeded males in every category and this was particularly true in the 'Periphery and Northeast'. This particular category might be a little extreme but there was always a significant majority of female Scots migrants. In the age-band classifications of life-time migrants one sex tended to dominate in percentage terms regardless of the census year or population category. Table 2.7 shows that there was generally a greater proportion of males in the migrants under 5 years, and indeed this was always true of migrants under 15 years. Thereafter the domination of one sex was not so marked. Males tended to have greater percentages in the age-bands 15–24 years.

Females predominated in the 25–44 years age-band, and while this was reversed in the subsequent one (45–60 years), there was again a greater percentage of female migrants in oldest age age-band (60 years and over). However, although the proportions in age-bands differed according to sex,

Table 2.7. The Percentage of Male and Female Migrants in Selected Age-Bands by Year and Population Category

POPULATION CATEGORY	GENDER	SAMPLE SIZE	AGE-BAND IN YEARS						
			<5	0–15	15–19	20–24	25–45	45–59	>60
1861									
Central Lowlands									
	Male	3,418	5.4	20.5	8.9	12.3	34.7	15.8	7.8
	Female	4,039	4.8	17.0	7.9	11.9	38.8	15.6	8.8
Periphery & Northeast									
	Male	2,284	5.3	21.6	8.6	11.1	32.0	17.2	9.5
	Female	2,587	3.7	18.3	8.9	9.4	35.0	15.6	12.8
Highlands									
	Male	1,681	5.7	23.3	9.6	9.9	32.5	16.0	8.9
	Female	1,768	5.7	23.0	8.4	9.2	34.0	15.6	9.8
Borders									
	Male	1,602	6.7	23.2	9.4	7.8	33.3	17.4	8.9
	Female	1,868	4.7	18.6	9.5	10.9	33.0	15.8	12.2
1891									
Central Lowlands									
	Male	5,035	3.9	18.1	10.0	12.4	36.0	16.7	6.8
	Female	5,561	3.3	15.4	8.9	12.5	37.4	16.1	9.7
Periphery & Northeast									
	Male	5,326	5.0	21.5	9.4	8.8	32.4	16.7	11.2
	Female	7,214	4.0	16.7	10.3	10.6	33.0	16.5	12.9
Highlands									
	Male	5,531	3.8	20.2	10.3	9.6	31.9	16.9	11.1
	Female	6,268	4.0	20.1	9.5	8.7	33.1	16.6	12.0
Borders									
	Male	2,438	4.6	21.3	10.1	8.4	33.0	16.5	10.7
	Female	2,939	3.5	18.0	9.1	10.0	32.7	17.2	13.0

within each sex the age-band percentages in all population categories were remarkably similar and a variation of even four percentage points was uncommon except amongst the oldest. Nevertheless, it was also the case that there were proportionally more male migrants in the younger age-bands than females, which inevitably means that in the life-time population female migrants tended to be older.

However, when one compared the categories over time other patterns in the age-bands emerged. The most obvious was the decline in the percentage of migrants under 5 years, apparent in all categories except 'Periphery and Northeast'. Here the percentage of female children actually increased over time. When all children under 15 years were considered all categories showed a decline in 1891. This meant that the 'Periphery' must have attracted families with very young migrant children. The decline in the proportion of young migrants could reflect several different scenarios, such as declining fertility, changing migration patterns or changing mortality rates which would be reflected in an ageing migrant population. The proportion of migrants aged 15–19 years of both sexes increased between the two samples. In 1861 only females in the 'Borders' peaked at this age-band, but by 1891 this age-band represented the peak for both sexes in 'Highlands' and males in the 'Borders'. This implies either migrants were moving at a younger age in 1891 in the declining counties, or that there was a movement out of counties in these categories by people in the older age-band, which then inflated the younger one. Hereafter, the changes in the higher adult age-bands became more complicated and no clear patterns could be discerned, except in the oldest group where improving age-specific mortality probably helped to increase the proportion in this age-band.

ASSUMPTIONS MADE CONCERNING THE DATA SOURCES

This discussion is in two parts. It will consider first the published sources, that is the census tabulations, and those derived from the detailed annual reports. The second part will discuss the migrant samples which were derived from the enumeration books. These samples have enabled both the migrant and the native age-structures to be calculated and, as already noted, this has radically altered the method of estimating population movement from that of Baines.

In the analysis of the available material, mention has already been made of the manual conversion of the tallies from registration to civil counties, of adjustments necessary to resolve boundary discrepancies and the risks of spurious migration. The Detailed Annual Reports also provided information on both births and age-specific mortality using the county-of-residence framework. In consequence it was necessary to apply an arithmetical conversion of vital data from the registration county framework to that of the civil counties. It has therefore been assumed that incidence of births and deaths occurred evenly throughout any county, although this is clearly unrealistic and the differences between urban and rural districts might have been quite large.

A further problem arises with the census in that the county-of-birth and age-structure of the population tallies are recorded in early April, whereas the births and deaths are tabulated annually from January to December. As the published Census was the major source of information, it was decided to convert other source material from the Detailed Annual Reports to conform to the April-to-March year. The April to March year was computed using ¾ of the present year's births and ¼ of those of the subsequent year. Clearly this process slightly modifies the effects of abnormally high or low years.[51] As has already been noted, all babies are natives at birth, even if their parents are migrants or immigrants. This substantially eases the application of fertility data.

The problems already mentioned with regard to births, that is the April to March year, the differing county frameworks, and lack of 1911 data also affected age-specific mortality, and were resolved in a similar manner to that described for births. There were however far more significant conceptual problems associated with the application of age-specific mortality data. The age-structure of the population was divided into sixteen five year age-bands except for those over 75 years. Initially the age-specific mortality was also divided into sixteen age-bands. However, this ignored the essentially dynamic nature of demography. For example the highest mortality was in the youngest and the oldest age-groups, but the youngest age-group was difficult to identify. Was it the existing 0–4 year olds or those to be born in the next five years? If one shifted the ages along one band to accommodate both the newly born and the 0–4 year olds, the age-specific mortality was nowhere near high enough for the final age-band which now included both those between 70–74 years as well as those over 75 years.

Clearly this was not a satisfactory solution, but it was also necessary to keep the problem in perspective, as the object was not to reproduce the entire demographic regime, but to measure population movement. Clearly a solution needed to be found that was a compromise between the kind of gross inaccuracy cited above and potentially time consuming work that might achieve a high degree of precision for mortality, but very little gain of accuracy in estimating migration. The solution finally adopted was to process the population under 5 years on a one year interval basis. For those over 5 years old less precision was required, as age-specific mortality did not fluctuate so much (indeed age-specific mortality was not even provided in greater detail than five year age-bands for those over five years old). These older people (over 5 years old) were computed in five year periods. These two different procedures will now be considered along with the problem posed by those children whose 5th birthday occurred during a five year period and were not entirely 'caught' by either method.

In the published census the age-structure of the total population was tabulated by one year intervals for the under 5 year olds, and migrant and native age-structure could therefore be calculated. The population patterns of young children could be mirrored fairly accurately by processing the data annually. At the start of each year the age of the existing child migrant population was increased by a year. Births were added to each county. These were assumed to remain natives of their county for the first three months and had the 3 month age-specific mortality for that county and year deducted from them. As has already been argued, there were probably very few migrants that young, although any that moved into a 'Central Lowlands' category county[52] would have a higher survival rate in this model than would have been the case in reality, as the age-specific mortality in the 'Central Lowlands' category counties was particularly high in the less–than–3 months age-band compared with the subsequent 9 months.[53] This high young infant mortality was presumably a reflection of considerable post-natal mortality. There is no detailed analysis of the extent to which this occurred in Scotland and whilst acknowledging that the problem exists it has not been compensated for.

The age-structure of the migrant population under five years old in a county-of-residence was assumed to remain constant throughout the ten year period. A migrant age-structure was applied for those migrants over 3 months and where there was a shortfall in the migrant population these were assumed to be current. In the census year the migrant age-structure ratios were applied to all migrant populations. The number of migrants in each county-of-residence from each county-of-birth was assumed to remain the same for the subsequent decade, although the age of existing migrants was increased every year in the computer model in order to mirror reality. For migrants under five years of age this means that the migrant population was re-created every year. Thus the current migrant age-structure was partly a result of the age-specific mortality of the previous year and of the original age-structure created by the migrant ratios for the previous census.[54] These current migrants were then deducted from the native population of their county-of-birth, and the age-specific mortality applied to all populations (migrant and native) in the county-of-residence.

The results of these computations were then carried forward to form the basis of the calculations for the subsequent year.

Age-specific mortality was applied to the over 5 year olds in five year age-bands as originally planned using similar methods to those described above. The results were not entirely satisfactory as there tended to be some bunching of ages, particularly in the older groups. This might have been caused by people generalising their ages in the census enumeration or when registering deaths, or even by mistakes in both. Since many people had been born before births were officially recorded this problem was inevitable, and there is evidence of bunching in the age-bands 35–44, 45–54 and 55–64 years in both sexes.

Clearly the methods adopted concerning age-specific mortality produce a problem of linking the system of yearly estimates for the under 5 year olds to the five year system for those over 5 years. This meant that every year a certain proportion of the under 5 year olds turned 5 years and were not caught until the next five year period began. These children had all had at least one year of age-specific mortality applied to them and for the oldest it had been applied every year, but most within this age-group would not have had the correct number of deaths applied. However, the age-band 5–9 years has a low age-specific mortality (in many counties the lowest of any age-band) and the error is therefore minimised. A special check was made to see if this 5–9 years age-group contained too many children, as a result of too few deaths being applied. But in fact the age-structure of the total population at the end of a five year period, when this group were finally incorporated back into the system, always appeared logical.[55] Furthermore, the fact that the run is only from census to census means that errors are not cumulative in the long term. It must be remembered that this model has not altered the total number of deaths in any way, but rather has adjusted their distribution within age-groups in order to mirror more accurately a dynamic situation.

The Migrant Age-Structures Derived from the Samples

The migrant samples were used to expand the information in the birthplace tabulation in the census by providing more detailed information on the age and sex of migrants. This information was also used to calculate current migration. The samples were therefore critical to the estimations of population movement, for which the recording of age and sex was necessary. It has already been noted that the migrant samples have external validation, as they have been 'held' by the above and below 20 years tabulations provided in the original census. This means that the migrant age-structure for the under 20 year olds applies to only four age-bands of the total migrants in that category and for those over 20 years twelve age-bands are applied. The breakdown of the population by sex into above and below 20 years means that the sixteen age-bands do not have to be applied to the whole population at the start, as the above and below 20 years groups can be analysed separately. The migrant age-structure is also 'held' during computation by the published age-structure of the population in the census.

The ages of migrants were recorded by sex in sixteen five-year age-bands. The actual age was noted enabling the under 5 year olds to be sub-divided by year and those less than a year by month. As the age-structures for 1861 and 1891 differed, an estimated migrant age-structure was computed for the censuses 1871 and 1881 and it was also projected on to 1901 and 1911 for both the sixteen five year age-bands and the one year bands for those under 5 years. This projection of the migrant data was not ideal; it would have been much more satisfactory if actual numbers could have been obtained for 1911, but as it was impossible to refer to the enumeration books after 1891 a more accurate migrant age-structure could not therefore be produced. It is possible that the age-structure of the migrant population in 1861 was exceptional and that population movement in the previous decade was unusually large due to the potato famine in the Highlands. A second scenario has therefore been considered in which the age-structure of the migrant population did not change after 1891. This alternative migrant age-structure has been used to compare the results with those achieved by projecting the age-structure, but when the entire project was re-calculated the differences between the two sets of estimates were generally insignificant.

With regard to those migrants that were less than a year old, the samples were small and there did not appear to be significant differences between the two sample years, the population categories or the sexes. Moreover, very few migrant babies were less than three months old. This was not surprising, as even if a baby migrated on its day of birth, the chance of it being enumerated within three months are low. This is possible if for example a wife returned to her mothers home to have a baby and then returned to her husband crossing a county boundary and thus rendering the baby a migrant. It can however be argued that the number of very young migrants would probably increase steadily after the first few months of life. This is an important argument as it has affected the approach adopted on age-specific mortality for very young migrants.

The migrant age-structure can be computed by selecting the correct year and category of age-structure ratios calculated from the samples. This ratio is applied to the migrant population in the county-of-residence by county-of-birth tabulation, which already lists the county-of-birth of all migrant and immigrant groups resident in a county by sex and two age-bands. It is assumed that all migrants conform to the migrant age-structure of their county-of-residence once they leave their county-of-birth. This is not unreasonable, as a migrant in a textile mill is likely to experience very different health hazards to those in farm work or general labouring. However, this assumption implies that long distance migrants may well have a very different age-structure from those migrants who moved to counties adjoining their county-of-birth. This also means that the migrant age-structure of two adjacent counties-of-birth can be very different despite their being in the same population category when considered as counties-of-residence. This is because out-migrants are being attracted to counties-of-residence in differing migrant age-structure categories. In parts of Scotland where several adjacent counties are in different population categories the current migrant age-structure of each county is likely to be very different. As already stated the age-structure of the county-of-residence by county-of-birth tabulation has been expanded from two to sixteen age-bands. This is the revised census of the Scots-born population only, an aggregated version of the original data.

It has already been stressed that as calculations are only made from census to census there is the advantage that errors are not cumulative, but there is also a disadvantage in that long term changes in the migrant age-structure of certain counties are not necessarily carried across censuses. The standardised age-structure categories recreate the same ratios from the migrant population of every county-of-birth. A county-of-birth with an exceptionally large outflow of current migrants in one decade would subsequently have an ageing migrant population if this outflow was not continued. It is recognised that this problem probably does exist, but in the Scottish context it is somewhat ameliorated by the fact that the birthplace tabulation is in two age-bands, that is above and below twenty years. An ageing migrant population would have relatively few young migrants in a census, and the number would not have increased ten years later. For older migrants this ageing problem would mean that more migrants would die than the model predicts, and the current migrant population would be underestimated.

It has proved possible to establish the native-born age-structure of a county by deducting the aggregate outsider age-structure (migrants and immigrants) from the total county age-structure derived from the census. As has already been noted, new-born babies are by definition natives even if their parents are migrants or immigrants and for the purposes of this analysis they are not considered capable of becoming migrants until they are at least three months old.

METHOD OF ESTIMATING POPULATION MOVEMENT

This section will describe how the basic measures of population movement are calculated. The degree of confidence that can be applied to the results is shown through the effects of applying standard errors to the data. The following is a brief summary of the method.

The migrant age-structure ratios are applied to the county-of-residence by county-of-birth tabulations for all censuses. It is assumed that the actual number of migrants and the migrant age-structure for each county-of-residence remain the same for the ten years after the census to which it was applied. This is important because as already noted the migrant age-structure for children under 5 years has to be created every year and for those over 5 every five years. The current migrant age-structure in the model is the difference between the newly applied migrant age-structure and the previous one (with the correct amendments for age applied). The previous migrant population will have had age-specific mortality applied in exactly the same proportion as the native population. This computer model therefore predicts the maximum population for the next census and the difference between this prediction and the actual census represents emigration and immigration. This model does not predict the current migrant population, but rather creates a hypothetical one from the ratios of the migrant age-structure which it is hoped bears some relation to reality. This hypothetical current migrant population and the life-time migrant population have had age-specific mortality applied to them. It has already been noted that although the correct total age-specific mortality has been applied to every county-of-residence, children between 5–9 years have had slightly less than their correct number of deaths applied and consequently all other age-bands must have had slightly above their allocation. It has been stressed that as age-specific mortality is low in this age-band the consequences are not likely to be serious. Minor errors that do occur probably result in slightly fewer current migrants being estimated in the age-band 5–9 years as less migrants and natives will die. This will mean that slightly too many emigrants in this age-band will be predicted but in all other age-bands a very slight reduction will occur. However, this will not have any overall affect on the aggregate estimations of emigration by county-of-birth.

This system of measuring both migration and emigration is net of returns. A migrant that emigrates, but is replaced by a current migrant in the same age-band from the same county-of-birth will not show up in the current migrant data, whereas the emigrant will appear as a loss from the county-of-birth and not from the county-of-residence. Moreover, when the data is aggregated a returning emigrant or migrant cancels out the effect of a new emigrant or current migrant despite the fact that the returning person is probably older. This means that one should not expect to find evidence of much mobility in older age-bands, even though it is quite possible that the elderly were continuing to migrate albeit in relatively small numbers.

It should be noted that whether the results are for current migration or emigration, the age-band of movement has errors contained within it. The computer model predicts the number in each age-band at the subsequent census. The number in each age-band that have moved is the difference between the actual numbers in the subsequent census and the number predicted by the model. This method of estimating both current migration and emigration therefore calculates the age at moving as the age they would have been if they had remained within either their county-of-birth (current migration) or Scotland (emigration). Clearly because measurement is over a decade, some 9 year olds could have migrated at less than a year and some 24 year olds at 15 years. Nevertheless, it should be noted that whereas for children less than 5 years old, the numbers stated represent the absolute minimum that could have left, for all other age-bands, some of their number should probably be incorporated in the previous age-band. This problem, together with already mentioned problems of age-bunching, probably accounts for many of the anomalies in estimates for older age-bands. The problem of the actual age of leaving the county-of-birth has been reduced by recalculating the data. It is assumed that half the population of most age-bands moved five years earlier than estimated by the model. This assumption is probably not fully justified, as movement did not occur uniformly but was spasmodic. With regard to emigration, certain years in each decade are known to have been peak or slump years from the evidence of passenger lists.[56] However, such detailed information is not available for current migration. Despite these reservations, this method of measuring movement permits a more accurate estimate of the actual age-band when people leave, rather than just their age at the end of the decade after they had departed. In the county-of-birth estimates for both current migration and emigration, it has been assumed that in any age-band, excluding those less than 5 years and those over 75 years, half the people recorded as moving went when they were still in the previous age-band. This age adjustment has therefore been made to the number of migrants and emigrants in each county. Children under 5 years, as already argued, were already correctly recorded for the second five year period of the decade, but half the previous 5–9 years age-band needed to be added to account for the first five years. These adjustments assume that the population recorded in any age-band was equally likely to move in the first or second five year period of a decade, and that the fact that they were 5 years younger in the first five year period made no difference to their propensity to move. The age-band over 75 years was treated separately as it could not be assumed that everybody in this age-band would have been below 75 years five years earlier. Therefore for this age-band only a quarter of the population were adjusted by five years. This factor cannot be supported by evidence, but if it was increased significantly more then the age-band 70–74 years became too large in relation to nearby age-bands. It should be noted that these adjustments make no difference to the total population loss from a county.

The risks attached to projecting the migrant age-structure beyond 1891 have already been considered. The computer model was therefore re-run to see the effects of using the 1891 migrant age-structure ratios, rather than the projected ratios, for the census tabulations of 1901 and 1911. The results suggest that the different migrant age-structure ratios made absolutely no difference to the 1891–1901 aggregated percentages for both current migrants and emigrants and only a slight difference to the aggregate figures for 1901–1911, although, within certain age-bands it did make differences to the number of people leaving.

Standard Errors

The value of calculations, whether they be of current migration or emigration, are only as good as the estimates themselves. In order that the reliability of information can be assessed, the standard errors have been presented in most tables of estimates of population movement. A measure of reliability of the estimates of both emigration and migration is of immense importance to the conclusions in this study.

Thus in order to test the results thoroughly, the method of estimating standard errors[57] adopted in this study represent a 'worst case' scenario. There were four published data sources used in this study (the age-structure of the county population, the birthplace enumeration, and annual numbers of births and deaths). The fifth source was the age-structure ratios of the migrant population by population category. This information has been created from two very large samples, but nevertheless probably held the greatest risk of error. This was because it is impossible to repeat a sample even from the same background population and sampling errors in any age-band could fluctuate at random. The standard error therefore measures the accuracy of population parameters from sample statistics.[58]

Two standard errors were calculated for both sexes in each age-band of the migrant age-structure ratio for every census year. It was therefore the ratios of the migrant age-structure that had the standard errors applied to them. Every age-band in each of the four population categories had a different amount of standard error. This was because the standard error reflected not only the extremes in the ratios of migrant age-structure, but also the number of samples taken. This was a problem, because some samples of the migrant population categories were large, both numerically and as a proportion of the total population, but they were derived from a relatively small number of sampled places. Moreover, the closeness of the fit of the individual migrant population categories to the published above and below 20 years gender proportions, although important as a criterion in the original sampling, was not measured in the standard errors.

The standard errors were applied to the migrant age-structure and this revised the proportion of natives and migrants in each age-band of every county, (the total population of each county in an age-band had been derived from the census). The data were then processed. The range of errors was calculated in the final estimates of both emigration and migration. Thus standard errors that were applied to data in a county-of-residence unit of measurement were finally calculated for estimates on a county-of-birth framework. This had the effect of concentrating errors in certain age-bands and counties-of-birth, often a different population category to that of the county-of-residence. The estimates with standard errors applied therefore represent extremes in variability.

The original intention was to skew the age-structure ratios in two separate models, one flattening and the other peaking the migrant ratios. However, this proved unworkable because there was not a large enough margin for error that would permit their application. This indicates how tightly the migrant age-structure ratios were held by the published data.[59] A second method of measuring the accuracy of the migrant age-structure ratios using standard errors was devised. In this model two standard errors were added to each age-band of the migrant age-structure to create one extreme scenario and vice versa for the other. The data were then rerun in exactly the same manner as in the previous tests in order to provide estimates of movement. The migrant age-structure for each population category in every census had two standard errors added or deducted from each age-band. This was a source database and it means that the entire computation of estimates of both emigration and migration occurred after the database had been adjusted. Variations based on these procedures will over-estimate the likely variability appreciably. This clearly represents a 'worst case' situation and has made the test a very rigorous one.

County-of-birth estimates of the proportion lost through current migration or emigration showed that there was very little variation when standard errors were applied. Small counties invariably showed the greatest fluctuations and their results should always be treated with extreme caution. Ideally every estimate should be accurate to $\pm 2\%$. Some showed a slightly larger error, but in most cases the fluctuation was less than $\pm 2\%$. For example in the estimates of current migration, the predicted loss of female migrants in Aberdeen in 1891–1901 is 9,721, which changes by only 0.37% when two standard errors are added and by 0.94% with two standard errors deducted. The standard errors on individual age-bands are sometimes unsatisfactorily large, particularly in counties with small populations. As has already been argued, these are a result of the sampling method used rather than the inadequacy of the sample itself. The two standard errors were applied to the county-of-residence migrant age-structure and the effects were then measured in the county-of-birth. This means that errors were likely to be concentrated in certain counties and age-bands. For example in current migration from Argyll, the resulting degree of variability in the data for females aged 30–39 years suggests that little significance can be attached to the results, but the estimates for younger females and of the total female migrants were considerably more reliable.[60] However, this discussion is considering a degree of accuracy that the results do not possess. The results are the product of various generalisations and simplifications that are required in order to make computation practical and it is not claimed that the results are accurate to a few people. Evidence of errors that could result from mis-recording of the original data are clearly seen in otherwise unexplained bunching, and in the results from the highest age-bands, which particularly in small population counties are often clearly absurd.

The Assumptions Made in Presenting the Estimates of Population Movement — Current Migration Population

Current migrants are assumed all to be migrants who arrived in a county-of-residence between two censuses. In the model described above hypothetical current migrants are created by calculating the migrant age-structure. The failings of this method have already been considered, and the model creates rather than predicts current migration. This is adequate for computation of the emigration estimates, but the assessments of current migration have been calculated differently. The estimated migrant population in any census year is considered to be the life-time migrant population, since those people arrived before the census enumeration. As no more migrants are incorporated into the model there are no current migrants. The native and life-time migrant populations have the county-of-residence age-specific mortality rates applied for the subsequent 10 years. The difference between this life-time migrant population predicted by the computer model and the actual migrant population obtained from the next census represents the current migrants who have arrived in the last 10 years. Clearly age-specific mortality complicates this estimation. The entire mortality for a county-of-residence is being applied to the native and life-time migrant population, because no allowance is being made for deaths amongst the current migrants. The estimated current migrant population is therefore too low and age-bands with the highest age-specific mortality reveal the highest under-estimates. This is however almost impossible to compute because the current migrant population in any county-of-birth is the sum of the current migrant populations in every county-of-residence. Nevertheless, the intention of this study is to show trends and not to determine precise numbers of currents migrants. Therefore despite their acknowledged problems these estimates do have some validity.

The Validity of Using Population Categories as a Unit of Measurement for Migration: A Regional Perspective

The population categories are not geographical regions, but are counties with common demographic characteristics. It is therefore necessary to show that the estimates of migration in the present study are not just a product of the way the counties have been organised into population categories.

The first part of Chapter 3 addresses this problem and analyses long-distance life-time migration using geographical regions as the unit of measurement; these regions are unique to that particular section of the discussion. These geographical regions consist of Highlands, Northeast, West Lowlands, East Lowlands and the South. The regions are considered in more detail in Chapter 3 and the counties within each region are listed in Table 3.2. These regions are not the same as those in the Scottish census, which were used by Flinn and by Anderson and Morse,[61] and it should be emphasised that they do not correspond to the population categories already considered.

Emigration and Immigration

Throughout this research the term emigration has been used to describe what is in fact current emigration. However, unlike migration where migrants can continue to move several times (although no longer measured), past emigrants cease to complicate models once they have left Scotland unless of course they return. All emigration estimations should therefore be assumed to reflect current movement within the given decade despite the word current being omitted.

The basic method of estimating emigration has already been considered in some detail. The hypothetical current migrant population model does have some advantages for the estimation of emigration. This is because the age-specific mortality of any county has been applied not only to the native population and life-time migrants but also to the current migrants, which makes the estimation of emigration more accurate. The accuracy of estimation of emigration could undoubtedly be improved still further if a better method of creating the hypothetical current migrant population could be devised. This would doubtless involve estimating back from the subsequent census, as well as projecting forward from the earlier one as done in this research.[62] However, this improvement would necessitate considerably more complicated computer programming.

Immigration has inevitably been caught by the computer model. Outsiders almost invariably show an increase in numbers when the estimated and actual censuses are compared and this represents immigration.

Comparisons of Measurement of Current Migration and Emigration

It can be seen that the appendices for emigration loss were tabulated in a similar way to those of current migration. This was in order that comparisons can be made. However, care must be exercised when making such comparisons because estimates of percentages do not use the same baselines. Whereas estimates of migration use only natives in the county-of-birth as the baseline, those of emigration use the total county-of-birth population as a framework of measurement. It is being argued that for an accurate measurement of the percentage lost through current migration, only those natives left in the county-of-birth at the end of the decade under consideration plus of course current out-migration, are the baseline. When emigration losses from Scotland as a whole are being computed, it cannot be ascertained whether an emigrant has just left his county-of-birth or is already a life-time migrant. The baseline for these percentage calculations is therefore the entire county-of-birth population, regardless of which county it is at present residing in at the end of the decade under consideration, plus current emigration.

It has been argued that this revised method of estimation provides a more accurate model of current migration than that of Baines', which in turn should provide better estimates of emigration. The Scottish data covers a longer period than the comparable English study and has a finer breakdown of the age of residents. Nevertheless, it is intended that this analysis should be compared with Baines' work on England and Wales and percentage losses are probably the most satisfactory way of measuring county-of-birth losses comparatively. Baines' method of estimating out-movement[63] is quite different from those described for this study. His baseline for all percentage calculations (current migration and emigration) is the mean native population[64] which Baines has defined as the entire county-of-birth population regardless of where it resides in England and Wales. The population that has been lost through emigration or migration is only partially included within these estimates. This method has the virtue of making direct comparisons between estimates of current migration and emigration possible, because they use the same baseline, but it can seriously under-estimate losses from individual counties because the relationship between the present native population and current migration is not being explored. The Scottish study has argued that the baseline is the county-of-birth population (native or total) at the end of the decade, that is the subsequent census plus the people who have left. In effect, it means that without current migration or emigration these people would have been in their county-of-birth and/or Scotland. By not including these measurements of loss in his baseline, Baines' estimates of percentage losses will inevitably appear far greater than those in Scotland regardless of whether they really are or not. In Chapter 5 when the findings in this study are compared with those of Baines' the Scottish data have been recalculated to make it directly comparable.

In concluding this section, it should be noted that when this research was started it was expected that one age-structure would suffice, regardless of gender, for migrants. This was clearly incorrect and four age-structure categories were created for both sexes and these changed over time. It should be noted that this laborious sampling process has provided considerable information on migrants and has also enabled migrant age-structures to be created. A current migrant age-structure can now be predicted with a fair degree of accuracy by the computer model, and has eliminated the need to rely on an estimate, as used in Baines' English study, which would in turn mean that other measurements such as emigration would then dependent on the accuracy of that estimate. It can therefore be concluded that the Scottish migrant samples will avoid one source of potential error when estimating population movement.

Notes

1. Flinn *et al. Scottish Population History*. p. 455.
2. Baines. *Migration in a Mature Economy*. p. XIV, and pp. 90–125.
3. Anderson and Morse. 'The People', p. 16.
4. Baines. *Migration in a Mature Economy*. pp. 121–2.
5. *Eighth Decennial Census of the Population of Scotland taken 3d April 1871 with Report,* Vol. I, p. XIV.

6. In addition to Edinburgh for Midlothian, the Census also assigned Elgin for Moray, Forfar for Angus, Haddington for East Lothian, and Linlithgow for West Lothian.

7. Flinn. *Scottish Population History*. p. 85.

8. Civil Registration Act, 1854, 17 & 18 Vic, c 80. Both the changes and the differences in boundaries were listed in the 'Explanation of Difference between the Civil and Registration counties' found in the first volume of each decennial census.

9. This data has been reproduced in Appendix 4.

10. Baines. *Migration in a Mature Economy*. pp. 178–212.

11. Information on the age-structure of the county populations occurs in various tabulations in the different censuses:

    1861 Census, Vol. II, 'Ages of the People in the Registration counties and Groups of Districts in Scotland in 1861', pp. 2–3.

    1871 Census, Vol. II, 'Table X, Ages of the People in the Registration Counties in Scotland in 1871', pp. 8–9.

    1881 Census, Vol. II, 'Table XI, Ages of the People in Quinquennial Periods in the Registration Counties and Groups of Districts in Scotland in 1881', pp. 4–5, (for those over 5 years and for young children), 'Table XII 'Education Statistics in Scotland and its Registration Divisions in 1881', pp. 79–80.

    1891 Census, Vol. II, 'Table XI, Ages of the People in Quinquennial Periods in the Civil Counties and Parishes of Scotland in 1891', pp. 4–5, (for those over 5 years and for young children), 'Table XII 'Education Statistics in Scotland in 1891', pp. 63–4.

    1901 Census, Vol. II, 'Table I (1) Ages of the people under 15 years in the Civil Counties and Parishes of Scotland in 1901', pp. 3–5, and 'Table I (2) Ages and Condition as to Marriage of the People in the Civil Counties and Parishes of Scotland in 1901 at Quinquennial Periods from 15 years upwards', pp. 37–43.

    1911 Census, Vol. II, 'Population of the Counties by Sex and Conjugal Condition in Quinquennial Age Groups', pp. 227–35.

12. *1861 Census,* Vol. II, pp. 2–3, *and 1911 Census,* Vol. II, pp. 227–35.

13. *1871 Census,* Vol. I, p. XIV.

14. The enumeration books are preserved in the General Register Office for Scotland, New Register House, Edinburgh. I would like to thank the staff at New Register House for their help.

15. No further instructions on county-of-birth questions for the benefit of the Enumerators were printed in the enumeration books seen (1861–91).

16. The registration district's enumeration books listed in the 'Explanation of differences between the Civil and Registration counties' were used in all five census years to check for mis-recording of birthplace information

(1861–91). enumeration books were also used to create samples of the migrant population. All the enumeration books used are listed in the bibliography.

17. Information on the conversion from post to pre-revision boundaries is available in Shennan, *Boundaries of the Counties and Parishes in Scotland,* and *1891 Census,* Sup. to Vol. I, pp. 83–137.

18. Flinn. *Scottish Population History.* p. 90.

19. *(7th–56th) Detailed Annual Reports.* (Edinburgh, 1865–1912).

20. The report notes a completely revised system for this year. Craufurd Dunlop, J. 'Report to the Registrar General', *Fifty-seventh Annual Report of the Registrar General for Scotland 1911,* (Edinburgh, HMSO 1914), [cd-7332], pp. VII–IX.

21. Thirty-nineth Detailed Annual Report of the Registrar General of Births, Deaths and Marriages in Scotland [Abstracts of 1893], (Edinburgh, HMSO 1895) [c-7914].

22. This table is provided separately for males and females and is entitled 'Male (Female) deaths at different Ages in Scotland in…'.

23. Baines. *Migration in a Mature Economy.* p. 95.

24. The districts investigated were Reay (Caithness and Sutherland), Croy and Dalcross (Inverness and Nairn), Kirkliston (Edinburgh and Haddington) and Roberton (Selkirk and Roxburgh).

25. The 1881 Census 'Instructions to Registrars…' was the oldest seen.

26. 1901 Census, Preliminary Report, p. 3.

27. Brock 'Spurious Migration' p. 81.

28. Urquhart and Logie-Wester becomes part of Ross and Cromarty in the boundary amendments of 1891.

29. In theory each county could have been allocated a proportion of the city. For arguments against this see Brock, 'Spurious Migration ' p. 87, fn.16.

30. Flinn. *Scottish Population History.* p. 87.

31. This was feasible because details of the amendments were in *1891 Census,* sup. to Vol. I, pt.II, Table IV. and also because the enumeration books for the 1891 Census were available.

32. In Nairn this was because the problem of Urquhart and Logie-Wester was resolved.

33. *1851 Census,* Vol. II, pp. 1038–40.

34. *1901 Census,* Vol. II, pp. 341–9.

35. *1861 Census,* Vol. II, p. 2 and 331 for the age and birthplace of males from Shetland.

36. *1911 Census,* Vol. II, p. LVII.

37. Baines. *Migration in a Mature Economy.* p. 96–7.

38. See Brock, 'Scottish Migration' Vol. II. Appendix I, pp. 37–40 or 50–1.

39. Baines, *Migration in a Mature Economy*, pp. 90–125

40. In order to test the accuracy of the results, two standard errors were computed for each migrant age-structure ratio for every census year. The intention was to skew the age-structure ratios in two separate models by two standard errors. This proved impossible because there was not a large enough margin for error that would permit their application, thus indicating how tightly the migrant age-structure ratios are held by the data.

41. The effects of applying two standard errors have been shown on all the final estimates.

42. Baines, *Migration in a Mature Economy*. pp. 108–25.

43. Flinn, *Scottish Population History*. p. 383.

44. Landers, 'Mortality and Metropolis' pp. 59–76.

45. Nicholas and Oxley, 'The Living Standards' (1993) pp. 723–49. This debate on the relative health of urban and rural dwellers is by no means over. See also Floud, Wachter and Gregory, *Height, health*, Voth and Leunig, 'Did Smallpox'; Jackson, 'The Heights': Nicholas and Oxley, 'The Living Standards' (1996).

46. In the Scottish context Floud, Wachter and Gregory have shown that Scottish male rural dwellers were slightly taller than comparable urban dwellers in 1815 but argues that by 1850 this may have changed. Floud, Wachter and Gregory, *Height, health*, p. 203.

    No evidence can be found to support the idea that migrants were healthier than the natives. Voth and Leunig, 'Did Smallpox'; Jackson, 'The Heights': p. 541. Indeed tuberculosis was noted as a serious problem for Highlanders in urban areas, but the slow progress of the disease meant that some returned to the Highlands with the infection and it was also the largest single cause of death in the Highland counties, (P.Gibb; Doctoral studies at the University of Glasgow, on the Highlands and Islands medical service, January 1987). The disease may originally have been contracted in a migrant situation but was by no means a strictly Lowland problem, as the migrants introduced the disease to areas where it was previously unknown.

47. The population density per square mile in 1891 in selected 'Central Lowlands' counties.

Edinburgh (Midlothian)	1,186.1
Lanark and Renfrew	1,178.1
Selkirk	103.8

48. Selected counties in the 'Periphery and Northeast' with extreme population densities per square mile in 1891.

Clackmannan	607.2
Nairn	56.2
Peebles	42.5

49. Selected counties in the 'Highlands' with extremes in population densities per mile in 1891:

    Orkney   80.9
    Sutherland 10.8

50. Selected counties in the 'Borders' with extremes in population densities per mile in 1891:

    Roxburgh   80.4
    Kirkcudbright 44.4

51. In 1911 the format of the Detailed Annual Report was completely changed and did not provide data on births in a usable form and it proved impossible to obtain the necessary information elsewhere. As only the first 3 months of 1911 were required in order to create the April 1910 to March 1911 year, 1/4 of the births tabulation for 1910 was added instead of 1/4 of 1911 in order to provide data for the year April 1910–March 1911.

52. There is an over-simplification of the mortality situation: certain 'Periphery and Northeast' counties such as Forfar (Angus) also had high mortality rates.

53. A new born baby that was a native of a 'Central Lowlands' category county and moved to a different category of county experienced the reverse of the situation described in the text.

54. In the census year the migrant age-structure ratios were applied to all migrant populations. The number of migrants in each county-of-residence from each county-of-birth was assumed to remain the same for the subsequent decade, although the age of existing migrants was increasing every year in the computer model in order to mirror reality. For migrants under five years of age this means that the migrant population was recreated every year.

55. A visual check was made to ensure that the 5 to 9 years age-band was not too large in numbers, as a result of having rather less than the correct amount of age-specific mortality applied to it and thus distorting the data. The age-structure of the child population is that of a gradual decrease in numbers with age, which is caused by mortality and should be expected. However, this pattern is complicated by a decline over time in infant mortality coupled with declining fertility in proportion to the total population. Furthermore, out-migration and emigration affect the numbers of children in any age-band. Checks were made for every estimated census of the largest population of both sexes, invariably the native-born. In these numbers in the 5 to 9 age-band exceeded those in the preceding age-band (0 to 4 years) in a total of 16 cases out of 320 age-structures checked. However, there were also 35 cases where the 5 to 9 age-band had lower numbers than the subsequent age-band (10 to 14 years), i.e. a result which could not have been affected by the mortality calculations. This check was applied both to the data estimating emigration and to that used for current migration. Moreover, when the young were aggregated by year, age-band and sex, the total

number in each age-band declined with increasing age as would be expected. This evidence suggests that the adjustments made to the data in this study in order to accommodate problems of age-specific mortality do not seriously affect results.

56. The spasmodic nature of emigration can be seen in the table of annual overseas emigration in Flinn, *Scottish Population History*. Table 6.1.4 pp. 446–7.

57. Hammond and McCullagh, *Quantitative Techniques in Geography,* pp. 144–58.

58. *Ibid,* p. 145.

59. The operation involved re-running the entire computer programme twice, with the revised age-structure ratios so that the effects of these two extreme situations on the results could be measured. However, this method of checking the accuracy of the data proved impossible. The migrant age-structure ratios were used to expand the published birthplace census tabulation from two to sixteen age-bands for each sex. The total number of migrants from any county-of-birth in a county-of-residence remained the same, but the number of migrants in an age-band was reduced or exaggerated by two standard errors. In some age-bands this exaggeration meant that too many migrants were predicted for the total number in that age-band in the county-of-residence. This total number for each county-of-residence was derived from the age-structure of the population tabulation obtained from the published census. This excess of migrants in an age-band meant that the native population of the county was forced into negative numbers, an impossible situation. The skewed migrant age-structure ratios could not therefore be used because there was not a large enough margin for error that would permit their application, thus indicating how tightly the migrant age-structure ratios were held by the data.

60. See Appendix 9, in some years errors are virtually as great as the totals for females from Argyll in the age-bands 30–34 and 35–39 years. However, the errors in female migrants under 20 years and the total numbers lost are very small.

61. The regions used by Anderson and Morse in 'The People' are those originally devised by Flinn *et al. Scottish Population History.* p. XXIII, Map 3.

62. Clearly this proposal for better programming would improve the current migrant estimates as well. It would no longer be necessary to estimate these separately.

63. Baines, *Migration in a Mature Economy,* Appendix I, pp. 283–98.

64. *Ibid.* p. 283.

3

Life-Time and Current Migration within Scotland

Migration, in this research inter-county migration, can be divided into two types: lifetime, which includes all migrants regardless of the length of time they have been resident outside their county-of-birth, or current that consists of those migrants that have moved recently, within a specified number of years (in the present study during the preceding decade). Before analysing the computed estimates of current migration, it is worth considering to what extent existing knowledge — in this case the published census — can provide us with new data on Scottish mobility. Thus this chapter begins by expanding information on migration from the 'cleaned' but 'unprocessed' census material,[1] and because of this the estimates may differ slightly from those calculated directly from the published census. It will therefore attempt to provide an overview of life-time movement, but it will also show the drawbacks of this data source.[2] Despite these constraints the census still supplies useful aggregate material on population movement within Scotland and provides a coarse age-structure of the migrant population. The second part of the chapter will consider the computed estimates of current migration providing first an overview, then regional issues and the age and gender of migrants.

The Scale Of Life-Time Migration: A Regional Perspective

In Chapter 1 it was shown that well before 1861, levels of out-migration within Scotland were significant, and they probably rose to unprecedented levels during the Highland famine. Yet Table 3.1 shows that in the period 1861–1911, the proportion of life-time migrants living outside their county-of-birth increased from slightly over a fifth to more than a quarter of the total Scottish-born population. Indeed the proportions of migrants increased steadily until 1901, although there was a slight decline in the subsequent census.

The total Scottish-born population rose steadily throughout the period 1861–1911 and the migrant population also increased. However, there was

93

Table 3.1. Life-Time Migration in Scotland Recorded in the Census

CENSUS YEAR	MALES			FEMALES		
	Total Scots-born	Scots living outside their county-of-birth	% of migrants in the Scots-born population	Total Scots-born	Scots living outside their county-of-birth	% of migrants in the Scots-born population
1861	1,309,398	294,602	22.50	1,474,402	333,441	22.58
1871	1,448,424	345,946	23.88	1,613,107	390,182	24.19
1881	1,618,027	400,238	24.74	1,772,586	452,239	25.51
1891 (pre)*	1,761,820	444,042	25.20	1,921,506	496,679	25.85
1891 (post)*	1,761,820	447,456	25.40	1,921,506	500,518	26.05
1901	1,959,654	504,029	25.72	2,120,993	558,898	26.35
1911	2,092,443	530,293	25.34	2,270,030	596,667	26.28

* pre- or post-revision census

a marked gender imbalance in the total population, in that the number of females vastly exceeded males even though the proportions of each sex leaving their county-of-birth were very similar. Although the percentage of females migrating always slightly exceeded males, the huge excess of females in the total population means that proportions lost inadequately reflect the greater number of female migrants. In every census year there were at least forty thousand more female life-time migrants than male, and in 1911 the excess was over sixty thousand females. Yet this excess of female migrants may not have been as apparent to contemporaries as it appears on paper, since the proportions of males to females lost were so similar. In 1861 there were 112.6 females for every 100 males in the Scottish population, and 113.2 female migrants for every 100 males. By 1911 the gender imbalance in the total population had been reduced to 108.5 females, but the ratio of female migrants to males had remained remarkably consistent at 112.6. We are therefore looking at a Scottish-born population where nearly three quarters of the population remain in their county-of-birth, but a sizeable minority migrate. This minority was not however spread evenly across Scotland, but concentrated in certain regions, counties and indeed parishes.[3]

INTER-REGIONAL LIFE-TIME MIGRATION

It could be argued that a considerable proportion of inter-county migration 'caught' by the census was in fact local movement that happened to cross a county boundary and not long distance movement. Moreover, the fact that the subsequent analysis uses population categories as the unit of measurement, and that these categories are based on demographic rather than geographical criteria means that the accident of certain counties being grouped together might over-emphasise the role of migration. This discussion of regional migration in Scotland is intended to reveal the true extent of long distance movement.[4] The regions are defined in Table 3.2. As noted in Chapter 2, these regions are not the same as those used in the Scottish census,[5] nor do they correspond to the population categories devised in the present study to explain the migrant age-structure samples.

When Scottish population movement is only considered at this inter-regional level, (in other words inter-county migration that remains within the region is ignored), then two types of long distance migration become apparent. These can be classified as either a rural to urban regional movement or as movement within the 'urbanising' regions. Urban counties in this context refers to counties with considerable urban growth; there were no totally urbanised counties. The counties comprising the West and East Lowlands were predominantly urban counties. However, Kinross, which was classified as within the East Lowland region, was not an urbanising county, but was included to create a geographical entity.

Table 3.2. Inter-Regional Life-Time Migration by Gender:
The Native-Born Population and the Proportion of Migrants

	1861		1911	
REGION	MALE	FEMALE	MALE	FEMALE
HIGHLAND COUNTIES	266,687	309,275	244,979	280,163
Argyll, Caithness, Inverness, Perth, Orkney,	*19.29%*	*19.80%*	*26.58%*	*29.16%*
Ross & Cromarty, Shetland and Sutherland				
NORTHEAST	173,561	196,184	238,942	265,918
Aberdeen, Banff, Elgin (Moray), Kincardine	*9.44%*	*9.21%*	*16.74%*	*16.83%*
and Nairn				
WEST LOWLANDS	394,679	432,772	886,830	941,380
Ayr, Bute, Dunbarton, Lanark, and Renfrew	*6.86%*	*6.55%*	*7.58%*	*7.98%*
EAST LOWLANDS	348,577	395,577	585,826	636,267
Angus (Forfar), Clackmannan, East Lothian	*13.48%*	*12.86%*	*14.25%*	*13.90%*
(Haddington), Fife, Kinross, Midlothian				
(Edinburgh), Stirling and West Lothian (Linlithgow)				
SOUTHERN COUNTIES	125,894	142,594	135,866	146,030
Berwick, Dumfries, Kirkcudbright, Peebles,	*15.54%*	*15.56%*	*28.18%*	*26.32%*
Roxburgh, Selkirk and Wigtown				

Total population in roman script.
Proportion of population that were life-time migrants in italics.

In Table 3.2 migrants from a region are shown as a percentage of the total number of people born in that region regardless of where they lived within Scotland. The greatest proportion of regional movement per head of population was from rural to urban regions and the largest flows were from the Highland and Southern counties. In 1861, almost 20% of Highland-born people were living elsewhere in Scotland and by 1911 this had increased to between 27% and 29% for males and females respectively, but as Devine has shown, some temporary migration would be included in those figures.[6] The Southern counties also experienced high out-migration, which between 1861 and 1911 increased by over 80% for males and by nearly 70% for females. This therefore suggests an increasingly mobile population, with a significant increase in the life-time migrant population over a fifty year period and in the case of the Northeast region almost a doubling of the proportions leaving from just over 9% to nearly 17%

The West Central Lowlands had the lowest proportion of migrants to other regions in relation to its total population, although the enormous population concentrated in this region meant that its natives still formed a significant proportion of the population of other regions. For example, in 1911 migrants from the West Lowlands represented more than 8% of the total adult male population in the East Lowlands and 6% in the Southern counties, 8% of adult females in the East Lowlands and 5% in the Highland counties. The census has only two age classifications (above and below 20 years) and so in this context 'adult' refers to everybody over 20 years old. Furthermore, even in 1861 11% of adult Scots males in the Highland counties had been born in other regions of Scotland, mainly the East Lowlands, but large numbers also came from the West Lowlands and Northeast regions. By 1911 this in-migration had risen to 17%. This movement was not restricted to males, as adult female migrants were also involved in these counter-flows. In 1861 they represented 9% of the population of the Highland counties and by 1911 this had increased to 17%.[7] Thus although most of the migration was towards the Central Belt, one should clearly not ignore the significant counter-flows. In the example of the West Lowlands this represented both urban to rural in the case of the Highland and the Southern County regions, but also inter-urban to the East Lowlands.

There are measurable gender differences in the life-time migration. At a regional level female migrants almost invariably exceeded the number of males in numerical terms (as Table 3.3 suggests), but as a proportion of the population (Table 3.2) they were frequently lower. However, the proportions of both sexes in any given region were generally fairly close, and although between 1861 and 1911 the proportions migrating increased, female life-time migration grew more than male. The proportions of migrants of both sexes in each region were much closer to each other than to the same sex in another region. This suggests that the regional factors were more significant than gender at the regional level of analysis.

Table 3.3. Life-Time Migrants by Age, Gender and Region-of-Birth

Region	Highland Counties		Northeast		East Lowlands		West Lowlands		Southern Counties	
Year	1861	1911	1861	1911	1861	1911	1861	1911	1861	1911
Males <20 yrs	10,251	9,953	4,256	6,303	14,436	20,239	11,161	23,825	4,715	6,154
Females <20 yrs	11,005	10,415	4,352	6,377	14,091	20,204	10,590	23,860	4,490	5,846
Males >20 yrs	41,183	55,158	12,133	33,698	32,540	63,223	15,912	43,439	14,844	32,129
Females >20 yrs	50,227	71,371	13,717	38,384	36,770	68,215	17,756	51,230	17,692	32,585

See Table 3.2 for counties in each region

Table 3.3 provides a breakdown by two age-bands of migrants who had left their region-of-birth. This shows that there was an increase in the numbers leaving in every category over the fifty year period, with the notable exception of young Highlanders. This increased volume of migration is not surprising in a region like the West Lowlands, where the population more or less doubled over the period and indeed the number of life-time migrants rose even faster. However, elsewhere population growth was less or non-existent, yet the volume of migration increased. Thus one has a situation in the Highland and Southern regions of counties that (except for Peebles and Selkirk) had negative population growth, and yet the volume of life-time migrants still rose.

The entire Scottish-born population was much younger than today and the proportion of the population under twenty years comprised almost half the total population — indeed, depending on the decade, 39–52% of males and 42–46% of females were under twenty-one years old (see Appendix 2[c]). Amongst the younger age-group the number of each sex migrating was much closer and the gender ratios remained fairly consistent. One can conclude that the forces promoting migration remained relatively constant over time. However, the ratio of those under 20 years to adult migrants varied considerably between regions. At one extreme young life-time migrants from the West Lowlands comprised almost 40% of all migrants in 1861 and about a third of the total in 1911, this being fairly close to the proportion of young people in the total Scottish population. Yet in contrast young migrants from the Highland region represented only 19% and 14% of the total migrant population in 1861 and 1911 respectively.

The dividing of migrants in census tabulations at 20 years is unfortunate, in that the younger group comprised two separate movements, firstly those of children with their parents and secondly independent young adult movement. Nevertheless, when the data from 1861 and 1911 are compared, the number of young life-time male migrants consistently exceeded females from the East Lowlands and the Southern counties and the reverse was true in the Highland counties and the Northeast. Amongst the adults, female life-time migrants invariably exceeded males. This meant that in every region the majority of life-time migrants were female and in every region except the Southern counties (1911) this majority was overwhelming. However, with this age-band being so broad it is impossible to make any meaningful conclusions as to when people left their region-of-birth.

Table 3.1 shows that the proportion of migrants in the total Scottish population increased until 1901, but the percentages of the population leaving individual regions changed markedly between 1861 and 1911. There was also a very significant increase in migrants from the Northeast (Table 3.2) where the percentage nearly doubled, but both the Highland and the Southern county regions retained their positions as the major regions of out-migration. In 1861 the Highland counties lost the highest proportion of both sexes through migration, but by 1911 a higher proportion of males were leaving the Southern counties than the Highlands. The two lowland regions were both areas with massive population growth and yet although the numbers of out-migrants increased, the proportions of out-migrants remained remarkably consistent over the fifty year period. Nevertheless the East Lowlands experienced greater migrant losses than the West in proportion to their population, and both areas were also attracting vast numbers of migrants this did not as previously shown, stem out-migration.

Thus it can be concluded that although the regions used in this discussion are quite large, a significant volume of inter-regional migration can be measured. Undoubtedly some of the inter-county migration still represents purely local movement between adjoining counties that straddle a regional border, but a considerable proportion of the movement is over a long distance. The greatest percentages of regional migration are from rural to urbanising regions (the Central Lowlands), but there are also significant counter-flows by both sexes. Finally, the factors promoting regional out-migration were remarkably consistent, in that migration was gender specific and sustained over time.

THE COUNTY-OF-BIRTH POPULATION

Leaving aside the regions, let us now consider inter-county life-time migration. In the total adult Scottish population there was a significant majority of females. This is not only observed at a national level[8] and with regard to the Scots-born population, but it is also true of every individual county.[9] However, it is also clear that the difference in numbers between males and females narrows over time. This is particularly noticeable in Shetland, where in 1861 there was the extraordinarily high ratio of 147.0 females for every 100 males, but this vast female majority was considerably reduced to 133.1 by 1911.[10] In Shetland some men were possibly away at the Greenland Fisheries in the 1860s and 70s, and the navy was also an important employer[11] so men could have been away on temporary employment. The subsequent rise in herring fishery may have enabled men to stay at home for longer periods, but its impact is largely unknown.[12]

The age-structure of the Scottish population was altering nationally between 1861 and 1911, and this is reflected in the decreasing proportion of persons less than twenty years old. The vast majority of counties were experiencing a declining death rate by the 1881 census.[13] This would have the effect of decreasing the percentage of the population that was less than twenty years old. This is apparent at the national level (Appendix 2[c]), and also in both the native and the migrant populations (Appendix 3[n] and 2[m] respectively)[14]. It is fortunate for the purposes of this study that this problem of a decreasing proportion of young in the population does not have to be estimated in the calculations, and can be resolved by the above and below twenty years age-bands.

In the censuses up to and including 1891, the number of Scots males over the age of twenty is not only less than females of the same age, but also less than Scots of both sexes under 20 years. Adults are less likely ever to numerically exceed the young in counties-of-birth with rapid growth, as in these counties newcomers, whether migrants or immigrants, have children which become natives of their parents' adopted county-of-residence and the young population therefore expands very fast. For example, in Dunbarton Scottish-born children always exceeded the adults, and this reflects the enormous population growth of that county (Table 2.3). Moreover, in most counties-of-birth, even those with some population growth, a decline in the proportion of young in the population is common. This decline in the young can be found for example in Forfar (Angus) by 1901 and in Dumfries by 1881. As indicated earlier, the declining proportion of the population under 20 years was the result of limiting fertility and improving mortality rates.[15]

It is important to appreciate that a declining county-of-residence population does not necessarily reflect massive emigration, as it can also reveal high levels of migration. The census not only records the total population by county-of-residence, but also the total population resident in Scotland by county-of-birth. Thus the natives of many counties with declining populations can be found in other parts of Scotland, and so the total county-of-birth population (resident anywhere in Scotland) was not falling. Indeed any decrease in the adult population by county-of-birth was very unusual.[16] Nevertheless, four counties-of-birth, namely Argyll, Perth, Shetland and Sutherland do experience an absolute decline in their populations. This means that not only the native population within the county-of-birth was declining, but also their total population anywhere Scotland was in decline. This could reflect long term population decline in the county, possibly due to out-migration leading to an ageing population, and/or massive emigration.

As already noted, Table 3.1 shows that the percentage of Scottish life-time migrants within Scotland increased nationally until 1901 and thereafter decreased slightly. Nevertheless, the percentage of migrants born in some counties decreased much earlier. For example a decrease in the percentage of Dunbarton-born migrants was observed as early as the 1881 enumeration, and in Linlithgow (West Lothian) a decrease occurred only a decade later. In contrast in many counties, such as Elgin (Moray) and Berwick, the proportion of migrants rose steadily throughout the period (1861–1911).[17] In both Dunbarton and Linlithgow (West Lothian), the population was growing very fast, the stimulus being rapid industrialisation, and these new opportunities would have encouraged the native population to stay.[18] In contrast both Berwick and Elgin (Moray) were experiencing a declining population by 1911.[19]

We have already observed that the percentage of migrants in the total county-of-birth population is remarkably similar for both males and females, although in absolute terms there is always a significant majority of females. An absolute majority of male migrants in the county-of-birth population is exceedingly rare, and only in Forfar (Angus) does it occur in every census (see Appendix 2[t]). In most counties with high out-migration, work for females was probably less likely to be available. In Angus however, the textile industry was an important employer of female labour and males may have been less likely to find work. In 1861 male out-migration also exceeded female in Sutherland.[20]

Migrants from a county were normally attracted to a particular county or region regardless of gender. Out-migrants from Argyll, for example, were most likely to go to Lanarkshire, rather than Dunbartonshire which was closer and also attracting incomers. However, the county of destination for migrants from Linlithgow (West Lothian), Perth and Sutherland was gender specific. In each case the males moved to Lanarkshire and with the exception of Perth where females went to Forfar (Angus), it was Edinburgh that attracted the females. [21] Moreover, this pattern was a long-standing tradition in Perth and Linlithgow in that it'had existed since 1861, but in Sutherland it changed over time.[22] This gender specific movement reveals that potential migrants had a detailed knowledge of the relative advantages of different destinations.

High levels of out-migration from the counties attracting in-migration were also apparent, it frequently being a higher proportion of the total county-of-birth population than in counties normally considered the focus of out-migration. For example, as can be seen in Appendix 2[p], the migration-attracting counties of Dunbarton, Stirling and Linlithgow (West Lothian) all had levels of out-migration in excess of 33%, while in contrast counties experiencing out-migration such as Ross and Cromarty or Sutherland were losing a much lower proportion of their population. This was perhaps the most significant aspect of migration, as it shows that a high proportion was no longer from remote rural areas to urban development, but was instead inter-urban migration. As noted earlier it is incorrect to describe any Scottish county as urban, as all retain some rural areas, although clearly some counties have more urban growth than others. In this context the counties of the Central Lowlands are considered to be industrialising counties and therefore counties with considerable urban development. However, inter-urban migration may not involve the same level of positive planning as previously. Migrants within an urban environment may well not even be aware of crossing a county boundary, especially if it occurs in a town that straddles two counties, the most obvious example of this being Glasgow (in the counties of Lanark and Renfrew), and it may well have implications for the age at which people migrate.

The percentage of the migrants under twenty years was noticeably higher in the Scottish-born migrant population (see Appendix 2[p]) than in the total migrant population, which includes immigrants from outside Scotland. There is therefore a greater proportion of Scots-born migrants under 20 years than in other immigrant groups. In the Scottish population there was always a greater percentage of males under twenty years than females, although the difference appears to narrow over time (see Appendix 2[p]). There was moreover a greater number of females than males in the total population. The importance of this becomes clearer when one compares the percentage and absolute data for migrants in Appendices 2[p] and [t] for every county. At a more general level Table 3.1 shows that in 1861, for example, 22.5% of Scots males were migrants, that is 294,602 males; for females the figures were 22.6% and 333,441. Thus almost 39,000 more females had migrated than males, but the percentage of each sex migrating was approximately equal. The percentage of migrants less than twenty appears to suggest a pattern of far more males migrating young than females (see Appendix 2[m]), but in fact 30.8% equal 90,826 individuals for young male migrants, while for females 26.9% equals 89,662, a difference of 1,164 or just over 1%, which is nowhere near as great a difference as the percentages imply.

Scottish Out-Movement to the Rest of Britain

This analysis of regional migration within Scotland is particularly interesting when compared with Scottish emigrants in England and Wales. Table 3.4 shows that the number of Scottish life-time emigrant males moving south peaked in 1901, but for females 1911 was higher. In that year 7.2% of males and 6.6% of females of Scottish birth lived south of the border. This represents over 320,000 Scots. Work by Baines on England and Wales,[23] and supported subsequently in this study, suggests that the decade ending in 1911 was one of high emigration and low current migration from England, Wales and Scotland. Since the population of these countries were emigrating overseas, there were probably less Scots moving south of the border. This may mean that by 1911 one is observing a fairly elderly Scots-born population that had been resident in England and Wales for a long time.

Table 3.4. The Number of Scots and their Percentage of the
Total Population Enumerated in the Censuses of England and Wales
and Ireland Between 1861 and 1911.

Census Year	Scots-Born Resident in England and Wales				Scots-Born Resident in Ireland			
	Males	Females	Total	Percentage of total population of England and Wales	Males	Females	Total	Percentage of total population of Ireland
1861	*	*	169,202	0.84	*	*	16,861	0.29
1871	*	*	213,254	0.94	*	*	20,318	0.38
1881	132,483	121,045	253,528	0.98	12,155	10,173	22,328	0.43
1891	144,886	137,385	282,271	0.97	14,737	12,586	27,323	0.58
1901	163,443	153,395	316,838	1.01	15,404	14,697	30,101	0.68
1911	161,242	160,583	321,825	0.93	20,030	18,456	38,486	0.87

* A breakdown of the Census enumeration not available

The only detailed census information available is from 1911 and as just argued above the people 'caught' in this census may have been fairly long-time residents. Nevertheless, even a cursory glance at Appendix 4 suggests that above-average proportions of Scottish movement[24] come from all the Southern counties region (Berwick, Dumfries, Kirkcudbright, Peebles, Roxburgh, Selkirk (males) and Wigtown), parts of the East Lowlands (Angus (males) East Lothian (females) and Midlothian) and the Northeast (Aberdeen, Moray and Nairn). Although movement from the south of Scotland may be explained, at least in part, by their geographical proximity to England, there does also appear to be a bias towards greater movement out of the eastern counties. This could be accounted for by traditional trading links with England along this coast dating back to at least the mid-fifteenth century.[25] The three regions of high emigration into England also had high proportions of migrants within Scotland in 1911. However, a high proportion of life-time migrants from a region does not necessarily imply large flows into England and Wales. The Highland counties region for example, despite the highest migration levels within Scotland, had relatively little movement south of the Border except for males from Perth and Shetland. Clearly in 1911 migratory patterns within Scotland were not necessarily reflected in movement across the Border, although it should be noted that the West Lowlands not only have the lowest migration rate within Scotland, but also have lower rates of movement south than the other Scottish regions.

The decision to consider movement into England and Wales as emigration rather than migration was made for ease of computation. Nevertheless, this section has highlighted two other reasons that justify this decision. Firstly, there was geographical inconsistency in the movement south from Scotland. Although the highest proportions of population movement into England and Wales came from the closest counties, regional patterns vary in a way that cannot be related to distance, the clearest examples of this being Shetland and Aberdeen, which both have high levels of male emigration. Secondly, the evidence from migrants to England in 1911 (Appendix 4) and also earlier censuses (Table 3.4) suggests that there were markedly different gender balances between the two out-migrant populations (in Scotland and in England and Wales). Bearing in mind that there was a female majority in Scotland, there were also far more female out-migrants within Scotland than males, indeed in 1911, as already noted, there were 112.6 female migrants for every 100 males. The evidence suggests that this pattern was not repeated in England and Wales, where Scottish-born male residents slightly exceeded females in numbers and one finds in 1881 only 91.4 female emigrants for every 100 males, rising to 99.6 in 1911.

Table 3.4 also shows the volume of Scots in Ireland. When compared with the numbers going to England and Wales, Scots in Ireland appear insignificant, only about a tenth of the number going south, and yet the proportions of Scots in relation to the two native populations were by 1911 very similar. As in England and Wales the number of Scots-born males exceeded females, but the number of females increased steadily over the fifty year period, but males, whilst also increasing, spurt suddenly in the final decade. Thus one can see that female emigrants rose from 83.7 per 100 males in 1881 to 92.1 in 1911. It is not known whether this increase in male migration was linked to the growth in the Belfast shipyards in that decade.[26] Indeed very little is known about the Scots in Ireland and it has been assumed that many of the Scots-born are in fact of Irish parents who happened to be in Scotland when their child was born. These people would therefore be part of a continuing pattern of interconnected links between the two countries. However, this is almost entirely hypothesis and needs further investigation.

This reworking of the census tabulations has shown that the Scots were a fairly mobile people, but it cannot tell us anything about the decade in which a migrant moved and the coarse age-bands in the census mean that very little is known about a migrants' age. We do not know for example if young migrants were moving as children or in their late teens. These problems will be addressed by examining the author's estimates of current migration.

The Structure of the Current Migrant Population 1861–1911

As in the discussion of life-time migration, this section will begin with a general overview and then move on to the particular to tease out the differences between individual demographic population categories as opposed to the geographical region considered in the first part of this discussion. Finally some general points concerning individual counties will be considered. It will look first at the proportion of the population leaving and then at the age at which people left. Evidence of return migration will be discussed, and to conclude the main points highlighted.

AN OVERVIEW OF CURRENT MIGRANTION

Current migration at the national level is shown in Table 3.5 and despite its coarse scale, demonstrates several important points. Firstly, from earlier discussion, it should be expected that the excess of females in the population and the greater number of female life-time migrants would result in considerably more female current migrants than males. Secondly,

Table 3.5. Scottish Current Migration 1861–1911

Decade	Current Migrants*			Proportion of the native population**		Proportion of the total current migrant population	
	Males	Females	Total	Males	Females	Males	Females
Scotland							
1861–1871	-95,309	-104,900	-200,209	-7.80	-7.73	47.6	52.4
1871–1881	-107,722	-119,123	-226,845	-7.95	-8.09	47.7	52.3
1881–1891	-99,825	-107,072	-206,897	-6.88	-6.82	48.2	51.8
1891–1901	-120,256	-128,375	-248,631	-7.46	-7.41	48.4	51.6
1901–1911	-93,119	-110,479	-203,598	-5.49	-6.04	45.7	54.3
Highlands							
1861–1871	-20,613	-24,565	-45,178	-9.39	-9.72	45.63	54.37
1871–1881	-18,287	-22,487	-40,774	-8.64	-9.39	44.85	55.15
1881–1891	-17,352	-18,873	-36,225	-8.57	-8.29	47.90	52.10
1891–1901	-18,684	-21,199	-39,883	-9.56	-9.74	46.85	53.15
1901–1911	-9,018	-13,080	-22,098	-5.11	-6.57	40.81	59.19
Borders							
1861–1871	-9,531	-9,874	-19,405	-9.86	-9.10	49.12	50.88
1871–1881	-10,486	-11,030	-21,516	-10.98	-10.48	48.74	51.26
1881–1891	-10,905	-10,362	-21,267	-11.78	-10.29	51.28	48.72
1891–1901	-11,001	-11,316	-22,317	-12.80	-11.97	49.30	50.70
1901–1911	-7,219	-7,811	-15,030	-9.15	-9.08	48.03	51.97
The Periphery and Northeast							
1861–1871	-31,573	-33,611	-65,184	-8.72	-8.32	48.44	51.56
1871–1881	-35,779	-37,787	-73,566	-9.04	-8.72	48.64	51.36
1881–1891	-32,369	-33,285	-65,654	-7.94	-7.44	49.30	50.70
1891–1901	-44,011	-43,023	-87,034	-10.01	-8.97	50.57	49.43
1901–1911	-28,345	-32,908	-61,253	-6.64	-6.92	46.28	53.72
Central Lowlands							
1861–1871	-33,592	-36,850	-70,442	-6.47	-6.55	47.69	52.31
1871–1881	-43,170	-47,819	-90,989	-6.93	-7.23	47.45	52.55
1881–1891	-39,199	-44,552	-83,751	-5.48	-5.89	46.80	53.20
1891–1901	-46,559	-52,837	-99,396	-5.45	-5.88	46.84	53.16
1901–1911	-48,536	-56,681	-105,217	-4.99	-5.54	46.13	53.87

*   See Appendix 8 for range of standard errors

**   The proportion is calculated as current migrants over the sum of the native population in the subsequent census plus current migrants (that is the total native population at the end of the decade if nobody had moved out). Current migrants are still considered as such even if they were resident in another county in the same population category. (This is to avoid the problem of the population categories not being homogeneous geographic units).

the proportions of current migrants of both sexes were generally very similar, except in the final decade; this too was suggested by the life-time data. Males therefore showed a comparable proportion of the population loss through current migration to that of females without reflecting the same number of individuals. Thirdly, the female bias in the total current migrant population narrowed between 1861 and 1901, there being 52.4% of female migrants in the former year but by the latter it had shrunk to 51.6%, and then in the final decade the gender difference widened again and the lowest proportion of males in the fifty year period was recorded at 45.7%. The ration of male to female losses are, however, sufficiently close to suggest that roughly the same proportions of population are migrating regardless of decade.

There was a fluctuating pattern of current migration with two troughs interspersed with two peaks. The first decade (1861–1871) cannot be described as a trough, because the lack of quantifiable knowledge of the previous decade prevents direct comparisons. All that can be deduced is that current migration for the decade 1861–71 is lower than the following decade, but closer to the subsequent peak in percentage terms than later ones. There were two decades of high current migration, 1871–81 and 1891–1901. The first peak in out-migration, 1871–81, had the highest proportion of current migrants. This is quite early in the study period and thereafter the overall impression is that the proportion of current migrants became less significant over time. This is not incompatible with the earlier statement that the life-time migrant population was increasing until 1901 because the life-time population included all the earlier movement. Moreover, despite the fact that the national population was increasing, the total native population as a proportion of the national population was declining (due to increased migration). This means that using the native population as a baseline for the proportion of out-migrants lost gives a baseline that is itself diminishing in relation to the total Scottish population.[27] Therefore the impression of the decreasing significance of current migration as a population pattern is not without foundation.

THE AGGREGATE CURRENT MIGRATION BY POPULATION CATEGORY-OF-BIRTH

So far the population categories — discussed in Chapter 2 — have been used for computational purposes as categories-of-residence. It has been argued that the population category was likely to affect the type of migrants it attracted, so that a county such as Forfar (Angus) tended to draw female in-migrants because of the attraction of work in the textile factories in

Dundee. Indeed, the computer estimations of both migration and emigration were based on this premise of categories-of-residence. As has already been mentioned that the actual population categories were groups of counties with similar characteristics of population growth or decline, rather than a regional grouping. Hereafter the population categories used in the discussion will be categories-of-birth rather than categories-of-residence. It is not unreasonable to argue that current migrants from a category that had rapid population expansion were quite likely to have different age-structures from those in a declining one, which was remote from centres of population growth. It should however be noted that when current migration was measured by category-of-birth, it included all migration, including that which occurred within the category. This was to avoid the problem of the categories not being geographic units. It means that migration between two counties within the same category was still being classed as current migration. The aggregation of estimates into categories will thus enable an overview of population patterns to be discussed, before considering some of the individual counties. The complex results from thirty two counties[28] in five decades for both sexes and in sixteen age-bands would be too detailed to summarise in an overview.

The discussion will now be widened to consider aggregate current migration by population category. It can be seen in Table 3.5 that although the generalised statements in the previous discussion remain valid there are differences between the individual population categories and when the categories are compared against the average which is Scotland as a whole. Hunt's analysis of regional wage variations has been used to explain the economic situation in each category and this may begin to account for the differing patterns of current migration.[29] The social conditions in each category also had important implications for population movement, but no comparative research on social conditions is known and indeed in some areas even the basic research is lacking. It should be noted that although the study period included the agricultural depression between 1875 and 1900, this has been shown to be a prosperous time for the Scottish agricultural labour force with wages and conditions improving.[30] Large scale rural–urban migration and emigration cannot therefore be directly linked to this depression, although locally it may be significant.

1. The 'Borders' and 'Highlands'

These two categories contained relatively small and decreasing proportions of the total Scottish population (Table 2.4). It was therefore not entirely surprising that these categories did not conform to the fluctuating pattern of troughs and peaks in current migration that were apparent in the national data (Table 3.5). These categories were both rural areas with employment mainly in agriculture, although there was some employment in textiles in the south.[31]

In the Highlands the proportion of out-migrants in the native population was above the national average, except for male migrants in 1901–11. However, current migration fell over time, both in volume and as a proportion of the native population, with the notable exception of the decade 1891–1901. Indeed the difference between the total number of migrants in the highest and lowest decades for out-migration was over 100%. This was the largest range in any population category and so clearly current migration patterns from the Highlands were changing far more than elsewhere. Moreover, the migration was more gender specific than in the other categories, in that it involved the highest ratios of female migrants. Males in particular appear to be highly sensitive to factors either within the Highlands that were forcing the men to migrate, or to attractions outwith the Highlands, but clearly these factors did not affect female out-movement in a similar way.

Unfortunately Hunt's regional wage analysis combines counties in the Highlands category with those in the Northeast and also Angus, which in this study are in the 'Periphery'.[32] However, with regard to agricultural wages, Hunt noted that there were variations, Perth and Kinross having higher wages, while in the Northwest crofting and payment in kind were common. This region (even when the Northeast was included) was one of the lowest wage areas in Britain and indeed in 1907 labourers in Caithness, Orkney and Shetland were the worst paid.[33] Clearly there was a financial incentive to encourage long distance out-migration.

The crofting communities of the west experienced two decades of relative stability, the 1860s and 70s, when their sheep were sold for high prices and the fishing industry grew rapidly.[34] This, Richards has argued, raised expectations which were not thereafter fulfilled.[35] Sometimes local casual work was available,[36] but a crofter's income was mainly supplemented by temporary migration.[37] Nevertheless, Devine has shown that estate policy, if strictly enforced, could cause subtle, but in the long-term substantial, out-migration or emigration.[38] Moreover, in some areas crofters were being deprived of their hill pasture for animals as it was fenced for deer forests. As the animals also spoilt the crofter's crops, deer forests were a serious threat to their fragile economy,[39] and increased crofter dependence on external earnings. However, deer forests may have encouraged the growth of a tourist industry and provided some people with employment in local towns. In agriculture there was a series of bad seasons between 1856–1890, recalling the earlier potato famine, and accommodation remained squalid, so 'the majority of inhabitants... continued to endure an existence of poverty and insecurity'. It is however, important to note that the declining population in this part of the Highlands cannot be solely attributed to high levels of out-migration. Anderson and Morse have shown that although maternal fertility was high, delayed marriage and very high levels of permanent celibacy also reduced natural increase.[40]

The majority of the foregoing discussion referred to the North and Western Highlands. The inland counties of Kinross and Perth although part of this category cannot be included in this analysis because, as already noted, the counties had relatively high wages. These counties were however, close to the more prosperous Central Belt where the prospects were even better.

In the 'Borders' the proportion of current migrants consistently exceeded the national average. Indeed the proportion of the native population migrating was generally higher than for any other category. This pattern occurred despite the declining populations of the counties in this category, and indeed the volume of current migrants generally increased until 1901 (although the female current migrant population did not rise in the decade 1881–91). Moreover, the proportion of male to female migrants was generally very close and in the decade 1881–91 male current migrants actually exceeded females. Indeed in that decade male migrants went against the national trend of a trough in migration. In the 'Borders' current male migration increased until 1901, both in volume and as a proportion of the population. Moreover, male current migrants formed a consistently higher proportion of the male native population than, was the case for females, unlike in the 'Highlands' where the reverse was true.

This pattern of out-migration in the 'Borders' is difficult to account for, as Hunt's study of regional wages shows this region[41] to be one of high agricultural wages (the staple economic activity), but 'it lacked the substantial industrial centres of the kind in which urban wages were usually high and well-paid occupations commonplace'.[42] There was however increased employment in textiles, which provided work for women and may account for the slightly lower proportion of female migrants.[43] The nearby 'Central Lowlands' category county of Selkirk in particular was growing very fast. In the dairy farming counties of the Southwest (Dumfries, Kirkcudbright and Wigtown) male employment in agriculture fell more heavily than in Scotland as a whole, particularly in Wigtown, whereas female employment fell more extensively in Dumfries and Kirkcudbright than the national average.[44] In the Border counties of Berwick and Roxburgh mixed farming prevailed and Robson has also shown that here social changes were also underway; the employment of bondagers was becoming less common and money wages were taking over. This meant that agricultural workers were no longer protected from steep price rises.[45] This was likely to make them more willing to move in bad times. Thus the 'Borders' generally had the highest proportions of out-migration to other parts of Scotland and at the same time emigration to England and Wales in 1911 was also exceptionally high (Appendix 4). This region was consequently experiencing massive out-movement, and at the same time a high level of female celibacy[46] which made population decline inevitable. Moreover, Robson cites evidence that even in the late eighteenth century the inhabitants of the Border counties had always been very mobile.[47] There was clearly a strong tradition of out-migration.

2. The 'Periphery and Northeast'

In this category the proportion of current migrants also consistently exceeded the national average. In the decade 1861–71 the current migration losses by volume were almost as high as those in the 'Central Lowlands' category, though they represented the loss of a higher proportion of the native population. However, the volume of current migrants failed to increase thereafter as rapidly as in the 'Central Lowlands'. This was because although the proportion lost through current migration in the 'Periphery' was consistently higher, the extraordinary population increase in the 'Central Lowlands' category meant that the volume of current migrants could increase, despite the lower proportions lost.

The 'Periphery' had fluctuating rates of current migration loss, but when out-migration was calculated as a proportion of the native population it was clear that the impact of these fluctuations increased over time. For example the largest migration losses by volume were in 1891–1901 and the lowest were in the subsequent decade. As with the 'Borders' the ratio of male to female out-migrants was generally close to unity. Male current migrants generally exceeded females as a proportion of the native population, although more females left than males, but in 1891–1901, the decade of high out-migration, male migrants exceeded females in all measurements.[48]

The counties forming this category were very disperse and cannot be related directly to Hunts' regional work. Nevertheless, it is possible to show that agricultural wages in this category were below the British average in 1867–70, but improved over time and were above the British average by 1898.[49] This suggests that increasing employment in industry may have been forcing agricultural wages upwards, and Carter considers that real wages in the Northeast rose by 30%.[50] This was because farm labour was in short supply due to a decline in crofting, the traditional source of additional farm workers. At the start of the period (1861) this region was experiencing agricultural improvement, farms were being enlarged by incorporating crofts, and displaced farmers and their offspring were increasingly unable to find other small farms to rent.[51] Crofts were only encouraged if they were useful as a method of reclaiming land. After 1870 crofting, which relied on family labour, declined, because crofters were unable or unwilling to continue paying the rents and their families were no longer prepared to stay.[52] There was therefore movement from the land throughout the period.[53]

The pattern for industries other than agriculture is not so clear. Campbell has shown that in 1886 wages in the granite industry (Aberdeen) were high, but in the jute industry (Angus) they were low.[54] The latter is particularly important because a quarter of all new jobs in Tayside were in textiles.[55] By comparison Aberdeen city had a much more diversified economic base. As Smith has pointed out she was the least specialised of the major Scottish cities, being an entreport for the Northeast region through both rail links and coastal shipping. She also had paper and textile mills as well as a fishing industry,[56] although by 1900 the once flourishing textile industry was declining.[57] After a crisis in the 1880s the herring fisheries flourished to an all time peak, benefiting the Northeast coastal villages and Angus. The white fisheries based in Aberdeen city were also very successful, but here profits were greatest from the larger steam boats and everywhere the number of traditional line boats fell and independent fishermen must have needed to adjust to the changing environment as employees of company-owned trawlers.[58]

3. The 'Central Lowlands'

In contrast to the other categories, the proportion of current migrants from the 'Central Lowlands' was always below the national average. The 'Central Lowlands' had the highest levels of population growth (every county had demographic growth in excess of 50% and sometimes much higher) and yet the increase in volume of current migration from the lowest (1861) to the highest (1911) was only 49%, which suggests that the proportion of current migrants was declining over time. Indeed the proportion of out-migration was high in the first two decades and greatest in the decade 1871–81, while it was lowest in 1901–11. The proportion of current migrants to the native population did not fluctuate wildly and indeed in the decades 1881–1901 were remarkably similar. The proportion of male to female out-migrants remained remarkably constant throughout the period although there was a slight increase in female migration vis-à-vis male.

The 'Central Lowlands' was attracting migrants from every other region, as the rapid population growth shows. Thus current migration was above the national average in three of the four population categories and the lowest levels of current out-migration were found in this category. The 'Central Lowlands' corresponds approximately to region twelve in Hunt's study.[59] In this region wages improved relative to the other regions both in agriculture and industry, so that 'by the early twentieth century it was one of the four highest-wage regions in Britain'.[60] Clearly for natives of this category nowhere else in Scotland was able to offer better prospects, while at the same time it was extremely attractive to migrants from other regions. As Hunt has noted the 'long term demand for labour was buoyant and wages were characterised by long-term improvement relative to other parts of Britain'.[61] However, Lee has found that only in the Lothians was service provision comparable to that in the Southeast of England, and the professional classes were under-represented in Fife, Stirling and the larger counties comprising part of the former Strathclyde region (Dunbarton, Lanark and Renfrew).[62] Therefore despite their relative prosperity, the counties of the Central Lowlands category did not generally offer as good employment prospects for all classes as were available elsewhere in Britain.[63]

Rural-urban migration still occurred in all the population categories because rural incomes remained below urban ones, and so migration had the effect of shifting people to high wage areas. Indeed as it has been observed 'the rural-urban migrant could expect to benefit from lower urban prices for everything except rent and sometimes from greater employment opportunities for his family'.[64] However it is important to remember that despite better prospects in urban areas a migrant's motives for moving were not just pull factors.

AGGREGATE CURRENT MIGRANT LOSSES BY COUNTY-OF-BIRTH

It is not proposed to analyse every county in great detail, but instead to highlight the main features of current migration patterns with examples. The aggregate computer estimates for every county-of-birth are tabulated in Appendix 5 and these should be referred to throughout this discussion.

The first point to notice is that the estimated percentage losses vary considerably according to the size of the county. As already noted, in a county that was small in area and did not contain a major town, many local moves could involve crossing a county boundary. It is perhaps surprising therefore that in Kinross only about 25% of the native population migrated in any decade despite its small size. In a county with a small population, migration can fluctuate wildly due to the booms and recessions of the major employer if it is a single industry, for example woollen textiles in Selkirk.[65] Clearly results from these small counties should be treated very cautiously. The larger the physical size of a county, the less likely there are to be violent fluctuations in the results, particularly if it contained a major town. Moreover, a big county with a large population was likely to have a broader based economy, so a marked difference from the normal trend would be more significant.

Five estimates of the percentage loss are provided for both males and females in every county, one for each decade from 1861–1911. These estimates are provided in Appendix 5 and it can be seen that the application of two standard errors plus or minus makes very little difference to the estimate. The estimates for Argyllshire males in 1891–1901 for example vary by only 1.1% and 0.6% when standard errors are deducted or added. The estimates of current migration losses have been mapped according to sex for every county and in each decade to provide an overall picture of movement in Scotland (see Appendix 7). These maps should be used in conjunction with the map showing population density in Scotland (Appendix 6). This is important because a county that reveals high losses may in fact have a very low density of population and although such losses would be very relevant in the local or regional context, the numbers involved could be insignificant in an analysis of movement in Scotland as a whole. Kirkcudbright and Wigtown are good examples of counties with a high percentage of losses through current migration but low population densities. Their population loss was therefore very significant locally and within the region of the Southwest, but not so nationally where the greatest volume of current migration was within the 'Central Lowlands'. This is noteworthy, as the greatest volume of current migration was always from the urban-based population of the 'Central Lowland' counties even though there were far greater percentage losses in other parts of the country.[66] The extraordinarily high proportion of the Scottish population concentrated in this area makes this inevitable. Rural-urban migration, although significant, was never the dominant form of inter-county migration in the period 1861–1911.

The maps in Appendix 7 show that there are no clear regional current migration patterns. The information was therefore replotted to show the relationship of the individual county-of-birth to the national average for both sexes (Table 3.5), and this is shown in Map 3.1. It was not unusual for a county to remain in the same relationship to the average throughout the period 1861–1911. Indeed in almost half the counties current migration was consistently above the national average for both sexes (Argyll, Ayr, Berwick, Bute, Clackmannan, Dunbarton, East Lothian, Inverness,

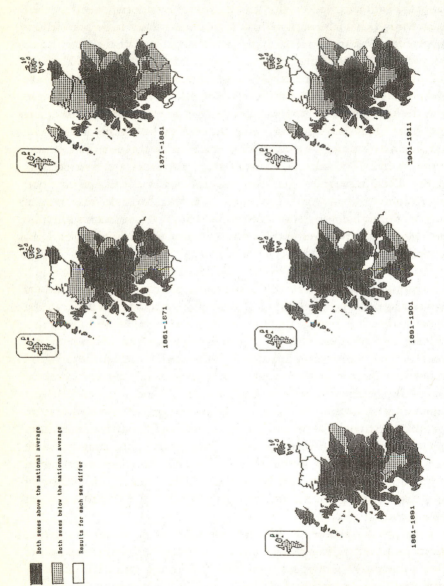

Both sexes above the national average

Both sexes below the national average

Results for each sex differ

1861-1871

1871-1881

1881-1891

1891-1901

1901-1911

Map 3.1. Current Migration: The Relationship of the Proportion Lost by County-of-Birth to the National Average (see Table 3.5).

Kincardine, Kinross, Moray, Nairn, Peebles, Perth and West Lothian) while in Aberdeen, Lanark and Renfrew and Shetland it was always below. The majority of counties (where measurement was possible)[67] were always above the national average, but this was because Lanark and Renfrew were consistently below the national average and their very large populations distorted the national average. It is interesting that all the population categories had some counties above and others below the national average in most decades, and so the proportion of migrants was not directly linked to the demographic characteristics of the county-of-birth. The categories with declining populations had generally high rates of out-migration, but within the 'Highlands' Shetland was consistently below average and Orkney and Ross and Cromarty were also low in three of the five decades. Likewise in the 'Borders' both Dumfries and Roxburgh were low in two decades. In the 'Periphery and Northeast' Aberdeen had a consistently low proportion of out-migrants. Indeed, the 'Central Lowlands' was the only category with a below average proportion of migrants, and yet Dunbarton, Fife and Linlithgow (West Lothian) were consistently above the national average.

It is possible to gain an overview of county migration from Map 3.1. although the proportion of out-migrants lost can be more clearly shown by referring back to Appendix 7. For example Kincardine has high rates of out-migration for both sexes in every decade, probably because it was adjacent to two counties with more industrial growth (Aberdeen and Angus). Perth has consistently higher out-migration than the national average but this out-migration was decreasing, perhaps suggesting that the peak in out-migration had passed. It has already been noted that current migration from Lanark and Renfrew was low, as it was also from Aberdeen. Probably these counties offered the best opportunities in their immediate area and so there was less incentive to migrate. Many counties-of-birth show a marked increase in the percentage of current migrants leaving in the decades 1871–1881 and 1891–1901.[68] This pattern is of interest especially when compared with emigration and will be taken up again subsequently.

It was anticipated that the maps of migration loss would show regional variations according to decade. This proved not to be the case, and indeed a few individual counties seem to follow unique patterns. For example, current out-migration from Roxburgh was high in the decade 1861–1871 when it was low in the surrounding counties, and the reverse occurred in the subsequent decade. In 1881–1891 Roxburgh again exhibited higher levels of out-migration, (both in relation to itself in the previous decade and also with regard to nearby counties), but in this decade increased out-migration was a common feature in all the border counties. In 1891–1901 migration out of Roxburgh was lower than nearby counties, but in the final decade (1901–11) it shared a decline in out-migration which was common throughout the 'Borders' counties. Roxburgh was adjacent to the far more prosperous county of Selkirk, which may begin to account for this unique out-migration pattern, but this is not the whole story because during sampling, migrants from Roxburgh were found in the most obscure places throughout Scotland.

Although current migration from a few counties such as Roxburgh fluctuate in a distinctive way, the results for most counties showed fluctuations that conformed to one of several patterns, and these will now be discussed. It should be noted that while either sex may predominate in current migration from different counties, peaks or troughs in the estimates are generally reflected in both sexes in the same decade. Shetland was a notable exception to this, with each sex having quite different decades of high losses.[69]

The clearest current migrant pattern is one of steadily declining losses. Ayr is an example of a county which had the highest current migration losses in the decade 1861–71 and thereafter the percentage loss was progressively less severe. This is not entirely surprising as Ayr was a county with a growing population and with expanding industrial development, and thus increasingly able to hold its population. Dunbarton, Fife, Linlithgow and Stirling, all counties with rapid population growth, had (with minor blips) migration patterns similar to that of Ayr, and for the same reasons. What is perhaps more surprising is that both Argyll and Perth also conform to this migrant pattern, because both counties were experiencing absolute population decline.[70] This raises the important point that counties-of-birth can share current migrant patterns without experiencing the same population expansion or decline. As has already been mentioned some of the counties-of-birth with the greatest population growth also had very high rates of out-migration. All that can accurately be said about these estimates is that the aggregate percentages show that the greatest proportion of the total population chose to leave the county-of-birth in question in decade 1861–71 and that subsequently this percentage continued to decline. In contrast Kincardine experienced the reverse of this pattern, there being an increasing percentage of out-migration in almost every decade. In Kincardine crofting was declining because, as Carter writes, 'Capitalist agriculture moves in to replace a family farming system that has lost the capacity to resist the intrusion'.[71] Carter assumed considerable emigration, but it can be seen that migration was also an important out-movement from this county.

Edinburgh (Midlothian), in contrast to all the other counties-of-birth, showed very little variation in the percentage loss of current migrants for both sexes, the estimates oscillating between 6.4% and 6.8%, except in the first decade when it was lower (5.9% for male and 5.5% for female migrants). Lanark and Renfrew also showed very little variation. These are the counties with very large populations and attracting vast in-migration, It should be noted that whilst the volume of out-migration is high, it represents only a small proportion of the total population. The consistency of the numbers leaving suggests that this is the migration equivalent of 'natural wastage', that is the percentage of the native population that will leave a prosperous county regardless of outside influences.

Some counties-of-birth lost consistently greater percentages of one sex than the other through current out-migration. Male current out-migration generally exceeded female in some 'Northeast' and 'Border' counties as well as Perth,[72] whereas female current out-migration usually exceeded male in most of the 'Highland' and the more western of the 'Central Lowlands' counties.[73] Where there was a gender bias, it appears to be related to availability of work in the county-of-birth. However, the greater the population loss of one sex, the smaller the subsequent native population of that sex will be. Therefore the loss can be less than that of the opposite sex in actual numbers, but still form a greater percentage. There is however some validity in this method of measurement, because if excessive population loss is confined to one sex its significance for the total population is greater, unless compensated by in-migration.

While the aggregate current migrant percentage estimates do show significant current migrant losses in all counties-of-birth in any decade, and therefore provide a useful tool for analysing overall trends, they also conceal a lot of information. For example, almost all the counties-of-birth experience current return migration and for some it is very significant. Since the aggregate figures disguise these important patterns, the current migrant age-structure will now be considered in more detail.

THE AGE-BAND OF DEPARTURE FOR CURRENT MIGRANTS

There are two important issues that arise from the estimates of current migration losses by age-band of departure: the first is the differences between categories and the second is the change over time. Table 3.5 showed that each population category was quite distinctive in its current migrant profile. It is not therefore surprising that the four categories have produced different migrant age-structure patterns, and these will now be considered individually using Appendix 8. Return migration will be mentioned when appropriate, but is considered in more detail later in this chapter.

1. The 'Highlands' and 'Borders'

We have already seen from Table 3.5 that the ratio of female current migrants from the 'Highlands' was far greater than for males; indeed it was almost invariably the highest in any category[74] and was always well above the national average. Nevertheless, both sexes produced remarkably similar age-band profiles with high losses in young children and the greatest loss in the age-band 20–24 years. The estimates of child migrants were however lower than in the other population categories (discussed below). The 'Highlands' was the only category where the number of adult migrants in the age-band with the greatest volume consistently exceeded that of the highest one for children and so the volume of child emigration was clearly less than for other categories. With regard to adult migrants there was relatively little out-migration of people over 30 years, but far more young adult females (aged 15–24 years) were migrating than males. Superficially this would appear to produce a very unbalanced young adult sex ratio in the county-of-birth, but Devine has argued that the Highland counties sex ratio in the age group 25–29 years was 'virtually identical' to the Scottish norm.[75] This will be considered in more detail subsequently.

The age-bands exhibit pronounced differences in numbers of current migrants, perhaps because of the distance from areas of attraction. This would mean that people only moved when essential, thus tending to concentrate current migrants into specific age-bands. Even at this aggregate level return migration is evident in the older age-bands and it becomes increasingly important over time.[76] Indeed when the 1901–1911 data was re-run using a slightly different migrant age-structure,[77] the revised figures produced an increase in the number of young migrants, but did not reduce the high levels of return migration. This suggests that the evidence of return migration is not simply an artefact created by the migrant age-structure, but evidence of temporary migration.

The 'Borders' had a far greater proportion of children under 5 years as current migrants than 'Highlands'. Child migrants were the numerically dominant group in the first four decades (1861–1901) for males and this was also true for females up to 1891. There was a trough in the migrant losses in the age-band 10–14 years. Females had a second peak in migration in the age-band 20–24 years, while for males this second peak was not very pronounced in 1861–71, but thereafter became more so. The peaks in migration from the 'Borders' were generally not as pronounced as those from the 'Highlands', implying that migration was more evenly spread throughout the age-bands, perhaps because many of the counties in the 'Borders' were not so remote from centres of attraction as those in the north. As in the north out-migration was hardly apparent after 30 years of age. Clearly, children must have been moving with their parents, but as the results were net of returns, for adults return migration must have frequently cancelled out departures, a situation that must also have occurred in the north. Furthermore, some child migrants from the 'Borders' probably had parents born in other parts of Scotland or possibly England or Ireland.

2. The 'Periphery and Northeast'

As in the 'Borders' children under 5 years formed the largest proportion of current migrants in any single age-band. For males this was true throughout the period, and for females until 1891. Over time there was an increasing similarity in the numbers leaving in each age-band up to 25 years. Females formed the majority of the adult migrants and although most current migration was completed by 30 years, males in particular did show a low level of mobility thereafter. Return migration increased at the end of the period.

3. The 'Central Lowlands'

Discussion of migrants from the 'Central Lowlands' has been left to last because the current migrant age-structure was quite unlike any other. The volume of current migrants was enormous because the bulk of the Scottish population was born in this category. Nevertheless, the proportion of current migrants were consistently below the national average. In 1861–71 the majority of the current migrants were less than 5 years and thereafter the numbers in each age-band dropped so quickly that current migration was negligible after 24 years for males and after 29 years for females. There was no second adult peak of current migrants. For males this pattern changed only slightly with time, but for females there was a gradual change and more adult out-migration occurred in the age-bands up to thirty years.[78] Small amounts of return migration were recorded.

The four categories revealed different current migrant age-structures. Nevertheless, there was some obvious affinity between all except the 'Central Lowlands' classification. The three similar categories had two ages of increased current out-migrant activity. The first involved young children and gradually tailed off as the children became older. The age-band 10–14 years was consistently the one when least child migration took place. Thereafter, there was an upsurge in migration again either of older family parties or of independent migrants. This new tide of migrants rose to a peak in the age-band 20–24 years and large scale movement appeared to end by the age of 29 years. The age-band 25–29 years probably involved large numbers of married migrants, but there appears to be a very sharp fall-off in out-migration thereafter. This is not however, supported by evidence from the enumeration returns which suggests that individuals were continuing to migrate when much older than the tables indicate. This was certainly true of a family from Maybole, Ayrshire (see Table 3.6): using the children's birthplaces as evidence it appears that the parents were about 37 years old when they migrated to Argyllshire, only to return between nine and twelve years later. Members of the family who, by this second move were rendered return migrants were aged approximately 47 years (the parents) and 22, 15 and 13 years (the three oldest children). The parents were well above the age for mass exodus of migrants on their initial departure and their movement was probably masked by those returning. Finally, the older children would as young return migrants would have cancelled out a similar number of young out-migrants.

Table 3.6. *Out- and Return Migration Identified from the Birthplaces of the Family Resident in Maybole, Ayrshire.*[79]

NAME	STATUS	AGE	OCCUPATION	BIRTHPLACE
David McClymont	Head (married)	49	Woollen Weaver	Maybole, Ayr
Mary McClymont	Wife (married)	49	—	Maybole, Ayr
James McClymont	Son (unmarried)	24	Shoemaker	Maybole, Ayr
Mary McClymont	Daughter (unmarried)	17	Machinist Shoes	Maybole, Ayr
Maggie McClymont	Daughter (unmarried)	15	Machinist Shoes	Maybole, Ayr
David McClymont	Son (unmarried)	12	Scholar	Campbelltown, Argyll
John McClymont	Son (unmarried)	10	Scholar	Campbelltown, Argyll
William McClymont	Son (unmarried)	8	Scholar	Campbelltown, Argyll
Robert McClymont	Son (unmarried)	6	Scholar	Campbelltown, Argyll
Joseph McClymont	Son (unmarried)	3	—	Campbelltown, Argyll

In the 'Central Lowlands', the proportions of current migrants were not particularly high and yet the estimates by age-band show almost entirely child current migration, especially in the earlier decades of this study. This appears to illustrate the limitations of the method used in this study to estimate current migration. Since this method used the county-of-birth as the measure of migration, it ignored all intervening moves. In an area of rapid growth, frequent inter-county migration for some migrants was probably inevitable, especially as the areas of greatest expansion were quite close. This secondary migration cannot be measured. It is clearly a mistake to consider county-of-birth as anything other than a transient location, an accident of time for some migrants. Table 3.7 provides an example of inter-urban county mobility; it shows that the children of the family enumerated as living in Bathgate, Linlithgow (West Lothian) had been born in four different counties in the Central Lowlands, but were actually enumerated as living in a fifth county. Some of the children were already seasoned migrants, the eldest daughter having lived in at least four counties excluding the one in which she was born. In this example the mother and two of her siblings were born in the same place. However, it is possible that the family unit never actually lived in Newton, but that the mother was returning to her parental home to give birth to some of her children. Nevertheless, this does not alter the point that the family migrated across county boundaries quite frequently.

Table 3.7. Inter-County Migration within the Central Lowlands Identified by the Birthplaces of a Family Resident in Bathgate, Linlithgow (West Lothian).[80]

NAME	STATUS	AGE	OCCUPATION	BIRTHPLACE
William Brown	Head(married)	40	Miner	Muirkirk, Ayr
Marion Brown	Wife(married)	40	-	Newton, Edinburgh (Midlothian)
Jane Brown	Daughter (unmarried)	17	-	Newton, Edinburgh (Midlothian)
Thomas Brown	Son (unmarried)	13	-	Dysart, Fife
William Brown	Son (unmarried)	10	-	Portseaton, Haddington (East Lothian)
Robert Brown	Son (unmarried)	7	-	Newton, Edinburgh (Midlothian)
Marion Brown	Daughter (unmarried)	1	-	Cambusneathan, Lanark

The 'Central Lowlands' category estimates showed that the first move for many migrants occurred at under 5 years and thereafter numbers tailed off sharply. All the children cited in Table 3.7 for example, had become migrants before the age of five. This would give the 'Central Lowlands' a migrant age-structure similar to that of the 'Highlands' with its dramatic peaks and falls, which seems most unlikely. Much more reasonable would be a current migrant age-structure similar to that of the 'Periphery and Northeast', with which it shares some population features. It is therefore probable that after the first two age-bands, out-migration and return-migration were already beginning to cancel each other out, hence the very dramatic apparent decline in out-migration. However, it is also the case that many outsiders, both migrants and immigrants, must have had children born in this category and in this situation the parents would be recorded under their county- or country-of-birth. The problems of age-structure of both emigrants and migrants from the 'Central Lowlands' will be considered subsequently.

Are we therefore seeing changes in the current migrant age-structure between 1861 and 1911? The following discussion probably applies to all categories of migrant age-structure, but was scarcely evident in the data for the 'Central Lowlands'. The migrant age-structures for 1861–71 and

1871–81 differed very little in the relationship between age-bands. However, thereafter there was a gradual but steady decline in the proportion of young children so that by 1891–1901 (with the exception of 'Central Lowlands') the number of migrants in the age-band 20–24 years had fundamentally altered the relationship between that age-band and those less than 5 years. The evidence of the life-time migrant samples supports this analysis, in that there were less young migrants in the total migrant population in 1891 than in 1861.[81] However, these comments must be treated with caution, as the migrant age-structure used in the computation after 1891 was projected from that year, and reference to the 1901–1911 results using the 1891 age-structure shows less change in the relationship between children and young adults. There are two possible reasons why the projected estimates might be more accurate. The first is demographic; the declining fertility rates plus improving age-specific mortality meant that there were less young people in proportion to the total population (as shown in Appendix 2[c]). The second is that it has already been established that migration patterns were changing and therefore the volume of children vis-à-vis other age-bands might be altering. The proportion of migrants in the life-time population was increasing until 1901 (Appendix 2[t]), but clearly the young were not increasing proportionally (Appendix 2[c]).[82] Indeed even in the 'Central Lowlands' the volume of young migrants did not increase significantly after 1871. It appears that by 1911 less young children were migrating in proportion to the total population.

THE AGE OF CURRENT MIGRANTS BY COUNTY-OF-BIRTH

The population category age-bands have provided an overview of the data on the age of current migrants and now the discussion will turn to the individual counties, and the difference between child and adult migration, (see Appendix 9).

1. Child Migrants

In many counties the number of young migrants under 5 years old was approximately the same for both sexes.[83] This is to be expected as young children migrate because of a family decision to move and therefore roughly equal numbers of both sexes seems rational. Despite the fact that the two sexes were calculated totally independently with their own age-specific mortality rates applied, the estimates for most counties showed similar results. There were however certain counties where the sex ratio of young children migrating never balanced[84] and a pattern seemed to emerge. The counties where the number of current migrants of both sexes under

5 years were similar tended (with the notable exception of Shetland)[85] to be those which were the greatest distance from the areas attracting migrants.[86] The counties which were losing young males in greatest numbers were those which were, or were close to, migrant attracting locations. The excess of male child migrants over females was far greater than can be accounted for by the difference in number of births. The male bias in migrants of less than 5 years tends to correspond to the 'Central Lowlands', 'Periphery and Northeast' and 'Borders' categories, but certainly does not include all the counties within these categories. Clearly this interesting feature of young migration needs further investigation. The fact that some counties have roughly equal numbers of migrants under 5 years and others never do suggests that it is not just an artefact of the method, especially, since as already noted, male and female migrants have their own age-specific rates applied to them.

Current migrants aged 5–9 years occurred in roughly the same numbers in both sexes in most counties,[87] perhaps the reverse of what might have been expected considering the findings for those under 5 years. Whereas migrants in the younger age-band would have needed fairly constant supervision and been unable to work, those aged 5–9 years were capable of simple jobs and so different migration patterns according to gender might have been anticipated.

Bearing in mind that the majority of people had probably begun to work before the age of 15 it is perhaps surprising that the age-band 10–14 years represents a dip in the numbers leaving. If people had to leave home to find work their move was generally fairly local. Information in the enumeration books on birthplace and surnames suggests that some young 'independent' adults may be related to older people living nearby, but frustratingly these connections cannot be proved. Indeed, the younger farm labourers living in bothies on the Carse of Gowrie often continued to live in the parish were they were born and therefore probably near their parental home. The unusual surname of a young maid in a big house near Kelso linked her to a middle-aged couple of the same name, presumably her parents, living in an estate cottage. Young migrants living a long way from home often lived with another member of their family or with people from the same area as themselves. These people may have left home, but had family support or friends nearby if necessary. Thus it appears that whilst many young teenagers worked, independent long distance migration was unusual and movement as part of a family unit was generally made with younger children. However, counties in the 'Central Lowlands' do not conform to this pattern. In this category the slump in current migration was non–existent; here inter–urban migration could involve quite short distances, opportunities were practically on the doorstep, and so migration was not a major decision as it was from further afield. Indeed families or even young independent teenagers might not even be aware of having crossed a county boundary.

2. Adult migrants

The number of female migrants generally exceeded males in all age-bands up to 30 years. For adults greatest out-migration generally occurred in the age-band 20–24 years, though this was not always apparent for males. Beyond thirty years of age the numbers of migrants were generally too small to investigate, or increasing return migration made it difficult to interpret the figures. However, in years of very high out-migration some counties showed losses in almost every age-band.[88] This was probably the 'real' current out-migration situation, as in years of massive out-migration, return migration was probably low. A county where this situation occurred was Forfar (Angus) which had a large population of over a quarter of a million and in the decade 1891–1901 current out-migration was unusually high.[89] Both sexes show losses through migration in all age-bands. Male migrants in the age-bands 30–49 years show fairly consistent losses equivalent to about a third of the losses of a young male adult age-band (for example those aged 15–19 years). This middle-aged male migration (30–44 years) represented a loss of at least 5% of the native population in those age-bands. Females in the age-bands 30–39 years exhibited less tendency to migrate than males (although these data are far less reliable than those used for the male estimates),[90] but there was a blip in the age-bands 40–49 years, when out-migration almost trebled from the previous low. This could be accounted for by the evidence from the migrant samples which suggested that this increased migration probably reflected mothers moving with older children. The evidence for females from Angus was less good, but it can be supported by evidence from several other counties, all of which show similar out-migration patterns in the older age-bands.[91]

RETURN MIGRATION

Return migration measures movement back to the county-of-birth, but not necessarily the place-of-birth. By definition return migrants must be older than out-migrants. Return migration was in evidence in the majority of counties. In many it occurred in every decade, although it does appear to become increasingly significant in the later decades. The estimates for every county suggest that return migration became an important feature in the age-structure of current migration over 30 years. The migrant samples also provided plenty of evidence of this phenomenon. Unfortunately the range of standard errors in the age-bands 30–39 years was generally high in most counties, which worked against accurate quantification. Nevertheless, by the age of 40 years there was fairly reliable evidence of return migration in most counties. Return migration was net and would therefore have been balanced by some current migration, and so the percentage that returned was probably an under-estimate. Interestingly Baines concluded despite the totally different method of estimating migration, that 30% was a realistic minimum return migration rate.[92] In Argyll there was plenty of evidence of return migration in the samples, some of it related to the growth of Oban. In 1861 a carpenter returned with his young family having spent several years in Lanark and Renfrew,[93] and in 1891 return migration was still apparent in a labourer's family.[94] Recent research on the island of Gigha has shown that out-migrants normally went either to the Clyde towns or the mainland of Argyll, and those who migrated from the island 'generally embrace the first opportunity of returning to it'.[95] However, return migrants were not just members of the working classes; for example a prosperous solicitor returned to Wick in Caithness having spent at least twelve years in Edinburgh.[96]

Return migration appeared to increase in a decade after unusually high out-migration. This apparent return is interesting because the method of computation used is not cumulative and the results are therefore independently calculated, yet they still suggest that high out-migration may lead to increased return migration a decade later. This may reflect the migrants' disillusionment with what he found, or maybe a downturn in the economy which made the migrant destination less attractive. It is clear from evidence of the birthplaces of children in the enumeration books that many migrant families moved several times before returning to their county-of-birth. For example Table 3.8 shows that a young married couple living in Wick were both born in the rural parish of Canisbay in Caithness, but it is not clear whether they moved south before or after marriage. However, the eldest son was born in the Northeast (Elgin) and the younger ones even further south in Edinburgh. This may indicate stage migration. They returned to their county-of-birth, but to a rather larger town than the parish where they were born. Nevertheless they appear to have retained links with their birthplace in that their two lodgers come from Canisbay. Moreover, the children, as a result of their parent's mobility, have migrated from the 'Central Lowlands' to the 'Highlands', an urban to rural movement.

So far return migration has been referred to in terms of decreasing or increasing flows, but there is also a second interpretation which is

Table 3.8. *Return Migration to Wick, Caithness*
by a Family from Canisbay, Caithness in 1861

NAME	STATUS	AGE	OCCUPATION	BIRTHPLACE
Donald Weir	Head (married)	33	Merchant	Canisbay, Caithness
Ann Weir	Wife (married)	33		Canisbay, Caithness
illegible Weir	Son (unmarried)	7	Scholar	Elgin, Elgin (Moray)
Peter Weir	Son (unmarried)	6	Scholar	Edinburgh, (Midlothian)
Donald Weir	Son (unmarried)	3	Scholar	Edinburgh, (Midlothian)
Jessie Miller	Servant (unmarried)	19	Domestic servant	Edinburgh, (Midlothian)
David Shearer	Lodger (unmarried)	25	Shopman	Canisbay, Caithness
William Shearer	Lodger (unmarried)	18	Shopman	Canisbay, Caithness

theoretically possible. It has already been argued that in- and out-migration cancel each other if both occurred in the same age-band. It is also possible that the volume of return migration was fairly constant, which would mean that in-migration would appear greatest in decades when there was least out-migration, and that decades apparently showing high return migration may instead be registering less out-migration.

Conclusion

This chapter has provided an overview of the life-time migrant population. It has highlighted the two major regional trends, rural-urban and inter-urban movement. Rural-urban movement provided the greatest proportions of regional migration and this movement had a small but significant counter-flow of urban-rural migrants. However, the huge population resident in the urban counties meant that inter-urban was the more important flow by volume. The percentage of Scottish migrants in the population increased between 1861–1901, but individual counties do not necessarily conform to the national trends. Indeed a declining civil county population did not necessarily reflect massive emigration, but may simply have indicated out-migration. Counties where population growth was most significant had a far greater proportion of their population under 20 years. There was a changing age-structure in the Scottish population over time and marked gender differences in the age-structure. Although the high ratio of females to males decreased gradually over the fifty year period, this imbalance between the sexes could make some migration statistics misleading and disguise the fact that in every census a significant majority of adult migrants were female.

The computer estimations of current migration have shown that between 5.5% and 8.1% of the native population were current migrants in each decade and that far more females migrated than males. However, there was far more spatial variation than these bald figures suggest and when the data are divided into population categories, the proportion of migrants was highest amongst those born in the 'Borders', while the 'Central Lowlands' was the only one with a below average proportion of migrants, although the very large population concentrated in this latter category meant it still contained the largest volume of current migrants. The age-structure of the current migrant population was unexpectedly young, and in most categories the greatest number of migrants in any age-band were children. However, in the 'Highlands' child migrants assumed a less significant role than in the other categories, while in contrast in the 'Central Lowlands' the vast majority of all current migrants were children. Nevertheless, the age-structure of the migrant population changed over time and by 1911 there were fewer child migrants. It was not clear if this reflects demographic changes or a new migrant trend. Return migration was in evidence in every county-of-birth and although it cannot be computed an estimate of 30% return migrants may well be realistic.

Notes

1. The 'cleaned' census is the county-of-residence by county-of-birth tabulation. It is an amended version of the published information which has been corrected for spurious migration; county boundaries have been standardised and it includes the two 1891 tallies (before and after the county boundary changes). The two 1891 data sets are necessary in order that migration can be compared over time. The 'processed' census tabulation is the expanded county-of-residence by county-of-birth tabulation, that has had the age-structure expanded from 2 to 16 age-bands.

2. The limitations of the census as a source of information on migration have been considered in Chapter 2.

3. Anderson and Morse 'The People' p. 10.

4. The movement of immigrants such as English and Irish into these regions is important in population terms, but for the purposes of this discussion of Scottish movement, such immigrants have been excluded from the calculations.

5. The regions used by Anderson and Morse in 'The People' and by Flinn *et al.* in *Scottish Population History* are based on those in the census.

6. Devine. *The Great Highland Famine*. p. 147 and idem. Appendix 8, pp. 317–9.

7. 3,999 men, members of the Royal Navy, were included in the enumeration of Ross and Cromarty (1911 census, Vol. II, p. 431). Some of the men were not Scots, only those born in Scotland were included in this regional calculation. This substantial addition of outsiders significantly alters the total

male population in Ross and Cromarty creating an increase of 8.6% over the previous census (1901), whereas in fact the county experienced a decline of 4.2%. Brock 'Migration' Vol. II, p. 52.

8. The 1911 census tabulates the national excess of females over males for each census. It should be noted that this includes everybody resident in Scotland and not just Scots. In 1861 there are 111.2 females for every 100 males, but by 1891 this had declined to 107.2 females and by 1911 to 106.2 females per 100 males. Census of Scotland 1911 Report on the Twelfth Decennial Census. Vol. II London, 1913 p. XXII.

9. In the 1861 census it is noted that in Linlithgow (West Lothian) there were only 94.4 females for every 100 males. (Census of Scotland Population Tables and Report Vol. I 1862, p. XXIII). However, this calculation is for the county-of-residence, and therefore includes outsiders. A similarly low ratio is calculated for subsequent censuses. If the data is recalculated for county-of-birth, Linlithgow-born still show a low ratio of females to males but it is no longer less than one and is never the lowest in Scotland, (the ratios per 100 males are: 107.4 (1861), 106.1 (1871), 104.5 (1881), 101.7 (1891), 103.5 (1901) and 103.0 (1911)). The lowest ratios of females to males are in Selkirk in 1861–81 (104.5 females in 1861, 105.0 in 1871 and 103.3 in 1881), in Haddington (East Lothian) (100.3 females in 1891 and 101.6 in 1911) and in Peebles (103.3 females in 1901).

10. This data for Shetland is calculated by county-of-birth. For every 100 males there were 147.0 females in 1861, 145.1 (1871), 143.8 (1881), 142.6 (1891), 133.2 (1901) and 133.1 (1911). The ratios for Shetland females are also calculated in the censuses of 1861 and 1911; these are for the county-of-residence and include outsiders. In these calculations the change in sex ratios is more dramatic, falling from 142.6 in 1861 to 118.7 in 1911. (Census of Scotland Population Tables and Report Vol. I 1862, p. XXIII and Census of Scotland 1911 Report on the Twelfth Decennial Census of Scotland. Vol. II, 1913 p. VIII). It is clear that however the data is calculated there is an enormous majority of females both within and from Shetland.

11. Smith. *Shetland Life*. pp. 157–8.

12. Coull, *The Sea Fisheries*. pp. 206–11.

13. Flinn. *Scottish Population History*. p. 380–1. These data are probably calculated in registration rather than civil counties but for the purposes of this analysis the difference is unimportant.

14. Appendices 2 and 3 are not directly comparable and should only be used together with caution. Appendix 3 considers age-structures using the county-of-residence as the framework but Appendix 2 uses the county-of-birth.

15. Anderson and Morse. 'The People' pp. 22–42.

16. A slight decline in the adult population when collated by county-of-birth is found in: Caithness (1911), Kinross (1911), Kirkcudbright (1881), Orkney (1911) and Ross and Cromarty (1911)

17. Other counties-of-birth in which the percentage of migrants continued to increase throughout the study period were: Aberdeen, Argyll, Banff (females only), Bute, Caithness (females only), Clackmannan, Dumfries, Edinburgh (Midlothian), Forfar (Angus), Inverness, Kincardine, Kirkcudbright, Lanark, Nairn, Orkney, Perth (females only), Roxburgh, Selkirk (females only) and Wigtown.

18. The population of Dunbarton increased by 28.0% between 1871–1881, and that of Linlithgow by 21.4% a decade later (calculated from data in Brock. 'Scottish Migration' Vol. II. Appendix I, p. 21 and 41 respectively).

19. The total population of the civil counties of Berwick and Elgin (Moray).

	1851	1861	1871	1881	1891 (pre)	1891 (post)	1901	1911
Berwick	36,297	36,613	36,486	35,392	32,406	32,290	30,824	29,643
Elgin.	38,959	42,695	43,128	43,788	43,453	43,471	44,800	43,427

20. The published 1851 census tabulation of county-of-residence by county-of-birth does not distinguish males and females. It is therefore impossible to deduce whether the findings for males in Sutherland reflects the end of an earlier migration pattern or an abnormal situation in 1861.

21. Census of Scotland 1911 Report on the Twelfth Decennial Census, vol II 1913 p. XCIII.

22. An analysis of all the censuses has shown that for the counties of Linlithgow and Perth, these differing migration routes dependent on sex have existed since 1861 when the study began. For Sutherland however the situation has changed over time. In the 1861 and 1871 census tabulations, the majority of both sexes migrated to Edinburgh, but by 1881 Lanark became the preferred destination for males and this pattern continued thereafter.

23. Baines. *Migration in a Mature Economy.* p. 95.

24. The average percentage of Scots moving south is shown under the field 'As a % of the total born in county' Scotland

25. Galloway, & Murray, 'Scottish Migration to England' pp. 29–38.

26. Cullen. *An Economic History.* pp159–62.

27. See Table 2.3.

28. There are only thirty-two counties in this research instead of the normal thirty-three, because Lanark and Renfrew have been combined into one county. See Chapter 2 for details.

29. Hunt, *Regional Wage Variations.*

30. Devine 'Scottish Farm Labour' p. 248.

31. Lee *The British Economy* p. 132.

32. The 'Highlands' category is part of region thirteen. Hunt. *Regional Wage Variations.* pp. 8–9.

33. *Ibid.* pp. 53–56.

34. Hunt. *The Making of the Crofting Community*, pp. 107–8.

35. Richards. *A History of the Highland Clearances. Vol. 2*. p. 489.

36. Devine. *The Great Highland Famine*. p. 287.

37. Devine. *Clanship to the Crofters' War*. pp. 135–45, MacPhail *The Crofters War*. p. 5 for detailed breakdown of earnings of Lewis fishermen in the 1870s and Brock. 'The Militia' for impact of service in the Militia on temporary employment throughout the period.

38. Devine. *The Great Highland Famine*. pp. 238–41.

39. Orr. *Deer Forests Landlords and Crofters*. pp. 119–32.

40. Anderson and Morse, 'High Fertility, High Emigration' Pt.II. pp. 323–31.

41. Hunt's analysis includes the counties of Peebles and Selkirk in region eleven, as well as all the 'Borders' counties. Hunt. *Regional Wage Variations*. pp. 8–9.

42. *Ibid*. pp. 47–50.

43. Lee. *The British Economy*. p. 136.

44. Campbell. 'Agricultural Labour in the South-West', pp. 67–8.

45. Robson, 'The Border Farm Worker' pp. 91–4.

46. Anderson and Morse, 'High Fertility, High Emigration' Pt.II. pp. 332–3

47. Robson, 'The Border Farm Worker' p. 91.

48. It should be noted that in the 'Periphery and Northeast' category male current migrants exceeded females in a decade of particularly high out-migration. However, in the 'Borders' category, the decade when the proportion of male migrants exceeded females was not a decade of exceptionally out-migration. Very high out-migration is therefore not in itself a cause of reversal of normal trends. See Table 3.5.

49. Table 1–4 recalculated. Hunt. *Regional Wage Variations*. pp. 63–4.

50. Carter. *Farm Life in Northeast Scotland*, p. 86. Carter considers the Northeast to include the counties of Aberdeen, Banff, Elgin, Kincardine and Nairn.

51. Harper. *Emigration from North-East, Vol. 1*, p. 166.

52. Carter. *Farm Life in Northeast Scotland*. pp. 95–6.

53. Harper. *Emigration from North-East, Vol. 1*, p. 166.

54. Campbell. *The Rise and Fall*, p. 82.

55. Lee, 'Regional Growth and Structural Change' p. 448.

56. Smith 'Aberdeen Harbour' p. 103.

57. Tyson 'The Economy of Aberdeen' pp. 22–3.

58. Coull, *The Sea Fisheries*. pp. 126–52.

59. The counties of Ayr, Clackmannan and Haddington which are in the 'Periphery and Northeast' population category in this study are also included in region twelve in Hunts' analysis. Hunt. *Regional Wage Variations*. pp. 8–9.

60. *Ibid*. pp. 50–3.

61. *Ibid*. p. 177

62. Strathclyde region comprised of Argyll, Ayr, Bute, Dumbarton, Lanark and Renfrew. Only the last three were in the 'Central Lowlands' population category, Ayr and Bute being in the 'Periphery' and Argyll in the 'Highlands'.

63. Lee, 'Modern Economic Growth'. pp. 5–35.

64. Baines 'The Labour Supply'. p. 156.

65. There are slight problems with data from Galashiels in Selkirk in 1861 (see Brock 'Scottish Migration'. Vol. II Appendix I Selkirk). The rapid growth of the woollen textile industry in Galashiels reduced current out-migration in Selkirk, but later falling prices and decreasing demand in the woollen industry caused very high out-migration in the decade 1891–1901; indeed Lenman has calculated that the population of Galashiels 'fell by a quarter'. Lenman, *An Economic History.* p. 187.

66. The urban counties of Scotland referred to here are the same as those already used in the earlier discussion on inter-regional migration, (Ayr, Clackmannan, Dunbarton, Edinburgh (Midlothian), Fife, Forfar (Angus), Haddington (East Lothian), Kinross, Lanark & Renfrew, Linlithgow (West Lothian) and Stirling.

67. Only counties where both male and female proportions of current migrants were above or below the national average were considered. Only a very few counties had to be omitted, the largest number being four in the decade 1901–11 because the two sexes did not reveal common trends.

68. Counties-of-birth that showed a marked increase in current migration in the decades 1871–1881 and 1891–1901: Banff, Berwick, Caithness, Clackmannan, Dumfries, Fife (females only), Kirkcudbright and Ross and Cromarty.

69. The peak losses of males from Shetland occurred in the decade 1891–1901, when the county lost 8.9% of the population, but in the subsequent decade departures fell to only 0.8%. The female losses followed an entirely different pattern, the greatest out-migration being in the decade 1861–1871 (4.6%) and thereafter there was a steady reduction in losses until the decade 1901–1911, with only a minor blip in 1891–1901.

70. In Perth current migration declines from approximately 14% to 7% and in Argyll from 12% to 8% (the latter having a blip in 1891–1901). Out-migration therefore remains at a significant level equal for example to that of more industrially prosperous Ayr (12%–7%).

71. Carter, I. 'Dorset, Kincardine and Peasant Crisis:' p. 483–8.

72. Male current out-migration generally exceeds female in: Banff, Berwick, Dumfries, Forfar (Angus), Kirkcudbright, Perth, Roxburgh and Wigtown.

73 Female current out-migration generally exceeds male in: Argyll, Bute, Dunbarton, Inverness, Kincardine, Lanark and Renfrew, Linlithgow (West Lothian), Orkney, Stirling and Sutherland.

74. In the decade 1891–1901 the female to male ratio from the 'Central Lowlands' population category was marginally higher but the two categories were so close as to be within the margin of error. (Table 3.5).

75. Devine. *The Great Highland Famine*. p. 289.

76. During computation return migration is easily identified, because whereas out-migration is always negative, return migration is positive.

77. After 1891 it was no longer possible to refer to the enumeration books in order to construct a migrant age profile. Two alternative profiles were constructed the first projecting changes from between the 1861 and 1891 sample on to 1911, and the second assuming that after 1891 the age structure did not change. The estimates provided assume an age profile that was continuing to change, but the data was also reworked using the 1891 profile. The two age profiles made very little difference to the estimates and for that reason have not been provided.

78. The significance of the 1901–11 estimations is open to question. If the projected migrant age-structure is used, then female current migration in the age-band 15–19 years is more or less equally important as child migration 0–4 years. However, if instead the 1891 migrant age-structure is used for calculations, children continue to dominate current out-migration.

79. Maybole, Ayr, 1891, RD. 605, ED. 7, p. 19, sch. 81 (23 Carrick Place)

80. Bathgate, Linlithgow, 1861, RD. 662, ED. 4, sch. 120, p. 25, (Cochraine Street),

81. The migrant samples had to fit the published migrant age-structure, this was known to have changed between 1861 and 1891. See Chapter 2.

82. This improvement was not entirely unexpected, as increasing life expectancy would inevitably lead to a greater proportion of older people in the population. Nevertheless, improved infant mortality rates would also increase the survival prospects for children.

83. The larger counties where migrants under 5 years were roughly the same in numbers for both sexes were: Berwick, Caithness, Inverness, Orkney, Ross & Cromarty and Sutherland.

84. Counties where there were always more current male migrants under 5 years than females: Aberdeen, Banff, Edinburgh (Midlothian), Elgin (Moray), Forfar (Angus), Fife, Lanark and Renfrew, Perth, Roxburgh and Shetland.

85. Shetland has a most unusual migrant pattern with very little migration to nearby counties and very close links with Leith, Edinburgh (Midlothian). In the enumeration books for Shetland it was not uncommon to see just 'Leith' stated as the birthplace.

86. This discussion is supported by the 1861 evidence of Devine, who showed that the male majority which occurred naturally at birth was still present in the 0–9 years sex ratio in the remote West Highland parishes he selected. Devine. *The Great Highland Famine*. Table 12.2. pp. 289–90.

87. The roughly equal numbers of current migrant males and females in the age-band 5–9 years occurs in every county-of-birth except Forfar (Angus) and up to 1881 in Fife where the age-band 10–14 years was when sexes were more or less equal.

88. The counties with unusually high current out-migration in one decade and the decade in which this occurred: Clackmannan (1891–1901), Angus (1891–1901), Kirkcudbright (1871–81) and Selkirk (1891–1901).

89. It is not possible to account for this sudden increase in migration. Dundee was the main industrial centre and textiles the most important area of growth. Walker does not analyse the economic fluctuations in Dundee manufacturing, but in the decade under consideration there was a serious strike in 1895 in the jute industry which may account for some out-movement. The jute industry was the largest employer in Dundee. Walker. *Juteopolis,* pp. 167–73.

90. It should be noted that Appendix 9, shows that the standard errors for females in the age-bands 30–44 years are greater than those for males. However, even the extremes computed using the standard errors do not exhibit as high current out-migration for females as the more reliable male estimates.

91. Counties which had very high levels of current migration in a decade, which has meant that almost every age-band contains out-migrants include: Ayr (1861–71), Linlithgow (West Lothian) (1871–81), Roxburgh (1861–71), Selkirk (1891–1901) and Wigtown (1891–1901)

92. Baines. *Migration in a Mature Economy.* p. 104.

93. This move to Oban was current return migration for the parents; their three young children had been born in Lanark or Renfrew.

    Oban, Kilmore and Kilbride, Argyll, 1861, RD. 523, ED. 3, sch. 93, p. 16

    Tweedale Street (2 rooms with Windows)

94. Return migration in Oban. The husband had been born in Fife but his wife came from this parish. The wife had obviously returned before (perhaps only for a holiday or to give birth) as two of their children were born in Argyll and three in Glasgow.

    Oban, Kilmore and Kilbride, Argyll, 1891, RD. 523, ED. 5, sch. 186, p. 29.

    18 Burnside Street (2 rooms with Windows).

95. Storrie, 'They go much from home' p. 110 and fn.41.

96. A professional family the head of which was a return migrant. He had previously lived with his large family in Edinburgh.

    Wick, Caithness, 1891, RD. 43, ED. 1, sch. 24, p. 5

    High Street, (9 rooms with windows).

97. Wick, Caithness, 1861, RD. 43, ED. 4, sch. 9, p. 2, (Louisburgh Road).

4

Scottish Current Emigration 1861–1911

This chapter which analyses the computer estimations of emigrant losses can be compared with the latter part of Chapter 3 which considered current migration. Direct comparisons can therefore be made between the two forms of population movement and a deliberate attempt has been made to keep the layout fairly similar. Thus it will begin by providing an overview of Scottish emigration and will show that there was considerable variation in losses depending on the decade. The analysis has then been expanded to consider emigration by the population category in each decade, emphasising the considerable diversity of experience, before discussing individual counties. Having analysed aggregate losses, the age of emigrants at departure will be examined, both by population category and also by county-of-birth. Finally, the issues concerning emigration raised in this chapter are analysed and brought together. Reference will be made to similarities and differences between current migration and emigration, but a wider discussion of these two forms of population movement will be reserved for Chapter 6.

It should be noted that Scotland was fortunate throughout this period (as indeed was England and Wales), in that there were no bars to emigration. These limitations could take the form of restrictions in the receiving counties,[1] whether colonial or foreign, social barriers such as language, race or religion, or restrictions in the parent country such as male liability for military service, which could delay the departure of males. Scots overseas emigration regardless of gender was therefore totally unimpeded except by cost.

A Comparison of Estimates of Emigration from Scotland

The estimates of emigration made in this study make many assumptions and complete accuracy is impossible. Indeed it is known that minor errors are brought into the estimates during computation, these being a product of the computer language used, and they have been analysed in Appendix 1.

This study has however attempted to estimate the losses from each county and also the age profile of the emigrant population, which has not been quantified before. Nevertheless, it is possible to compare these findings with previously published aggregate estimates of emigration and Appendix 10 tabulates published estimates of net emigration and those calculated in this study. The estimates of net emigration are all close, although when this study was compared with the other estimates, it gave slightly higher emigration losses in 1871–81 and 1891–1901 and lower ones in the intervening decade. There is remarkable agreement between all three estimates in the final decade.

AN OVERVIEW OF CURRENT EMIGRATION FROM SCOTLAND

The overall aggregate losses through Scottish current emigration (Table 4.1) in each decade will be considered first because such an overview can illustrate several general points. Although not all the results in this table are directly comparable to those in Table 3.5 it is nevertheless instructive to compare the two tables where possible.[2] Table 4.1 shows that emigration was gender specific and in all measures of current emigration male emigrants exceeded females in every decade. This was in contrast to the pattern for current migration where there was also a gender bias, but here the volume of female out-migration invariably surpassed that of males and the proportion of females migrating was sometimes higher too. Far more males emigrated than females, both as a proportion of the population and also in actual volume, and this low female participation was particularly true of 1891–1901 a decade of low emigration.

The proportion of Scots that emigrated fluctuated between decades. There is a pattern to the emigration flows with two decades of increasing emigration building up to a peak in 1881–91 followed by a trough and then a second peak in 1901–11. By comparing Tables 3.5 and 4.1 it can be seen that in aggregate the proportion emigrating fluctuated far more between decades than for those migrating. Moreover, the proportion of out-migrants tended to be highest when emigration was lowest and vice versa. However, this generalisation is an over-simplification, since in the first decade considered (1861–71), the total numbers of migrants and emigrants were remarkably similar (200,209 and 197,364 respectively). Thereafter, the difference between the volume of current migration and that of emigration widened steadily over time regardless of whether emigration or out-migration was the dominant population movement. Current emigration was high in the decades 1881–91 and 1901–11 and current out-migration in 1871–81 and 1891–1901. Although the greatest

Table 4.1. Scottish Current Emigration in each Decade 1861–1911

Decade	Current Emigrants			Proportion of the total Scots-born population*		Proportion of the total current emigrant population	
	Male	Female	Total	Male	Female	Male	Female
Scotland							
1861–1871	−115,745	−81,619	−197,364	−7.40	−4.82	58.65	41.35
1871–1881	−116,853	−89,351	−206,204	−6.74	−4.80	56.67	43.33
1881–1891	−162,892	−114,226	−277,118	−8.46	−5.61	58.78	41.22
1891–1901	−103,085	−62,837	−165,922	−5.00	−2.88	62.13	37.87
1901–1911	−188,014	−137,286	−325,300	−8.24	−5.70	57.80	42.20
Highlands							
1861–1871	−19,219	−11,811	−31,030	−6.60	−3.62	61.94	38.06
1871–1881	−16,653	−11,596	−28,249	−5.80	−3.60	58.95	41.05
1881–1891	−21,124	−13,238	−34,362	−7.35	−4.16	61.47	38.53
1891–1901	−13,677	−8,376	−22,053	−4.94	−2.73	62.02	37.98
1901–1911	−23,424	−14,754	−38,178	−8.60	−4.92	61.35	38.65
Borders							
1861–1871	−12,576	−10,094	−22,670	−9.52	−6.97	55.47	44.53
1871–1881	−10,965	−10,805	−21,770	−8.24	−7.41	50.37	49.63
1881–1891	−11,319	−9,575	−20,894	−8.39	−6.63	54.17	45.83
1891–1901	−10,086	−8,120	−18,206	−7.69	−5.79	55.40	44.60
1901–1911	−9,172	−8,494	−17,666	−7.22	−6.26	51.92	48.08
Periphery and Northeast							
1861–1871	−30,682	−19,056	−49,738	−6.64	−3.82	61.69	38.31
1871–1881	−29,224	−21,018	−50,242	−5.76	−3.85	58.17	41.83
1881–1891	−47,695	−32,216	−79,911	−8.61	−5.48	59.69	40.31
1891–1901	−25,978	−13,964	−39,942	−4.52	−2.28	65.04	34.96
1901–1911	−57,773	−38,830	−96,603	−9.40	−5.95	59.80	40.20
Central Lowlands							
1861–1871	−53,267	−40,658	−93,925	−7.85	−5.61	56.71	43.29
1871–1881	−60,012	−45,931	−105,943	−7.44	−5.41	56.65	43.35
1881–1891	−82,754	−59,197	−141,951	−8.73	−6.01	58.30	41.70
1891–1901	−53,344	−32376	−85,720	−4.94	−2.88	62.23	37.77
1901–1911	−97,645	−75,208	−172,853	−7.71	−5.70	56.49	43.51

★ The proportion is calculated as current emigrants over the total population born in Scotland in the subsequent census plus current emigrants (that is the total population at the end of the decade if nobody had moved out).

number of emigrants left Scotland in the final decade, which is to be expected because the Scottish-born population was increasing,[3] the highest proportion of the male Scottish-born population left in the decade 1881–1891, while for females emigrating the decade 1901–1911 was of greater significance.[4] This finding was not expected, as Baines had speculated that for England and Wales emigration in the final decade before the First World War was likely to be markedly higher than in all previous decades,[5] whereas the evidence for Scotland suggests that the decade 1881–91 was equally important. The measurement of emigration (as with current migration) was net of returns. It cannot therefore automatically be assumed that a decade with a low proportion of emigrants reflects low current emigration, as it may indicate a high rate of return.

AGGREGATE SCOTTISH EMIGRATION BY POPULATION CATEGORY

The analysis of current out-migration patterns in Scotland in Chapter 3 showed that the demographic experience of the population categories produced differing migration patterns. This section will use the same categories to consider and compare aggregate emigration rates.

When Table 4.1 is compared with the corresponding table for current migration (Table 3.5), it is clear that at the national aggregate level the fluctuations between decades for current migration were less than those for emigration. However, once the framework was expanded to that of population category the fluctuations in current migration exceeded those of emigration. Table 4.1 shows that three of the four categories were fairly similar in their emigration patterns, but the fourth (Borders) exhibited a very different one. The categories with common emigration characteristics will be considered first. These exhibited a pronounced majority of male emigrants and involved a fluctuating proportion of the Scottish population according to the decade. The proportions of the population in these three categories that emigrated in each decade varied relatively little and for the decade 1891–1901, which experienced a low level of emigration, there was remarkable similarity.

Direct comparisons between measurements of emigration and migration are useful but can be misleading, as the proportion of migration is measured against the native population of the county-of-birth and emigration against the total population from a county-of-birth. This is because emigrants did not necessarily emigrate from their county-of-birth and may have migrated first. Comparisons of the volume of emigration and current migration were safer, although the same caveat concerning emigration still applies.

1. The 'Highlands'

The pattern of 'Highland' emigration did not copy the national one in that the numbers leaving in 1861–71 were higher than those in the subsequent decade giving a pattern of three peaks interspersed by two troughs. The number of emigrants from the 'Highlands' tended to increase over time, but the proportion of the population lost was generally below the national average (except for males in 1901–11). In the decades of high emigration this increasing population movement was in contrast to the pattern for out-migration, where the volume of current migration was falling slightly over time (except in 1891–1901). Nevertheless migration remained the more significant movement, a far larger number of Highlanders migrated than emigrated in every decade except in the last (1901–11). Furthermore, the growth in the volume of emigration should be considered in relation to a declining total population; indeed as noted earlier four counties-of-birth were experiencing absolute population decline. There were three decades of high emigration, 1861–71, 1881–91 and 1901–11, and the strength of these peaks increased over time. Male emigrants generally exceeded females by the largest ratio in the 'Highlands', and it was only in the decade with a low proportion of emigrants, 1871–81, that female emigration exceeded 40% of the total. It is therefore the case that there was a marked gender bias in the patterns of 'Highland' mobility because the category recorded the highest proportions of males emigrating and the lowest proportions migrating and the situation for females was reversed — lowest proportions emigrating and highest migrating.

2. The 'Periphery and Northeast'

The 'Periphery and Northeast' also had a lower proportion of emigrants than the national average, except in the decades 1901–11 and 1881–91 (the latter being males only). There were two pronounced peaks in emigration, 1881–91 and 1901–11. Although demographic growth in this category was less than 50%, when the decades 1861–71 and 1901–1911 are compared the volume of emigration doubled for females and was almost as high for males. However, it was only in the two decades of high emigration (1881–91 and 1901–11) that the numbers emigrating exceeded those migrating. The high proportion of male to female emigrants was not as pronounced as in the 'Highlands'. However, the male:female ratio of emigrants did vary considerably from 58:42 in 1871–81 to 65:35 in 1891–1901, the latter being the lowest ratio of females emigrating in any category or decade. It should be noted that these extremes in male:female ratio occurred in the two decades of low emigration, which suggests that a high or low ratio of females was not directly related to the low proportion of emigrants leaving.

3. The 'Central Lowlands'

Unlike the other population categories so far considered, the numbers emigrating from the 'Central Lowlands' generally surpassed those migrating by a considerable margin (except in the decade 1891–1901). Indeed as a proportion of population in this category emigrants almost invariably exceeded the national average. Male emigration was above the national average in the first three decades and the volume of male emigration always exceeded that of current migration. Indeed in decades 1881–91 and 1901–11 there were approximately twice as many male emigrants as current migrants. The percentage of females in the emigrant population was close to or above the national average in every decade, but when compared with migration the volume of female emigration was not so remarkable and in two decades (1871–81 and 1891–1901) the volume of current migration was greater than that of emigration, in the latter decade by as much as 63%. The proportion of the population emigrating in each decade did not fluctuate markedly, and indeed the proportion of emigrants leaving in the decades 1861–81 and 1901–11 were remarkably similar. Nevertheless, two decades did show distinctive features. In 1891–1901 a much lower proportion of the population emigrated and indeed it had the lowest number of emigrants, while in contrast 1881–91 had the highest proportion of the population emigrating, even if not the greatest volume of emigrants. These two decades 1881–1901 are particularly interesting for studies of population movement, because despite the fluctuations in the proportions emigrating, there were no similar or compensating fluctuations in the proportion migrating.

4. The 'Borders'

The numbers leaving the 'Borders' through migration and emigration were remarkably similar with emigration exceeding migration in three of the five decades (1861–81 and 1901–11). Moreover, whereas the numbers migrating increased until 1901, those emigrating declined steadily throughout the period. As already noted the 'Borders' exhibited a pattern of emigration that was quite different from the other categories. As in the 'Central Lowlands' female emigration was above the national average in every decade, while male emigration was lower in 1881–91 and 1901–11. The 'Borders' had an emigration pattern that was quite distinctive in three ways. Firstly, the largest number and the highest proportion of emigrants were found in the decade 1861–71 and thereafter, the 'Borders' experienced a relatively steady fall in emigrants in both measures, whereas the other categories recorded their greatest volume and highest emigration rates much later. Secondly, there were no marked fluctuations between decades in the proportion of the population lost through emigration. Thirdly, although male emigrants still predominated, the ratio of male to female emigrants was very close to unity especially in the decades 1871–81 and 1901–11, and the range was much narrower than in the other population categories.

This different emigration pattern clearly needs to be accounted for. The counties which comprise the 'Borders' are adjacent or close to the border with England, and as already noted, movement into England in this study was defined as emigration. The counties-of-birth of the Scottish life-time population in England and Wales in 1911 are shown in Appendix 4 and this clearly demonstrates that the highest proportions were born in the counties comprising the 'Borders'. Although the orientation of population movement could have changed prior to 1911 and only recently re-directed itself towards England, it seems more likely that this emigrant population from the southern Scottish counties probably reflected a long standing pattern from a region where emigration (as defined in this study) was as easy as migration. Indeed the almost equal numbers of males and females suggests a combination of both migrant and emigrant movement, because whereas in the migrant population females generally exceeded males both in volume and proportion (Table 3.5), in emigration males normally always exceed females. This is not to argue that there was no genuine overseas emigration from the 'Borders', but that it was buried amongst the emigrants to England. Indeed the fact that this category recorded a consistently high proportion of emigrants when other categories experienced decades of relatively low emigration, supports the argument that much of the emigration was into England. Furthermore, Baines has argued from the opposite perspective that emigration from the northern English counties into Scotland was also similar to migration in character.[6] Finally, there were excellent reasons for emigrating only a fairly short distance south. Although, the 'Borders' was an area with agricultural wages that were above the national average, out-movement was considerable because there were even better wages in agriculture in the four closest English counties of Cumberland, Durham, Northumberland and Westmoreland,[7] while in the industrial Northeast wages generally 'were always amongst the highest in Britain'.[8]

To conclude this analysis of the population categories, three of the four categories showed very similar emigration profiles with noticeably higher ratios of male to female emigrants. The fourth category, the 'Borders', had a quite distinctive profile which was probably related to its close proximity to England. When this analysis of how individual categories related to the national average is compared with that for current migration it is clear that total population movements in the three categories with similar emigration profiles have a consistent pattern. Current migration rates were above average and emigration rates were generally below average in the 'Highlands' and the 'Periphery and Northeast' categories, while in the 'Central Lowlands' the pattern was reversed. This interesting model suggests that emigration and current migration could be inversely related and this will be explored in more depth subsequently. Only in the 'Borders' were there high proportions of both current migrants and emigrants.

THE AGGREGATE CURRENT EMIGRANT LOSSES FROM THE COUNTY-OF-BIRTH

In order to avoid repetition it is not intended to consider every county-of-birth, but to follow the practice already adopted in Chapter 3 for current migration and highlight the main features. The aggregate computer estimates of the proportion of emigrants lost by county-of-birth are tabulated in Appendix 5, together with estimates of standard errors, and these should be referred to throughout this discussion. This Appendix also contains the estimates of current migration so that both forms of mobility can be compared. The information on emigration has been mapped in Appendix 11.

There was no obvious regional dimension to emigration in Appendix 11, and therefore Map 4.1 has been created to clarify the situation. This illustrates the relationship of the individual counties-of-birth to the national average proportion of emigrants for both sexes (Table 4.1) and shows that it was very unusual for a county to remain either above or below the national average throughout the period 1861–1911. The only three counties that showed this degree of consistency were Fife, Inverness and West Lothian. These counties had lower proportions of emigrants than the national average in every decade. No county was consistently above the national average for both sexes, that is even including those in the 'Borders' category which, as already noted, had a high proportion of emigrants. The majority of counties (where measurement was possible)[9] were always below the national average. This was because the counties with the biggest populations, Midlothian (Edinburgh), Lanark and Renfrew,[10] were generally above the national average for the proportion of emigrants and the very large populations in these counties distorted the national averages. The relationship of the counties-of-birth to the national average for emigration is the reverse of the pattern found for current migration (Map 3.1). In current migration the majority of counties were consistently above

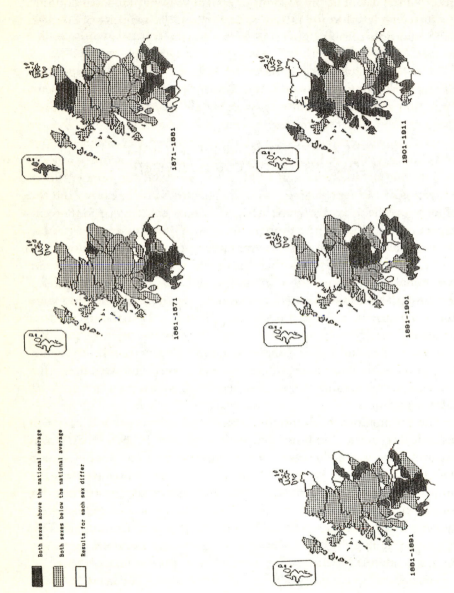

Map 4.1. Emigration: The Relationship of the Proportion Lost by County-of-Birth to the National Average (see Table 4.1).

the national average, and the county with largest population, Lanark and Renfrew, was much lower than the national average and thereby again distorted the data. The proportions of emigrants from individual counties fluctuated far less than for current migration, and the majority of counties had proportions of emigrants leaving that were generally below the national average.

Map 4.1 (emigration) complements Map 3.1 for current migration, although the framework of analysis is different. Map 4.1 shows that as with migration individual counties go against the dominant trend in their category, although far less frequently. Thus in the 'Highlands', although most counties had proportions of emigrants that were below average, Argyll, Ross and Cromarty, Shetland and Sutherland all exceeded the national average in only one decade, whilst in Orkney and Shetland the proportion of emigrants of each sex differed enough to cause one to be above and the other below the national average in four out of five decades.[11] As one would expect, in the 'Borders' the proportion of emigrants was generally above the national average, but every county had one decade with an anomalous result, where the proportions of each sex changed but in opposite directions. In the 'Periphery and Northeast' all the counties experienced several decades below the national average, but had estimates that were above average in at least one decade. Finally, although the 'Central Lowlands' experienced an above average proportion of emigrants, the counties of Fife and Linlithgow (West Lothian) were consistently below average, and Dunbarton and Stirling were also generally low. It can be seen from this that individual counties varied considerably from the norm of their category.

The proportions of emigrants lost do not vary as much between individual counties as do those for current migration (Appendix 5). This is because there was no intrinsic reason why more or less people should emigrate, as opposed to migrate, from a small county. Moreover, the proportions lost through emigration were generally lower than for migration, although of course it must remembered that the baselines were different (native population for migration, total population for emigration). Indeed, excluding the 'Border' counties where emigration was unusually high, it is unusual for emigration to reach 10% even for males.

The national emigrant pattern has already been discussed and consisted of two decades of increasing emigration peaking in 1881–91 followed by a trough and then a second peak. However, many individual counties reveal a pattern of three peaks interspersed by two troughs. Indeed this pattern predominates at the level of the individual county-of-birth in both sexes, but within this pattern differences between the counties do emerge. The variations cannot be classified as regional trends and probably relate to economic circumstances abroad as well as those within the county-of-residence, which may or may not be the county-of-birth. This is in contrast to current migration where the economic situation in the county-of-birth was likely to be a push factor. However, sometimes a county-of-birth experienced a decade of high population losses through both emigration and current migration. This indicates that events in the county-of-birth had precipitated the out-movement. For example, in the county of Selkirk in the decades 1881–91, the proportion of both out-migrants and emigrants was high which suggests that there may have been a crisis in the economy of that county.[12]

When emigration estimations were considered in aggregate, male and female results appeared to follow similar patterns, although there were far less female emigrants. This was also generally true at the county level. The major exception was Kincardine, a county with below average levels of emigration[13] except in the decade 1891–1901. The proportion of male emigrants followed the 'normal' pattern of peaks and troughs, but in contrast female emigration was relatively high in the normally low decade 1871–81 and low in the final decade. Indeed in Kincardine female emigration as a proportion of the total population peaked in the decade 1871–81 and steadily declined thereafter. However, Kincardine also followed a distinctive pattern with regard to current migration, suggesting the presence of some special factors in that county.

Several counties had emigration patterns where the two sexes did not conform in individual decades. These minor differences between the sexes are clearly emphasised in Map 4.1 and give the impression that gender discrepancies in proportions leaving certain counties through emigration increased over time. This is in contrast to the pattern for current migration where there were very few counties in which the proportions of migrants of both sexes did not agree in their relationship to the national average and the number of counties where discrepancies occurred did not grow (Map 3.1). This would suggest that there was more likely to be gender conformity in relation to the national average in current migration than was the case in emigration. However, the proportions emigrating from individual counties were generally much closer to the national average and therefore it was more likely that the sexes would not conform. With current migration the proportions lost from individual counties were widely dispersed from the national average and therefore both sexes were more likely to agree.

The marked peaks in the aggregate proportions of emigrants (Table 4.1) were not apparent in every county. This was particularly true of female emigrants. Thus in the decade 1881–91 the proportion of female emigrants was low from Midlothian. The male peak in emigration could reflect males travelling ahead to investigate opportunities before bringing out their families. Indeed there is evidence to support this; Robert Louis Stevenson, when travelling to the United States by ship in 1879, met married emigrant males intending to assess their prospects in that country before bringing out their families.[14] However, the lack of female emigrants could also imply better opportunities for females in the mother-country; certainly work opportunities in Angus and Midlothian (Edinburgh) were good for females.[15]

It has already been noted that certain counties did not conform to the general pattern of peaks and troughs in emigration. Shetland lost the highest proportion of its population in the decade 1871–81 and Roxburgh in 1891–1901,[16] these being decades when most counties experienced low emigration. However, this high loss through emigration was not complemented by an unusually high proportion of out-migrants in that decade. This suggests that the high level of emigration cannot necessarily be related to strictly local events. Nevertheless, in the case of Shetland there may be a link between high emigration and low migration in the decade under consideration. Smith states that for Shetlanders 'the availability of assisted passages to such places as New Zealand, energetically canvassed by emigration agents in 1874 and 1875' was a decisive factor when considering emigration vis-à-vis migration.[17] Both Roxburgh and Shetland had decades with above average proportions of emigrants and others where emigrant levels were very low, but these counties also had atypical migration patterns which have already been considered in Chapter 3.

It has been noted that the proportion of male emigrants invariably exceeded that of females. Nevertheless, in East Lothian (Haddington) the proportion of females to males was close in every decade except 1891–1901 and females exceeded males in 1881–91. It is possible that family emigration was particularly high from this county making the female proportions more similar to those of males. But it is also the case that male and female emigrants could have moved separately and to different countries. As Appendix 4 showed, females from East Lothian were attracted to England and Wales in greater numbers than males, although not in markedly larger numbers than from many other counties such as Midlothian (Edinburgh) and Inverness.

The proportion of current migrants from Midlothian and Lanark and Renfrew fluctuated far less than from any other county, but this was certainly not the case for emigration. The only county-of-birth with a relatively stable proportion of emigrants was Stirling and even here a lack of fluctuation was only found amongst the males. Moreover, the proportion of emigrants from Stirling was low, below the national average for both sexes, except in the decade 1891–1901, whereas the proportion of current migrants from Stirling was above average. Clearly, a stable proportion of either migrants or emigrants in every decade from an individual county was most unusual and was never consistent enough to include both forms of population movement.

It is the counties with largest populations (Lanark and Renfrew and Midlothian) that had emigration rates above the national average and provided the bulk of the emigrants. This was in complete contrast to migration where their rates were low and indeed these counties were important magnets for migrants. Nowhere else in Scotland was attractive enough to native-born residents of these counties and they found their greatest opportunities abroad. It is therefore not entirely surprising that these counties had a consistently higher proportion of emigrants than the majority of counties (except of course the 'Borders').

A COMPARISON OF SCOTTISH EMIGRATION TO ENGLAND AND WALES OR OVERSEAS

This chapter has argued that some Scottish population movement to England and Wales resembled current migration in the sex ratios, despite being classified as emigration. Baines has estimated Scottish immigration into England and Wales[18] and if these figures are deducted from total emigration from Scotland, overseas emigration can be calculated. Table 4.2 shows the proportions of the total Scottish population that went either to England and Wales or overseas. In this context overseas destinations include Ireland, but as can be seen in Table 3.4, the life-time Scottish immigrant population in Ireland was only about 10% or less of that in England and Wales.

Table 4.2 shows that in every decade and regardless of gender (except for females in 1891–1901) overseas emigration exceeded that within Britain.[19] Male emigration overseas was markedly higher, but female movement was almost equally spread between the two destinations and only in the decade 1881–91, which it has been argued was one of exceptionally high emigration, did the proportion of female emigrants going overseas differ markedly from those to the rest of Britain. The peaks and troughs in emigration have already been briefly analysed. It is useful to consider the response of emigrants to a changing situation. In the decades 1861–81 the proportions emigrating to both destinations were approximately the same, but in the subsequent decade, one of high

*Table 4.2. The Proportion of the Scottish Population Emigrating
to Overseas Destinations or to England and Wales[1]*

Decade	Total Current Emigrants		Overseas Destinations[2]				England and Wales[3]			
			Proportion of the total Scots-born population[4]		Proportion of each sex		Proportion of the total Scots-born population[4]		Proportion of each sex	
	Male	Female	Male	Female	Male	Female	Male	Female	Male	Female
1861–1871	-115,745	-81,619	-4.72	-2.48	63.7	36.6	-2.68	-2.34	51.4	48.6
1871–1881	-116,853	-89,351	-4.28	-2.61	60.5	39.5	-2.46	-2.19	51.1	48.9
1881–1891	-162,892	-114,226	-6.56	-3.81	61.9	38.1	-1.90	-1.80	50.0	50.0
1891–1901	-103,085	-62,837	-2.85	-1.15	70.2	29.8	-2.14	-1.73	53.9	46.1

1 Baines. *Migration in a Mature Economy*. Table 4.5 p. 115. Baines did not calculate his data beyond 1901.

2 The proportion of Scots-born population emigrating abroad has been calculated by deducting Baines' estimate of Scottish movement into England and Wales from the total emigrant population estimated in this study.

3 The proportion of Scots-born population emigrating to England and Wales has been calculated by Baines. Ireland is not included in this calculation, but as Table 3.4 showed it was relatively insignificant in emigration terms compared with that to England and Wales.

4 The proportion is calculated as current emigrants over the total population born in Scotland in the subsequent decade plus total current emigration. (That is the total population at the end of the decade if nobody had moved out).

emigration, far more emigrants of both sexes were going abroad. In the decade of low emigration, 1891–1901, the proportion going to England and Wales increased slightly for males and not at all for females. Unfortunately, it is impossible to assess emigration to England and Wales using Baines' work in the final decade.[20] However, Flinn has also estimated emigration to the United Kingdom,[21] and his calculations suggest that emigration south in 1901–11 was considerably lower than in the previous decades. For males the troughs in overseas emigration may have created a slight increase in emigration to England and Wales, but there was no evidence that female emigration was similarly affected.

The proportion of the population going overseas fluctuated according to the decade, but the proportion emigrating to England and Wales declined over time. For females this decrease was steady throughout the period. There was also evidence of decline for males, but it was complicated by the marked drop in the proportion of emigrants in the decade 1881–91.

Nevertheless, 1891–1901 did have less male emigrants than 1871–81. Flinn's estimates of movement south in 1901–11 imply that the male flow south was even lower than in 1881–91. This declining movement to England and Wales was not just in the proportions of emigrants, as Baines estimates show fluctuations in the volume leaving and they were higher in the years of lower Scots total emigration. Moreover, his estimates of Scottish male emigrants in England and Wales fluctuate more than those for females. This may suggest that men were more likely to see emigration south as an alternative to movement overseas in decades when opportunities overseas were less good. Women were less inclined to move overseas and therefore made no such choice. Therefore, the largest emigration flows south were in the years of high current migration.

In order to estimate emigration in this study it was necessary to consider as emigration all movement out of Scotland, including that to the rest of the United Kingdom, but in view of the previous discussion, should movement to England and Wales really be considered emigration? Table 3.5 showed that nationally female current migration invariably exceeded that of males. In Baines' estimates of Scottish movement into England and Wales male movement exceeded female in three of the four decades considered, but the volume was generally fairly close and the ratio of male to female emigrants was not typical of an emigrant population. This is supported by the data from the 1911 census (Appendix 4) which shows a very slight male majority amongst Scots resident in England and Wales which is significant bearing in mind the large female majority in the Scottish population. Movement to England and Wales was therefore probably a mixture of both emigration and migration. Movement from the Border counties to the north of England probably did resemble current migration, but then the 'Borders' contained only a small proportion of the Scottish population. Thus despite the fact that Appendix 4 showed that the highest proportions of emigrants to England and Wales came from the 'Borders' counties in 1911, life-time emigrants from these counties comprised only 13% of males and 14% of females. This supports a 'migrant' type emigration pattern from these counties as females are predominant. The vast majority of Scots emigrants had had travelled far greater distances when they moved south, and the total movement to England and Wales was not typical of current migration. An emigrant-type population probably moved a greater distance and indeed Anderson and Morse have observed that emigration south was at first 'focused on London and the Southeast and Lancashire' and after 1870 there was more movement to the heavy industry and mining towns of England and Wales.[22] Therefore, if distance can be used as an additional criterion much of the movement should be considered emigration. Finally, as with out-migration we should not assume that it was only the poorer classes who emigrated south, since professionals could also benefit from such a move. For example Duncan MacArthur emigrated to Wakefield in Yorkshire from the Island of Iona, Argyllshire to practice as a medical doctor.[23] At a more general level Cage has highlighted in importance of Scottish doctors in England. They were often as pioneers in their field.[24] Indeed, medics also emigrated overseas as well and Richards has stressed their impact in colonial Australia.[25]

THE CURRENT EMIGRANT AGE-STRUCTURE

The method by which the emigrant age-structure has been computed has been discussed in Chapter 2. Here it will suffice to note that the age-band shown is that in which the emigrant is assumed to have left Scotland. However, it is not assumed that the emigrant was previously a resident of his county-of-birth, but could have lived anywhere in Scotland. For example, Duncan MacArthur mentioned above left Iona to go to University and study to become a doctor, and probably went to Glasgow.[26] He was therefore a migrant before becoming an emigrant. The analysis of this section will begin with a brief overview of the current emigrant age profile. The discussion will then be widened using the population categories, and finally interesting features of individual counties-of-birth will be considered. This is the same system as was used to analyse current migration.

Table 4.3 shows the proportion of the total population lost in each age-band, together with the standard errors. A fairly high proportion of emigrants were young children, as was found for current migration. The proportion of girls appears to exceed that of boys, but this is only because far fewer females emigrated and there were proportionally less adults. In fact young boys exceeded girls in volume in every decade. The decades of very high emigration, 1881–91 and 1901–11, involved proportionally far fewer children. The age-band of maximum adult departures was one age-band younger for males (20–24 years) than for females (25–29 years). A larger proportion of elderly females emigrated than males, but return emigration was a significant component of the emigration patterns of both sexes and this is the reason why the age-bands up to 45 years add up to more than 100% and those above 45 years are frequently negative. This represents return migration.

The youngest emigrants, those less than 5 years, frequently exceeded a quarter of the total emigrant population. As with migration, the birth of a child or several young children appears to be the catalyst that encouraged

Table 4.3. The Proportion of Scots Emigrating by Age-Band at Departure (with 2 standard errors applied ±)[27]

Decade	Gender	Standard Errors ±	<5	<10	<15	<20	<25	<30	<35	<40	<45	>45
1861–1871												
	Males	+2SE	25.1	4.9	-0.2	15.1	26.4	19.6	7.8	2.4	1.0	-2.1
			24.9	**4.9**	**0.1**	**15.2**	**26.1**	**19.6**	**8.4**	**2.7**	**0.9**	**-2.8**
		-2SE	24.6	5.1	0.7	15.2	25.5	19.7	9.5	3.3	0.6	-4.2
	Females	+2SE	31.5	6.7	-2.3	3.1	13.1	21.4	17.8	8.3	3.3	-2.9
			31.4	**6.6**	**-2.1**	**2.6**	**12.0**	**21.8**	**19.0**	**8.7**	**3.3**	**-3.3**
		-2SE	31.3	6.6	-1.7	1.6	9.9	22.6	21.5	9.3	3.3	-4.4
1871–1881												
	Males	+2SE	26.1	8.0	1.8	13.7	24.0	17.8	7.8	2.1	-0.2	-1.1
			26.0	**8.0**	**2.0**	**13.8**	**23.9**	**17.7**	**8.2**	**2.4**	**-0.2**	**-1.8**
		-2SE	26.0	8.1	2.4	14.0	23.5	17.6	9.0	2.9	-0.2	-3.3
	Females	+2SE	30.6	10.2	2.6	5.8	12.8	16.7	12.5	5.2	2.5	1.1
			30.5	**10.2**	**2.7**	**5.3**	**11.7**	**16.9**	**13.8**	**5.9**	**2.7**	**0.3**
		-2SE	30.5	10.2	3.0	4.4	9.5	17.2	16.3	7.1	2.9	-1.1
1881–1891												
	Males	+2SE	18.6	9.1	4.4	13.0	23.5	19.5	9.4	3.6	1.0	-2.1
			18.8	**9.1**	**4.5**	**13.1**	**23.5**	**19.4**	**9.5**	**3.7**	**1.1**	**-2.7**
		-2SE	19.0	9.1	4.6	13.4	23.6	19.3	9.8	4.0	1.1	-3.9
	Females	+2SE	24.4	12.6	6.4	7.7	12.5	15.9	11.9	4.9	2.4	1.3
			24.4	**12.6**	**6.4**	**7.4**	**11.6**	**15.9**	**13.0**	**5.6**	**2.5**	**0.6**
		-2SE	24.5	12.7	6.5	6.7	9.8	15.8	15.2	7.0	2.7	-0.9
1891–1901												
	Males	+2SE	22.3	6.4	2.8	16.8	28.7	20.6	5.6	0.5	0.7	-4.4
			22.7	**6.3**	**2.7**	**17.3**	**29.1**	**20.4**	**5.6**	**0.6**	**1.0**	**-5.7**
		-2SE	23.4	6.1	2.5	18.1	29.9	20.1	5.3	0.9	1.6	-7.9
	Females	+2SE	32.6	9.6	5.0	9.1	11.4	15.3	10.6	3.6	3.0	-0.2
			32.7	**9.7**	**4.9**	**8.5**	**9.6**	**14.7**	**12.8**	**5.2**	**3.4**	**-1.5**
		-2SE	33.0	9.9	4.7	7.3	6.1	13.7	17.1	9.1	4.3	-5.2
1901–1911												
	Males	+2SE	15.6	7.7	4.7	15.4	25.8	20.4	9.0	3.4	1.9	-3.9
			15.9	**7.6**	**4.5**	**15.7**	**26.2**	**20.2**	**8.7**	**3.4**	**2.2**	**-4.4**
		-2SE	16.4	7.4	4.2	16.3	27.0	19.9	8.2	3.5	2.6	-5.5
	Females	+2SE	19.6	9.8	6.8	11.5	15.4	15.9	11.5	6.5	5.2	-2.2
			19.6	**9.8**	**6.7**	**11.2**	**14.5**	**15.5**	**12.6**	**7.6**	**5.5**	**-3.0**
		-2SE	19.8	10.0	6.6	10.7	12.9	14.6	14.9	9.9	5.9	-5.3

the family to emigrate. Child emigration declined amongst older children, thus following an exceedingly similar pattern to that of out-migration, with the age-band 10–14 years appearing least likely to involve movement abroad. Thereafter the proportions emigrating increased, as already noted. Adult males were most likely to emigrate in the age-bands 20–29 years, and thereafter emigration tailed off rapidly, so that the age-band 15–19 years invariably lost far more male emigrants than 30–34 years. Female emigration was far less concentrated and peaked in an older age-band, for example a slightly higher proportion generally emigrated when aged between 30–34 years than between 20–24 years.

THE EMIGRANT AGE-STRUCTURE BY POPULATION CATEGORY

Since the aggregate emigration age profile does not reflect the variety of experience in the individual population categories (Appendix 12), these will now be considered. Appendix 12 can be compared to the current migrant age-structure shown in Appendix 8. The age-structure of the emigrant population was similar to that of current migration in that it varied according to category and gender. The migrant and emigrant age profiles for the same population category were however quite dissimilar. Moreover, the age profile fluctuated according to whether it was a high or low emigration decade. When emigration was considered in aggregate the standard errors were generally very low, but this assumes far greater importance when analysed by age-bands. For the purposes of this discussion it will suffice to note that it is the relative importance of individual age-bands for emigrant departure that is being considered, and where the results are anomalous this will be stated. The categories for the age-structure of emigrants will be considered in the same order as for current migration. This is because as with migration, the 'Central Lowlands' age profile for emigrants was quite different from the other categories and therefore it will be considered last. A brief summary of the main points concerning emigration that have already been established will be provided for each category, so that the new information can be placed in context.

1. The 'Highlands'

This category generally had a below average proportion of emigrants, although in the decades of high emigration the proportion increased over time and this was despite a declining population. Male emigrants exceeded females by a ratio of approximately 6:4. This category had an emigrant age profile that fluctuated according to the decade. At the most general level the emigrant age-structure included very few young children. Thereafter there was generally a gradual and fairly steady increase in male emigrants aged over 10 years. The peak age for male emigrants was generally in the age-band 25–29 years, but the age-bands either side were also important.

The age-profile of female emigration was quite different from that of males. Female emigration was concentrated in the age-band 30–34 years with the age-bands either side being considerably less important. Research by Anderson and Morse has identified the Highlands as a region of comparatively late marriage and high rates of permanent celibacy, with the median age of marriage in all the counties being in the late twenties, the oldest in Scotland. The male emigrants may have been leaving as single men, but this does suggest that the women were leaving at about the time of, or just after, they might have got married.[28] This argument assumes that the females were emigrating directly from their county-of-birth, the high rates of out-migration suggesting that some must have migrated before they emigrated, in at least a two stage movement. Male emigration over the age of 35 years fell rapidly and then remained at a fairly low level. Female emigration also decreased but generally less steeply than for males. The estimates suggest that in every decade, even allowing for the problems of age bunching, a proportion of the emigrants were quite old when they emigrated.

When the emigrant age profile is compared with that for current migration, three important points become clear. Firstly, it is clear that a very much higher proportion of young children were involved in current migration than in emigration, although the proportion of child movement was lower both for emigration and current migration than in any other population category. Secondly, the volume of current migrants of each sex may have differed but the pattern was remarkably similar, as both sexes experienced peak losses in the age-band 20–24 years. However, for emigration the age profiles of the sexes were different. Most males left in the age-band 25–29 years and females five years later. Adult emigrants were generally older than migrants. Thirdly, because current migration estimates are net of returns, it appears to have virtually ceased after 29 years, whereas emigration (which is also estimated net of returns) continued throughout middle age. It is possible that there was more return migration than return emigration, as it was cheaper for a migrant to return than an emigrant. This would have had the effect of disguising late current out-migration. The fact that older out-emigrants were measurable despite return emigration means that there were considerable numbers of older people leaving Scotland, but it does not necessarily mean that current out-migration had ceased or was even low.

When the emigrant age-profile is considered in more detail, it cannot be generalised because there was not a consistent age-structure within each sex as there was for current migration. The age profile of emigrants was influenced by the peaks and troughs in emigration, each decade tending to fit one of two patterns, and provided quite distinctive age profiles for both sexes. The volume of child emigration increased markedly in decades of high emigration, whereas in the decades where the troughs occur child emigration became negligible. This pattern of child emigration occurred in both sexes, and was not an artefact of the method because the two sexes and each decade were calculated independently. This suggests a big increase in family movement in decades of high emigration.

In adult emigration it was the male age profiles that varied the most. In the two decades of high emigration (1861–71 and 1881–91) the number of emigrants in the age-bands with greatest volume increased dramatically, whereas the male age-structure in the trough decades (1871–81 and 1891–1901) had by comparison a flattened appearance. In the decades of high emigration, the volume of emigration was up in most age-bands but this increase was most pronounced in young adult males. The final decade 1901–11 had a high volume of emigration by both sexes and for males it was above the national average. However, this decade did not produce the pronounced increase in young adult male emigrants that the previous discussion might lead one to expect. Whether the projected migrant age-structure or the 1891 one is used, it is quite clear that a large proportion of the increase in male emigration in this decade was due to males over the age of 30 years. Indeed, evidence of this is found in the age-band 30–34 years which was equal to the 'normal' peak age-band 25–29 years. This pattern of an increase in older emigrants was also apparent in female emigration.

2. The 'Borders'

Emigration from the 'Borders' was above the national average, but volume and proportion declined steadily over time. The proportion of male to female emigrants was very close, much closer than in any other category, and the proportions of emigrants leaving did not closely follow the pattern of peaks and troughs in emigration. Moreover, the proximity to England and the unusual emigrant patterns have already led to the argument that emigration in the 'Borders' was a combination of 'true emigration' and 'current migration' across the border.

As with the 'Highlands' it is very hard to distinguish a general emigrant age profile as the age-structure appears to differ in each decade. There was a large proportion of child emigrants in every decade and more children aged 5–14 years than in the other categories. Adult male emigration was spread across three age-bands (15–29 years). There was a wide range of errors in the estimates for females which made the patterns less clear. Male emigration was negligible after 35 years except in the final decade. In contrast female emigration continued throughout middle-age in every decade but was more pronounced in the final one (1901–11).

Child emigration appeared to decrease over time both in volume, as one would expect in relation to declining emigration, but also in relation to adult emigrants. This does not necessarily indicate a change in the age at which people were emigrating, as it may be no more than evidence of the declining birth and mortality rates in Scotland. In the decade 1861–71 there was a peak in adult male emigration in the 20–24 years age-band. The age-bands either side of this peak were also high. This pattern was repeated subsequently, but the age-bands 15–29 years shared a decreasing volume of male emigrants. In the final decade adult male emigration was spread across a broad range of age-bands of 10–34 years and emigration in this decade contained many older males, in contrast to the previous decades. Female emigration retained much the same pattern throughout the period with some emigration in most age-bands, but a peak in 30–34 years.

When the age profiles for emigration are compared with those for current migration three interesting differences appear: Firstly, although child movement formed a far larger proportion of emigrants in the 'Borders' than in the 'Highlands', the age-band with the greatest volume (0–4 years) often had only a third of the volume of the peak adult emigration. This contrasts with the situation for current migration, in which the volume of children was very much higher; indeed the 0–4 years age-band exceeded any other in volume in the first three decades. Therefore, although children were an important component of both population movements, they were far less significant as emigrants. Secondly, peak adult male movement, in both emigration and current migration, was in the age-band 20–24 years. Female current migration was also highest in this age-band, but for emigration the greatest losses were 10 years later (30–34 years). There was a slight secondary peak in emigration in the age-band 20–24 years in the decades 1861–81, but thereafter this age-band was remarkable for its lack of female movement. This raises the question of whether there was a current migrant-type emigrant pattern from this category, because one would have expected an increase in female emigration aged 20–24 years, a peak age-band in current migration. Thirdly, there was some slight evidence of current migration in older males but this was hardly apparent in emigration, except in the final decade (1901–11) when (as with the 'Highlands') the emigration of older males was noticeable. For females current migration amongst the old was not in evidence, although it could have been hidden as measurements are net of returns, but in every decade some older females were emigrating, especially in the final decade.[29]

As with the 'Highlands', the emigrant gender age profiles in the 'Borders' were distinctive and yet, despite marked differences, the 'Borders' age profiles were more similar to emigration from the 'Highlands' than to current migration from the 'Borders' category. This age profile clearly raises a question concerning the hypothesis that emigration from the 'Borders' into England resembled migration. The larger proportion of females is typical of a migrant gender division, and yet the emigrant age structure does not altogether support this.

3. The 'Periphery and Northeast'

The proportion of emigrants from the 'Periphery and Northeast' was generally below the national average, but it achieved the highest proportion of emigrants in 1901–11 and males also exceeded the national average in 1881–91. The difference in the ratio of male to female emigrants was fairly high, only the 'Highlands' category being greater. The proportion of child emigrants was larger in the 'Periphery' than in the other categories discussed so far. Indeed in several decades the volume in the age-band 0–4 years for both sexes was nearly as large as that of the peak female adult age-band. Male emigration was almost always highest in the age-band 20–24 years,[30] but for females the peak was ten years later[31] so that at this age male emigration was generally much lower than female.[32] There was a little emigration by both sexes in later life and this became more significant over time. When the current migrant and emigrant age profiles are compared the two types of population movement superficially appear to be closely inversely related. However, when the decade 1891–1901 is considered (it was generally exceptionally high for current migration and low for emigration) the proportion of males to females does not suggest an inverse relationship, the ratio for males to females being unusually high in both population measures.

In the 'Periphery and Northeast' the proportion of current migrants was above the national average, but in contrast emigrants were generally below average except in 1901–11. Again three points emerge when comparing the age profiles for current migration and emigration. Firstly, child current migration dominated the age-structure at the start of the period, but the volume remained fairly constant, which in a growing population meant that children were a decreasing proportion of the migrant population over time. In contrast the volume of child emigration gradually increased over time (except in the decade 1891–1901) although not as a proportion of the total emigration. Secondly, adult current migration was greatest in the age-band 20–24 years and this was also the most popular age-band for male emigration. In contrast, female emigration increased after 25 years and was generally highest in the age-band 30–34 years. Thirdly, although a small amount of both current out- and return migration was recorded amongst older people, the net volume of emigration in later life was far higher.

4. The 'Central Lowlands'

Emigration from the 'Central Lowlands' was above the national average, but the proportions did not fluctuate as markedly as in some other categories. Moreover, the proportion of male to female emigrants was closer than in the other population categories except 'Borders', which also experienced above-average emigration. Nevertheless, the age profile of the 'Central Lowlands' was quite different to all the others. There were far more child emigrants; indeed in all the decades up to 1901, emigrants aged 1–4 years exceeded in volume any other age-band. However, there was a second peak in adult emigration at 20–24 years.[33] This was the only population category where, in most decades, the age-band with the greatest losses of adult emigrants was the same for both sexes. It should be noted that the adult age-band of peak emigration (20–24 years) was too young to account for the large child emigrant population, bearing in mind that the median age at first marriage for females ranged between 22.7 and 24.7 years.[34] This problem will be considered in more detail subsequently. For older emigrants, male movement remained more important than female,[35] although there was evidence of movement in both sexes. The lack of adult emigrants generally may be accounted for by return emigrants cancelling out those leaving.

When current migration and emigration are compared, it is the 'Central Lowlands' which shows below average current migration and above average emigration. With this in mind three important points emerge. Firstly, young children aged 0–4 years formed the greatest volume of movement in both emigration and current migration. It was only in the decade 1901–11 that this pattern had changed enough for other age-bands to become more significant.[36] Secondly, the age-structure for male current out-migrants was that of a steady decline in volume after the 0–4 years age-band. This was only slightly modified over time. In female current migration, child migrants also dominated but never to the same extent as for males. This pattern changed over time, so that by 1901–11 the first four age-bands were much closer in volume due to more adult migration. In contrast, the emigrant age-structure had two peak age-bands of emigration (0–4 years and 20–24 years) and these altered in their relationship to each other as adult emigration increased over time. The trough in emigration between the two peak age-bands meant that older children (5–14 years) were far more likely to migrate than emigrate. Thirdly, in both current migration and emigration some mobility both outward and return was seen, although net movement was far higher amongst emigrants.

It can be seen that the population categories have produced some interesting and quite distinctive emigration age structures and before proceeding to the individual counties, these profiles will be considered. It is hoped that by considering the general emigrant age-structure now, too much repetition can be avoided later. Moreover, counties that are exceptions to the general trends can be more easily identified.

THE AGE OF EMIGRANTS

This section will begin by considering child out-movement. The arguments in this discussion are relevant to both current migration and emigration. The reasons for differences in the age profiles of each sex will then be examined. Thirdly, possible reasons why elderly emigrants are more common than elderly current migrants will be discussed as will transient emigration. Finally reasons for differences in the age profiles of emigrants in the peaks and troughs of emigration are analysed.

1. Child Emigrants

Children and young adults comprised a surprisingly large proportion of all emigrants. Indeed Table 4.4 shows that when the proportion of the total Scottish population under 20 years is compared with the proportion of emigrants in the same age-band males conformed very well with the national age-structure, except in 1871 and to a lesser extent 1891. In contrast female emigrants failed to agree, being slightly below the national average in the decade 1861–71 and above thereafter, and increasing steadily until 1901. This in part reflects the lack of adult female emigrants. A far greater proportion of the much smaller total female emigrant population left as children, probably within a family unit.

At a regional level, the age profiles of child emigration followed those of current migration in some respects. Certainly the patterns of child movement were similar in that very few children moved from the 'Highlands', but they dominated in the 'Central Lowlands'. There are four possible reasons for the huge numbers of mobile children, particularly from the 'Central Lowlands' and apparently without accompanying adults.

Firstly, in categories such as 'Central Lowlands', the age-bands that would have included the child's parents would have also included considerable return movement. Both emigration and current migration is calculated net,

*Table 4.4. The Proportion of Emigrants Under 20 years
Compared with the Scottish Population 1871–1911*

Census year or decade ending	Proportion of the total Scottish population <20 years[1]		Proportion of the Scottish emigrant population <20 years[2]	
	Male	Female	Male	Female
1871	49.4	44.1	45.1	42.7
1881	49.0	44.5	49.8	48.7
1891	48.2	43.9	45.5	50.9
1901	48.4	42.0	49.0	55.8
1911	43.6	40.5	43.6	47.4

1 Taken from Appendix 3[p].

2 Calculated from Brock 'Scottish Migration', Vol. I, p. 313, Table 8.4.

these returning Scots would have cancelled out some of those leaving. It was only in the decade 1901–11 that female emigration in the age-band 40–44 years, a suitable age for the movement of mothers, remained high (Table 4.3).

Secondly, some children, particularly those born in the 'Central Lowlands' counties, were undoubtedly travelling with parents who were born elsewhere in Scotland,[37] their parents having migrated earlier. This may account for the relative lack of child migrants and emigrants in the 'Highlands'. In that category female emigration was concentrated in the 30–34 year age-band, an age when one might have expected accompanying children.

Thirdly, it may also be the case that some of the Scots-born children who were migrating or emigrating were travelling with English- or Irish-born parents. Certainly there were large concentrations of both nationals in the counties that comprise the 'Central Lowlands' category.[38] Appendix 14 shows the volume of current immigrants into Scotland. The Irish in particular appear to fluctuate in volume following the same peaks and troughs as the Scottish national emigrant pattern.[39] It is possible that many young adult Irish who arrived in Scotland married, had children and then emigrated when there was an upturn in emigration from Scotland. This would have had the effect of increasing the volume of Scottish-born child emigrants and reducing immigration from Ireland (which is also calculated net) in years of high out-movement.

Finally there was some assisted emigration of children from Scotland. Harper estimates that nearly 7,000 Scottish orphans were sent abroad by the Quarrier Homes in the period 1872–1930,[40] and this was only one of several philanthropic organisations encouraging child emigration. Nevertheless, in every decade this study has estimated that between about

45,000 and 60,000 children aged 0–10 years emigrated from Scotland. The assisted movement of children can therefore account for only a very small proportion of child emigration.

2. Adult Emigrants

It has already been established that far more males emigrated than females, but it was also clear that in the age-band of maximum volume adult emigration was gender specific. Whereas the majority of males emigrated at 20–24 years (Table 4.3), females emigrated when they were much older and except in the 'Central Lowlands' category the maximum number left in the age-band 30–34 years.[41] However, the enormous population in that category meant that nationally the largest volume of adult females left in the age-band 25–29 years.

It is interesting to consider why these marked differences between the adult male and female emigrant age-structures have arisen. Erickson studied British emigration to the United States,[42] the most popular overseas destination for Scots,[43] and has shown that marital status of male emigrants from Great Britain altered between the 1850s and the 1880s. Single men had always outnumbered married men, but in 1854 the ratio was 2:1, whereas by the 1880s, a decade of high emigration, this ratio had increased of 8:1.[44] Clearly, this study cannot identify the marital status of emigrants, and the Scottish ratio may never have conformed exactly to the British one. However, the mean and mode of the average age of marriage for males in Scotland[45] was older than the peak male adult age-band for emigration, and so even in the peak age-band a large majority of males probably would not have been married. Moreover, if married men were leaving with wives, there would have been far more females of a similar age travelling. This age profile for males does not change markedly over time; indeed the proportion of males leaving in the age-band 20–24 years in 1861–71 was not exceeded until 1891–1901, and therefore it seems possible that by 1861–71 the higher proportion of unmarried adult male emigrants was already in existence. However, Andersons research suggests that for some Englishmen emigration offered the opportunity to escape from an unsatisfactory marriage.[46] It is not known whether the same was true in Scotland, but it seems quite likely that it was.

Female emigration age profiles also need to be accounted for. If females had emigrated with their husbands, they would have been about the same age or younger than their husbands[47] and so the peak in older females is unlikely to be accounted for solely by the emigration of married couples. It seems more likely that many men were going abroad alone first and were later joined by their wives or fiancees, hence the marked difference in age.

Indeed Erickson has identified this pattern of the males leaving first and considered it arose after the 1850s. In the 1850s she found family parties of emigrants were more common, but by the 1880s on any ship to the United States there was a complement of Scottish wives and children travelling alone,[48] their husbands having probably left earlier.[49] In this study the evidence seems to support Erickson's findings for the later period.

Erickson's work suggested that the emigrant age profile had changed between the mid 1850s and 1880s. This study suggests that for Scotland at least, the 1880s emigrant age profile may have already existed in the decade 1861–71, as there was no firm evidence in the emigrant age-structures of a changing pattern of emigration. There are several reasons why Ericksons' 1880s age profile may have existed in Scotland two decades earlier. Firstly, the transport for emigration had changed rapidly after Ericksons' first sample. The change to steamship for journeys to the U.S.A occurred in the late 1860s.[50] The faster speed and cheaper costs of the steamships[51] made it feasible for one member of a family to travel ahead to investigate the possibilities abroad. Secondly, improved postal services meant information could be sent home easily, family contacts could be maintained over long distances, and many authors have stressed the importance of letters as a means of disseminating information.[52] Thirdly, the 1850s may have been a decade of exceptional emigration from Scotland. In the West Highlands Devine has shown that the long term effects of the famine were still being felt through emigration[53] and work by Anderson and Morse also indicates that the decade 1851–61 was one of exceptional population mobility.[54] Indeed Erickson has also speculated that emigration between 1846 and 1854 was probably the highest of the century in England and Scotland, with the exception of the decade of the 1880s.[55]

3. Older Emigrants

It was because movement has been calculated net of return migration that current migration age profiles appeared to have a marked cut-off at 29 years, and although out-migration continued above that age it was unusual for it to be large enough to be significant. Current emigration appears to have continued until old age, although age-bunching has caused problems in this set of data. However, some emigration of the elderly was genuine and not an artefact of the method. The process of one member of a family going abroad first and then others coming later may also account for some older emigrants, as they may have been going to join younger members of their family who had become established abroad.[56] Return emigration was also apparent amongst the elderly and this will be discussed below as an aspect of transient emigration.

Some emigrants were therefore travelling to join relatives abroad and yet it has been argued that unlike in Ireland, there is no evidence in the records of Scottish banks of remittances being sent back to pay for the journey. However, the agents of one major transatlantic shipping company are known to have booked passages with money advanced from the United States[57] and so perhaps the money was it was still being transferred but not using conventional banks.

TRANSIENT OR TEMPORARY EMIGRATION

Clearly, some emigrants went abroad intending to stay but later changed their mind, creating return emigration. However, some return emigration was undoubtedly a product of the method of estimating emigration used in this study. This cannot distinguish emigrants, that is those moving abroad permanently, from those going abroad for a limited period. In the 1880s Erickson found these transient people in many different groups, as commercial men, gentlemen and also building, iron, steel and engineering workers,[58] while Harper found temporary migration to the USA amongst Aberdeen granite workers.[59] Transient emigrants could also be colonial civil servants, merchants, military personnel or others working in the colonies. Many of these people had their families with them[60] but ultimately intended to retire to Britain. It should be noted that these people working abroad may have intended to return to Scotland, but if they died whilst still abroad then they became true emigrants. Finally some people who were merely visiting overseas would have been picked up in the system. Stevenson recorded visitors to the United States even amongst the poorer steerage passengers.[61] Both long term temporary emigrants and short-term visitors were classified as emigrants in this study. Likewise their return was recorded as return emigration, and it is therefore not surprising that many older Scots could appear as either out or return emigrants in the data.

THE EFFECT OF THE DECADE OF DEPARTURE ON THE AGE-STRUCTURE OF THE EMIGRANT POPULATION

The pattern of peaks and troughs in emigration was tabulated in Table 4.1 and expanded in the accompanying text. Table 4.3 showed that in the low emigration decade, 1891–1901, the age-bands of peak male departures (0–4 and 20–24 years) had above average proportions of emigrants and for females the children were also high. However, this pattern was not necessarily repeated in the individual population categories; for example the age-bands of peak adult emigration were less pronounced in decades of low emigration in the 'Highlands' (Appendix 12). This alternating pattern of age profiles is interesting, although it must be remembered that the coarse framework of analysis (the decade), which was dictated by the raw material (the Census), was not necessarily the ideal framework for analysis; it disguises the fluctuations that occurred annually in the numbers of emigrants leaving.[62] The 'trough' decades reflect the minimum number of emigrants that had decided to leave whatever the circumstances, or for whom economic considerations were unimportant. Indeed work by Erickson shows that years of low emigration had proportionally more emigrants in the trades and professions because they were 'relatively insensitive to the short-term forces governing' emigration and formed 'a higher share of a reduced number of emigrants'.[63] In contrast, in the 'peak' decades opportunities for the unskilled increased, although obviously it was not just the young who were unskilled and so the largest increases were spread across several age-bands and not confined to the peak age-bands. Indeed the ratios of married to unmarried male emigrants calculated by Erickson were all estimated in years of exceptionally high emigration. The ratios of single to married emigrants may well have been less extreme in decades of low emigration. Certainly the proportion of males aged 20–24 years tended to decrease more than in other age-bands.

It should be born in mind that the age-structure of the emigrant population described by Erickson was for an overseas destination and many Scots emigrants were in fact moving south into the rest of Britain. In England and Wales Baines assumed that the Scottish immigrant population had the same age profile as the native migrant population. This had less children and more young adults than the Scottish current migrant population, and in that respect Baines' estimation for Scottish immigrants was closer to the computed emigrant population in this study. With regard to overseas emigration, although the United States was the most popular destination for Scots, it was not the only one and Flinn has found that the gender ratios of emigrants varied according to the country of destination.[64] One may speculate that the age profile of emigrants differed as well. Certainly for the years 1912–3 Flinn has shown that the skilled, unskilled and middle classes were attracted to different countries.

EMIGRATION FROM SCOTLAND BY COUNTY-OF-BIRTH

The previous discussion has considered the emigration patterns in the age profiles of the categories. The individual counties will now be analysed to see how they fitted the general trends. This analysis of emigration from counties-of-birth has focused on the peak age-band of adult departure of both sexes, as a method of distinguishing differing emigration patterns within counties. This section compares counties that followed the emigrant age profile proposed by Erickson (that is of adult males leaving at an earlier age than females) with those counties that have different profiles. The pattern that Erickson identified was for movement to the United States, but whether, for example, it occurred in Scottish movement to the rest of Britain is unknown. This method of comparing counties could therefore identify counties with common emigrant destinations and this will be considered as the analysis proceeds.

Three main emigration groupings have been identified. The first, has the peak age-band of male emigration younger than that of females, the second had the peak age-band of both sexes coinciding, while the third type had the reverse pattern of the first group. The groupings were not always as distinctive as the three classifications suggest and some counties formed a transitional group in which the analysis became blurred over time. Not every county will be discussed in detail, although Appendix 13 provides estimates for every county.

The first type of county includes all those which exhibited a peak emigration pattern similar to that described by Erickson,[65] which was of peak male emigration being younger than that of females. The present study has shown that the greatest volume of male emigrants occurred one or more age-bands younger than females. There were not many counties where age-bands with the highest volume of emigration from each sex remained consistent throughout the study. The relationship between the age-bands of maximum emigration varied according to the county. In Inverness peak adult male emigration was in the age-band 25–29 years and for females it was five years later.[66] Child emigration was fairly low especially in the decade 1891–1901. In Aberdeen[67] adult emigration was similar but slightly younger than that in Inverness, but in the former more children were moving. In Shetland peak male adult emigration was younger (in the age-bands 20–24 years) but in contrast female movement was much older, 30–34 years.[68]

Dumfries also had young peak male emigration, and the age-bands 15–24 years both had a high volume of emigrant males. In the final decade male emigration peaked much later at 30–34 years.[69] Emigration overseas from Dumfries was probably an important component of population movement because in decades of high overseas emigration the volume of emigration from Dumfries was markedly higher. However, this county also had a high proportion of emigrants to England and Wales (Appendix 4), but as the proportion of emigrants moving south was declining nationally (Table 4.2), it is likely that emigration south of the border had most impact on the estimations at the start of the study. Whilst this analysis provides possible reasons for the changing pattern, it cannot entirely account for it and it is possible to speculate that peak male emigration overseas occurred at a later age as time progressed. Female emigration from Dumfries was much older than for males and consistently peaked in the age-band 30–34 years,[70] and in this county there were also fairly high rates of child emigration. It could be assumed that the children were offspring of the older females and it suggests that they emigrated directly from Dumfries. But it was also possible that the Dumfries-born females may have migrated before having children, and the younger children were born to outsiders.

This pattern of a peak in male emigration one or two age-bands before that of the females was apparent, but not consistent, in many counties. It should however be noted that the age-bands are coarse, and the change in age may not be as large as the age-bands suggest. If emigrants became on average only a year older or younger, it could still affect the age-band of peak departures. In Midlothian (Edinburgh) the age-bands of maximum departures for each sex also became closer over time until they were the same. Male emigration remained consistently highest in the age-band 20–24 years, whereas peak female emigration in 1861–71 was five years older, but by 1901–11 it was younger and coincided with that of males. Child emigration under five years was higher than that of adults. This pattern was also found in Forfar (Angus).[71]

The counties so far considered share common characteristics in terms of emigrant age profiles, but they come from very different population categories and demographic experiences. Moreover, the emigrants from these counties were not attracted to the same destinations. The counties analysed in this first group include those with very different proportions moving south of the Border.

This brings us to the second type of emigration age profile, which consists of a small group of counties in which the peak age-band of departure was the same for both sexes. Lanark and Renfrew were an example of this pattern and despite quite large standard errors the age-bands of peak emigration were generally consistent.[72] The adult age-band of maximum departure was 20–24 years, but there were always far more male emigrants than females. It has already been noted that within Scotland these counties offered the best prospects, hence their high in-migration. For natives there were unlikely to be better prospects elsewhere in Scotland.[73] Moreover, these counties contained the main emigration ports and it is possible that natives were better informed of opportunities abroad than elsewhere in Scotland. Clearly, as both sexes were leaving in greatest numbers in the same age-band, many young married people may have left together, but even if the males did leave first, the fact that they were better informed about prospects meant that their wives or fiancees were soon able to join them. Certainly, as females often marry slightly younger than males, a delay of a year or more between the sexes departing would not be apparent in the calculations.[74] Nevertheless, far more young adult males left than females and so clearly many males were independent or possibly travelling with their parents. The emigration of young children from this county was greater in volume than that of females in the largest age-band, although not as high as that of adult males. This evidence supports the hypothesis that many of the young children were accompanying parents who were outsiders, either in-migrants or immigrants.

The third type of county to be considered is that where female adult emigration was younger than that of males. This age profile of the sexes was the reverse of that proposed by Erickson. Stirling was an example of a county where female peak emigration in the age-band 15–19 years was consistently younger than male (20–24 years). This pattern was also apparent, but the age-bands not so consistent, in West Lothian.[75] The counties were both in the 'Central Lowlands' population category, with heavy industry and mining attracting in-migrants, and they probably had less work for females. Certainly, there was a higher proportion of female current migration than of males in both counties (Appendix 5). Indeed West Lothian (Linlithgow) was the only county in Scotland that had a male majority in the population. These counties had proportions of emigrants that were below the national average and in 1911 there were relatively few life-time emigrants from either West Lothian or Stirling resident in England and Wales (Appendix 4). There was also a younger peak of female than male emigration found in Banff.[76]

Ericksons' suggested age pattern for adult emigrants assumed that the age profile of female emigration was largely a response to the earlier emigration by males. Flinn has analysed female emigrants' occupations in 1912–13 and just over half were wives or did not state an occupation. Clearly, the rest were not all independent emigrants, as many would have been daughters, sisters or fiancees of emigrants, but there was some independent emigration.[77] Harper has analysed organised female emigration from the Northeast and found that domestic servants were particularly in demand.[78] Although the numbers involved are not significant in national terms[79] it might begin to account for the younger female peak emigration in the smaller Northeast counties, where numbers leaving were low. Finally, one cannot exclude the possibility that some older single women were emigrating to find husbands or to improve their own career opportunities. Indeed Anderson cites contemporary beliefs that the British Mormon

Church was systematically recruiting single women to go out to America and become additional wives.[80]

It has already been noted that young child emigration (aged 0–4 years) was low from the 'Highlands' and highest in the 'Central Lowlands'. The 'Borders' counties were also distinctive in their young emigrant age profile, compared with the rest of Scotland. This age-structure was even more noticeable when the counties were considered separately. Counties other than the 'Borders' experienced a sharp drop after the age-band 0–4 years and the age-band 10–14 years was lower or at best equal to the 5–9 years age-band. In contrast, in the 'Borders' counties the volume of emigrants in each of these three age-bands was often approximately equal, and if the 5–9 year age-band did decline the subsequent one increased again. This appears to be the most distinctive difference between the 'Borders' and the rest of Scotland. This, it could be argued, is further evidence of the mixed nature of emigration thought to have occurred in this area.

Having considered the age-structure of emigration by county-of-birth, the discussion will now consider issues that have arisen in the analysis. This will not repeat the discussion on the age profile in the population categories but will concentrate on new issues.

The age-band of peak emigration in both sexes was used as a criterion for grouping counties. Attempts were made to find reasons to account for the wide gap in peak age-bands between the sexes that occurred in some counties but not in others. The rural counties appeared to be more likely to have males emigrating much earlier than females, but this was not true of the smaller counties in the Northeast. The ratios of males to females did not appear to be important, but this was difficult to ascertain because the volume of males fluctuated so much. The volume of life-time immigrants in England and Wales in 1911 (Appendix 4) was an imperfect measure because one has no idea how old the Scots were, how recently they had emigrated or even if this pattern was typical of earlier censuses. Nevertheless, even in the 'Borders' counties, with high emigration south, there was no obvious link between the counties in peak age-band of emigration. Appendix 13 shows that the age-bands of maximum male emigration from Berwick were much older than from Dumfries.

The counties where peak emigrant age-bands for both sexes were close or coincided, were usually industrialised counties (where less than 15% of the population was employed in agriculture in 1881).[81] However, also included in this group were the smaller counties in the Northeast, which employed considerably more than 15% in agriculture, while Fife, an important industrial and mining county had to be omitted.

RETURN EMIGRATION

Return emigration was apparent in the estimates of emigrant losses and it was equally obvious in this study in the samples taken to establish a migrant age-structure. However, as with return migration, it remains impossible to quantify. Baines estimated that nearly 50% of outward passengers on the North Atlantic routes returned. This would have included transient emigrants, visitors, and others who, in both Baines' study and this one, have sometimes inevitably been measured. Baines concluded that as return movement increased after 1870, a 40% return emigration for England and Wales was reasonable.[82] Furthermore, estimates by Anderson and Morse for Scotland are only slightly more cautious, suggesting that a third of emigrants returned.[83] Moreover, Hollingsworth's study on much more recent population movement in Scotland supports these conclusions for the earlier period, as he deduced that approximately 35–45% of emigrants from Scotland returned. Interestingly, Hollingsworth used the same definition of emigration as this study, in considering movement to England or Wales as emigration.[84] We have therefore only rather imprecise estimates of what was clearly a very significant population movement. In this study there are two sources of evidence of return emigration. Firstly, there are the estimated emigrant age profiles and secondly, the samples from the enumeration books. Exactly the same problems arise with measurement of return emigration as with return current migration. The estimations are net of returns and as return emigrants must overall be older than out-emigrants, it is therefore only as emigrants become older that the significance of return emigration can be appreciated. For example Table 4.5 tabulates a family from Melrose who emigrated to Australia with two children and returned with four. The youngest Scots-born child was no more than seven years old when she became a return emigrant. Her return

Table 4.5. Out- and Return Emigration Identified from the Birthplaces of the Children of a Family Resident in Ladhope, Roxburgh in 1871

NAME	STATUS	AGE	OCCUPATION	BIRTHPLACE
James Coldwell	Head (married)	33	Wool scourer	Roxburgh, Melrose
Elizabeth Coldwell	Wife (married)	40		Roxburgh, Melrose
Jane Coldwell	Daughter	11		Roxburgh, Melrose
Maggie Coldwell	Daughter	7		Midlothian, Edinburgh
Mary Coldwell	Daughter	4		Australia
Elizabeth Coldwell	Daughter	2		At sea, Cape Horn

Ladhope, Roxburgh, 1871, RD. 799-2, ED. 9, sch. 52, p. 10.

trip to Australia was too rapid to be recorded by the system used in this study. Even if the emigration had been over different decades so that her return had been 'caught', it would undoubtedly have been swamped by the larger volume of outward movement.

When the enumeration samples were taken in order to establish a migrant age-structure, examples of return emigration were noted because they were interesting, but without any expectation that they would have any great significance. Return emigration could only be identified if the family in question had children born abroad, and if these children were still young enough to be part of the family unit. There were therefore probably far more return emigrants in the samples than were pin-pointed, especially of people who had lived outside Scotland a long time and whose children had grown up or remained abroad. Moreover, there was no way single people who emigrated and then returned could be identified and this group could have been quite large.

Although return emigrants were noted from enumeration books in each census year (1861–91), it was only in 1891 that sufficient return emigrants were recorded to create a small sample. This was because the enumeration books for that year were used more extensively. This sample will enable the length of time abroad, and pattern of settlement on returning to Scotland to be examined.

First, the length of time that emigrants had left Scotland will be considered. It has already been argued that the samples from the enumeration books were unlikely to identify return emigrants who had been away a long time. The length of absence of short term return emigrants also presented problems if the eldest or only child was born outside Scotland, as it was impossible to be sure that the parents had not themselves been child emigrants. In the 1891 samples, there were sixteen families where the maximum length of absence from Scotland could be measured, and this ranged from two to eleven years, but many stayed away less than five years.[85] Clearly, this sample is very small, but it shows how mobile people had become in the short term.

The 1891 samples showed that many emigrant families returned to their county-of-birth.[86] Their emigration from Scotland was not therefore a stage in a series of movements after leaving the county-of-birth. Moreover, this was true both of movement abroad and south to the rest of Britain. Thus in 1891 there were many examples of emigrants returning to the county-of-birth of the head of the household (normally the male). For example in the north of Scotland, a family from Shetland (the head was a cooper) returned from New Zealand,[87] three families from Caithness (hotel keeper, pedlar and mason) returned from England,[88] America[89] and Canada,[90] two families from Ross and Cromarty (builder and grocer) returned from England[91] and Australia,[92] and finally two families from Aberdeen (a tramway conductor and a retired fleet surgeon) returned from England.[93] In the Central Lowlands and south the same pattern for some returning emigrants was apparent; for example in Lanark two miners families returned from the USA[94] while in Berwick two families (joiner and farmer) returned from Canada[95] and New Zealand.[96] Clearly, this returning to the county-of-birth can only be identified in family parties and indeed it is possible that this phenomenon was restricted to family parties, which were possibly more likely to have strong extended family connections than a single emigrant. However, it also appears to be the case that social class and emigrant destination were not important determinants in this pattern of movement.

The sample from 1861 was very small and evidence from this enumeration was not so clear. It was possibly the case, as Baines has suggested, that 'the rate of return rose sharply in the 1870s' as a result of the introduction of steamships.[97] However, this would not have prevented emigrants to England and Wales returning to their county-of-birth in 1861 and these return emigrants were not in evidence either. The evidence from the 1891 enumeration suggests that emigration was not regarded as an alternative to out-migration, as many families, if they chose to return, did so to their county-of-birth. Erickson has discussed the mobility of certain tradesmen in the 1880s, citing both the building-trades workers and miners as being over-represented as emigrants in relation to the total employed in those trades in Scotland.[98] The samples from the enumeration books however provided some evidence of return emigrants in both occupations from North America and indeed in 1891 nearly a quarter of the return emigrants were miners. This was the most numerous occupation recorded.[99]

The returning flow of emigrants would have had important repercussions in Scotland. Although there has been very little research, it has been argued that the evidence does not suggest that returning emigrants were necessarily less prosperous than those that remained abroad.[100] Indeed the poor, the failures, were unlikely to be able to pay the necessary fares in order to return. Moreover, many may have left Scotland with the specific intention of returning. Return emigrants were not therefore those who had been unsuccessful abroad, and they were an important source of information to potential emigrants, widening the horizons of those left behind. Such people, by their mere presence, could be an encouragement to others to leave.

Conclusion

It is evident that the highest proportion of emigrants came from urban counties, which was where the majority of the Scottish population lived in the second half of the nineteenth century. The residents of these highly populous counties were emigrating because there were no better opportunities within Scotland, whereas those born in rural counties were more likely to migrate to urban counties than to emigrate.[101] However, individual counties did not necessarily conform to patterns of movement in their population category in every decade.

The current migrant and emigrant populations were not the same populations and had some distinctive elements within them. Females showed a greater propensity to migrate than males, whereas males were more likely to emigrate. Males appeared more willing than females to change their direction of movement, to emigrate to England and Wales rather than overseas, or to migrate within Scotland in decades of low emigration. Furthermore, analysis of the county-of-birth and county-of-residence of return emigrants suggests that for many families migration was not an alternative to emigration.

In many counties males emigrated markedly earlier than females, but in the larger urban counties peak adult emigration of both sexes either coincided throughout or became closer over the period. Although it is probably quite correct to state that the 'largest proportion of out-migration and emigration took place between the ages of 15 and 25 years',[102] the majority of current migrants and a sizeable proportion of emigrants were considerably younger.

Notes

1. In the second half of the nineteenth century, Tranter has noted increasing restrictions imposed by the receiving countries on 'undesirables'. They were unwilling to take paupers, the destitute, lunatics, the deaf and dumb and certain types of criminal. However, this selectivity did not affect the majority of emigrants. Tranter. *Population and Society*. p. 134.

2. In order that comparisons can be made emigration losses have been tabulated in a similar way to those of current migration. However, care must be exercised when making such comparisons because estimates of percentages do not use the same baselines. Whereas estimates of migration use only natives in the county-of-birth as the baseline, those of emigration use the total county-of-birth population as a framework of measurement. It is being argued that for an accurate measurement of the percentage lost through current migration, only those natives left in the county-of-birth at

the end of the decade under consideration plus of course present out-migration, are the baseline. When emigration losses from Scotland as a whole are being computed, it cannot be ascertained whether an emigrant has just left his county-of-birth or is already a life-time migrant. The baseline for these percentage calculations is therefore the entire county-of-birth population, regardless of which county the person is at present residing in at the end of the decade under consideration, plus current emigration. See Chapter 2.

3. The Scottish-born population resident in Scotland rose from 3,061,531 in 1871 to 4,362,473 in 1911. The 1911 figure is not the same as that quoted in the census of that year (1911 Census, Vol. II, Table XXXVIII, pp. 502–23). The estimate provided is more rigid than that in the census and includes only those born in Scotland.

4. Table 3.5 shows that for current out-migration the greatest proportion of the native population (both male and female) left in the decade 1871–81, which was earlier than the peaks for both sexes in emigration.

5. Baines. *Migration in a Mature Economy.* p. 95.

6. Baines. *Migration in a Mature Economy.* pp. 121–2 and Appendix 6, p. 307.

7. Hunt. *Regional Wage Variations.* pp. 43–7.

8. *Ibid.* p. 170.

9. Only counties where both male and female proportions of emigrants were above or below the national average were considered. In the decades 1881–91 and 1901–11 a third of the counties were omitted because the two sexes did not reveal common trends.

10. The county of Edinburgh (Midlothian) agreed with Lanark and Renfrew in some decades but there was nowhere near the same degree of consistency in the relationship to the national averages for both emigration and current migration.

11. In Orkney and Shetland the proportions of male and female emigrants only conformed to the national average in one decade (1871–81) when emigration was below average for Orkney and above for Shetland. In the majority of decades the proportion emigrants was consistently above average for males and below average for females from Orkney. This was also true for Shetland except in the decade 1891–1901 when the pattern was reversed. See Appendix 5. Many Shetland males worked in the merchant navy or in the Greenland whaling industry, so they would therefore have been transient emigrants unless they died or settled abroad. For reasons for the Shetland emigration see Smith, *Shetland Life.* pp. 157–9.

12. A slump in the wool trade due to foreign competition may account for this movement out of Selkirk. Campbell cites evidence from the Royal Commission of 1886 with regard to a woollen manufacturer from Galashiels who stated that 'trade was very bad' and that 'we get no profits'. Campbell. *The Rise and Fall.* p. 69.

13. See Appendix 13 Kincardine and Table 4.1.

14. Stevenson, *The Amateur Emigrant*. p. 8 and 33 respectively.

15. In the decade 1861–71 in Dundee the linen industry was reaching its peak. This employed large numbers of males, but the jute-based industries which were still growing employed mainly females. Walker cites a newspaper report from 1864 which states that female workers were preferred in the jute industry. *Glasgow Free Press* 1864 cited in Walker. *Juteopolis*. pp. 33–4.

16. A decline in the woollen trade in 1891–1901 caused the population of Hawick to decline from 19,204 to 17,303 which suggests that there were serious economic problems in Roxburgh. Lenman. *An Economic History*. p. 187.

17. Smith. *Shetland Life*. p. 159.

18. Baines. *Migration in a Mature Economy*. Table 4.5. p. 115.

19. The estimates in Table 4.2 for the proportions of total emigrants moving to other parts of Britain are lower than those of Anderson and Morse. They estimated that 'about half' of Scots who emigrated moved south, but included Ireland in their calculations. However, Table 3.4 (which shows lifetime emigration) suggests that emigration to Ireland was insignificant when compared with movement to England and Wales and is therefore unlikely to markedly increase the present estimation of British emigration. See Anderson and Morse. 'The People' p. 17.

20. Baines did not calculate his data beyond 1901. Baines. *Migration in a Mature Economy*. Table 4.5 p. 115.

21. Flinn's estimates of Scottish emigration are to the United Kingdom, which includes Ireland, but they are still probably higher than Baines, Flinn. *Scottish Population History*. Table 6.1.2. p. 442.

22. Anderson and Morse. 'The People' p. 17.

23. MacArthur. *Iona* p. 125.

24. Cage. 'The Scots in England' p. 43.

25. Richards. 'Australia' p. 134.

26. MacArthur discusses the educational achievements of several men from Iona, several of whom went to Glasgow University. It is not clear whether Duncan MacArthur was amongst them. MacArthur. *Iona* p. 125.

27. See Chapter 2 for details of how standard errors were calculated.

28. Anderson and Morse 'High Fertility, High Emigration' pp. 326–31.

29. There are quite large standard errors in the middle-aged female age-bands, but despite this it is clear that some emigration was occurring. See Appendix 12.

30. In the decade of very high male emigration (1901–11) most males left in the age-band 25–29 years (this was regardless of the migrant age-structure used, although it should be noted that in every decade emigration in the age-bands either side of the adult peak tended to be high. This group of age-bands shifted upwards in age over time, so that in 1861–71 the age-

bands 15–29 years were the most important years for adult male emigration, by 1891–1901 it was 20–39 years, and in the subsequent decade 20–34 years. See Appendix 12

31. The standard errors in female emigration are such that it is probably wiser to consider the age-bands 25–34 years as the peak age-band for emigration, although the majority of data do suggest that it is within the age-band 30–34 years. See Appendix 12.

32. In the decade of very high emigration (1901–11) the volume of male emigrants in the age-band 30–34 years was still higher than that of females.

33. Differences in the standard errors do not affect these conclusions for male emigrants, but for females there is disagreement. In 1861–71 the peak age-band of female loss ranges from 20–34 years; in 1871–81 and 1881–91 it was 20–29 years and in 1891–1901 15–24 years. It is only in the decade 1901–11 that all three sets of data show female emigration concentrated in the 20–24 age-band. See Appendix 12.

34. Anderson and Morse 'High Fertility, High Emigration' Table 2. p. 328.

35. In the decade 1901–11 older female emigrants were more in evidence and indeed there was a another minor peak of female emigration in the age-band 40–45 years, which occurred regardless of the migrant age-structure used. See Brock, 'Scottish Migration'. Vol. II. Appendix XXVI, pp. 258–9.

36. The significance of the 1901–11 estimations is open to question. If the projected migrant age-structure is used, then female current migration in the age-band 15–19 years as important as child migration 0–4 years. (See Appendix 8). Likewise, in emigration the volume of male emigration in the age-band 20–24 years was significantly greater than that of young children, while adult female emigration in the same age-band not. However, if instead, the 1891 migrant age-structure is used for calculations, children continue to dominate current out-migration, but estimates of emigration are not significantly altered. (See Appendix 12).

37. The migrant samples provided plenty of evidence of this pattern and individual schedules from the enumeration books have been used as evidence.

38. Anderson and Morse have noted that the English were 'particularly concentrated in the cities'. The peak immigration of Irish into Scotland occurred in the decade 1841–51, and in 1851 18.2% of Glasgow's population were Irish-born. Thereafter the rate of Irish immigration slowed down but the life-time population decreased only slowly. Anderson and Morse. 'The People' p. 18.

39. See Table 4.1.

40. Harper. *Emigration from North-east. Vol. 1*, p. 130.

41. It has already been argued that the effects of high levels of both immigration and migration into the 'Central Lowlands' category may have produced a distinctive age profile for both migrants and emigrants. Moreover, return

movement may have complicated the estimates. It is impossible to estimate whether there was an underlying pattern of emigration that was similar to the other categories, although it may be apparent in individual counties.

42. Erickson. 'Who were'.

43. Although the United States was the most popular overseas destination for Scots, more people emigrated to other parts of Britain. Flinn. *Scottish Population History.* Tables 6.1.2 and 6.1.7 compared pp. 442 & 451.

44. Erickson. 'Who were'. p. 371.

45. See Table 5.2.8 for average age at first marriage. Flinn. *Scottish Population History.* p. 331.

46. Anderson, 'Emigration and marriage breakup' pp. 104–9.

47. The mean and mode age for first marriage of females was approximately two years younger than for males. See Table 5.2.8 for average age at first marriage. Flinn. *Scottish Population History.* p. 331.

48. The proportion of children in the emigrant population also fluctuated, there being a far higher proportion in the decades of relatively low emigration, and especially in 1891–1901. In that decade the transatlantic economy was depressed and the British one boomed. For adult males this was not an attractive time to emigrate overseas, but children could still join fathers or parents abroad.

49. Erickson. 'Who were'. p. 371.

50. Baines has estimated that whereas in 1862 only about 20% of emigrants travelled by steamship to the U.S.A, by 1870 virtually everybody did. Baines has used evidence from Carrothers, *Emigration from the British Isles* p. 213. Jones, 'Background to Emigration', pp. 54–5, Hyde, *Cunard,* p. 59. Baines. *Migration in a Mature Economy.* p. 77.

51. Hyde lists steamship prices from Liverpool dropping as early as 1863. Some Scots used Liverpool as a port for embarkation (Harper) and undoubtedly Scottish ports would have had to follow suit to remain competitive. Hyde. *Cunard.* p. 64. and Harper. *Emigration from North-East. Vol. 1,* p. 21–2.

52. See Smith on the influence of letters in Shetland. Harper also quotes extensively from published and unpublished letters form emigrants born in the Northeast. Smith. *Shetland Life.* p. 159. Harper. *Emigration from North-East. Vol. 1 & 2.*

53. Devine. *Great Highland Famine.* pp. 275–84 and Appendix II pp. 327–32.

54. Anderson and Morse. 'The People' p. 22.

55. Erickson. 'Who were'. p. 359.

56. This is based on the oral evidence of Mrs. A. Hepburn, (National Centre for Training and Education in Prosthetics and Orthotics, University of Strathclyde, 28th. August 1989) many of whose family moved from Glasgow to Saskatchewan, Canada in the late nineteenth century. An unmarried adult son emigrated first and later his brothers joined him. When they prospered they returned to Lanarkshire to collect first their fiancees and then later

their retired father. Harper also cites similar patterns of family movement from the north-east to Canada. Harper. *Emigration from North-East. Vol. I,* pp. 209–10.

57. Ferenczi and Willcox, *International migrations, Vol. II,* p. 255.

58. Erickson. 'Who were'. p. 371.

59. Harper. *Emigration from North-East. Vol. I,* pp. 254–9.

60. Duncan describes the lifestyle of British-born young men in commerce in India, who married British-born ladies, but only to returned to Britain permanently to retire. Duncan, *The Simple Adventures of a Memsahib.*

61. Stevenson. *The Amateur Emigrant.* p. 47.

62. See Table 6.1.4 for UK overseas emigrants of Scottish Origin 1853–1938. Flinn. *Scottish Population History.* p. 447.

63. Erickson. 'Who were'. p. 370.

64. Flinn. *Scottish Population History.* p. 452.

65. Erickson. 'Who were'. p. 371.

66. Adult male emigration from Inverness was high in the decade 1861–71 and embraced the age-bands 15 to 34 years. In contrast female adult emigration in the same decade was comparatively low. However, in the subsequent decade when young adult male emigration was much lower, adult females continued to leave. One can speculate that these females were joining males who had already left. Certainly the numbers of emigrants of each sex in this decade (1871–81) were much closer than in any other. See Appendix 13.

67. The estimates for female emigration from Aberdeen peak in the age-band 25–29 or 30–34 years, the application of standard errors provides differing estimates. The broad age-bands make this inaccuracy appear more serious than it is See Appendix 13.

68. In Shetland emigration was highest in volume in the decade 1871–81 for both sexes and possible reasons for this have already been considered. However, even in this decade of high emigration relatively few young adult females were involved, peak adult male emigration still being much younger than female. Emigration was particularly low for both sexes in 1891–1901. See Appendix 13.

69. In the decade 1901–11 there was a second younger peak at 15–19 years. (Appendix 13).

70. Kirkcudbright, another county with high emigration to England and Wales, followed almost the reverse of the pattern in Dumfries, in that peak male emigration was consistent and female movement fluctuated wildly. See Appendix 13.

71. Both Edinburgh and Forfar had some problems with standard errors in estimates of emigration, but they do not affect the overall trends. (Appendix 13).

72. In the decades 1861–81 there is some slight disagreement with peak female emigration in that the estimates with two standard errors deducted peak in the subsequent age-band. However, it was decided to use Lanark and Renfrew as an example because the combined unit had such a large population and was therefore significant in that it had a distinctive age profile. See Appendix 13.

73. There was a below average proportion of life-time emigrants from Lanark and Renfrew in England and Wales in 1911. See Appendix 4.

74. Flinn. *Scottish Population History.* Tables 5.2.8 and 5.2.9 pp. 331–2.

75. In West Lothian in both 1861–71 and 1891–1901, male emigration did not peak until the age-band 30–34 years. The estimates for 1901–11 were anomalous due to disagreement in standard errors. (Appendix 13).

76. In 1861–71 female adult emigration from Banff peaked in a much older age-band 30–34 years.

77. Flinn. *Scottish Population History.* p. 453.

78. Harper. *Emigration from North-East. Vol. 2.* pp. 231–88.

79. It is impossible to distinguish what proportion of the female emigrants in Table I were Scots but in Table II the volume was very small, although could possibly be significant in individual decades and age-bands. Harper. *Emigration from North-East. Vol. 2.* p. 287.

80. Anderson, 'Emigration and marriage breakup' pp. 105–6.

81. Erickson. 'Who were', Table 11, p. 377.

82. Baines. *Migration in a Mature Economy. p. 279.*

83. Anderson and Morse. 'The People' p. 16.

84. Hollingsworth. *A study based on the Scottish.* p. 132.

85. Maximum length of absence of sixteen return emigrant families: 2–4 years (eight), 5–7 years (five) and 8 years and over (three).

86. In 1891, fifteen out of a total of twenty one families had emigrated and then returned to the county-of-birth of the head of the household and a further four to an adjoining county.

87. Lerwick, Shetland, 1891, RD. 5, ED. 5, sch. 208, p. 35.

88. Wick, Caithness, 1891, RD. 43, ED. 2, sch. 2, p. 1.

89. Wick, Caithness, 1891, RD. 43, ED. 6, sch. 188, p. 37.

90. Wick, Caithness, 1891, RD. 43, ED. 7, sch. 74, p. 19.

91. Dingwall, Ross and Cromarty, 1891, RD. 62, ED. 2, sch. 28, p. 5.

92. Stornoway, Ross and Cromarty, 1891, RD. 88, ED. 4, sch. 19, p. 4.

93. Aberdeen, Aberdeen, 1891, RD. 162, ED. 8, sch. 176, p. 41.
    Aberdeen, Aberdeen, 1891, RD. 168–2, ED. 36, sch. 240, p. 54.

94. Larkhall, Lanark, 1891, RD. 638–1, ED. 4, sch. 14, p. 6.
    Larkhall, Lanark, 1891, RD. 638–1, ED. 4, sch. 54, p. 15.

95. Eyemouth, Berwick, 1891, RD. 739, ED. 1, sch. 199, pp. 41–2.

96. Cockburnspath, Berwick, 1891, R.D. 731, E.D. 1, sch. 119, p. 25.

97. Baines, *Migration in a Mature Economy, p. 279*.

98. Erickson, 'Who were', p. 365.

99. Of the 22 return emigrant families recorded in 1891, the heads of household in five families were miners and three were in the building trade (two joiners and a builder). The joiners had been in Canada and all the other families in the USA.

100. Baines, *Migration in a Mature Economy,* p. 29.

101. Erickson has shown that in the 1880s 'farm labourers and pre-industrial tertiary workers were least well represented amongst the emigrants to the USA'. Nevertheless, it is probably also the case that some farm workers were buried in passenger lists under the description 'general labourer'. Erickson, 'Who were', p. 368.

102. Anderson and Morse. 'The People' p. 22.

5

An Exceptionally Mobile Population? Scottish Population Movement in the Wider Context

'The Scots are notoriously migratory' observed Bisset–Smith in 1909[1] and indeed the evidence so far presented seems to agree with this statement. However, estimates of movement alone cannot define mobility and we must consider whether the period (1861–1911) is unique in terms of Scottish history and how it compared with its nearest neighbour, England and Wales. It is not intended to repeat the survey in Chapter 1, but instead to consider to what extent there was a tradition of out-movement within Scotland, analysing first migration and then emigration. This data will then be compared with other quantitative research on Scotland and to investigate whether the Scots were really more mobile than the English and Welsh. Baines has shown that the Irish and the Norwegians had a greater propensity to emigrate than the Scots,[2] but he has analysed a longer time period (1850–1930) than this study. His analysis will be reconsidered in the light of further evidence, putting both emigration and migration together to assess mobility.

A TRADITION OF MIGRATION?

There are no national studies of Scottish migration in the early nineteenth century to compare with this study. Nevertheless, it does appear that Scottish internal migration had altered since the early nineteenth century when, as Tranter has argued, migration was more diffuse and localised. Towns were generally small and were administrative and commercial centres, industry was small scale and as industrial and agricultural activity were closely linked industry was spatially scattered. The volume of migration in the first half of the nineteenth century is difficult to ascertain, but for the decade 1831–41 it has been shown that many parishes experienced population gains or losses in excess of 10%. While this may not indicate movement on a scale found in this study, it is nevertheless significant.[3] More importantly, it has been argued that there was a massive outflow of migrants in the 1850s.[4] Migration in the second half of the century was different in that movement was as Tranter observes 'increasingly concentrated towards a relatively small number of highly specific regions' such as Lanark and Renfrew, and that the frequency of internal migration increased towards the end of the century.[5] Although, this secondary movement cannot be measured in the present study, evidence presented in Chapter 3 suggested that there was considerable inter-county movement within the 'Central Lowlands'.

Migration in the Twentieth Century

No studies are known that consider twentieth century aggregate migration in Scotland.[6] Flinn has estimated decennial population change which exhibits relatively low rates of population growth in the period up to 1939 and an actual decline in the total population of Scotland between 1921–31.[7] In this decade emigration was 110.5% of natural increase;[8] this means that movement out of Scotland exceeded natural increase and clearly reflects massive emigration (including movement into England and Wales). As the Scottish economy was depressed throughout much of this period,[9] especially in comparison with other parts of Britain, the traditional migrant attracting region, the 'Central Lowlands', was unlikely to encourage in-migration.[10] It therefore seems improbable that in the period up to 1939, the proportion of current migrants exceeded levels attained in the period 1861–1911.

The most thorough study of the age and nature of migration in mid-twentieth century Scotland is that of Hollingsworth, who analysed movement between 1939 and 1964. He used national registration and medical cards as a data source and it is the only work known to consider twentieth century Scottish current migration in detail. His work is on a much finer framework than was possible in the present study. He concluded that mobility in Scotland was so great that by the age of 25 years almost all adults no longer lived at their place of birth.[11] This is a level of detail that the present study cannot hope to achieve, but it does indicate that high levels of mobility are not just a feature of the nineteenth century. However, many of these twentieth century moves would have been fairly local in nature and not crossing a county boundary.

Hollingsworth's most relevant work is on the current migrant age-structure. He identified ages when people were most likely to move, and his superior data source enabled him to locate all local migrations, rather than just county-of-birth and current residence. Hollingsworth was unable to calculate the volume of migration for young children, though he estimated that it was initially high but decreased as children got older.[12] Although it is a pity that more results were not possible these conclusions do correspond quite well with the findings of the present research. In 1939–64 the lowest rates of child migration occurred at 12 years. Hollingsworth attributed this to the fact that although child migration was within a family unit this tended to involve younger children, and independent migration was restricted by the necessity of school attendance. The present research also found child migration dipped in the age-band 10–14 years, although movement would not have been so restricted by a minimum school leaving age. In the late nineteenth century a lack of experience, if distance was involved, and an inability to gain adequate employment or accommodation may well have been powerful deterrents to young people moving alone.

Hollingsworth did not distinguish male and female migrants, arguing that they exhibit similar patterns. He found maximum frequency of migration occurred at 22 years.[13] In the present study, despite being computed separately, both sexes also generally peaked in the age-band 20–24 years. However, there were far more female migrants than males in many counties, a phenomenon that had evidently disappeared by the time of the later study. Indeed, Hollingsworth states that 'the two sexes have almost identical rates of migration, chiefly because married couples and their children usually move together'.[14] He identified a gradual decline in migration levels from 22 to about 45 years, after which there was little further change in the migration rate. However, there is one new factor that might have affected the twentieth century study — public sector housing. It has been argued that people in such housing may be less likely to move than those in the private sector and in Scotland a high proportion of housing was rented from local authorities.[15] This would undoubtedly reduce the mobility of potential migrants aged between 22–45 years, a situation that could not have restricted nineteenth century migration, when such housing was not available.[16] Nevertheless, mobility did decline sharply after 30 years although it has been argued that some of this decline might have been exaggerated, because movement is measured net and return migration became more significant.

Hollingsworth also identified return migration arguing that it was very frequent. He pointed out that when changing jobs a migrant might only consider two locations, the present one and his place of birth which suggests a desire for a fairly quick return, but on the other hand he also found evidence of migrants returning after a fifty year gap to retire.[17] His evidence suggests that this form of movement may have increased in the twentieth century.

Hollingsworth's research and this study together span a period of a hundred years and one might well expect changes in life-style over time to affect migration patterns. It is therefore rather remarkable how similar the two sets of findings are, and adds credence to the results of the present one. Current migration patterns with respect to age seem to have remained remarkably constant, possibly because, regardless of the century, major changes in life-style that are likely to promote out-migration, such as marriage and the arrival of children, occur at very roughly similar stages in peoples lives. The larger proportion of female current migrants found in the nineteenth century study is the most noticeable difference that has occurred over time. It could be argued that a mature economy is one that fulfils the employment needs of both sexes equally, and thus creates a balanced society in terms of numbers of each sex migrating, and current migration would not have a sex bias. This had occurred by the mid twentieth century but was certainly not apparent before 1911.

To conclude this discussion of Scottish migration over time: it has been argued that current out-migration in the late nineteenth century may well have involved an unprecedentedly high proportion of the Scottish population. This statement does however need qualification because the data outwith this period (both before and after) are less satisfactory and the decade prior to this study (1851–61) is known to have had high total mobility. We can therefore say that out-migration in 1861–1911 was high, and possibly historically the highest in terms of the proportion of the total population in the period up to 1939.

A TRADITION OF EMIGRATION?

Baines has calculated that there was an overall increase in overseas emigration from Scotland (despite fluctuations) in the period 1825–53.[18] However, measurement was on the basis of numbers leaving Scottish ports and one cannot be certain that they were all Scots, while on the other hand Scots emigrating from English ports would have been missed. Certainly, emigrants from the Northeast Scotland are known to have left from Liverpool and London as well as Scottish ports.[19] Nevertheless, the volume of overseas emigration undoubtedly did increase markedly after 1853 although there were some fluctuations. Emigration overseas was therefore on an unprecedented scale. However, emigration in the present study does not just comprise overseas emigration; movement to other parts of Britain is also included. Unfortunately there is no quantitative research on Scottish out-migration to England and Wales before 1841, but the evidence thereafter suggests that this movement was also increasing in volume.[20]

The decade 1851–61 probably had very high emigration from Scotland, the volume of which can only be interpreted from various sources as the methods of recording movement changed.[21] Nevertheless estimates suggest that approximately 231,000 left Scotland in the decade 1851–61, and that this figure was not exceeded again until 1881–91[22] — although the two calculations are not directly comparable because the 1851–61 estimation is gross and the 1881–91 one is net of returns. However, if this was the case then the much smaller population in Scotland at the earlier date would mean that the proportion emigrating was far larger.

The Changing Age-Structure and Gender of Scottish Emigrants 1773–1986

The age profile of emigrants has generally not been considered in detail by historians, and Table 5.1 tabulates such information as is available from previous research on Scottish emigrants. This study has estimated various age-bands so that the proportions in each age-band can be compared. Several age-bands have therefore been used more than once.

The earliest study of emigrants in the period 1773 to 1776[23] has shown a high ratio of male to female emigrants but, as Table 5.1 shows, it is no higher than that found in this study for overseas emigrants. The proportion of emigrant children in the eighteenth century study was compared with the national average, which showed that there were relatively few children emigrating.[24] Far more children were emigrating by the late nineteenth century. When we considered the latter in more detail as we did when discussing Table 4.4, it was observed that young Scottish male emigrants (under 20 years) accounted for approximately the same proportions as in the native population whilst for females the proportions lost were generally higher. However, it should be noted that Bailyn was measuring purely outward movement, whereas the present study was net of returns. Although this study cannot distinguish the age-structures of UK and overseas emigrants, there probably was a difference, because as Table 4.2 showed, the gender ratios of UK and overseas emigrants differed significantly. It is also possible that more child emigrants moved within Britain than overseas, as the gender ratios for those emigrating overseas were so unbalanced. Flinn provides some information on emigration in 1912–3. This showed that the proportion of child emigrants had fallen and this decline may well be true of overseas emigration which the present study (1861–1911) cannot separate. Indeed Table 4.3 shows that the proportion of young emigrants varied according to whether the decade was one of high or low emigration, the proportion of children was lower in decades of high emigration, and Flinn's work was on years with high emigration. Bailyn's work on 1773–6

Table 5.1. *The Age Profile and Gender of Scottish Overseas Emigrants*

Years Studied	1773–6[1]		1861–1911[2]		1912–3[3]	1984–6[4]	
Source	Bailyn		This study		Flinn	Findlay & Garrick	
	Male	Female	Male	Female	Gender not specified	Male	Female
Gender ratio	6.3	3.7	5.7–6.2 *6.0–7.0*	3.8–4.3[5] *3.0–4.0*[6]		5.7	4.3
Age in Years							
0–14	20.1%	29.9%	28–36%	36–45%		12.4%	16.6%
<18			★	★	26.0%		
15–25	38.1%	32.6%	36–46%	14–25%		15.7%	34.3%
25–44	35.7%	33.5%	27–34%	36–53%		44.7%	43.4%
>29	25.7%	23.5%	1–12%	20–28%			
>45	6.0%	4.1%	★	★		27.2%	5.7%

1 Calculated from Bailyn. *Voyagers to the West*. Table 5.5, p. 132.

2 This study includes emigration to the rest of the United Kingdom as well as overseas. The other studies only consider overseas emigration. This is the only study where estimates were net of returns. Estimations have been made for all age-bands to provide comparisons, both the highest and lowest proportions found in the study are shown. It was not possible to estimate those under 18 years, because our estimates were in five year age-bands. Return migration meant that those over 45 years could be positive or negative. This was because of the high proportions of return migrants in the older age-bands. Age-bands that cannot be estimated have been shown thus ★.

3 Gender not stated for age-band. Flinn. *Scottish Population History*. p. 452.

4 Calculated from Findlay and Garrick 'Scottish emigration' Table IV, p. 183.

5 The ratio of male to female emigrant losses for all emigration both within Britain and Overseas 1861–1911 (Table 4.1).

6 The ratio of male to female emigrant losses for overseas emigration 1861–1901 (Table 4.2) in italics

and Flinn's on 1912–3 are difficult to compare because the age-bands are different, but it appears that the volumes of child and teenage movement were surprisingly similar. The present study (1861–1911) appears to show higher proportions of young emigrants. Nevertheless, this statement must be treated with caution for two reasons: firstly, estimates in the present study (1861–1911) are net, which would exaggerate the proportion of young emigrants in the population, because return emigrants were likely to affect older age-bands far more than the younger ones: and secondly, this work considers emigration to include migration to the rest of the British Isles, and both the other studies only measured overseas movement.

The proportion of male emigrants over 29 years was considerably higher in Bailyns' eighteenth century study than in the present one. There was moreover relatively little difference in the proportions lost by each sex in the earlier work. However, it cannot be argued that this evidence reflected changes in emigration patterns, although this may be the case, because the present study is net of returns and there could have been a considerable movement amongst older males. Bailyn concluded that many of the emigrant males were unmarried.[25] Erickson's work on nineteenth century emigration has already been considered and also showed that single male emigrants predominated in the 1850s and that this pattern became even more pronounced over time.[26] Bailyn's eighteenth century analysis and its confirmation in subsequent research suggests that the pattern of predominantly male overseas emigration from Scotland was long standing. We therefore have some evidence of consistency over time in the sex ratios and age-structure of Scottish emigrants prior to 1900.

Emigration in the Twentieth Century

No studies are known that analyse emigration in the inter-war years. The work of Hollingsworth used the 1961 published census, external data and the international port survey.[27] Unfortunately the results were not presented in such a way that they could be incorporated in Table 5.1. Nevertheless, as with his research on current migration, there were both marked similarities and some differences between his findings and those in this study. Male emigrants still predominated and the proportions of male to female emigrants going to England and Wales were remarkably similar to those estimated in the present study (Table 4.2). Males were particularly dominant in the age-band 25–44 years.[28] Nevertheless, single emigrants were still in evidence. However, the direction of Scottish emigration had changed. Using the National Register Hollingsworth found 74% of Scots emigrated to the rest of Britain and Northern Ireland and only 26% went abroad. This was a most remarkable turnabout in population movement, as in the present study over half of emigrants went overseas (Table 4.2). One can only speculate on possible reasons for this change in the direction of movement. Scotland's economic growth was poor, regional income per head was lower and unemployment much higher than in other parts of Britain.[29] Furthermore, the demography of Britain had altered; fertility had declined, the population was ageing and the labour market was no longer expanding.[30] Jobs were available for Scots in other parts of Britain, especially the south-east, where an improved lifestyle was possible. A huge increase in Scottish emigration to England and Wales had occurred in the 1920s,[31] and the post war movement was therefore a continuation of that trend. Moreover, movement abroad was becoming less easy, as some overseas countries were beginning to specify the skills they required from potential emigrants.[32] The USA applied a quota system, but this was not a restriction for Scots, who preferred Canada (although some may have moved on to the United States subsequently). Nevertheless, emigration to Canada fluctuated. It showed a marked inverse relationship with unemployment in that country.[33] Potential emigrants were clearly aware of economic advantages both within Britain and abroad.[34] In the late nineteenth century emigration was encouraged by the receiving countries and in the 1950s and 60s a similar policy was adopted by ex-colonies such as Australia, Canada, Rhodesia and South Africa, which attracted 300,000 Scots in twenty years. This active recruitment changed to much more restrictive policies in the 1970s, when only those with specific skills continued to be encouraged and the political situation in Africa made it less attractive.[35]

By the 1980s Findlay and Garrick's research shows that overseas emigration had changed considerably. They found that although some settler emigration continued, there has been a switch to that of skilled transient movements[36] 'whose outstanding characteristic is their readiness to move from one country to another and back again for the purposes of employment'.[37] This raises two important points: temporary emigration and the export of skills. Both these issues have their origins in our period or even earlier. Without being able to measure temporary migration it appears to have increased over time from about the 1860s. It began in part as a response to the transport revolution. The growth of railways coupled with the change from sailing to steam ships meant that the time lost and costs forfeited in terms of lost wages when travelling were reduced. Moreover, wage differences were such as to make the journey financially viable. The rise in temporary emigration was also in response to the information revolution which enabled potential emigrants to be aware of opportunities in other countries. The export of highly qualified Scots was also not new. In the eighteenth century the Scots provided 'a disproportionate number of skilled and educated emigrants: merchants, doctors, ministers and educators in the New World'.[38] Thomas has calculated that in 1910 62.5% of Scottish male adult emigrants to the United States were classified as skilled,[39] and confirming that this was not just an aberrant finding, Flinn estimated that only 29% of all Scottish overseas emigrants were unskilled in 1912–3. It therefore appears that the majority of emigrants going abroad in our study probably had some skills. The emigration of skilled workers was therefore certainly not a new trend in emigration, although the level of skill found in most recent studies may be higher. Indeed the Toothill

Report correctly summed up this loss in 1960 when it observed that 'emigration generally means the loss of the more skilled and younger parts of the population...It has gone on at as high proportionate rates through some of the most prosperous periods of our history and we think it likely to continue in some measure, for we could find no direct relationship between it and unemployment rates'.[40]

The link therefore between emigration and unemployment is not proven. Indeed Lindsay argues that the emigrants are much more likely to be influenced by economic factors outside Scotland.[41] and in the nineteenth century, Erickson found that the relationship between skilled and unskilled emigrants to the United States depended on the state of the American economy.[42] Flinn calculated that the proportion of skilled emigrants was directly related to the country of destination. Thus skilled artisans were more likely to go to South Africa or the United States and the unskilled to Canada and Australasia. The middle class was particularly attracted to South Africa.[43]

Transient emigration, which has been identified as a characteristic of recent emigration, was also an unquantifiable but nevertheless important element of the present study. For England and Wales Baines has estimated that approximately 40% of emigrants returned.[44] Late twentieth century emigration appears therefore to be an extension of a historically important trend, which modern modes of transport have made even easier. The age profile of emigrants in this late twentieth century study has been tabulated in Table 5.1 where it can be compared with the present study. There was still a predominance of males, but far less so than in the earlier time periods.[45] The age profile was generally older, but an interesting gender reversal had occurred in the age-bands 15–25 years. This meant that whereas in the present study male emigrants formed a much higher proportion of this age-band, in the 1980's it was the females that exceeded males.

The majority of emigrants in the Findley and Garrick study were concentrated in the age-band 25–44 years, a far higher proportion than was found in the present study. This probably reflects the longer training period necessary today to acquire professional skills. Over a quarter of late twentieth century male emigrants were over 45 years, but only 6% of females. These estimations are not net of return emigrants and so permit considerably more precision than is possible in the present study. It is possible that a similar gender imbalance between older emigrants occurred in the period 1861–1911 and that this has not been possible to identify.

The volume of emigration between 1861 and 1911 was in certain decades (1881–91 and 1901–11) probably on a previously unprecedented scale. This included a high volume of overseas emigration which continued up to the First World War and resumed again thereafter, only to decline in the later 1920's.[46] This meant that whereas in the present study emigration accounted for between 10.6% and 46.8% of natural increase, in the decade 1921–31 emigration exceeded natural increase.[47] Emigration declined in the 1930s and it was not until the 1970's that Scotland's out-migration was again in excess of natural increase.[48] The present study was preceded by a decade of exceptionally high emigration and the subsequent inter-war years also incurred greater out-movements, but it has examined a time-span which included four decades[49] with very high proportions of emigrants. The period 1861–1911 — whilst not including the greatest losses through emigration- was one in which Scotland experienced sustained high population losses.

This comparison of Scottish emigration, both before and after the present study, suggests that the emigrant age-structure has changed over time, though possibly no more than the national age-structure. Nevertheless, three other elements in emigration have remained remarkably consistent; the unusually high level of emigration, the constant gender imbalance amongst emigrants which meant that the male emigrants always exceeded females in volume, and the high proportion of skilled emigrants. In contrast, the regions exporting population have varied.

Findlay and Garrick have argued that the 'continued loss of population by both internal and international migration has become an increasingly important force in determining Scotland's total population change. The small gains by natural increase have been erased by population losses through overseas emigration in five of the last eight years' (1978–86).[50] This phenomenon is not new; in Chapter 1 it was noted that between 1600 and 1650 losses through emigration are thought to have depressed the natural rate of population increase.[51] In the late nineteenth century, it has also been observed that emigration was one of several factors that accounted for the relatively low population growth of the period,[52] and as already mentioned in the 1920s population loss through emigration exceeded natural increase.

Emigration does appear to have become a tradition, one indeed that has damped population growth for centuries, and there is some truth in the observation that there is an acceptance of emigration as a fact of Scottish life.[53] One must however, question whether it is correct to refer to emigration as a loss. Scotland never appears to have experienced a population shortage. Unemployment was apparent even in the most prosperous decades in the late nineteenth century, and Scotland appears incapable of sustaining her population growth.

SCOTTISH MOBILITY COMPARED WITH
THAT OF ENGLAND AND WALES

Clearly there is plenty of evidence of both emigration and migration of Scots, but in order to establish whether the Scots were exceptionally mobile it is necessary to compare out-movement with another country. England and Wales, Scotland's nearest neighbour presents the most obvious comparison. Geographically linked to Scotland and with an economy based on similar industries maturing only slightly ahead of Scotland, it produced more or less the same social problems.

It appears quite reasonable at first sight to compare the Scottish inter-county migrant age patterns with those in England and Wales. There are however risks attached in that Scottish counties and their southern counterparts are not really directly comparable. Although the average land area of English and Scottish counties is fairly similar (2,851 sq.km. 2,387 sq.km respectively), the average population of each county was very different. In 1881 for example the mean population of the Scottish counties was less than a quarter that of the English counties (113,199 and 488,117 respectively). While acknowledging the artificiality of these average measurements because counties vary enormously both in population and area, the measurements are nevertheless useful benchmarks for comparison.

Clearly not all the Scottish population was thinly distributed in large counties as these statistics suggest. As the population density map (Appendix 6) shows, for the most part population had become increasingly concentrated in the Central Lowlands. Thus the distribution of the population can be described spatially as like a sandwich with two thinly populated outer areas (Highlands and Borders) comprising the bread, and the filling being the more densely populated Central Lowlands. This area of attraction represented almost a third of the counties of Scotland and was contiguous.[54] In contrast the pattern of population growth in England and Wales was spatially very different. Vast almost empty areas did not exist, and continuing the bakery theme, the counties could be likened to a fruit bun, the dough being the areas of out-migration, and the fruit being the several quite separate areas of attraction. We now have two distinct patterns, Scotland having a far smaller population in the 'average' county, and a central zone attracting in-migration, whereas England and Wales had a far larger more evenly spread population and several magnets for in-migration. The Scottish situation was inherently more likely to produce a greater volume of migration per head of population. This was because the county, although covering a similar sized area, was effectively a much finer mesh when applied as the unit of measurement to a much less dense population.

It is therefore four times more likely that population movement will be recorded as migration in Scotland than in England and Wales.[55] Moreover, once the Scots migrant was within the zone of high in-migration, he was more easily able to indulge in inter-urban migration. It seems reasonable to speculate that the Scots Lowland dweller was likely to have a more accurate knowledge of income opportunities than his southern counterpart, for whom the opportunities were possibly greater, but also more dispersed.

Baines deliberately avoided discussing the results from English and Welsh counties with small populations because he considered that these presented an increased risk of error. The county with the smallest population in England was Rutland (population in 1861 approximately 22,000),[56] but in the same year in Scotland, six out of the total of thirty-three counties had smaller populations.[57] This means that 18% of Scots counties had populations that were less than the smallest of those designated by Baines as too small to analyse. This emphasises the argument that differences in baseline between England and Scotland should be born in mind when comparing data at the county level of analysis.

The Age-Structure and Gender of Scottish Migrants Compared with those from England and Wales

The age profiles and gender ratios of the native populations of the two counties was distinctive. In 1861 the imbalance between the sexes in the Scottish native population was far greater than in England and Wales, although by 1901 the situation was reversed.[58] This imbalance is important when considering mobility. Moreover, in those English counties which were attracting migrants approximately 50% of the native population was under twenty years.[59] This proportion was generally exceeded throughout Scotland, where young males ranged from 59% of the male native population in 1871 to 53% in 1911, and females from 53% in 1881 to 49% in 1911 (Appendix 3[n]).

In 1861 rapidly expanding counties such as Dunbarton and Midlothian had proportions of males under 20 years old in the native population that were as high as 66% and 61% respectively of the total native population. Moreover, these high proportions were not restricted to areas of population growth. Indeed the lowest recorded percentage of young males, in Ross and Cromarty, was still almost 49%. Thus in high in-migration counties the proportion of males under 20 years in the native total population was over 60%, at least 10% higher than Baines' estimate. The proportion of young native females in the high in-migration counties varied more, but was still higher than in England and Wales. In Scotland as a whole, females under 20 years averaged 51% of native females, a percentage which equalled the English and Welsh counties with high in-migration, but there was a variety of experience; in Dunbarton the proportion was as high as 61% but in Shetland it was only 37%. By 1911 the percentage of young natives, both male and female, had declined nationally to 53% and 49% respectively. These proportions are closer not only to each other, but also to the English norm. The decline in the national percentage of natives was in part a reflection of the falling death rate but it may also reflect increased migration. The percentage of young natives in the population of counties with considerable in-migration remained high. This was partly because children born of in-migrants or immigrants were natives of that county. Thus in 1911 young natives in Dunbarton still constituted 65% of males and 62% of females. Conversely, the counties with high out-migration experienced an ageing population. Evidence of this can be found across Scotland. In 1911 in Sutherland only 42% of males and 37% of females were less than twenty years and natives, in Orkney there were 40% and 33% respectively and in Berwick 44% and 41% (Appendix 2[c]). Furthermore, when one considers the total county-of-birth population in these counties of high out-migration the percentage of the population under 20 years falls even lower.[60] High percentages of young natives in Scotland reflect not only native fertility, but also adult incomers having families once they arrived. As has already been noted, these children would be considered not as migrants into, but as natives of the county despite their parents being born elsewhere (they could be migrants or immigrants).

Approximately a quarter of the migrant population in England and Wales was less than twenty years[61] compared with about half of the native population. Moreover, the proportion under 20 years in both categories declined over time. By 1911 the percentage of young migrants under 20 years was about 20% of the life-time migrant population. Using the 1861 and 1871 censuses Baines calculated that there was a greater percentage of female life-time migrants less than 20 years in counties attracting in-migration (27.1% females as opposed to 25.5% for males).[62] The Scottish population revealed a higher proportion of young migrants throughout the period, males under 20 years ranging from 31% to 26% and females from 27% to 23% (Appendix 2[m]). The proportion of young migrants from individual Scottish counties could be much higher; Lanark was attracting in-migration, but between 34% and 47% of its out-migrants were under 20 years (Appendix 2[m]). The finer 'mesh' of the Scottish county may well be a factor in explaining the high proportion of young migrants within Scotland when compared with England and Wales, but it is impossible to attribute the greater percentage of young natives in Scotland to this factor.

As previously argued the county unit of measurement is more likely to record movement in Scotland than further south in England and Wales. Scotland therefore has a higher proportion of young people in its population.

The method by which Baines estimated current migration has already been discussed in Chapter 2. Here it will suffice to note that in Baines' work the current migrant age–structure ratio was standardised and calculated prior to estimation, whereas in the Scottish study a life-time migrant age–structure ratio was applied and the current migrant age–structure computed. Baines justified his age–structure through other evidence, while in this study of Scotland it was necessary to look for reasons to justify the results.

Table 5.2 charts the Scottish current migrant age–structure in selected age-bands so that it can be compared with the proportions calculated by Baines for England and Wales.[63] The most obvious difference is the much higher proportion of Scots children under five years who were migrating. There was at least three times more movement of young males than in England and Wales, and almost as great a proportion of young females. If the information contained in Appendix 8 is aggregated it can be seen that the movement of the very young was greatest in the 'Central Lowlands', and least in the 'Highlands' category which contained the most remote counties, but even here it never fell to anywhere near the levels predicted for England and Wales. This pattern of a greater proportion of young current migrants in Scotland was continued in the 5–14 years age-band, and indeed it was estimated that nationally at least 50% of the male current migrants were less than 15 years of age, compared with Baines estimate of only 20%. When each population category was considered, all tended to have lower proportions of child migrants in the decade 1891–1901, and 'Highlands' was generally the lowest. In contrast in 1881–1891, a relatively low migration decade (which generally seemed to result in a higher proportion of children migrating), as many as 76% of males and 65% of females in 'Central Lowlands' counties were less than 15 years old. Clearly in Scotland a very much larger proportion of migration was of young children than in England and Wales. All subsequent secondary migration cannot be identified by the computation methods used, but the evidence of birth-places of children, which has already been discussed, suggests that it was probably considerable.

It is inevitable that as the proportion of child migrants in Scotland vastly exceeds that predicted for England and Wales, the proportion of adults amongst Scottish migrants must be lower, and that is indeed the situation. It has already been observed that the majority of the Scottish population

Table 5.2. The Percentage of Scottish Current Migrants in Selected Age-Bands Compared with the Current Migrant Age-Structure for England and Wales estimated by Baines★

BAINES ESTIMATES OF ENGLISH AND WELSH CURRENT MIGRATION★

Decade	Gender	Total	Selected Age-Bands			
			% lost <5 yrs	% lost 5–14 yrs	% lost 15–24 yrs	% lost 25–34 yrs
all	both	not applicable	4.0	15.0	53.0	28.0

SCOTTISH CURRENT MIGRANT POPULATION

Decade	Gender	Total	Selected Age-Bands			
			% lost <5 yrs	% lost 5–14 yrs	% lost 15–24 yrs	% lost 25–34 yrs
1861–1871	Male	-95,309	16.9	37.4	27.3	10.7
	Female	-104,900	14.9	33.6	31.8	20.9
1871–1881	Male	-107,722	15.9	39.6	28.5	9.5
	Female	-119,123	13.9	34.7	33.6	17.9
1881–1891	Male	-99,825	16.9	45.1	32.0	7.6
	Female	-107,072	15.2	41.0	40.6	13.8
1891–1901	Male	-120,256	13.2	39.1	31.1	10.3
	Female	-128,375	11.8	35.0	39.7	12.7
1901–1911	Male	-93,119	15.4	51.6	43.5	8.1
	Female	-110479	12.4	41.9	53.3	8.9

★ Baines. *Migration in a Mature Economy.* p. 107. Baines assumed that all current migration took place before the age of 34 years and his total losses therefore equal 100%. In parts of Scotland not all current migration was completed by 34 years, whereas in others the proportion was apparently in excess of 100%, due to the effect of return migration in older age-bands.

lived within the 'Central Lowlands' and only a relatively small proportion in the two categories with declining populations, the 'Borders' and the 'Highlands'. The Scottish current migrant age-structure was therefore disproportionately influenced by the 'Central Lowlands' and 'Periphery' categories. It was only when the migrant population was disaggregated that, in the 'Highlands' at least, some similarities with the age-structure south of the border appear. It has already been argued that the migrant-attracting counties within Scotland are contiguous, unlike in England and Wales, and that this could encourage movement by making it easier. This certainly might induce people with younger children to move, and indeed many counties, including some not actually in the 'Central Lowlands' category, but included within the 'Periphery' and 'Borders' were also either close to or were themselves migrant-attracting locations. Most counties within the 'Highlands' were geographically much more remote than anywhere in England and Wales, despite improving transport facilities. One must conclude that this category's similar migrant age-structure to that of England and Wales is simply a coincidence. Indeed it has already been noted that in the 'Highlands', the census was picking up some temporary migration. This was supported by the computer estimates of current migration which include high levels of return migration.[64]

Before finishing this comparison of the estimates of the age of current migrants in Britain, we will return to the analysis of the life-time migrant population, because evidence in it supports the findings of this comparative approach. In Scotland over the period under consideration male migrants under 20 years declined from 31% to 26% and females from 27% to 23% of the total migrant population.[65] In England and Wales they also declined from 25% to 20%,[66] and there were clearly less young migrants than in Scotland, as would be expected, but particularly for females the differences were not very large. Baines' ratios of child to adult current migrants involved a far smaller proportion of children under 15 years. This implies a very high level of young adult out-migration in the age-band 15–19 years in England and Wales, considerably more than was found in Scotland.

There has been a second estimate of current migration in late nineteenth century England and Wales, that of Friedlander and Roshier,[67] which so far has not been considered. This is because the study was attempting to identify current migration flows and much of the analysis is not comparable with this study of Scotland. However, this second study of England did estimate the age-structure of current migrants and the estimates are very different from those of Baines, in that it assumes a far larger proportion of migrant children. Friedlander and Roshier calculated the age structure by projecting the age distributions from 1851 to 1911, a procedure that Baines claims was spurious, because there was more than one possible solution.[68] Their current migration age-structure was estimated prior to calculating the volume of migration, as indeed was that of Baines. It was only in the current Scottish study that the life-time age-structure was applied and the current migrant structure actually calculated. Nevertheless, this second age structure for England and Wales provided by Friedlander and Roshier (Table 5.3) is very interesting because it more closely resembles that of this Scottish study. The current migrant age-structure estimated by Friedlander and Roshier[69] was common to both sexes and was estimated in ten year age-bands, but these age-bands differ from those used by Baines (Table 5.2).

Table 5.3 showed that both studies calculated that about half of all current migrants were under 20 years, but the Scottish estimates still

Table 5.3. The Percentage of Scottish Current Migrants in Selected
Age-Bands Compared with the Current Migrant Age-Structure for
England and Wales Estimated by Friedlander and Roshier*

FRIEDLANDER AND ROSHIER'S ESTIMATES OF ENGLISH
AND WELSH CURRENT MIGRATION*

Decade	Gender	Total	Selected Age-Bands in Years			
			% lost <10 yrs	% lost 10–9 yrs	% lost 20–9 yrs	%lost 30–9 yrs
all	both	not applicable	34.00	15.00	28.00	23.00

SCOTTISH MIGRANT POPULATION

Decade	Gender	Total	Selected Age-Bands in Years			
			% lost <10 yrs	% lost 10–9 yrs	% lost 20–9 yrs	% lost 30–9 yrs
1861–1871	Males	-95,309	41.4	23.2	27.7	1.7
	Females	-104,900	35.8	25.1	37.2	-0.7
1871–1881	Males	-107,722	41.6	25.9	26.4	0.7
	Females	-119,123	35.1	27.6	35.5	-2.0
1881–1891	Males	-99,825	46.2	29.5	28.0	-2.2
	Females	-107,072	39.6	34.5	38.4	-8.9
1891–1901	Males	-120,256	38.3	26.3	29.4	1.3
	Females	-128,375	31.7	31.4	37.7	-6.8
1901–1911	Males	-93,119	47.4	37.1	40.1	-9.2
	Females	-110479	34.6	41.7	48.4	-19.0

*   Friedlander and Roshier. 'A Study of Internal. part I' Table II. pp. 272–3. Friedlander
and Roshier assumed that all current migration took place before the age of 39 years
and total losses therefore equal 100%. In parts of Scotland not all current migration
was completed by 39 years, whereas in others the proportion was apparently in excess
of 100%, due to the effect of return migration in older age-bands

exceeded that proposed for England and Wales. This was despite the fact
that the Scottish study always assumes the numbers involved to be an
under-estimate. For migrants under 20 years, the English estimates (which
were applied to both sexes) were more similar to the proportions of
Scottish female current migrants than males. This may in part reflect
the considerable female majority in the Scottish population, which as has
already been shown can distort proportions. Both studies had a lower
proportion of current migrants in the 10–19 years age-band and the
subsequent age-band (20–29 years) was higher. The Friedlander and
Roshier study assumed current migration to have totally finished by 40
years of age, while in Scotland the vast majority of net movement was

completed by 30 years. It is interesting that the estimates by both Baines (Table 5.2) and Friedlander and Roshier (Table 5.3) predicted far more current migrants in the age-bands 25–40 years. This suggests that either current migration in England and Wales involved a far greater proportion of adults than in Scotland, or that there was less return migration cancelling outward movement.

Baines has been quite critical of the research of Friedlander and Roshier,[70] pointing out that the 'current migrant group contains too many children. This age distribution implies that over 40% of current migrants were children under 10 (net of returns). Yet only 25% of the population of England and Wales were under 10 years old in 1861'.[71] However, in Scotland there was an even higher proportion of young current migrants than in the study by Friedlander and Roshier. Although it is possible that the age-structure of the current migrant population in Scotland was very different from that in England and Wales, one must consider whether Baines might have misinterpreted the evidence. The national age structure is of a life-time population, whereas current migration in all the studies measures the first movement outside the county-of-birth, and ignores all subsequent moves. It therefore has a very different age structure. This is an important reason why, in the estimates for Scottish current migration, there appeared to be very few parents migrating with their children, as for many adults this was not their first move. If one now considers the life-time migrant age-structure for Scotland in 1861,[72] male migrants under 20 years comprised only 30.8% of the Scottish migrant population. Yet this same age-band (less than 20 years) comprised 52.0% of the entire national population, despite only 30.8% of male life-time migrants being under 20 years in 1861, and 30.6% in 1871. In the intervening decade (1861–71) males under 20 years comprised 64.6% of total male current migrants. This suggests that the current migrant population can be remarkably young, without the life-time migrant population appearing distorted in the same direction. The life-time migrant population had a markedly lower proportion of migrants under 20 years than the national age-structure, despite very high current migration. Baines appears to have assumed that child current migration should be markedly lower than the national age-structure. This evidence shows that in Scotland this was certainly not the case. Nevertheless, there is no intrinsic reason why Scottish and English current migration should have the same age-structure.

Unfortunately, the Friedlander and Roshier calculations of current migration in England and Wales were not presented in a way that made it feasible to make comparisons with Scotland. This section therefore will now return to comparing Scottish estimates with those of Baines. Although the age-distribution of current migrants differed north and south of the border, the ratio of males to females was more or less the same. In Scotland, depending on the decade, between 46% and 48% of current migrants were males (Table 3.5), which was only very slightly lower than in England and Wales where between 47% and 50% of the internal migrants were men.[73] The proportions migrating were therefore remarkably similar.

It is a great pity that Baines' work does not include an emigrant age profile, and no other study is known that does include one. However, it is possible to estimate the gender ratio of emigrants and this suggests that the English and Welsh emigrant population contained a higher proportion of males (approximately 63%)[74] than in Scotland where the percentages of males vary according to decade from 57–62% (Table 4.1). The higher proportion of males in the English emigrant population may reflect a long standing bias, in that Bailyn's study of emigrants to North America in 1773–6 also revealed a similar pattern.[75] He also found marked differences in the age-structure of emigrants, with far less family emigration from England.[76]

To conclude this section on the age profile of both migrants and emigrants: the vast majority of all current migrants in Britain were under 30 years of age but there was a markedly higher proportion of out-movement in the age-band 25–40 years in England and Wales compared to Scotland. The two studies of the age at which the English migrate disagreed on the proportion of children involved. Nevertheless, the Scottish current migrant population was even younger than either of the English estimates. A substantial proportion (12–17%) of Scots migrants were less than five years and about half of all current migrants were less than 20 years. As migrants were so young in Scotland and the main counties of attraction so close to each other, it is possible to speculate that secondary migration was much higher in Scotland than in England and Wales. At the same time we should not ignore the fact that return movement was an important component of migration in both countries.

Mobility by County-of-Birth Compared: Migration

Baines' estimates of population movement by county in England and Wales[77] are difficult to compare with Scotland, because as it has already been argued that the much smaller average population in the Scottish counties means that one would need to find far greater levels of out-migration if the actual degree of movement in both countries was similar. Moreover, direct comparisons between counties north and south of the Border are difficult because no two counties are alike.

It was therefore decided to compare migration in some of the largest and fastest-growing migrant-attracting counties in each country. It would have been preferable to have compared some counties with declining populations as well, but it was impossible to find similar ones in both countries. To compare current migrant proportions counties with rapid demographic growth were chosen. In Scotland, Edinburgh and Lanark plus Renfrew were selected as counties with very large populations that were expanding.[78] It was difficult to establish which counties were comparable in England and Wales and so two counties, Lancashire and London plus Middlesex, have been chosen based on the estimates of Hunt[79] and Friedlander and Roshier.[80]

Table 5.4. Mean Native Population in Selected Counties in England and Scotland in 1866 and 1896

Year	Sex	Scotland		England and Wales	
		Edinburgh (Midlothian)	Lanark & Renfrew	Lancashire	London & Middlesex
1866	Male	104,370	303,935	1,053,846	1,140,845
	Female	119,235	331,077	1,107,894	1,285,714
1896	Male	164,590	545,245	1,715,385	2,020,732
	Female	180,796	577,333	1,856,757	2,235,714
% growth 1866–1896		54%	76%	65%	75%

Table 5.5. The Proportion of Current Migrants in Selected Counties in England* and Scotland**

County	Scotland **				England and Wales *			
	Edinburgh (Midlothian)		Lanark & Renfrew		Lancashire		London Middlesex	
Area in acres[81]	234,325		726,153		1,201,888		*223,541*	
Decade	Males	Females	Males	Females	Males	Females	Males	Females
1861–1871	5.3	4.9	3.0	3.4	3.9	3.8	7.1	7.0
1871–1881	6.2	6.0	4.6	4.8	3.6	3.4	6.4	6.4
1881–1891	5.9	6.1	3.2	3.7	3.1	3.2	7.1	7.6
1891–1901	6.2	5.7	3.3	3.6	3.9	3.7	8.2	8.4
1901–1911	5.8	5.6	3.7	4.0				

*   Estimates for English and Welsh counties derived from Baines. *Migration in a Mature Economy.* pp. 283–98. Appendix 2 'Net migration of natives into other counties…(% of mean decade population)'.

**   Estimates derived from Brock 'Scottish Migration' Vol. II Appendix XXVI, pp. 293–9.

All the counties chosen experienced population growth in excess of 50% (Table 5.4). Nevertheless, the percentage of migrants lost (Table 5.5) does not appear to relate directly to population growth, since Lanark plus Renfrew and London plus Middlesex, which had the greatest population growth, had the lowest and highest proportions of migrant losses respectively amongst the counties considered. When all four counties are considered, the percentage of migrant losses divides the counties into two types. In one group are Edinburgh and London plus Middlesex which reveal percentage losses which were generally in excess of 5%, although London's rates were higher, and in the other group are the counties of Lanark plus Renfrew and Lancashire which had much lower migrant losses of approximately 3–4%.

Of the counties considered Edinburgh (Midlothian) and London plus Middlesex were probably most similar to each other. As Lee has observed both had some industry, but employment was not so concentrated in these occupations as in the purely industrial counties, and both had important roles as capital cities with larger professional and service sectors.[82] These counties both had a higher proportion of current out-migrants than the more strictly industrial counties. London plus Middlesex was clearly losing a greater proportion of its population despite being more than ten times larger than Edinburgh (Midlothian). London generated growth in adjoining counties as it was the centre of a group of suburban counties,[83] whereas smaller Edinburgh had adjacent counties with independent flourishing economic growth; Dunbarton, Fife, Lanark, Linlithgow (West Lothian), Selkirk and Stirling were all within 40 miles of Edinburgh (Midlothian). It is possible that the more industrial economies of the surrounding counties were so different from Edinburgh that they held very little attraction to its inhabitants. In contrast the expanding suburbs of London may even have offered its inhabitants better prospects.

Lanark plus Renfrew had approximately a third the population of Lancashire but the two counties did have some common industries. The proportion of migrants from Lancashire varied very little and was very similar to that of Lanark plus Renfrew except that in the latter there was a marked increase in the decade 1871–1881. As the most thriving counties in their region it is possible that nowhere else offered their inhabitants better prospects and this discouraged out-migration.

As Table 5.5 shows London plus Middlesex combined is remarkably similar in area to Edinburgh (Midlothian) and so arguments concerning the impact of differences in county size are not relevant here. Unfortunately, this is not true for Lanark plus Renfrew combined which is only just over half the area of Lancashire. One should therefore expect a greater proportion of current migrants from the former, but in fact the losses are very similar. There is no evidence in the rapidly growing counties of a higher proportion of current migrants within Scotland; indeed there appears to be less than in England and Wales, but the current migrants in Scotland were younger.

Mobility by County-of-Birth Compared: Emigration

It has already been established that Scottish emigration was proportionally higher than that in the rest of Britain. Indeed 'between 1861 and 1913 about 1.46 million Scots natives were recorded in the non–European emigration statistics, the equivalent of 30.7 per cent of the population in 1911'.[84] It therefore seemed of interest to see whether the industrial or commercial character of the county rather than the country-of-birth influenced the proportions of current emigrants. Table 5.6 shows that the influences on emigration were quite different and the grouping of county by its economy was not appropriate, because the county emigrant losses formed groupings that had national rather than economic criteria. Scotland had at least twice the proportion of emigrants of the English counties. The principle of grouping by type of county had relatively little obvious effect. Indeed, if the predominantly industrial counties of Lancashire and Lanark plus Renfrew are compared (Tables 5.5 and 5.6), the latter had a slightly lower proportion of current migrants, but generally more than three times the percentage of emigrants.[85] Yet both these counties contained major

Table 5.6. A Comparison of the Proportion of Emigrants in the Population of Selected Counties in England and Wales★ and Scotland★★

	Scotland★★				England and Wales★			
County	Edinburgh (Midlothian)		Lanark & Renfrew		Lancashire		London & Middlesex	
	Males	Females	Males	Females	Males	Females	Males	Females
Decade								
1861–1871	10.1	8.1	10.7	7.5	3.0	2.3	3.9	3.6
1871–1881	9.8	7.5	10.2	7.3	1.9	1.2	4.0	3.2
1881–1891	10.9	4.2	11.1	8.0	4.2	2.5	4.7	2.9
1891–1901	7.2	6.0	6.2	3.2	1.8	0.4	3.1	1.1
1901–1911	8.5	5.4	9.7	7.2				

★ Estimates for English and Welsh counties derived from Baines. *Migration in a Mature Economy.* pp. 283–98. Appendix I 'Net migration of natives into other counties. (% of mean decade population)'.

★★ Estimates derived from Brock 'Scottish Migration' Vol. II, Appendix XXVI, pp. 293–9.

emigration ports and so it could be argued that their residents were subject to very similar influences. Scottish emigration, in the counties examined, was therefore on a completely different scale to that in England and Wales, but it is still necessary to consider whether or not the two countries shared common emigration characteristics.

Baines noted that about 35% of permanent emigrants from England and Wales had been born in London, the West Midlands or Lancashire, and another 25% had been born in other urbanised counties. He therefore argued that the majority of emigrants were people 'born and brought up in an urban environment'.[86] In Scotland this pattern of mainly urban-born emigrants also prevailed. If the counties which comprise the 'Central Lowlands' were defined as urban counties[87] (and this excludes counties such as Ayr, Clackmannan and Forfar (Angus) which also have large urban populations), then, as shown in Table 5.7 between 48% and 53% of total net emigration was of people born in urban counties. Indeed less than a quarter of all emigration in any decade was from the overwhelmingly rural counties, that is those that were losing population and comprise the two declining population categories ('Highlands' and 'Borders'). Scotland's emigrants were undoubtedly urban in origin.

Table 5.7. *The Proportion of Total Emigrant Losses from Each Population Category*

Decade	Population Category			
	Highlands	Borders	Periphery & Northeast	Central Lowlands
Proportion of the total native population born in that category n 1861 and 1911[88]	21.0%–12.3%	8.8%–5.6%	29.7%–26.8%	40.5%–55.3%
1861–1871	15.7	11.5	25.2	47.6
1871–1881	13.7	10.5	24.4	51.4
1881–1891	12.4	7.6	28.8	51.2
1891–1901	13.3	11.0	24.1	51.6
1901–1911	11.8	5.4	29.7	53.1

Baines also found that people born in the rural counties of England and Wales were 'only marginally more likely to emigrate than natives of urban counties'.[89] Table 5.7 shows the proportion of total emigrant losses each population category sustained, and for comparative purposes the proportion of the total population born in that category. This illustrates the fact that Scottish emigration from the urban counties of the 'Central Lowlands' was generally above the national average (except for males in the last two decades), but the 'Borders' also experienced high levels of emigration, whereas emigration from the 'Periphery' increased over time and the

'Highlands' was almost invariably below average (except for males in the decade 1901–1911). It is difficult to argue that this pattern represents a straightforward rural–urban divide. However, geography and information networks may provide a clue. The population categories with above-average emigration are those in the south of the country. The 'Central Lowlands' contained the capital Edinburgh, the major port of Glasgow, and the vast majority of the population and industry. They were therefore a major centre of urban development and information. The 'Borders' were far more rural, but much closer to England than the 'Central Lowlands'. Emigration was cheap and easy, and so probably was information. In contrast the 'Highlands' was extremely remote and isolated, and emigration involved the additional costs of getting to a major port. In this hypothesis the 'Periphery and Northeast' provides an intermediate category, not as isolated as the Highlands but not as much in the information hub as the 'Central Lowlands'.

The volume of emigration fluctuated in both England and Scotland according to decade, and except in 1861–71 the losses always moved in the same direction in the corresponding decade.[90] This was because the United States was the most popular overseas destination for emigrants of both countries and as Thomas has argued, the 'British and American development was complementary and characterised by alternating decades of investment and migration'.[91] In the decade 1891–1901 emigration was generally low. In England and Wales Baines attributes this in part to a high level of return emigration.[92] Although the rate of return emigration to Scotland has not been studied, the samples from the enumeration books for the years up to and including 1891 provided plenty of evidence of transient movement. There was a marked fall in the proportion of emigrants going abroad in the decade 1891–1901, but the volume of males moving to England and Wales increased. The 'Borders' in particular had well above average levels of emigration in that decade and due to its location emigrants from the category were most likely to move south. This could be taken as evidence of males moving south when the prospects overseas were less good.

Baines concluded that rural–urban stage emigration was relatively rare in England and Wales.[93] This may well also be true in Scotland, but it was very difficult to prove, although in this study it has been argued that the low volume of adults migrating and emigrating from the 'Central Lowlands' may in part be a reflection of the parents being born in different counties. It has also been shown that current migration within Scotland involved a high proportion of young children, and it has been proposed that this may have led to considerable secondary migration, particularly as the counties with most industrial expansion were contiguous and relatively small in area. These same young migrants may have emigrated as adults and led to a higher proportion of rural-urban or urban-urban stage emigration than was found by Baines, especially as the proportion of emigrants was so much higher in Scotland. Nevertheless, most of the remote rural northern counties[94] had high proportions of current migrants, well above the national average, but relatively low and below average proportions of emigrants. This suggests that the mobile rural population in the north preferred out-migration to emigration. It was only in the final decade (1901–11) that the proportion of male emigrants from counties such as Argyll, Caithness, Orkney, Ross and Cromarty and Sutherland equalled the national average.[95]

The county of Shetland may however provide some evidence of rural-urban stage emigration. This county had a high proportion of emigrants in several decades and generally low levels of current out-migration. It was therefore behaving like a 'Central Lowlands' county and this may be a reflection of its close links with Leith, Midlothian. Nevertheless, it is also the case that many Shetland-born males served in fishing fleets and the merchant navy,[96] and as the high proportion of emigrants was restricted to males, it is also possible that the figures may reflect not only some transient emigration, but also men dying abroad and thus becoming emigrants who had nevertheless intended to return to Shetland. It is a pity that Baines does not provide more information on the age of emigrants from England and Wales, as it is possible that it differed considerably from that found in Scotland.

The Scots: an Emigration-Prone Nation?

Although not top of the league of European emigrant-prone nations, Scotland is placed second by Anderson and Morse[97] and third by Baines. Baines has shown that the Irish and the Norwegians had a greater propensity to emigrate than the Scots,[98] but he has considered a longer time period (1850–1930) than this study. When the data is recalculated to include only the study period 1861–1911, the averages produce a different result. Thus the Irish remain the most emigrant prone nation (10.26 losses per 1,000 population) and the Norwegians remain second (6.56) with the Scots third (6.14).

Baines estimates are for overseas movement, and so for Scotland (and indeed Ireland) the estimate does not include the measurement of the substantial emigration to other parts of Britain. However, Baines' table also under-estimates the emigration from other countries in that it also excludes movement within Europe and research has shown that France in particular was attracting huge numbers of Italians, Poles, Austro-Hungarians and

Spaniards.[99] Scotland is not therefore alone in having its total losses under–represented. However, in comparison with Ireland and Norway there is one factor that is not being taken into consideration immigration.

Baines' calculations are not as easy to reproduce as his footnotes suggest, but it is presumed that the estimations are made as a proportion of the total population. In the cases of both Ireland and Norway — both overwhelmingly rural countries — this is probably a valid procedure, as they had relatively few immigrants. For example immigrants into Ireland (both those from other parts of Great Britain and foreigners) increased from 1.3% in 1861 to 3.6% in 1911,[100] and foreigners resident in Norway are unlikely to exceeded these proportions. The situation is not the same in predominantly urban Scotland where approximately 9% of the total population were immigrants.[101] If the data is reworked using only the Scottish native population, then the average annual rates per 1,000 leaving would increase by a factor of almost 0.9, enough to make Scotland a clear second, above Norway, in rank order.

Conclusion

It was already known that Scottish overseas emigration exceeded that of England and Wales.[102] It is also clear that Scots were proportionally more likely to emigrate within Britain as well, thus increasing the overall level of emigration from Scotland. Yet when considering migration it was the English and Welsh that were more mobile. For the latter there were more opportunities available within their country, thus encouraging migration and dampening emigration. When the three countries (England and Wales and Scotland) were compared national influences were far more significant for emigration than regional ones, but the latter did appear to influence migration. But by far the most important contrast was in the scale of emigration, the proportion of Scottish emigration vastly exceeding that south of the border: indeed the Scots were a 'notoriously migratory' population. They exceeded all, except the Irish, in the proportion of the population that went overseas and large numbers of Scots also moved into England and Wales.

Finally, when Scottish patterns of migration and emigration were compared over time, it was clear that migration patterns remained very similar throughout the nineteenth and twentieth centuries in terms of age of departure, but that the gender imbalance gradually disappeared. There was however, marked differences but it should be remembered that although this period had fairly sustained high levels of emigration, the decades of greatest population loss from Scotland were outwith the period 1861–1911.

When out-migration patterns for Scotland where compared with those for England and Wales, several points emerged despite the limited sampling base. Factors influencing migration seemed to relate to the economic character of the county and regardless of country, prosperous industrial counties being better able to 'hold' their population. With regards to emigration it appeared that the national propensity to emigrate was more significant than the nature of the county and the populations of the Scottish counties were overall more likely emigrate than those of English ones.

In Chapter 1 it was argued that levels of migration and distances travelled increased over time. This chapter has shown that the period 1861–1911 continued this pattern reinforcing the re-distribution of the population that was already underway, so that the vast majority of the population was concentrated in the Central Belt. The major redistribution appears to have slowed down in the late nineteenth century, but Hollingsworth's work shows that very high levels of local mobility continued.

Chapter 1 also highlighted the remarkably high levels of emigration from Scotland that appear to have been ongoing for at least three centuries, despite changes in the areas of attraction. This chapter has also been shown that high levels of emigration were maintained, albeit with dramatic fluctuations in the numbers leaving during the period 1861–1911. In this chapter it can be seen that the gender and age structure of emigrants was remarkably consistent over time and that it was only in the late twentieth century that this changed, when temporary emigration as opposed to settler emigration became the dominant out-movement.

Notes

1. Bisset-Smith, 'A Statistical Note' quoted by Flinn. *Scottish Population History.* p. 459.

2. Baines, Emigration from Europe. p. 3

3. This can be compared with the life-time migrant population of Scotland as a whole, which increased from 22.5% in 1861 to about 26% in 1911. See Appendix 2[p].

4. Anderson and Morse. 'The People'. pp. 19–22.

5. Tranter. *Population and Society.* pp. 142–3.

6. The Census of Scotland for 1921–51 provided birthplace information but not in a usable form. (No census taken in 1941).
   Census of Scotland 1921, Report on the Thirteenth Decennial Census of Scotland, Vol. II, Tables 50–7, pp. 179–209. Census of Scotland 1931, Report on the Fourteenth Decennial Census of Scotland, Vol. II, Tables 40–7, pp. 101–20. Census 1951 Scotland, Vol. II, Tables 32–4, pp. 49–53.

7. Flinn. *Scottish Population History*. Table 5.1.1 p. 302.

8. *Ibid*. Table 6.1.1 p. 441.

9. Hobsbawn, *Industry and Empire,* pp. 308–9.

10. Unemployment in Britain varied, and was highest in the manufacturing regions including Scotland. Lee. *The British Economy since 1700*. pp. 258–60.

11. Hollingsworth. *Migration. A study*. p. 95.

12. *Ibid*. p. 91 and 97

13. This age of maximum frequency of migration was influenced by the fact that national service caused males to be exceptionally mobile. However, in the present study the highest volume of adult movement is still in the same age-band even without the distorting influence of military service.

14. Hollingsworth. *Migration. A study* p. 101.

15. Hollingworth cites the findings of Cramond. and Marshall. 'Housing and Mobility' p. 35.

16. In the period 1861–1911, housing tied to a job was uncommon except in mining and agriculture.

17. Hollingsworth. *Migration. A study* p. 96.

18. It is assumed (because he does not acknowledge it) that Baines calculated this using Carrier and Jeffrey, *External Migration*. and Mitchell. *Abstract of British Historical Statistics*. Baines. *Migration in a Mature Economy*. Appendix 3, p. 300.

19. Harper. *Emigration from North-East. Vol. 1,* pp. 21–2.

20. Flinn. *Scottish Population History*. Table 6.1.2 p. 442.

21. Total emigration out of Scotland in the decade 1851–61 can be estimated by using data from both Baines and Flinn. It is estimated that approximately 231,000 people left Scotland. Baines. *Migration in a Mature Economy*. appendices 3 & 5, pp. 300 and 304 respectively and Flinn. *Scottish Population History*. Table 6.1.2 p. 442.

22. See Table 4.1.

23. These emigrants came primarily from the Highland counties of Argyll, Inverness, Perth and Ross and Cromarty, but also from Renfrew. There was a secondary out-movement from Berwick, Dumfries, Kirkcudbright and Wigtown. Bailyn. *Voyagers to the West. pp. 108–12*. Flinn has also considered emigration in 1774–5, Flinn. *Scottish Population History*. pp. 443–52.

24. Bailyn has only made estimates of the national proportions in each age-band by combining the data for both sexes. It was clear in the present study that the male and female proportions in each age-band differed markedly, see Table 5.1. Bailyn. *Voyagers to the West. pp. 127–8*.

25. Bailyn. *Voyagers to the West. p. 131*.

26. Erickson. 'Who were'. p. 371.

27. Hollingsworth. *A study based on Scottish*. pp. 104–5.

28. Calculated from Hollingsworth. The proportions of male to female emigrants aged 25–44 years were 57.2% to 42.8% respectively. *Ibid*. p. 123.

29. Lee. *The British Economy*. pp. 257–8.

30. Jones, *A Population Geography* p. 268.

31. Lee. *The British Economy*. pp. 256.

32. Jones. *A Population Geography,* p. 261.

33. *Ibid,* pp. 262–3.

34. Fluctuations in the volume of emigrants were also found in the present study. Mobility varied according to the economic prospects on both sides of the Atlantic. This will be considered subsequently in Chapter 6.

35. Lindsay 'Migration and Motivation' p. 156

36. Scottish professional and managerial emigrants comprised 52.7% of all employed Scottish emigrants in 1980–85 and 62.3% in 1986. Findlay. and Garrick. 'A Migration Channels Approach. 'Table 5, p. 18.

37. Findlay and Garrick 'Scottish emigration' p. 177.

38. Smout, Landsman and Devine, 'Scottish Emigration'. p. 99.

39. Thomas used unpublished data made available by the Bureau of the Census, Washington. Thomas. *Migration and Economic Growth*. Table 43, p. 149.

40. *Toothill Report on the Scottish Economy,* The Scottish Council (Development and Industry) (1961) quoted in Lindsay 'Migration and Motivation' p. 155.

41. Lindsay 'Migration and Motivation' p. 156.

42. Erickson. 'Who were'. p. 367.

43. Flinn. *Scottish Population History.* p. 453.

44. Baines. *Migration in a Mature Economy*. p. 279. This is somewhat higher than the 30% assumed in this study for Scotland.

45. Male emigration from Scotland in the period 1984–6 comprised 56% of the total, thus maintaining the traditional male preponderance in emigration. This was not however, the case in England and Wales were females achived a slight majority of 51.1%. Findlay and Garrick 'Scottish emigration'.p. 183 Tables III and IV.

46. Flinn. *Scottish Population History.* Table 6.1.4. p. 447.

47. Baines. *Migration in a Mature Economy.* Table 3.2. p. 61.

48. Lee. *The British Economy*. p. 256.

49. The decades with high proportions of emigrants were 1861–71, 1871–81, 1881–91 and 1901–11.

50. Findlay and Garrick 'Scottish Emigration' p. 182.

51. Smout, Landsman & Devine, 'Scottish Emigration'.pp. 85–6.

52. Anderson and Morse 'High Fertility, High Emigration'.

53. Lindsay 'Migration and Motivation' p. 155.

54. These magnet counties of the Central Lowlands were Ayr, Clackmannan, Dunbarton, Edinburgh (Midlothian), Fife, Forfar (Angus), Lanark, Linlithgow

(West Lothian), Renfrew, Stirling and parts of Haddington (East Lothian) and Lowland Perth

55. This argument assumes that the distance involved in a migratory movement had no influence on whether to migrate or not.

56. Mitchell and Deane, *Abstract of British Historical Statistics* p. 20. Radnor , the second smallest county, had a population in 1861 of 25,000 and was the only other one below 47,000.

57. In 1861 the Scottish counties with smaller populations than Rutland, England (population approximately 22,000 in 1861) were Bute (16,331), Clackmannan (21,450), Kinross (7,977), Nairn (10,065), Peebles (11,408) and Selkirk (9,926).)

58. Mitchell and Deane. *Abstracts*. p. 6.

Females per 1,000 Males in England & Wales and Scotland

	England & Wales	Scotland
Census Year		
1861	1,053	1,112
1871	1,054	1,096
1881	1,055	1,076
1891	1,063	1,072
1901	1,068	1,057
1911	1,068	1,062

59. Baines. *Migration in a Mature Economy*. p. 102.

60. The Percentage of the native and total population less than 20 years in 1911 compared (Appendices 3[n] and 2[c]).

61. Baines. *Migration in a Mature Economy*. p. 102, fn.33. In 1861 and 1871 'in the seventeen most important counties of in-migration' (in England and Wales) 25.5% of males and 27.1% of females were less than twenty years.

62. *Ibid*. p. 102, fn.33.

63. *Ibid*. p. 107.

64. It is possible that the migrant age–structure was incorrect for some counties. This would also result in high return migration.

65. See Appendix 2[m].

66. Baines. *Migration in a Mature Economy*. p. 102. The percentage of the current migrant population who were under 20 years in England and Wales, was calculated from the 'seventeen most important counties attracting in-migration'. If the findings in Scotland are at all relevant here, it seems likely that the percentage would probably fall slightly if all 52 counties were included as the 'Central Lowlands' category had the highest proportion of migrant children.

67. Friedlander and Roshier. ' A Study of Internal Migration'.

68. Baines. *Migration in a Mature Economy*. p. 124.

69. Friedlander and Roshier.' A Study of Internal Migration. part I' Table II.₁, pp. 272–3.

70. Ibid. pp. 239–279.

71. Baines. *Migration in a Mature Economy.* p. 123.

72. See Appendix 2[m] and [c].

73. Baines. *Migration in a Mature Economy.* p. 121.

74. *Ibid.* Table 6.1, p. 144 recalculated.

75. Bailyn, *Voyagers to the West,* Table 4.4, p. 111.

76. *Ibid.* pp. 126–203.

77. Baines. *Migration in a Mature Economy.* Appendix I, pp. 282–98.

78. Scottish counties with small populations such as Selkirk were avoided because they were small even though they experienced even higher rates of growth.

79. Hunt's study of migration suggested that both Lancashire and London plus Middlesex, were in regions that had consistently high rates of decennial net migration, except in 1901–11. Hunt. *Regional Wage Variations.* Table 7–1, p. 247.

80. Friedlander and Roshier.' A Study in Internal. part I' p. 262.

81. The county areas are taken from *The Concise Oxford Atlas,* pp. VII–XL. The acreages of counties are those current when the atlas was published. The Scottish study had county boundary changes in 1891, and the English and Welsh boundaries were also revised (Baines. *Migration in a Mature Economy.* p. 95) and therefore acreages may differ slightly from those of the study period.

82. This argument is supported by the findings of Lee. Lee.' Modern Economic Growth and Structural Change'. pp. 21–2.

83. Lee has argued that as London grew it generated growth in the neighbouring counties of Essex, Kent and Surrey. Lee. *The British Economy.* p. 140.

84. Anderson and Morse 'High Fertility, High Emigration' p. 9.

85. There was slightly less than three times the proportion of male emigrants in the decade 1881–1891.

86. Baines. *Migration in a Mature Economy.* p. 279.

87. The 'Central Lowlands' comprised counties with at least 50% population growth during this study. The counties in this category were: Dunbarton, Edinburgh (Midlothian), Fife, Lanark, Linlithgow (West Lothian), Selkirk, Stirling and Renfrew.

88. See Table 2.5 for a breakdown of the proportion of the native population by population category in every census year.

89. This statement does not contradict with the previous paragraph if one assumes the unstated fact that the majority of the English and Welsh population lived in an urbanising county. Baines. *Migration in a Mature Economy.* p. 279.

90. See Table 4.1 and Baines. *Migration in a Mature Economy.* Table 2.1 p. 10.

91. Baines. 'The labour supply'. p. 160.

92. Baines. *Migration in a Mature Economy.* p. 280.

93. *Ibid.* p. 281.

94. This discussion relates to the 'Highlands'. The 'Borders' could not be included in this analysis, because as has already been argued, some emigration in the category was localised movement more similar to current migration.

95. See Table 4.1 and Appendix 5

96. Smith. *Shetland Life and Trade,* pp. 157–9.

97. Anderson and Morse, 'The People' p. 15.

98. Baines, *Emigration from Europe.* p. 3

99. Hoerder, *Labour Migrations.* p. 150.

100. Census of Ireland 1911, General Report, H.M.S.O, London [cd 6663] 1913, Table 25, p. 30.

101. Census of Scotland 1911, Vol. II, p. XXII.

102. Baines, *Migration in a Mature Economy* p. 10.

6

Total Scottish Population Movement 1861–1911: An Overview and Conclusions

Up to now we have examined separately current migration within and emigration from Scotland. Yet it seems likely that the two movement are similar and how they relate together is important. Moreover the impact of both movements is undoubtedly going to affect the population profile of a county or region. In this chapter we will consider the two forms of mobility together, looking first at the relationship between emigration and migration, and then secondly at the impact of population movement on the county-of-birth.

THE RELATIONSHIP BETWEEN CURRENT EMIGRATION AND MIGRATION

Scottish emigration losses created a pattern of peaks and troughs in movement. These phases corresponded to similar ones in England and Wales, as already mentioned in Chapter 1. The links between fluctuating rates of emigration and business cycles in Britain and the United States, and Thomas's explanation of the relationship between current migration and emigration have already been considered in Chapter 1. It is the work of Thomas[1] that will be used in this study to provide a basis to explore Scottish mobility, although it is recognised that aspects of Thomas's thesis with regard to population movement in England and Wales have already been questioned by Baines.[2]

Thomas identified an inverse relationship between emigration and migration. He considered that in certain decades British urban expansion could absorb rural migration, while in others the same rural-born population emigrated overseas. His theory therefore assumed a mobile rural-born population that moved either within Britain or abroad according to the economic climate. Inter-urban migration, which has been identified in this study, was not considered by Thomas. This section will therefore consider the links between emigration and migration, and attempt to determine whether there was one mobile population. It has already been shown that nationally the proportion of both current migrants and emigrants varied according to decade and there appeared to be an inverse relationship between the two sets of data. If this was indeed the situation then combining the two sets of calculations should provide estimates that lack the obvious peaks and troughs apparent in both separate population movements (Table 6.1).

Table 6.1 shows the proportion of the population lost when all population movement (current migration and emigration) was combined. There were fluctuations in both forms of population movement. The proportion of emigrants in the population increased, while in contrast current migration fell, but overall the first three decades (1861–91) had higher proportions of out-migration than the subsequent two (1891–1911) regardless of gender. After 1891 the proportion of Scots involved in any form of out-movement was declining. Clearly over time there was considerably less movement within Scotland, which was not compensated for by increased emigration.

If emigration and current migration were inversely related and part of the same mobile population, the proportions moving from each category should remain fairly consistent regardless of whether the decade had high or low emigration and migration. This is not apparent in the proportions lost from the national estimates and indeed inspection shows that for males the fluctuations relate closely to those apparent in estimates of emigration (Tables 4.1 and 6.1). This means that increased current migration in decades of lower emigration did not compensate for the lower proportion emigrating. This was particularly true in the decade 1891–1901, which experienced higher than normal proportions of current migrants and lower proportions of emigrants, but nevertheless remained a decade of low overall net mobility.[3] The pattern for females was different, as in the first three decades overall movement tended to resemble current migration, but thereafter the pattern fitted emigration. These differing patterns between the sexes are not entirely surprising as males predominated in emigration, which is therefore likely to be the more significant form of movement, while for females current migration was more important.

Having considered the main trends in movement at the national level, the analysis will now consider the individual population categories. However, it should be born in mind that in order to measure this mobility, a new degree of artificiality has had to be created. Whereas emigration has previously been assumed to be from anywhere in Scotland, it is now being

Table 6.1. The Total Volume of Movement (both Current Migration and Emigration) by Decade, Population Category and Gender

Population Category	Decade	Males		Females	
		Proportion Lost*	Approximate Numbers Lost	Proportion Lost*	Approximate Numbers Lost
Scotland					
	1861–1871	13.5	–211,054	11.0	–186,519
	1871–1881	12.9	–224,575	11.2	–208,474
	1881–1891	13.7	–262,717	10.9	–221,298
	1891–1901	10.8	–223,341	8.8	–191,212
	1901–1911	12.3	–281,133	10.3	–247,765
Highlands					
	1861–1871	13.7	–39,832	11.1	–36,376
	1871–1881	12.2	–34,940	10.6	–34,083
	1881–1891	13.4	–38,476	10.1	–32,111
	1891–1901	11.7	–32,361	9.6	–29,575
	1901–1911	11.9	–32,442	9.3	–27,834
Borders					
	1861–1871	16.8	–22,107	13.8	–19,968
	1871–1881	16.1	–21,451	15.0	–21,835
	1881–1891	16.5	–21,835	13.8	–22,224
	1891–1901	16.1	–21,087	13.9	–19,436
	1901–1911	12.9	–16,391	12.0	–16,305
Periphery & Northeast					
	1861–1871	13.5	–62,255	10.6	–52,667
	1871–1881	12.8	–65,005	10.8	–58,805
	1881–1891	14.5	–80,064	11.2	–65,501
	1891–1901	12.2	–69,989	9.3	–56,987
	1901–1911	14.0	–86,118	11.0	–71,738
Central Lowlands					
	1861–1871	12.8	–86,859	10.7	–77,508
	1871–1881	12.8	–103,182	11.1	–93,750
	1881–1891	12.9	–121,953	10.5	–103,749
	1891–1901	9.3	–99,903	7.6	–85,213
	1901–1911	11.6	–146,181	10.0	–131,889

⋆ The proportion is calculated as (current emigrants plus migrants) divided by (the total population born in Scotland in the subsequent census plus current emigrants), that is the total population at the end of the decade if nobody had moved out. The current emigrants could have left their county-of-birth decades before.

considered as originating from a particular population category, which was clearly not always necessarily the situation. This is necessary in order that the overall losses due to mobility can be estimated. It should be remembered that the calculations in Table 6.1 are aggregates of estimates for current migration and emigration, and that these were measured completely independently. The estimates for current migration were probably slightly low, but this does not affect the calculations for emigration. Finally the proportions lost in each age-band are subject to errors and can be checked against Appendices 8 and 12.

TOTAL MOVEMENT FROM EACH POPULATION CATEGORY

The highest proportions of total out-migration in every population category were in or before the decade 1881–91. The various categories did reveal some consistency in their mobility patterns. The 'Borders' experienced well above average levels of out-movement in every single decade. Even allowing for the artificiality of the measurement, it is clear that not every emigrant departed abroad directly from their county-of-birth, and some would have already migrated. Nevertheless. the 'Borders' was haemorrhaging its population and losing approximately a sixth of its males and an eighth of its females in every decade except the final one, when the proportions leaving fell. Over the entire period male out-movement exceeded the national average by almost a quarter and female by 40%. Population losses from the 'Highlands' was not on the same scale as from the 'Borders' and there were only two decades (1861–71 and 1891–1901) when out-movement exceeded the national average. Unlike the previous two population categories which were experiencing population decline, the 'Periphery and Northeast' still had some growth. Yet levels of out-migration from this category were always close to or above the national average and exceeded it in the later decades (1881–1911). Out-movement from the Central Lowlands was consistently below the national average, and although in decades of high emigration it was close to the national average, it was well below the national average in 1891–1901. The lower levels of movement thereafter suggest that within Scotland a 'modern' population distribution had already been achieved.

Having provided a general overview, it is still important to consider the population categories individually, looking firstly at the two categories experiencing population decline, then the 'Periphery' where some population growth was apparent, and finally at the Central 'Lowlands'.

The 'Highlands'

Table 6.1 shows that over time there was a steady decline in the numbers and proportions of females leaving the 'Highlands'. The situation for males was more complicated with peaks in the decades of higher emigration. Nevertheless, the overall trend for males was also down when the two peak emigration decades are compared (1871–81 and 1891–1901). It has already been argued that whereas the volume and proportion of current migrants, although above the national average, was decreasing over time, the proportion of emigrants during the same period was increasing in the decades of peak emigration, but remained generally below average. This category was experiencing a declining total native population and the proportions leaving were also decreasing.[4] This suggests that the peak out-movement from this population category may have occurred at or before the start of the present study. The pattern of mobility in the present study (1861–1911) of below average emigration and above average migration in the 'Highlands' category is in complete contrast to slightly earlier studies by Levitt and Smout[5] and Flinn,[6] where emigration was the main type of out-movement, suggesting that the entire direction of out-movement had recently changed.

The 'Borders'

The population losses from the 'Borders' were higher than from any other population category in the first four decades, albeit with some fluctuations in the proportions of males leaving. The final decade (1901–11) did show a marked decrease in total mobility for males, but this must be kept in perspective as losses in this decade were still well above the national average. Moreover, these high population losses were reinforcing the steady demographic decline. Indeed Table 6.1 shows that unlike the other population categories male and female out-movement were extremely similar in volume.[7] Movement from this category involved a far higher proportion of the total population than that from the 'Highlands'.

It is known that a considerable volume of emigration from the 'Borders' was into England and Wales in 1911[8] and it is thought that this may have been typical of the pattern throughout the study period (1861–1911). The 1911 evidence suggests that movement overseas was not necessarily any greater than from the other population categories (excluding the 'Central Lowlands'), because the numbers going to England and Wales were sufficiently high to account for much of the emigration.[9] In this category the mobile population could choose between migration, emigration south (which in terms of distance was similar to migration), or emigration overseas, and this wide choice might account for the relative lack of fluctuations in the proportions of emigrating (Table 4.1). However, even the relatively easy access to areas of greater economic potential cannot alter the fact that the 'Borders' category was experiencing massive out-movement throughout the entire period 1861–1911.

The 'Periphery and Northeast'

Total mobility from the 'Periphery and Northeast' was well below the national average in the first two decades (1861–81), but thereafter it exceeded the national average for both sexes.[10] The fluctuations in the proportions leaving were pronounced, and inspection shows that for both sexes the pattern of total movement closely followed that of emigration. Far more males were involved in out-movements than females. There was a marked fall in mobility in the decade 1891–1901, so clearly current migration was not entirely compensating for lower emigration. Indeed the proportion of both sexes emigrating almost halved even though the proportion of males migrating increased by a quarter and females by a fifth. This suggests that for some, migration was an alternative to emigration, but it also reveals a keen awareness of the economic situation abroad. Thus despite the fact that this category comprised counties with some population growth, the total out-movement indicates increasing mobility over time in relation to the national average. Indeed, in the final decade the 'Periphery and Northeast' was losing a higher proportion of males than any other, and for females it was only exceeded by the 'Borders'.

The 'Central Lowlands'

The proportions of the population leaving this category were never above the national average (Table 6.1). Although the proportion of emigrants lost was almost invariably above the norm, total movement was lower, because current migration was low. With the exception of the decade 1891–1901 there was a remarkable consistency in the proportion of the population that was mobile, and this pattern was very similar to that of emigration. Indeed the decade 1891–1901 is interesting in that, unlike the other categories, current out-migration did not increase. This was probably because nowhere else in Scotland offered better prospects and therefore the options for current migration were limited. However, it is recognised that secondary migration could have increased, and cannot be readily identified in this study.[11]

The 'Central Lowlands' experienced rapid population growth, but it was also the most important source of 'true' overseas emigrants.[12] Indeed this category provided over half the total number of emigrants in every decade except the first (1861–71).[13] Thus it was people born in a predominantly urban environment that comprised the bulk of the Scottish overseas emigration and not, as Thomas suggested, a mobile rural population. It is instructive to compare the vastly increased current out-migration from the 'Periphery and Northeast' in the decade 1891–1901 with that of the 'Central Lowlands'. In the former category migrants could move to the more prosperous Central Lowlands and therefore for some of the mobile population migration and emigration were alternative options. In the 'Central Lowlands' such a choice was not available and total mobility in this category was therefore reduced by a far greater proportion.

Overview

This analysis provides only relatively little support for Thomas's argument that movement to a major urban area was an alternative to emigration in decades of low emigration. However, the counties with some of the highest losses through emigration (excluding those in the 'Borders') were the largest urban counties in the 'Central Lowlands'. This urban-born population did not regard migration as a substitute for emigration. When considering the other population categories care must be taken in defining the migrant populations. Out-migration from the 'Periphery and North-east' counties cannot generally be classified as rural-urban movement, although some migration from the northeast and counties on the fringe of the central Lowlands undoubtedly fell within that classification.[14] Several of the 'Periphery and Northeast' counties had considerable urban development and indeed Ayr, Clackmannan and Forfar (Angus) all had less than 15% of males employed in agriculture in 1881.[15] Not all migration was to the Central Lowlands, but rural-urban migration was only possible from counties in the declining population categories and the northeast, and from parts of the remaining 'Periphery' counties. Elsewhere migration into the 'Central Lowlands' could be defined as inter-urban rather than rural-urban. Moreover, inter-urban movement also took place within the 'Central Lowlands'. In the period 1861–1911 rural-urban movement was no longer the dominant form of migration (although even within urban counties such as Lanark, rural pockets still existed). The natives of the urban counties of the 'Central Lowlands' were most likely to emigrate and migrants from outwith this category could replace them as workers. This pattern of predominantly urban-born emigrants was not unique to Scotland, as Baines identified a similar pattern of urban emigration from England and Wales.[16]

However, emigration in this context did not just embrace overseas movement, as Scots could also move south to England and Wales. The estimates for movement south (Table 4.2) suggest that this increased in decades of low overseas emigration such as 1891–1901 and decreased in the high emigration decades. Emigration to England and Wales was therefore performing the same compensating function as current migration in decades of low emigration. However, it should be noted that emigration south was declining over time. For some emigrants, movement into England and Wales may in fact reflect stage emigration, with emigration into England and Wales when the economic situation abroad was poor, followed by movement overseas later. Emigration south was high in the decade 1891–1901 and low subsequently, but as the estimates were also net, a Scot going abroad having previously been resident in England would simply disguise a new arrival from Scotland moving south.[17]

THE EFFECTS OF MOBILITY ON THE AGE-STRUCTURE OF THE POPULATION

Both emigration and current migration have been estimated net of returns. This means that return movement was incorporated in the estimates, which has the effect of making both movements appear to be composed of almost entirely young people. While the majority of outward movement was probably amongst the young this was clearly not the whole story, as return movement inevitably involved older people than outward movement and this has meant that its effects are disproportionately concentrated on the older age-bands thus disguising older outward movement. This is an inevitable result of the method of estimation used which has to taken into account throughout this study.

Children comprised a large proportion of the aggregate Scottish mobility, but as a proportion of the total native population in the relevant age-bands they were relatively unimportant. For example in the decade 1861–71 Aberdeen-born male mobility in the under 5 years age-band amounted in volume to over two and half thousand children,[18] about 14.2% of the native population.[19] There were approximately four hundred fewer males moving in the age-band 25–29 years than in the young children, yet in percentage terms it was considerably larger (24.2%). Child movement was therefore not particularly important in its own right but it steadily eroded the potential adult native population.

In counties attracting in-migration such as Dunbarton and Linlithgow (West Lothian), this out-movement of native children was not significant,[20] but in counties that failed to attract migrants it was very important. Thus in these counties, when adult movement increased, the majority of losses were from age-bands that were already severely depleted. In consequence

Anderson and Morse could write that 'by far the largest proportion of out-migration and emigration took place between the ages of 15 and 25' and 'even in relatively good years like the 1870s, more than a quarter of boys aged 15–19 at the start of the decade had left by its end from the Highlands and Islands, from the North-East and the South-West; more than a fifth had gone from the Borders; one in ten had left the country altogether'.[21] Clearly, although these statements are correct they ignore the earlier childhood mobility.[22]

The discussion will now consider movement of young adults, which as Anderson and Morse have noted experienced the greatest impact from mobility, because for males the peak age-bands of departure for both emigration and migration often coincided. For females peak out-migration generally preceded emigration. Counties that were failing to attract in-migrants were losing their most economically-active age groups (assuming that their economies were capable of sustaining them, which may well have not always been the case). However, the expanding urban counties gained an economically active group of migrants that may well have been able to replace their own native emigrant losses. Superficially this suggests that high proportions of native emigrants might have created labour shortages that permitted the easy assimilation of in-migrants into the Central Lowlands. However, as the decades of highest in-migration were also the decades of low emigration, this pattern may not be as simple as it at first appears and needs further investigation. Moreover, it should be noted that migrants were predominantly female and emigrants male.

There was a second source of replacement of labour: immigrants. Scotland was losing more males than females, and although the sex ratio of English and Welsh immigrants was almost unity, Irish and foreign-born current immigrants were predominantly male.[23] Moreover, Irish current immigrants were generally young adults, exactly the same sort of age-group as many of the economically-active Scots emigrants leaving. Nevertheless, there was an imbalance here too in that immigration into Scotland from Ireland was highest in decades of low Scottish emigration.[24]

Most Scots emigrated when the American economy was thriving and the British economy weak, so demand to replace workers may not have existed. Indeed Treble has shown that huge variations in the demand for labour occurred in the construction industry which related closely to downturns in the British economy.[25] In-migration and immigration was greatest in decades when the British economy was prospering, and it was at this stage in the cycle that the workforce needed replacing or expanded.

The Effects of both Out-Migration and Emigration by County-of-Birth

It has been argued throughout the present study that it cannot be assumed that emigrants had just left their county-of-birth. It might therefore seem meaningless to consider total mobility from a county-of-birth. However, with the notable exception of the 'Borders', counties that had a high proportion of emigrants had lower proportions of migrants and vice versa. Those emigrating were therefore less likely to have been involved in long term migration before emigrating if they came from a county where emigration rates were high. (Short term migration before emigration was very unlikely to be caught by this study).

Map 6.1.[26] illustrates the relationship between the individual counties-of-birth and the national average with regard to the proportion of mobile natives of both sexes (Table 6.2). It is not proposed to consider the individual counties in detail, because as discussed above the data lack sufficient precision,[27] but instead to highlight regional trends. Map 6.1. indicates that it was very unusual for a county to retain the same relationship to the national average throughout the period. Clearly, the border counties with their consistently high losses were almost invariably above average, and Fife, Lanark and Renfrew, with very low proportions of migrants remained below average.

The Highlands had generally below average mobility, but at the county level there appears to be a regional split. Map 6.1. shows that the northern counties[28] were generally below the national average except in the decade of low emigration (1891–1901). In this decade a much lower national average meant that the high levels of current migration from these northern counties pushed their mobility above the national average, except in Shetland and Sutherland. The more southern counties of Argyll and Perth were more likely to exceed the national average in total out-movement, and indeed they were both experiencing an absolute decline in population.[29] These counties were much closer to the industrial centres of the Central Lowlands and had been subject to lowland influences for the longest time.

In the Northeast and East there was also a regional dimension to mobility. The smaller counties of Banff, Elgin (Moray), Kincardine and Nairn had generally high mobility, while Aberdeen and Forfar (Angus) were invariably lower. However, the latter counties both contained a large city, which was also a regional centre. Rural-urban movement was therefore more likely to remain within the county, as no easily accessible adjacent county offered better prospects. Further south mobility from Ayr was high, but only in the decades of high emigration. Haddington (East Lothian)

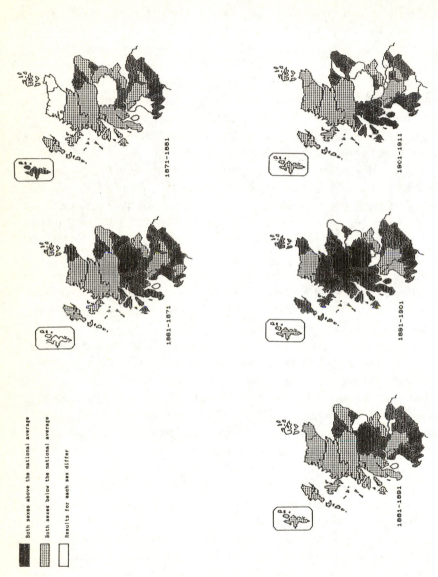

Both sexes above the national average

Both sexes below the national average

Results for each sex differ

1861-1871

1871-1881

1881-1891

1891-1901

1901-1911

Map 6.1. Total Movement: The Relationship of the Proportion Lost by County-of-Birth to the National Average (see Table 6.1).

Table 6.2. Total Out-Movement as a Proportion
of the Population of the County-of-Birth*

COUNTY-OF-BIRTH	DECADE	MALE	FEMALE
Aberdeen			
	1861–1871	10.16	7.20
	1871–1881	10.74	8.85
	1881–1891	13.49	9.64
	1891–1901	10.93	8.05
	1901–1911	13.96	10.31
Argyll			
	1861–1871	13.73	12.25
	1871–1881	10.77	9.91
	1881–1891	12.47	10.19
	1891–1901	10.37	8.98
	1901–1911	13.25	11.63
Ayr			
	1861–1871	16.80	14.40
	1871–1881	12.74	11.33
	1881–1891	14.91	12.02
	1891–1901	10.06	9.13
	1901–1911	13.90	10.76
Banff			
	1861–1871	14.13	11.27
	1871–1881	16.08	13.22
	1881–1891	14.17	13.13
	1891–1901	15.03	11.80
	1901–1911	11.52	11.44
Berwick			
	1861–1871	16.68	14.71
	1871–1881	16.60	15.64
	1881–1891	17.95	15.23
	1891–1901	15.22	13.83
	1901–1911	12.36	12.07
Bute			
	1861–1871	12.66	12.03
	1871–1881	12.06	11.66
	1881–1891	14.43	9.97
	1891–1901	12.34	11.11
	1901–1911	15.66	11.94
Caithness			
	1861–1871	13.64	11.37
	1871–1881	13.07	10.99
	1881–1891	13.04	10.18
	1891–1901	14.99	12.97
	1901–1911	11.49	8.79

Table 6.2 (cont)

County-of-Birth	Decade	Male	Female
Clackmannan			
	1861–1871	15.53	12.40
	1871–1881	18.48	15.53
	1881–1891	15.63	12.63
	1891–1901	10.87	7.61
	1901–1911	16.37	14.18
Dumfries			
	1861–1871	14.61	11.59
	1871–1881	15.04	14.28
	1881–1891	16.08	13.76
	1891–1901	14.71	12.66
	1901–1911	11.92	11.70
Dunbarton			
	1861–1871	19.13	17.23
	1871–1881	14.92	13.48
	1881–1891	16.56	15.14
	1891–1901	13.01	11.86
	1901–1911	14.14	13.65
Edinburgh (Midlothian)			
	1861–1871	13.16	11.49
	1871–1881	13.54	11.80
	1881–1891	14.14	9.22
	1891–1901	11.73	10.51
	1901–1911	12.56	9.95
Elgin (Moray)			
	1861–1871	18.24	15.79
	1871–1881	13.84	12.52
	1881–1891	17.34	12.23
	1891–1901	12.82	11.27
	1901–1911	13.98	12.09
Fife			
	1861–1871	12.79	9.32
	1871–1881	12.24	10.15
	1881–1891	11.31	9.51
	1891–1901	7.59	6.06
	1901–1911	8.12	7.34
Forfar (Angus)			
	1861–1871	10.73	6.38
	1871–1881	11.97	8.74
	1881–1891	13.78	9.93
	1891–1901	13.25	7.95
	1901–1911	13.78	10.05

Table 6.2 (cont)

County-of-Birth	Decade	Male	Female
Haddington (East Lothian)			
	1861–1871	16.08	14.98
	1871–1881	14.80	14.46
	1881–1891	17.09	15.76
	1891–1901	15.97	13.43
	1901–1911	11.84	12.34
Inverness			
	1861–1871	12.70	9.91
	1871–1881	10.36	10.06
	1881–1891	13.06	9.77
	1891–1901	11.63	9.66
	1901–1911	11.78	7.67
Kincardine			
	1861–1871	16.81	15.04
	1871–1881	16.62	16.09
	1881–1891	14.12	12.30
	1891–1901	16.45	14.60
	1901–1911	19.63	16.22
Kinross			
	1861–1871	18.97	16.76
	1871–1881	16.89	13.29
	1881–1891	15.95	14.32
	1891–1901	11.57	9.47
	1901–1911	13.38	12.33
Kirkcudbright			
	1861–1871	10.86	9.00
	1871–1881	23.24	21.54
	1881–1891	17.87	14.61
	1891–1901	17.50	15.70
	1901–1911	16.11	13.82
Lanark & Renfrew			
	1861–1871	11.36	9.30
	1871–1881	12.22	10.27
	1881–1891	11.94	10.01
	1891–1901	8.15	6.03
	1901–1911	11.48	9.79
Linlithgow (West Lothian)			
	1861–1871	21.75	20.14
	1871–1881	19.64	19.18
	1881–1891	15.48	15.31
	1891–1901	13.38	13.16
	1901–1911	13.24	13.25

Table 6.2 (cont)

County-of-Birth	Decade	Male	Female
Nairn			
	1861–1871	14.97	12.36
	1871–1881	15.66	14.39
	1881–1891	18.60	11.88
	1891–1901	13.30	13.32
	1901–1911	16.44	12.37
Orkney			
	1861–1871	13.40	9.62
	1871–1881	8.95	7.13
	1881–1891	14.45	9.78
	1891–1901	13.40	10.73
	1901–1911	11.61	7.85
Peebles			
	1861–1871	17.93	17.25
	1871–1881	17.36	15.07
	1881–1891	17.10	14.55
	1891–1901	16.65	14.87
	1901–1911	14.72	13.87
Perth			
	1861–1871	15.84	13.12
	1871–1881	12.89	11.39
	1881–1891	15.24	11.44
	1891–1901	12.02	9.85
	1901–1911	12.31	10.71
Ross & Cromarty			
	1861–1871	11.60	9.60
	1871–1881	12.89	10.45
	1881–1891	11.58	9.26
	1891–1901	11.45	9.32
	1901–1911	11.03	8.71
Roxburgh			
	1861–1871	23.14	19.80
	1871–1881	13.62	12.10
	1881–1891	14.78	12.44
	1891–1901	16.88	13.77
	1901–1911	13.09	11.98
Selkirk			
	1861–1871	7.53	4.30
	1871–1881	6.09	4.42
	1881–1891	27.83	25.68
	1891–1901	15.65	12.76
	1901–1911	10.58	9.79

Table 6.2 (cont)

COUNTY-OF-BIRTH	DECADE	MALE	FEMALE
Shetland			
	1861–1871	13.54	7.29
	1871–1881	17.17	12.38
	1881–1891	13.12	6.59
	1891–1901	9.49	6.34
	1901–1911	10.26	5.04
Stirling			
	1861–1871	15.90	14.87
	1871–1881	13.28	13.12
	1881–1891	14.09	13.06
	1891–1901	10.10	10.03
	1901–1911	12.29	12.29
Sutherland			
	1861–1871	10.70	10.91
	1871–1881	12.23	11.37
	1881–1891	12.46	9.80
	1891–1901	9.76	8.61
	1901–1911	11.08	9.20
Wigtown			
	1861–1871	18.35	14.43
	1871–1881	13.60	12.59
	1881–1891	16.74	13.55
	1891–1901	16.96	14.55
	1901–1911	11.85	10.88

★ The proportion is calculated as (current migration plus emigration) over (native population anywhere in Scotland in the subsequent census plus emigrants), that is the total population if nobody had emigrated. The estimates of emigration do not assume that emigrants have just left their county-of-birth experienced high population losses throughout the period, which peaked in 1891–91

In the Central Belt it has already been noted that mobility from Fife and Lanark and Renfrew was consistently below the national average, whereas the remaining counties which straddled the area from east to west were generally high. This belt of above average mobility counties included Edinburgh (Midlothian). The proportion of emigrants from Edinburgh was frequently lower than that from Lanark and Renfrew, but current migration was much higher. However, Fife and Lanark and Renfrew combined were physically much larger than any other counties in the Central Belt and the proportions of migrants were lower.[30] These less mobile native populations may reflect not just the economic strength of their county-of-birth, but also its physical size. Nevertheless, when the proportion of total losses from these counties are compared, Fife undoubtedly had the most contented native population in Scotland,[31] the natives of Lanark and Renfrew[32] being much more likely to emigrate, but less inclined to migrate than those in Fife.[33]

To conclude, it seems that Scotland does not appear to fit the thesis of Thomas very satisfactorily, despite the fact that emigration from Scotland fits the classic pattern of peaks and troughs. It does not appear to be the case that migration was considered an adequate substitute for emigration in decades with an economic downturn in the USA. Although there was still plenty of evidence of rural–urban migration in Scotland, the majority of Scottish movement in this period was inter-urban, because the majority of the population lived in urbanising counties. Except in the 'Borders' where classifications of emigration probably included some migration-type movement, the inhabitants of Scottish rural counties preferred migration to emigration, and the proportion of emigrants was by and large below the national average. This contrasts with the situation in England and Wales, where rural dwellers were marginally more likely to emigrate than natives of urban counties.[34]

A far higher proportion of the population emigrated in Scotland than in England and Wales, and less migrated. Overall Scotland probably had a more mobile population. Once a Scot was within the Central Lowlands, he was part of a contiguous belt of twelve counties each experiencing some industrial growth. There was nowhere else in Scotland with better opportunities, and in any case the majority of the population lived within this area. The greatest increase in the proportion of male current migrants in decades of low emigration occurred in the 'Periphery and Northeast', but many of these counties were not predominantly rural. They were growing industrially or were in close proximity to the counties that were expanding.[35] This suggests that the economic cycle may have influenced some rural–born migrants thus supporting Thomas' thesis, but this was only a relatively small proportion of the mobile population.

Migration within Scotland was not the only alternative to emigration. Emigration to England and Wales or to British colonies may have been substitute for US emigration in decades when overall emigration was low. However, the proportion of Scots emigrating to England and Wales did decrease over time, possibly because as Hunt has shown, the wage differentials between the two countries were diminishing. Indeed, by the end of the nineteenth century Central Scotland was one of Britain's high–wage areas.[36] In Scotland some counties (for example those in the northeast) had increased proportions of emigrants in decades of high emigration. However, sudden marked increases to new and sustainable levels did not occur, these being only temporary aberrations.[37] This sustained pattern of emigration probably still supports Baines' argument that 'in the main, emigrants were not fleeing from problems at home nor were they going blindly overseas'. They were 'going to parts of the world which they knew something about'.[38] Indeed return emigrants, letters and published information enabled prospective emigrants to find out about places before they left. If emigration was a planned event, it seems unlikely that many potential emigrants would migrate as an alternative to emigration unless forced to leave their county-of-birth. It was therefore probably only the most mobile elements in the population that would migrate if emigration was unwise, which is why all population categories showed some increase in migration (Table 3.5) in decades of low emigration, but the proportions never equalled the loss in emigration (Table 4.1) and the resulting movement was frequently not rural-urban.

It has been argued that most emigrants left from the urban Central Lowlands and this would have enabled migrants and immigrants to find jobs within the cities. Nevertheless, the decades of greatest emigrant losses did not correspond to the decades of high in-migration or immigration, whereas it did relate to the cycles in British employment demand. In-migration and immigration was greatest when the British economy was thriving, and in the downturn emigration increased.

Conclusions

Since summaries have been provided with every chapter this section will just provided a brief overview of the main conclusions concerning Scottish population movement, both emigration and migration, between 1861 and 1911.

The counties of Scotland have been grouped into four categories based on their demographic characteristics. Some of these categories contained counties that were widely separated geographically and/or had quite different characteristics in other respects. Although these population categories were an essential tool in the estimation and analysis of mobility, it is now more appropriate to consider population movement in terms of geographical regions or type of county (rural or urban).

The physical and demographic characteristics of the counties-of-birth influenced the type of out-movement. A low density of population reflected a lack of economic development, which made out-movement more likely. The rural counties tended to have declining populations[39] and lost a greater proportion of their population through migration. This was generally rural–urban movement, but there was some inter-rural and even urban–rural mobility. The counties with expanding populations had some economic development and most have been classified as urban.[40] Inter-urban movement was the dominant form of migration in terms of volume, because the majority of the population was already concentrated in the urbanising counties. Many counties with declining populations had their natives scattered across Scotland, which is evidence of out-migration, but only a very few counties-of-birth experienced absolute decline in the total number of native-born.

Counties-of-birth with high proportions lost through emigration had quite different characteristics, but it must be remembered that emigrants may not have emigrated directly from their county-of-birth, but migrated first. The proportion of urban-born emigrants exceeded those from the rural counties, except for those in the 'Borders'. For the rural-born, migration to the nearest industrial centre offered either an alternative to unemployment or improved opportunities. The urban population in the most prosperous counties was unlikely to be able to improve its position within Scotland and opportunities were likely to be better outside Scotland. The largest proportions of total losses (emigration and migration) were from the counties bordering on to England. Dunbarton and Linlithgow (West Lothian) also experienced high losses from their native population, but in these counties, unlike the Border counties, high rates of in-migration and immigration more than compensated for the native out-movement and their respective populations grew rapidly.

The pattern of mobility from the two regions most remote from major industrial development was very different. In the Highlands and Islands the proportion of the population migrating was high, but the proportion emigrating was generally lower and overall mobility was normally below average and decreasing over time. These counties were the most remote from centres of economic growth. It was Argyll and Perth, the two counties closest to areas of industrial development that experienced the greatest population losses. In contrast the southern counties with declining populations experienced a very much greater population loss through both migration and emigration, although the proximity to England probably increased the proportion of natives classified as emigrants. There was a veritable haemorrhage of the population.

The counties experiencing some demographic growth[41] were generally those with relatively high rates of economic growth. Their proportions of emigrants were frequently below the national average while the proportions of migrants were generally above average. In decades of low emigration there was increased migration, because there were more prosperous industrial counties relatively close, but this movement was insufficient to compensate for the decrease in emigration. The Central Lowlands experienced the greatest industrial expansion and attracted an increasing proportion of in-migrants over time, while the overall proportion of out-migrants was below average because nowhere else in Scotland was equally attractive. However, the proportion of emigrants in the native population of this area was generally above average.

The changing structure of the Scottish population cannot be attributed solely to mobility. Fertility declined and mortality improved over time and this combined with heavy out-movement meant that the age-structure of the counties with declining populations altered in relation to the national average. The period of greatest population loss from the Highlands and Islands was probably at the beginning of or before this study in the aftermath of the Highland famine. In the other counties the highest proportions of total losses were generally not later than the decade 1881–91. Scotland had become a mature industrial economy and the reorganisation of the distribution of the population through migration was slowing down well before the First World War.

Population mobility in Scotland varied according to the demographic, economic and spatial characteristics of the county-of-birth. These features appeared to influence the native's decision whether to migrate or emigrate, but the type of movement was also gender specific, males being more likely to emigrate and females to migrate. Moreover, although both males and females migrated at approximately the same ages, peak adult female emigration was markedly older than male. Population movement is often considered to be concentrated in the young adult age-bands and indeed these age-bands did contain the highest proportions, but the majority of current migrants and a sizeable proportion of emigrants were considerably younger. The estimations can only identify the first move, and in the most prosperous counties children under 5 years provided the highest volume of migrants by age-band, and child migration was markedly higher than Baines found in England and Wales. Child emigrants were less important than migrants but still significant. Both migration and emigration were estimated net of returns and both forms of mobility involved a considerable proportion of return movement. This made mobility appear to end at 29 years, and disguised the movement of older people. Furthermore, it is thought that secondary migration was very common, although it cannot be measured by this study. Young children cannot migrate alone, and the fact that there were far less migrants in their parents' age-bands suggests that either it was not the parents' first move or that they were immigrants.

It has already been argued that the economic characteristics of the county-of-birth were significant, but the international economic cycles were also very important in that they influenced the volume of emigration from Scotland. Emigration therefore appeared in decades of peaks and troughs. Nationally migration appeared to have an inverse relationship with emigration, which was more marked amongst males than females. Thomas has attributed this inverse relationship to the movement of the rural-born population, but in Scotland, where the majority of migration was inter-urban, this hypothesis had only very limited applicability. Moreover, Scots emigration into England and Wales increased in decades of low overseas emigration providing an alternative to internal migration.

The proportion of Scots migrating was probably not as high as in England and Wales, although secondary migration might have been greater as the initial age of first migration was much younger and economic development was mainly confined to a broad band of adjacent and easily accessible counties. The lack of adequate comparative data outside the study period makes it is impossible to be certain which decade experienced the greatest proportion of migrants, but it was probably between 1851–61. The age of migrants did not change markedly over time, even when compared with post-1945 studies. This is probably because the major changes always tend to affect people at the same stages in their lives. However, whereas in this study female migrants exceeded males in volume, more recent mid-twentieth century research found the sex ratio to be unity.[42]

Scottish emigration was predominantly from urban and industrialised counties. Indeed Scotland appears to have a more urban bias to emigration losses than England and Wales.[43] Not only did the majority of the Scottish population live in urbanising counties, but overseas emigration from these counties was disproportionately high. Emigrants came mainly from the Central Lowlands, a high wage region which attracted considerable immigration as well as in-migration. The explanation for this mainly urban overseas emigration is not immediately obvious although it is argued that emigrants were not fleeing from problems within Scotland. Instead, it is more likely that emigrants with appropriate skills and experience of a technically advanced urban and industrial environment considered that they could benefit from emigrating, perhaps perceiving that the opportunities for further advancement at home were severely curtailed.

It may be that emigration was less attractive to the rural population because the enlargement of farms in Scotland had not only restricted the access to land, but also reduced the opportunities for acquiring the capital to buy land abroad. It was only in the northeast that farmers with sufficient capital to emigrate were still being evicted.[44] The agricultural labourer was therefore less likely to be able to benefit from emigration, except in the Border counties where movement into England was easy. Elsewhere rural-urban migration offered advantages without the expense of emigration.

The three countries experiencing greatest losses through emigration were Ireland and Norway, which were overwhelmingly rural countries, and Scotland whose population losses through emigration were unique in that they were from a mature, highly industrialised, urbanised country, one moreover that was still in its economic heyday. These largely urban emigrants had benefited from improving standards of living, and their out-movement was not a response to destitution but rather a reflection of economic choice.

In the period 1861–1911 the proportion of Scottish emigrants was generally very high by international measures, exceeded by only Ireland in terms of trans-Atlantic emigration, but this study also classified migration to England and Wales as emigration, inflating the volume of out-movement still further. Nevertheless, this period did not achieve the highest proportions of emigrants from Scotland. The seventeenth century may well have experienced greater losses and in the mid-nineteenth century the period during and immediately after the Highland famine, losses were also very high, and inflated still further by military casualties in the Crimean War. In the twentieth century emigration exceeded natural increase in the decades 1921–31 and 1971–81, although the proportions lost may not have been as great as earlier. What is being argued is that without ever ranking as the leading exporter of population in a specified time span, Scotland achieved centuries of exceptionally high emigration and in this feat alone she may well be unique. Whether this out-movement is just a reflection of a country unable to sustain its population growth or whether it represents the aspirations of a people born in a country of limited resources and determined to take advantage of any opportunity regardless of location, is an interesting topic for speculation. Nevertheless, overall it is justifiable to describe the Scots as an exceptionally mobile people.

Notes

1. Thomas. *Migration and Economic Growth.*
2. Baines. *Migration in a Mature Economy.* pp. 213–78.
3. It has been argued by Baines that this decade experienced high return emigration in England and Wales. This may also have been true in Scotland.
4. The proportion of males leaving fluctuated, but if the three decades of greatest loss are considered (1861–71, 1881–91 and 1901–11), the proportion lost decreases over time (Table 6.1).
5. In 1840–2 Levitt and Smout found high emigration and relatively low migration except on the fringes of the Highlands such as Southern Argyll. Levitt and Smout. *The State of the Scottish Working Class.* pp. 237–40.
6. Flinn appears to consider all Highland out-movement after 1846 emigration. Flinn, *Scottish Population History.* p. 438.
7. In the decades 1871–91, female out-movement was slightly greater than male, the only population category in which this occurred.
8. See Appendix 4.
9. The age of emigrants in England and Wales is not known and so it is impossible to estimate when they might have arrived. Moreover, people who went south may have emigrated overseas subsequently, and this cannot be measured.
10. The 'Periphery and Northeast' population category experienced proportions of current migration that were well above the national average, whereas emigration was generally below.
11. In the 'Central Lowlands' category the majority of out-migrants were children, so if their parents were indulging in secondary migration, this would become apparent in an increased level of mobility amongst children in this decade. There was no evidence of increased child out-migration, which suggests that their parents were not moving. However, there may have been secondary movement amongst young adults and this cannot be identified. See Appendix 8.
12. It has already been argued that emigration from the 'Borders' included an element of purely local movement.
13. Table 4.1 recalculated.

14. Counties with more than 15% of the population employed in agriculture in 1881 have been classified as rural. The rural counties in the 'Periphery and Northeast' category were Aberdeen, Banff, Elgin (Moray) and Kincardine in the northeast and also Bute, Haddington (East Lothian) and Peebles. Erickson. 'Who were'. Appendix B, Table 11, p. 377.

15. Erickson, 'Who were'. Appendix B, Table 11, p. 377.

16. Baines, *Migration in a Mature Economy.* p. 279.

17. A Scot emigrating to England and then moving abroad could not be identified in the present study, because the movement was outside Scotland. The estimates of Scottish movement into England are those of Baines and as his estimations are also net of returns, which means that a person leaving cancels out a new arrival.

18. See Appendices 9 and 13.

19. The formula used was (emigrants plus current migrants) over (native population). The native population refers to the native population plus emigrants, that is the total native population if nobody had emigrated.

20. Lawton found that in Scotland the central area had the most youthful population, a product of high in-migration. 'The highest younger working-age populations were still in urban/industrial counties: central Scotland, Aberdeen and Forfar' in 1911. Lawton, 'Population' p. 16.

21. Anderson. and Morse, 'The People'. p. 22.

22. The estimates of losses in the present study (Table 6.1) are higher than some of those calculated by Anderson and Morse. This is because the present study is measuring all population loss, including that of adult emigrants who left their county-of-birth as child migrants.

23. See Appendix 14. It should be noted that these estimates are net of returns. The pattern for Irish immigrants suggests that there are least arrivals in decades of high Scottish emigration. This may mean that more Irish are emigrating overseas rather than coming to Scotland. Alternatively the Irish resident in Scotland may be re-emigrating later in decades of high out-movement, thus cancelling out new arrivals because the calculations are net. In 1901–11 Irish immigration was markedly lower than previously and female immigrants exceeded males.

24. See Appendix 14, and Table 4.1.

25. Treble, The Occupied Male Labour Force', p170.

26. Only counties-of-birth where both male and female proportions in the mobile population were above or below the national average were considered. In the decade 1901–11 a quarter of the counties were omitted because the two sexes did not reveal common trends.

27. The estimates of emigration do not assume that emigrants have just left their county-of-birth.

28. The Highland counties with below average total mobility were Caithness, Inverness, Orkney, Ross and Cromarty, Shetland and Sutherland.

29. See Brock, 'Scottish Migration' vol II, Appendix XXXI, pp. 311, 313 and 325.

30. High proportions of current migrants were most likely in the smaller counties, because although the size of the county did not influence the decision to move, a greater amount of movement could be measured.

31. If the proportions from total population loss from Fife are averaged (see Table 6.2) the proportions for 1861–1911 are 10.45% and 8.48% for males and females respectively.

32. If the proportions from total population loss from Lanark and Renfrew are averaged (see Table 6.2), the proportions for 1861–1911 are 11.03% and 9.08% for males and females respectively.

33. See Appendix 5.

34. Baines, *Migration in a Mature Economy*. p. 279.

35. It should be noted that although the largest proportional increase in migration in a low emigration decade (1891–1901) was from the 'Periphery and Northeast' category, some additional movement also came from rural counties in the 'Highlands'.

36. Hunt, 'Wages' p. 64.

37. For example the sudden increase in mobility in 1871–81 from Kirkcudbright, both emigration and current migration. See Appendix 5.

38. Baines, *Migration in a Mature Economy*. p. 282.

39. The rural counties were those with more than 15% of the population employed in agriculture in 1881. The only ones that did not have declining populations were counties in the northeast (Aberdeen, Banff, Elgin (Moray), Kincardine and Nairn) and also Bute, Haddington (East Lothian) and Peebles. Erickson. 'Who Were'. Table 11, p. 377.

40. Counties with 15% or less of the population employed in agriculture in 1881 have been defined as urban. These include: Ayr, Clackmannan, Dunbarton, Edinburgh (Midlothian), Fife, Forfar (Angus), Lanark, Linlithgow (West Lothian), Renfrew, Selkirk and Stirling. Erickson. 'Who Were'. Table 11, p. 377.

41. The counties fringing the Central Lowlands were Ayr, Bute, Clackmannan, Forfar (Angus), Haddington (East Lothian) and Peebles.

42. Hollingsworth, *Migration. A study* p. 101

43. Baines, *Migration in a Mature Economy*. 279.

44. Harper, *Emigration from North-East. Vol. I,* 156–90.

Appendix 1

Using SPSS-X to Estimate Scottish Population Movement 1861–1911[1]

This Appendix will discuss the computer methods used in this research.[2] There will therefore some repetition of discussion found elsewhere in the book, but here it will be presented from the perspective of the programming problems that were involved. This appendix divides into two parts. The first two sections (1A and 1B) will consider how the expanded data base was created: the remaining sections (1C–1E) how the files inter-relate and how they were checked for errors. Appendix 1A will discuss the problems involved in checking, cleaning and standardising the data. An example will be used to show how the data sets were linked and processed in order to create a more detailed data base and includes an illustration of how the files were linked and (1B) the actual SPSS-X programming involved. Appendix 1C indicates by diagram and key how the files linked together in order to estimate emigration between two censuses and (1D) analyses the points in the computer programme where the processed data was checked against the original material. This emphasises how insignificant the errors were that crept in. Finally, (1E) considers how standard errors were computed and applied.

APPENDIX 1A: USING SPSS-X TO ESTIMATE SCOTTISH POPULATION MOVEMENT

Inevitably the creation of the computer model involved many programmes, and space alone prevents all of these from being discussed here. It is therefore proposed to consider the creation of the data sets because many of the concepts used in their programming were used thereafter in the computation of data. The discussion will therefore concentrate on the method whereby data sets were created in order to estimate the volume and the age-structure of emigration from Scotland by county-of-birth. The printed census tabulation was inadequate because it provided only two age-bands for migrants, which was unsatisfactory for estimating an age-structure and it was therefore necessary to incorporate several data sets into the study. These data sets consisted of the published county-of-birth by county-of-residence and age-structure tabulations in the census[3] and the published annual report tables of births and deaths.[4] The final data set was created from a manuscript source, which enhanced the census information and provided a migrant age-structure. We will now consider problems inherent in the original data and data cleaning. The processing of data using the cross-linking facilities of SPSS-X[5] will be considered, using as an example the creation of the 1861 data set, and finally the advantages of using SPSS-X will be explored.

Problems Inherent in the Scottish Material

The Scottish published data contained several incompatibilities; measurement was on differing county frameworks before and after 1891 and the detailed information provided varied over time. Moreover, in 1891 there was a major county boundary reorganisation, which together with the differing county units, created spurious migration, that is the movement of boundaries rather than people. Finally, all the Scottish census data before 1891 contained an additional serious difficulty, in that they were tabulated on the recently-devised Registration county framework, but people still recorded their county-of-birth in the traditional Civil Counties. This created another source of spurious migration which was overcome by manually converting the county-of-birth tabulation to a Civil county framework before entering it on to the computer. This meant that all subsequent mathematical calculations using the other published data sets, which were also organised by Registration counties, had to be either adjusted in advance to the Civil County, or a conversion formula applied when needed.

Standardisation and Checking of Data

The first priority of this research was therefore to correct and standardise counties on all the data sets. It proved impossible to standardise all the county-of-residence by county-of-birth tabulations to the civil county unit of measurement in any year. To resolve this problem two 1891 county-of-residence tabulations were created, one before and the other after boundary reorganisation. All data was standardised to these two 1891 censuses. This meant that there were therefore seven rather than six county-of-residence tabulations. It has been assumed that the age-structure and vital data remain the same when adjustments are made for differing county populations. All the data for each county at every census year were typed into the computer. The codes were standardised for counties so that all units such as counties could be used later for key variable matching and revising. The year was given an additional code to indicate whether it referred to the pre- or post-county boundary revision set of records.

Data Cleaning

In order to aid data cleaning, all totals were recorded from the original data, although they were not needed for the final analysis. This enabled the computer to check the data for any year by comparing these original totals with those derived from the data cross-tabulation facilities of SPSS-X through sort cases and compute or aggregate commands either across age groups or counties. Several errors in the published material were quickly identified, and later this method of checking was used when cleaning the data to check for discrepancies and again after processing to check that the total population had not been altered. The county-of-residence by county-of-birth tabulation was also checked for enumeration errors. The percentage of natives and the most significant migrant populations in any county were compared between census years to see if there were marked percentage fluctuations from the normal trend, as this could indicate an Enumeration Error.[6] Although such errors have been found in the English census,[7] none were found in Scotland. The final stage was to standardise the age-structure based upon sixteen age-bands to ensure compatibility with the published mortality data. The age-structure of the population tabulations varied in the age-band information provided. This meant that each census year had to be standardised separately, and an additional pre-boundary revision tabulation created, before the files could be combined. All the published material provided more detailed information than was required. Since the primary interest was in Scottish population movement, the categories of birthplace outside Scotland were reduced. The number of age-bands in the age-structure tabulations were also reduced to sixteen, consisting of 15 five year-bands and over 75 years. Children under 5 years were divided into five age-bands. The annual reports of deaths were combined into 5 year aggregate totals, except for children less than five years for whom annual mortality information was retained. The categories of age at death were also reduced to 16 age-bands, and in addition deaths for the under five year olds were reduced to five age-bands. These data sets have all been deposited in the ESRC archive at Essex University.

The prime aim was to establish a migrant age-structure, and as this was not provided in the published material, it was necessary to sample a manuscript source. In all 78 settlements were sampled from the 1891 Census Enumeration Books, which represented 4.6% of the total Scottish migrant population. A further sample of 50 settlements was taken in 1861

(3.2% of the migrant population), this being partly a selective sample of the 1891 sample. The two sets of samples showed that there were some changes in the age-structure of the migrant population, so the same migrant age-structure could not be used throughout the period for estimating migration. Moreover, four distinct categories of migrant age-structure emerged depending on whether the population in the county-of-residence was experiencing rapid growth, average growth or decline, the last being distinguishable between northern and southern counties. To determine whether the samples were an accurate representation of the categories of migrant populations, the ages of the sample migrants were aggregated by sex and category into two age-bands (above and below 20 years) to check against the printed census. The proportion in each category in each year was within 1.0% of the national migrant average calculated for each category from the corresponding census. An age-structure in sixteen bands and for both sexes was computed for the four categories of county of residence in the years 1861 to 1891. These were projected on to 1901 and 1911 using the cross-linking facilities of SPSS-X such as input programme, LAG and table-match files. These manuscript samples have provided an age-structure in sixteen age-bands for the migrant population and have been used to enhance the original printed census, in order to create a data set in sixteen age bands for all populations in the county-of-residence.

The Processing of Data

The preceding discussion on data preparation should provide some indication of the volume of data. This has led to a need for access to larger amounts of data than are normally available to an on-line user. The problem has been resolved by removing into system files the relevant material from the large data sets and matching files using key variables. This operation is perhaps best described in an example. The published 1861 county-of-residence by county-of-birth tabulation needed to be expanded from two to sixteen age-bands for each sex. The expansion of the material involved three large data sets, the county-of-residence by county-of-birth tabulation (B), the age-structure of the population by county (C) and the much smaller national migrant age-structure estimated from the migrant samples (A). Figure A1.1 illustrates how the files link together and Appendix 1c provides a listing of the programme.[8] The three large data-sets are indicated alphabetically on the tables and in the text, as also is the outfile (D).

The 1861 county-of-residence by county-of-birth tabulation was selected from the data set and saved on a new system file (B). It was sorted on a county-of-residence framework. The migrant population was then selected from every county, sorted so that the counties were separated into

Figure A1.1 — Expanding the 1861 County-of-Residence by County-of-Birth Tabulation from 2 to 16 Age-Bands.

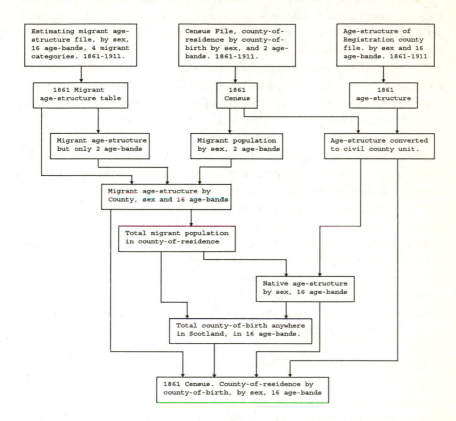

boom, average and declining (north and south) and again this file was saved. The four 1861 estimated migrant age-structure categories were selected, added together and saved (A). A second version was then aggregated into two age-bands (above and below 20 years) for each sex, matched as a table with the previous file and also with the migrant population file. By matching the four migrant age-structures to the appropriate counties, it was possible to compute an age-structure for every migrant population in each county. This file was saved and a second was created which aggregated the migrant age-structure in every county. The 1861 age-structure of every county was then selected from the data-set file (C), converted to the Civil County unit using the total county population from the original county-of-residence tabulation and saved. This file contained the age-structure of the total population of every county, and by deducting the total migrant population, a native county population was constructed.

By creating these system files, it was now possible to provide three of the four sets of information required for each sex and, in sixteen age-bands, a native, migrant and total population for every county. The native and migrant files were added and the cases sorted by county-of-birth, rather than as previously by county-of-residence. This enabled the total county-of-birth population to be computed and provided the final file (D) required from the 1861 census so that the cases could be sorted and added. The data were then aggregated and this enabled checks to be made with the original census.

Normally, analysis of large data sets on a mainframe computer can only be carried out overnight. However, in this study, despite the large data sets, material could be processed whenever convenient. This was achieved by making considerable use of the complex file features of SPSS-X. The cross-linking procedures described have created multiple save files, but the on-line computing time was kept to a minimum.

APPENDIX 1B: THE CREATION OF THE REVISED
1861 CENSUS FROM 2 TO 16 AGE-BANDS

Key

`*** and italic text`	A programme comment. Not a fuctional part of programme, but a note explaining what the programme is doing.

Variable Names	*Details*
YR	Year of census.
Census	County-of-residence by county-of-birth tabulation (2 age-bands for each sex), unit of measurement civil county.
Age-structure	Age-structure of county-of-residence, all tabulations standardised to 16 age-bands, unit of measurement registration county.
COUNTY	County-of-residence (county code nos. same as used in census).
FROM	County-of-birth (county code nos. same as used in census).
COUNTY or FROM	Renfrew and Lanark Counties which because of boundary 21, 23 problems were combined as 'COUNTY 41' or 'FROM 41'.
FROM 34-38	People born outside Scotland.
FROM 39	Total population in county-of-residence.
FROM 40	Total population in county-of-birth.

```
         *** TO ACCESS 1861 CENSUS FILES.
GET FILE='DISK08:[XYZ111.CENSUS]CENSUSHALFY.SAV'/MAP
         *** entire census 1861-1911
SELECT IF YR=18611
         *** Last number refers to whether the data were standardised to the
                 pre- or post 1891 boundary revision.
LIST CASES=50
SAVE OUTFILE=CEN61.SAV
/KEEP=YR, COUNTY, FROM, M19L, M20M, F19L, F20M/MAP
         ***1861 census saved.

         *** TO ACCESS 1861 ESTIMATED AGE-STRUCTURES FILES.
                 (3 age-structures according to the nature of population
                       growth in a county).
GET FILE='DISK08:[XYZ111.SAMPLES]TAGGSAMTOTAL.SAV'/MAP
SELECT IF YR=1861
LIST CASES=10
RECODE YR (1861=18611)
COMPUTE MTOT19L=SUM.4(ADML5 TO ADML20)
COMPUTE MTOT20M=SUM.12(ADML25 TO ADMG75)
COMPUTE FTOT19L=SUM.4(ADFL5 TO ADFL20)
COMPUTE FTOT20M=SUM.12(ADFL25 TO ADFG75)
         *** Additional age-bands created to make data compatible with
                 census.
LIST
SAVE OUTFILE=TAGGTOT.SAV
/KEEP=TYPE TO FTOT20M/MAP
         *** estimated migrant age-structure saved.

         ***TO REMOVE NATIVE-BORN FROM THE COUNTY-OF-RESIDENCE AND
                 REORGANISE 1861 CENSUS BY COUNTY INTO MIGRANT AGE-STRUCTURE
CATEGORIES.
GET FILE=CEN61.SAV/MAP
SELECT IF COUNTY NE FROM
         *** removal of native-born.
LIST CASES=10
SELECT IF NOT (ANY (FROM, 39, 40))
         *** removal of population totals.
LIST CASES=10
RECODE COUNTY(1, 2, 3, 4, 5, 6, 13, 15, 19=1
(27, 30, 31, 32, 33=2)
(7, 8, 9, 10, 11, 12, 16, 20, 22, 26, 28=3)
(14, 17, 18, 24, 25, 29, 41=4)INTO MCT
         ***counties recoded into migrant age-structure categories.
SORT CASES BY MCT YR COUNTY FROM
         *** counties 'SORTED' according to migrant age-structure
categories.
LIST CASES=50
         *** check.
         *** MIGRANT AGE-STRUCTURE CALCULATED
                 using 3 estimated migrant age-structures.
MATCH FILES FILE=*/TABLE=TAGGTOT.SAV/RENAME TYPE=MCT/BY MCT YR/MAP
COMPUTE MB5=ADML5*M19L/MTOT19L
COMPUTE MB10=ADML10*M19L/MTOT19L
COMPUTE MB15=ADML15*M19L/MTOT19L
COMPUTE MB20=ADML20*M19L/MTOT19L
COMPUTE MB25=ADML25*M20M/MTOT20M
COMPUTE MB30=ADML30*M20M/MTOT20M
COMPUTE MB35=ADML35*M20M/MTOT20M
COMPUTE MB40=ADML40*M20M/MTOT20M
COMPUTE MB45=ADML45*M20M/MTOT20M
COMPUTE MB50=ADML50*M20M/MTOT20M
COMPUTE MB55=ADML55*M20M/MTOT20M
COMPUTE MB60=ADML60*M20M/MTOT20M
COMPUTE MB65=ADML65*M20M/MTOT20M
COMPUTE MB70=ADML70*M20M/MTOT20M
COMPUTE MB75=ADML75*M20M/MTOT20M
```

```
COMPUTE MO75=ADMG75*M20M/MTOT20M
COMPUTE FB5=ADFL5*F19L/FTOT19L
COMPUTE FB10=ADFL10*F19L/FTOT19L
COMPUTE FB15=ADFL15*F19L/FTOT19L
COMPUTE FB20=ADFL20*F19L/FTOT19L
COMPUTE FB25=ADFL25*F20M/FTOT20M
COMPUTE FB30=ADFL30*F20M/FTOT20M
COMPUTE FB35=ADFL35*F20M/FTOT20M
COMPUTE FB40=ADFL40*F20M/FTOT20M
COMPUTE FB45=ADFL45*F20M/FTOT20M
COMPUTE FB50=ADFL50*F20M/FTOT20M
COMPUTE FB55=ADFL55*F20M/FTOT20M
COMPUTE FB60=ADFL60*F20M/FTOT20M
COMPUTE FB65=ADFL65*F20M/FTOT20M
COMPUTE FB70=ADFL70*F20M/FTOT20M
COMPUTE FB75=ADFL75*F20M/FTOT20M
COMPUTE FO75=ADFG75*F20M/FTOT20M
LIST CASES=10
SORT CASES BY YR COUNTY FROM
        *** Counties 'SORTED' into 'normal' numeric order.
LIST CASES FROM 900 TO 980
        *** these cases include the counties of Berwick, Peebles, Selkirk
                and Roxburgh, used as check because three of four categories
                of migrant age-structure were found in these counties.
SAVE OUTFILE=CENA61.SAV
/KEEP=YR, COUNTY, FROM, MB5, MB10, MB15, MB20, MB25, MB30, MB35, MB40,
MB45, MB50, MB55, MB60, MB65, MB70, MB75, MO75, FB5, FB10, FB15, FB20,
FB25, FB30, FB35, FB40, FB45, FB50, FB55, FB60, FB65, FB70, FB75, FO75/MAP
        *** Migrant age-structure saved.

        *** TO CREATE TOTAL MIGRANT AGE-STRUCTURE FOR COUNTY-OF-RESIDENCE.
GET FILE=CENA61.SAV
        *** migrant age-structure
SELECT IF NOT (ANY (FROM, 21, 23, 39, 40))
        ***precaution these not wanted.
list cases=10
AGGREGATE OUTFILE=*
/PRESORTED
/BREAK YR, COUNTY
/MGL5, MGL10, MGL15, MGL20, MGL25, MGL30, MGL35, MGL40, MGL45, MGL50,
MGL55, MGL60, MGL65, MGL70, MGL75, MGO75, FGL5, FGL10, FGL15, FGL20,
FGL25, FGL30, FGL35, FGL40, FGL45, FGL50, FGL55, FGL60, FGL65, FGL70,
FGL75, FGO75=SUM(MB5 TO FO75)
        *** aggregate the total migrant population in county-of-residence
                by age-bands.
LIST CASES=10
SAVE OUTFILE=MIG61.SAV
/KEEP=YR, COUNTY, MGL5, MGL10, MGL15, MGL20, MGL25, MGL30, MGL35, MGL40,
MGL45, MGL50, MGL55, MGL60, MGL65, MGL70, MGL75, MGO75, FGL5, FGL10,
FGL15, FGL20, FGL25, FGL30, FGL35, FGL40, FGL45, FGL50, FGL55, FGL60,
FGL65, FGL70, FGL75, FGO75/MAP
        *** the total migrant population in county-of-residence by age-
                bands saved.

        *** ACCESSING THE 1861 AGE-STRUCTURE OF THE TOTAL POPULATION OF
                COUNTY-OF-RESIDENCE TABULATION FILE AND CONVERTING THE DATA
                FROM A REGISTRATION TO A CIVIL COUNTY UNIT OF MEASUREMENT.
GET FILE='DISK08:[XYZ111.AGESTR]AGESTRHALFC.SAV'/MAP
SELECT IF YR=18611
        *** removing 1861 information from data-base.
LIST CASES=10
SORT CASES YR COUNTY
LIST CASES=10
SAVE OUTFILE=AGESTRTOT61X.SAV
/KEEP=YR, COUNTY, MTOT, ML5, ML10, ML15, ML20, ML25, ML30, ML35, ML40,
ML45, ML50, ML55, ML60, ML65, ML70, ML75, MG75, FTOT, FL5, FL10, FL15,
FL20, FL25, FL30, FL35, FL40, FL45, FL50, FL55, FL60, FL65, FL70, FL75,
```

```
FG75/MAP
       ***1861 total age-structure file saved.

      *** ADJUSTING REGISTRATION COUNTY BASED AGE-STRUCTURE OF THE
            POPULATION (1861) TO THE CIVIL COUNTY UNIT OF MEASUREMENT.
GET FILE=CEN61.SAV/MAP
       *** 1861 census in civil county framework.
SELECT IF FROM=39
       *** total population.
LIST CASES=10
SORT CASES BY YR COUNTY
LIST CASES=10
MATCH FILES FILE=AGESTRTOT61X.SAV/FILE=*/BY YR COUNTY/MAP
       *** match files 1861 age-structure with census.
LIST CASES =10
COMPUTE M19LTOT=SUM.4(ML5 TO ML20)
COMPUTE M20MTOT=SUM.12(ML25 TO MG75)
COMPUTE F19LTOT=SUM.4(FL5 TO FL20)
COMPUTE F20MTOT=SUM.12(FL25 TO FG75)
COMPUTE MAB5=ML5*M19L/M19LTOT
COMPUTE MAB10=ML10*M19L/M19LTOT
COMPUTE MAB15=ML15*M19L/M19LTOT
COMPUTE MAB20=ML20*M19L/M19LTOT
COMPUTE MAB25=ML25*M20M/M20MTOT
COMPUTE MAB30=ML30*M20M/M20MTOT
COMPUTE MAB35=ML35*M20M/M20MTOT
COMPUTE MAB40=ML40*M20M/M20MTOT
COMPUTE MAB45=ML45*M20M/M20MTOT
COMPUTE MAB50=ML50*M20M/M20MTOT
COMPUTE MAB55=ML55*M20M/M20MTOT
COMPUTE MAB60=ML60*M20M/M20MTOT
COMPUTE MAB65=ML65*M20M/M20MTOT
COMPUTE MAB70=ML70*M20M/M20MTOT
COMPUTE MAB75=ML75*M20M/M20MTOT
COMPUTE MAO75=MG75*M20M/M20MTOT
COMPUTE FEB5=FL5*F19L/F19LTOT
COMPUTE FEB10=FL10*F19L/F19LTOT
COMPUTE FEB15=FL15*F19L/F19LTOT
COMPUTE FEB20=FL20*F19L/F19LTOT
COMPUTE FEB25=FL25*F20M/F20MTOT
COMPUTE FEB30=FL30*F20M/F20MTOT
COMPUTE FEB35=FL35*F20M/F20MTOT
COMPUTE FEB40=FL40*F20M/F20MTOT
COMPUTE FEB45=FL45*F20M/F20MTOT
COMPUTE FEB50=FL50*F20M/F20MTOT
COMPUTE FEB55=FL55*F20M/F20MTOT
COMPUTE FEB60=FL60*F20M/F20MTOT
COMPUTE FEB65=FL65*F20M/F20MTOT
COMPUTE FEB70=FL70*F20M/F20MTOT
COMPUTE FEB75=FL75*F20M/F20MTOT
COMPUTE FEO75=FG75*F20M/F20MTOT
LIST VARIABLES=YR COUNTY FROM M19LTOT M20MTOT MTOT MAB5 MAB10 MAB15 MAB20
MAB25 MAB30 MAB35 MAB40 MAB45 MAB50 MAB55 MAB60 MAB65 MAB70 MAB75 MAO75
F19LTOT F20MTOT FTOT FEB5 FEB10 FEB15 FEB20 FEB25 FEB30 FEB35 FEB40 FEB45
FEB50 FEB55 FEB60 FEB65 FEB70 FEB75 FEO75
SAVE OUTFILE=CENAGE61TOT.SAV
/KEEP=YR, COUNTY, FROM, MAB5, MAB10, MAB15, MAB20, MAB25, MAB30, MAB35,
MAB40, MAB45, MAB50, MAB55, MAB60, MAB65, MAB70, MAB75, MAO75, FEB5,
FEB10, FEB15, FEB20, FEB25, FEB30, FEB35, FEB40, FEB45, FEB50, FEB55,
FEB60, FEB65, FEB70, FEB75, FEO75/MAP
       *** 1861 total age-structure by county-of-residence in civil county
            framework saved.

      *** TO CREATE NATIVE AGE-STRUCTURE.
MATCH FILES FILE=CENAGE61TOT.SAV/FILE=MIG61.SAV/BY YR COUNTY/MAP
       *** match 1861 total age-structure by county-of-residence and
            migrant age-structure (both in civil county frameworks)
```

```
COMPUTE FROM=COUNTY
        *** in CENAGE61TOT.SAV 'FROM' equalled the total population, now
             equals county-of-residence.
LIST CASES=10
DO REPEAT AA1=MAB5 TO MAO75
/BB1=MGL5 TO MGO75
/CC1=MB5, MB10, MB15, MB20, MB25, MB30, MB35, MB40, MB45, MB50, MB55,
MB60, MB65, MB70, MB75, MO75
COMPUTE CC1=AA1-BB1
END REPEAT
DO REPEAT DD1=FEB5 TO FEO75
/EE1=FGL5 TO FGO75
/FF1=FB5, FB10, FB15, FB20, FB25, FB30, FB35, FB40, FB45, FB50, FB55,
FB60, FB65, FB70, FB75, FO75
COMPUTE FF1=DD1-EE1
END REPEAT
        *** for every age-band, total age-structure of county-of-residence
             minus total migrant age-structure equals native age-
             structure.
LIST VARIABLES=YR COUNTY FROM MB5 MB10 MB15 MB20 MB25 MB30 MB35 MB40
MB45 MB50 MB55 MB60 MB65 MB70 MB75 MO75 FB5 FB10 FB15 FB20 FB25 FB30 FB35
FB40 FB45 FB50 FB55 FB60 FB65 FB70 FB75 FO75
SAVE OUTFILE=CENAGE61N.SAV
/KEEP=YR, COUNTY, FROM, MB5, MB10, MB15, MB20, MB25, MB30, MB35, MB40,
MB45, MB50, MB55, MB60, MB65, MB70, MB75, MO75, FB5, FB10, FB15, FB20,
FB25, FB30, FB35, FB40, FB45, FB50, FB55, FB60, FB65, FB70, FB75, FO75/MAP
        *** native age-structure saved.

        *** TO CALCULATE TOTAL POPULATION OF COUNTY-OF-RESIDENCE IN 16 AGE-
             BANDS.
ADD FILES FILE=CENA61.SAV/FILE=CENAGE61N.SAV/MAP
        *** 'ADD' Migrant and native age-structure files.
SORT CASES BY YR FROM COUNTY
        *** 'SORT' cases on county-of-birth not county-of-residence.
SELECT IF NOT (ANY (FROM, 21, 23))
        *** precaution.
LIST CASES=10
SELECT IF NOT (ANY (COUNTY, 21, 23))
        *** precaution.
LIST CASES=10
        *** check.
AGGREGATE OUTFILE=*
/PRESORTED
/BREAK YR, FROM
/MAB5, MAB10, MAB15, MAB20, MAB25, MAB30, MAB35, MAB40, MAB45, MAB50,
MAB55, MAB60, MAB65, MAB70, MAB75, MAO75, FEB5, FEB10, FEB15, FEB20,
FEB25, FEB30, FEB35, FEB40, FEB45, FEB50, FEB55, FEB60, FEB65, FEB70,
FEB75, FEO75=SUM(MB5 TO FO75)
        *** 'AGGREGATE' total county-of-birth population anywhere in
             Scotland by age-bands.
LIST CASES=10
        *** check.
COMPUTE COUNTY=FROM
        *** county code lost in 'AGGREGATE' process.
LIST CASES=10
        *** check.
COMPUTE FROM=40
        *** code for total county-of-birth population anywhere in Scotland
             by age-bands.
SORT CASES BY YR COUNTY FROM
        *** 'SORT' cases back into county-of-residence.
SELECT IF NOT (ANY (COUNTY, 34, 35, 36, 37, 38))
LIST VARIABLES=YR COUNTY FROM MAB5 MAB10 MAB15 MAB20 MAB25 MAB30 MAB35
MAB40 MAB45 MAB50 MAB55 MAB60 MAB65 MAB70 MAB75 MAO75 FEB5 FEB10 FEB15
FEB20 FEB25 FEB30 FEB35 FEB40 FEB45 FEB50 FEB55 FEB60 FEB65 FEB70 FEB75
FEO75
SAVE OUTFILE=FROM61.SAV
```

```
/KEEP=YR, COUNTY, FROM, MAB5, MAB10, MAB15, MAB20, MAB25, MAB30, MAB35,
MAB40, MAB45, MAB50, MAB55, MAB60, MAB65, MAB70, MAB75, MAO75, FEB5,
FEB10, FEB15, FEB20, FEB25, FEB30, FEB35, FEB40, FEB45, FEB50, FEB55,
FEB60, FEB65, FEB70, FEB75, FEO75/MAP
        *** total county-of-birth population anywhere in Scotland by age-
            bands saved.

        *** TO COMBINE ALL FILES
                (all files have already been sorted to year and county-of-
                residence, but they do not have common names for age
                variables).
ADD FILES FILE=CENA61.SAV
        *** migrant age-structure.
/FILE=CENAGE61N.SAV
        *** native age-structure.
/FILE=CENAGE61TOT.SAV/RENAME=(MAB5=MB5)
        *** age-structure in civil county units, this is also the total
                population in 16 age-bands of county-of-residence.
/RENAME=(MAB10=MB10)
/RENAME=(MAB15=MB15)
.....
/RENAME=(FEB75=FB75)
/RENAME=(FEO75=FO75)
/FILE=FROM61.SAV/RENAME=(MAB5=MB5)
        *** total county-of-birth population anywhere in Scotland by age-
            bands.
/RENAME=(MAB10=MB10)
/RENAME=(MAB15=MB15)
......
/RENAME=(FEB75=FB75)
/RENAME=(FEO75=FO75)/MAP
SORT CASES BY YR COUNTY FROM
        *** reorganise cases by year county-of-residence and county-of-
            birth.
LIST VARIABLES=YR COUNTY FROM MB5 MB10 MB15 MB20 MB25 MB30 MB35 MB40 MB45
MB50 MB55 MB60 MB65 MB70 MB75 MO75 FB5 FB10 FB15 FB20 FB25 FB30 FB35 FB40
FB45 FB50 FB55 FB60 FB65 FB70 FB75 FO75
SAVE OUTFILE=CENSUSAGEC61.SAV
KEEP=YR, COUNTY, FROM, MB5, MB10, MB15, MB20, MB25, MB30, MB35, MB40,
MB45, MB50, MB55, MB60, MB65, MB70, MB75, MO75, FB5, FB10, FB15, FB20,
FB25, FB30, FB35, FB40, FB45, FB50, FB55, FB60, FB65, FB70, FB75, FO75/MAP
        *** file checked against original county-of-residence by county-of-
            birth tabulation from census, file now contains same
            information as original but in 16 age-bands instead of 2.
```

APPENDIX 1C: THE FILES USED TO ESTIMATE EMIGRANTS FROM SCOTLAND FROM ONE DECENNIAL CENSUS TO THE SUBSEQUENT ONE.

Key to Figure A1.2 on Page 249

For convenience this diagram applies to the decennial census period 1861–1871, but every estimation was computed in the same way.

1   subsequent census, data file (1871)

2–4   expanding the county-of-residence by county-of-birth tabulation from 2 to 16 age-bands.

5   original census, data file (1861)

6–8   expanding the county-of-residence by county-of-birth tabulation from 2 to 16 age-bands.

9   Creating file for those less than 5 years: needs special migrant age-structure and total age-structure. (1861)

10   Total migrant age-structures estimated from samples for every census year samples calculated for migrant categories.

11   Migrant age-structure estimated from samples in 5 year age-bands except for those over 75 years, computed for both census years, counties matched to migrant categories.

12   Migrant age-structure estimated from samples for those less than 5 years computed for census in question, and counties matched to migrant region. Re-applied to those under 5 years every year.

13   Total age-structure of the county, adjusted in order to standardise data and converted to civil counties, but taken from original censuses.

14   Total age-structure of county in 5 year age-bands except for those over 75 years, for both census years.

15   Total age-structure of county for those less than 5 years.

16   Total deaths by year in counties, those without age stated spread across age-bands. Data adjusted to civil counties and corrected from January-to-December to April-to-March year to make it compatible with census.

17   Deaths for those over 5 years organised by sex into 5 year age-bands and in 5 year time periods, so that two time periods occur between every census.

18   Deaths for those less than 5 years organised by sex into 6 age-bands (less than 3 months, 3 months to 1 year and by year thereafter up to, but not including, 5 years). The deaths retain a one year time period, so that ten time periods occur between every census.

19   Births by sex and county, which must by definition be native-born. Data recorded annually and adjusted to civil counties. It has been corrected from January-to-December to April-to-March year to make it compatible with census.

20–4   The data for children under 5 years computed annually. Births and deaths applied, and the assumed migrant age-structure. Children that reach 5 years aggregated as native or migrant of every county and entered into file 30.

25–9   The data for children under 5 years computed annually. Births and deaths applied, and the assumed migrant age-structure. Children that reach 5 years aggregated as native or migrant of every county and entered into file 31.

30   Data for those over five years old computed every 5 years. Deaths applied and also the assumed migrant age-structure.

31   Data for those over five years old computed every 5 years. Deaths applied and also the assumed migrant age-structure. Total estimated population (migrants and natives) created for next census by including information from file 29.

32   Estimated census (file 30) would be the projected census if everybody had stayed in Scotland. File 4 is the actual subsequent census, and the difference between the two is emigration.

33   The final checking file. The original census plus births plus immigrants created by the migrant age-structure categories (but immigrants unlike Scots cannot to be deducted from the native population) minus deaths minus emigrants should equal the subsequent census.

Figure A1.2 — The Linking of SPSS-X Files to Create an Estimated 1871 Census from the 1861 Census and to Compare it with the Actual 1871 Census in Order to Calculate Emigration

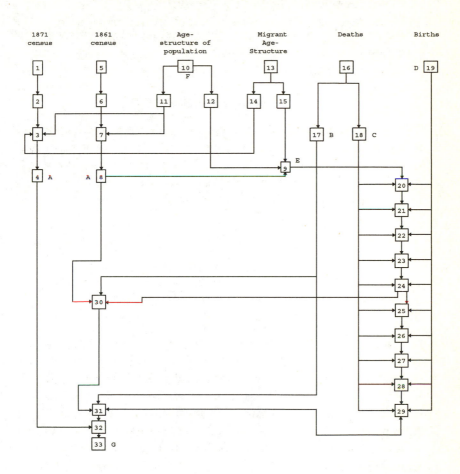

APPENDIX 1D: POINTS IN COMPUTATION WHERE DATA WAS CHECKED AGAINST ORIGINAL CENSUS

This section also refers to Figure A1.2, page 249.

a Census manually converted from civil to registration counties with the exception of Lanark and Renfrew which were combined (see Brock, 'Scottish Migration' Vol. II Appendix I, pp. 37–40 and 50–1 respectively). This was to avoid spurious migration. Census compared with original data file. 100% correct, that is total population the same.

b Deaths per 5 year age-band and in 5 year periods. 'age not known' spread across all age-bands at point (16) and checked. Data converted from registration to civil counties at point (17). Converted to April-to-March year; slight discrepancy to be expected as original measures 1861–1910 and computed measures April 1861 to March 1911 (January to March 1911 estimated, see Chapter 2).

	Male	Female
Total deaths from original data	1,168,759	1,284,420
Total deaths from computed data	1,170,059	1,285,765
% difference between original and computed data	+0.111	+0.105

c Deaths in 6 age-bands (less than 3 mths, greater than 3 mths and less than 1yr, less than 2 yrs, less than 3 yrs, less than 4 yrs and less than 5 yrs) and in 1 year periods. 'age not known' spread across all age-bands at point (16) and checked. Data converted from registration to civil counties at points (18). Converted to April-to-March year: slight discrepancy to be expected as original measures 1861–1910 and computed measures April 1861 to March 1911 (January to March 1911 estimated, see Brock, 'Scottish Migration and Emigration' Vol. II, Appendix III, pp. 68–9).

	Males	Females
Total deaths from original data	704,114	602,518
Total deaths from computed data	703,950	602,363
% difference between original and computed data	–0.023	–0.026

d Births in 1 year periods. Data converted from registration to civil counties at point (19). Converted to April-to-March year: slight discrepancy to be expected as original measures 1861–1910 and computed measures

April 1861 to March 1911 (January-to-March 1911 estimated. See Chapter 2 and Brock, 'Scottish Migration and Emigration' Vol. I, ch. IV, p. 153)

	Males	Females
Total births from original data	3,172,966	3,019,042
Total births from computed data	3,175,213	3,021,665
% difference between original and computed data	+0.071	+0.087

e Computed native and migrant age-structure for population under 5 years. Checked against under 5 population estimated at (8); 100% correct.

f Age-structure of the total population from census; 'age not known' spread across all age-bands. Data converted from registration to civil counties at points (2) and (6).

g The final check was made separately for every census run (see below). The original census plus births plus immigrants minus deaths minus emigrants equals the subsequent census.

Census Decade	Sex	Actual	Predicted	Percentage Difference
1861–71	Male	1,603,143	1,603,219	+0.005
	Female	1,756,875	1,757,490	+0.035
1871–81	Male	1,799,475	1,797,993	-0.082
	Female	1,936,098	1,934,167	-0.080
1881–91	Male	1,942,717	1,942,955	+0.012
	Female	2,082,930	2,084,065	+0.054
1891–1901	Male	2,173,755	2,172,725	-0.047
	Female	2,298,348	2,296,801	-0.067
1901–11	Male	2,308,839	2,308,949	+0.005
	Female	2,452,065	2,452,027	-0.002

APPENDIX 1E: THE ESTIMATION OF STANDARD ERRORS[9]

A measure of reliability of the estimates of both emigration and migration is of immense importance to the conclusions of this study. Thus in order to test the results thoroughly, the method of estimating standard errors[10] represent the 'worst case' scenario.

There were four published sources used in this study: the age-structure of the population, the birthplace enumeration and the annual numbers of births and deaths. The fifth source was the age-structure ratios of the migrant population by population category. This information had been created from two very large samples (4.3% of the total Scottish migrant population in 1891 and a further 3.1% from the 1861 enumeration) and as a result probably held the greatest risk of sampling error. The standard error therefore measures the accuracy of population parameters from sample statistics.

Two standard errors were calculated for both sexes in each age-band of the migrant age-structure ratio for every census year. It was therefore the ratios of the migrant age-structure that had the standard errors applied to them. Every age-band in each of the four population categories had a different amount of standard error. This was because the standard error reflected not only the extremes in the ratio of the migrant age-structure, but also the number of samples taken. This was a problem because some samples of the migrant population were large, both numerically and in relation to the total population, but they were derived from a relatively small number of sampled places. Moreover, the closeness of the fit of the individual migrant population categories to the published above and below 20 years proportions, although important as a criterion in the original sampling, was not measured in the standard errors.

The standard errors were applied to the migrant age-structure and this revised the proportion of natives and migrants in each age-band of every county, (the total population of each county in an age-band had been derived from the census). The data were then processed. The range of errors was calculated in the final estimates of both emigration and migration. Thus standard errors that were applied to data in a county-of-residence unit of measurement were finally calculated for estimates on a county-of-birth framework. This had the effect of concentrating errors in certain age-bands and counties-of-birth, often in a different population category to that of the county-of-residence. The estimates with standard errors therefore represent the extremes of variability.

The original intention was to skew the age-structure ratios in two separate models, one flattening and one peaking the migrant age ratios.

However, this proved unworkable because there was not a large enough margin for error that would permit their application. This indicates how tightly the migrant age-structure was held by the published data.[11]

A second method of measuring the accuracy of the migrant age-structure ratios was devised. In this model two standard errors were added to each age-band of the migrant age-structure to create one extreme scenario and vice versa for the other. The data was then rerun in exactly the same manner as in the previous investigation in order to provide estimates of out-movement

The migrant age-structure for each population category in every census had two standard errors added or deducted from each age-band. This was the source database and it means that the entire computation of estimates of both migration and emigration occurred after the database had been adjusted. Variations based on these procedures will over-estimate the likely variability appreciably. This clearly represents a 'worse case' situation and has made the test a very rigorous one.

Notes

1. I would like to thank Dr S.K. Tagg (Dept of Marketing) for the considerable amount of help he gave me with the computer analysis. I would also like to thank the staff of the Computer centre, especially Mr Oliver Allen. Finally, I am extremely grateful to Margaret Gowans and Anne Manzor for typing the data so accurately and to Serindar Hungan and Ann Mair in the Social Sciences Computing Lab. for their advice. These people were all members of the University of Strathclyde.

2. This appendix is based on a paper Brock and Tagg, 'Using SPSS-X'.

3. The county-of-residence by county-of-birth and age-structure of the population tabulations are always found in the *Census of Scotland, Vol. II.* 1861–1911, 1861 (1864, [63 C-226]), 1871 (1874, [C-841]), 1881 (1883, [C-3657]), 1891 (1893, [C-9637]), 1901 (1903, [CD 1481]), 1911 (1913, [CD 6896])

4. *(7th–56th) Detailed Annual Reports of the Registrar-General of births, deaths and marriages in Scotland* (Edinburgh, 1865–1912)

5. *SPSS-X Users Guide,*

6. An example of a marked fluctuation from the normal trend would be if in one particular census a county contained a considerably increased proportion of the adjoining county's population and there was a corresponding decrease in the losing county. If no historical reason could account for such a sudden movement then it would be assumed to be an enumeration error.

7. Baines. *Migration in a Mature Economy.* p. 78.

8. Examples of the original datasets and the final database can be seen in Figure 2 (A) to (D). Brock and Tagg 'Using SPSS–X' p. 21.

9. I would like to thank Dr R.Ahmad and Dr Mackenzie (University of Strathclyde) for their advice on the best method of applying standard errors.

10. Hammond & McCullagh, *Quantitative Techniques*, pp.144–58.

11. The operation involved re–running the entire computer programme twice, with the revised age–structure ratios so that the effect of these two extreme situations on the results could be measured. However, this method of checking proved impossible.

The migrant age–structure ratios were used to expand the published birthplace census tabulation from two to sixteen age–bands for each sex. The total number of migrants from any county remained the same, but the number of migrants in any age–band was exaggerated or reduced by two standard errors. In some age–bands this exaggeration meant that too many migrants were predicted for the total number in that age–band in the county–of–residence. This total number for each county–of–residence was derived from the age–structure of the population tabulations in the published census. This excess meant that the native population of the county was forced into negative figures, an impossible situation. The skewed migrant age–structures could not therefore be used because there was not enough margin for error that would permit their application, Thus indicating how tightly the migrant age–structure was held by the data.

Appendix 2
The Significance of Migration Patterns Upon the County-of-Birth Enumeration

Key

c   Percentage of people less than 20 years in entire population of county-of-birth

m   Percentage of total population living outside the county-of-birth who are less than 20 years old.

p   Percentage of total county-of-birth population no longer living in the county-of-birth, but still living within Scotland. (With reference to Table 3.4, it is clear that a significant proportion of the population movement in some Scottish counties is south into England, Wales and Ireland, this form of migration is not considered in calculations in this appendix).

t   Total population living outside county-of-birth.

★   The data considers only Scots resident in Scotland and does not include outsiders living in Scotland.

★★   Data adjusted so that the detached portion of Nairn (Urquhart and Logie-Wester) is included in Ross and Cromarty between 1861 and 1891 pre-revision censuses (see Brock 'Scottish Migration' Vol. II, App. I for either county).

★★★   Lanark and Renfrew were not converted to Civil Counties but remained Modified Registration Counties until the revision of boundaries (see Brock 'Scottish Migration' Vol. II, Appendix I for either county).

County-of-Birth		1861 Male	1861 Female	1871 Male	1871 Female	1881 Male	1881 Female	1891 Male	1891 Female	Pre-Revision 1891 Male	Pre-Revision 1891 Female	Post-Revision 1901 Male	Post-Revision 1901 Female	1911 Male	1911 Female
Scotland	c	51.98	45.29	52.42	46.18	52.00	46.52	51.02	45.77	51.02	45.77	48.22	43.74	46.27	42.22
	m	30.83	26.89	30.55	27.29	30.45	27.14	29.76	26.89	30.11	27.21	26.61	24.29	25.71	23.03
	p	22.50	22.58	23.88	24.19	24.74	25.51	25.20	25.85	25.40	26.05	25.72	26.35	25.34	26.28
	t	294,602	333,441	345,946	390,182	400,238	452,239	444,042	496,679	447,456	500,518	504,029	558,898	530,293	596,667
Aberdeen	c	51.73	44.37	52.28	45.09	51.12	45.34	49.91	43.71	49.91	43.71	46.50	41.45	44.60	39.63
	m	31.62	28.01	29.78	26.46	28.31	25.41	26.11	24.24	25.60	23.91	24.15	22.23	22.23	19.99
	p	13.72	13.13	14.73	14.58	16.13	16.28	17.74	17.63	17.27	17.19	19.63	19.13	20.02	19.56
	t	14,069	15,206	17,013	18,828	20,914	23,194	24,569	26,934	23,925	26,274	29,837	31,897	30,692	33,364
Argyll	c	40.92	35.01	39.08	33.16	38.02	32.12	38.55	32.65	38.55	32.65	36.46	31.63	33.30	29.36
	m	19.82	17.15	17.39	14.95	17.48	13.54	19.16	15.48	19.72	15.89	18.28	15.04	17.35	13.88
	p	31.04	36.56	33.29	39.28	33.35	40.27	33.94	40.74	34.66	41.33	36.25	41.55	37.69	42.94
	t	14,534	19,728	14,909	20,274	14,393	19,844	14,254	19,481	14,558	19,761	15,167	19,126	14,661	18,439
Ayr	c	53.34	47.75	52.27	47.18	50.23	45.65	48.60	44.16	48.60	44.16	45.01	41.97	43.63	40.56
	m	31.11	28.11	30.34	28.09	26.74	24.58	26.33	24.55	26.32	24.55	22.41	21.22	21.61	20.26
	p	22.80	22.73	26.63	26.63	27.45	28.17	28.91	29.44	28.89	29.43	28.92	29.46	28.84	29.03
	t	21,297	23,069	27,056	29,269	30,878	33,919	34,419	37,635	34,399	37,613	38,129	40,880	39,551	42,555

COUNTY-OF-BIRTH		1861		1871		1881		1891		1891 Pre-Revision		1901 Post-Revision		1911	
		MALE	FEMALE	MALE	FEMALE	MALE	FEMALE	MALE	FEMALE	MALE	FEMALE	MALE	FEMALE	MALE	FEMALE
Banff	c	49.39	42.85	48.85	43.59	46.34	41.12	44.82	39.68	44.82	39.68	41.76	37.18	39.09	34.85
	m	26.12	22.44	26.88	24.98	25.50	22.68	22.68	20.92	24.98	23.09	21.45	19.20	19.41	16.93
	p	26.69	26.00	29.42	28.95	34.29	33.47	34.02	34.70	36.19	36.96	39.75	39.53	37.37	40.60
	t	7,815	8,540	9,550	10,418	11,974	12,898	12,154	13,635	12,931	14,524	14,820	16,076	13,470	16,404
Berwick	c	46.24	40.62	46.41	41.50	44.15	39.94	40.50	37.19	40.50	37.19	36.16	32.05	31.63	28.65
	m	26.19	21.86	25.64	23.58	25.72	23.38	22.43	21.90	22.64	22.00	21.36	17.46	16.34	14.45
	p	30.20	31.68	32.72	33.06	36.25	37.25	40.10	40.22	40.28	40.34	44.24	44.50	44.75	46.07
	t	5,521	6,346	6,240	6,780	7,011	7,760	7,484	8,154	7,517	8,179	8,110	8,761	7,797	8,627
Bute	c	46.86	37.84	46.32	37.87	46.09	37.67	46.71	37.73	46.71	37.73	43.46	36.73	40.43	33.65
	m	29.24	22.77	28.01	22.20	27.61	22.89	28.25	22.33	28.25	22.33	26.60	21.20	24.05	19.04
	p	33.33	35.02	36.50	38.31	36.34	41.09	37.72	41.44	37.72	41.44	38.98	42.92	40.34	44.15
	t	2,182	2,881	2,453	3,175	2,539	3,443	2,704	3,552	2,704	3,552	2,883	3,660	2,910	3,639
Caithness	c	46.93	39.71	46.13	39.24	42.65	36.56	41.39	35.57	41.39	35.57	37.75	32.45	36.65	30.43
	m	17.86	16.23	19.77	17.68	18.66	16.15	16.49	15.43	16.49	15.43	16.05	14.37	12.79	10.99
	p	15.22	15.05	19.22	19.63	23.25	24.52	24.64	26.22	28.02	29.75	31.26	32.85	29.39	33.46
	t	3,080	3,475	4,052	4,701	4,962	6,020	5,136	6,379	5,136	6,379	6,511	7,882	5,661	7,625

County-of-Birth	1861		1871		1881		1891		1891 Pre-Revision		1901 Post-Revision		1911	
	Male	Female	Male	Female	Male	Female	Male	Female	Male	Female	Male	Female	Male	Female
Clackmannan														
c	54.07	48.14	51.93	45.99	50.68	46.26	48.62	46.42	48.62	46.42	44.48	41.72	39.71	37.02
m	36.19	31.42	29.32	26.59	30.34	27.76	28.13	26.93	28.84	27.91	25.84	25.29	23.04	22.31
p	35.03	36.05	34.73	36.49	39.09	38.77	39.22	37.86	36.74	34.80	39.92	37.09	43.18	40.48
t	3,448	3,835	3,704	4,219	4,782	5,028	5,141	5,266	4,816	4,840	6,466	6,291	7,106	7,050
Dumfries														
c	47.82	41.50	47.10	41.41	45.68	39.84	43.66	38.33	43.66	38.33	40.62	35.91	37.39	33.73
m	27.08	22.08	23.94	22.36	25.22	22.84	23.23	21.66	23.20	21.64	22.49	20.79	19.23	17.94
p	22.57	21.91	23.43	23.02	28.23	28.15	31.32	30.23	31.30	30.22	35.85	34.76	36.50	36.22
t	8,337	9,216	8,662	9,760	10,778	12,022	11,860	12,542	11,853	12,535	13,726	14,548	13,856	14,707
Dunbarton														
c	54.92	49.58	56.88	51.06	56.68	51.43	57.39	53.86	57.39	53.86	56.53	53.07	55.08	51.52
m	36.56	31.97	37.71	33.74	35.33	30.75	34.47	31.26	34.44	31.25	34.84	32.24	33.70	30.22
p	38.22	39.45	39.65	41.56	37.03	39.26	34.25	36.96	34.06	36.75	33.13	35.33	30.73	33.15
t	7,741	8,640	9,335	10,379	10,175	11,296	11,066	12,544	11,005	12,472	13,593	15,086	14,873	16,703
Edinburgh (Midlothian)														
c	55.30	47.26	56.82	49.86	58.00	52.76	57.23	50.36	57.23	50.36	53.15	48.42	48.86	45.01
m	36.16	30.34	35.58	31.56	38.56	34.22	38.20	34.32	38.17	34.31	35.57	31.70	31.23	28.44
p	20.62	20.92	20.00	20.40	19.77	20.42	19.99	20.34	19.98	20.33	20.71	20.96	21.81	21.57
t	20,013	23,628	22,329	25,609	26,090	29,523	30,664	34,747	30,640	34,727	36,407	39,984	42,227	45,746

County-of-Birth	1861		1871		1881		1891		1891 Pre-Revision		1901 Post-Revision		1911	
	Male	Female	Male	Female	Male	Female	Male	Female	Male	Female	Male	Female	Male	Female
Elgin (Moray)														
c	51.04	43.60	51.92	44.49	48.92	41.62	47.34	40.72	47.34	40.72	43.47	38.04	39.90	34.54
m	27.21	23.22	31.26	27.85	27.63	23.80	25.06	22.02	26.29	23.23	22.42	19.88	20.39	17.15
p	25.04	24.26	29.50	28.89	31.74	32.34	34.22	33.72	35.02	34.53	37.07	37.57	37.99	39.30
t	4,789	5,374	6,002	6,674	6,957	7,888	7,570	8,544	7,748	8,748	8,604	9,806	8,691	10,071
Fife														
c	48.76	42.24	47.61	41.44	45.88	40.92	45.18	40.55	45.18	40.55	43.50	39.18	44.28	40.62
m	27.29	24.44	26.02	23.36	23.77	21.64	22.28	21.61	22.25	21.66	20.89	19.42	21.39	19.18
p	21.16	20.67	24.62	23.17	26.85	25.54	26.88	25.71	26.74	25.61	26.02	25.89	22.81	23.61
t	16,351	18,007	20,598	21,596	24,160	25,312	25,415	26,435	25,287	26,334	27,143	29,252	25,830	28,839
Forfar (Angus)														
c	54.71	46.38	55.60	47.75	55.54	48.57	53.18	46.31	53.18	46.31	48.12	42.02	44.24	38.39
m	32.71	29.27	31.02	28.72	32.02	30.65	30.66	29.87	30.69	29.97	26.09	25.59	22.43	21.31
p	15.30	13.02	15.86	13.19	16.95	14.25	17.98	15.19	17.97	15.22	21.27	17.49	22.52	18.94
t	12,279	12,130	14,708	14,041	18,101	17,156	20,851	19,740	20,841	19,775	26,708	24,770	28,621	27,321
Haddington (East Lothian)														
c	45.47	40.17	45.38	40.40	43.90	39.07	41.74	38.81	41.74	38.81	37.15	35.72	36.75	34.07
m	24.43	21.05	24.80	22.62	24.25	21.74	23.55	21.99	23.60	21.98	21.74	20.07	19,07	17,05
p	34.23	36.26	36.84	39.22	39.06	42.46	42.95	44.06	43.02	44.09	46.72	47.86	44.73	47.14
t	6,730	7,764	7,640	8,661	8,491	9,637	9,516	9,806	9,530	9,813	10,412	11,041	10,236	10,956

County-of-Birth	1861		1871		1881		1891		1891 Pre-Revision		1901 Post-Revision		1911	
	Male	Female	Male	Female	Male	Female	Male	Female	Male	Female	Male	Female	Male	Female
Inverness														
c	43.37	37.68	42.39	36.68	41.42	35.67	41.15	35.16	41.15	35.16	38.57	33.17	36.71	30.69
m	22.66	19.95	21.45	20.23	20.02	17.45	19.95	16.88	20.18	17.01	18.24	15.98	18.03	14.77
p	23.55	22.78	26.55	26.49	26.54	28.68	29.37	30.52	29.27	30.47	31.35	34.13	32.18	34.88
t	10,573	11,838	12,198	14,102	12,391	15,245	13,893	16,318	13,847	16,286	14,799	18,275	14,548	18,353
Kincardine														
c	46.66	39.90	45.14	39.84	44.51	39.36	43.40	37.64	43.40	37.64	40.42	35.63	41.43	36.83
m	28.01	22.77	25.76	22.49	26.34	23.13	23.19	20.83	23.35	20.97	21.79	19.58	27.00	23.73
p	33.90	35.15	37.70	39.37	41.34	44.21	41.90	45.00	42.09	45.16	45.41	48.27	50.32	52.35
t	6,329	7,331	7,395	8,568	8,455	9,812	8,797	10,221	8,835	10,257	9,832	11,266	11,276	12,856
Kinross														
c	43.08	37.31	39.34	34.43	34.93	32.43	32.98	29.87	32.98	29.87	33.60	28.44	35.64	30.68
m	29.55	24.57	25.17	22.91	22.55	21.39	20.30	20.62	20.44	21.05	20.93	17.11	21.64	19.03
p	46.58	46.03	53.33	51.96	60.47	57.25	64.18	62.99	64.33	63.44	63.66	62.80	61.35	62.41
t	2,105	2,279	2,364	2,501	2,652	2,777	2,670	2,948	2,676	2,969	2,700	2,910	2,486	2,801
Kirkcudbright														
c	52.41	43.54	51.36	45.08	49.37	43.71	47.86	41.48	47.86	41.48	44.16	37.72	39.07	34.58
m	31.53	24.75	29.10	26.13	28.85	28.14	27.51	24.96	27.51	24.96	26.85	21.40	21.95	19.39
p	21.35	21.69	21.17	20.24	27.82	27.55	31.06	30.59	31.06	30.82	35.49	35.16	38.68	37.90
t	3,822	4,573	4,178	4,486	5,254	5,849	5,972	6,490	5,972	6,490	6,864	7,276	7,354	7,602

COUNTY-OF-BIRTH		1861		1871		1881		1891		1891 Pre-Revision		1901 Post-Revision		1911	
		MALE	FEMALE	MALE	FEMALE	MALE	FEMALE	MALE	FEMALE	MALE	FEMALE	MALE	FEMALE	MALE	FEMALE
Lanark	c	63.22	57.67	63.54	58.69	62.47	58.32	59.88	56.31	59.88	56.31	56.73	53.12	53.93	50.85
	m	46.94	43.18	46.48	41.84	46.98	42.68	44.53	38.95	44.53	38.95	39.56	34.42	38.40	34.31
	p	14.89	14.83	14.32	14.97	15.16	16.29	14.12	15.57	14.12	15.58	13.99	15.48	15.39	17.09
	t	30,783	33,258	36,794	41,215	49,111	55,918	55,167	63,933	55,172	63,937	67,877	79,419	87,918	103,392
Linlithgow (West Lothian)	c	52.10	46.64	56.79	51.80	54.42	50.16	51.57	48.23	51.57	48.23	50.58	48.63	50.57	48.39
	m	31.48	27.23	41.83	36.68	41.01	36.46	34.32	30.85	34.32	30.85	31.95	29.82	29.25	27.20
	p	35.30	39.35	39.55	43.83	43.97	48.45	42.43	46.51	42.43	46.51	40.41	45.33	36.84	42.36
	t	5,839	6,989	7,822	9,200	9,916	11,421	11,064	12,332	11,064	12,332	12,502	14,507	13,308	15,762
Nairn**	c	46.60	40.47	48.28	42.17	47.11	41.39	45.45	39.77	45.45	39.77	41.43	36.37	40.15	33.80
	m	27.64	25.27	29.05	27.25	27.41	23.30	26.86	24.38	27.76	25.09	23.28	21.85	24.02	19.29
	p	37.46	39.32	39.29	41.12	39.69	41.70	43.09	43.49	43.85	44.37	44.54	46.95	46.73	48.23
	t	1,476	1,777	1,625	1,971	1,711	1,987	1,858	2,203	1,891	2,248	1,950	2,302	1,994	2,296
Orkney	c	47.42	37.80	47.30	37.66	45.12	36.86	43.25	35.30	43.25	35.30	39.28	30.56	34.89	27.54
	m	22.23	14 55	24.74	19.08	19.41	14.54	19.80	14.23	19.80	14.23	17.62	14.10	13.30	10.12
	p	7.14	8.68	10.82	13.02	11.83	14.61	14.48	17.48	14.48	17.48	20.19	23.15	20.31	24.07
	t	1,039	1,546	1,621	2,380	1,844	2,731	2,212	3,211	2,212	3,211	3,071	4,128	2,865	4,023

County-of-Birth		1861 Male	1861 Female	1871 Male	1871 Female	1881 Male	1881 Female	1891 Male	1891 Female	1891 Pre-Revision Male	1891 Pre-Revision Female	1901 Post-Revision Male	1901 Post-Revision Female	1911 Male	1911 Female
Peebles	c	42.73	36.60	43.39	39.59	45.15	41.64	44.25	41,48	44.25	41,48	41.92	38.64	37.65	33.82
	m	23.72	19,10	25.50	23.19	27.45	24.63	26.18	24.23	26.27	24.33	25.22	23.24	22.21	19.78
	p	49.38	53.06	51.61	54.75	51.60	53.70	51.86	52.32	51.99	52.49	54.60	53.08	53.05	52.52
	t	3,111	3,581	3,455	3,864	3,588	3,930	3,759	3,953	3,769	3,966	4,115	4,131	3,890	3,989
Perth	c	41.68	36.40	41.14	36.02	40.36	35.68	39.51	35.13	39.51	35.13	37.43	33.26	35.77	31.73
	m	21.92	20.49	22.37	21.28	21.40	20.19	21.54	19.93	22.91	21.00	19.62	18.19	18.05	16.76
	p	30.66	30.40	35.24	34.72	37.07	37.33	39.70	38.58	41.25	40.20	41.24	40.05	40.19	40.33
	t	21,996	24,408	25,006	27,556	26,108	29,270	27,185	29,311	28,245	30,535	27,294	29,287	25,507	28,491
Renfrew***	c	56.28	49.07	57.27	50.67	57.34	51.68	56.78	51.24	56.78	51.24	52.38	47.78	49.31	45.38
	m	39.28	32.96	38.85	32.60	39.45	34.77	43.11	38.57	43.13	38.58	35.52	31.32	30.81	26.60
	p	31.65	32.37	31.22	32.20	30.81	31.74	33.07	34.13	33.09	34.14	30.06	30.80	26.81	27.43
	t	21,446	24,884	23,861	27,570	27,508	30,888	33,566	37,636	33,582	37,652	34,028	37,225	32,968	35,994
Ross & Cromarty**	c	43.58	38.20	43.21	37.62	41.09	35.26	39.80	34.34	39.80	34.34	38.29	32.98	36.80	31.98
	m	19.55	18.28	19.44	18.00	19.79	15.91	16.00	14.51	15.96	14.46	15.92	13.67	15.94	12.95
	p	17.91	16.61	19.94	19.66	23.53	23.37	24.65	24.67	24.61	24.60	26.73	28.18	26.37	27.22
	t	7,539	7,893	8,599	9,520	10,200	11,320	10,646	11,876	10,626	11,845	11,369	13,631	10,609	12,313

COUNTY-OF-BIRTH		1861 MALE	1861 FEMALE	1871 MALE	1871 FEMALE	1881 MALE	1881 FEMALE	1891 MALE	1891 FEMALE	1891 PRE-REVISION MALE	1891 PRE-REVISION FEMALE	1901 POST-REVISION MALE	1901 POST-REVISION FEMALE	1911 MALE	1911 FEMALE
Roxburgh	c	51.50	45.20	50.13	44.56	48.00	43.47	46.72	42.57	46.72	42.57	39.67	35.69	33.81	31.28
	m	31.61	26.93	35.16	30.24	30.61	26.54	31.17	29.18	31.41	29.45	23.42	21.27	17.42	16.69
	p	24.26	25.21	32.89	32.98	31.91	31.98	36.23	35.38	36.62	35.73	38.68	36.80	40.05	38.16
	t	5,654	6,423	8,183	8,935	8,255	8,923	10,111	10.517	10,220	10,621	9,894	10,276	9,706	10,207
Selkirk	c	52.63	48.02	52.76	49.21	58.55	55.10	59.28	54.32	59.28	54.32	49.80	46.08	39.48	35.48
	m	35.57	30.69	33.60	32.12	35.09	32.47	35.41	34.36	35.96	34.56	34.45	33.91	23.83	22.55
	p	43.16	44.34	37.40	37.40	27.15	26.90	30.87	31.31	30.97	31.25	40.17	37.38	39.81	38.08
	t	1,999	2,147	2,110	2,217	2,197	2,248	2,581	2,768	2,589	2,763	4,238	4,079	4,246	4,275
Shetland	c	50.14	34.93	51.02	34.38	47.51	32.25	44.47	31.23	44.47	31.23	41.82	29.84	39.60	28.83
	m	21.65	11.59	27.57	16.90	25.26	15.10	22.06	15.98	22.06	15.98	21.57	14.76	14.14	10.50
	p	5.09	6.42	8.31	9.49	10.89	12.42	13.45	13.84	13.45	13.84	15.92	15.44	14.71	15.22
	t	679	1,260	1,150	1,905	1,425	2,338	1,741	2,553	1,741	2,553	2,123	2,744	1,881	2,591
Stirling	c	50.78	45.51	50.69	45.63	51.25	46.28	50.02	45.98	50.02	45.98	47.67	44.66	48.35	45.20
	m	30.89	28.04	30.91	28.22	30.49	27.47	30.20	26.70	33.79	29.89	27.25	24.65	28.97	25.43
	p	33.92	36.40	35.57	38.74	34.41	39.03	34.45	38.45	38.04	42.15	33.42	38.09	31.56	36.54
	t	14,721	17,330	17,070	20,115	18,422	22,509	20,221	24,046	22,329	26,358	21,710	26,107	22,829	27,561

County-of-Birth		1861		1871		1881		1891		1891 Pre-Revision		1901 Post-Revision		1911	
		Male	Female	Male	Female	Male	Female	Male	Female	Male	Female	Male	Female	Male	Female
Sutherland	c	42.09	35.30	40.58	33.16	37.79	32.09	37.15	32.54	37.15	32.54	35.33	30.75	33.97	28.70
	m	17.13	15.80	18.35	15.92	17.04	16.10	17.82	15.30	17.82	15.30	17.17	14.21	15.17	12.26
	p	23.30	19.10	24.58	23.65	26.40	26.98	28.02	29.75	28.02	29.75	30.07	32.23	29.64	33.98
	t	3,030	2,867	3,167	3,511	3,315	3,827	3,373	4,145	3,373	4,145	3,617	4,315	3,264	4,234
Wigtown	c	52.77	45.12	49.19	41.19	47.38	40.21	45.63	39.68	45.63	39.68	39.31	35.70	35.64	32.68
	m	25.75	22.33	21.37	18.99	22.65	18.81	23.38	20.15	23.38	20.15	20.24	18.67	15.97	15.06
	p	23.06	23.35	27.07	27.39	28.74	28.15	32.30	30.82	32.30	30.82	38.52	36.44	38.80	37.41
	t	4,275	5,218	5,097	6,182	5,681	6,306	6,423	6,824	6,423	6,824	7,530	7,960	7,462	7,881

Appendix 3

The Percentage of Migrants and Natives in their Respective Populations Less Than 20 Years Old in the Civil Counties

Key

m Percentage of migrants less than 20 years in migrant population (migrants in this context includes both Scots and those born outside Scotland).

n Percentage of natives less than 20 years in native population (natives refers only to those still resident in their county-of-birth).

p Percentage of people less than 20 years in entire population.

* Data adjusted so that the detached portion of Nairn (Urquhart and Logie-Wester) is included in Ross and Cromarty between 1861 and 1891 pre-revision censuses (see Brock 'Scottish Migration' Vol. II, Appendix I for either county).

** Lanark and Renfrew were not converted to Civil Counties but remained Modified Registration Counties until the revision of boundaries (see Brock 'Scottish Migration' Vol. II, Appendix I for either county).

COUNTY-OF-BIRTH		1861		1871		1881		1891 PRE-REVISION		1891 POST-REVISION		1901		1911	
		MALE	FEMALE	MALE	FEMALE	MALE	FEMALE	MALE	FEMALE	MALE	FEMALE	MALE	FEMALE	MALE	FEMALE
Scotland	m	28.05	25.48	27.76	25.67	27.87	26.03	27.19	25.52	27.45	25.77	24.73	23.74	23.35	22.11
	n	58.12	50.66	59.29	52.20	59.09	53.16	58.19	52.35	58.15	52.31	55.56	50.70	53.26	49.06
	p	49.10	43.33	49.44	44.14	48.99	44.54	48.22	43.88	48.22	43.88	45.37	41.98	43.58	40.50
Aberdeen	m	26.18	22.43	28.09	24.96	30.50	27.80	29.95	27.42	31.00	28.35	29.00	26.84	29.38	27.41
	n	54.93	46.85	56.17	48.27	55.51	49.21	55.04	47.87	54.98	47.82	51.96	46.00	50.20	44.41
	p	50.53	43.40	51.96	44.95	51.73	46.06	51.30	44.88	51.33	44.90	48.37	43.02	46.71	41.56
Argyll	m	35.05	34.71	35.15	33.39	34.71	33.48	31.38	29.71	31.49	29.80	26.90	25.02	25.57	24.67
	n	50.42	45.30	49.90	44.93	48.31	44.66	48.51	44.45	48.54	44.45	46.80	43.42	42.94	41.02
	p	47.80	43.60	47.09	42.73	45.03	42.01	44.30	40.63	44.38	40.67	41.57	38.24	37.45	35.96
Ayr	m	27.09	26.71	24.85	23.90	27.39	27.35	28.57	27.32	28.61	27.36	28.15	27.70	26.08	25.37
	n	59.91	53.53	60.23	54.11	59.12	53.91	57.65	52.34	57.65	52.34	54.21	50.63	52.55	48.86
	p	51.49	47.34	51.71	47.65	51.63	48.10	50.75	46.89	50.75	46.89	47.64	45.08	45.92	43.06
Banff	m	32.94	29.50	35.46	29.51	37.04	31.76	38.96	33.16	39.47	33.96	35.75	31.28	35.11	30.93
	n	57.86	50.02	58.01	51.18	57.22	50.40	56.23	49.65	56.07	49.41	55.16	48.93	50.83	47.10
	p	52.04	45.48	53.05	46.47	52.58	46.26	52.20	45.82	52.28	45.87	50.60	44.79	47.04	43.20

County-of-Birth		1861		1871		1881		1891 Pre-Revision		1891 Post-Revision		1901		1911	
		Male	Female	Male	Female	Male	Female	Male	Female	Male	Female	Male	Female	Male	Female
Berwick	m	35.33	30.70	31.69	27.87	33.85	28.62	32.68	25.46	32.62	25.42	29.81	24.35	27.89	22.91
	n	54.92	49.31	56.51	50.36	54.63	49.77	52.59	47.47	52.54	47.46	47.91	43.75	44.01	40.78
	p	49.68	43.98	49.98	44.05	48.97	43.61	47.09	41.19	47.05	41.18	42.37	37.52	38.82	34.59
Bute	m	36.77	29.40	33.03	29.05	34.03	27.68	34.37	28.12	34.37	28.12	29.11	23.28	27.04	21.55
	n	55.67	45.96	56.84	47.60	56.64	47.98	57.89	48.64	57.89	48.64	54.23	48.40	51.50	45.20
	p	48.21	39.09	46.36	39.19	46.44	38.17	47.16	38.22	47.16	38.22	42.60	35.06	40.18	32.25
Caithness	m	29.08	26.51	26.09	24.90	30.08	30.67	29.83	28.91	29.83	28.91	28.52	31.73	31.92	31.11
	n	52.15	43.86	52.41	44.51	49.91	43.19	49.52	42.73	49.52	42.73	47.62	41.30	46.58	40.21
	p	49.53	42.16	49.76	42.82	47.75	42.00	47.54	41.50	47.54	41.50	45.54	40.39	45.07	39.30
Clackmannan	m	33.53	30.80	36.15	30.99	38.09	32.88	35.31	31.53	40.66	36.70	30.50	26.97	30.31	25.99
	n	63.71	57.57	63.97	57.14	63.73	57.97	61.85	58.29	60.11	56.29	56.87	51.41	52.38	47.02
	p	52.09	47.28	52.90	46.74	53.73	47.68	50.77	47.21	50.85	46.97	47.39	42.46	44.39	39.23
Dumfries	m	32.49	28.86	32.73	28.64	34.08	30.54	32.88	28.39	32.89	28.39	31.01	25.40	30.02	24.05
	n	53.86	46.96	54.18	47.11	53.73	46.50	52.98	45.55	52.99	45.55	50.75	43.96	47.83	42.69
	p	49.63	43.64	50.18	43.71	49.03	42.74	47.87	41.02	47.87	41.02	45.12	38.67	42.28	36.82

County-of-Birth	1861 Male	1861 Female	1871 Male	1871 Female	1881 Male	1881 Female	1891 Pre-Revision Male	1891 Pre-Revision Female	1891 Post-Revision Male	1891 Post-Revision Female	1901 Male	1901 Female	1911 Male	1911 Female
Dunbarton														
m	29.80	28.70	31.54	28.69	30.79	29.34	30.22	27.65	31.25	28.97	26.21	24.73	25.59	24.72
n	66.28	61.05	69.48	63.37	69.24	64.80	69.32	67.11	69.24	67.00	67.27	64.45	64.57	62.09
p	47.78	44.80	50.22	45.56	48.62	45.64	47.92	45.40	47.88	45.52	46.12	43.89	44.33	42.67
Edinburgh (Midlothian)														
m	25.66	22.02	26.85	23.99	26.08	23.19	23.97	22.89	23.97	22.89	21.10	18.77	19.65	16.35
n	60.28	51.73	62.13	54.55	62.79	57.52	61.99	54.46	61.99	54.46	57.74	52.85	53.78	49.56
p	46.77	40.00	47.33	41.49	47.21	42.43	46.65	41.69	46.65	41.69	43.26	38.66	41.59	36.65
Elgin (Moray)														
m	30.40	27.28	32.52	28.66	30.16	27.68	31.33	26.45	32.03	27.54	29.00	26.57	28.11	24.64
n	59.00	50.13	60.57	51.25	58.83	50.15	58.93	50.23	58.68	49.94	55.87	48.97	51.86	45.79
p	50.68	43.87	52.57	44.76	50.85	43.75	51.03	43.76	50.84	43.62	47.59	41.98	44.55	38.99
Fife														
m	32.76	27.30	33.16	28.07	37.37	31.22	35.79	31.46	36.49	32.05	33.03	29.97	29.07	28.95
n	54.52	46.87	54.66	46.89	54.00	47.53	53.59	47.10	53.54	47.05	51.46	46.09	51.04	47.25
p	51.02	43.76	51.21	43.82	50.90	44.44	49.60	43.62	49.54	43.54	46.55	41.84	43.61	41.54
Forfar (Angus)														
m	24.70	21.60	26.74	23.02	27.21	22.44	25.96	21.44	26.04	21.48	24.46	18.90	23.67	19.28
n	58.69	48.94	60.24	50.64	60.33	51.54	58.11	49.26	58.10	49.25	54.07	45.51	50.58	42.38
p	49.76	41.35	51.33	42.48	51.68	42.98	50.35	41.56	50.36	41.57	47.38	38.78	44.60	36.73

COUNTY-OF-BIRTH		1861		1871		1881		1891 Pre-Revision		1891 Post-Revision		1901		1911	
		MALE	FEMALE	MALE	FEMALE	MALE	FEMALE	MALE	FEMALE	MALE	FEMALE	MALE	FEMALE	MALE	FEMALE
Haddington (East Lothian)															
	m	32.30	27.38	32.07	25.93	34.08	28.31	32.50	26.44	32.32	26.41	34.51	27.35	32.20	28.70
	n	56.41	51.05	57.37	51.86	56.50	51.85	55.44	52.07	55.43	52.09	50.65	50.07	51.05	49.25
	p	49.76	43.71	50.41	43.62	49.87	43.92	48.40	43.01	48.38	43.04	44.68	41.14	43.31	40.29
Inverness															
	m	30.74	28.33	32.67	30.15	32.67	28.73	28.46	28.26	29.05	28.82	29.97	28.81	30.42	31.05
	n	49.74	42.91	49.95	42.60	49.15	42.99	49.96	43.19	49.82	43.11	47.86	42.08	45.57	39.22
	p	46.59	40.75	46.86	40.54	45.56	40.33	45.11	40.27	44.99	40.24	43.22	38.91	41.36	37.30
Kincardine															
	m	33.50	29.82	34.17	28.80	36.46	31.28	36.06	31.24	35.95	31.16	40.25	34.67	37.58	32.00
	n	56.23	49.18	56.86	51.10	57.32	52.22	57.97	51.39	57.96	51.37	55.92	50.61	56.04	51.21
	p	50.25	44.60	50.69	45.29	51.20	46.11	51.24	45.19	51.22	45.16	49.47	43.90	47.99	42.58
Kinross															
	m	37.22	30.90	37.85	30.75	38.03	31.77	36.70	31.12	37.35	32.08	33.26	31.70	30.33	28.43
	n	54.89	48.17	55.53	46.89	53.86	47.20	55.70	45.61	55.59	45.18	55.81	47.56	57.85	50.03
	p	48.48	41.91	48.64	40.55	46.85	40.70	46.26	38.69	45.92	38.46	43.66	39.21	42.24	37.75
Kirkcudbright															
	m	31.91	28.25	24.39	21.57	32.33	30.59	31.06	27.22	31.06	27.22	30.51	26.64	28.99	26.12
	n	58.08	48.74	57.33	49.89	57.28	49.63	57.03	48.76	57.03	48.76	53.69	46.57	49.87	43.85
	p	50.53	43.15	50.68	43.96	49.50	43.71	49.28	42.27	49.28	42.27	45.93	39.60	42.46	37.00

County-of-Birth		1861 Male	1861 Female	1871 Male	1871 Female	1881 Male	1881 Female	1891 Pre-Revision Male	1891 Pre-Revision Female	1891 Post-Revision Male	1891 Post-Revision Female	1901 Male	1901 Female	1911 Male	1911 Female
Lanark**	m	25.23	23.33	24.25	23.36	23.37	23.15	23.78	23.53	23.78	23.53	20.41	21.43	17.51	17.92
	n	66.07	60.19	66.39	61.66	65.23	61.37	62.40	59.52	62.40	59.52	59.53	56.55	56.75	54.26
	p	48.54	44.53	48.14	45.86	48.00	46.28	47.31	46.00	47.31	46.00	44.61	44.32	43.80	43.04
Linlithgow (West Lothian)	m	34.95	35.51	33.17	32.17	31.07	32.97	31.48	34.35	31.48	34.35	31.32	31.63	27.32	30.04
	n	63.36	59.23	66.58	63.60	64.93	63.03	64.29	63.34	64.29	63.34	63.22	64.22	63.01	63.97
	p	50.25	49.12	52.32	50.59	49.89	50.56	49.11	50.89	49.11	50.89	48.01	50.34	46.38	49.48
Nairn*	m	34.34	27.53	30.99	26.86	32.69	28.71	31.12	26.30	32.58	26.79	30.90	26.29	30.04	25.83
	n	57.95	50.33	60.73	52.59	60.08	54.32	59.54	51.62	59.27	51.49	56.01	49.21	54.29	47.30
	p	47.79	40.69	48.39	41.91	48.24	42.97	47.27	41.07	47.67	41.08	44.71	38.52	42.77	36.44
Orkney	m	28.04	28.33	27.83	25.83	26.37	28.53	28.03	25.57	28.03	25.57	22.46	26.63	27.25	29.23
	n	49.36	40.01	50.04	40.44	48.57	40.68	47.22	39.76	47.22	39.76	43.51	35.51	40.39	33.06
	p	47.35	39.20	48.49	39.56	46.72	39.89	45.57	38.88	45.57	38.88	40.68	34.93	39.30	32.79
Peebles	m	35.28	33.35	35.78	33.40	33.07	31.59	31.63	26.73	31.93	26.67	24.00	20.30	24.98	21.13
	n	61.27	56.38	62.47	59.42	64.02	61.36	63.72	60.39	63.74	60.42	62.00	56.07	55.10	49.36
	p	49.93	46.03	50.31	46.44	48.83	45.64	47.86	42.20	47.95	42.13	42.24	36.75	39.65	33.56

County-of-Birth		1861 Male	1861 Female	1871 Male	1871 Female	1881 Male	1881 Female	1891 Pre-Revision Male	1891 Pre-Revision Female	1891 Post-Revision Male	1891 Post-Revision Female	1901 Male	1901 Female	1911 Male	1911 Female
Perth	m	34.52	30.02	33.34	29.68	34.06	31.52	31.08	28.40	31.07	28.47	27.81	24.87	27.71	22.39
	n	50.41	43.35	51.35	43.86	51.54	44.91	51.34	44.67	51.16	44.62	49.92	43.34	47.68	41.85
	p	46.98	40.65	46.98	40.62	46.64	41.27	45.08	39.83	45.05	39.87	42.62	37.28	40.70	34.82
Renfrew**	m	27.65	26.41	27.36	27.03	27.34	26.91	25.63	24.98	25.62	24.97	24.99	24.30	25.33	25.10
	n	64.15	56.78	65.63	59.25	65.31	59.55	63.54	57.81	63.53	57.80	59.71	55.11	56.09	52.47
	p	48.93	44.06	48.95	45.34	48.90	45.45	48.92	44.80	48.92	44.80	46.08	42.89	43.58	41.11
Ross & Cromarty*	m	30.55	26.73	32.82	29.05	34.44	30.72	34.50	30.31	34.58	30.43	32.29	29.23	26.00	29.83
	n	48.82	42.16	49.13	42.42	47.64	41.16	47.59	40.83	47.58	40.82	46.45	40.55	44.27	39.10
	p	46.96	40.65	47.43	41.01	46.13	39.94	45.94	39.53	45.93	39.53	44.46	39.02	39.97	37.73
Roxburgh	m	27.99	28.85	30.61	27.78	30.81	27.82	30.43	25.69	30.65	25.78	28.60	21.91	25.72	18.42
	n	57.87	51.36	57.47	51.61	56.15	51.44	55.56	49.90	55.57	49.86	49.92	44.08	44.77	40.29
	p	47.48	44.40	49.67	44.49	48.36	43.83	48.31	41.88	48.35	41.87	43.56	36.70	38.54	32.54
Selkirk	m	31.52	27.72	39.74	35.26	34.38	28.79	33.04	28.58	33.41	29.02	21.85	18.17	22.33	20.24
	n	65.59	61.82	64.21	59.42	67.29	63.43	69.94	63.41	69.75	63.29	60.10	53.34	49.83	43.43
	p	50.11	45.74	49.40	44.57	50.31	44.56	49.76	43.06	49.66	43.09	44.47	37.12	37.91	32.39

COUNTY-OF-BIRTH		1861		1871		1881		1891 Pre-Revision		1891 Post-Revision		1901		1911	
		MALE	FEMALE	MALE	FEMALE	MALE	FEMALE	MALE	FEMALE	MALE	FEMALE	MALE	FEMALE	MALE	FEMALE
Shetland	m	41.34	45.95	29.62	42.69	24.25	40.39	25.93	35.43	25.93	35.43	25.00	33.33	23.63	30.67
	n	51.67	36.53	53.15	36.21	50.22	34.68	47.96	33.68	47.96	33.68	45.65	32.59	43.99	32.12
	p	51.36	36.67	52.39	36.33	48.18	34.87	46.17	33.74	46.17	33.74	43.66	32.63	41.27	32.04
Stirling	m	32.65	29.47	31.40	29.54	31.66	29.74	30.20	28.91	30.67	29.11	29.12	28.61	26.45	27.26
	n	60.98	55.50	61.61	56.64	62.15	58.33	60.43	58.02	59.98	57.70	57.92	56.98	57.29	56.58
	p	50.65	46.31	50.77	46.78	50.72	47.59	48.64	46.82	48.59	46.78	46.23	45.92	44.99	45.10
Sutherland	m	27.49	27.53	27.84	28.23	30.70	31.03	26.66	28.59	26.66	28.59	24.57	27.99	28.23	28.80
	n	49.67	39.91	47.83	38.50	45.23	38.00	44.67	39.84	44.67	39.84	43.14	38.62	41.88	37.17
	p	46.64	38.51	44.86	37.25	42.67	36.97	41.67	38.16	41.67	38.16	39.52	36.76	38.96	35.47
Wigtown	m	24.37	24.19	25.94	23.90	26.02	26.02	31.78	27.16	31.78	27.16	32.62	26.27	30.45	26.69
	n	60.87	52.07	59.51	49.58	57.35	48.59	56.24	48.38	56.24	48.38	51.25	45.46	48.10	43.21
	p	51.22	45.23	51.73	43.99	51.33	43.78	51.18	44.19	51.18	44.19	47.28	41.57	44.23	39.57

Appendix 4

The County-of-Birth of Scots Enumerated in England and Wales in the 1911 Census

BORN IN	RESIDENTS		VISITORS		AS % OF TOTAL BORN IN COUNTY*		RANK ORDER OF LOSSES	
	Male	Female	Male	Female	Male	Female	Male	Female
Scotland	159,744	158,852	1,498	1,731	7.15	6.60		
Aberdeen	13,046	13,437	95	153	7.89	7.38	7	9
Argyll	2,050	2,132	20	19	5.05	4.77	27	26
Ayr	7,727	6,917	76	71	5.38	4.55	25	28
Banff	2,107	2,333	19	25	5.57	5.51	24	19
Berwick	3,412	3,557	17	20	16.44	16.04	2	2
Bute	530	546	5	7	6.91	6.29	15	15
Caithness	1,292	1,403	13	9	6.35	5.83	18	17
Clackmannan	810	734	6	9	4.72	4.09	32	32
Dunbarton	2,415	2,215	30	33	4.81	4.27	31	31
Dumfries	7,739	8,586	39	52	17.00	17.54	1	1
Edinburgh (Midlothian)	22,042	22,982	208	310	8.39	9.89	6	6
Elgin (Moray)	1,785	2,148	19	20	7.31	7.80	11	8
Fife	6,104	5,588	48	66	5.15	4.42	26	29
Forfar (Angus)	10,245	8,558	96	102	7.53	5.66	10	18
Haddington (East Lothian)	1,587	1,743	12	18	6.53	7.04	17	10
Inverness	3,135	3,714	32	52	6.55	6.68	16	12
Kincardine	1,352	1,390	12	14	5.74	5.41	22	20
Kinross	256	196	3	6	6.05	4.35	19	30
Kirkcudbright	3,139	3,400	35	38	14.31	14.63	4	3
Lanark	34,826	32,673	391	301	5.81	5.17	21	23
Linlithgow (West Lothian)	1,401	1,376	25	22	3.80	3.62	33	33
Nairn	320	443	11	12	7.20	8.72	12	7
Orkney	824	923	15	11	5.62	5.29	23	21
Peebles	562	559	6	8	7.19	6.95	14	11
Perth	4,884	4,806	40	81	7.20	6.47	12	14
Renfrew	7,771	7,080	56	57	5.98	5.16	20	24
Ross and Cromarty	2,058	2,488	14	28	4.90	5.27	30	22
Roxburgh	4,297	3,884	24	33	15.13	12.77	3	4
Selkirk	898	783	9	14	7.84	6.63	8	13
Shetland	1,060	900	12	9	7.73	5.07	9	25
Stirling	3,760	3,657	46	48	5.00	4.68	29	27
Sutherland	572	791	10	5	5.02	6.00	28	16
Wigtown	2,371	2,850	14	26	11.03	12.01	5	5
County not stated	3,365	4,058	40	52				

* The total born refers to those Scots living in England, Scotland and Wales. Taken from the *1911 Census (E. & W.)*, Vol. IX, p.242 and the *1911 Census of Scotland*, Vol. X, pp.502–523.

273

Appendix 5

The Percentage of Current Migrants and Emigrants Leaving their County-of-Birth

Plus or minus two standard errors — see Appendix 1 for further information on how standard errors calculated.

County-of-Birth	Decade	MIGRANTS						EMIGRANTS					
		Standard Errors Deducted		Estimated Migrants		Standard Errors Added		Standard Errors Deducted		Estimated Emigrants		Standard Errors Added	
		Male	Female	Male	Female	Male	Female	Male	Female	Male	Female	Male	Female
Aberdeen	1861–1871	-4.88	-5.13	-4.94	-5.15	-5.04	-5.22	-5.91	-2.64	-6.00	-2.68	-6.04	-2.70
	1871–1881	-5.70	-5.73	-5.78	-5.79	-5.82	-5.82	-5.84	-3.86	-5.89	-3.90	-5.92	-3.92
	1881–1891	-5.67	-5.41	-5.73	-5.47	-5.76	-5.50	-8.90	-5.08	-8.93	-5.12	-8.94	-5.13
	1891–1901	-7.38	-6.67	-7.42	-6.73	-7.44	-6.75	-4.79	-2.31	-4.80	-2.36	-4.79	-2.37
	1901–1911	-4.17	-4.21	-4.20	-4.28	-4.22	-4.31	-10.85	-6.91	-10.84	-6.96	-10.82	-6.98
Argyll	1861–1871	-10.20	-12.55	-10.26	-12.44	-10.44	-12.54	-6.72	-3.91	-6.61	-3.97	-6.56	-4.00
	1871–1881	-8.38	-11.08	-8.53	-11.08	-8.61	-11.08	-4.99	-2.66	-4.85	-2.66	-4.79	-2.69
	1881–1891	-8.32	-10.57	-8.45	-10.59	-8.52	-10.59	-6.99	-3.50	-6.78	-3.41	-6.70	-3.40
	1891–1901	-10.72	-9.79	-10.84	-9.80	-10.91	-9.81	-3.16	-3.07	-2.84	-2.80	-2.72	-2.73
	1901–1911	-7.42	-9.31	-7.55	-9.34	-7.65	-9.37	-9.07	-6.58	-8.59	-6.11	-8.42	-5.95
Ayr	1861–1871	-11.76	-11.55	-11.74	-11.51	-11.85	-11.60	-7.50	-5.25	-7.81	-5.37	-7.93	-5.43
	1871–1881	-10.07	-10.49	-10.14	-10.51	-10.18	-10.52	-4.79	-3.03	-4.96	-3.15	-5.02	-3.21
	1881–1891	-9.51	-9.63	-9.59	-9.65	-9.64	-9.66	-7.90	-4.73	-7.97	-4.85	-7.98	-4.89
	1891–1901	-9.21	-8.95	-9.32	-8.96	-9.38	-8.97	-2.97	-2.20	-2.97	-2.34	-2.96	-2.39
	1901–1911	-6.90	-7.32	-7.04	-7.33	-7.12	-7.35	-9.04	-5.28	-9.00	-5.45	-8.96	-5.49
Banff	1861–1871	-11.28	-11.09	-11.48	-11.18	-11.69	-11.33	-5.52	-2.57	-5.48	-2.55	-5.46	-2.54
	1871–1881	-14.49	-13.57	-14.72	-13.74	-14.82	-13.82	-5.42	-2.98	-5.34	-2.93	-5.31	-2.91
	1881–1891	-7.88	-9.35	-8.08	-9.58	-8.17	-9.67	-8.94	-6.74	-8.88	-6.68	-8.85	-6.65
	1891–1901	-14.93	-13.01	-15.04	-13.24	-15.10	-13.32	-4.93	-2.89	-4.89	-2.83	-4.86	-2.81
	1901–1911	-4.28	-9.92	-4.31	-10.20	-4.34	-10.31	-8.96	-5.11	-8.95	-5.03	-8.93	-5.00

County-of-Birth	Decade	MIGRANTS						EMIGRANTS					
		Standard Errors Deducted Male	Standard Errors Deducted Female	Estimated Migrants Male	Estimated Migrants Female	Standard Errors Added Male	Standard Errors Added Female	Standard Errors Deducted Male	Standard Errors Deducted Female	Estimated Emigrants Male	Estimated Emigrants Female	Standard Errors Added Male	Standard Errors Added Female
Berwick	1861–1871	-11.61	-9.69	-11.62	-10.08	-11.79	-10.34	-8.79	-7.47	-8.60	-7.79	-8.52	-7.89
	1871–1881	-13.11	-13.76	-13.27	-14.09	-13.35	-14.22	-7.70	-5.74	-7.59	-5.96	-7.55	-6.04
	1881–1891	-12.31	-11.74	-12.52	-12.01	-12.62	-12.11	-10.30	-7.58	-10.26	-7.70	-10.25	-7.75
	1891–1901	-14.94	-14.54	-15.21	-14.70	-15.35	-14.77	-5.80	-4.67	-5.79	-4.72	-5.80	-4.76
	1901–1911	-8.56	-10.79	-8.92	-10.88	-9.12	-10.94	-7.29	-5.90	-7.35	-5.87	-7.39	-5.87
Bute	1861–1871	-13.67	-14.02	-13.75	-13.99	-13.99	-14.15	-2.49	-1.95	-2.82	-2.21	-2.95	-2.33
	1871–1881	-11.23	-15.03	-11.39	-15.10	-11.48	-15.13	-3.89	-1.00	-4.22	-1.32	-4.35	-1.45
	1881–1891	-11.82	-12.35	-11.94	-12.41	-12.01	-12.44	-6.33	-1.47	-6.53	-1.82	-6.60	-1.95
	1891–1901	-12.27	-12.86	-12.37	-12.90	-12.44	-12.92	-3.94	-2.44	-4.07	-2.89	-4.11	-3.06
	1901–1911	-9.81	-10.98	-9.91	-11.00	-9.98	-11.02	-9.73	-4.90	-9.73	-5.41	-9.71	-5.57
Caithness	1861–1871	-8.25	-8.62	-8.31	-8.63	-8.39	-8.69	-6.88	-4.09	-6.82	-4.09	-6.79	-4.09
	1871–1881	-9.22	-10.30	-9.30	-10.33	-9.34	-10.35	-5.73	-2.54	-5.64	-2.51	-5.61	-2.51
	1881–1891	-6.14	-7.06	-6.21	-7.07	-6.25	-7.08	-8.57	-4.88	-8.48	-4.84	-8.43	-4.82
	1891–1901	-13.76	-13.78	-13.81	-13.78	-13.85	-13.79	-4.60	-2.58	-4.47	-2.51	-4.41	-2.48
	1901–1911	-1.57	-6.22	-1.62	-6.19	-1.67	-6.20	-10.61	-4.69	-10.45	-4.60	-10.38	-4.56
Clackmannan	1861–1871	-10.48	-11.97	-10.42	-11.83	-10.68	-12.03	-8.15	-4.02	-8.59	-4.24	-8.73	-4.34
	1871–1881	-18.81	-16.02	-18.91	-16.04	-18.96	-16.05	-4.71	-4.12	-4.99	-4.34	-5.09	-4.44
	1881–1891	-12.03	-10.48	-12.15	-10.51	-12.21	-10.52	-7.78	-5.52	-7.89	-5.75	-7.92	-5.84
	1891–1901	-19.71	-17.04	-19.80	-17.05	-19.86	-17.06	4.77	6.51	4.66	6.12	4.63	5.98
	1901–1911	-14.27	-13.89	-14.42	-13.92	-14.51	-13.95	-7.54	-4.77	-7.52	-5.04	-7.48	-5.11

County-of-Birth	Decade	MIGRANTS						EMIGRANTS					
		Standard Errors Deducted		Estimated Migrants		Standard Errors Added		Standard Errors Deducted		Estimated Emigrants		Standard Errors Added	
		Male	Female	Male	Female	Male	Female	Male	Female	Male	Female	Male	Female
Dumfries													
	1861-1871	-5.94	-5.94	-5.93	-6.26	-6.06	-6.46	-10.41	-6.67	-10.28	-6.80	-10.22	-6.85
	1871-1881	-11.97	-11.35	-12.07	-11.58	-12.12	-11.66	-5.83	-5.24	-5.76	-5.38	-5.73	-5.43
	1881-1891	-9.83	-7.83	-9.97	-8.05	-10.04	-8.14	-9.17	-8.06	-9.17	-8.15	-9.18	-8.19
	1891-1901	-13.49	-12.96	-13.67	-13.07	-13.77	-13.12	-4.99	-3.09	-5.07	-3.16	-5.11	-3.20
	1901-1911	-8.41	-8.59	-8.66	-8.61	-8.80	-8.65	-6.10	-6.08	-6.27	-6.05	-6.37	-6.06
Dunbarton													
	1861-1871	-17.65	-18.62	-17.60	-18.43	-17.83	-18.58	-7.10	-4.66	-7.16	-4.64	-7.19	-4.63
	1871-1881	-12.91	-13.81	-13.01	-13.79	-13.07	-13.78	-5.97	-4.18	-6.07	-4.17	-6.13	-4.16
	1881-1891	-10.63	-12.73	-10.72	-12.73	-10.77	-12.73	-9.29	-6.55	-9.41	-6.55	-9.48	-6.54
	1891-1901	-13.58	-14.30	-13.67	-14.30	-13.72	-14.30	-2.56	-1.18	-2.71	-1.20	-2.79	-1.20
	1901-1911	-8.55	-10.10	-8.64	-10.13	-8.70	-10.14	-7.95	-6.55	-8.12	-6.62	-8.21	-6.66
Edinburgh (Midlothian)													
	1861-1871	-5.86	-5.50	-5.86	-5.53	-6.00	-5.65	-8.53	-7.31	-8.61	-7.17	-8.66	-7.11
	1871-1881	-6.56	-6.54	-6.62	-6.61	-6.66	-6.64	-8.21	-6.63	-8.32	-6.54	-8.38	-6.50
	1881-1891	-6.35	-6.59	-6.40	-6.64	-6.43	-6.66	-9.05	-3.81	-9.16	-3.76	-9.23	-3.74
	1891-1901	-6.74	-6.38	-6.79	-6.42	-6.82	-6.43	-6.17	-5.38	-6.32	-5.38	-6.39	-5.38
	1901-1911	-6.51	-6.34	-6.56	-6.37	-6.59	-6.38	-7.29	-4.83	-7.48	-4.88	-7.57	-4.91
Elgin (Moray)													
	1861-1871	-11.93	-11.40	-12.05	-11.47	-12.24	-11.62	-9.31	-7.18	-9.49	-7.25	-9.57	-7.27
	1871-1881	-11.19	-11.76	-11.34	-11.87	-11.41	-11.93	-5.49	-3.64	-5.60	-3.74	-5.64	-3.78
	1881-1891	-10.38	-9.89	-10.49	-9.99	-10.55	-10.04	-10.37	-5.16	-10.43	-5.26	-10.44	-5.30
	1891-1901	-12.53	-12.82	-12.58	-12.89	-12.62	-12.93	-4.10	-2.10	-4.13	-2.23	-4.13	-2.28
	1901-1911	-9.12	-10.00	-9.11	-10.05	-9.14	-10.08	-8.27	-5.51	-8.28	-5.70	-8.27	-5.75

County-of-Birth	Decade	MIGRANTS						EMIGRANTS					
		Standard Errors Deducted		Estimated Migrants		Standard Errors Added		Standard Errors Deducted		Estimated Emigrants		Standard Errors Added	
		Male	Female	Male	Female	Male	Female	Male	Female	Male	Female	Male	Female
Fife	1861–1871	-10.34	-8.65	-10.38	-8.64	-10.51	-8.73	-4.54	-2.27	-4.45	-2.22	-4.41	-2.20
	1871–1881	-10.11	-9.25	-10.22	-9.31	-10.27	-9.33	-4.34	-2.75	-4.27	-2.71	-4.24	-2.69
	1881–1891	-7.23	-6.55	-7.32	-6.60	-7.37	-6.63	-5.90	-4.53	-5.87	-4.50	-5.86	-4.48
	1891–1901	-7.49	-7.98	-7.56	-8.02	-7.60	-8.04	-1.63	.43	-1.64	.44	-1.64	.44
	1901–1911	-3.36	-4.27	-3.41	-4.31	-3.45	-4.33	-5.49	-4.03	-5.55	-4.04	-5.57	-4.04
Forfar (Angus)	1861–1871	-5.33	-3.91	-5.35	-3.91	-5.45	-3.98	-5.89	-2.76	-6.27	-2.95	-6.42	-3.03
	1871–1881	-6.18	-4.87	-6.23	-4.90	-6.26	-4.91	-6.57	-4.30	-6.82	-4.53	-6.92	-4.62
	1881–1891	-5.48	-4.42	-5.51	-4.42	-5.53	-4.43	-9.29	-6.00	-9.45	-6.25	-9.51	-6.34
	1891–1901	-8.41	-6.35	-8.43	-6.34	-8.45	-6.34	-6.37	-2.22	-6.47	-2.50	-6.49	-2.60
	1901–1911	-5.59	-4.99	-5.60	-4.96	-5.62	-4.96	-9.59	-5.79	-9.62	-6.07	-9.62	-6.16
Haddington (East Lothian)	1861–1871	-14.42	-14.41	-14.42	-14.47	-14.60	-14.65	-5.73	-5.16	-6.09	-5.23	-6.20	-5.28
	1871–1881	-14.71	-15.86	-14.84	-15.98	-14.91	-16.02	-4.53	-3.81	-4.68	-3.95	-4.73	-4.01
	1881–1891	-16.25	-12.21	-16.41	-12.32	-16.50	-12.36	-6.59	-8.43	-6.63	-8.57	-6.63	-8.63
	1891–1901	-17.16	-18.82	-17.39	-18.89	-17.51	-18.92	-5.45	-1.25	-5.35	-1.46	-5.29	-1.53
	1901–1911	-9.79	-11.29	-10.10	-11.37	-10.27	-11.42	-6.17	-5.71	-6.01	-5.96	-5.92	-6.04
Inverness	1861–1871	-9.12	-9.64	-9.25	-9.70	-9.41	-9.83	-5.79	-2.21	-5.64	-2.19	-5.59	-2.18
	1871–1881	-6.45	-8.38	-6.59	-8.48	-6.66	-8.53	-5.60	-3.77	-5.46	-3.70	-5.40	-3.68
	1881–1891	-9.71	-8.79	-9.78	-8.84	-9.82	-8.87	-6.01	-3.36	-5.85	-3.25	-5.79	-3.21
	1891–1901	-9.39	-11.82	-9.41	-11.80	-9.45	-11.80	-5.07	-1.11	-4.84	-.93	-4.75	-.88
	1901–1911	-6.68	-8.16	-6.64	-8.08	-6.66	-8.06	-7.62	-2.36	-7.31	-2.07	-7.20	-1.97

County-of-Birth	Decade	MIGRANTS Standard Errors Deducted		Estimated Migrants		Standard Errors Added		EMIGRANTS Standard Errors Deducted		Estimated Emigrants		Standard Errors Added	
		Male	Female	Male	Female	Male	Female	Male	Female	Male	Female	Male	Female
Kincardine	1861-1871	-14.79	-15.99	-15.08	-16.14	-15.39	-16.35	-6.59	-3.90	-6.46	-3.81	-6.41	-3.77
	1871-1881	-16.15	-17.78	-16.49	-18.07	-16.64	-18.19	-5.83	-4.42	-5.70	-4.32	-5.64	-4.28
	1881-1891	-12.24	-13.59	-12.53	-13.95	-12.66	-14.09	-6.43	-3.84	-6.33	-3.72	-6.28	-3.67
	1891-1901	-17.47	-17.85	-17.66	-18.21	-17.74	-18.35	-5.47	-3.60	-5.38	-3.48	-5.33	-3.44
	1901-1911	-21.62	-21.84	-21.72	-22.22	-21.78	-22.36	-6.85	-3.09	-6.77	-3.01	-6.73	-2.99
Kinross	1861-1871	-22.54	-20.15	-22.57	-20.01	-22.95	-20.28	-6.36	-5.29	-6.21	-5.39	-6.15	-5.45
	1871-1881	-28.53	-24.59	-28.77	-24.67	-28.89	-24.71	-1.34	.78	-1.10	.83	-1.00	.81
	1881-1891	-23.02	-25.81	-23.30	-25.90	-23.47	-25.95	-6.02	-1.79	-5.69	-1.59	-5.55	-1.53
	1891-1901	-22.86	-18.99	-23.12	-19.11	-23.29	-19.18	-1.24	-1.18	-.72	-.74	-.52	-.62
	1901-1911	-10.49	-16.29	-10.81	-16.41	-11.03	-16.49	-9.86	-5.82	-9.12	-5.34	-8.85	-5.39
Kirkcudbright	1861-1871	-6.04	-3.27	-6.01	-3.78	-6.12	-4.03	-6.25	-5.78	-6.13	-6.06	-6.08	-6.15
	1871-1881	-11.77	-11.85	-11.86	-12.18	-11.91	-12.31	-15.02	-12.65	-14.98	-12.77	-14.97	-12.82
	1881-1891	-10.56	-9.45	-10.71	-9.73	-10.79	-9.85	-10.44	-7.54	-10.46	-7.70	-10.48	-7.77
	1891-1901	-13.08	-12.02	-13.28	-12.16	-13.39	-12.23	-8.38	-7.31	-8.46	-7.38	-8.50	-7.42
	1901-1911	-11.51	-10.70	-11.81	-10.68	-11.98	-10.69	-8.45	-6.91	-8.60	-6.91	-8.69	-6.93
Lanark & Renfrew	1861-1871	-2.97	-3.39	-2.96	-3.37	-3.04	-3.44	-8.76	-6.48	-8.88	-6.39	-8.94	-6.35
	1871-1881	-4.44	-4.69	-4.47	-4.71	-4.49	-4.72	-8.33	-6.25	-8.43	-6.19	-8.49	-6.16
	1881-1891	-3.21	-3.68	-3.23	-3.70	-3.25	-3.71	-9.14	-6.90	-9.25	-6.87	-9.31	-6.85
	1891-1901	-3.20	-3.59	-3.22	-3.61	-3.24	-3.62	-5.21	-2.83	-5.34	-2.82	-5.41	-2.81
	1901-1911	-3.78	-4.14	-3.80	-4.16	-3.81	-4.17	-8.14	-6.21	-8.29	-6.24	-8.36	-6.25

County-of-Birth	Decade	MIGRANTS								EMIGRANTS							
		Standard Errors Deducted		Estimated Migrants		Standard Errors Added		Standard Errors Deducted		Estimated Emigrants		Standard Errors Added	
		Male	Female	Male	Female	Male	Female	Male	Female	Male	Female	Male	Female
Linlithgow (West Lothian)													
	1861-1871	-20.46	-22.69	-20.44	-22.56	-20.62	-22.69	-7.32	-4.52	-7.36	-4.52	-7.38	-4.52
	1871-1881	-21.35	-23.55	-21.45	-23.56	-21.50	-23.56	-5.11	-3.91	-5.13	-3.91	-5.14	-3.92
	1881-1891	-14.83	-15.59	-14.95	-15.61	-15.01	-15.62	-5.92	-6.02	-5.97	-6.01	-5.99	-6.01
	1891-1901	-14.50	-18.85	-14.64	-18.88	-14.71	-18.90	-3.47	-.47	-3.53	-.49	-3.56	-.51
	1901-1911	-9.93	-13.32	-10.08	-13.38	-10.17	-13.41	-6.55	-4.76	-6.63	-4.77	-6.66	-4.77
Nairn													
	1861-1871 -12.73	-13.54	-12.96	-13.68	-13.29	-13.97	-6.14	-3.21	-6.52	-3.34	-6.66	-3.39	-8.58
	1871-1881	-11.39	-9.70	-11.62	-9.92	-11.74	-10.04	-8.17	-8.33	-8.40	-8.52	-8.48	-2.02
	1881-1891	-14.65	-15.13	-14.77	-15.23	-14.84	-15.29	-9.53	-1.65	-9.72	-1.92	-9.79	-5.88
	1891-1901	-12.84	-13.13	-12.84	-13.11	-12.87	-13.12	-5.47	-5.46	-5.59	-5.78	-5.62	-5.93
	1901-1911	-13.41	-12.05	-13.28	-11.89	-13.28	-11.86	-8.87	-5.34	-9.02	-5.79	-9.04	
Orkney													
	1861-1871	-5.51	-6.54	-5.52	-6.54	-5.56	-6.56	-8.63	-3.74	-8.64	-3.76	-8.64	-3.77
	1871-1881	-3.67	-4.58	-3.71	-4.59	-3.73	-4.59	-5.79	-3.17	-5.75	-3.16	-5.73	-3.16
	1881-1891	-5.00	-5.88	-5.04	-5.89	-5.06	-5.90	-10.44	-4.90	-10.38	-4.87	-10.35	-4.86
	1891-1901	-9.29	-9.66	-9.33	-9.67	-9.36	-9.68	-5.76	-2.80	-5.65	-2.72	-5.61	-2.70
	1901-1911	-2.48	-4.16	-2.55	-4.19	-2.60	-4.21	-9.97	-4.80	-9.73	-4.68	-9.64	-2.64
Peebles													
	1861-1871	-22.83	-22.74	-22.83	-22.75	-23.10	-22.97	-3.82	-4.48	-4.22	-4.52	-4.36	-4.60
	1871-1881	-18.99	-18.04	-19.20	-18.16	-19.31	-18.20	-6.37	-5.13	-6.62	-5.34	-6.71	-5.45
	1881-1891	-17.89	-15.36	-18.11	-15.47	-18.23	-15.51	-7.12	-6.14	-7.22	-6.39	-7.25	-6.48
	1891-1901	-21.85	-17.73	-22.11	-17.82	-22.26	-17.86	-4.34	-4.88	-4.32	-5.23	-4.30	-5.36
	1901-1911	-9.81	-11.46	-10.21	-11.57	-10.44	-11.64	-10.03	-7.85	-9.90	-8.17	-9.83	-8.28

County-of-Birth	Decade	MIGRANTS Standard Errors Deducted Male	Female	Estimated Migrants Male	Female	Standard Errors Added Male	Female	EMIGRANTS Standard Errors Deducted Male	Female	Estimated Emigrants Male	Female	Standard Errors Added Male	Female
Perth													
	1861-1871	-13.50	-12.77	-13.65	-12.78	-13.86	-12.91	-6.41	-3.90	-6.24	-3.94	-6.18	-3.97
	1871-1881	-11.60	-11.90	-11.84	-12.02	-11.95	-12.07	-5.08	-3.18	-4.85	-3.09	-4.76	-3.08
	1881-1891	-11.85	-9.61	-12.06	-9.77	-12.16	-9.83	-7.89	-5.34	-7.60	-5.13	-7.49	-5.07
	1891-1901	-8.95	-7.89	-9.17	-8.08	-9.28	-8.16	-6.91	-5.25	-6.48	-4.84	-6.32	-4.71
	1901-1911	-6.40	-8.22	-6.60	-8.43	-6.72	-8.52	-9.02	-6.19	-8.44	-5.52	-8.24	-5.30
Ross & Cromarty													
	1861-1871	-6.23	-6.80	-6.33	-6.87	-6.45	-6.96	-6.66	-3.94	-6.54	-3.91	-6.49	-3.89
	1871-1881	-8.54	-8.27	-8.63	-8.33	-8.67	-8.36	-6.20	-3.79	-6.12	-3.74	-6.07	-3.73
	1881-1891	-6.16	-6.23	-6.18	-6.23	-6.20	-6.24	-7.02	-4.52	-6.96	-4.48	-6.93	-4.46
	1891-1901	-7.85	-9.90	-7.79	-9.84	-7.79	-9.82	-5.66	-1.66	-5.61	-1.61	-5.58	-1.59
	1901-1911	-3.83	-2.81	-3.70	-2.64	-3.69	-2.59	-8.50	-6.94	-8.44	-6.87	-8.41	-6.85
Roxburgh													
	1861-1871	-17.16	-16.14	-17.13	-16.31	-17.26	-16.49	-10.92	-6.97	-10.76	-7.75	-10.69	-8.00
	1871-1881	-7.23	-6.77	-7.36	-7.01	-7.42	-7.10	-8.73	-6.91	-8.68	-7.35	-8.67	-7.51
	1881-1891	-14.68	-13.18	-14.80	-13.31	-14.87	-13.36	-4.10	-2.43	-4.16	-2.80	-4.19	-2.94
	1891-1901	-6.54	-6.02	-6.78	-6.12	-6.90	-6.18	-12.90	-9.92	-13.00	-10.06	-13.06	-10.13
	1901-1911	-7.69	-7.87	-7.97	-7.94	-8.13	-7.99	-8.15	-7.09	-8.33	-7.02	-8.43	-7.01
Selkirk													
	1861-1871	-10.61	-9.13	-10.52	-9.98	-10.78	-10.48	-0.12	1.52	-.18	2.84	-.23	3.15
	1871-1881	-6.64	-5.57	-6.76	-5.95	-6.82	-6.09	-0.72	-.15	-.85	.21	-.93	.35
	1881-1891	-10.78	-12.22	-10.90	-12.43	-10.96	-12.51	-21.06	-17.74	-21.16	-17.65	-21.21	-17.62
	1891-1901	-24.21	-19.96	-24.32	-20.03	-24.38	-20.07	4.61	3.47	4.42	3.48	4.31	3.47
	1901-1911	-8.14	-9.63	-8.39	-9.66	-8.54	-9.68	-5.36	-3.26	-5.36	-3.39	-5.36	-3.46

County-of-Birth	Decade	MIGRANTS Standard Errors Deducted Male	Female	Estimated Migrants Male	Female	Standard Errors Added Male	Female	EMIGRANTS Standard Errors Deducted Male	Female	Estimated Emigrants Male	Female	Standard Errors Added Male	Female
Shetland	1861-1871	-4.51	-4.60	-4.52	-4.61	-4.55	-4.62	-9.64	-3.06	-9.61	-3.05	-9.60	-3.05
	1871-1881	-3.99	-4.47	-4.03	-4.47	-4.04	-4.48	-13.99	-8.64	-13.96	-8.63	-13.94	-8.63
	1881-1891	-4.75	-3.71	-4.79	-3.72	-4.81	-3.72	-9.23	-3.40	-9.17	-3.38	-9.15	-3.37
	1891-1901	-5.71	-3.95	-5.75	-3.96	-5.78	-3.97	-4.70	-3.00	-4.59	-2.96	-4.55	-2.94
	1901-1911	-.78	-1.88	-.83	-1.91	-.86	-1.92	-9.77	-3.52	-9.62	-3.45	-9.56	-3.42
Stirling	1861-1871	-15.75	-14.23	-15.62	-14.44	-15.76	-5.84	-3.99	-5.83	-3.98	-5.84	-3.97	
	1871-1881	-11.46	-14.62	-11.57	-14.63	-11.63	-14.63	-5.11	-2.99	-5.13	-2.99	-5.15	-2.99
	1881-1891	-11.14	-12.05	-11.24	-12.07	-11.29	-12.08	-6.28	-5.03	-6.31	-5.04	-6.33	-5.04
	1891-1901	-6.02	-8.37	-6.14	-8.41	-6.21	-8.42	-5.94	-4.61	-6.00	-4.61	-6.03	-4.61
	1901-1911	-7.95	-10.17	-8.05	-10.19	-8.11	-10.21	-6.60	-5.45	-6.70	-5.48	-6.74	-5.50
Sutherland	1861-1871	-6.01	-8.46	-6.13	-8.54	-6.27	-8.66	-6.19	-4.10	-6.08	-4.06	-6.03	-4.04
	1871-1881	-7.00	-7.69	-7.08	-7.74	-7.13	-7.78	-7.09	-5.61	-7.01	-5.58	-6.98	-5.57
	1881-1891	-6.66	-8.63	-6.65	-8.60	-6.67	-8.60	-7.79	-3.43	-7.73	-3.42	-7.70	-3.41
	1891-1901	-9.02	-8.63	-8.94	-8.50	-8.94	-8.47	-3.17	-2.49	-3.11	-2.47	-3.07	-2.46
	1901-1911	-3.14	-7.07	-2.96	-6.82	-2.93	-6.75	-9.26	-4.66	-9.13	-4.60	-9.08	-4.57
Wigtown	1861-1871	-10.45	-10.35	-10.51	-10.50	-10.65	-10.64	-10.89	-6.07	-10.70	-6.46	-10.62	-6.59
	1871-1881	-10.09	-7.28	-10.23	-7.49	-10.30	-7.57	-6.08	-6.98	-5.97	-7.19	-5.92	-7.26
	1881-1891	-11.33	-9.50	-11.47	-9.65	-11.54	-9.71	-8.74	-6.53	-8.73	-6.65	-8.73	-6.70
	1891-1901	-15.47	-14.22	-15.65	-14.32	-15.75	-14.36	-6.26	-4.38	-6.26	-4.40	-6.27	-4.42
	1901-1911	-8.79	-8.39	-9.06	-8.47	-9.21	-8.51	-6.14	-5.48	-6.13	-5.40	-6.13	-5.38

Appendix 6
Population Density in Scotland by County-of-Birth in 1891

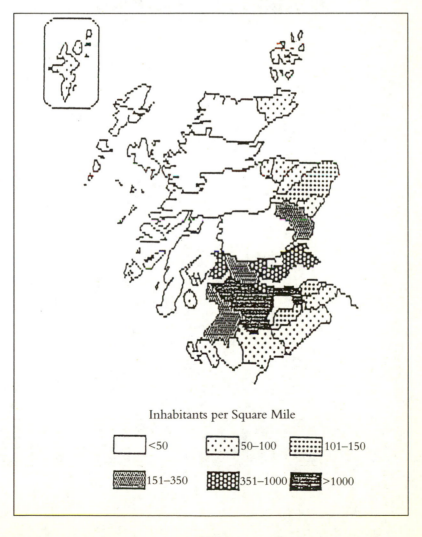

Inhabitants per Square Mile

<50   50–100   101–150

151–350   351–1000   >1000

Appendix 7

Maps to Show the Proportion of Current Migrant Losses to the County-of-Birth by Decade and Gender.

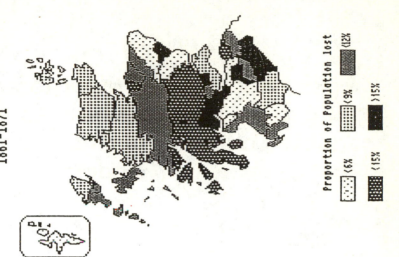

FEMALE MIGRANTS FROM COUNTY-OF-BIRTH 1861-1871

Proportion of Population lost

<6% <9% <12% <15% >15%

MALE MIGRANTS FROM COUNTY-OF-BIRTH 1861-1871

Proportion of Population lost

<6% <9% <12% <15% >15%

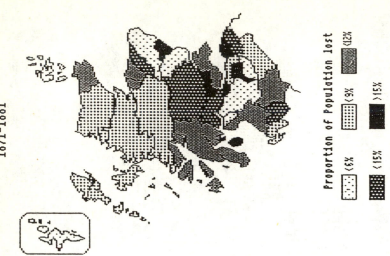

FEMALE MIGRANTS FROM COUNTY-OF-BIRTH
1871-1881

Proportion of Population lost

<6%   <9%   <12%
<15%   >15%

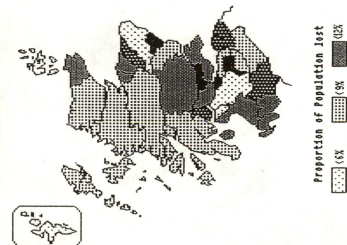

MALE MIGRANTS FROM COUNTY-OF-BIRTH
1871-1881

Proportion of Population lost

<6%   <9%   <12%
<15%   >15%

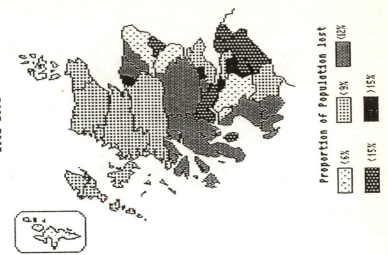

FEMALE MIGRANTS FROM COUNTY-OF-BIRTH
1881-1891

Proportion of Population lost

<9% <6% <12%

<15% >15%

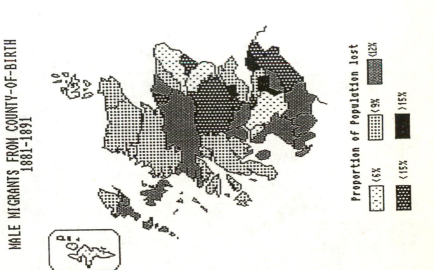

MALE MIGRANTS FROM COUNTY-OF-BIRTH
1881-1891

Proportion of Population lost

<9% <6% <12%

<15% >15%

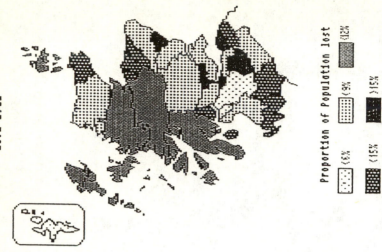

FEMALE MIGRANTS FROM COUNTY-OF-BIRTH
1891-1901

Proportion of Population lost

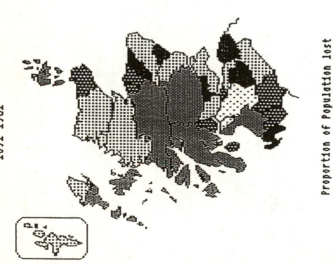

MALE MIGRANTS FROM COUNTY-OF-BIRTH
1891-1901

Proportion of Population lost

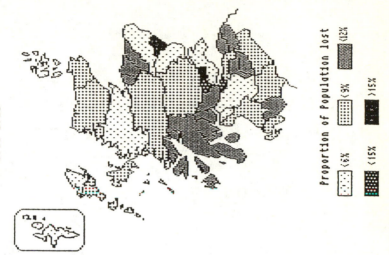

FEMALE MIGRANTS FROM COUNTY-OF-BIRTH 1901-1911

Proportion of Population lost

<6%   <9%   <12%

<15%   >15%

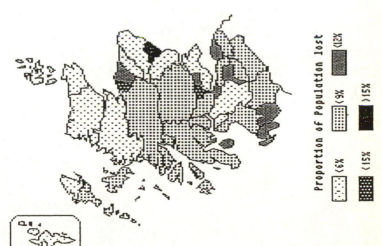

MALE MIGRANTS FROM COUNTY-OF-BIRTH 1901-1911

Proportion of Population lost

<6%   <9%   <12%

<15%   >15%

Appendix 8

Current Migrant Losses by Age-Band of Departure, Decade, Population Category and Gender

Estimates shown with two standard errors added or deducted.*

Key

* See Appendix 1 for further information on the calculation of standard errors.

Three estimates are provided for each calculation.

The top estimate has been calculated with two standard errors added to every age-band in the migrant age-structure according to population category.

The middle estimate is the original measurement with the correct application of the migrant age-structure.

The bottom estimate has been calculated with two standard errors deducted from every age-band in the migrant age-structure according to population category.

HIGHLANDS   Age-Band in Years

	Total	<5	<10	<15	<20	<25	<30	<35	<40	<45	<50	<55	<60	<65	<70	<75	75+
1861-1871																	
Male	-20979.6	-4569.83	-2883.12	-1517.45	-3713.94	-5489.55	-2119.43	338.64	-190.85	-444.25	-266.04	-82.78	-25.91	214.15	389.21	-12.92	-625.98
	-20612.5	-4418.04	-2824.21	-1599.18	-3682.05	-5317.87	-2124.88	57.40	-287.65	-374.09	-267.29	-73.92	46.96	289.28	487.65	52.98	-566.72
	-20378.5	-4378.16	-2984.05	-1784.97	-3636.07	-4955.71	-2155.20	-509.35	-526.76	-214.80	-250.93	-51.96	194.52	448.78	679.62	175.09	-448.36
Female	-24847.6	-4622.94	-3072.89	-2030.18	-4730.69	-7556.36	-9827.66	730.54	881.18	199.88	185.54	-2.29	-103.70	-39.86	149.25	-138.57	-848.65
	-24565.2	-4494.30	-2966.49	-2117.57	-4521.48	-7122.30	-4005.75	240.17	768.82	202.84	112.52	.81	-89.66	32.98	278.50	-63.39	-841.09
	-24533.9	-4514.95	-3035.23	-2282.45	-4098.70	-6290.50	-4368.48	-740.55	581.70	222.17	-17.57	23.72	12.77	176.88	529.10	86.68	-823.49
1871-1881																	
Male	-18443.5	-4353.07	-2875.30	-1554.27	-3694.26	-5421.04	-1901.02	712.72	265.59	-28.60	4.71	71.12	103.91	367.07	389.31	-30.04	-599.46
	-18286.5	-4341.71	-2980.60	-1592.78	-3690.20	-5321.05	-1890.53	519.48	103.01	3.37	-8.13	140.09	259.35	416.03	445.29	21.80	-559.09
	-17969.2	-4325.19	-2966.89	-1660.49	-3645.55	-5119.61	-1886.79	133.85	-20.75	83.20	-6.98	307.64	514.33	478.65	548.37	102.98	-495.79
Female	-22558.0	-4266.99	-2865.36	-1917.73	-5000.04	-7958.47	-8630.27	1384.33	1124.19	405.56	278.58	234.26	69.89	26.77	111.42	-157.73	-726.37
	-22487.3	-4251.82	-2868.42	-1965.53	-4774.07	-7479.31	-3719.13	827.14	1182.27	367.03	235.60	288.06	156.65	83.16	228.51	-78.67	-718.78
	-22318.5	-4230.01	-2892.39	-2044.57	-4301.44	-6569.43	-3918.73	-257.35	697.65	289.23	188.58	436.26	286.46	179.46	440.68	72.64	-705.69
1881-1891																	
Male	-17475.6	-4186.10	-3018.67	-1890.10	-3946.35	-5546.86	-1930.02	825.91	509.72	294.75	203.45	18.56	423.78	627.36	448.62	3.85	-479.56
	-17351.8	-4222.61	-3021.09	-1876.06	-3973.24	-5551.42	-1904.04	748.90	443.72	276.46	166.34	339.05	506.25	595.68	453.98	41.06	-456.71
	-17134.8	-4309.50	-3048.84	-1826.23	-3969.73	-5556.90	-1892.53	596.60	338.71	254.51	134.20	651.43	874.76	531.11	450.53	78.37	-443.33
Female	-18935.4	-4060.85	-2984.86	-2427.61	-5515.13	-8147.23	-3062.53	2435.11	2219.98	823.87	596.08	721.94	520.55	289.14	242.19	-67.55	-518.45
	-18872.9	-4068.54	-3008.24	-2427.20	-5290.01	-7658.90	-3050.31	1825.34	1817.62	751.13	602.12	840.42	629.03	329.21	340.65	10.27	-515.53
	-18751.2	-4094.20	-3075.18	-2404.92	-4804.74	-6748.66	-3060.64	669.13	1014.79	589.21	679.17	1141.64	840.93	370.80	495.42	149.84	-513.77
1891-1901																	
Male	-18794.4	-3854.84	-3022.24	-1990.79	-4087.21	-5744.96	-2217.88	495.53	364.12	276.88	91.55	53.10	436.60	660.38	349.78	-88.43	-536.17
	-18684.1	-3951.58	-3006.96	-1913.77	-4151.26	-5867.13	-2163.30	553.56	358.67	192.93	19.55	298.56	658.86	562.40	302.89	-59.80	-515.73
	-18533.2	-4174.09	-3006.70	-1721.81	-4199.64	-6102.53	-2106.45	669.96	342.40	40.30	-80.18	790.75	1043.73	360.73	189.23	-55.85	-523.08
Female	-21239.1	-3671.80	-2893.25	-2568.79	-5924.91	-8557.51	-3142.34	2470.39	2157.57	419.18	163.71	624.00	442.03	103.87	-1.25	-251.23	-607.82
	-21199.4	-3708.17	-2943.52	-2514.19	-5685.44	-8025.03	-2977.99	1815.67	1563.40	283.14	192.17	789.87	584.60	121.70	77.40	-171.55	-601.47
	-21142.4	-3791.68	-3063.79	-2379.32	-5158.43	-7043.11	-2696.89	605.79	378.03	-22.84	345.79	1212.60	651.64	93.17	165.84	-41.88	-597.36
1901-1911																	
Male	-9115.73	-3062.72	-2640.44	-1839.85	-3558.72	-5114.28	-1404.17	1577.66	1493.35	1331.25	976.03	776.48	1120.98	1240.83	601.99	-45.70	-460.62
	-9018.11	-3201.66	-2622.65	-1702.05	-3744.06	-5351.01	-1327.12	1778.86	1511.16	1191.63	882.99	1096.54	1390.70	1070.67	485.16	-29.17	-448.11
	-8932.51	-3520.33	-2588.87	-1373.52	-3822.07	-5813.88	-1238.53	2177.44	1590.81	927.91	741.91	1173.30	1849.27	720.70	229.24	-61.89	-481.99
Female	-13108.6	-2914.84	-2490.57	-2443.39	-5865.11	-6336.03	-2211.73	3846.48	3226.61	1031.44	675.60	1300.57	1011.63	475.74	207.11	-160.32	-469.77
	-13078.7	-2976.17	-2562.07	-2333.37	-5631.95	-7015.23	-1934.86	3132.45	2444.57	871.25	764.51	1540.17	1204.63	483.46	267.44	-77.83	-456.73
	-13078.1	-3104.21	-2717.22	-2095.81	-5113.50	-6663.02	-1442.06	1713.95	886.70	498.89	1063.22	2111.08	1550.02	405.29	296.88	48.80	-435.15

BORDERS   Age-Band in Years

	Total	<5	<10	<15	<20	<25	<30	<35	<40	<45	<50	<55	<60	<65	<70	<75	75+
1861-1871																	
Male	-9678.61	-2677.40	-1603.83	-968.63	-1340.92	-1529.57	-758.83	-64.46	-51.73	-240.26	-237.71	-174.14	-81.72	131.84	192.83	-16.22	-257.70
	-9530.79	-2580.25	-1574.85	-1023.55	-1293.61	-1454.57	-792.32	-184.90	-126.12	-219.03	-218.25	-131.51	-25.54	142.93	195.38	-7.29	-237.33
	-9533.19	-2541.42	-1674.40	-1130.97	-1181.90	-1298.16	-870.14	-652.52	-297.87	-166.57	-150.23	-5.63	115.13	155.75	172.26	-6.24	-200.19
Female	-10115.1	-2520.70	-1643.15	-1205.47	-1059.57	-2235.04	-982.27	266.29	287.70	140.95	67.67	-107.74	-47.32	92.93	64.60	-103.61	-330.51
	-9873.98	-2453.50	-1810.61	-1224.28	-1804.54	-2139.47	-1020.98	148.46	251.42	120.15	95.63	1.51	-9.25	66.01	112.34	-55.06	-351.81
	-9517.49	-2458.55	-1682.40	-1253.68	-1736.85	-2012.40	-1063.19	-20.39	193.20	62.53	227.78	390.45	117.31	-56.09	181.72	38.21	-445.14
1871-1881																	
Male	-10548.6	-2818.24	-1847.37	-1169.16	-1518.54	-1686.23	-751.16	-16.63	-69.09	-218.00	-211.05	-125.11	-19.71	113.00	135.87	-50.75	-295.68
	-10486.3	-2782.82	-1858.70	-1227.11	-1515.60	-1630.47	-764.62	-118.07	-123.98	-197.27	-204.58	-76.40	46.49	120.47	145.37	-30.01	-288.97
	-10360.5	-2720.58	-1888.08	-1334.22	-1480.65	-1518.20	-804.20	-333.06	-243.41	-146.80	-168.41	42.78	190.15	128.10	146.62	-1.64	-221.88
Female	-11142.7	-2632.58	-1818.15	-1330.14	-2051.93	-2427.65	-1011.65	335.08	328.42	68.35	-.61	-80.24	-50.43	19.26	-9.93	-141.86	-338.65
	-11030.1	-2609.24	-1830.07	-1357.12	-1984.09	-2277.23	-1032.57	160.36	245.46	37.16	13.99	.58	-18.92	4.26	39.72	-90.74	-338.64
	-10723.0	-2572.79	-1656.49	-1396.50	-1866.29	-2019.45	-1056.56	-121.58	93.60	-28.65	90.62	259.27	69.19	-70.70	116.32	7.07	-370.06
1881-1891																	
Male	-10985.5	-2888.74	-2063.78	-1345.11	-1716.09	-1874.21	-765.98	-.29	-86.22	-177.73	-144.14	-42.39	106.05	190.55	148.85	-35.83	-277.43
	-10905.2	-2866.28	-2049.55	-1392.62	-1765.02	-1858.33	-769.61	-62.75	-121.05	-160.41	-153.45	20.92	184.96	181.62	157.55	-5.15	-244.03
	-10752.7	-2832.66	-2023.84	-1476.58	-1844.84	-1031.72	-788.08	-187.58	-168.04	-114.53	-152.88	152.16	335.56	157.98	164.39	44.26	-186.26
Female	-10454.6	-2670.86	-2000.74	-1542.87	-2233.04	-2512.88	-844.75	653.61	555.21	132.02	79.47	135.35	108.79	54.55	15.80	-102.53	-281.91
	-10361.9	-2648.19	-2013.13	-1570.19	-2148.21	-2311.06	-832.11	447.18	422.28	95.04	85.87	190.62	134.49	46.57	59.02	-53.47	-266.57
	-10133.1	-2610.19	-2037.28	-1611.05	-1976.28	-1933.64	-796.87	67.00	176.73	38.18	126.69	336.26	184.40	-3.41	118.37	37.21	-249.25
1891-1901																	
Male	-11111.5	-2667.23	-2039.87	-1230.69	-1742.95	-2110.56	-832.52	-33.80	-177.84	-177.79	-119.43	19.49	189.26	174.06	65.35	-94.55	-332.44
	-11001.6	-2653.59	-2003.53	-1267.66	-1857.53	-2150.37	-813.17	-43.00	-168.69	-172.58	-148.82	107.58	289.92	147.01	72.44	-51.01	-288.34
	-10799.9	-2622.59	-1929.98	-1336.06	-2090.37	-2234.93	-787.90	-49.46	-136.32	-150.73	-191.57	270.96	465.66	89.59	83.52	24.04	-213.72
Female	-11375.7	-2327.03	-1810.61	-1303.47	-2340.17	-2944.60	-1027.54	640.55	491.23	-105.13	-128.25	131.40	79.18	-88.94	-124.51	-182.56	-335.30
	-11315.9	-2304.12	-1825.55	-1329.95	-2237.66	-2677.66	-961.56	363.92	284.79	-157.58	-139.92	152.89	99.21	-87.27	-84.94	-132.56	-297.76
	-11191.9	-2257.60	-1652.43	-1379.96	-2016.64	-2150.39	-829.32	-166.57	-103.44	-231.86	-151.42	175.66	115.49	-105.55	-34.07	-41.09	-222.75
1901-1911																	
Male	-7357.23	-2007.59	-1608.23	-772.07	-1540.94	-2280.79	-700.19	291.86	68.87	137.17	202.62	351.19	510.97	367.40	109.28	-120.23	-366.57
	-7219.32	-1997.65	-1585.01	-801.57	-1709.24	-2377.91	-662.08	349.09	123.21	134.48	158.19	459.54	626.76	315.48	106.55	-65.70	-313.46
	-6975.29	-1961.16	-1474.83	-684.70	-2057.14	-2573.77	-589.35	468.09	256.32	139.33	81.73	647.42	814.24	209.34	104.40	30.29	-225.50
Female	-7846.84	-1855.08	-1536.66	-1075.50	-2431.82	-3339.12	-635.50	1340.26	1043.32	181.24	142.26	550.50	391.52	46.98	-31.66	-129.29	-305.28
	-7810.86	-1828.76	-1555.63	-1102.04	-2321.50	-3035.07	-732.42	1032.56	762.43	132.61	138.34	551.06	415.30	62.84	-1.25	-82.49	-246.36
	-7768.62	-1758.63	-1590.27	-1174.52	-2076.19	-2418.66	-527.92	434.69	229.91	79.28	130.57	488.70	419.48	82.66	30.72	1.35	-119.80

PERIPHERY & NORTHEAST   Age–Band in Years

	Total	<5	<10	<15	<20	<25	<30	<35	<40	<45	<50	<55	<60	<65	<70	<75	75+
1861–1871																	
Male	-32128.7	-8857.63	-5609.27	-3186.44	-4176.42	-6689.77	-1862.40	-186.86	-669.19	-1002.36	-758.37	-410.67	-303.16	60.20	361.17	-77.53	-779.97
	-31573.4	-8534.21	-5518.70	-3378.48	-4172.54	-4414.25	-1057.13	-524.27	-811.95	-909.46	-762.25	-406.76	-206.44	153.29	473.71	1.34	-703.23
	-3184.0	-8358.07	-5539.71	-3769.82	-4149.59	-3901.75	-1877.07	-1223.65	-1087.31	-692.57	-741.88	-384.79	-3.92	353.50	692.26	149.44	-549.02
Female	-34057.4	-8158.18	-5558.38	-6021.04	-5333.58	-6456.20	-3381.85	282.65	447.27	-82.44	28.13	-157.12	-310.31	-284.66	42.07	-184.61	-949.16
	-33611.2	-7946.61	-5387.21	-4155.54	-5126.10	-5970.44	-3568.28	-265.24	362.81	-36.14	-58.81	-167.16	-285.61	-182.80	190.72	-90.66	-835.90
	-33556.0	-7980.21	-5500.66	-4409.63	-4714.74	-5071.36	-3954.92	-1358.45	201.23	72.89	-202.68	-128.82	-147.27	-28.24	484.78	102.17	-920.10
1871–1881																	
Male	-35890.9	-9410.13	-6323.97	-3850.64	-4900.90	-5286.19	-2109.78	-223.84	-675.39	-966.09	-800.33	-525.73	-286.30	115.88	279.08	-164.08	-862.43
	-35778.8	-9332.00	-6375.54	-3984.83	-4927.07	-5117.24	-2082.47	-485.52	-803.40	-915.97	-824.34	-432.61	-125.19	159.77	357.89	-88.75	-800.51
	-35336.9	-9188.77	-6513.59	-4251.51	-4937.47	-4778.32	-2069.27	-1023.00	-1039.35	-784.27	-832.23	-235.60	107.66	258.10	506.88	39.20	-685.33
Female	-37918.5	-8570.29	-6032.65	-4684.73	-6360.38	-7339.65	-3517.96	626.58	732.71	-203.04	-218.78	-226.69	-366.24	-390.81	-144.45	-296.78	-805.31
	-37786.8	-8540.06	-6032.33	-4769.58	-6131.21	-6783.94	-3625.02	-21.46	471.81	-222.79	-280.41	-178.58	-288.93	-322.21	7.49	-185.36	-684.25
	-37473.5	-8496.14	-6051.90	-4913.61	-5614.57	-5749.03	-3981.38	-1294.27	-38.46	-250.58	-353.72	-13.16	-112.36	-201.20	299.27	42.27	-644.66
1881–1891																	
Male	-32570.0	-9274.03	-6570.65	-4078.88	-5182.74	-5502.09	-1867.65	311.78	-102.20	-307.36	-283.76	-179.18	200.96	607.47	491.76	-79.90	-753.53
	-32369.1	-9306.39	-6573.62	-4115.15	-5261.33	-5484.75	-1818.54	166.09	-190.87	-316.81	-336.60	38.33	448.02	571.28	512.54	-12.43	-709.65
	-31984.6	-9369.13	-6622.37	-4176.48	-5349.96	-5449.23	-1779.43	-70.62	-336.27	-299.52	-387.78	476.76	907.45	504.03	542.34	84.88	-659.09
Female	-33418.1	-9507.51	-6279.81	-5336.65	-7181.91	-7857.04	-2709.99	2109.57	1895.54	369.74	185.83	367.31	196.96	-31.45	30.83	-182.19	-687.29
	-33285.3	-9514.05	-6304.77	-5348.13	-6906.33	-7054.09	-2702.34	1366.93	1423.28	289.94	177.25	501.24	325.83	19.34	172.92	-61.60	-657.31
	-32971.9	-9548.29	-6375.17	-5337.92	-6323.27	-5953.23	-2754.34	-59.43	501.60	139.29	238.73	851.93	586.37	82.74	424.06	178.00	-624.98
1891–1901																	
Male	-44219.3	-9102.04	-7042.72	-4776.67	-6593.07	-7504.35	-3457.13	-928.96	-1068.67	-999.82	-972.62	-846.61	-154.47	423.37	104.29	-343.96	-1035.90
	-44010.7	-9258.84	-6997.47	-4691.04	-6759.41	-7695.61	-3367.44	-856.74	-1104.54	-1113.61	-1084.69	-453.98	216.96	284.14	135.12	-279.86	-992.67
	-43650.9	-9569.42	-6926.05	-4505.56	-6997.39	-8069.79	-3262.74	-715.72	-1129.14	-1297.11	-1233.62	323.97	890.02	9.31	17.84	-213.81	-970.90
Female	-43139.7	-8102.14	-6385.82	-5995.88	-8041.15	-9642.16	-3624.00	1889.82	1543.73	-551.02	-776.15	-89.13	-166.43	-486.01	-463.77	-540.79	-908.82
	-43023.1	-8153.36	-6444.79	-5918.86	-8529.48	-8930.85	-3402.09	1036.10	767.57	-754.63	-771.09	118.30	16.01	-456.61	-323.70	-397.97	-877.59
	-42755.8	-8276.30	-6581.66	-5728.51	-7854.54	-7845.94	-3058.70	-575.46	-753.88	-1181.21	-643.42	639.71	370.77	-457.63	-99.66	-120.44	-808.92
1901–1911																	
Male	-28563.6	-8176.15	-6820.93	-4715.39	-9600.68	-10451.7	-2242.81	1222.55	1008.49	1015.02	800.55	582.48	1227.82	1649.43	762.81	-222.11	-920.35
	-28345.2	-8435.40	-6710.33	-4503.28	-9369.79	-9712.03	-2101.94	1547.46	1040.52	792.41	643.75	1158.07	1727.50	1370.19	595.83	-165.12	-886.26
	-28028.2	-8949.47	-6542.68	-4084.92	-8682.09	-8398.68	-1914.97	2188.19	1186.85	396.37	412.38	2283.51	2615.03	812.82	246.10	-129.58	-901.12
Female	-33037.7	-7206.58	-6029.49	-6198.30	-9680.68	-10451.7	-2506.43	4454.29	3569.76	467.80	.01	992.26	752.90	110.03	-148.02	-222.90	-740.62
	-32907.7	-7293.17	-6121.10	-6033.35	-9369.79	-9712.03	-2096.85	3450.01	2447.84	208.00	113.86	1337.84	1035.19	127.16	-27.76	-269.00	-704.58
	-32634.8	-7481.62	-6317.93	-5670.75	-8682.09	-8398.68	-1408.44	1592.73	251.47	-323.38	505.66	2163.54	1561.90	61.96	120.96	15.97	-625.25

CENTRAL LOWLANDS   Age-Band in Years

	Total	<5	<10	<15	<20	<25	<30	<35	<40	<45	<50	<55	<60	<65	<70	<75	75+
1861-1871																	
Male	-34269.2	-12718.01	-8027.56	-4719.45	-3834.02	-2385.71	-465.45	214.13	-290.29	-684.45	-553.70	-347.16	-216.59	168.62	446.03	-47.37	-828.27
	-33592.4	-12241.0	-7894.07	-5038.46	-3654.79	-2020.11	-389.96	-140.55	-473.04	-611.53	-563.42	-329.94	-112.48	248.94	554.55	35.09	-752.66
	-33606.7	-11976.3	-8349.10	-5681.97	-3876.30	-1329.24	-290.46	-859.38	-829.71	-444.62	-553.78	-274.73	108.22	415.73	753.92	184.80	-603.84
Female	-37439.9	-12072.5	-7893.97	-5455.55	-5446.52	-4904.70	-2188.17	899.59	1000.82	195.07	121.81	-158.03	-210.19	-29.88	134.19	-282.38	-1149.51
	-38049.5	-11726.1	-7634.93	-5886.81	-5210.55	-4249.10	-2381.02	235.74	841.08	182.45	49.57	-127.15	170.79	32.13	297.94	-169.90	-1132.02
	-38967.2	-11733.3	-7817.15	-6126.37	-4743.86	-2897.04	-2784.17	-1061.98	530.23	164.25	-52.27	17.18	-61.22	129.24	610.78	54.96	-1116.53
1871-1881																	
Male	-43371.6	-14618.7	-10150.0	-6929.97	-5178.92	-2375.63	-442.26	-26.08	-506.34	-877.27	-760.62	-564.08	-301.26	152.48	308.55	-175.27	-926.20
	-43170.2	-14510.0	-10198.3	-7146.53	-5240.53	-2141.29	-353.02	-289.85	-666.13	-856.69	-806.47	-455.43	-125.65	180.13	382.65	-90.04	-853.26
	-42763.2	-14296.6	-10339.3	-7366.52	-5304.79	-1674.47	-213.54	-820.45	-966.60	-792.02	-859.93	-228.36	213.68	240.04	516.79	54.84	-725.99
Female	-47932.8	-13866.5	-8958.78	-8196.80	-7433.37	-5368.16	-2219.85	1036.99	1062.99	-146.62	-227.08	-251.91	-343.06	-285.75	-166.93	-448.36	-1119.62
	-47819.0	-13798.6	-9961.14	-8351.37	-7146.75	-4621.57	-2299.53	245.91	697.14	-220.28	-292.76	-180.65	-259.78	-221.51	4.99	-319.04	-1094.11
	-47542.0	-13685.5	-9999.26	-8623.18	-6543.80	-3204.86	-2485.80	-1295.25	-24.82	-364.16	-371.84	36.80	-73.57	-119.41	326.75	-62.66	-1052.42
1881-1891																	
Male	-39401.0	-14998.0	-10906.0	-7281.10	-4859.69	-1111.37	608.63	357.11	-133.51	-460.91	-421.81	-335.26	88.02	572.21	440.39	-137.50	-822.23
	-39198.7	-15081.9	-10867.4	-7228.86	-4976.95	-1062.26	711.93	233.41	-251.54	-505.26	-507.31	-95.26	364.98	521.26	458.64	-53.57	-758.60
	-38821.5	-15262.1	-10045.2	-2392.40	-5114.43	-868.89	852.11	-16.07	-457.12	-563.58	-626.87	381.97	877.31	424.13	482.13	75.14	-667.59
Female	-44866.4	-14088.8	-10578.1	-9101.76	-7740.64	-4330.73	-663.74	2079.36	1776.68	-22.43	-129.07	158.68	-25.11	-202.40	-176.39	-435.59	-986.42
	-44552.3	-14091.2	-10627.8	-8135.90	-7397.05	-3511.33	-799.60	1146.83	1154.56	-158.71	-184.01	301.87	124.55	-139.17	-2.08	-291.49	-861.87
	-44290.1	-14124.1	-10784.2	-9133.38	-6647.30	-1975.39	-731.87	-649.15	-71.86	-430.61	-157.91	667.66	426.00	-54.59	304.57	-12.11	-915.83
1891-1901																	
Male	-46791.9	-14813.9	-11685.2	-8116.99	-5741.78	-1743.60	27.84	-517.04	-831.80	-965.53	-887.84	-756.55	-66.87	537.06	206.98	-380.10	-1056.49
	-46559.3	-15139.4	-11530.9	-7935.36	-5947.01	-1956.72	156.41	-437.79	-889.69	-1114.58	-1040.81	-333.24	349.16	380.33	154.63	-291.46	-982.97
	-46156.3	-15800.2	-11285.2	-7530.13	-6228.29	-2378.56	326.39	-281.54	-959.51	-1369.90	-1275.40	493.91	1102.98	73.92	34.82	-174.32	-897.18
Female	-52946.3	-13698.7	-11155.8	-10513.8	-9461.64	-5464.68	-1084.18	2227.81	1705.93	-846.62	-946.13	-76.10	-252.90	-634.71	-690.41	-815.62	-1238.73
	-52836.7	-13779.1	-11261.8	-10392.4	-9043.73	-4534.76	-788.88	1126.81	725.17	-1096.16	-967.93	144.67	-26.54	-579.44	-512.04	-646.18	-1204.33
	-52602.9	-13967.4	-11506.0	-10095.1	-8125.93	-2813.43	-297.77	-967.11	-1206.95	-1598.64	-895.16	684.27	409.29	-533.95	-225.48	-326.18	-1137.41
1901-1911																	
Male	-48799.6	-14958.1	-13432.2	-10731.6	-7816.00	-2668.97	149.96	284.14	-59.08	-139.03	-125.36	-161.53	705.35	1375.23	464.09	-482.89	-1183.73
	-48536.2	-15584.5	-13129.1	-10247.9	-8121.69	-3227.34	308.89	621.55	-36.95	-418.14	-350.00	493.15	1296.26	1067.83	293.44	-394.59	-1107.00
	-48129.2	-16860.9	-12587.9	-9226.32	-8576.82	-4329.45	513.43	1326.36	69.96	-921.88	-711.71	1759.90	2353.78	463.19	-60.35	-300.33	-1040.23
Female	-56810.1	-13695.5	-13848.9	-12607.2	-7213.46		-687.66	4207.98	3159.81	-489.03	-699.45	688.25	347.62	-381.23	-573.15	-914.49	-1290.81
	-56680.4	-13368.1	-12893.4	-12121.9	-6197.45		-122.88	2889.14	1725.83	-847.32	-647.47	1041.27	692.63	-328.05	-497.78	-718.75	-1244.96
	-56442.3	-14230.1	-13299.5	-12881.1	-11053.2	4336.74	865.99	415.72	-1095.42	-1559.05	-373.91	1669.97	1332.85	-328.10	-257.57	-380.59	-1151.49

Appendix 9

Current Migrant Losses by Age-Band of Departure, County-of-Birth, Decade and Gender

Estimates shown with two standard errors added or deducted.*

Key

* See Appendix 1 for further information on the calculation of standard errors

Three estimates are provided for each calculation.

The top estimate has been calculated with two standard errors added to every age-band in the migrant age-structure according to population category.

The middle estimate is the original measurement with the correct application of the migrant age-structure.

The bottom estimate has been calculated with two standard errors deducted from every age-band in the migrant age-structure according to population category.

Age-Band in Years

ABERDEEN

	TOTAL	<5	<10	<15	<20	<25	<30	<35	<40	<45	<50	<55	<60	<65	<70	<75	75+
1861-1871																	
MALE	-5226.50	-1557.19	-977.12	-479.95	-575.97	-635.84	-244.28	-68.47	-162.49	-215.92	-145.29	-44.94	-41.72	2.95	56.10	-13.62	-122.75
	-5115.90	-1501.77	-963.60	-503.74	-576.13	-603.37	-252.81	-124.95	-175.00	-191.05	-142.69	-48.68	-26.89	24.93	78.09	.02	-108.26
	-5054.51	-1472.79	-1027.93	-554.31	-574.72	-536.67	-277.62	-247.35	-197.68	-132.54	-133.17	-56.18	6.14	75.04	124.92	27.85	-77.52
FEMALE	-6080.61	-1338.08	-984.52	-741.53	-792.70	-860.76	-545.41	-122.80	-76.30	-105.15	-31.30	-37.43	-99.57	-132.16	-28.49	-23.67	-158.74
	-5995.65	-1311.32	-954.79	-755.02	-767.88	-814.81	-582.19	-199.23	-71.59	-75.96	-50.58	-50.52	-88.32	-108.28	-2.56	-9.58	-153.94
	-5970.91	-1334.36	-970.51	-780.24	-716.17	-729.33	-684.79	-360.22	-57.08	-11.46	-87.44	-73.38	-61.09	-56.60	52.39	21.89	-142.52
1871-1881																	
MALE	-6718.41	-1742.10	-1158.50	-663.92	-788.37	-852.04	-395.48	-164.99	-223.56	-237.67	-183.79	-100.52	-65.48	-4.74	36.36	-29.96	-143.65
	-6673.98	-1720.92	-1175.22	-685.28	-789.35	-830.09	-402.05	-211.18	-235.34	-218.33	-180.85	-89.34	-41.86	8.77	52.68	-19.07	-135.85
	-6576.83	-1671.62	-1217.05	-731.78	-785.87	-784.93	-427.12	-310.38	-255.04	-170.93	-167.05	-84.93	6.23	39.93	86.28	.01	-122.57
FEMALE	-7371.83	-1532.66	-1128.91	-952.41	-1141.70	-1174.76	-640.60	-70.61	-17.91	-106.28	-80.51	-72.67	-112.88	-139.96	-41.32	-25.36	-133.30
	-7336.76	-1533.49	-1126.92	-959.02	-1109.07	-1120.59	-669.56	-153.07	-34.60	-91.36	-91.37	-71.23	-99.25	-123.77	-17.32	-8.40	-128.75
	-7255.77	-1539.04	-1125.45	-967.79	-1036.26	-1028.47	-743.01	-319.77	-65.02	-55.88	-103.86	-57.17	-67.19	-90.93	31.60	29.34	-116.87
1881-1891																	
MALE	-6970.10	-1708.39	-1228.42	-709.46	-887.37	-995.71	-460.89	-171.39	-198.04	-165.85	-147.18	-99.22	-25.68	49.03	55.75	-30.93	-156.33
	-6931.65	-1788.44	-1243.62	-733.85	-893.40	-993.87	-464.98	-196.46	-205.26	-155.66	-145.10	-64.67	12.10	48.51	61.87	-23.59	-155.14
	-6853.36	-1759.96	-1266.37	-757.68	-895.17	-988.56	-484.97	-251.10	-213.48	-125.97	-128.91	7.81	84.38	49.51	73.05	-15.46	-160.46
FEMALE	-7324.64	-1624.67	-1182.95	-1034.85	-1393.76	-1365.81	-574.48	137.91	187.00	-25.34	-68.60	-37.45	-49.16	-89.88	-21.93	-16.90	-113.83
	-7298.73	-1630.21	-1185.03	-1051.23	-1355.31	-1306.84	-590.44	45.51	115.65	-27.08	-64.05	-12.87	-28.78	82.21	-.86	3.47	-108.47
	-7201.98	-1646.38	-1192.08	-1046.95	-1271.59	-1216.22	-945.46	-132.47	17.90	-26.34	-36.23	56.65	15.51	-71.80	38.84	40.27	-93.64
1891-1901																	
MALE	-9825.34	-1921.62	-1439.26	-909.60	-1288.58	-1478.70	-823.49	-407.10	-357.44	-245.60	-256.16	-226.37	-91.91	11.75	3.01	-79.48	-225.78
	-9791.83	-1925.88	-1448.92	-1060.61	-1307.53	-1511.01	-821.98	-397.65	-357.17	-252.51	-258.34	-157.38	-32.69	-8.18	-4.97	-76.33	-230.63
	-9732.32	-1922.39	-1484.43	-1011.99	-1329.10	-1572.39	-834.28	-381.19	-347.29	-256.13	-245.55	-15.16	76.65	-47.64	-24.84	-82.35	-254.43
FEMALE	-9757.00	-1686.90	-1256.32	-1281.77	-1889.51	-1905.92	-796.41	126.78	144.07	-180.22	-260.26	-153.85	-122.63	-163.59	-106.38	-84.67	-159.42
	-9720.76	-1699.01	-1264.48	-1294.01	-1844.63	-1833.90	-781.27	21.69	39.01	-190.15	-243.75	-104.63	-93.39	-165.50	-87.46	-58.19	-151.04
	-9629.71	-1730.09	-1284.03	-1219.15	-1745.93	-1729.88	-783.21	-172.12	-164.30	-248.20	-180.24	25.38	-32.67	-180.20	-56.26	-.52	-128.27
1901-1911																	
MALE	-5402.30	-1725.86	-1286.39	-768.97	-1002.22	-1202.15	-463.09	32.96	104.11	246.84	160.86	88.36	206.08	266.53	141.96	-24.44	-177.66
	-5373.91	-1742.12	-1293.52	-758.67	-1032.47	-1271.94	-451.45	90.51	117.02	221.88	157.31	192.33	285.58	219.15	110.52	-26.80	-191.33
	-5337.41	-1762.22	-1328.56	-748.34	-1068.86	-1404.98	-447.93	203.48	155.67	182.99	169.53	403.48	427.00	122.59	43.27	-47.36	-237.16
FEMALE	-6178.61	-1516.45	-1066.15	-1102.99	-1894.38	-1879.30	-381.04	741.60	665.82	159.82	-49.02	85.46	115.68	26.21	10.96	-19.08	-75.94
	-6137.92	-1533.50	-1080.14	-1070.02	-1850.65	-1812.35	-338.75	624.96	503.81	114.42	-1.98	171.11	159.52	12.91	21.96	8.66	-67.88
	-6034.73	-1574.46	-1110.47	-993.05	-1751.61	-1730.26	-294.85	423.16	192.04	23.50	136.21	385.42	244.55	-35.30	29.82	66.26	-45.71

Age-Band in Years

ARGYLL

	TOTAL	<5	<10	<15	<20	<25	<30	<35	<40	<45	<50	<55	<60	<65	<70	<75	75+
1861-1871																	
MALE	-3482.93	-779.20	-441.30	-168.58	-764.60	-1281.96	-426.01	210.37	89.61	5.99	-2.17	-.56	11.85	61.28	104.57	13.08	-135.30
	-3417.11	-745.04	-431.45	-195.38	-762.07	-1212.79	-415.89	148.10	53.84	16.02	-7.33	-.10	28.70	74.99	125.57	23.04	-123.32
	-3392.53	-730.63	-467.22	-249.29	-756.14	-1116.86	-397.87	27.75	-13.21	37.42	-15.22	1.28	61.28	102.43	165.54	58.76	-100.51
FEMALE	-4495.54	-888.66	-499.76	-220.11	-1152.90	-2077.37	-889.28	484.82	447.71	200.29	136.70	50.72	36.19	76.89	79.07	-36.99	-224.68
	-4453.53	-856.16	-475.51	-244.49	-1075.86	-1920.70	-945.15	292.30	397.42	191.98	119.63	49.89	41.17	90.33	113.28	-13.64	-218.01
	-4498.58	-857.19	-483.55	-291.42	-923.48	-1813.95	-1056.22	-49.11	297.86	176.86	87.16	50.41	48.70	116.95	180.68	32.76	-205.04
1871-1881																	
MALE	-2709.36	-708.51	-460.11	-251.36	-784.74	-1218.08	-341.48	358.47	225.92	113.06	92.67	69.40	76.99	115.38	103.73	8.33	-109.00
	-2683.16	-704.26	-462.33	-264.10	-790.17	-1194.13	-329.17	319.42	197.18	112.88	83.47	86.74	105.47	116.25	114.12	22.16	-98.67
	-2632.35	-696.43	-466.72	-288.56	-797.16	-1147.04	-308.06	244.19	144.09	114.31	68.64	120.48	158.50	124.36	133.26	46.45	-80.64
FEMALE	-3666.55	-723.53	-454.27	-284.68	-1195.47	-2100.34	-801.70	657.54	585.16	252.51	193.88	148.88	109.02	81.81	50.62	-38.66	-158.33
	-3667.42	-718.99	-454.47	-276.81	-1127.49	-1947.25	-827.09	473.55	497.70	238.45	182.98	161.22	117.61	97.18	84.38	-14.95	-153.44
	-3667.07	-710.70	-456.61	-299.26	-991.38	-1848.70	-878.58	112.01	324.28	210.71	164.94	189.96	153.52	126.15	149.40	31.49	-144.18
1881-1891																	
MALE	-2584.97	-711.83	-529.36	-366.74	-790.96	-1122.03	-304.07	354.68	239.26	140.64	117.97	88.02	111.15	149.98	106.16	12.34	-72.38
	-2560.85	-719.85	-525.88	-366.63	-811.31	-1120.55	-288.37	341.36	219.27	129.89	104.00	120.36	149.19	141.30	106.33	24.00	-63.98
	-2517.65	-738.13	-521.33	-283.67	-828.97	-1117.05	-262.11	225.46	183.60	110.87	80.97	183.03	218.55	124.59	105.19	42.52	-51.17
FEMALE	-3356.95	-740.41	-569.85	-496.62	-1288.79	-2006.29	-658.29	801.72	654.18	288.03	232.59	239.21	164.63	102.91	55.31	-20.18	-93.09
	-3354.71	-740.12	-572.72	-489.11	-1232.71	-1863.93	-652.45	615.03	533.94	249.58	229.37	284.11	196.01	119.88	87.42	2.70	-91.72
	-3349.58	-740.53	-580.66	-501.90	-1118.11	-1583.90	-643.72	250.80	285.79	211.90	228.96	319.41	257.99	150.04	147.25	46.63	-89.54
1891-1901																	
MALE	-3285.78	-662.65	-534.71	-389.04	-785.68	-1098.74	-378.97	191.58	115.77	42.98	33.06	19.50	72.72	125.73	63.34	-17.28	-83.41
	-3241.04	-684.15	-524.76	-353.64	-805.79	-1121.77	-360.35	203.14	104.49	19.64	10.93	68.33	121.65	105.82	55.40	-6.38	-73.59
	-3201.60	-731.13	-506.83	-317.10	-835.24	-1166.90	-331.48	225.60	66.59	-23.76	-27.00	162.34	209.47	66.76	37.94	8.77	-59.94
FEMALE	-2925.83	-638.52	-519.16	-451.70	-1152.15	-1763.46	-512.42	805.54	628.72	186.75	165.59	243.46	160.39	64.33	3.66	-51.16	-95.70
	-2923.26	-643.39	-526.07	-444.44	-1103.49	-1624.55	-472.95	621.61	477.78	180.98	166.00	276.37	201.04	80.24	32.07	-23.32	-95.14
	-2920.42	-654.26	-542.31	-427.11	-1000.57	-1357.03	-400.22	266.34	179.05	107.04	176.13	349.83	279.48	105.41	81.50	11.11	-94.80
1901-1911																	
MALE	-2006.89	-552.05	-500.75	-368.94	-746.23	-1022.64	-270.68	338.55	260.95	174.38	153.66	122.97	176.44	224.04	100.72	-19.27	-78.05
	-1990.34	-584.06	-486.33	-340.52	-773.52	-1067.94	-246.66	376.16	258.07	140.77	126.71	187.12	236.49	191.08	80.03	-9.74	-67.99
	-1941.20	-653.59	-453.11	-276.74	-815.66	-1155.78	-246.58	449.58	258.32	77.80	60.07	310.37	343.03		36.95	.73	-55.43
FEMALE	-2532.51	-504.21	-469.87	-466.29	-1148.28	-1711.03	-440.04	662.99	647.75	159.07	157.32	286.59	189.69	70.36	-4.70	-64.16	-97.68
	-2524.75	-513.24	-479.82	-450.19	-1107.09	-1578.33	-371.12	679.37	467.41	129.18	164.23	328.04	239.94	66.01	20.43	-42.69	-96.89
	-2515.32	-531.82	-501.27	-415.95	-1018.02	-1323.83	-241.99	328.06	111.35	65.79	190.43	420.11	33.90	107.49	60.22	-4.49	-96.30

Age-Band in Years

AYR

	TOTAL	<5	<10	<15	<20	<25	<30	<35	<40	<45	<50	<55	<60	<65	<70	<75	75+
1861-1871																	
MALE	-10026.0	-2473.90	-1571.30	-1052.44	-1331.21	-1385.72	-843.78	-140.73	-212.05	-290.61	-283.96	-253.07	-180.41	-38.05	70.76	-24.30	-215.22
	-9812.1	-2388.52	-1549.58	-1138.59	-1335.46	-1290.11	-816.23	-225.72	-269.51	-285.78	-295.79	-247.83	-154.90	-26.60	94.27	-3.86	-197.97
	-9835.1	-2281.31	-1631.56	-1311.25	-1341.47	-1102.02	-564.51	-392.50	-382.98	-274.29	-311.69	-229.65	-101.19	-6.66	132.93	31.00	-166.09
FEMALE	-10579.9	-2429.57	-1538.62	-1119.09	-1653.07	-1970.84	-981.88	64.46	99.81	-84.50	-137.59	-204.94	-151.71	-36.43	-15.96	-112.49	-287.62
	-10408.0	-2355.12	-1492.64	-1172.27	-1570.55	-1770.14	-1030.66	-115.60	31.45	-124.45	-156.28	-195.40	-152.60	-36.21	20.64	-83.04	-285.11
	-10533.7	-2333.28	-1526.81	-1274.31	-1413.40	-1385.45	-1101.36	-460.32	-102.02	-186.24	-180.97	-149.48	-146.32	-46.87	88.27	-26.05	-289.11
1871-1881																	
MALE	-9246.9	-2325.60	-1514.47	-903.56	-1328.25	-1485.47	-570.35	29.86	-111.14	-247.78	-235.29	-219.35	-130.55	19.71	60.65	-49.86	-225.45
	-9208.4	-2302.54	-1518.57	-961.46	-1351.76	-1428.18	-530.46	-36.86	-165.85	-257.48	-260.57	-186.96	-78.47	19.78	77.78	-23.80	-203.06
	-9135.3	-2258.08	-1529.26	-1075.65	-1392.24	-1294.97	-455.87	-166.32	-271.19	-274.01	-303.06	-120.05	21.61	19.24	106.34	21.78	-162.87
FEMALE	-10155.9	-2256.05	-1485.89	-1039.24	-1717.63	-2172.21	-975.09	290.40	257.97	-83.82	-119.60	-123.09	-124.99	-72.58	-82.75	-156.43	-288.96
	-10180.6	-2237.44	-1485.95	-1077.25	-1625.49	-1928.63	-982.01	48.79	126.20	-136.81	-143.78	-111.71	-107.74	-62.23	-34.23	-118.73	-282.61
	-10138.3	-2202.28	-1487.58	-1149.24	-1448.24	-1456.45	-982.76	421.11	-134.75	-224.82	-182.55	-58.58	-67.82	-48.65	58.07	-45.23	-275.32
1881-1891																	
MALE	-9032.6	-2372.09	-1756.16	-1238.63	-1685.81	-1783.83	-549.97	293.55	96.11	-78.06	-64.73	-68.84	38.09	166.25	139.49	-16.39	-171.64
	-8892.8	-2391.42	-1731.97	-1254.29	-1736.23	-1769.99	-503.71	263.68	52.44	-105.90	-105.22	-.62	121.88	165.72	143.00	-14.35	-144.61
	-8892.5	-2431.89	-1685.33	-1282.51	-1827.69	-1742.08	-419.98	206.38	-28.62	-155.52	-176.04	129.90	277.03	125.54	146.69	68.18	-96.58
FEMALE	-9848.2	-2270.15	-1742.14	-1500.29	-2117.25	-2444.14	-847.10	775.38	586.69	49.27	56.53	119.81	53.83	14.06	-44.31	-124.47	-214.00
	-9637.3	-2263.00	-1746.27	-1516.44	-2023.63	-2172.18	-809.32	478.17	384.20	-.55	34.37	150.02	94.44	13.89	10.74	-82.60	-209.09
	-9608.7	-2250.33	-1755.53	-1545.25	-1836.29	-1639.68	-731.84	-100.08	-13.94	-97.99	-1.07	219.49	174.15	64.27	111.50	-2.89	-203.25
1891-1901																	
MALE	-9703.6	-2056.06	-1636.10	-1074.95	-1764.45	-2106.58	-740.79	173.57	-42.93	-221.27	-150.32	-123.51	27.31	196.58	88.74	-67.88	-205.03
	-9633.4	-2120.42	-1585.38	-1043.83	-1849.39	-2157.26	-680.27	196.29	-70.29	-278.93	-216.74	-10.19	150.00	150.68	77.90	-29.37	-166.16
	-9508.0	-2251.21	-1485.09	-977.88	-2007.33	-2254.46	-570.34	242.13	-116.30	-384.32	-336.85	201.34	373.37	62.67	55.51	38.25	-97.49
FEMALE	-9848.2	-1910.62	-1608.33	-1406.63	-2168.55	-2856.06	-861.27	929.39	629.91	-110.23	-42.64	173.42	60.30	-66.05	-156.28	-202.52	-252.11
	-9840.3	-1915.15	-1618.54	-1401.08	-2073.69	-2342.08	-751.97	575.87	336.30	-179.56	-74.77	206.84	124.23	-35.95	-93.41	-154.87	-244.49
	-9627.6	-1924.72	-1639.77	-1387.79	-1878.87	-1723.36	-536.94	-114.14	-240.37	-313.13	-131.38	278.53	244.30	15.63	20.62	-65.15	-231.09
1901-1911																	
MALE	-7484.5	-1882.48	-1742.41	-1321.58	-2018.44	-2320.05	-570.74	688.77	379.57	126.84	207.72	202.02	342.45	491.54	203.36	-73.34	-196.99
	-7392.6	-1986.72	-1662.82	-1243.07	-2136.30	-2242.65	-496.87	775.72	371.35	39.97	120.99	362.94	506.93	412.04	164.92	-29.35	-149.77
	-7231.8	-2195.05	-1502.99	-1082.80	-2360.46	-2677.98	-362.69	946.72	365.67	-120.69	-38.44	660.13	803.68	260.55	91.70	47.70	-66.93
FEMALE	-8250.3	-1886.05	-1694.56	-1724.36	-2487.17	-2931.38	-690.90	1528.34	1039.09	37.61	152.97	485.38	273.21	27.82	-124.99	-206.97	-248.35
	-8233.4	-1897.69	-1711.09	-1699.26	-2401.36	-2596.44	-516.41	1112.26	648.82	-34.65	11.75	538.41	371.10	72.56	-57.21	-154.62	-237.58
	-8213.8	-1718.55	-1745.22	-1649.72	-2219.09	-1933.07	-177.57	299.55	-121.40	-171.33	96.04	633.26	551.21	152.21	63.57	-57.30	-216.45

Age-Band in Years

BANFF

	TOTAL	<5	<10	<15	<20	<25	<30	<35	<40	<45	<50	<55	<60	<65	<70	<75	75+
1861-1871																	
MALE	-3033.41	-795.13	-518.12	-277.83	-393.85	-481.20	-185.79	-24.38	-88.88	-128.13	-75.26	-1.51	-12.25	4.09	23.26	-12.82	-71.51
	-2970.41	-788.99	-512.19	-285.95	-392.56	-469.05	-199.82	-59.07	-92.02	-108.66	-71.21	-4.95	-3.31	19.88	43.55	-4.27	-61.69
	-2912.90	-753.02	-542.47	-303.88	-388.82	-443.21	-234.84	-136.93	-97.21	-63.05	-60.60	-12.56	17.21	56.49	75.44	14.30	-39.94
FEMALE	-3285.76	-678.96	-541.78	-459.63	-504.93	-562.95	-336.28	-37.55	-17.46	-23.69	33.95	28.89	-29.63	-70.89	-2.94	7.55	-69.46
	-3219.29	-689.67	-528.84	-463.43	-495.64	-550.03	-358.09	-76.46	-4.97	2.93	21.96	16.16	-21.03	-53.81	11.88	14.64	-66.90
	-3187.11	-684.73	-535.66	-470.24	-475.58	-527.77	-408.66	-161.53	21.02	61.05	-1.75	-2.48	-.84	-16.00	44.47	31.61	-59.96
1871-1881																	
MALE	-3990.32	-909.24	-602.24	-334.82	-463.55	-566.38	-281.70	-133.44	-165.54	-164.03	-124.29	-58.28	-46.82	-21.99	9.07	-27.17	-99.79
	-3958.63	-897.42	-613.42	-344.39	-460.82	-557.70	-285.10	-162.19	-167.10	-145.99	-117.37	-54.25	-35.07	-10.31	19.84	-21.70	-95.64
	-3887.04	-869.10	-641.02	-366.26	-452.29	-538.29	-328.96	-226.28	-167.95	-103.04	-98.16	-44.52	-9.58	16.69	43.09	-11.76	-88.64
FEMALE	-4111.64	-751.27	-554.51	-462.38	-613.05	-679.07	-395.11	-99.15	-57.14	-80.46	-57.24	-48.49	-78.89	-107.21	-34.74	-12.89	-80.04
	-4085.64	-753.57	-553.20	-463.23	-600.21	-668.60	-418.11	-135.83	-54.38	-62.43	-61.63	-48.87	-69.91	-95.54	-21.28	-3.10	-75.75
	-4025.20	-760.50	-551.68	-462.51	-572.04	-658.68	-476.55	-213.10	-46.62	-21.63	-64.69	-42.75	-68.27	-70.51	8.05	20.51	-64.03
1881-1891																	
MALE	-2097.28	-787.96	-487.35	-183.12	-316.85	-454.13	-150.28	17.00	3.09	36.14	33.44	52.70	67.96	72.64	66.85	5.94	-73.36
	-2071.82	-780.17	-498.57	-191.10	-315.83	-454.99	-161.90	1.26	5.73	51.59	43.37	67.82	83.71	75.95	70.92	7.01	-76.63
	-2017.33	-759.58	-527.96	-210.42	-308.60	-456.31	-193.05	-34.36	14.82	89.37	70.67	101.32	114.98	83.84	79.13	6.17	-87.43
FEMALE	-2747.96	-713.88	-487.69	-405.57	-652.88	-711.15	-252.05	140.08	159.85	74.86	36.54	37.68	25.62	-15.23	25.01	26.41	-35.57
	-2719.31	-717.33	-488.18	-402.34	-638.95	-704.13	-270.06	109.39	150.48	83.63	43.75	51.86	35.82	-11.89	34.04	36.43	-31.83
	-2648.39	-727.02	-490.38	-392.08	-607.81	-707.99	-322.66	50.46	136.44	105.89	69.79	93.01	58.91	-7.52	52.42	60.60	-20.45
1891-1901																	
MALE	-3995.05	-866.54	-590.00	-312.73	-477.29	-650.84	-375.61	-216.62	-157.83	-49.65	-76.98	-76.88	-16.79	15.58	14.39	-32.75	-124.72
	-3977.55	-862.13	-603.12	-318.92	-479.56	-665.30	-384.12	-214.02	-151.25	-41.71	-65.34	-45.62	5.88	8.86	10.33	-36.51	-135.02
	-3943.27	-847.58	-639.64	-335.97	-474.87	-692.63	-409.08	-210.25	-132.09	-18.94	-31.27	21.82	48.58	-4.96	3.57	-50.99	-164.23
FEMALE	-3780.42	-748.32	-490.59	-440.86	-842.38	-909.06	-318.20	110.43	136.33	5.23	-86.17	-58.87	-30.56	-54.45	-11.19	2.49	-44.25
	-3752.18	-754.03	-483.71	-431.61	-826.19	-904.52	-326.33	84.44	105.49	-2.48	-67.57	-27.64	-18.24	-59.78	-5.72	15.04	-39.33
	-3678.01	-769.01	-501.24	-407.79	-789.72	-922.83	-365.74	40.98	49.88	-14.27	-10.79	55.77	8.96	-76.41	3.57	45.10	-24.46
1901-1911																	
MALE	-1023.80	-685.78	-456.72	-194.20	-313.63	-178.78	-151.12	89.18	162.84	289.93	206.82	138.74	176.19	168.28	106.38	7.91	-89.84
	-1015.04	-683.96	-467.25	-196.64	-320.39	-507.97	-155.19	113.65	174.00	289.03	218.84	181.29	201.75	148.60	92.22	1.44	-105.26
	-1006.93	-674.01	-498.42	-206.49	-323.18	-566.06	-174.92	161.40	203.09	293.05	252.74	271.21	247.34	106.65	61.81	-18.16	-144.98
FEMALE	-2758.64	-655.88	-414.07	-416.96	-857.04	-1066.80	-234.66	362.71	357.46	143.47	-23.22	13.77	58.89	23.52	36.25	25.90	-11.98
	-2727.96	-663.09	-419.90	-402.59	-941.68	-1069.45	-232.77	342.05	303.95	124.24	13.61	65.74	75.34	8.74	35.31	38.80	-6.26
	-2644.12	-681.00	-432.59	-388.31	-906.31	-1109.13	-256.35	318.21	205.57	88.02	115.13	198.32	108.94	-32.60	27.99	68.92	11.07

BERWICK

Age-Band in Years

	TOTAL	<5	<10	<15	<20	<25	<30	<35	<40	<45	<50	<55	<60	<65	<70	<75	75+
1861-1871																	
MALE	-1715.83	-484.30	-287.51	-166.87	-284.34	-329.90	-148.19	16.86	13.56	-27.96	-30.23	-20.85	-4.84	35.45	43.43	-3.86	-56.28
	-1697.18	-466.98	-282.96	-176.98	-255.28	-314.78	-153.51	-7.38	-1.41	-23.42	-26.43	-12.72	6.31	37.68	44.31	-1.63	-52.00
	-1684.83	-461.18	-303.13	-196.74	-234.01	-283.46	-166.17	-60.82	-35.82	-12.27	-13.10	11.31	33.94	40.18	40.67	-.27	-44.16
FEMALE	-1563.50	-453.51	-285.19	-212.95	-348.20	-435.26	-163.37	113.82	109.18	65.21	47.39	10.09	12.25	31.16	21.41	-17.88	-67.74
	-1538.77	-441.47	-289.45	-215.98	-335.67	-414.40	-173.77	65.81	101.65	62.82	51.93	28.69	19.50	28.21	31.41	-8.31	-69.77
	-1472.91	-443.57	-303.56	-220.44	-317.70	-383.67	-188.69	41.08	89.06	55.43	73.79	94.43	42.65	11.51	47.58	10.64	-81.46
1871-1881																	
MALE	-1898.85	-516.36	-338.13	-214.53	-303.75	-555.74	-146.20	22.57	7.27	-25.29	-26.17	-9.97	9.18	31.83	33.58	-7.51	-59.62
	-1886.10	-509.79	-339.09	-224.80	-300.34	-345.40	-148.34	3.37	-3.55	-21.60	-25.37	-.53	22.21	32.93	35.41	-3.20	-54.22
	-1860.37	-497.87	-344.51	-243.92	-298.69	-324.73	-155.10	-37.05	-26.76	-12.35	-19.60	22.26	50.16	33.90	35.74	2.95	-44.62
FEMALE	-2166.04	-488.47	-339.53	-256.32	-409.63	-489.01	-210.97	70.81	67.89	13.72	1.93	-10.86	-6.47	5.05	-1.23	-29.90	-73.01
	-2144.46	-484.39	-341.45	-260.84	-393.95	-465.89	-214.50	35.43	50.05	7.36	2.76	2.02	-1.07	3.13	8.58	-20.02	-71.70
	-2085.27	-477.87	-345.67	-267.33	-365.56	-407.13	-218.53	-27.73	17.09	-5.57	12.36	43.83	13.79	-8.00	24.62	-.71	-72.88
1881-1891																	
MALE	-1614.95	-454.07	-303.04	-156.39	-277.29	-367.02	-134.27	32.91	8.01	-14.56	-9.43	7.29	31.68	47.25	35.92	6.11	-55.82
	-1599.33	-450.65	-301.47	-164.53	-286.06	-364.10	-132.82	21.66	2.53	-12.29	-11.95	19.86	47.44	45.10	37.24	.03	-49.23
	-1589.66	-444.34	-298.91	-179.30	-300.58	-359.00	-133.18	-.77	-7.84	-5.72	-13.53	45.61	77.49	39.89	38.06	10.15	-37.67
FEMALE	-1670.14	-450.83	-324.85	-232.14	-392.91	-483.21	-148.00	161.05	133.94	39.25	27.36	37.47	27.65	15.69	5.95	-23.32	-63.23
	-1653.63	-447.38	-326.83	-236.70	-376.41	-443.07	-146.46	116.19	105.52	32.94	28.67	48.03	34.06	15.84	15.04	-13.59	-59.52
	-1612.59	-441.70	-330.71	-243.60	-343.11	-366.99	-141.88	32.11	52.17	22.81	35.91	75.05	46.76	10.73	28.81	4.65	-53.77
1891-1901																	
MALE	-1853.90	-442.76	-340.47	-214.67	-349.48	-458.05	-172.01	35.86	3.45	-5.06	3.87	22.04	52.14	53.73	26.76	-11.70	-57.54
	-1833.24	-440.21	-335.34	-220.81	-366.60	-465.43	-166.70	35.70	3.99	-5.97	-2.60	39.80	72.13	47.76	26.76	-4.00	-48.72
	-1795.34	-434.21	-325.27	-232.42	-405.50	-480.67	-158.58	36.98	7.31	-5.78	-12.63	72.99	107.67	35.61	26.38	9.27	-36.48
FEMALE	-1893.50	-362.76	-271.31	-182.15	-432.07	-611.13	-213.75	148.57	112.71	-7.43	-9.62	36.56	23.52	-8.26	-18.52	-33.82	-63.73
	-1802.31	-359.83	-273.84	-185.74	-412.95	-558.80	-189.70	95.87	69.99	-18.25	-12.73	41.83	29.53	-6.60	-9.73	-24.13	-57.46
	-1659.02	-353.98	-277.87	-192.26	-372.19	-455.87	-172.13	-5.53	-11.27	-35.06	-16.31	49.65	37.87	-6.74	3.37	-5.65	-44.84
1901-1911																	
MALE	-965.87	-305.80	-230.24	-86.06	-255.94	-424.54	-118.59	92.99	48.58	50.16	58.06	77.55	100.66	79.35	30.52	-19.04	-63.93
	-942.38	-305.58	-224.88	-89.97	-281.90	-441.37	-110.86	104.15	55.99	47.48	50.14	99.22	122.87	68.65	28.11	-9.74	-54.70
	-901.07	-302.60	-214.36	-98.67	-334.40	-474.97	-96.41	130.05	74.98	44.24	36.76	137.02	159.79	47.03	23.72	6.35	-39.58
FEMALE	-1241.00	-276.96	-222.65	-159.60	-462.73	-686.44	-175.62	291.09	225.40	52.49	43.52	113.22	80.78	18.94	-1.05	-24.80	-56.73
	-1233.32	-274.63	-225.56	-161.93	-443.62	-631.61	-155.59	229.36	168.83	44.02	44.97	117.87	89.38	23.14	5.51	-15.80	-47.48
	-1221.90	-288.14	-231.06	-168.39	-401.13	-522.04	-117.62	109.38	60.56	33.91	48.66	117.72	99.84	29.31	13.85	.71	-27.52

BUTE

Age-Band in Years

	TOTAL	<5	<10	<15	<20	<25	<30	<35	<40	<45	<50	<55	<60	<65	<70	<75	75+
1861-1871																	
MALE	-694.45	-206.61	-127.13	-68.89	-100.80	-117.95	-39.26	8.65	-5.38	-14.30	-10.58	-4.84	-3.39	4.00	11.14	-.19	-18.94
	-680.69	-198.31	-124.84	-74.92	-101.13	-110.39	-37.95	.31	-9.16	-12.17	-11.03	-4.95	-1.20	6.15	14.10	1.90	-17.11
	-676.06	-193.56	-132.54	-67.05	-101.49	-95.41	-35.95	-16.42	-16.14	-7.23	-11.38	-5.07	3.23	10.72	19.88	5.82	-13.47
FEMALE	-842.94	-205.81	-128.71	-79.31	-158.42	-233.86	-111.70	31.36	35.28	13.13	14.11	6.41	-.09	.60	7.10	-3.62	-29.58
	-831.85	-199.34	-123.81	-83.96	-150.71	-215.46	-117.51	11.63	31.35	14.32	10.68	4.80	.93	3.25	11.67	-.76	-28.91
	-833.63	-198.93	-126.50	-92.88	-135.27	-179.70	-129.65	-29.06	23.71	17.38	4.06	1.89	3.08	8.82	20.89	5.13	-27.50
1871-1881																	
MALE	-576.54	-196.96	-130.80	-77.15	-101.16	-106.36	-21.81	30.21	14.46	2.23	2.04	1.99	4.01	10.71	11.10	-1.10	-17.97
	-571.08	-195.89	-131.35	-80.53	-102.21	-101.79	-20.13	24.41	11.05	2.90	1.16	4.25	7.80	11.47	12.79	.73	-16.57
	-562.39	-193.96	-133.00	-87.00	-103.35	-92.72	-17.58	12.93	4.87	4.75	.11	8.00	14.95	13.15	15.98	3.86	-14.18
FEMALE	-860.05	-212.04	-147.27	-112.29	-186.07	-244.70	-102.03	56.88	54.39	16.96	12.52	9.49	3.01	-.12	1.90	-6.26	-24.80
	-878.04	-210.80	-147.29	-115.17	-178.24	-225.59	-105.06	34.58	44.82	16.16	11.07	10.65	5.39	2.18	6.45	-3.07	-24.12
	-873.23	-208.57	-147.82	-120.39	-162.07	-189.02	-111.96	-9.31	26.01	14.90	6.31	13.98	10.46	6.56	15.21	3.30	-22.72
1881-1891																	
MALE	-609.40	-200.25	-148.30	-102.66	-116.36	-105.23	-21.37	28.81	16.46	7.04	4.66	2.80	9.18	16.66	12.24	.03	-13.13
	-605.53	-202.21	-147.02	-102.80	-118.70	-104.75	-19.32	26.59	14.05	5.99	2.91	7.63	14.64	15.55	12.47	1.56	-12.10
	-598.43	-206.47	-144.99	-102.51	-121.96	-103.82	-16.39	22.20	9.98	4.43	.38	17.18	24.59	13.40	12.64	3.76	-10.85
FEMALE	-713.27	-194.66	-143.40	-116.50	-184.86	-229.38	-74.70	84.91	72.32	23.29	19.23	22.86	14.97	7.65	4.73	-3.88	-15.75
	-711.36	-194.57	-144.05	-117.26	-176.71	-208.45	-72.78	60.79	58.45	20.18	17.99	25.63	18.73	9.42	9.11	-.61	-15.49
	-706.92	-194.64	-145.62	-118.19	-159.84	-168.62	-70.17	14.16	25.27	13.99	17.02	33.39	26.17	12.14	17.05	5.71	-14.95
1891-1901																	
MALE	-641.43	-185.00	-149.57	-105.21	-118.51	-105.13	-25.61	18.61	10.10	2.47	.75	-1.03	8.89	17.85	8.90	-3.54	-15.39
	-637.50	-190.60	-146.44	-101.60	-122.62	-109.00	-22.56	20.53	8.81	-.85	-2.48	6.61	16.49	14.69	7.64	-2.03	-14.10
	-631.18	-202.41	-140.68	-94.13	-128.96	-116.46	-17.78	24.31	7.15	-6.63	-7.73	22.09	30.05	8.40	4.73	-.24	-12.69
FEMALE	-722.37	-171.75	-144.02	-131.64	-186.92	-232.61	-64.14	103.10	81.40	15.14	10.82	25.38	15.99	2.75	-4.71	-11.49	-19.67
	-721.13	-172.86	-145.58	-130.04	-186.88	-210.90	-57.24	76.03	58.29	10.50	10.84	30.70	21.87	4.50	-.64	-8.14	-19.60
	-718.54	-175.31	-149.16	-126.31	-171.80	-189.73	-44.70	24.51	12.70	.87	13.14	43.36	33.26	6.58	5.95	-2.13	-19.77
1901-1911																	
MALE	-477.04	-154.11	-137.63	-97.72	-115.09	-105.75	-16.02	36.19	26.52	16.55	14.17	10.06	22.17	32.83	13.38	-5.76	-16.85
	-473.09	-162.60	-132.79	-90.62	-121.02	-114.76	-12.05	42.71	26.26	10.75	9.47	21.39	32.54	27.23	10.03	-4.25	-15.39
	-467.87	-180.31	-123.45	-75.32	-130.76	-132.35	-5.85	55.36	26.73	-.12	1.39	43.22	51.02	16.18	3.09	-2.73	-13.98
FEMALE	-570.34	-136.24	-127.45	-127.38	-197.56	-234.46	-49.12	100.46	99.35	18.37	16.08	40.24	26.89	8.08	-3.55	-13.29	-20.77
	-569.12	-138.35	-129.52	-123.57	-189.82	-211.73	-36.58	100.91	88.67	12.09	16.88	47.23	34.66	9.81	.34	-9.74	-20.60
	-567.86	-142.79	-133.99	-115.43	-172.99	-168.60	-13.25	45.25	8.69	-1.35	21.38	63.57	49.11	11.02	5.86	-3.73	-20.60

Age–Band in Years

CAITHNESS

	TOTAL	<5	<10	<15	<20	<25	<30	<35	<40	<45	<50	<55	<60	<65	<70	<75	75+
1861-1871																	
MALE	-1560.61	-238.79	-165.19	-115.36	-254.95	-385.96	-175.96	-29.52	-49.43	-55.34	-39.23	-28.21	-19.14	.78	13.15	-4.24	-33.21
	-1544.10	-232.50	-181.70	-118.05	-253.39	-356.83	-176.09	-44.00	-50.98	-52.92	-39.83	-27.18	-15.64	3.98	18.38	-.97	-30.38
	-1532.48	-231.25	-166.63	-123.37	-249.40	-338.70	-177.16	-72.75	-71.18	-47.34	-60.02	-24.78	-8.70	10.70	28.29	4.86	-25.05
FEMALE	-1831.96	-242.72	-167.54	-128.38	-300.05	-480.05	-279.70	-24.21	-6.72	-32.98	-29.94	-32.14	-27.95	-15.83	-3.79	-14.64	-44.52
	-1818.62	-236.21	-182.67	-132.89	-289.04	-455.94	-286.25	-46.30	-12.57	-36.55	-34.52	-31.39	-26.97	-13.41	2.44	-11.09	-45.24
	-1814.99	-235.12	-165.21	-141.39	-285.31	-409.14	-299.23	-90.02	-24.70	-43.26	-42.42	-28.59	-24.43	-9.08	14.05	-4.26	-46.88
1871-1881																	
MALE	-1687.21	-256.25	-181.24	-119.20	-279.46	-406.80	-189.55	-24.17	-43.02	-52.27	-45.22	-35.83	-18.09	3.79	9.40	-9.31	-39.98
	-1679.34	-257.21	-182.00	-120.14	-278.58	-400.41	-187.96	-35.32	-50.11	-52.19	-47.24	-30.79	-11.35	4.81	12.76	-6.18	-37.42
	-1684.19	-260.28	-184.95	-120.82	-273.91	-387.46	-186.25	-57.08	-62.95	-51.52	-49.59	-20.28	.77	6.92	18.59	-1.71	-33.69
FEMALE	-2136.82	-262.14	-184.75	-140.06	-371.13	-597.15	-327.69	-5.01	9.44	-42.06	-42.03	-33.97	-31.10	-21.14	-11.71	-24.09	-54.22
	-2135.39	-260.81	-185.14	-143.25	-354.80	-561.79	-329.05	-38.67	-8.47	-49.07	-46.90	-31.64	-28.51	-19.06	-4.73	-19.30	-54.19
	-2128.86	-258.60	-187.31	-148.61	-320.81	-493.72	-332.25	-103.47	-44.64	-63.60	-54.04	-24.35	-23.13	-16.33	7.26	-10.84	-54.63
1881-1891																	
MALE	-1046.76	-218.44	-155.10	-86.71	-255.00	-395.46	-143.20	54.38	33.12	17.17	11.00	9.83	29.61	45.96	32.15	1.86	-27.93
	-1039.67	-221.70	-154.68	-84.34	-256.58	-396.35	-141.05	49.63	27.99	14.54	7.46	20.45	40.57	43.29	32.44	4.55	-25.88
	-1028.51	-229.76	-155.00	-77.39	-255.47	-398.12	-139.63	40.42	19.42	9.76	2.52	41.92	59.64	37.67	32.03	7.38	-23.89
FEMALE	-1366.36	-242.54	-178.81	-141.16	-377.48	-596.46	-241.86	153.71	138.36	39.21	27.70	41.00	29.70	18.57	13.00	-10.63	-40.74
	-1366.29	-242.91	-180.56	-141.34	-360.73	-558.17	-238.79	108.77	107.33	32.02	26.87	48.63	36.99	21.27	20.08	-5.24	-40.52
	-1363.59	-244.22	-185.52	-140.33	-324.73	-465.31	-234.08	23.51	44.94	15.91	29.28	67.83	50.92	23.67	30.81	4.04	-40.53
1891-1901																	
MALE	-2301.89	-246.52	-216.38	-184.72	-403.38	-581.92	-298.56	-61.48	-61.59	-65.17	-67.97	-58.72	-15.76	18.45	4.40	-17.69	-44.89
	-2294.71	-254.53	-215.98	-178.07	-407.82	-591.32	-293.52	-56.52	-63.87	-73.37	-75.57	-39.99	1.37	10.83	1.10	-15.21	-42.23
	-2285.39	-273.89	-216.50	-161.07	-410.27	-609.17	-286.89	-46.29	-85.92	-88.85	-87.43	-2.63	30.93	-4.73	-7.28	-14.52	-40.57
FEMALE	-2576.31	-252.98	-218.79	-217.67	-526.87	-798.69	-383.97	72.23	58.37	-61.18	-59.79	-9.38	-15.07	-26.85	-29.50	-41.55	-64.61
	-2575.20	-255.86	-222.88	-213.54	-506.47	-748.81	-384.67	19.20	8.64	-75.76	-62.96	-.18	-5.10	-25.28	-22.50	-35.19	-64.05
	-2576.10	-262.32	-232.72	-203.74	-462.08	-653.35	-328.18	-79.36	-91.09	-107.60	-62.66	24.28	13.44	-26.74	-14.18	-25.40	-64.20
1901-1911																	
MALE	-231.56	-150.59	-127.57	-69.84	-248.69	-410.21	-95.25	169.09	155.44	129.27	97.54	81.64	104.19	106.60	54.75	.70	-30.65
	-223.67	-159.06	-126.77	-59.62	-254.00	-427.83	-88.96	184.79	156.20	117.95	89.85	105.77	124.95	95.18	45.03	2.03	-29.16
	-217.12	-180.40	-125.84	-33.75	-257.03	-462.38	-81.55	216.10	161.27	96.11	77.71	153.58	159.74	67.47	23.60	-.86	-30.91
FEMALE	-1001.21	-166.83	-141.31	-121.35	-446.76	-731.74	-224.15	303.94	247.68	62.06	47.58	107.49	78.16	35.54	12.70	-19.62	-44.58
	-1000.46	-171.74	-147.49	-112.73	-426.19	-682.23	-197.78	238.28	178.61	48.97	52.67	124.66	95.34	37.77	18.29	-13.11	-43.98
	-1005.43	-181.72	-160.90	-94.36	-380.54	-588.61	-148.07	117.44	40.24	17.98	71.84	167.41	126.24	34.69	21.16	-4.28	-43.96

Age-Band in Years

CLACKMANNAN

	TOTAL	<5	<10	<15	<20	<25	<30	<35	<40	<45	<50	<55	<60	<65	<70	<75	75+
1861-1871																	
MALE	-832.11	-325.19	-177.71	-58.34	-90.73	-102.61	-23.17	9.49	-8.37	-18.48	-15.86	-14.10	-7.97	7.45	18.75	1.46	-26.72
	-809.37	-310.25	-172.60	-70.04	-81.32	-88.00	-18.30	-2.99	-16.25	-17.29	-17.13	-13.56	-4.52	9.89	22.96	4.62	-24.55
	-815.13	-306.02	-188.50	-93.48	-92.01	-59.13	-8.83	-27.00	-31.30	-14.83	-19.08	-12.20	2.19	14.59	30.68	10.34	-20.55
FEMALE	-1003.67	-332.12	-182.72	-79.35	-156.50	-219.55	-96.30	42.79	46.96	10.98	2.74	-7.20	-3.50	8.44	9.64	9.63	-38.27
	-984.72	-319.17	-173.33	-88.65	-146.01	-189.32	-102.31	15.91	38.15	7.52	-.24	-6.36	-3.10	10.21	15.52	5.69	-37.66
	-997.95	-319.29	-180.74	-107.10	-124.90	-130.31	-114.02	-36.80	20.50	.64	-5.47	-3.70	-1.95	13.29	26.72	1.93	-36.75
1871-1881																	
MALE	-1743.08	-405.32	-292.02	-220.51	-256.10	-244.38	-106.45	-17.59	-34.31	-46.48	-40.25	-34.56	-20.16	2.51	9.98	-5.98	-31.44
	-1737.40	-403.55	-292.21	-228.23	-258.57	-236.15	-101.43	-28.59	-41.65	-48.00	-43.98	-30.14	-13.25	2.56	12.74	-2.37	-28.59
	-1726.78	-400.79	-293.62	-236.81	-261.57	-219.95	-92.41	-43.86	-55.37	-50.64	-50.31	-21.34	-.44	2.66	17.63	3.79	-23.72
FEMALE	-1517.99	-377.18	-285.06	-213.86	-278.03	-311.34	-136.14	59.90	56.76	3.00	-1.66	-1.44	-2.91	2.03	.38	-15.15	-37.29
	-1516.76	-374.60	-285.08	-219.30	-265.48	-278.18	-137.82	26.37	39.14	-2.26	-4.73	.96	-.06	4.41	6.96	-10.51	-36.60
	-1514.34	-369.79	-266.04	-229.37	-239.70	-213.61	-141.22	-38.98	3.85	-13.14	-9.60	7.19	5.82	8.44	19.17	-1.71	-35.58
1881-1891																	
MALE	-1106.15	-374.01	-269.77	-171.03	-201.22	-181.88	-33.82	48.45	21.70	-.86	.10	-.67	15.36	36.32	27.15	.41	-24.38
	-1101.35	-378.94	-266.77	-170.75	-206.34	-180.76	-27.88	44.60	15.47	-5.11	-5.35	9.46	27.30	33.25	27.37	4.36	-21.26
	-1089.59	-380.07	-261.66	-168.50	-213.50	-178.73	-18.09	37.25	4.18	-12.94	-14.76	29.02	49.06	27.32	27.31	10.80	-16.27
FEMALE	-1016.23	-347.86	-256.63	-205.91	-243.83	-242.35	-57.62	130.52	108.87	30.69	25.70	34.15	23.38	15.87	7.44	-10.63	-28.01
	-1014.67	-347.58	-257.95	-207.52	-231.25	-208.82	-54.08	91.12	82.22	25.07	24.36	39.54	29.80	19.07	14.22	-5.69	-27.68
	-1012.10	-347.40	-261.56	-209.78	-204.64	-142.38	-47.66	14.93	29.08	13.16	23.51	52.03	42.34	24.14	26.14	3.39	-27.39
1891-1901																	
MALE	-2411.62	-399.00	-341.75	-180.96	-355.27	-354.59	-182.07	-75.62	-88.78	-99.51	-83.44	-70.40	-33.04	8.58	.60	-18.10	-38.29
	-2403.45	-413.20	-333.46	-272.57	-385.76	-363.49	-173.82	-71.09	-92.52	-106.30	-93.77	-52.38	-14.65	1.08	-1.70	-13.40	-33.42
	-2389.60	-442.82	-317.54	-254.15	-383.29	-380.65	-159.67	-62.10	-98.48	-127.42	-111.94	-17.97	18.69	-13.36	-6.92	-6.23	-25.75
FEMALE	-2195.30	-348.55	-311.51	-315.90	-375.18	-377.92	-175.63	30.17	10.17	-73.68	-58.94	-21.10	-25.98	-31.86	-36.09	-37.86	-45.43
	-2193.72	-350.78	-314.08	-312.98	-360.79	-335.87	-158.71	-13.14	-28.72	-85.60	-64.86	-16.77	-18.21	-28.82	-28.13	-31.66	-44.62
	-2191.53	-355.62	-319.93	-306.29	-330.54	-254.30	-126.33	-96.74	-105.76	-109.86	-74.30	-6.34	-3.39	-24.36	-14.23	-20.19	-43.35
1901-1911																	
MALE	-1586.65	-354.30	-328.35	-252.45	-339.50	-348.85	-104.44	56.79	18.17	-12.25	-2.19	-1.37	34.96	73.61	29.82	-14.65	-35.64
	-1575.09	-377.45	-315.05	-233.63	-355.57	-371.61	-93.26	66.59	16.43	-28.35	-16.45	27.50	62.94	59.22	21.88	-8.97	-29.39
	-1557.09	-425.78	-289.04	-93.58	-383.04	-415.76	-74.39	97.14	14.94	-58.46	-41.96	82.48	113.36	31.43	5.85	-.57	-19.72
FEMALE	-1680.07	-304.60	-302.16	-318.64	-392.79	-399.87	-114.33	161.99	106.56	-33.45	-17.26	37.75	16.32	-9.77	-27.33	-37.77	-44.72
	-1676.58	-309.07	-306.40	-310.74	-360.79	-352.02	-86.87	103.25	47.29	-46.93	-20.21	48.17	31.62	-4.44	-17.89	-30.21	-44.31
	-1671.66	-318.31	-315.49	-294.04	-345.54	-259.61	-34.60	-5.55	-69.85	-74.75	-22.47	71.30	60.73	3.60	-2.26	-16.72	-44.09

Age-Band in Years

DUMFRIES

	TOTAL	<5	<10	<15	<20	<25	<30	<35	<40	<45	<50	<55	<60	<65	<70	<75	75+
1861-1871																	
MALE	-1827.61	-627.02	-389.92	-142.55	-303.18	-414.29	-168.57	50.01	50.92	-14.97	-20.49	-6.38	14.54	70.92	78.94	8.28	-64.86
	-1786.09	-602.47	-329.54	-155.49	-288.12	-383.52	-180.35	15.16	29.75	-7.04	-13.09	6.43	29.98	72.45	78.39	10.20	-58.82
	-1788.39	-597.51	-355.35	-180.72	-253.38	-350.55	-207.83	-63.24	-18.80	13.18	11.56	44.14	68.43	71.42	68.06	8.68	-47.47
FEMALE	-2252.78	-619.96	-391.82	-263.05	-476.89	-622.58	-247.90	122.73	122.63	77.43	51.75	-3.34	13.43	52.39	37.58	-19.17	-85.99
	-2179.51	-602.75	-383.63	-267.07	-462.82	-599.14	-256.53	94.53	115.18	73.11	62.70	31.63	24.56	41.37	48.51	-6.05	-93.31
	-2059.45	-606.09	-404.42	-272.87	-446.27	-570.08	-260.56	61.15	106.60	61.30	109.39	154.63	60.81	-5.55	56.99	18.23	-124.11
1871-1881																	
MALE	-3779.40	-778.57	-541.22	-397.39	-548.59	-846.35	-325.92	-54.45	-70.72	-108.95	-103.42	-75.26	-39.01	5.48	19.48	-24.54	-89.96
	-3762.35	-768.49	-544.03	-411.80	-547.71	-632.30	-330.60	-84.40	-87.10	-104.12	-102.28	-61.57	-19.69	8.60	23.26	-18.02	-82.09
	-3727.08	-751.05	-551.72	-438.05	-539.84	-603.70	-343.02	-147.58	-122.67	-92.60	-94.55	-28.19	22.29	13.58	26.14	-8.59	-68.34
FEMALE	-4049.94	-740.68	-537.64	-432.77	-679.19	-825.71	-404.36	7.90	19.31	-40.98	-56.50	-73.42	-57.51	-31.61	-31.20	-56.09	-109.51
	-4017.15	-734.00	-541.24	-439.37	-661.40	-788.17	-411.74	-36.10	-3.64	-51.78	-52.00	-48.65	-48.01	-35.88	-15.56	-40.25	-109.37
	-3928.23	-723.90	-549.30	-448.19	-631.90	-726.83	-422.27	-112.21	-46.64	-75.89	-28.84	31.22	-20.20	-56.54	10.34	-9.50	-117.55
1881-1891																	
MALE	-2902.73	-743.60	-517.07	-309.49	-477.35	-596.01	-246.39	11.41	-16.03	-40.01	-31.50	-3.72	39.41	61.77	47.57	-6.19	-75.53
	-2679.21	-737.01	-513.84	-323.20	-490.79	-591.54	-247.10	-6.93	-22.86	-34.24	-33.85	14.78	62.18	59.00	49.79	2.35	-65.94
	-2834.90	-725.39	-507.98	-347.31	-512.42	-584.13	-253.62	-43.59	-35.83	-19.35	-32.70	53.34	105.59	51.49	50.76	15.75	-49.43
FEMALE	-2565.45	-689.71	-499.15	-348.52	-594.37	-733.15	-237.58	204.25	179.36	63.78	44.06	55.81	45.61	26.15	15.21	-21.38	-75.76
	-2534.61	-683.44	-503.05	-356.14	-570.47	-679.95	-234.95	151.03	145.72	54.25	47.65	73.41	51.85	21.80	26.25	-7.46	-71.40
	-2458.63	-673.09	-510.69	-366.96	-521.80	-580.79	-225.98	55.41	84.95	39.91	64.78	120.41	64.08	1.52	39.10	17.81	-67.27
1891-1901																	
MALE	-3920.34	-781.17	-627.39	-444.10	-637.35	-775.25	-345.20	-40.84	-78.89	-76.75	-57.67	-14.34	38.81	38.06	10.71	-30.44	-98.52
	-3888.45	-778.65	-617.23	-454.20	-669.77	-767.15	-339.82	-43.48	-75.98	-75.57	-67.10	11.65	68.43	30.17	13.20	-17.60	-85.36
	-3830.21	-772.74	-596.66	-472.55	-732.62	-812.26	-332.91	-45.14	-66.06	-69.91	-81.24	59.83	120.03	13.35	17.20	4.53	-63.05
FEMALE	-4122.36	-721.97	-598.14	-469.08	-813.12	-988.34	-395.04	131.62	101.64	-54.85	-61.39	17.22	6.26	-41.35	-46.66	-57.36	-101.91
	-4104.40	-714.39	-602.59	-507.14	-787.71	-912.37	-376.16	63.66	46.40	-65.83	-65.83	21.16	8.77	-42.82	-36.49	-43.17	-89.93
	-4067.38	-698.99	-610.59	-522.65	-716.65	-761.62	-337.83	-65.22	-56.52	-83.00	-71.10	22.46	6.14	-52.73	-25.26	-17.69	-66.13
1901-1911																	
MALE	-2325.68	-630.17	-521.61	-290.80	-504.73	-696.16	-211.23	102.51	34.82	48.84	68.70	105.66	152.62	115.41	34.74	-32.96	-101.52
	-2284.66	-630.39	-507.34	-297.08	-554.31	-725.82	-198.46	120.83	50.23	46.25	54.05	139.39	188.68	99.65	33.34	-17.30	-86.58
	-2212.68	-626.03	-477.65	-310.70	-656.50	-785.43	-174.32	163.98	67.82	43.91	28.36	198.03	247.60	67.84	31.72	10.29	-61.90
FEMALE	-2450.98	-594.23	-499.21	-358.79	-720.46	-943.47	-233.58	372.87	293.94	48.96	36.07	159.18	114.97	11.35	-9.20	-36.78	-92.60
	-2441.63	-585.33	-505.20	-366.10	-687.14	-854.49	-203.64	286.13	215.03	34.50	33.97	156.92	119.13	15.28	-1.02	-23.36	-74.30
	-2433.16	-561.73	-516.06	-392.56	-612.88	-672.60	-145.76	117.63	65.74	19.08	29.37	131.35	113.96	19.65	6.48	.31	-35.16

DUNBARTON

Age-Band in Years

	TOTAL	<5	<10	<15	<20	<25	<30	<35	<40	<45	<50	<55	<60	<65	<70	<75	75+
1861-1871																	
MALE	-3082.99	-1060.47	-679.48	-449.81	-382.37	-239.40	-57.26	20.41	-20.94	-48.68	-50.47	-46.24	-32.25	.62	31.33	-1.63	-66.17
	-3035.07	-1015.30	-670.37	-487.57	-388.27	-203.17	-43.38	-6.84	-38.16	-46.36	-54.83	-46.69	-25.03	5.82	40.60	5.94	-60.65
	-3045.79	-977.76	-706.19	-563.50	-402.88	-131.97	-16.32	-58.91	-70.58	-41.04	-62.49	-47.27	-11.19	15.99	58.59	20.00	-50.28
FEMALE	-3331.27	-1035.42	-657.34	-471.48	-526.41	-500.07	-209.37	100.75	103.24	18.37	-1.55	-27.34	-20.47	7.02	11.03	-28.09	-94.15
	-3297.93	-1003.27	-635.75	-496.66	-500.80	-425.24	-224.58	32.49	79.85	11.04	-9.43	-28.65	-21.22	10.44	23.96	-16.70	-81.43
	-3339.31	-994.16	-647.61	-645.44	-449.88	-278.70	-254.67	-102.01	33.54	-3.36	-24.51	-30.22	-22.19	16.98	49.38	-.17	-86.29
1871-1881																	
MALE	-2600.79	-1012.16	-665.15	-600.00	-322.58	-149.36	23.18	63.67	9.76	-35.99	-34.84	-36.72	-18.25	20.17	28.33	-8.34	-62.72
	-2588.29	-1003.16	-666.99	-423.67	-333.09	-124.50	39.59	44.74	-6.28	-38.90	-42.90	-27.77	-3.09	20.37	34.03	-.29	-56.41
	-2564.35	-985.27	-671.99	-470.74	-352.15	-75.38	70.75	8.20	-36.17	-43.81	-57.16	-10.62	25.19	20.96	44.56	14.26	-45.00
FEMALE	-2784.62	-937.65	-611.33	-419.38	-462.03	-416.75	-128.23	164.62	144.59	16.31	4.02	-2.24	-10.62	-4.03	-10.10	-38.36	-83.44
	-2796.66	-930.79	-610.62	-435.66	-434.58	-334.65	-131.03	82.38	101.99	5.45	-3.90	.99	-4.73	1.55	5.09	-27.29	-80.90
	-2800.21	-917.55	-610.15	-466.99	-379.33	-173.91	-136.93	-79.36	17.43	-16.22	-18.45	8.87	7.37	12.11	34.56	-5.57	-76.08
1881-1891																	
MALE	-2564.76	-937.25	-731.01	-490.04	-402.50	-175.05	45.19	109.94	47.05	-6.55	-5.78	-13.38	13.68	57.48	42.71	-3.56	-47.68
	-2551.01	-1007.88	-722.37	-501.90	-418.00	-169.17	61.81	102.60	33.71	-15.97	-17.85	6.93	38.37	51.37	43.43	4.93	-41.02
	-2525.86	-1029.91	-706.78	-508.46	-445.10	-157.25	92.09	88.54	9.28	-33.07	-39.22	45.56	83.97	39.93	44.35	19.74	-29.57
FEMALE	-3121.43	-959.21	-738.52	-655.32	-632.33	-481.81	-106.10	256.29	196.09	23.05	23.74	42.03	18.01	4.35	-11.65	-36.31	-63.75
	-3121.31	-958.17	-740.24	-560.22	-604.02	-397.05	-94.89	160.83	131.64	6.84	16.97	51.10	32.20	12.55	5.71	-23.90	-62.66
	-3120.80	-956.75	-744.85	-568.68	-546.17	-231.61	-73.89	-26.19	3.93	-19.69	5.70	71.24	60.37	27.66	38.72	.18	-60.76
1891-1901																	
MALE	-4382.14	-1141.11	-979.80	-817.96	-668.23	-318.97	-73.10	-.14	-53.97	-99.69	-78.39	-73.66	-23.63	42.32	16.54	-26.57	-65.77
	-4344.51	-1180.00	-955.44	-796.60	-691.70	-336.30	-54.55	8.31	-63.39	-119.27	-98.30	-37.97	13.60	28.03	12.31	-16.84	-56.20
	-4313.46	-1258.93	-909.79	-751.94	-732.75	-369.85	-22.11	24.28	-79.86	-155.31	-133.87	29.68	82.12	1.01	3.69	.19	-40.03
FEMALE	-4610.03	-1064.96	-968.01	-1014.00	-874.65	-550.66	-141.46	238.06	152.97	-74.62	-50.06	17.62	-12.28	-43.34	-66.02	-73.00	-84.81
	-4608.80	-1071.02	-973.53	-843.70	-806.25	-454.66	-106.29	127.47	58.84	-97.92	-61.15	30.60	9.61	-33.44	-45.75	-58.00	-83.70
	-4606.86	-1094.09	-985.83	-986.62	-779.49	-288.17	-39.59	-88.44	-127.09	-144.63	-78.00	59.28	52.32	-15.88	-7.89	-29.04	-81.73
1901-1911																	
MALE	-3194.07	-1097.42	-1027.42	-827.91	-595.76	-125.85	124.69	134.75	60.75	-8.13	14.30	4.54	60.23	133.51	51.49	-29.85	-65.97
	-3171.25	-1166.52	-985.19	-775.09	-630.24	-173.15	147.03	164.40	55.85	-39.01	-12.39	59.29	113.53	107.17	36.86	-19.17	-54.61
	-3132.07	-1307.24	-902.51	-566.22	-691.07	-265.09	185.37	221.10	49.09	-96.13	-60.11	162.90	211.17	57.08	7.96	-2.10	-36.25
FEMALE	-3801.93	-977.76	-985.59	-1064.28	-840.37	-393.20	45.26	401.24	256.93	62.57	-23.49	67.53	33.34	-14.20	-70.80	-68.58	-93.64
	-3795.10	-990.17	-996.28	-1042.23	-808.25	-289.24	105.49	267.13	124.27	-91.36	-30.63	110.78	68.90	-17.45	-47.45	-68.75	-93.11
	-3783.13	-1015.94	-1019.07	-995.71	-740.14	-98.75	219.45	6.68	-136.89	-149.30	-38.94	161.29	137.66	9.38	-5.30	-35.06	-92.65

Age-Band in Years

EDINBURGH (MIDLOTHIAN)

	TOTAL	<5	<10	<15	<20	<25	<30	<35	<40	<45	<50	<55	<60	<65	<70	<75	75+
1861-1871																	
MALE	-5697.66	-2403.09	-1470.34	-790.65	-637.02	-385.29	-26.32	111.15	20.95	-73.48	-58.11	-22.16	-2.28	72.28	118.15	4.52	-155.97
	-5560.10	-2311.07	-1444.68	-850.42	-634.79	-319.37	-19.67	38.83	-15.60	-56.43	-56.04	-15.01	21.40	86.10	136.71	19.18	-141.33
	-5559.54	-2266.12	-1538.83	-870.91	-625.27	-186.73	-11.46	-110.51	-89.46	-17.11	-43.94	6.76	73.94	119.56	168.34	44.56	-112.36
FEMALE	-5982.03	-2303.02	-1498.42	-1009.47	-1011.60	-902.97	-305.40	351.24	354.83	180.05	152.85	69.44	38.30	57.27	77.22	-23.53	-207.80
	-5845.97	-2237.63	-1449.74	-1049.18	-969.50	-791.25	-346.67	226.45	331.15	184.72	145.21	85.94	52.40	68.50	110.87	.21	-207.43
	-5817.46	-2246.05	-1490.99	-1123.80	-890.02	-584.35	-425.78	-12.06	287.13	194.74	145.08	152.26	91.10	79.53	173.08	47.60	-214.92
1871-1881																	
MALE	-7551.45	-2868.72	-2000.09	-1397.32	-974.62	-358.54	13.32	116.34	23.42	-61.38	-49.61	-19.96	14.41	83.67	98.69	-11.65	-159.42
	-7511.08	-2843.24	-2009.58	-1440.87	-985.39	-316.26	24.58	63.97	-5.94	-53.16	-53.98	1.85	48.99	89.57	111.12	3.39	-146.12
	-7428.54	-2782.45	-2036.86	-1525.82	-995.77	-231.95	39.25	-43.00	-82.45	-54.46	-54.46	49.06	117.68	101.58	132.19	28.55	-122.63
FEMALE	-8179.93	-2695.74	-1947.59	-1623.06	-1387.49	-873.81	-269.89	323.72	320.86	93.84	63.36	37.61	6.93	-.02	11.95	-53.97	-186.66
	-8144.12	-2682.56	-1948.05	-1650.57	-1340.10	-752.33	-269.92	186.57	262.53	86.36	57.70	59.03	25.50	10.15	43.65	-28.99	-183.28
	-8054.51	-2681.10	-1953.95	-1698.00	-1242.19	-526.83	-333.88	-77.22	149.24	72.30	60.16	124.40	68.55	21.70	102.09	20.64	-180.42
1881-1891																	
MALE	-8434.46	-3128.20	-2304.17	-1618.11	-1002.73	-108.98	124.50	-5.71	-82.46	-130.48	-110.06	-60.54	3.68	100.00	83.67	-23.38	-151.50
	-8394.60	-3140.63	-2294.54	-1633.56	-1028.95	-97.22	143.07	-30.51	-102.74	-135.95	-125.35	-36.69	55.14	90.89	87.76	-6.93	-138.41
	-8318.67	-3185.52	-2285.30	-1660.25	-1064.95	-74.79	167.98	-80.96	-138.37	-140.35	-145.83	50.78	151.37	73.25	93.30	19.28	-118.32
FEMALE	-9714.39	-2949.12	-2281.59	-2033.99	-1616.14	-733.59	-154.11	282.49	249.30	-45.40	-61.42	-5.90	-26.99	-54.09	-41.48	-79.81	-181.76
	-9682.20	-2947.86	-2269.97	-2042.02	-1555.25	-588.59	-141.54	124.61	144.12	-70.71	-67.73	20.81	-2.70	-47.02	-10.37	-52.12	-176.06
	-9606.09	-2951.05	-2292.34	-2048.26	-1423.40	-319.05	-127.05	-176.82	-60.91	-119.09	-64.34	91.70	46.44	-41.43	42.92	2.06	-165.49
1891-1901																	
MALE	-10208.2	-3202.74	-2575.98	-1895.60	-1230.96	-166.30	57.10	-167.60	-228.36	-243.51	-206.19	-163.36	-27.00	90.46	38.04	-68.54	-197.50
	-10160.6	-3273.26	-2536.73	-1851.04	-1279.15	-225.44	83.79	-154.62	-237.95	-270.15	-236.80	-83.98	52.72	61.33	30.36	-46.98	-180.62
	-10075.4	-3415.21	-2469.68	-1786.47	-1354.10	-302.70	122.24	-128.00	-248.64	-314.68	-284.97	69.66	197.49	4.50	12.62	-19.99	-157.46
FEMALE	-10364.8	-2866.34	-2363.07	-2219.77	-1816.31	-760.33	-51.38	393.87	305.42	-152.68	-173.64	-10.28	-38.12	-110.17	-117.61	-138.50	-215.92
	-10338.3	-2879.82	-2382.53	-2229.30	-1739.67	-588.10	3.09	197.71	131.07	-198.53	-178.41	27.72	-.52	-102.18	-85.30	-106.41	-207.09
	-10279.7	-2911.72	-2426.41	-2178.62	-1571.80	-266.41	94.40	-174.64	-209.78	-287.29	-166.93	119.07	70.14	-98.85	-34.28	-45.51	-189.05
1901-1911																	
MALE	-10682.1	-3007.90	-2650.39	-1978.77	-1433.76	-453.02	-28.89	-203.30	-285.38	-255.19	-197.97	-165.98	39.16	211.26	52.14	-111.01	-233.07
	-10626.6	-3130.38	-2579.98	-1863.91	-1514.19	-570.63	6.12	-133.07	-259.08	-311.97	-248.95	-32.66	161.89	150.27	22.04	-87.77	-212.58
	-10534.3	-3376.86	-2450.93	-1667.02	-1648.74	-801.88	56.32	6.21	-234.70	-413.82	-333.57	222.13	382.51	31.35	39.34	-58.66	-187.31
FEMALE	-11336.8	-2687.42	-2437.18	-2546.71	-2275.67	-1192.04	-98.48	624.70	448.01	-221.32	-239.51	51.07	-.16	-130.91	-170.92	-196.34	-243.95
	-11309.2	-2714.55	-2494.18	-2470.43	-2183.65	-988.76	14.48	378.79	179.39	-292.25	-238.11	107.82	57.92	-121.98	-136.78	-157.27	-269.64
	-11256.4	-2770.44	-2541.05	-2382.51	-1981.15	-612.32	214.21	-83.93	-346.59	-431.73	-205.63	237.72	162.48	-123.00	-89.22	-84.59	-218.68

Age-Band in Years

ELGIN (MORAY)

	TOTAL	<5	<10	<15	<20	<25	<30	<35	<40	<45	<50	<55	<60	<65	<70	<75	75+
1861-1871																	
MALE	-2001.44	-565.15	-392.62	-254.00	-276.67	-278.72	-106.26	-5.55	-39.71	-55.44	-28.95	-1.30	.44	16.01	26.48	-1.40	-38.61
	-1986.23	-553.24	-386.21	-255.87	-274.74	-269.92	-110.42	-25.03	-45.01	-47.70	-27.42	-.99	5.36	22.91	33.85	2.84	-34.45
	-1943.09	-554.61	-401.50	-259.85	-269.02	-251.60	-120.90	-66.30	-54.53	-29.61	-22.76	-.20	15.98	36.47	49.01	10.36	-26.02
FEMALE	-2159.51	-516.80	-393.97	-316.85	-334.80	-375.67	-219.43	-.43	19.12	-.26	19.52	14.03	-6.57	-18.76	9.67	4.27	-42.47
	-2128.06	-506.93	-384.20	-322.48	-327.08	-360.00	-228.87	-21.70	22.21	6.85	12.99	11.81	-2.30	-11.35	17.93	8.03	-43.15
	-2113.20	-511.25	-389.56	-332.53	-312.05	-330.61	-249.89	-66.34	28.23	23.08	1.07	8.52	7.62	4.13	34.55	16.06	-44.21
1871-1881																	
MALE	-1927.09	-549.40	-362.24	-182.21	-217.08	-237.79	-98.88	-40.25	-59.67	-63.16	-47.80	-26.23	-11.81	7.75	15.84	-7.81	-46.33
	-1913.52	-548.06	-365.91	-183.15	-214.64	-232.45	-102.27	-55.47	-64.58	-57.97	-46.66	-21.48	-4.38	11.44	20.95	-4.68	-44.00
	-1884.97	-545.69	-376.75	-183.90	-204.97	-221.60	-112.64	-87.36	-72.95	-45.51	-42.34	-11.05	9.96	19.73	30.92	-.03	-40.78
FEMALE	-2234.50	-485.31	-342.74	-235.14	-318.05	-388.20	-221.56	-20.81	3.77	33.73	-28.30	-21.52	-30.34	-35.84	-6.87	-9.42	-50.44
	-2223.22	-494.98	-343.25	-238.41	-305.66	-366.04	-228.40	-47.38	-3.79	-32.46	-31.93	-19.39	-26.02	-31.48	.53	-4.50	-50.05
	-2198.90	-495.74	-347.06	-242.35	-276.79	-327.23	-246.87	-99.58	-18.77	-29.18	-35.36	-10.91	-16.24	-23.60	14.21	5.54	-48.97
1881-1891																	
MALE	-1717.20	-514.35	-355.78	-195.50	-252.31	-288.17	-104.85	-3.08	-12.45	-9.89	-13.48	-4.23	19.97	36.45	29.16	-3.21	-45.49
	-1706.30	-515.72	-359.61	-194.00	-250.70	-285.56	-107.09	-10.03	-14.89	-7.65	-13.23	7.11	31.12	35.28	30.04	-1.71	-45.39
	-1685.98	-519.20	-371.21	-189.02	-240.47	-292.38	-116.38	-24.36	-17.28	-1.79	-8.93	31.16	51.00	32.90	30.47	-2.09	-48.39
FEMALE	-1873.11	-468.37	-333.66	-267.53	-402.78	-488.57	-187.30	97.84	107.48	28.62	9.32	21.87	15.88	-.03	12.75	.00	-38.62
	-1863.49	-470.24	-336.48	-265.91	-386.85	-444.79	-190.31	66.10	87.65	25.91	11.21	30.94	22.38	1.39	18.29	5.25	-38.04
	-1842.38	-475.69	-344.80	-259.36	-349.85	-405.54	-202.71	7.41	48.62	20.01	22.03	56.34	35.58	.94	26.21	15.16	-36.71
1891-1901																	
MALE	-2109.95	-496.06	-361.12	-211.44	-296.18	-363.01	-171.10	-56.68	-39.73	-17.53	-38.91	-32.78	8.78	28.73	13.55	-16.63	-61.84
	-2101.94	-500.08	-366.13	-207.43	-296.22	-373.44	-171.83	-52.63	-39.21	-20.41	-37.82	-12.61	25.02	21.81	9.65	-16.90	-63.69
	-2091.55	-509.30	-381.03	-196.78	-286.82	-393.53	-179.14	-44.40	-34.53	-24.37	-34.53	29.61	52.88	7.07	-.64	-23.17	-72.87
FEMALE	-2419.58	-458.85	-333.27	-300.66	-512.84	-585.93	-233.59	88.64	97.09	-13.58	-47.76	-8.25	-3.25	-20.77	-10.90	-19.56	-52.12
	-2412.08	-463.57	-339.03	-293.12	-492.79	-561.84	-226.35	52.80	60.21	-23.98	-42.20	7.25	5.37	-22.92	-7.47	-13.59	-50.82
	-2395.93	-475.01	-353.00	-274.34	-446.78	-517.12	-219.93	-9.89	-12.91	-47.02	-19.63	49.46	21.90	-33.32	-6.55	-3.33	-48.26
1901-1911																	
MALE	-1426.83	-428.95	-334.05	-216.11	-307.39	-386.38	-147.56	25.09	57.67	91.02	47.85	29.85	74.00	86.19	41.63	-7.58	-52.11
	-1422.03	-435.62	-339.21	-208.45	-309.25	-407.66	-146.61	43.00	62.66	82.85	45.45	58.44	94.67	71.79	31.26	-9.54	-55.80
	-1423.24	-450.57	-354.35	-189.82	-301.74	-449.35	-152.37	78.90	77.50	66.15	46.03	117.32	129.95	41.10	7.54	-20.63	-69.91
FEMALE	-1743.61	-383.19	-277.77	-274.40	-558.70	-662.03	-180.69	234.45	222.70	58.03	-4.67	48.59	50.28	18.08	12.84	-8.75	-38.36
	-1737.81	-390.52	-285.98	-261.03	-536.72	-635.73	-165.89	193.81	167.52	43.73	10.11	73.94	63.05	12.50	12.75	-2.80	-36.54
	-1727.52	-406.59	-303.85	-231.15	-486.54	-597.10	-145.97	126.50	57.79	10.47	55.68	140.11	65.94	-8.85	3.06	6.00	-33.01

Age-Band in Years

F I F E

	TOTAL	<5	<10	<15	<20	<25	<30	<35	<40	<45	<50	<55	<60	<65	<70	<75	75+
1861-1871																	
MALE	-7411.16	-1613.98	-1046.63	-619.43	-982.65	-1233.00	-559.38	-120.08	-223.06	-276.99	-219.07	-155.84	-119.93	-34.75	33.38	-44.86	-194.67
	-7309.12	-1560.45	-1027.40	-650.41	-980.77	-1181.09		-189.77	-256.91	-263.22	-222.97	-155.11	-102.52	-17.40	58.35	-26.69	-177.30
	-7270.14	-1538.19	-1078.79	-713.02	-973.46	-1077.58	-552.50	-330.52	-321.14	-231.42	-226.39	-152.30	-66.98	19.54	107.06	7.69	-142.15
FEMALE	-6651.24	-1437.75	-950.01	-634.11	-1070.82	-1504.19	-797.24	60.68	91.96	-42.85	-35.28	-67.29	-84.45	-81.92	-10.74	-70.04	-237.09
	-6771.42	-1397.25	-917.16	-662.14	-1024.68	-1396.27	-835.84	-56.71	67.91	-42.53	-52.86	-67.75	-77.34	-46.01	19.94	-50.51	-232.22
	-6777.49	-1403.26	-939.06	-715.32	-832.03	-1188.44	-915.61	-291.50	19.57	-39.33	-83.84	-61.96	-59.14	-14.50	60.63	-10.79	-222.92
1871-1881																	
MALE	-7532.06	-1626.96	-1090.54	-643.41	-1096.15	-1402.18	-582.25	-54.99	-157.29	-221.62	-193.30	-143.86	-86.00	4.49	38.24	-54.84	-211.38
	-7489.36	-1618.55	-1097.11	-662.50	-1099.44	-1368.95	-585.13	-109.26	-187.69	-216.04	-201.37	-122.83	-52.61	11.84	55.21	-38.04	-196.90
	-7402.83	-1602.66	-1116.62	-698.94	-1095.81	-1302.56	-579.37	-218.33	-243.27	-200.09	-209.79	-79.22	10.57	28.31	86.99	-10.14	-172.51
FEMALE	-7595.41	-1459.54	-1013.82	-759.81	-1327.34	-1797.69	-880.75	154.01	171.71	-47.32	-59.18	-59.18	-83.63	-80.80	-42.51	-87.09	-222.45
	-7573.97	-1453.99	-1013.98	-775.70	-1270.86	-1672.36	-900.43	13.03	109.82	-57.81	-73.07	-49.22	-80.70	-67.16	-11.62	-64.53	-217.39
	-7525.43	-1445.51	-1018.70	-802.91	-1153.33	-1435.21	-946.76	-263.19	-12.95	-77.73	-91.48	-18.09	-36.04	-43.18	46.49	-19.48	-207.37
1881-1891																	
MALE	-5503.68	-1502.58	-1059.55	-1024.24	-1061.68	-1391.58	-440.39	219.88	114.86	44.19	22.78	18.38	88.14	159.44	111.02	-18.99	-163.36
	-5463.85	-1513.32	-1059.17	-1024.43	-1094.56	-1390.78	-429.94	195.25	93.67	38.75	10.96	65.28	139.83	150.59	113.94	-5.51	-154.39
	-5391.38	-1537.66	-1065.71	-1019.48	-1104.57	-1389.04	-421.52	145.40	58.47	33.43	-2.12	159.82	234.02	133.48	116.90	12.23	-145.03
FEMALE	-5418.80	-1411.37	-1038.80	-665.03	-1396.12	-1730.42	-573.98	612.99	543.12	185.73	127.51	152.88	98.12	38.81	31.03	-38.32	-152.96
	-5397.93	-1413.51	-1044.71	-666.19	-1341.92	-1606.49	-574.62	452.04	440.79	170.51	129.14	183.05	127.47	51.33	59.52	-14.95	-149.39
	-5351.10	-1420.99	-1061.55	-662.41	-1221.12	-1377.40	-587.62	142.95	238.67	139.07	147.59	258.93	166.40	68.79	109.04	30.46	-141.69
1891-1901																	
MALE	-6349.87	-1398.70	-1097.54	-749.00	-1250.01	-1589.33	-589.12	124.74	71.68	36.19	-1.11	-12.46	92.68	166.81	84.50	-44.50	-184.71
	-6310.17	-1430.72	-1088.19	-727.34	-1276.02	-1626.39	-580.66	141.10	63.28	11.88	-23.26	62.75	163.15	138.23	71.91	-33.33	-176.56
	-6245.76	-1499.15	-1077.04	-676.70	-1307.60	-1698.54	-558.81	173.26	56.11	-29.94	-54.05	212.07	288.85	81.08	42.47	-24.30	-173.25
FEMALE	-7324.37	-1286.16	-1026.89	-952.94	-1846.99	-2045.92	-766.60	484.25	401.16	-30.24	-79.78	45.32	12.54	-61.13	-73.42	-108.13	-189.43
	-7304.77	-1296.36	-1039.09	-937.48	-1585.24	-1905.50	-722.93	312.60	246.35	-68.49	-77.59	86.38	50.09	-54.24	-46.95	-81.92	-184.59
	-7282.03	-1320.00	-1067.92	-900.00	-1450.97	-1649.33	-652.91	-9.81	-58.87	-147.67	-50.56	189.56	122.78	-52.80	-6.09	-32.54	-174.70
1901-1911																	
MALE	-3121.69	-1259.26	-1090.63	-799.27	-1117.16	-1289.87	-240.54	520.75	461.03	409.75	320.34	248.46	331.99	363.69	175.58	-22.17	-154.39
	-3084.39	-1311.12	-1070.35	-754.36	-1152.76	-1343.36	-215.24	579.75	464.62	293.33		346.82	313.47		142.48	-14.23	-149.22
	-3036.60	-1419.55	-1036.43	-556.01	-1201.31	-1467.25	-182.98	695.93	483.62	293.85	252.81	540.18	565.43	212.17	72.15	-14.55	-154.67
FEMALE	-4220.91	-1143.07	-1001.59	-1045.77	-1670.66	-1903.47	-359.27	1069.72	873.77	270.47	167.82	323.85	246.84	103.31	91.30	-53.33	-131.23
	-4199.72	-1160.53	-1019.92	-1013.86	-1612.42	-1771.19	-289.43	878.04	665.83	229.86	194.76	390.61	302.70	108.35	52.34	-27.61	-127.26
	-4158.46	-1197.80	-1059.55	-944.44	-1483.24	-1534.18	-190.47	524.67	256.74	142.37	278.67	550.10	406.88	98.61	74.72	17.71	-119.25

Age–Band in Years

FORFAR (ANGUS)

	TOTAL	<5	<10	<15	<20	<25	<30	<35	<40	<45	<50	<55	<60	<65	<70	<75	75+
1861-1871																	
MALE	-4484.91	-1363.39	-872.34	-472.71	-535.85	-543.98	-203.24	-33.63	-106.82	-133.77	-89.69	-55.44	-36.62	18.61	54.93	-10.29	-110.46
	-4409.44	-1322.70	-850.78	-690.94	-534.61	-509.51	-199.40	-80.33	-129.28	-124.17	-90.50	-52.85	-24.88	30.33	71.38	.16	-101.26
	-4395.84	-1322.26	-892.98	-527.41	-528.04	-440.10	-194.06	-173.40	-171.37	-102.10	-86.81	-46.48	-1.54	55.14	102.76	18.73	-83.92
FEMALE	-3830.05	-1186.84	-783.93	-471.55	-541.78	-651.38	-347.41	70.40	103.36	17.79	17.69	-1.31	-9.06	.85	25.65	-12.42	-100.12
	-3760.18	-1132.25	-735.51	-494.36	-523.25	-592.97	-365.26	14.35	94.53	15.42	8.23	3.18	-2.34	11.13	43.78	-2.88	-101.97
	-3763.54	-1136.56	-754.42	-536.85	-483.15	-480.49	-401.72	-97.13	75.47	12.14	-7.05	16.16	13.15	30.53	77.79	15.34	-106.74
1871-1881																	
MALE	-5920.99	-1620.52	-1168.18	-824.24	-805.14	-662.05	-253.72	-41.92	-100.57	-132.09	-112.56	-83.92	-86.88	25.24	40.13	-23.68	-120.69
	-5895.74	-1621.36	-1172.44	-831.76	-803.20	-639.72	-248.00	-76.82	-121.25	-130.12	-117.21	-68.61	-16.21	29.16	50.27	-14.61	-113.86
	-5846.99	-1628.00	-1189.03	-841.09	-785.82	-594.73	-242.28	-145.38	-158.63	-124.28	-121.05	-36.27	21.33	37.34	67.62	-2.25	-104.47
FEMALE	-5328.04	-1415.13	-1039.73	-844.92	-837.19	-779.46	-394.78	80.69	118.46	-11.95	-25.25	-13.61	-20.83	-14.45	6.93	-29.48	-107.34
	-5313.08	-1409.07	-1042.33	-858.75	-806.92	-708.94	-400.99	12.04	85.91	-22.44	-31.23	-3.28	-11.81	-8.22	22.15	-19.96	-109.24
	-5284.03	-1399.96	-1056.15	-880.05	-735.97	-576.21	-416.72	-117.85	19.41	-45.14	-34.91	26.02	7.05	-.40	46.22	-4.11	-115.27
1881-1891																	
MALE	-5564.14	-1655.75	-1249.16	-868.88	-797.20	-569.03	-168.99	-10.65	-49.94	-76.36	-82.69	-67.89	12.86	84.63	62.83	-16.15	-111.66
	-5543.33	-1678.27	-1248.11	-856.15	-797.40	-570.46	-162.15	-25.48	-64.97	-84.63	-94.04	-34.23	47.03	76.17	63.90	-8.36	-106.16
	-5511.84	-1733.84	-1255.25	-817.51	-774.72	-574.41	-160.29	-53.99	-89.44	-99.33	-108.99	34.47	106.43	58.39	61.73	-2.09	-102.79
FEMALE	-5111.93	-1455.48	-1110.33	-945.04	-878.04	-679.84	-271.80	171.53	190.02	-4.66	-28.18	21.86	13.59	1.12	8.01	-35.89	-108.90
	-5103.26	-1458.24	-1121.19	-944.19	-833.41	-593.69	-260.80	85.07	125.20	-24.78	-30.62	39.50	27.11	3.28	20.04	-26.19	-110.36
	-5091.42	-1467.42	-1152.21	-933.78	-728.09	-434.02	-245.58	-73.11	-6.49	-71.10	-21.63	88.31	52.43	-1.83	32.37	-12.92	-116.35
1891-1901																	
MALE	-9123.83	-1671.05	-1390.00	-1088.16	-1202.92	-1113.16	-610.37	-378.80	-353.74	-341.76	-336.67	-283.68	-117.45	14.45	-15.63	-77.68	-177.21
	-9102.44	-1721.21	-1377.56	-1027.63	-1215.01	-1152.69	-598.37	-361.28	-359.86	-370.15	-363.66	-218.31	-58.36	-12.25	-26.97	-69.85	-169.09
	-9078.79	-1835.20	-1360.56	-928.29	-1208.59	-1232.01	-591.65	-324.59	-362.81	-423.51	-405.14	-67.58	43.17	-67.14	-56.96	-70.51	-167.42
FEMALE	-7909.47	-1415.03	-1182.92	-1142.59	-1253.66	-1136.03	-571.23	-1.02	24.73	-247.37	-251.34	-101.54	-95.98	-113.35	-99.15	-121.68	-191.32
	-7909.16	-1429.06	-1212.92	-1120.84	-1188.96	-1016.88	-524.23	-119.06	-95.06	-288.20	-258.01	-77.68	-75.34	-114.98	-87.45	-108.92	-191.56
	-7922.56	-1460.61	-1280.79	-1068.67	-1041.40	-795.79	-439.27	-330.74	-338.11	-381.21	-248.59	-8.63	-38.40	-134.06	-83.89	-94.32	-198.09
1901-1911																	
MALE	-5866.14	-1385.30	-1254.22	-940.55	-1182.70	-1192.25	-393.31	82.39	83.00	44.16	-11.40	-15.84	153.35	266.20	103.31	-57.24	-165.80
	-5841.99	-1462.39	-1231.02	-868.59	-1209.24	-1279.35	-371.67	146.10	86.66	-6.55	-51.25	87.53	242.71	212.10	67.81	-50.17	-156.67
	-5830.40	-1636.44	-1190.23	-760.28	-1225.59	-1450.84	-350.74	273.29	113.63	-103.72	-116.45	291.20	394.48	101.29	-12.04	-58.96	-158.61
FEMALE	-6096.01	-1160.91	-1063.30	-1077.58	-1375.47	-1377.15	-447.01	438.22	378.37	-82.90	-113.28	98.23	59.19	-18.09	-48.69	-114.79	-190.73
	-6100.74	-1185.66	-1091.37	-1033.34	-1299.05	-1237.22	-365.38	272.87	187.69	-132.11	-105.68	142.75	98.54	-20.93	-39.94	-109.40	-190.92
	-6136.48	-1236.85	-1152.29	-940.28	-1127.45	-976.70	-211.65	-20.28	-197.98	-249.11	-56.58	262.22	166.97	-53.40	-54.07	-89.13	-199.90

Age–Band in Years

HADDINGTON (EAST LOTHIAN)

	TOTAL	<5	<10	<15	<20	<25	<30	<35	<40	<45	<50	<55	<60	<65	<70	<75	75+
1861-1871																	
MALE	-2239.17	-570.88	-348.15	-213.37	-381.79	-494.13	-194.63	43.73	12.67	-27.91	-32.40	-28.63	-11.06	28.39	46.36	-.62	-66.76
	-2206.69	-546.38	-342.11	-232.23	-379.07	-469.33	-191.37	14.93	-6.25	-24.72	-32.98	-24.10	-.67	32.31	51.97	4.79	-61.46
	-2207.71	-530.54	-363.50	-268.83	-372.20	-420.10	-166.07	-43.86	-45.23	-17.51	-30.58	-10.61	22.47	38.68	59.32	13.13	-51.78
FEMALE	-2305.54	-575.99	-356.74	-245.84	-500.61	-701.67	-267.27	156.04	148.82	66.92	37.70	.62	7.09	34.33	25.76	-25.05	-89.65
	-2273.39	-557.57	-345.76	-257.24	-475.17	-646.73	-304.73	97.50	129.13	60.25	36.18	10.66	10.47	34.52	36.82	-14.44	-89.32
	-2262.62	-554.55	-357.32	-278.73	-428.74	-544.22	-335.95	-12.17	91.27	45.40	40.09	46.23	21.93	28.86	62.44	6.22	-93.38
1871-1881																	
MALE	-2321.02	-561.73	-383.15	-242.27	-415.23	-518.58	-188.68	59.91	17.05	-28.28	-29.50	-20.68	2.65	36.75	41.53	-5.35	-66.19
	-2308.99	-575.71	-383.96	-255.76	-420.24	-502.39	-181.19	39.32	1.52	-28.83	-34.39	-10.26	18.47	36.67	45.35	1.72	-59.34
	-2284.46	-564.12	-386.20	-282.14	-428.10	-470.47	-168.11	-1.62	-29.12	-28.49	-40.90	12.06	49.69	35.74	50.57	13.62	-46.92
FEMALE	-2490.84	-566.20	-375.79	-271.41	-535.89	-736.15	-293.44	170.36	148.48	36.36	18.34	5.29	3.45	18.50	5.58	-35.46	-82.85
	-2483.36	-561.57	-376.17	-280.10	-509.19	-669.90	-298.13	100.33	112.00	25.99	14.36	14.31	9.82	20.66	19.66	-24.01	-81.44
	-2461.25	-552.97	-377.27	-296.20	-457.05	-542.62	-305.18	-33.80	40.99	5.15	11.09	41.15	24.56	20.33	44.96	-2.00	-81.61
1881-1891																	
MALE	-2497.55	-588.84	-428.82	-291.90	-480.80	-594.40	-208.47	69.42	17.65	-27.68	-20.24	-14.71	19.58	60.81	44.51	6.41	-57.24
	-2481.72	-592.93	-423.27	-296.36	-494.17	-581.18	-196.83	60.47	6.15	-34.23	-31.09	4.47	43.31	55.10	45.34	2.39	-48.89
	-2452.42	-601.39	-412.65	-304.54	-518.39	-574.81	-176.17	43.05	-15.26	-45.27	-49.60	41.59	57.56	43.78	45.93	17.85	-33.88
FEMALE	-1755.53	-529.08	-392.00	-316.98	-534.55	-680.36	-182.94	319.76	255.97	90.68	79.02	88.24	64.23	46.05	21.11	-21.96	-63.03
	-1748.52	-527.69	-393.06	-320.80	-510.11	-611.16	-176.89	237.72	202.49	80.63	76.80	99.82	76.99	51.81	35.83	-10.11	-60.91
	-1731.10	-525.25	-395.40	-327.51	-461.28	-476.18	-163.93	78.65	97.90	61.16	75.41	126.57	102.09	59.91	62.44	12.49	-57.97
1891-1901																	
MALE	-2520.87	-548.56	-440.53	-303.92	-518.22	-641.21	-217.52	88.05	22.01	-28.39	-11.65	-4.65	37.84	80.58	40.54	-15.90	-59.34
	-2499.31	-563.60	-427.88	-297.07	-541.25	-654.90	-201.39	94.00	14.85	-43.07	-29.06	25.59	72.07	67.76	36.92	-5.05	-46.23
	-2460.05	-593.98	-402.96	-282.58	-584.30	-681.23	-172.18	106.04	2.92	-89.56	-60.35	84.88	134.58	43.27	29.70	14.20	-28.49
FEMALE	-2807.64	-490.09	-420.37	-388.14	-648.34	-823.72	-298.04	239.08	162.99	-29.81	-11.10	50.23	24.06	-6.76	-30.40	-53.35	-77.86
	-2801.31	-491.09	-422.83	-386.62	-622.76	-745.08	-288.75	146.44	85.72	-48.75	-20.00	59.58	40.79	1.02	-13.38	-39.86	-74.63
	-2788.94	-483.23	-427.99	-383.07	-570.18	-581.39	-211.36	-34.25	-65.58	-84.77	-35.61	77.84	71.97	14.11	17.50	-14.52	-68.41
1901-1911																	
MALE	-1447.23	-431.57	-379.06	-241.84	-467.65	-615.56	-136.23	212.95	127.20	62.36	80.61	80.33	115.60	147.89	67.88	-15.20	-54.97
	-1420.62	-453.32	-360.86	-224.94	-499.29	-647.02	-116.54	236.02	125.46	40.47	58.73	123.13	159.45	126.37	57.17	-3.21	-42.25
	-1373.23	-496.81	-324.38	-190.31	-559.69	-707.91	-90.70	281.60	124.99	.19	18.76	202.19	238.59	85.45	36.90	17.89	-19.97
FEMALE	-1584.02	-369.13	-346.60	-315.42	-598.87	-810.90	-179.48	445.71	313.95	41.86	65.13	153.20	97.51	30.56	-10.62	-41.94	-58.99
	-1576.21	-371.56	-350.80	-309.81	-576.35	-723.75	-135.04	334.63	209.66	23.80	61.72	168.32	124.98	43.04	7.48	-27.61	-55.92
	-1563.79	-375.75	-359.48	-298.84	-528.46	-551.72	-49.36	117.66	5.45	-10.12	56.92	198.77	175.97	65.60	39.91	-.73	-49.63

Age-Band in Years

I N V E R N E S S

	TOTAL	<5	<10	<15	<20	<25	<30	<35	<40	<45	<50	<55	<60	<65	<70	<75	75+
1861-1871																	
MALE	-3505.95	-787.93	-499.96	-238.46	-560.23	-836.67	-341.34	2.87	-72.06	-105.47	-55.06	-8.17	-1.24	37.61	61.61	-4.14	-96.32
	-3437.43	-766.54	-487.70	-243.29	-554.44	-813.16	-347.38	-42.10	-88.73	-91.28	-52.55	-6.77	9.80	50.91	77.70	5.18	-87.08
	-3387.61	-770.31	-513.65	-253.40	-539.83	-785.22	-363.29	-134.70	-119.34	-58.25	-43.75	-1.06	32.67	79.95	109.37	22.10	-81.91
FEMALE	-4264.91	-802.13	-566.85	-390.27	-706.40	-1083.96	-612.90	15.64	58.67	-11.73	13.00	-1.70	-27.24	-35.06	14.00	-9.70	-118.21
	-4206.29	-782.85	-548.77	-401.83	-685.38	-1039.87	-635.97	-37.15	58.23	-6.07	.59	-.82	-18.34	-20.64	33.46	-.45	-120.45
	-4176.83	-790.13	-559.83	-422.93	-640.73	-955.53	-684.32	-144.55	56.14	8.54	-20.71	4.10	1.74	7.97	70.48	17.87	-124.94
1871-1881																	
MALE	-2446.08	-696.73	-451.45	-206.61	-515.26	-780.06	-252.29	126.40	63.43	29.22	38.33	50.57	65.61	86.96	77.31	4.90	-87.60
	-2418.76	-698.46	-456.24	-206.91	-509.81	-768.04	-255.60	97.29	50.40	37.73	40.17	62.76	81.61	92.81	66.17	10.79	-83.24
	-2363.59	-704.06	-470.81	-204.92	-490.41	-741.34	-267.85	34.71	57.52	37.51	48.66	88.99	110.77	105.21	102.04	17.89	-78.35
FEMALE	-3532.88	-710.11	-473.81	-286.47	-709.55	-1145.42	-569.03	134.67	179.76	48.90	33.34	37.27	16.15	.13	30.49	-8.61	-110.58
	-3511.01	-708.44	-474.96	-292.60	-680.83	-1090.61	-581.24	73.75	156.92	45.37	27.85	47.00	26.21	7.69	45.09	.03	-112.26
	-3467.15	-707.02	-482.02	-300.81	-616.68	-980.23	-610.70	-42.25	110.10	37.51	26.08	75.75	47.43	18.60	68.46	15.31	-116.68
1881-1891																	
MALE	-3637.98	-720.72	-544.32	-375.15	-898.32	-951.84	-401.15	17.32	-2.20	-10.65	-24.14	-12.90	42.61	78.67	58.68	-5.10	-88.71
	-3820.51	-729.73	-547.47	-367.50	-695.83	-954.51	-401.74	5.31	-9.97	-12.09	-27.60	11.06	65.02	73.99	59.42	-1.81	-87.05
	-3592.55	-753.11	-559.26	-345.42	-676.84	-958.97	-410.68	-18.06	-20.43	-13.25	-27.69	61.58	102.85	63.57	57.24	-3.37	-90.70
FEMALE	-3613.82	-684.19	-506.99	-403.77	-892.97	-1328.16	-580.84	254.41	276.02	88.19	44.83	79.13	63.36	33.69	44.10	-6.31	-94.36
	-3601.44	-686.57	-513.71	-401.51	-857.02	-1284.94	-578.00	183.07	225.15	75.46	48.06	99.25	76.28	34.52	52.90	1.56	-95.95
	-3580.46	-693.78	-533.00	-391.56	-774.75	-1151.61	-578.70	55.60	121.79	44.32	70.42	155.09	100.50	26.01	58.76	11.80	-101.37
1891-1901																	
MALE	-3380.40	-646.32	-518.74	-358.11	-689.23	-956.63	-403.53	21.61	38.46	40.26	-8.63	-9.08	70.68	102.02	50.33	-17.13	-96.33
	-3387.28	-663.05	-521.93	-341.56	-690.53	-977.80	-399.80	32.18	37.53	28.64	-17.25	29.61	102.47	86.00	41.11	-16.43	-96.48
	-3356.80	-705.43	-533.58	-297.42	-673.69	-1018.62	-402.74	54.76	43.01	6.64	-26.07	109.44	154.21	51.34	16.80	-27.53	-107.71
FEMALE	-4720.23	-663.84	-541.48	-509.88	-1089.15	-1551.10	-688.07	234.83	252.77	1.69	-54.89	41.34	33.88	-7.86	-4.01	-47.15	-127.28
	-4718.31	-672.39	-554.35	-496.55	-1043.31	-1471.58	-660.14	149.43	164.56	-24.73	-48.37	88.69	50.27	-13.20	.15	-39.18	-127.61
	-4725.40	-691.95	-585.49	-464.11	-938.53	-1329.04	-612.27	2.72	-14.69	-86.66	-11.89	145.97	78.44	-40.41	-10.24	-32.78	-132.47
1901-1911																	
MALE	-2107.42	-567.72	-518.53	-420.07	-692.92	-899.04	-301.84	181.84	215.36	211.67	124.45	97.83	180.59	199.95	93.65	-9.07	-83.67
	-2160.59	-592.64	-522.03	-392.71	-695.42	-939.81	-294.58	217.26	222.30	189.26	110.09	149.54	220.61	171.04	72.50	-10.65	-85.14
	-2194.21	-655.67	-532.88	-322.25	-677.63	-911.96	-293.87	286.66	245.60	145.02	89.47	254.30	283.95	109.02	23.41	-27.53	-101.78
FEMALE	-3005.48	-557.39	-483.28	-490.64	-1082.41	-1501.88	-482.94	543.32	506.40	151.03	61.73	189.94	156.84	74.98	45.78	-29.32	-107.62
	-3011.34	-572.54	-501.09	-464.46	-1030.78	-1418.02	-436.30	436.27	378.21	120.13	81.09	230.21	181.96	66.07	44.75	-21.58	-106.46
	-3044.40	-603.84	-542.42	-408.12	-913.62	-1267.49	-351.54	250.74	117.79	41.08	150.37	339.16	222.44	23.41	16.26	-19.63	-108.99

Age-Band in Years

KINCARDINE

	TOTAL	<5	<10	<15	<20	<25	<30	<35	<40	<45	<50	<55	<60	<65	<70	<75	75+
1861-1871																	
MALE	-2222.39	-583.00	-366.60	-157.27	-255.61	-340.67	-126.56	-20.50	-72.84	-108.57	-71.95	-6.86	-17.79	-8.08	13.32	-18.14	-68.27
	-2170.12	-571.15	-363.18	-165.54	-254.69	-329.69	-136.34	-47.43	-74.41	-92.70	-69.47	-13.68	-10.70	4.53	24.44	-10.76	-59.26
	-2121.10	-557.14	-390.66	-183.71	-252.24	-306.61	-161.22	-108.40	-76.66	-55.60	-62.46	-21.88	5.86	33.87	49.47	5.44	-39.14
FEMALE	-2578.62	-488.49	-390.94	-312.52	-382.07	-464.79	-275.00	-34.15	-21.41	-25.71	23.73	17.22	-36.14	-73.48	-14.02	-6.67	-84.00
	-2540.52	-481.49	-380.55	-314.89	-373.08	-453.65	-295.59	-70.16	-11.33	-1.39	13.33	6.71	-29.06	-58.59	-1.09	.07	-79.74
	-2511.31	-503.95	-385.21	-319.24	-354.22	-434.41	-342.92	-148.47	10.09	51.57	-7.49	-13.66	-12.29	-25.60	27.52	16.48	-69.52
1871-1881																	
MALE	-2394.48	-669.51	-438.95	-238.03	-310.29	-366.68	-138.04	-12.14	-48.91	-60.09	-40.80	.11	-4.67	4.66	21.35	-15.20	-74.48
	-2388.42	-658.90	-447.65	-246.76	-309.55	-362.52	-148.34	-33.88	-49.34	-45.83	-35.12	2.76	4.86	13.69	29.37	-10.55	-70.65
	-2309.04	-633.31	-468.63	-266.99	-306.99	-349.57	-174.27	-82.80	-48.58	-10.01	-19.97	9.02	25.77	34.63	47.19	-1.18	-63.25
FEMALE	-2753.93	-579.71	-437.97	-384.74	-489.38	-518.09	-251.18	18.53	36.28	4.72	14.00	6.70	-30.71	-66.49	-15.13	-1.56	-59.20
	-2731.50	-582.00	-436.89	-384.91	-480.66	-513.53	-271.87	-11.38	40.81	22.94	11.82	6.47	-22.73	-56.39	-4.39	6.35	-55.13
	-2678.63	-588.41	-435.21	-383.61	-461.74	-513.04	-323.38	-74.86	52.23	63.82	11.44	11.01	-3.82	-34.51	19.59	25.88	-44.03
1881-1891																	
MALE	-1767.69	-589.22	-363.18	-137.82	-223.29	-315.72	-114.62	-10.18	-22.71	.39	.67	13.86	20.33	26.09	25.67	-11.58	-66.40
	-1747.24	-582.01	-371.97	-145.57	-223.46	-315.98	-123.27	-22.15	-20.57	12.70	8.52	24.34	32.24	29.34	29.22	-10.17	-68.45
	-1701.65	-562.86	-394.74	-164.79	-221.38	-316.27	-146.03	-49.56	-13.70	43.05	29.67	47.47	56.95	37.34	36.99	-8.68	-75.10
FEMALE	-2049.03	-533.66	-356.42	-292.02	-472.37	-496.80	-164.46	102.37	116.72	56.54	21.97	15.88	2.98	-31.33	3.77	12.43	-34.63
	-2024.93	-536.39	-356.01	-289.47	-464.38	-489.58	-181.73	82.41	113.76	66.03	29.01	27.09	11.14	-31.05	10.80	20.58	-31.05
	-1984.32	-543.98	-355.55	-281.68	-446.65	-516.62	-230.21	43.16	111.87	89.47	51.81	56.32	30.17	-22.59	26.34	41.14	-20.30
1891-1901																	
MALE	-2549.63	-595.14	-406.55	-225.49	-327.87	-440.56	-232.55	-100.64	-71.35	.01	-18.81	-26.84	-3.16	8.01	8.73	-24.80	-92.61
	-2534.40	-589.91	-414.40	-231.59	-331.69	-450.80	-239.29	-100.20	-67.00	7.17	-9.37	-5.88	12.05	4.64	7.25	-26.48	-99.60
	-2501.88	-573.37	-436.67	-248.68	-335.60	-471.37	-259.03	-101.34	-55.25	27.06	16.55	33.32	44.69	-1.58	4.07	-32.59	-118.11
FEMALE	-2713.04	-540.97	-362.56	-355.53	-642.01	-671.71	-221.48	105.95	124.72	36.02	-45.20	-39.18	-20.51	43.17	-11.23	3.06	-29.24
	-2688.45	-544.69	-363.30	-349.75	-634.44	-679.14	-232.88	94.71	109.87	33.84	-28.29	-14.84	-11.54	-47.05	-7.78	12.44	-25.12
	-2622.84	-554.83	-366.34	-334.67	-617.37	-714.97	-273.76	77.34	85.30	33.19	19.91	49.49	9.08	-58.24	-.55	36.32	-12.25
1901-1911																	
MALE	-3099.67	-829.91	-640.55	-499.73	-462.99	-432.42	-230.99	-66.49	-25.01	87.99	45.62	4.60	34.02	39.95	19.58	-25.42	-97.93
	-3090.11	-820.93	-651.54	-507.87	-469.73	-453.71	-234.42	-70.03	-17.13	89.47	57.44	36.96	53.91	28.12	11.03	-30.85	-110.83
	-3071.76	-790.50	-684.48	-533.56	-477.12	-486.02	-248.57	-37.85	3.17	98.05	89.44	105.71	92.00	3.97	-7.09	-45.90	-143.00
FEMALE	-3389.60	-741.44	-519.06	-640.93	-916.63	-754.40	-176.76	203.23	215.73	82.35	-54.80	-41.49	2.48	-17.03	-.54	6.94	-17.26
	-3343.45	-747.46	-522.23	-629.83	-910.26	-770.74	-182.99	201.47	187.50	69.33	-24.73	-1.44	13.21	-28.66	-1.46	17.44	-12.53
	-3270.29	-783.97	-529.71	-602.20	-894.45	-831.55	-218.55	208.55	137.87	46.21	56.15	100.66	36.71	-58.89	-4.42	44.46	2.84

Age-Band in Years

KINROSS

	TOTAL	<5	<10	<15	<20	<25	<30	<35	<40	<45	<50	<55	<60	<65	<70	<75	75+
1861-1871																	
MALE	-616.39	-178.03	-103.09	-42.16	-88.00	-120.65	-43.08	4.84	-8.39	-14.63	-10.60	-7.66	-3.85	5.76	12.51	.11	-19.46
	-603.07	-170.64	-100.26	-47.29	-88.05	-112.95	-41.23	-3.57	-13.17	-13.41	-11.16	-7.35	-1.60	7.69	15.47	2.28	-17.81
	-601.69	-168.70	-107.85	-57.59	-87.82	-97.71	-37.83	-19.99	-22.20	-10.76	-11.86	-6.59	2.76	11.59	21.07	6.20	-14.61
FEMALE	-587.97	-180.01	-98.98	-52.33	-116.89	-178.09	-78.05	38.58	40.01	16.53	11.05	3.60	3.38	8.26	8.83	-3.67	-22.30
	-578.33	-181.99	-94.42	-56.65	-110.21	-161.47	-83.15	21.58	35.19	15.29	9.33	4.14	4.06	9.98	12.89	-1.15	-21.75
	-583.29	-162.23	-97.71	-64.93	-96.86	-129.10	-93.38	-12.10	25.41	12.87	6.21	5.63	5.71	13.41	20.68	3.83	-20.72
1871-1881																	
MALE	-704.56	-187.94	-108.99	-59.80	-121.33	-163.48	-61.58	9.14	-3.67	-12.18	-9.79	-6.83	-.25	10.16	12.17	-1.14	-19.05
	-700.29	-167.14	-109.43	-62.37	-122.21	-159.12	-59.58	3.12	-7.87	-12.31	-11.26	-4.06	3.97	10.59	13.96	.93	-17.51
	-692.06	-165.76	-110.83	-67.19	-122.96	-150.46	-56.31	-3.60	-15.62	-12.27	-13.46	1.51	11.77	11.50	17.19	4.37	-14.94
FEMALE	-680.62	-159.83	-105.37	-72.13	-144.72	-207.33	-88.66	45.33	43.26	10.20	6.44	5.88	3.39	5.15	4.63	-6.13	-20.73
	-679.19	-158.90	-105.44	-74.51	-137.26	-189.22	-90.50	25.78	33.59	7.86	4.95	7.52	5.35	6.81	8.56	-3.42	-20.35
	-676.26	-157.24	-106.05	-78.84	-121.94	-154.14	-94.36	-12.33	14.26	3.06	2.78	11.68	9.37	9.68	15.83	1.74	-19.77
1881-1891																	
MALE	-456.84	-141.88	-98.88	-51.52	-117.37	-163.60	-45.17	41.45	28.62	14.61	12.45	10.77	18.49	27.27	20.03	2.11	-14.22
	-452.71	-143.34	-95.88	-51.67	-119.80	-163.26	-42.78	38.99	23.49	12.98	10.25	16.45	24.95	25.76	20.07	3.99	-12.90
	-445.59	-146.47	-94.23	-51.51	-123.33	-162.53	-39.15	34.20	17.99	10.13	6.83	27.61	36.61	22.80	19.83	6.75	-11.12
FEMALE	-607.02	-149.32	-109.54	-88.68	-161.80	-217.75	-76.91	73.66	62.43	17.34	14.50	19.96	14.55	10.03	5.46	-5.18	-15.77
	-605.48	-148.30	-110.07	-89.20	-154.33	-198.60	-75.18	51.05	47.19	14.10	13.63	23.12	18.34	11.95	9.50	-2.18	-15.49
	-602.63	-148.46	-111.52	-89.78	-138.72	-161.78	-72.41	7.25	16.65	7.26	13.06	30.58	25.75	15.05	16.74	3.50	-15.00
1891-1901																	
MALE	-467.84	-136.15	-110.46	-79.45	-135.56	-169.94	-46.63	47.12	34.56	23.09	19.94	17.91	26.50	33.18	20.19	1.17	-13.29
	-463.47	-140.28	-108.48	-76.77	-139.30	-173.76	-43.43	48.37	32.84	19.54	16.63	26.30	34.88	29.61	18.57	3.01	-11.80
	-454.66	-149.16	-105.00	-70.62	-145.06	-181.08	-38.34	52.56	30.27	13.03	11.13	42.57	49.88	22.57	15.07	5.48	-9.96
FEMALE	-409.08	-110.90	-83.16	-63.55	-145.45	-208.49	-56.65	58.84	78.97	19.96	17.03	30.79	22.41	10.85	3.52	-6.74	-16.33
	-407.31	-111.69	-84.15	-62.37	-136.60	-189.37	-50.84	74.07	58.24	16.03	17.19	35.68	28.13	12.89	7.35	-3.65	-16.22
	-404.20	-113.47	-86.45	-59.55	-124.05	-152.91	-40.29	27.01	17.13	7.66	19.25	47.01	39.18	15.80	13.74	1.95	-16.21
1901-1911																	
MALE	-194.17	-117.36	-106.09	-79.40	-113.19	-125.42	-11.94	72.26	58.73	46.00	41.27	35.04	42.29	47.78	25.30	.95	-10.37
	-189.82	-124.34	-102.86	-73.57	-117.51	-133.11	-8.27	78.31	58.31	40.76	37.16	45.49	52.08	42.13	21.72	2.65	-8.77
	-183.61	-139.16	-96.78	-60.74	-124.07	-148.21	-2.61	90.00	58.35	30.95	30.02	65.52	69.49	31.03	14.49	4.83	-6.75
FEMALE	-333.14	-105.55	-102.50	-111.87	-176.04	-212.30	-38.48	134.83	106.04	36.03	32.67	50.67	37.47	20.37	9.39	-3.25	-10.62
	-331.17	-107.52	-104.58	-108.72	-169.78	-194.67	-29.30	109.80	80.89	32.11	34.69	57.38	44.83	22.34	12.56	-.34	-10.67
	-328.27	-111.61	-109.05	-102.02	-156.20	-161.22	-12.25	61.81	31.17	23.48	40.91	72.61	58.67	24.52	17.16	4.68	-10.96

Age-Band in Years

KIRKCUDBRIGHT

	TOTAL	<5	<10	<15	<20	<25	<30	<35	<40	<45	<50	<55	<60	<65	<70	<75	75+
1861-1871																	
MALE	-1014.85	-367.15	-204.42	-109.04	-116.36	-109.11	-67.97	-6.96	12.07	-21.96	-26.10	-18.95	-5.38	28.68	31.87	-1.57	-32.50
	-994.76	-356.24	-199.98	-112.64	-102.98	-102.30	-78.82	-23.67	.75	-19.13	-20.20	-8.66	4.78	28.90	28.50	-2.62	-30.46
	-1000.42	-359.09	-215.60	-118.93	-66.75	-86.75	-102.40	-63.48	-27.99	-11.90	-2.45	21.17	31.73	27.14	15.57	-6.33	-27.19
FEMALE	-742.94	-328.70	-208.10	-140.05	-178.30	-166.69	-31.58	73.32	69.78	61.26	42.80	3.48	17.54	42.23	27.17	-1.49	-25.60
	-693.76	-320.44	-206.10	-138.66	-177.33	-170.68	-31.57	74.43	70.28	58.54	54.85	32.29	26.08	31.80	31.31	5.18	-33.70
	-597.54	-323.74	-221.45	-134.17	-184.09	-192.41	-20.98	94.59	75.90	49.98	98.35	131.69	53.99	-6.10	31.27	16.40	-63.97
1871-1881																	
MALE	-1842.43	-435.04	-294.68	-208.07	-210.14	-189.14	-130.25	-61.83	49.18	-84.20	-62.76	-43.33	-22.84	-.59	5.48	-16.37	-48.18
	-1834.30	-429.97	-296.43	-215.53	-205.90	-193.54	-138.43	-77.69	-56.54	-59.73	-58.77	-35.94	-13.24	.85	5.48	-14.56	-44.36
	-1817.82	-420.48	-301.25	-227.85	-192.33	-181.98	-157.03	-112.53	-74.54	-49.62	-46.75	-14.78	8.94	2.19	1.59	-13.50	-37.90
FEMALE	-2158.07	-445.81	-335.61	-260.29	-315.61	-283.77	-146.40	-40.80	-29.32	-34.41	-42.69	-53.37	-37.65	-18.23	-17.36	-27.43	-49.32
	-2133.77	-441.07	-339.15	-282.82	-311.56	-278.52	-148.64	-47.41	-34.10	-40.29	-36.50	-35.19	-32.74	-24.29	-11.07	-19.40	-50.92
	-2067.12	-434.29	-346.87	-284.55	-307.75	-277.20	-148.94	-51.69	-41.41	-53.97	-13.88	23.96	-16.46	-46.17	-2.97	-4.24	-60.88
1881-1891																	
MALE	-1603.53	-447.29	-317.81	-202.45	-197.55	-184.95	-94.67	-35.90	-34.18	-37.11	-33.05	-6.60	16.88	15.10	9.84	-9.48	-43.94
	-1590.58	-438.86	-316.38	-213.49	-204.08	-182.08	-100.80	-47.82	-35.01	-29.56	-30.56	-.17	25.32	15.45	11.64	-5.62	-38.55
	-1566.05	-424.14	-313.67	-232.18	-213.25	-177.00	-115.69	-71.55	-37.04	-12.88	-22.28	14.99	41.79	14.26	12.69	-.07	-29.24
FEMALE	-1608.77	-420.49	-305.88	-194.02	-250.07	-243.92	-88.50	9.16	12.60	-13.42	-22.48	-12.06	-3.35	-6.88	-9.00	-18.52	-42.15
	-1587.97	-414.23	-309.16	-200.37	-240.22	-225.94	-67.88	5.47	-4.83	-18.31	-19.00	-2.82	-3.80	-12.95	-5.51	-11.65	-39.36
	-1536.51	-403.52	-315.39	-209.58	-219.86	-193.93	-82.85	-17.95		-24.64	-6.22	23.37	-5.16	-33.24	-4.97	-.02	-37.74
1891-1901																	
MALE	-1928.55	-473.89	-378.97	-258.62	-244.10	-226.92	-106.97	-43.76	-60.05	-43.20	-34.15	2.48	28.94	2.64	-8.09	-19.91	-58.99
	-1910.15	-462.99	-373.84	-272.82	-264.52	-229.35	-109.30	-54.66	-53.90	-34.70	-34.55	8.49	37.52	2.09	-3.84	-12.83	-50.93
	-1876.67	-440.81	-382.31	-296.96	-305.48	-236.36	-115.62	-62.75	-39.15	-16.51	-33.44	18.67	50.46	-.70	3.75	-.50	-36.95
FEMALE	-1870.32	-385.31	-305.88	-194.78	-314.19	-369.58	-144.60	16.49	18.94	-32.64	-42.07	2.74	3.83	-24.28	-20.77	-25.43	-55.03
	-1858.02	-377.94	-305.99	-203.69	-298.57	-337.66	-140.33	-2.82	5.19	-37.62	-42.89	.21	-2.02	-28.64	-19.48	-19.26	-46.53
	-1833.44	-362.63	-311.31	-221.21	-263.35	-271.87	-129.11	-37.65	-17.09	-39.54	-43.64	-12.38	-20.00	-42.23	-23.81	-9.32	-28.30
1901-1911																	
MALE	-1586.41	-390.76	-324.74	-171.02	-193.66	-234.05	-90.09	-50.35	-73.95	-31.93	-16.49	35.80	64.37	9.43	-14.21	-28.92	-75.82
	-1561.05	-378.97	-318.05	-188.18	-228.14	-243.46	-88.64	-47.81	-57.95	-21.44	-19.55	41.03	72.58	7.02	-8.23	-18.52	-64.73
	-1516.37	-344.09	-302.07	-223.25	-303.51	-263.83	-83.86	-35.01	-20.79	.07	-24.87	46.09	80.74	.38	3.95	.21	-45.73
FEMALE	-1491.50	-351.14	-299.20	-190.22	-347.22	-436.75	-124.60	109.29	95.65	9.93	-.26	71.35	52.65	-6.46	-5.42	-15.94	-53.15
	-1488.62	-341.12	-302.95	-201.99	-326.80	-393.52	-117.03	81.28	61.28	6.10	-3.60	57.78	42.44	-7.83	-6.48	-11.22	-37.60
	-1492.53	-315.36	-309.29	-231.49	-280.39	-299.74	-100.12	26.48	36.56	10.08	-13.47	10.16	11.07	-12.13	-15.09	-4.46	-5.33

Age-Band in Years

LANARK AND RENFREW

	TOTAL	<5	<10	<15	<20	<25	<30	<35	<40	<45	<50	<55	<60	<65	<70	<75	75+
1861-1871																	
MALE	-9328.15	-8651.66	-3020.94	-1630.09	-591.83	534.81	506.28	98.01	-60.55	-172.11	-112.55	-28.37	-8.21	82.38	143.19	-1.48	-205.04
	-9070.37	-8674.49	-2987.09	-1737.32	-603.54	637.67	526.22	-10.97	-103.33	-144.13	-109.65	-23.49	21.42	109.20	173.64	19.99	-184.48
	-9104.80	-8595.67	-3152.03	-1954.74	-619.20	845.90	558.97	-216.52	-187.12	-79.33	-94.72	-7.79	85.75	165.55	230.89	59.31	-143.03
FEMALE	-11428.0	-4433.60	-2923.87	-1858.05	-1154.91	-219.46	-115.68	33.65	93.81	-63.39	-35.33	-63.14	-109.03	-75.36	6.72	-77.44	-312.89
	-11200.5	-4309.42	-2823.85	-2036.55	-1109.32	-56.87	-182.17	-125.71	66.90	-55.85	-57.65	-78.03	-94.40	-52.62	52.38	-48.13	-309.18
	-11252.1	-4330.32	-2883.57	-2184.67	-1014.67	251.21	-258.85	-440.14	15.05	-37.10	-90.17	-45.01	-55.71	-13.25	140.41	11.26	-306.48
1871-1881																	
MALE	-17172.2	-6161.31	-4396.77	-3174.20	-1608.51	297.45	238.24	-313.24	-401.69	-451.33	-380.94	-276.07	-183.08	-34.79	41.36	-77.03	-290.33
	-17108.3	-6120.76	-4422.44	-3246.04	-1622.70	369.82	258.91	-390.63	-440.48	-438.85	-388.22	-247.49	-136.12	-22.42	64.87	-54.14	-270.61
	-16975.9	-6040.09	-4497.09	-3383.59	-1624.38	512.40	286.00	-549.98	-513.24	-405.46	-390.54	-185.78	-43.09	5.00	108.41	-15.97	-236.91
FEMALE	-19197.9	-5787.36	-4333.64	-3813.40	-2517.92	-675.82	-342.42	-50.30	21.33	-245.08	-233.07	-207.49	-216.91	-190.29	-103.93	-149.59	-351.93
	-19150.8	-5766.00	-4337.02	-3864.60	-2445.14	-488.77	-367.71	-246.87	-62.06	-258.44	-250.96	-187.67	-192.33	-169.67	-55.79	-113.46	-344.30
	-19041.4	-5735.17	-4361.67	-3946.86	-2279.28	-142.01	-433.92	-630.26	-227.04	-283.67	-268.29	-122.44	-135.69	-135.50	34.21	-40.91	-330.93
1881-1891																	
MALE	-14638.9	-6527.52	-1761.12	-3207.96	-1160.74	1315.44	945.66	-144.24	-233.88	-281.01	-236.85	-174.39	-33.11	104.69	88.41	-66.19	-286.13
	-14574.9	-6554.60	-1762.19	-3222.24	-1180.37	1331.07	962.43	-185.51	-260.92	-262.42	-250.47	-105.76	43.38	94.76	95.81	-45.70	-272.20
	-14453.6	-6614.66	-1794.85	-3234.38	-1172.59	1368.54	968.04	-270.73	-305.45	-254.61	-259.66	34.37	185.43	76.26	106.28	-18.15	-257.42
FEMALE	-17631.2	-6022.48	-4516.24	-3917.99	-2343.49	126.71	327.95	190.45	207.53	-247.23	-271.96	-148.43	-167.86	-199.25	-123.37	-165.45	-360.05
	-17582.8	-6029.07	-4542.44	-3922.82	-2233.11	343.75	338.50	-50.16	44.94	-286.05	-278.60	-102.97	-127.37	-185.53	-76.90	-123.63	-351.36
	-17473.4	-6057.54	-4615.76	-3905.16	-1975.55	734.12	327.91	-508.20	-275.98	-364.24	-260.51	21.27	-44.06	-173.18	.60	-42.53	-334.58
1891-1901																	
MALE	-17794.3	-6314.43	-4897.97	-3319.39	-1375.81	1089.97	845.96	-655.45	-636.25	-541.92	-524.21	-440.21	-178.43	21.07	-42.27	-187.91	-415.91
	-17726.8	-6416.38	-4857.67	-3255.26	-1414.06	996.57	659.89	-636.26	-644.47	-572.09	-552.28	-310.59	-58.01	-21.70	-56.83	-169.48	-406.17
	-17611.4	-6633.98	-4842.29	-3104.64	-1427.69	845.71	648.79	-598.46	-644.71	-618.19	-581.64	-50.45	159.84	-106.35	-92.62	-155.74	-408.94
FEMALE	-20950.8	-5791.11	-4573.46	-4286.90	-3079.78	-508.79	137.50	199.32	191.93	-526.38	-610.60	-303.52	-293.73	-376.93	-312.63	-313.96	-489.80
	-20904.9	-5830.02	-4626.27	-4238.59	-2927.25	-270.51	201.97	-97.07	-88.81	-603.43	-597.52	-218.67	-228.14	-371.73	-270.00	-262.45	-476.36
	-20807.4	-5923.62	-4750.21	-4088.26	-2577.51	141.22	281.56	-648.44	-645.09	-762.79	-517.88	.63	-99.99	-387.94	-213.67	-165.51	-450.11
1901-1911																	
MALE	-24249.3	-7030.86	-6333.23	-5344.35	-3022.29	210.06	271.40	-681.96	-598.03	-399.00	-414.60	-382.83	-5.65	241.56	9.64	-243.89	-525.30
	-2417A.8	-7276.21	-6250.08	-5159.07	-3081.88	12.23	289.43	-654.55	-574.66	-473.39	-466.16	-183.67	178.71	144.77	-43.90	-228.07	-518.29
	-24069.2	-7778.76	-6123.40	-4760.46	-3122.40	-384.23	274.44	-330.28	-502.03	-602.91	-533.74	269.48	506.40	-49.07	-159.46	-230.57	-541.40
FEMALE	-27938.0	-6469.92	-5922.03	-6718.65	-5315.41	-1764.28	-76.97	736.40	619.25	-483.15	-663.78	-156.20	-149.25	-328.79	-336.92	-369.80	-536.48
	-27887.0	-6557.23	-6019.92	-6568.60	-5109.51	-1487.83	82.09	375.04	174.87	-614.81	-624.77	-21.95	-51.76	-338.60	-299.93	-307.39	-517.31
	-27791.1	-6742.44	-6230.53	-6241.54	-4648.56	-1021.01	331.61	-277.17	-702.02	-690.13	-662.39	321.37	127.41	-406.61	-274.67	-195.02	-478.54

Age-Band in Years

LINLITHGOW (WEST LOTHIAN)

	TOTAL	<5	<10	<15	<20	<25	<30	<35	<40	<45	<50	<55	<60	<65	<70	<75	75+
1861-1871																	
MALE	-3106.18	-987.68	-690.63	-568.55	-463.52	-275.74	-78.70	39.80	3.48	-22.29	-23.97	-20.63	-11.49	12.46	32.42	1.07	-52.13
	-3072.03	-948.33	-684.12	-600.10	-471.11	-249.62	-69.80	17.74	-10.18	-19.72	-26.83	-20.61	-5.19	16.83	39.69	6.99	-47.65
	-3075.69	-905.13	-707.62	-663.64	-486.31	-198.37	-52.52	-24.82	-36.17	-14.24	-31.55	-20.05	7.23	25.31	53.18	17.96	-39.14
FEMALE	-3459.48	-989.03	-688.07	-600.02	-600.75	-519.47	-216.90	106.55	106.46	32.74	14.07	-9.73	-6.40	14.69	15.53	-22.79	-80.57
	-3434.30	-972.17	-671.30	-620.03	-587.82	-459.39	-231.94	50.06	67.03	27.44	8.18	-9.71	-6.22	18.14	27.00	-14.47	-78.09
	-3460.31	-958.18	-677.15	-661.58	-547.15	-342.23	-281.54	-64.90	46.65	16.66	-2.54	-7.53	-4.94	24.05	49.53	2.02	-73.69
1871-1881																	
MALE	-3461.91	-1148.50	-797.17	-577.61	-393.03	-89.69	-3.06	-32.68	-66.94	-93.54	-82.93	-71.35	-45.44	31.83	13.22	-13.19	-58.73
	-3451.08	-1134.76	-797.56	-603.76	-405.46	-65.86	12.75	-48.35	-60.16	-96.61	-90.89	-63.96	-32.53	25.60	18.28	-6.02	-52.76
	-3430.07	-1110.90	-799.26	-556.32	-429.24	-18.67	42.99	-76.59	-104.97	-101.68	-104.99	-49.70	-8.17	14.02	27.61	7.11	-41.78
FEMALE	-3744.66	-1124.16	-785.18	-647.29	-561.52	-343.61	-127.33	77.05	66.97	-33.18	-35.86	-34.37	-33.78	-17.39	-18.14	-43.07	-83.80
	-3744.40	-1115.57	-783.61	-684.90	-537.88	-266.76	-126.45	5.43	28.59	-44.65	-44.71	-32.69	-29.50	-13.14	-4.45	-32.83	-81.28
	-3742.46	-1098.80	-780.90	-699.19	-491.02	-116.31	-124.65	-135.16	-47.31	-67.33	-60.97	-27.45	-20.50	-5.50	22.00	-12.71	-76.64
1881-1891																	
MALE	-2650.80	-894.32	-688.21	-395.26	-287.28	-48.90	60.10	1.94	-48.93	-85.06	-69.71	-63.42	-24.74	31.83	26.38	-12.76	-54.24
	-2637.31	-1004.42	-678.30	-402.11	-306.30	-41.02	78.96	-4.64	-59.36	-95.06	-83.15	-43.85	-.61	25.60	27.55	-3.92	-46.69
	-2612.45	-1024.33	-659.49	-415.86	-342.01	-24.97	114.21	-17.87	-82.24	-113.02	-107.23	-6.85	44.27	14.02	29.53	12.05	-33.17
FEMALE	-2624.65	-929.06	-657.49	-490.25	-440.89	-262.27	-11.59	193.68	142.00	-18.21	-11.13	14.30	-2.21	-8.27	-21.30	-45.93	-76.02
	-2623.04	-927.73	-658.72	-496.91	-414.28	-176.16	2.62	101.91	79.07	-33.75	-19.77	21.71	10.71	-.63	-3.91	-33.20	-74.02
	-2619.10	-925.43	-661.64	-509.42	-380.92	-7.70	29.91	-78.19	-45.35	-64.55	-35.10	38.23	36.38	13.54	29.50	-6.20	-70.16
1891-1901																	
MALE	-3179.46	-981.06	-785.99	-575.69	-506.90	-288.09	-15.47	57.47	-8.06	-62.14	-40.90	-38.81	5.66	66.99	33.99	-19.75	-60.69
	-3160.23	-995.02	-762.31	-557.76	-533.55	-284.39	4.95	65.72	-17.92	-81.46	-60.79	-3.42	43.43	52.45	29.29	-9.10	-50.36
	-3125.08	-1063.08	-716.13	-521.58	-583.04	-315.36	42.27	81.30	-35.41	-116.82	-96.62	63.16	113.30	25.19	20.14	9.77	-32.16
FEMALE	-4076.86	-943.52	-839.63	-946.72	-792.59	-574.07	-147.71	248.74	158.94	-89.82	-42.60	27.18	-2.73	-32.96	-57.88	-72.22	-89.28
	-4072.98	-948.38	-943.51	-840.70	-783.42	-476.11	-111.41	136.40	64.01	-93.03	-53.43	39.99	19.78	-22.32	-36.75	-56.56	-87.54
	-4064.97	-958.72	-851.84	-827.52	-704.01	-285.02	-41.84	-83.51	-123.06	-138.85	-72.00	67.48	63.78	-2.87	3.28	-26.08	-84.20
1901-1911																	
MALE	-2582.02	-857.54	-780.67	-590.83	-528.91	-289.82	34.63	147.06	64.08	-7.06	21.93	15.76	67.59	139.46	58.88	-25.64	-60.94
	-2557.71	-911.85	-743.62	-538.53	-565.64	-333.72	57.97	175.12	58.52	-37.40	-4.88	69.00	120.42	113.66	45.08	-13.65	-48.17
	-2514.22	-1020.62	-670.76	-453.23	-633.75	-418.67	99.57	228.51	49.83	-93.35	-53.41	168.95	217.75	65.04	18.65	7.22	-25.95
FEMALE	-3322.16	-824.04	-827.62	-878.15	-803.57	-542.96	-25.18	429.53	276.41	-45.91	-3.58	107.06	51.28	-11.92	-57.89	-78.97	-86.66
	-3312.85	-834.08	-835.33	-860.29	-775.15	-436.28	36.06	292.52	142.79	-74.20	-11.60	129.60	87.81	3.40	-32.83	-59.97	-85.28
	-3295.23	-855.12	-851.73	-822.59	-715.59	-229.33	152.33	24.86	-119.56	-130.05	-23.35	176.61	158.26	31.09	14.14	-22.98	-82.22

Age-Band in Years

N A I R N

	TOTAL	<5	<10	<15	<20	<25	<30	<35	<40	<45	<50	<55	<60	<65	<70	<75	75+
1861-1871																	
MALE	-384.67	-141.37	-82.92	-46.58	-55.83	-63.43	-15.61	10.49	-1.40	-6.69	1.20	8.76	7.20	9.31	10.85	1.38	-10.21
	-373.75	-138.71	-90.73	-54.86	-61.29	-61.29	-17.18	4.88	-2.61	-4.15	2.07	9.02	8.53	11.44	12.88	2.35	-9.14
	-386.16	-141.35	-95.12	-45.62	-52.25	-56.70	-20.92	-7.00	-4.64	1.79	4.35	9.60	11.37	16.20	17.02	4.10	-7.00
FEMALE	-458.26	-151.34	-108.50	-70.98	-70.19	-85.89	-48.04	12.23	18.08	9.79	15.13	12.65	4.74	-.41	6.02	5.55	-9.11
	-447.22	-147.80	-104.95	-72.93	-69.48	-82.65	-50.69	7.44	20.09	12.24	13.41	12.45	6.49	2.21	10.51	6.39	-9.77
	-442.04	-149.49	-107.12	-76.34	-67.17	-77.20	-56.58	-2.76	23.96	17.65	10.35	12.21	10.31	7.61	15.30	8.08	-11.01
1871-1881																	
MALE	-345.68	-131.38	-87.86	-42.55	-47.36	-50.72	-12.90	4.97	-.79	-1.91	1.53	5.65	7.76	9.80	9.40	1.00	-10.32
	-341.97	-132.25	-88.80	-41.51	-45.80	-49.89	-14.59	.95	-1.76	-.16	2.41	6.97	9.38	10.90	10.68	1.49	-9.99
	-334.29	-134.53	-91.83	-38.75	-40.90	-48.12	-19.00	-7.47	-3.30	3.82	4.88	9.95	12.40	13.29	13.13	1.83	-9.79
FEMALE	-309.93	-123.37	-80.30	-40.13	-53.81	-74.54	-34.84	18.76	26.53	13.72	11.90	11.94	7.81	3.15	8.64	4.11	-9.51
	-306.06	-123.29	-80.73	-41.02	-51.31	-70.53	-36.49	14.10	26.03	14.45	11.44	13.04	9.10	4.19	10.05	4.81	-9.90
	-298.30	-123.57	-82.62	-41.81	-44.46	-64.00	-41.14	5.35	24.88	15.92	11.81	16.43	11.79	5.78	12.18	6.00	-10.66
1881-1891																	
MALE	-427.54	-134.26	-100.59	-66.48	-65.12	-58.48	-19.86	-1.13	-.78	2.15	-.01	2.26	8.34	10.09	7.61	-.12	-11.15
	-425.24	-135.77	-101.83	-64.51	-63.12	-59.45	-21.61	-2.83	-.95	3.10	.74	4.75	10.35	9.97	7.72	-.24	-11.56
	-421.37	-139.96	-105.59	-59.01	-56.28	-61.57	-26.68	-6.31	-.61	5.35	3.26	10.34	13.64	9.57	7.46	-1.59	-13.37
FEMALE	-516.73	-133.89	-102.55	-87.86	-105.40	-112.51	-50.17	19.56	27.26	9.48	2.90	7.43	6.84	3.01	6.81	1.94	-9.96
	-514.53	-134.57	-103.92	-86.84	-100.97	-108.06	-50.71	14.44	23.55	8.68	3.88	9.99	8.06	2.71	7.13	2.40	-10.30
	-510.49	-136.50	-108.44	-83.86	-89.66	-101.37	-53.30	6.32	15.89	6.34	8.29	17.53	10.36	.70	6.09	2.50	-11.35
1891-1901																	
MALE	-358.65	-109.92	-83.30	-49.14	-52.24	-52.52	-20.93	-8.76	-.25	7.66	-1.15	-1.33	9.56	11.57	6.29	-1.59	-12.81
	-357.69	-112.17	-84.82	-46.23	-50.03	-55.57	-22.62	-7.82	.47	7.77	-.69	2.70	12.21	10.06	5.21	-2.26	-13.78
	-357.83	-118.40	-89.29	-38.09	-38.00	-62.00	-28.07	-5.76	2.95	7.76	1.46	11.51	16.13	6.51	2.15	-5.37	-17.32
FEMALE	-392.88	-116.90	-85.79	-70.91	-93.77	-93.53	-30.05	30.81	39.63	13.26	-.50	8.74	9.08	3.59	6.49	-.22	-12.81
	-392.45	-118.67	-88.50	-67.98	-87.47	-89.63	-29.75	25.29	32.54	11.27	2.39	13.09	10.48	1.98	5.46	-.04	-12.93
	-393.14	-122.78	-95.14	-60.70	-72.00	-84.81	-30.99	17.86	17.67	5.42	11.99	25.65	12.68	-3.81	.55	-1.02	-13.71
1901-1911																	
MALE	-347.94	-103.47	-96.06	-83.89	-77.92	-64.98	-23.96	2.05	17.01	26.98	11.38	8.21	20.15	20.05	9.45	-1.18	-11.76
	-348.12	-107.28	-98.49	-79.31	-74.92	-70.21	-25.30	6.17	16.95	25.83	11.49	13.59	23.30	16.93	6.80	-2.46	-13.20
	-351.92	-117.93	-104.31	-66.72	-64.92	-62.00	-30.36	14.60	24.37	23.54	13.03	25.21	27.49	9.80	.17	-7.43	-18.11
FEMALE	-331.64	-94.96	-74.07	-72.49	-109.74	-110.84	-28.35	42.81	52.76	21.40	1.14	14.51	16.11	9.41	11.06	1.41	-11.79
	-332.67	-97.77	-77.65	-67.49	-101.86	-107.27	-26.44	37.67	42.66	18.42	5.68	20.04	17.24	6.19	8.39	1.12	-11.58
	-337.60	-103.62	-85.44	-56.63	-83.51	-103.25	-24.09	32.67	21.42	9.56	20.10	36.33	18.21	-4.38	-1.39	-1.66	-11.93

Age-Band in Years

ORKNEY

	TOTAL	<5	<10	<15	<20	<25	<30	<35	<40	<45	<50	<55	<60	<65	<70	<75	75+
1861-1871																	
MALE	-786.43	-120.70	-85.94	-66.65	-107.03	-134.33	-74.03	-29.37	-33.96	-34.88	-29.25	-23.82	-18.25	-8.55	-.89	-4.50	-14.18
	-780.88	-117.15	-84.75	-68.93	-107.00	-130.49	-73.41	-34.39	-36.85	-34.44	-30.09	-25.69	-17.09	-7.52	1.03	-3.10	-13.00
	-778.75	-114.39	-87.20	-73.11	-106.74	-122.96	-72.45	-44.30	-42.33	-33.37	-31.46	-23.74	-14.60	-5.38	4.72	-.51	-10.73
FEMALE	-1117.14	-131.96	-98.08	-88.24	-176.16	-261.72	-156.26	-26.29	-17.62	-28.67	-26.35	-26.45	-22.44	-13.62	-7.01	-11.23	-25.06
	-1113.02	-129.07	-96.09	-90.36	-168.55	-247.23	-159.73	-38.53	-22.15	-30.96	-29.04	-26.96	-22.61	-12.75	-3.89	-9.17	-24.92
	-1113.52	-127.95	-96.90	-94.35	-153.40	-218.96	-166.65	-65.71	-31.28	-35.41	-34.01	-27.44	-22.65	-11.15	2.14	-5.10	-24.73
1871-1881																	
MALE	-532.71	-100.85	-62.81	-27.01	-82.16	-127.38	-54.84	-3.06	-12.08	-17.87	-15.56	-12.21	-6.43	2.09	4.84	-2.81	-14.77
	-523.70	-100.59	-63.44	-28.36	-82.42	-124.43	-53.25	-7.23	-14.94	-18.00	-16.79	-10.38	-3.53	2.38	6.16	-1.32	-13.54
	-523.79	-100.23	-65.18	-30.04	-82.20	-118.59	-51.01	-15.40	-20.20	-17.97	-18.72	-6.72	1.86	3.04	8.60	1.21	-11.43
FEMALE	-768.21	-106.92	-66.84	-35.91	-150.04	-204.41	-129.43	26.07	25.91	-4.72	-6.92	-6.34	-6.85	-3.13	-1.98	-10.62	-25.27
	-767.40	-106.38	-67.00	-37.48	-142.28	-245.54	-130.94	6.44	15.80	-7.76	-9.14	-5.23	-5.31	-1.78	1.91	-7.87	-24.85
	-765.64	-105.50	-67.85	-40.19	-124.76	-209.00	-134.20	-31.84	-4.39	-13.96	-12.72	-2.08	-2.09	.53	9.13	-2.60	-24.13
1881-1891																	
MALE	-696.39	-113.84	-87.01	-64.36	-127.34	-175.41	-76.81	1.22	-7.44	-13.77	-13.07	-11.57	-2.39	8.17	5.76	-3.73	-14.81
	-693.28	-115.02	-86.94	-63.90	-128.44	-175.54	-75.20	-.55	-9.81	-15.25	-15.05	-7.17	2.56	7.05	5.95	-2.29	-13.67
	-687.71	-117.82	-87.39	-62.39	-129.22	-175.73	-72.92	-3.99	-13.94	-17.82	-18.16	1.52	11.55	4.88	6.03	-.22	-12.08
FEMALE	-949.68	-112.57	-86.30	-75.50	-213.53	-341.27	-155.62	51.01	41.61	-5.37	-6.24	2.47	-1.33	-3.74	-4.98	-12.85	-25.47
	-948.77	-112.67	-86.89	-75.63	-204.56	-319.72	-153.42	26.18	24.42	-9.68	-7.85	5.49	2.38	-1.93	-.54	-9.42	-24.93
	-947.11	-113.10	-88.56	-75.37	-185.84	-276.36	-149.80	-21.91	-9.84	-18.68	-9.64	12.94	9.71	.84	7.35	-2.90	-23.93
1891-1901																	
MALE	-1252.86	-135.57	-111.04	-89.00	-185.22	-263.11	-147.68	-53.90	-56.01	-55.76	-50.10	-43.82	-22.79	-1.03	-3.82	-11.39	-22.00
	-1249.26	-138.15	-110.80	-87.07	-188.82	-287.59	-144.93	-51.79	-57.56	-60.12	-54.40	-34.82	-14.09	-4.47	-4.85	-9.60	-20.22
	-1243.53	-143.42	-109.75	-82.59	-194.08	-276.28	-140.99	-47.78	-59.87	-68.09	-61.58	-17.24	1.65	-11.15	-7.22	-7.27	-17.86
FEMALE	-1469.99	-131.01	-113.92	-119.50	-295.88	-447.98	-215.19	37.05	22.37	-41.61	-36.39	-10.67	-14.21	-20.09	-22.33	-25.45	-34.19
	-1467.60	-132.07	-115.17	-118.00	-285.90	-419.69	-204.59	6.17	-5.40	-49.60	-39.24	-6.31	-8.27	-18.15	-16.98	-20.98	-33.44
	-1465.30	-134.49	-118.14	-114.41	-264.86	-365.56	-184.88	-53.09	-60.49	-66.08	-42.58	4.45	3.17	-15.68	-7.94	-12.65	-32.07
1901-1911																	
MALE	-299.49	-86.00	-65.55	-28.06	-124.21	-213.06	-63.37	61.57	48.70	36.02	30.49	24.29	35.13	44.37	21.38	-3.58	-17.60
	-294.19	-89.56	-64.43	-24.70	-129.27	-221.45	-58.96	69.00	48.24	29.83	26.04	37.27	46.95	37.80	17.15	-1.98	-16.12
	-286.18	-97.37	-62.87	-17.25	-136.95	-237.48	-51.99	83.46	48.54	18.44	18.77	62.47	68.08	24.85	6.38	-.48	-14.78
FEMALE	-557.73	-83.26	-64.72	-52.20	-243.10	-407.12	-121.80	169.02	128.63	25.87	22.75	52.88	36.26	13.66	.36	-13.02	-21.95
	-555.19	-84.73	-66.35	-49.31	-234.69	-379.23	-106.93	131.07	90.32	18.97	24.60	62.26	46.84	16.47	5.36	-8.33	-21.51
	-551.23	-87.63	-69.88	-43.06	-216.39	-326.37	-79.38	59.00	14.61	4.24	31.64	83.66	66.81	19.66	12.79	-.02	-20.74

Age-Band in Years

PEEBLES

	TOTAL	<5	<10	<15	<20	<25	<30	<35	<40	<45	<50	<55	<60	<65	<70	<75	75+
1861-1871																	
MALE	-973.43	-285.83	-185.24	-104.94	-178.11	-225.52	-79.83	34.24	16.08	-2.55	-5.72	-5.63	.41	15.51	23.21	1.02	-30.52
	-958.62	-254.18	-182.88	-114.43	-177.98	-213.65	-77.21	21.12	7.56	-.99	-6.09	-4.16	4.84	17.53	26.23	3.76	-28.08
	-958.31	-245.47	-172.95	-133.43	-177.34	-190.20	-72.35	-4.98	-9.58	2.41	-5.71	.45	14.35	20.97	30.83	8.29	-23.59
FEMALE	-952.50	-284.17	-167.95	-124.36	-238.33	-329.04	-123.14	100.32	93.00	48.33	32.43	13.94	13.97	23.27	17.65	-8.23	-40.15
	-940.41	-255.96	-162.81	-130.12	-226.44	-302.48	-132.37	71.06	83.79	46.14	31.51	17.33	15.24	24.10	23.59	-3.59	-39.42
	-940.01	-253.85	-166.70	-141.15	-204.10	-251.86	-149.40	15.39	66.07	41.47	31.82	28.87	19.12	23.67	34.46	5.47	-39.40
1871-1881																	
MALE	-805.54	-276.37	-185.57	-121.37	-188.32	-183.72	-41.77	61.55	37.59	13.97	10.39	10.09	15.74	25.50	23.69	1.01	-25.93
	-799.80	-275.38	-186.02	-128.02	-170.92	-176.38	-38.03	52.78	30.90	13.84	8.42	14.45	22.53	25.65	25.44	4.09	-23.16
	-788.65	-269.57	-187.21	-141.12	-175.38	-161.66	-31.24	35.55	17.90	14.06	5.62	23.52	35.73	25.70	28.12	9.44	-18.14
FEMALE	-753.78	-261.35	-174.46	-128.22	-209.58	-261.13	-73.20	121.62	105.11	48.44	36.61	26.72	21.04	22.15	12.93	-8.88	-31.58
	-751.77	-259.24	-174.53	-132.40	-198.99	-233.40	-76.59	89.98	89.64	45.43	35.57	30.46	24.28	23.99	18.93	-4.24	-30.66
	-745.53	-255.33	-174.74	-140.30	-178.45	-179.70	-82.59	28.75	59.34	39.41	34.89	40.47	31.30	26.28	30.00	4.74	-29.59
1881-1891																	
MALE	-778.30	-258.90	-183.13	-113.40	-156.40	-165.51	-34.54	50.98	26.71	5.60	5.69	4.76	14.98	28.51	20.40	-1.50	-22.55
	-772.01	-260.51	-180.87	-115.70	-161.89	-163.76	-29.81	47.24	21.94	3.19	1.90	12.26	24.35	26.45	20.70	1.96	-19.47
	-760.34	-283.90	-176.61	-119.96	-171.82	-160.29	-21.40	39.99	13.06	-.89	-4.51	25.69	41.84	22.44	20.94	8.04	-13.97
FEMALE	-661.26	-235.62	-172.15	-134.27	-196.19	-226.13	-47.38	129.61	103.28	36.11	31.41	34.98	24.80	17.28	7.43	-9.24	-24.98
	-659.17	-235.03	-172.62	-136.13	-186.70	-198.49	-45.23	96.21	81.61	32.21	30.54	39.46	30.13	19.98	13.49	-4.53	-24.08
	-654.06	-233.66	-173.61	-139.43	-167.76	-144.81	-40.81	31.13	39.05	24.70	29.81	49.49	40.66	24.38	24.67	4.56	-22.61
1891-1901																	
MALE	-979.29	-253.10	-204.54	-146.07	-191.53	-198.05	-57.09	35.03	11.27	-6.46	-1.28	.65	15.51	29.69	15.17	-5.60	-22.89
	-971.17	-259.65	-199.23	-143.17	-200.29	-203.15	-51.21	37.14	8.74	-11.61	-7.40	12.30	28.16	25.01	13.86	-1.67	-18.96
	-956.45	-272.77	-188.94	-137.03	-216.55	-213.05	-40.73	41.44	4.60	-20.85	-18.27	34.11	51.23	16.04	11.22	5.20	-12.10
FEMALE	-793.77	-214.17	-180.15	-161.26	-217.98	-239.66	-53.96	126.51	92.68	14.22	16.93	35.89	23.05	7.65	-3.93	-15.00	-24.58
	-791.49	-214.45	-181.33	-160.83	-208.82	-210.01	-44.62	91.03	63.91	8.49	15.13	40.38	30.00	10.88	2.28	-10.09	-23.46
	-786.96	-215.10	-183.78	-158.72	-189.95	-151.76	-26.48	21.74	7.61	-2.25	12.30	49.20	43.07	16.46	13.63	-.67	-21.25
1901-1911																	
MALE	-401.42	-194.40	-165.48	-98.34	-142.92	-156.59	-5.35	88.66	57.32	34.58	39.13	37.49	48.05	56.37	26.06	-5.21	-20.79
	-391.68	-203.01	-157.78	-91.49	-154.59	-168.54	1.42	96.94	56.86	27.08	31.73	52.87	63.72	48.63	22.20	-.94	-16.38
	-374.49	-219.84	-142.47	-77.70	-178.16	-191.80	13.53	113.35	57.10	13.38	18.31	81.34	91.91	33.83	14.91	6.56	-8.75
FEMALE	-474.89	-157.73	-144.30	-127.14	-192.34	-224.59	-24.08	164.58	118.00	21.23	26.94	56.62	36.37	11.24	-3.40	-14.56	-21.74
	-471.90	-158.51	-145.97	-125.07	-184.24	-195.34	-9.72	126.11	82.08	15.66	26.73	62.63	45.92	15.45	2.50	-9.64	-20.47
	-466.03	-159.74	-149.40	-121.09	-166.94	-137.71	17.79	51.03	11.88	5.52	27.10	73.56	63.55	22.95	12.89	-.40	-17.84

PERTH

Age-Band in Years

	TOTAL	<5	<10	<15	<20	<25	<30	<35	<40	<45	<50	<55	<60	<65	<70	<75	75+
1861-1871																	
MALE	-7393.22	-1709.70	-1076.20	-597.20	-1285.74	-1780.41	-654.25	144.2	-31.29	-150.91	-117.61	-30.55	-22.22	44.54	117.17	-17.58	-237.51
	-7262.45	-1842.48	-1063.16	-641.50	-1284.31	-1714.58	-656.69	47.44	-70.12	-129.47	-119.35	-34.00	4.71	73.68	151.48	8.34	-212.36
	-7171.00	-1595.74	-1131.94	-732.71	-1260.03	-1583.93	-671.00	-152.03	-143.31	-82.11	-117.23	-40.01	61.20	136.57	220.83	59.93	-159.57
FEMALES	-7862.37	-1632.90	-1120.97	-816.09	-1487.05	-2118.71	-995.46	301.51	303.25	108.46	115.72	41.52	-25.73	-30.96	38.75	-56.31	-307.42
	-7591.51	-1582.10	-1055.69	-843.49	-1419.49	-1982.31	-1063.75	123.52	275.29	129.22	92.85	33.50	-13.85	-3.39	82.13	-28.26	-295.70
	-7503.58	-1604.22	-1107.48	-896.04	-1285.29	-1719.66	-1206.21	-235.38	221.72	176.24	50.27	23.85	15.04	53.49	170.57	30.66	-271.14
1871-1881																	
MALE	-6015.67	-1619.47	-1025.74	-513.31	-1149.84	-1653.18	-529.46	274.32	106.17	-12.00	2.09	43.60	54.24	113.21	131.97	-16.49	-221.98
	-5952.33	-1600.49	-1038.43	-543.06	-1157.29	-1616.67	-526.57	206.46	75.90	6.56	-1.71	65.27	97.09	126.86	153.10	5.08	-204.42
	-5817.06	-1558.10	-1089.56	-605.26	-1168.02	-1544.06	-531.24	66.14	21.44	53.42	-.44	109.05	181.71	159.15	195.88	45.35	-171.51
FEMALES	-6746.32	-1554.96	-1057.92	-776.88	-1507.07	-2001.91	-845.34	486.33	455.64	182.15	135.30	97.25	21.66	-25.09	14.86	-47.19	-223.15
	-6713.30	-1551.41	-1055.68	-791.99	-1443.58	-1947.50	-887.06	303.32	389.77	170.26	123.01	107.75	45.23	-1.23	56.07	-17.09	-213.17
	-6634.16	-1547.01	-1052.48	-818.85	-1315.73	-1696.12	-983.22	-61.47	262.26	191.95	107.05	139.83	96.99	46.30	139.36	47.13	-190.15
1881-1891																	
MALE	-5716.95	-1599.93	-1106.96	-661.54	-1239.66	-1675.59	-531.11	315.31	177.02	102.55	96.14	90.28	133.93	200.21	153.07	-2.62	-166.04
	-5661.09	-1600.00	-1111.79	-673.62	-1260.04	-1673.21	-520.82	285.91	157.34	104.49	86.94	139.04	193.37	193.62	158.18	14.42	-156.53
	-5549.61	-1595.32	-1125.04	-700.60	-1292.77	-1680.18	-512.24	223.79	125.56	119.17	80.54	238.34	306.55	183.45	168.24	42.91	-144.02
FEMALES	-5088.39	-1445.57	-1026.41	-844.65	-1574.84	-2019.72	-594.52	803.86	696.94	301.69	230.69	232.73	156.16	67.10	60.99	-5.88	-126.95
	-5051.44	-1447.91	-1027.84	-846.14	-1519.11	-1894.08	-605.87	622.35	591.54	296.21	234.34	266.02	192.07	85.28	97.75	24.38	-120.41
	-4960.39	-1455.70	-1032.31	-844.60	-1404.90	-1666.57	-646.71	267.53	388.49	290.84	256.45	348.26	266.33	117.31	169.79	88.84	-103.35
1891-1901																	
MALE	-3977.92	-1383.64	-949.05	-438.54	-977.01	-1414.99	-384.48	351.56	252.41	212.54	181.21	138.72	197.69	249.43	154.80	-13.72	-174.85
	-3924.13	-1384.43	-940.03	-429.26	-1013.50	-1451.00	-363.62	365.43	242.95	193.41	163.83	218.71	275.50	221.02	143.17	1.04	-167.35
	-3821.41	-1422.38	-930.48	-412.67	-1074.14	-1521.31	-336.04	390.19	232.80	166.48	143.21	375.06	420.12	166.72	119.55	22.60	-161.93
FEMALES	-3894.20	-1223.34	-873.59	-707.60	-1476.78	-1679.47	-391.65	984.11	800.17	292.82	186.75	255.92	192.31	69.58	30.59	-25.27	-108.73
	-3855.28	-1231.19	-880.18	-695.77	-1426.46	-1757.09	-385.88	782.69	648.05	268.48	203.50	310.25	239.65	81.59	62.96	6.41	-102.28
	-3757.31	-1250.19	-895.26	-666.56	-1320.59	-1542.33	-338.57	435.43	354.98	224.63	258.22	439.07	334.08	96.96	123.43	73.52	-84.12
1901-1911																	
MALE	-2733.16	-1087.63	-860.20	-503.51	-1027.58	-1467.78	-370.31	492.77	411.67	391.22	343.08	256.42	318.35	361.85	185.55	-19.51	-157.57
	-2683.60	-1123.39	-843.21	-475.58	-1075.08	-1539.12	-340.19	551.01	413.62	352.90	320.18	361.30	410.05	311.55	154.33	-8.48	-153.50
	-2595.38	-1192.19	-817.43	-421.21	-1155.49	-1676.39	-295.25	664.08	427.27	287.93	289.45	565.98	577.95	213.56	91.90	3.74	-157.28
FEMALES	-3823.89	-1013.75	-815.21	-813.94	-1679.04	-2101.60	-410.72	1091.98	870.36	278.79	158.96	288.44	231.77	94.61	23.98	-36.80	-91.73
	-3882.04	-1025.78	-826.29	-790.74	-1635.89	-1984.17	-346.80	914.47	674.60	238.01	188.32	361.08	299.58	101.04	51.30	-4.92	-85.66
	-3777.85	-1052.62	-850.06	-739.04	-1542.67	-1783.49	-248.09	582.34	297.98	160.56	274.06	529.97	401.64	100.53	98.27	61.41	-69.64

Age–Band in Years

ROSS AND CROMARTY

	TOTAL	<5	<10	<15	<20	<25	<30	<35	<40	<45	<50	<55	<60	<65	<70	<75	75+
1861-1871																	
MALE	-2379.11	-490.27	-327.80	-170.06	-427.74	-650.53	-264.06	16.21	-43.95	-63.19	-15.84	10.27	15.63	44.39	50.97	.21	-63.33
	-2332.55	-484.59	-317.05	-166.08	-413.73	-636.04	-271.40	-16.58	-56.82	-53.90	-11.76	15.05	22.99	53.64	62.27	5.54	-58.09
	-2293.30	-503.54	-327.77	-157.48	-399.77	-605.73	-288.19	-83.39	-80.53	-32.54	-.65	25.62	37.81	73.62	83.76	14.02	-48.54
FEMALE	-2912.58	-488.54	-339.30	-202.86	-460.36	-798.33	-480.89	-14.84	30.78	-23.46	-10.11	-13.55	-22.43	-21.39	13.01	-.92	-69.37
	-2868.19	-484.73	-327.16	-211.47	-452.50	-776.56	-491.44	-35.14	34.39	-25.80	-17.06	-7.05	-15.10	-12.16	25.36	3.17	-74.93
	-2839.95	-487.35	-335.18	-226.90	-433.64	-734.82	-512.69	-76.11	39.20	-28.64	-27.36	7.84	.49	4.92	46.66	9.99	-86.39
1871-1881																	
MALE	-3146.92	-548.61	-409.44	-276.46	-533.14	-740.79	-339.42	-43.95	-67.64	-67.13	-52.10	-34.61	-.11	28.66	26.59	-12.90	-75.68
	-3129.29	-557.09	-410.73	-268.08	-523.47	-733.21	-345.44	-66.83	-77.79	-62.55	-49.17	-24.22	8.89	32.48	32.74	-10.71	-74.12
	-3095.73	-578.82	-418.28	-246.26	-493.23	-716.49	-361.52	-111.74	-94.46	-52.77	-38.69	-.65	23.24	39.84	41.97	-12.32	-75.55
FEMALES	-3388.17	-487.45	-339.41	-216.37	-575.18	-980.37	-568.64	-17.37	46.48	-36.24	-45.33	-24.35	-22.76	-22.24	7.61	-16.44	-90.11
	-3372.52	-485.92	-341.74	-220.85	-555.90	-944.68	-571.62	-47.23	32.32	-45.62	-48.57	-14.07	-16.71	-19.33	15.02	-13.10	-94.49
	-3345.02	-484.42	-351.82	-226.02	-509.58	-873.62	-579.61	-98.37	.85	-67.48	-45.98	14.75	-4.80	-18.84	22.02	-10.59	-105.32
1881-1891																	
MALE	-2150.97	-428.24	-303.82	-150.34	-452.07	-711.17	-292.06	15.30	23.06	28.96	-.72	5.64	60.99	75.85	46.88	-1.50	-67.74
	-2142.33	-436.97	-304.55	-138.86	-445.27	-715.48	-297.87	6.53	18.99	28.65	.18	23.96	73.35	71.83	45.79	-3.08	-69.53
	-2136.20	-460.33	-309.37	-107.53	-416.71	-722.99	-317.19	-9.00	15.93	26.94	8.06	64.95	89.70	61.07	38.16	-16.58	-81.30
FEMALE	-2415.31	-428.15	-311.55	-220.52	-618.08	-1024.03	-477.91	178.84	224.59	80.69	35.04	70.40	63.11	40.70	48.62	.80	-76.86
	-2410.21	-430.05	-317.93	-218.36	-592.08	-981.22	-473.80	136.36	189.31	67.95	40.01	87.87	70.86	38.04	50.24	2.81	-90.22
	-2410.41	-435.64	-336.21	-209.27	-527.33	-905.21	-468.88	67.18	114.23	33.44	65.03	137.46	83.56	21.76	40.12	-.44	-90.22
1891-1901																	
MALE	-2634.33	-413.07	-363.39	-295.57	-609.32	-865.55	-381.88	6.85	56.28	73.78	1.71	3.54	85.20	95.01	43.88	-5.06	-66.76
	-2633.81	-427.77	-387.95	-279.53	-604.63	-881.35	-382.70	15.58	58.58	65.67	-2.70	30.69	102.97	82.43	35.48	-8.85	-69.76
	-2655.02	-467.93	-380.98	-235.30	-576.66	-910.26	-393.10	34.96	34.96	47.11	-5.02	89.72	125.69	52.45	11.59	-30.32	-87.01
FEMALE	-3784.64	-421.14	-356.78	-334.35	-825.55	-1273.06	-633.06	102.56	161.71	-15.18	-68.25	17.90	18.10	-7.54	2.42	-39.90	-112.52
	-3790.30	-428.06	-368.74	-323.39	-788.34	-1216.78	-610.58	49.26	98.68	-36.75	-60.11	39.39	26.85	-16.55	-2.04	-38.85	-114.28
	-3818.90	-443.66	-397.83	-296.86	-701.13	-1116.10	-568.36	-32.45	-33.99	-94.85	-20.95	104.71	39.06	-52.14	-32.23	48.67	-123.46
1901-1911																	
MALE	-1134.00	-341.77	-334.47	-290.93	-509.95	-660.90	-215.83	165.06	231.83	238.75	123.63	105.58	179.62	168.57	79.48	3.39	-56.07
	-1138.46	-360.58	-341.26	-267.14	-502.83	-710.60	-216.07	192.27	241.19	224.81	116.38	138.76	201.03	147.24	61.63	-2.77	-60.52
	-1178.39	-412.79	-356.79	-201.98	-466.71	-768.75	-228.93	248.56	269.39	194.10	107.81	209.48	227.24	96.06	17.37	-31.91	-82.56
FEMALES	-676.93	-323.98	-279.86	-290.93	-702.68	-1056.13	-292.62	504.74	500.56	246.71	156.07	239.74	208.10	128.63	95.24	16.37	-51.82
	-682.60	-335.31	-294.72	-247.90	-662.03	-1000.43	-264.54	433.24	225.17	225.17	172.21	267.57	221.49	118.64	91.12	20.87	-48.15
	-953.07	-358.39	-327.18	-204.86	-569.08	-900.46	-214.44	315.11	221.86	157.83	228.94	346.42	235.44	75.19	60.57	19.46	-41.47

Age-Band in Years

ROXBURGH

	TOTAL	<5	<10	<15	<20	<25	<30	<35	<40	<45	<50	<55	<60	<65	<70	<75	75+
1861-1871																	
MALE	-3483.41	-867.75	-581.93	-462.51	-439.16	-350.02	-209.78	-90.08	-83.19	-106.57	-100.35	-65.81	-55.84	-2.16	21.94	-11.36	-58.84
	-3450.36	-837.25	-575.16	-482.51	-432.70	-330.12	-212.36	-115.20	-100.35	-104.88	-99.01	-77.79	-44.32	.61	24.06	-8.57	-54.79
	-3457.19	-813.97	-589.69	-521.91	-416.12	-289.17	-219.02	-169.63	-139.05	-100.89	-91.56	-54.14	-15.66	4.81	23.06	-6.25	-47.80
FEMALES	-3584.68	-786.33	-537.32	-455.47	-542.20	-537.96	-289.31	-35.28	-16.44	-43.13	-54.54	-79.56	-55.49	-14.66	-13.24	-40.17	-83.57
	-3539.36	-786.03	-527.17	-464.62	-527.11	-505.47	-298.15	-68.39	-30.44	-52.86	-52.97	-61.46	-49.50	-18.26	-1.00	-29.27	-86.65
	-3484.75	-760.54	-541.41	-481.02	-505.14	-453.11	-311.35	-124.47	-57.63	-76.89	-37.51	4.21	-27.41	-34.70	21.18	-7.65	-101.31
1871-1881																	
MALE	-1411.50	-717.90	-422.18	-182.36	-172.74	-112.72	5.51	53.10	37.31	.80	-.50	11.96	30.38	55.19	52.59	3.03	-52.75
	-1398.59	-709.54	-424.96	-201.07	-174.61	-94.79	7.99	32.57	24.53	4.19	-.16	22.69	44.83	55.15	54.08	7.61	-47.10
	-1373.47	-694.28	-431.53	-236.78	-174.30	-59.24	9.87	-10.25	-2.42	13.09	5.29	48.71	75.06	53.21	53.15	13.91	-36.95
FEMALES	-1450.01	-640.17	-389.93	-210.15	-309.60	-330.88	-63.77	171.65	152.67	71.52	52.00	30.13	31.40	44.75	24.35	-20.72	-63.26
	-1430.90	-634.52	-391.99	-219.96	-292.07	-284.03	-65.87	124.72	129.29	64.84	54.03	45.43	37.81	42.20	34.27	-10.87	-64.18
	-1378.46	-624.77	-396.55	-236.93	-259.58	-197.47	-65.26	40.58	86.24	52.00	66.97	92.59	53.73	27.05	47.97	7.14	-72.16
1881-1891																	
MALE	-3107.26	-834.58	-628.15	-472.51	-461.20	-355.46	-141.77	-21.58	-47.08	-67.70	-54.33	-33.77	4.79	40.71	35.05	-8.48	-61.19
	-3091.51	-835.75	-621.18	-481.32	-474.80	-350.86	-136.48	-33.13	-54.92	-68.69	-60.29	-18.19	24.26	37.23	36.73	-.73	-53.37
	-3062.00	-839.15	-607.81	-496.93	-498.44	-342.43	-129.20	-55.92	-69.63	-68.53	-68.57	12.94	60.95	29.64	38.33	12.33	-39.58
FEMALES	-2962.82	-763.07	-606.45	-546.26	-594.04	-529.25	-177.01	150.79	120.82	10.05	7.01	24.99	19.55	13.07	.39	-28.51	-64.91
	-2949.48	-758.62	-608.51	-552.41	-573.18	-471.68	-169.83	91.25	80.72	-.87	4.38	34.77	27.33	14.55	12.32	-17.47	-62.23
	-2917.27	-750.85	-612.60	-562.52	-531.29	-360.81	-154.10	-22.17	3.78	-20.68	3.40	59.46	42.47	12.31	31.92	3.30	-58.91
1891-1901																	
MALE	-1162.66	-577.85	-394.23	-126.12	-186.94	-207.79	8.70	79.98	32.44	12.05	23.54	42.86	73.93	78.10	42.60	-7.98	-55.95
	-1139.70	-581.77	-382.04	-128.06	-213.94	-218.35	18.23	80.69	30.93	8.00	14.06	65.93	100.00	69.56	41.66	1.81	-46.41
	-1097.87	-589.15	-357.52	-130.73	-266.10	-289.87	34.36	83.98	30.78	2.34	-1.57	108.81	146.38	52.39	39.34	18.78	-30.07
FEMALES	-1161.67	-565.58	-353.90	-180.40	-310.92	-381.50	-21.24	259.44	196.71	28.64	28.50	78.73	55.49	17.60	-3.66	-30.29	-59.49
	-1151.39	-502.54	-357.11	-184.08	-289.15	-296.25	-3.40	186.14	138.30	17.06	26.45	87.72	67.35	22.70	8.44	-16.75	-54.26
	-1130.42	-496.38	-363.09	-190.90	-243.33	-167.67	31.79	43.97	25.64	-1.82	24.44	103.11	87.46	29.15	28.19	2.90	-43.85
1901-1911																	
MALE	-1285.12	-393.01	-309.18	-125.77	-319.60	-490.35	-129.18	98.60	40.40	33.20	51.31	76.17	113.39	105.32	42.35	-17.36	-61.21
	-1258.11	-398.46	-297.05	-124.13	-354.33	-514.69	-117.40	113.90	47.45	25.62	37.72	105.33	144.10	90.94	38.50	-5.76	-49.88
	-1210.69	-406.99	-272.31	-121.28	-424.01	-562.95	-95.44	147.69	65.84	12.92	13.39	157.40	196.49	62.58	31.81	14.83	-30.66
FEMALES	-1436.47	-363.00	-307.03	-220.38	-490.47	-683.29	-154.53	323.08	243.89	34.82	40.81	125.72	65.4	17.74	42.35	-30.68	-56.28
	-1427.26	-360.61	-310.84	-222.11	-460.97	-611.60	-123.31	247.66	168.31	21.28	38.69	132.79	99.88	25.04	-8.31	-18.94	-47.86
	-1412.92	-353.48	-318.09	-227.91	-422.24	-468.07	-63.31	89.36	22.34	.19	35.28	138.29	122.27	37.44	21.45	3.03	-29.45

Age-Band in Years

SELKIRK

	TOTAL	<5	<10	<15	<20	<25	<30	<35	<40	<45	<50	<55	<60	<65	<70	<75	75+
1861-1871																	
MALE	-426.97	-214.51	-119.50	-60.67	-43.17	-16.12	-5.85	8.42	14.85	-2.76	-5.89	-3.89	2.73	18.60	17.38	-.71	-15.87
	-415.36	-207.28	-116.71	-63.80	-37.00	-12.04	-10.97	.48	9.59	-1.17	-3.15	.65	7.24	18.61	16.06	-.98	-14.88
	-419.44	-207.17	-125.54	-69.69	-22.66	-3.10	-22.23	-18.19	-3.52	2.90	5.16	13.80	19.05	17.48	10.64	-3.09	-13.28
FEMALE	-434.33	-199.73	-128.14	-89.28	-78.80	-42.11	.68	30.13	28.57	21.68	15.54	1.30	5.45	14.87	8.56	-5.12	-17.91
	-411.29	-194.62	-126.29	-89.15	-76.43	-41.03	.06	28.21	28.18	20.71	19.63	11.61	8.39	11.07	10.34	-2.13	-19.82
	-372.64	-196.19	-134.14	-88.06	-74.85	-43.84	2.98	31.36	29.47	18.03	35.09	47.45	18.05	-3.77	10.60	3.33	-28.13
1871-1881																	
MALE	-431.33	-221.03	-142.28	-86.73	-55.02	-14.31	5.60	16.90	17.08	6.17	3.61	8.10	13.07	17.78	15.48	.26	-16.01
	-427.37	-218.30	-143.07	-90.71	-53.60	-11.18	3.02	10.82	14.26	8.40	5.36	11.40	16.81	17.90	15.19	.87	-14.54
	-419.44	-213.64	-145.22	-97.74	-48.81	-4.94	-3.32	-2.48	7.58	13.67	10.70	20.03	25.36	17.34	13.01	1.05	-12.01
FEMALE	-396.25	-196.71	-132.93	-90.43	-72.99	-28.48	12.04	34.98	33.43	21.22	14.15	6.81	7.95	10.42	5.86	-4.80	-16.77
	-388.62	-194.98	-134.07	-91.99	-70.54	-23.89	11.02	29.75	31.13	20.17	16.41	13.00	9.83	11.07	7.95	-2.05	-16.95
	-360.22	-192.36	-136.57	-93.79	-65.69	-17.64	10.68	23.74	27.77	18.00	24.53	32.59	15.25	1.29	10.21	3.10	-19.32
1881-1891																	
MALE	-711.40	-247.23	-181.43	-126.28	-79.70	-22.16	-5.28	-8.52	-10.60	-13.23	-11.49	-1.92	6.26	7.00	5.24	-3.99	-18.06
	-706.77	-244.38	-180.48	-130.72	-82.75	-20.78	-6.59	-12.71	-13.00	-11.10	-11.00	.95	9.69	6.97	5.86	-2.45	-16.08
	-699.06	-239.44	-178.89	-138.39	-87.22	-18.53	-10.40	-21.07	-13.01	-6.28	-8.65	7.27	16.91	6.37	6.30	-.14	-12.68
FEMALE	-868.66	-242.70	-191.13	-163.45	-132.96	-64.50	-18.77	6.33	6.52	-7.84	-9.95	-5.20	-3.87	-5.03	-4.77	-9.78	-21.55
	-662.03	-240.34	-192.30	-165.88	-123.89	-55.79	-18.09	-.76	1.80	-9.89	-9.36	-2.27	-3.40	-6.40	-3.05	-7.12	-20.18
	-845.59	-236.48	-194.61	-169.45	-120.67	-39.81	-15.90	-12.80	-6.38	-12.98	-6.35	5.93	-2.55	-11.46	-1.51	-2.32	-18.27
1891-1901																	
MALE	-2034.40	-387.27	-318.66	-279.08	-223.45	-134.22	-109.13	-118.00	-114.19	-98.15	-84.04	-59.38	-33.41	-23.46	-19.71	-19.15	-32.91
	-2027.89	-368.01	-314.48	-262.27	-232.33	-136.45	-108.78	-119.45	-112.47	-97.21	-86.37	-54.28	-27.53	-24.67	-18.02	-15.87	-29.09
	-2016.07	-369.19	-305.75	-287.78	-251.26	-141.57	-109.07	-121.11	-107.96	-94.48	-89.76	-44.93	-17.66	-27.57	-15.10	-10.28	-22.59
FEMALE	-1715.96	-325.04	-289.21	-281.23	-235.24	-131.01	-72.53	-43.59	-39.56	-61.02	-56.45	-32.80	-29.28	-33.48	-27.72	-23.55	-33.25
	-1711.94	-322.56	-291.07	-283.91	-228.97	-113.70	-67.49	-55.50	-50.12	-65.66	-58.79	-33.49	-30.21	-34.48	-25.79	-20.29	-28.89
	-1703.82	-317.58	-294.50	-288.66	-213.01	-79.47	-57.40	-78.04	-69.58	-72.47	-62.74	-36.67	-33.91	-38.03	-24.08	-14.34	-23.14
1901-1911																	
MALE	-599.55	-239.41	-180.51	-58.57	-41.44	-20.89	17.32	-17.74	-31.36	-18.23	-9.98	8.70	26.71	16.08	-.07	-14.32	-35.85
	-588.30	-240.34	-174.48	-59.70	-57.69	-29.82	19.95	-13.70	-26.01	-17.45	-13.36	16.72	35.39	12.39	.47	-9.65	-31.03
	-568.74	-240.42	-162.22	-62.31	-91.22	-48.02	25.02	-3.18	-13.15	-15.16	-19.12	30.38	48.97	4.64	1.69	-1.54	-23.10
FEMALE	-745.28	-213.03	-163.33	-92.02	-109.78	-77.30	3.71	31.52	20.55	-32.00	-30.70	6.58	1.09	-18.88	-18.61	-20.04	-33.06
	-742.86	-210.95	-165.67	-94.09	-99.83	-53.81	12.01	11.95	2.05	-36.48	-32.66	4.06	.39	-18.73	-17.11	-16.58	-27.44
	-740.60	-205.23	-170.07	-99.80	-77.63	-5.57	28.13	-26.09	-32.42	-41.18	-36.73	-7.11	-4.86	-19.47	-16.64	-10.43	-15.48

Age-Band in Years

SHETLAND

	TOTAL	<5	<10	<15	<20	<25	<30	<35	<40	<45	<50	<55	<60	<65	<70	<75	75+
1861-1871																	
MALE	-604.76	-95.16	-70.10	-60.66	-83.30	-94.82	-53.53	-23.14	-25.83	-25.96	-21.58	-17.06	-13.32	-6.60	-1.05	-3.22	-9.62
	-600.98	-92.23	-69.38	-62.68	-83.47	-91.82	-53.01	-26.46	-27.66	-25.61	-22.20	-17.19	-12.57	-5.91	.27	-2.27	-8.79
	-599.12	-89.31	-71.06	-66.72	-83.68	-86.32	-52.20	-33.05	-31.09	-24.71	-23.22	-17.42	-11.10	-4.44	2.85	-.47	-7.17
FEMALE	-879.98	-94.14	-70.21	-64.99	-146.72	-228.05	-132.24	-18.25	-11.46	-20.35	-18.31	-18.76	-16.16	-9.50	-4.30	-8.43	-20.12
	-878.82	-92.08	-68.86	-66.55	-140.23	-213.94	-135.07	-29.36	-15.11	-21.93	-20.62	-19.42	-16.35	-8.82	-1.81	-6.73	-19.94
	-876.10	-91.02	-69.29	-69.51	-127.35	-190.28	-140.65	-51.29	-22.34	-24.86	-24.91	-20.32	-16.55	-7.63	2.95	-3.40	-19.67
1871-1881																	
MALE	-491.25	-101.58	-69.11	-44.84	-70.44	-84.52	-38.17	-8.01	-13.79	-17.12	-14.74	-11.65	-6.97	-.11	2.58	-2.32	-10.49
	-489.11	-100.66	-69.32	-46.57	-71.14	-82.09	-36.91	-10.86	-15.77	-17.30	-15.81	-10.42	-4.91	.06	3.56	-1.20	-9.57
	-484.84	-99.51	-69.98	-49.92	-72.12	-77.31	-34.82	-16.47	-19.39	-17.41	-17.58	-7.99	-1.05	.49	5.41	.75	-7.94
FEMALE	-772.39	-95.02	-84.58	-47.26	-147.81	-243.66	-123.42	14.80	14.98	-9.52	-10.27	-9.19	-9.35	-5.62	-3.90	-10.29	-22.28
	-771.00	-94.44	-84.60	-48.59	-140.52	-227.48	-124.62	-2.04	6.32	-12.08	-12.40	-8.60	-8.15	-4.41	-.53	-7.88	-21.79
	-770.49	-93.41	-84.91	-50.99	-125.81	-196.08	-127.27	-35.05	-10.94	-17.21	-16.04	-6.74	-5.62	-2.24	5.86	-3.17	-20.87
1881-1891																	
MALE	-565.56	-102.85	-74.57	-49.29	-87.68	-112.69	-51.09	-7.85	-14.46	-18.65	-16.33	-14.30	-6.53	3.32	2.74	-3.69	-11.64
	-563.23	-103.63	-74.15	-49.55	-89.32	-112.44	-49.37	-9.18	-16.38	-20.02	-18.21	-10.92	-2.58	2.42	3.02	-2.38	-10.55
	-558.96	-105.24	-73.63	-49.87	-91.88	-111.96	-46.60	-11.83	-19.82	-22.38	-21.37	-4.37	4.72	.76	3.49	-.20	-8.77
FEMALE	-614.80	-100.47	-76.69	-67.97	-167.67	-255.92	-101.38	67.27	55.47	13.13	10.64	15.34	9.94	5.77	2.26	-6.83	-17.68
	-613.96	-100.60	-77.16	-68.16	-160.57	-238.27	-99.87	46.15	41.35	10.16	9.59	17.94	13.26	7.49	6.01	-4.01	-17.25
	-612.26	-101.04	-78.47	-68.19	-145.93	-204.28	-97.40	5.11	13.31	4.06	8.46	24.09	19.79	10.33	12.89	1.42	-16.41
1891-1901																	
MALE	-667.47	-112.84	-93.47	-73.66	-117.87	-146.63	-66.47	-5.65	-12.37	-17.15	-15.26	-14.00	-3.51	8.01	3.07	-5.56	-14.12
	-684.26	-115.49	-92.65	-71.95	-120.45	-149.53	-64.06	-4.20	-13.68	-20.04	-18.03	-7.67	2.82	5.57	2.15	-4.19	-12.85
	-678.63	-121.16	-91.64	-68.08	-124.23	-155.08	-60.14	-1.44	-15.75	-25.24	-22.63	4.59	14.41	.88	.16	-2.21	-11.07
FEMALE	-620.72	-92.04	-72.83	-67.70	-175.12	-264.42	-97.28	78.70	60.01	5.75	4.96	18.49	11.32	2.19	-3.46	-10.73	-18.56
	-619.56	-92.80	-73.70	-66.59	-168.43	-245.50	-91.30	55.00	39.90	1.49	4.37	22.66	16.51	4.11	.45	-7.56	-18.16
	-617.44	-94.55	-75.77	-63.91	-154.30	-209.38	-80.46	9.28	.07	-7.37	4.65	32.29	26.56	7.05	7.31	-1.55	-17.37
1901-1911																	
MALE	-94.93	-61.34	-41.64	-5.34	-56.35	-104.19	-19.75	43.83	34.08	25.42	21.94	17.27	23.28	29.00	13.98	-2.73	-12.41
	-91.20	-63.65	-40.38	-2.69	-59.87	-110.23	-17.15	48.64	33.60	21.41	19.22	25.92	31.21	24.76	11.22	-1.67	-11.55
	-85.28	-68.48	-38.16	3.14	-65.34	-122.13	-13.46	57.90	33.34	14.08	14.81	42.73	45.58	16.49	5.62	-.55	-10.04
FEMALE	-282.18	-56.94	-40.96	-31.17	-151.43	-250.54	-65.21	120.89	92.69	23.70	20.02	37.88	26.27	10.81	2.00	-7.13	-13.06
	-280.27	-57.95	-42.05	-29.18	-146.18	-233.64	-56.50	95.79	67.61	19.72	22.09	44.84	33.78	12.91	5.35	-3.96	-12.91
	-276.93	-60.12	-44.40	-24.81	-134.77	-202.07	-40.79	47.89	18.01	11.16	28.42	60.69	48.23	15.69	10.62	1.93	-12.61

Age–Band in Years

STIRLING

	TOTAL	<5	<10	<15	<20	<25	<30	<35	<40	<45	<50	<55	<60	<65	<70	<75	75+
1861-1871																	
MALE	-5216.10	-1586.57	-1000.04	-600.26	-733.46	-750.96	-244.14	66.42	-25.01	-87.94	-83.65	-70.03	-45.16	17.02	70.18	-4.29	-138.22
	-5130.37	-1524.05	-983.70	-648.04	-738.31	-692.48	-226.89	9.90	-58.43	-80.50	-89.94	-69.68	-29.81	28.79	89.29	10.65	-126.37
	-5131.08	-1485.23	-1040.12	-746.51	-746.51	-577.39	-194.39	-98.88	-121.74	-64.38	-99.85	-67.87	.43	52.31	125.22	38.38	-103.61
FEMALE	-5953.51	-1663.91	-1048.12	-683.14	-995.23	-1216.43	-544.27	214.59	221.96	48.57	11.56	-40.26	-33.59	13.36	25.87	-55.37	-199.10
	-5888.15	-1611.71	-1010.83	-732.29	-941.90	-1079.05	-579.88	80.95	180.07	36.92	-3.50	-40.55	-32.39	22.61	53.42	-36.16	-193.85
	-5947.89	-1605.14	-1034.53	-807.54	-835.26	-810.69	-650.69	-182.73	96.82	14.42	-31.37	-37.82	-28.38	40.20	107.15	1.74	-184.09
1871-1881																	
MALE	-4621.79	-1581.99	-1058.03	-650.68	-729.01	-659.01	-127.30	177.70	69.32	-19.57	-22.61	-24.20	4.03	64.44	73.22	-10.48	-127.62
	-4594.77	-1571.27	-1061.53	-678.98	-740.85	-623.46	-106.73	138.87	40.15	-21.53	-34.40	-6.63	32.90	66.29	84.15	4.18	-115.92
	-4542.11	-1550.79	-1072.28	-733.97	-758.63	-553.37	-68.04	63.73	-14.07	-23.20	-53.70	27.88	66.94	70.35	104.02	29.98	-95.15
FEMALE	-6024.00	-1665.29	-1134.30	-843.45	-1104.08	-1231.91	-483.26	332.91	304.09	47.59	19.51	6.93	-13.00	-3.63	-10.05	-71.50	-174.57
	-6022.44	-1654.68	-1133.80	-857.96	-1047.65	-1082.81	-495.01	175.62	225.15	28.64	5.76	15.91	.15	8.16	19.97	-49.88	-170.01
	-6017.78	-1635.05	-1136.31	-913.44	-931.96	-792.95	-520.34	-132.81	68.05	-9.50	-17.33	38.33	27.49	29.67	77.19	-7.74	-161.67
1881-1891																	
MALE	-4697.14	-1600.92	-1180.48	-811.20	-845.05	-660.14	-121.14	183.82	78.44	-8.75	-10.70	-19.99	34.12	111.77	82.94	-8.60	-101.26
	-4870.19	-1616.72	-1170.31	-813.68	-866.02	-674.36	-97.82	168.94	55.49	-23.52	-30.45	17.90	78.90	101.09	84.29	6.02	-89.81
	-4821.46	-1650.59	-1154.21	-815.57	-898.00	-662.86	-58.28	140.12	14.19	-49.68	-43.96	91.03	161.34	80.82	85.47	30.13	-71.41
FEMALE	-5287.27	-1574.84	-1174.29	-975.73	-1176.72	-1184.83	-327.14	537.16	432.12	87.48	74.14	109.00	59.70	21.67	-4.86	-59.99	-130.34
	-5282.96	-1574.56	-1179.39	-981.67	-1119.47	-1031.02	-311.58	358.26	312.19	62.34	65.35	130.45	67.66	36.53	26.92	-36.58	-128.20
	-5274.01	-1575.86	-1193.46	-990.00	-999.47	-733.93	-285.23	10.10	74.15	10.87	55.11	180.36	143.03	61.49	65.30	8.22	-124.68
1891-1901																	
MALE	-2863.54	-1428.53	-1029.11	-480.26	-466.33	-316.66	121.59	242.14	137.35	43.68	47.01	31.23	97.25	172.87	95.89	-13.68	-97.99
	-2829.14	-1473.98	-1005.63	-455.10	-519.61	-344.32	151.77	257.42	123.23	13.72	17.06	94.25	161.79	146.67	85.61	1.94	-83.96
	-2769.14	-1568.69	-964.53	-401.03	-571.65	-396.25	203.08	287.20	100.96	-40.48	-34.49	214.72	279.04	96.07	63.63	26.03	-62.75
FEMALE	-3903.40	-1421.61	-1095.56	-870.26	-1015.08	-893.90	-42.02	707.25	535.06	68.14	67.80	180.37	110.70	23.32	-35.13	-66.26	-136.24
	-3895.07	-1430.97	-1105.83	-856.63	-955.49	-726.18	14.17	505.01	363.83	30.90	58.97	212.15	152.66	38.95	-1.50	-60.55	-135.15
	-3878.11	-1451.66	-1129.23	-823.22	-829.14	-404.26	118.00	115.75	26.54	-44.74	52.76	284.92	234.17	62.42	57.24	-13.16	-134.49
1901-1911																	
MALE	-4370.94	-1465.73	-1369.30	-1141.05	-1076.67	-719.58	-28.65	364.58	249.82	138.82	140.62	109.80	185.32	269.67	116.43	-36.01	-108.22
	-4333.69	-1548.09	-1325.42	-1077.27	-1119.28	-708.88	3.63	413.59	243.81	92.21	102.41	197.84	269.40	226.10	90.40	-21.05	-93.10
	-4274.09	-1717.44	-1241.64	-941.04	-1188.32	-746.31	55.88	508.07	238.11	35.43	35.43	365.87	421.55	141.97	37.99	-.11	-71.54
FEMALE	-5445.01	-1380.28	-1366.52	-1503.31	-1591.60	-1340.20	-176.73	914.86	664.89	75.45	93.79	271.37	164.47	33.92	-49.91	-109.43	-145.79
	-5433.67	-1400.63	-1385.88	-1468.53	-1533.10	-1170.35	-83.58	665.68	436.68	31.92	95.54	320.34	226.67	53.72	-16.02	-81.17	-144.91
	-5417.40	-1443.15	-1427.54	-1394.54	-1406.87	-845.57	90.74	246.50	-13.88	-59.03	114.47	430.00	345.02	81.90	39.41	-30.20	-144.67

SUTHERLAND

Age-Band in Years

	TOTAL	<5	<10	<15	<20	<25	<30	<35	<40	<45	<50	<55	<60	<65	<70	<75	75+
1861-1871																	
MALE	-650.24	-169.97	-113.53	-58.11	-162.34	-254.42	-87.17	42.15	15.44	8.15	24.71	23.80	24.63	34.93	31.19	7.36	-17.06
	-633.98	-167.78	-108.76	-55.91	-159.57	-249.21	-89.79	28.97	8.83	10.93	26.99	27.30	27.67	37.82	35.48	8.96	-15.90
	-621.75	-174.30	-110.71	-51.30	-152.65	-238.28	-95.21	3.12	-3.58	16.88	32.49	34.76	33.39	43.73	43.19	10.99	-14.26
FEMALE	-1075.14	-163.68	-111.21	-66.92	-183.37	-332.09	-203.09	-6.41	16.57	-8.24	-6.21	-5.48	-3.31	1.34	10.60	3.32	-16.96
	-1058.89	-159.10	-107.32	-89.02	-180.21	-324.27	-205.25	-9.76	18.12	-12.55	-8.63	-1.08	-.86	3.83	14.63	3.92	-20.95
	-1047.08	-159.76	-110.10	-74.98	-172.65	-309.08	-209.13	-16.29	19.87	-20.17	-11.81	8.23	4.72	7.99	20.09	4.33	-28.96
1871-1881																	
MALE	-709.77	-153.12	-106.41	-55.86	-158.09	-246.84	-94.45	21.57	10.48	7.69	9.03	8.66	18.92	26.93	20.73	1.70	-20.91
	-704.47	-155.61	-106.67	-53.20	-155.08	-243.75	-95.85	13.43	6.01	8.56	10.22	13.17	22.11	27.81	22.73	2.25	-20.60
	-695.61	-162.01	-108.57	-46.71	-145.55	-236.85	-99.73	-2.10	-1.83	9.90	14.01	23.23	26.78	29.13	25.44	.98	-21.73
FEMALE	-874.00	-167.03	-116.41	-77.97	-198.27	-337.88	-176.36	41.77	63.57	24.35	14.17	18.83	18.73	16.90	20.60	4.51	-21.71
	-869.30	-166.53	-119.37	-79.45	-191.41	-325.23	-177.02	32.26	58.32	19.62	13.80	24.10	20.93	17.27	22.75	4.92	-24.24
	-862.99	-166.12	-123.35	-81.01	-174.75	-301.82	-178.53	16.42	46.07	8.25	16.50	37.56	24.81	15.62	23.36	3.97	-29.97
1881-1891																	
MALE	-619.23	-148.36	-118.65	-84.44	-169.94	-239.07	-85.36	33.91	34.73	33.89	20.14	16.85	35.91	37.93	23.14	4.18	-16.10
	-617.28	-152.35	-119.76	-80.01	-166.65	-240.06	-86.84	30.91	32.79	33.26	20.36	25.02	39.83	36.43	22.77	3.65	-16.63
	-618.06	-163.30	-123.59	-67.83	-154.54	-211.38	-92.02	25.61	30.40	31.10	22.50	38.85	44.60	32.32	20.31	-.83	-20.27
FEMALE	-921.04	-157.64	-118.72	-88.74	-218.98	-355.62	-175.19	50.63	70.39	20.95	6.34	21.66	20.45	14.12	17.35	-.49	-27.53
	-920.65	-158.41	-121.36	-87.76	-208.91	-339.95	-172.92	36.37	57.39	15.34	8.09	27.98	22.85	12.72	17.29	-.32	-29.04
	-924.75	-160.65	-128.93	-83.92	-184.43	-311.64	-168.94	14.06	29.23	.18	17.15	45.99	26.36	5.57	11.71	-3.07	-33.43
1891-1901																	
MALE	-825.87	-135.07	-124.40	-102.70	-183.92	-247.44	-109.69	-2.15	16.60	22.31	-2.43	-.96	26.06	29.59	13.59	-1.76	-20.51
	-826.16	-143.73	-126.33	-95.92	-180.42	-253.03	-110.90	.77	17.39	19.56	-3.89	7.41	31.29	25.58	10.76	-3.20	-21.45
	-834.19	-159.60	-131.64	-76.97	-166.09	-253.83	-116.73	7.41	21.24	13.00	-4.79	25.80	37.37	15.89	2.63	-10.85	-27.03
FEMALE	-839.15	-138.03	-113.55	-97.84	-237.96	-370.83	-164.04	76.73	94.48	30.19	8.69	36.15	32.89	19.27	17.66	-3.27	-23.90
	-842.62	-140.73	-118.28	-93.53	-224.42	-351.87	-157.04	58.23	72.95	23.01	11.79	43.32	35.53	16.03	15.94	-3.24	-30.30
	-857.39	-146.80	-129.82	-83.06	-192.32	-317.41	-143.66	29.91	27.05	2.59	25.62	64.99	38.23	2.93	4.44	-7.43	-32.66
1901-1911																	
MALE	-234.09	-98.24	-93.66	-73.77	-139.61	-191.04	-55.21	52.88	76.59	78.53	39.97	35.34	61.09	56.66	27.17	3.42	-14.22
	-236.23	-104.14	-95.40	-65.52	-136.57	-200.91	-56.28	61.41	79.63	73.93	37.35	45.36	67.34	49.91	21.55	1.44	-15.35
	-251.16	-120.49	-99.03	-42.75	-123.20	-220.80	-62.99	79.09	88.73	63.47	33.79	66.87	74.20	34.09	7.52	-7.99	-21.68
FEMALE	-595.52	-102.93	-92.83	-87.93	-235.36	-363.69	-135.76	114.77	126.49	46.17	18.50	54.95	47.07	26.77	22.36	-3.38	-30.71
	-601.89	-107.37	-98.08	-80.14	-219.32	-344.52	-125.59	92.37	96.76	36.98	50.88	63.93	50.86	22.22	18.27	-3.78	-30.31
	-625.66	-116.25	-112.07	-63.58	-182.22	-309.48	-105.53	58.57	33.69	16.77	46.58	91.04	54.63	4.11	-.16	-10.27	-31.50

Age–Band in Years

WIGTOWN

	TOTAL	<5	<10	<15	<20	<25	<30	<35	<40	<45	<50	<55	<60	<65	<70	<75	75+
1861-1871																	
MALE	-1636.91	-331.25	-191.05	-87.84	-217.88	-328.26	-184.41	-34.30	-45.09	-68.81	-60.54	-42.15	-30.19	-1.05	16.65	-7.71	-45.22
	-1612.40	-317.31	-187.22	-95.93	-214.53	-313.84	-167.28	-53.81	-54.84	-64.56	-59.52	-38.77	-22.30	3.29	20.14	-4.67	-41.25
	-1602.36	-309.69	-200.71	-112.68	-206.47	-288.22	-174.72	-96.35	-76.41	-54.69	-54.68	-28.11	-3.10	12.21	24.89	-.07	-33.57
FEMALE	-1951.16	-332.20	-210.72	-133.96	-313.96	-472.55	-250.10	-8.31	2.64	-19.81	-20.87	-38.41	-35.05	-18.18	8.32	-24.90	-67.62
	-1922.59	-322.81	-204.26	-137.95	-301.82	-449.78	-260.97	-37.93	-5.23	-21.47	-20.88	-29.64	-29.90	-17.10	2.12	-16.60	-68.37
	-1892.84	-324.62	-211.56	-145.19	-282.84	-412.53	-281.61	-92.74	-20.73	-27.29	-16.24	5.49	-12.73	-19.24	22.70	.59	-74.29
1871-1881																	
MALE	-1616.41	-369.37	-251.16	-166.82	-283.31	-372.28	-154.30	23.99	6.22	-20.36	-18.99	-7.70	2.38	21.09	24.74	-5.36	-45.17
	-1604.93	-365.03	-253.39	-173.91	-284.03	-364.45	-155.23	8.06	-1.32	-16.02	-17.99	-1.05	12.38	22.94	27.14	-1.84	-41.20
	-1580.93	-356.09	-259.08	-187.61	-283.30	-348.55	-158.92	25.65	-17.03	-5.34	-12.60	14.78	33.70	26.22	30.01	3.59	-34.07
FEMALE	-1318.62	-317.46	-215.44	-150.61	-337.89	-488.29	-186.14	125.52	117.88	58.51	44.66	27.29	19.80	19.29	15.51	-7.72	-43.55
	-1303.79	-315.27	-216.23	-154.04	-325.11	-460.63	-191.81	91.71	103.85	57.03	45.70	36.98	24.95	19.11	23.51	-.20	-43.48
	-1263.93	-311.96	-218.10	-159.50	-301.49	-410.82	-201.56	29.48	78.33	54.78	53.80	67.67	38.34	12.96	36.35	14.38	-46.59
1881-1891																	
MALE	-1757.03	-409.20	-297.71	-204.27	-302.70	-370.77	-151.67	12.68	-6.95	-18.35	-15.83	-5.40	13.28	25.72	20.47	-5.57	-40.95
	-1744.59	-406.01	-298.67	-210.08	-300.28	-369.75	-152.32	3.47	-10.79	-15.63	-16.81	4.65	25.75	24.83	22.16	-1.17	-36.95
	-1720.16	-399.63	-295.47	-220.86	-320.16	-368.36	-156.39	-15.75	-17.70	-8.05	-15.80	25.29	49.74	22.70	24.53	6.10	-30.34
FEMALE	-1647.41	-346.75	-284.41	-221.88	-401.65	-523.35	-193.66	128.56	106.29	32.37	23.52	29.14	19.33	6.51	3.24	-10.81	-35.85
	-1636.17	-344.52	-265.58	-224.57	-387.93	-491.21	-192.99	90.93	84.85	27.84	23.98	37.19	24.95	7.32	10.92	-3.29	-34.05
	-1608.14	-341.03	-267.90	-228.40	-360.21	-431.12	-182.06	19.61	40.66	20.76	28.82	57.97	36.25	5.28	23.51	11.27	-31.56
1891-1901																	
MALE	-2246.06	-391.55	-298.81	-187.18	-325.00	-442.55	-217.05	-60.05	-74.79	-64.83	-55.02	-33.54	-4.56	1.54	-6.63	-24.52	-61.45
	-2230.07	-389.96	-295.07	-191.96	-340.70	-450.09	-215.58	-61.34	-73.72	-64.33	-58.62	-18.31	11.03	-2.57	-5.34	-18.39	-55.91
	-2199.79	-385.67	-288.22	-201.40	-370.67	-465.77	-215.15	-62.52	-69.21	-60.86	-62.69	10.66	41.12	-11.06	-3.16	-8.03	-47.17
FEMALE	-2327.82	-351.43	-284.43	-247.15	-469.87	-614.05	-252.91	84.44	61.22	-38.84	-43.47	-3.75	-9.82	-32.65	-34.90	-35.57	-54.34
	-2319.79	-349.42	-286.24	-243.30	-454.27	-572.78	-241.98	41.07	24.90	-47.98	-44.92	1.96	-9.42	-31.92	-27.66	-27.25	-49.57
	-2301.67	-345.61	-289.56	-252.94	-421.11	-493.35	-222.04	-42.14	-44.20	-62.45	-44.80	12.82	4.03	-33.00	-16.56	-11.14	-39.62
1901-1911																	
MALE	-1194.15	-287.83	-222.46	-98.41	-266.81	-435.89	-151.10	48.11	19.02	36.90	41.04	55.61	79.72	57.89	15.88	-21.95	-64.09
	-1172.91	-286.24	-217.70	-102.21	-290.56	-452.57	-146.73	58.03	27.48	36.57	35.83	74.57	98.53	49.22	14.84	-14.39	-57.57
	-1134.47	-280.65	-208.43	-110.79	-338.72	-486.59	-139.31	61.37	48.47	38.19	28.06	108.59	129.62	31.52	13.20	-1.39	-47.64
FEMALE	-1226.82	-269.75	-208.56	-146.51	-410.94	-589.17	-150.18	237.93	184.35	35.05	22.13	81.02	57.68	5.41	-7.68	-21.09	-46.52
	-1220.03	-267.07	-211.07	-148.51	-394.97	-544.44	-132.84	187.93	136.14	26.71	24.31	86.50	64.46	7.31	-2.39	-13.17	-38.93
	-1208.03	-259.92	-215.77	-154.16	-359.54	-456.20	-101.12	91.84	44.71	16.03	30.72	91.18	72.35	8.39	4.03	1.76	-22.34

Appendix 10

A Comparison of Estimations of Net Emigration in Published Literature and those Computed in this Study using the same Methods

Decade	Carrier & Jeffrey[1]	Flinn[2]	New Estimate[3]
1861–1871	–120,000	–116,872	–116,181
1871–1881	–93,000	–92,808	–96,221
1881–1891	–217,000	–218,274	–215,604
1891–1901	–53,000	–51,728	–54,304
1901–1911	–254,000	–253,894	–253,822

1   Carrier and Jeffrey, *External Migration*, p.14.

2   Flinn, *Scottish Population History*, p.441.

3   New estimate is calculated for each decade from April to April for all vital data, it is not clear whether this adjustment was made in the other studies.

Appendix 11

Maps to Show the Proportion of Emigrant Losses to the County-of-Birth by Decade and Gender

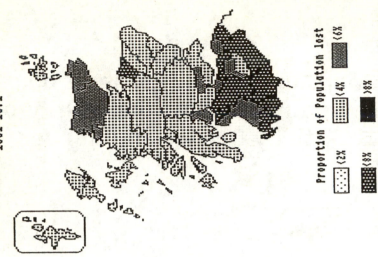

FEMALE EMIGRANTS FROM COUNTY-OF-BIRTH
1861-1871

Proportion of Population lost

<2%   <4%   <6%
<8%   >8%

MALE EMIGRANTS FROM COUNTY-OF-BIRTH
1861-1871

Proportion of Population lost

<2%   <4%   <6%
<8%   >8%

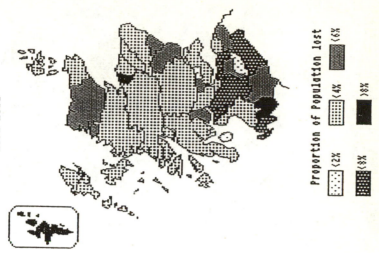

FEMALE EMIGRANTS FROM COUNTY-OF-BIRTH 1871-1881

Proportion of Population lost

<2% <4% <6% <8%

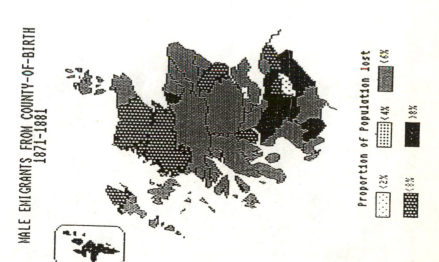

MALE EMIGRANTS FROM COUNTY-OF-BIRTH 1871-1881

Proportion of Population lost

<2% <4% <6% <8%

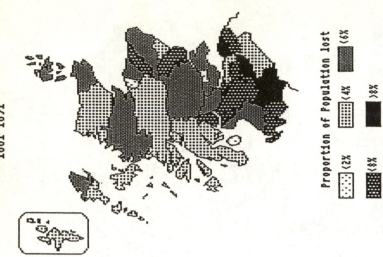

FEMALE EMIGRANTS FROM COUNTY-OF-BIRTH
1881-1891

Proportion of Population lost

<2% <4% <6%
<8% >8%

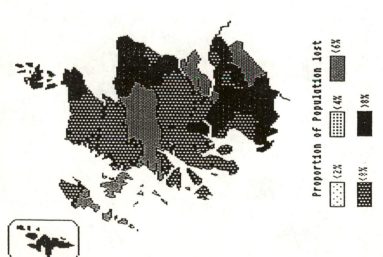

MALES EMIGRANTS FROM COUNTY-OF-BIRTH
1881-1891

Proportion of Population lost

<2% <4% <6%
<8% >8%

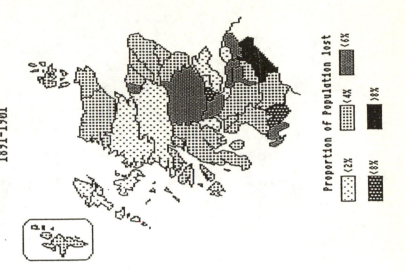

FEMALE EMIGRANTS FROM COUNTY-OF-BIRTH 1891-1901

Proportion of Population lost

<2% <4% <6% <8% >8%

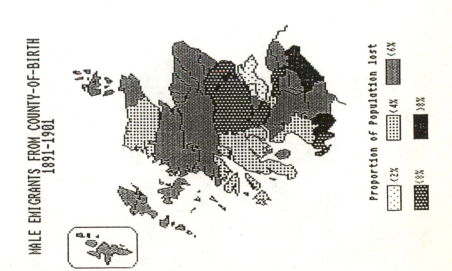

MALE EMIGRANTS FROM COUNTY-OF-BIRTH 1891-1901

Proportion of Population lost

<2% <4% <6% <8% >8%

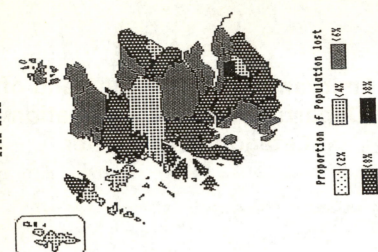

FEMALE EMIGRANTS FROM COUNTY-OF-BIRTH
1901-1911

Proportion of Population lost

<2% <4% <6%
<8% >8%

MALE EMIGRANTS FROM COUNTY-OF-BIRTH
1901-1911

Proportion of Population lost

<2% <4% <6%
<8% >8%

Appendix 12

Emigrant Losses by Age-Band of Departure, Decade, Population Category and Gender

Estimates shown with two standard errors added or deducted.*

Key

* See Appendix 1 for further information on the calculation of standard errors.

Three estimates are provided for each calculation.

The top estimate has been calculated with two standard errors added to every age-band in the migrant age-structure according to population category.

The middle estimate is the original measurement with the correct application of the migrant age-structure.

The bottom estimate has been calculated with two standard errors deducted from every age-band in the migrant age-structure according to population category.

HIGHLANDS   Age-Band in Years

	Total	<5	<10	<15	<20	<25	<30	<35	<40	<45	<50	<55	<60	<65	<70	<75	75+
1861-1871																	
Male	-19069.1	-499.53	28.95	-1529.56	-3672.15	-4564.87	-4897.50	-3146.07	-1127.55	-426.09	-.69	-113.52	-374.22	-415.23	-1038.97	91.63	2615.24
	-19219.5	-713.62	98.92	-1304.49	-3627.76	-4738.32	-4842.46	-2996.37	-1078.05	-489.10	44.03	-46.76	-426.39	-471.45	-1100.50	21.41	2551.40
	-19506.2	-1168.00	217.30	-839.54	-3507.02	-5067.35	-5002.18	-2675.37	-986.10	-641.62	125.36	88.34	-545.07	-596.40	-1235.62	-138.75	2385.85
Female	-11852.5	-571.59	135.81	-636.45	76.37	951.80	-2596.07	-4653.15	-2910.90	-1805.40	-1228.18	-880.65	-392.55	-76.64	-1142.84	67.26	3610.62
	-11810.6	-579.93	137.35	-623.01	-222.78	470.57	-2398.95	-4022.08	-2725.69	-1876.36	-1152.92	-571.89	-369.88	-113.50	-1237.59	-31.73	3507.74
	-11777.4	-598.18	109.03	-583.05	-777.98	-463.53	-1986.80	-2754.45	-2385.14	-2028.94	-990.02	-369.77	-343.00	-203.84	-1458.59	-249.05	3306.79
1871-1881																	
Male	-16476.1	8.73	-468.01	-2226.78	-2714.37	-2344.38	-3312.90	-2658.99	-839.65	-538.76	-617.53	-561.23	-592.76	-699.69	-1183.82	-18.99	2292.04
	-16652.0	-177.53	-450.69	-2010.56	-2581.05	-2456.92	-3389.44	-2541.72	-777.10	-573.29	-562.81	-572.18	-717.16	-725.26	-1228.85	-106.76	2219.32
	-17072.2	-620.39	-453.03	-1512.57	-2220.23	-2669.73	-3536.77	-2285.08	-656.79	-681.40	-458.79	-572.80	-986.68	-798.71	-1341.86	-316.11	2038.77
Female	-11571.2	55.52	-185.63	-1422.23	140.31	1963.92	-1720.99	-4500.71	-2726.18	-1826.87	-1508.60	-966.33	-705.52	-224.62	-1028.76	77.44	3008.06
	-11586.9	52.04	-226.13	-1402.63	-75.83	1452.21	-1613.37	-3802.00	-2433.47	-1859.28	-1427.41	-911.28	-747.64	-294.74	-1173.91	-51.44	2917.93
	-11789.5	35.57	-372.61	-1328.29	-411.95	446.67	-1381.08	-2384.06	-1890.75	-1969.13	-1235.07	-787.02	-851.87	-470.08	-1522.63	-353.18	2713.96
1881-1891																	
Male	-20916.7	-913.43	-592.89	-1841.06	-2694.11	-2896.82	-4573.43	-4301.46	-1501.54	-519.49	-675.55	-614.93	-469.95	-590.23	-872.54	150.14	1990.68
	-21123.8	-1046.77	-632.89	-1638.05	-2466.45	-2956.84	-4713.03	-4245.13	-1428.25	-500.84	-594.69	-707.14	-686.44	-578.36	-897.36	42.01	1908.48
	-21639.8	-1429.24	-744.48	-1106.40	-1866.37	-3089.57	-5021.33	-4107.40	-1278.36	-518.68	-441.25	-849.05	-1091.14	-589.63	-982.74	-226.75	1702.66
Female	-13136.1	-889.67	-494.45	-965.07	1019.69	2559.62	-2080.33	-5402.49	-3083.46	-1864.21	-1467.05	-1333.69	-1022.45	-299.51	-673.85	144.13	2416.67
	-13238.3	-911.91	-580.96	-918.70	834.59	2155.03	-2077.71	-4648.96	-2674.85	-1663.81	-1394.63	-1344.97	-1147.10	-417.01	-877.54	-16.68	2346.84
	-13584.4	-969.26	-827.38	-776.47	896.65	1156.63	-2053.62	-3062.71	-1925.42	-1753.38	-1183.40	-1314.81	-1421.27	-714.07	-1380.55	-409.53	2184.15
1891-1901																	
Male	-13403.6	143.02	-40.42	-2075.65	-2773.91	-1844.14	-2568.92	-2387.75	-282.42	69.69	-655.14	-632.79	-470.42	-691.92	-887.31	78.46	1616.02
	-13677.3	52.23	-151.83	-1895.49	-2433.65	-1828.00	-2764.57	-2389.67	-185.43	156.06	-535.80	-825.46	-761.48	-638.85	-809.57	-68.65	1485.35
	-14386.6	-294.63	-391.78	-1352.31	-1576.54	-1812.93	-3199.65	-2352.12	35.24	258.99	-307.34	-1143.78	-1392.38	-592.22	-990.84	-456.33	1182.07
Female	-8170.44	-151.28	-68.36	-1157.85	862.60	3487.29	-1147.37	-4942.85	-2595.99	-1045.57	-1181.40	-1183.39	-984.68	-172.06	-235.80	308.29	2023.79
	-8376.51	-208.70	-200.10	-1057.30	920.57	2947.56	-1303.48	-4146.10	-2051.94	-980.35	-1082.87	-1250.56	-1169.92	-342.04	-514.37	101.56	1961.63
	-9019.19	-331.95	-525.53	-813.68	1173.59	1887.71	-1559.27	-2420.02	-1069.38	-994.58	-788.18	-1268.22	-1614.23	-787.83	-1228.74	-430.63	1751.95
1901-1911																	
Male	-23055.3	-385.34	-895.04	-2473.41	-1950.49	-1340.48	-3650.94	-4211.50	-1702.68	-1179.19	-2309.63	-1865.17	-1311.91	-1364.44	-557.32	524.46	1598.01
	-23423.6	-470.61	-1093.25	-2269.72	-1477.89	-1273.69	-3915.10	-4267.51	-1586.77	-1033.39	-2173.00	-2145.34	-1607.96	-1268.47	-549.17	331.48	1437.63
	-24434.9	-824.98	-1489.34	-1586.25	-310.20	-1414.60	-4506.10	-4314.31	-1234.02	-828.93	-1902.63	-2602.08	-2524.44	-1175.77	-647.31	-209.92	995.99
Female	-14411.2	-436.71	-533.93	-1558.72	689.73	3165.23	-2246.98	-6529.84	-3649.49	-1527.18	-1889.30	-1838.98	-1548.78	-566.96	904.92	1302.73	1853.08
	-14754.5	-561.85	-723.66	-1365.47	942.54	2645.77	-2530.74	-5680.17	-2990.40	-1442.80	-1801.79	-1972.65	-1861.64	-812.27	544.26	1052.74	1813.63
	-15805.5	-802.85	-1138.84	-964.65	1570.67	1642.71	-2992.70	-3816.68	-1838.18	-1494.15	-1467.00	-2054.41	-2542.74	-1477.34	-419.88	379.29	1621.47

	Total	<5	<10	<15	<20	<25	<30	<35	<40	<45	<50	<55	<60	<65	<70	<75	75+
1861-1871																	
Male	-12480.0	-1643.24	-679.89	-1212.64	-2778.31	-3445.29	-2876.87	-1182.98	47.13	79.37	-77.11	-295.86	-81.71	330.93	123.70	243.55	969.19
	-12575.9	-1699.10	-681.73	-1159.78	-2672.69	-3496.15	-2983.47	-1197.59	6.81	86.33	7.94	-180.78	-20.73	284.95	18.72	172.60	938.78
	-12799.9	-1825.38	-690.48	-1045.22	-2430.93	-3577.23	-3203.49	-1286.54	-141.25	115.01	238.82	143.82	164.20	160.00	-262.87	-17.11	858.66
Female	-10272.7	-1450.11	-803.72	-900.61	-1044.50	-646.15	-1457.17	-2026.76	-1098.63	-418.68	-539.00	-714.82	-371.42	42.66	-166.84	170.12	1153.04
	-10094.2	-1457.99	-844.74	-841.68	-1142.32	-910.89	-1382.79	-1786.65	-1035.98	-447.81	-415.63	-483.63	-306.00	-63.35	-192.18	170.89	1026.82
	-9531.71	-1479.49	-931.18	-715.11	-1406.63	-1532.49	-1156.62	-1117.73	-881.23	-539.01	-34.10	284.53	-8.68	-417.63	-299.71	156.75	619.64
1871-1881																	
Male	-10922.4	-674.02	-666.48	-1617.23	-2446.97	-2526.33	-1982.02	-939.54	-73.99	-22.65	-146.43	-252.62	-246.51	-97.33	-214.41	124.94	859.19
	-10964.8	-669.90	-687.36	-1609.19	-2396.57	-2559.08	-2070.99	-963.15	-72.41	7.22	-85.09	-222.38	-240.20	-100.38	-257.65	89.84	653.43
	-11070.5	-685.68	-671.86	-1573.02	-2267.26	-2618.51	-2249.67	-1034.88	-108.60	65.06	56.01	-114.23	-191.56	-124.46	-380.12	-2.24	830.51
Female	-10392.9	-630.35	-915.99	-1509.65	-1170.35	-288.58	-1153.60	-1975.37	-1205.77	-580.68	-656.49	-791.66	-560.60	-215.91	-324.69	73.21	973.63
	-10804.9	-612.24	-941.59	-1493.58	-1258.05	-528.28	-1136.59	-1713.94	-1094.74	-597.64	-574.49	-681.23	-546.75	-293.95	-347.35	77.58	917.91
	-10453.8	-588.92	-994.50	-1443.06	-1465.15	-1052.95	-1057.83	-1128.22	-858.06	-646.56	-344.04	-241.79	-470.66	-527.21	-426.21	73.95	719.36
1881-1891																	
Male	-11335.1	-985.29	-679.43	-1143.89	-1977.74	-2539.51	-2427.40	-1527.36	-454.37	-35.85	-27.39	13.00	-6.68	-166.97	-164.15	147.57	650.29
	-11319.0	-926.64	-681.89	-1197.96	-1967.48	-2527.99	-2517.63	-1572.95	-407.51	54.59	43.50	-38.44	-67.53	-140.31	-164.88	131.42	664.72
	-11303.8	-815.49	-678.29	-1281.34	-1934.81	-2515.78	-2690.91	-1659.79	330.87	230.77	189.85	-120.19	-175.63	-107.32	-187.25	90.23	691.03
Female	-9683.59	-1186.93	-839.19	-746.49	-384.71	111.10	-1174.02	-2495.40	-1496.80	-513.06	-546.95	-668.04	-451.22	-168.72	-152.73	178.54	851.03
	-9574.51	-1145.60	-856.11	-778.41	-438.96	-83.13	-1201.12	-2205.00	-1299.17	-493.50	-494.03	-638.10	-508.33	-246.23	-203.43	168.65	847.95
	-9318.10	-1071.06	-885.89	-826.17	-546.09	-467.40	-1208.28	-1588.83	-881.32	-434.06	-365.58	-540.03	-623.60	-455.52	-346.01	130.64	791.89
1891-1901																	
Male	-10135.3	-829.64	-483.21	-1198.13	-2026.54	-2143.24	-1830.59	-1146.67	-489.38	-174.51	-120.63	139.47	85.25	-352.02	-303.24	123.06	614.76
	-10085.9	-701.88	-491.72	-1312.48	-2053.73	-2060.14	-1924.64	-1232.46	-402.36	-27.43	-46.35	-13.72	-56.30	-282.26	-241.76	132.73	648.61
	-10001.1	-453.44	-489.95	-1522.92	-2128.47	-2095.13	-1366.89	...	-225.62	251.92	65.78	-322.56	-344.28	-163.60	-124.82	154.81	718.33
Female	-8186.82	-900.01	-748.46	-715.26	-524.60	195.97	-984.21	-2376.36	-1422.78	-392.82	-363.27	-426.59	-311.85	-186.26	-73.18	260.36	782.51
	-8120.16	-836.14	-755.93	-792.48	-543.51	34.15	-1088.43	-2060.12	-1122.65	-327.60	-342.03	-516.73	-448.96	-252.74	-149.38	235.45	847.23
	-8003.14	-699.94	-761.72	-952.56	-561.51	-232.83	-1245.90	-1427.00	-502.12	-148.48	-323.55	-775.83	-763.77	-405.76	-338.41	167.67	968.57
1901-1911																	
Male	-9268.16	-661.11	-546.79	-877.83	-1133.55	-1206.63	-1556.46	-1488.35	-820.81	-356.76	-360.67	38.83	-13.63	-678.62	-409.68	200.06	603.84
	-9171.69	-471.44	-551.31	-1056.64	-1210.78	-1091.21	-1662.99	-1627.86	-687.28	-139.86	-284.58	-223.93	-239.02	-553.36	-270.72	238.96	660.29
	-8996.78	-63.30	-528.05	-1415.02	-1437.04	-895.31	-1830.20	-1634.67	-401.72	265.73	-166.57	-770.36	-711.13	-329.05	8.65	326.98	777.25
Female	-8493.53	-802.00	-715.26	-336.77	152.04	677.30	-1120.41	-2873.35	-1803.33	-722.40	-709.11	-633.14	-522.07	-404.59	128.74	491.22	699.62
	-8494.02	-711.76	-719.75	-458.56	194.96	565.30	-1292.59	-2525.90	-1391.60	-625.88	-747.87	-879.67	-766.36	-466.05	23.84	448.73	839.11
	-6555.49	-488.70	-718.26	-750.72	310.27	514.28	-1570.44	-1861.08	-551.16	-348.35	-891.59	-1561.63	-1329.49	-578.39	-219.16	347.47	1142.25

PERIPHERY & NORTHEAST   Age-Band in Years

	Total	<5	<10	<15	<20	<25	<30	<35	<40	<45	<50	<55	<60	<65	<70	<75	75+
1861-1871																	
Male	-31095.2	-6145.35	-1189.60	-587.36	-6577.52	-9983.06	-6463.78	-2505.12	-568.79	-71.90	18.21	326.69	58.01	-83.27	-281.86	565.25	2374.25
	-30682.6	-6129.06	-1254.73	-499.68	-6576.98	-10124.0	-6673.64	-2562.35	-371.72	145.94	94.86	243.87	68.15	51.95	-220.63	613.64	2511.77
	-29585.2	-6052.63	-1392.17	-397.44	-6585.35	-10383.9	-7157.69	-2790.05	27.23	659.52	252.59	44.97	116.56	390.03	-28.73	785.52	2917.09
Female	-19287.7	-4133.86	-1341.07	-941.02	-20.55	-386.63	-4158.05	-5333.53	-2793.36	-758.25	-247.42	-215.40	-781.20	-927.26	-708.01	580.53	2877.40
	-19055.5	-4255.52	-1340.55	-819.54	-146.77	-841.58	-4283.53	-5240.03	-2488.19	-353.01	-306.45	-384.72	-707.78	-761.74	-667.69	593.06	2958.51
	-18570.6	-4506.39	-1324.74	-508.25	-378.01	-1744.80	-4627.03	-5165.91	-1862.91	515.91	-462.26	-615.56	-553.60	-361.81	-529.51	660.69	3173.60
1871-1881																	
Male	-29491.0	-5486.73	-1440.24	-1263.68	-5709.72	-8743.00	-5989.69	-2472.17	-430.84	484.62	136.74	161.06	-186.10	-447.33	-602.27	310.90	2187.41
	-29224.6	-5365.45	-1546.79	-1275.45	-5669.32	-8854.00	-8223.51	-2510.63	-237.08	720.00	290.43	69.09	-242.04	-327.64	-557.12	299.42	2205.51
	-28526.0	-5037.98	-1780.56	-1558.66	-5629.28	-9066.22	-6736.49	-2678.22	151.26	1261.37	614.11	-114.56	-304.17	-43.29	-413.81	325.08	2287.37
Female	-21279.4	-3422.83	-1813.72	-2317.16	-1700.70	-595.05	-3474.51	-5009.75	-2479.45	-445.53	-358.15	-825.02	-873.92	-897.56	-607.36	789.18	2812.19
	-21016.2	-3516.38	-1596.34	-2214.08	-1809.60	-1280.35	-3697.86	-4639.83	-2029.83	-77.54	-309.34	-902.63	-840.86	-810.06	-681.64	765.72	2683.32
	-20398.2	-3718.71	-1539.90	-2011.16	-2267.10	-2701.54	-4269.52	-3997.38	-1101.27	725.73	-209.88	-1063.07	-752.71	-584.94	-645.48	842.82	2895.69
1881-1891																	
Male	-47818.4	-6329.45	-3031.41	-2262.36	-6912.43	-11552.7	-9937.62	-5707.69	-2067.92	-151.21	-148.03	-333.20	-583.02	-675.97	-506.38	390.02	1990.91
	-47695.0	-6087.55	-3209.18	-2596.40	-6808.42	-11570.4	-10178.3	-5760.70	-1889.62	116.89	98.60	-459.00	-728.51	-552.18	-453.18	315.15	1879.82
	-47315.0	-5480.68	-3613.41	-2774.42	-6658.10	-11605.4	-10680.1	-5928.00	-1533.83	714.92	616.19	-676.19	-943.30	-277.95	-338.05	203.60	1659.72
Female	-32482.0	-5748.47	-3015.83	-2606.01	-2502.37	-1369.35	-4669.61	-6781.57	-3373.67	-720.28	-997.37	-1913.27	-1540.84	-654.37	-311.92	1051.39	3053.51
	-32215.8	-5803.26	-2977.89	-2742.49	-2745.19	-2285.84	-5012.82	-6077.48	-2745.20	-418.53	-850.84	-1807.99	-1575.36	-382.92	-382.82	1030.61	3115.76
	-31500.3	-5935.18	-2881.18	-2601.78	-3250.34	-4174.38	-5860.97	-4790.45	-1454.68	258.77	-517.71	-1812.04	-1601.35	-837.64	-444.98	1074.44	3322.35
1891-1901																	
Male	-25968.1	-4989.38	-535.34	-494.18	-4321.82	-7848.69	-6988.37	-3274.33	-186.16	1355.38	813.52	62.50	-585.17	-648.91	-499.22	334.45	1837.87
	-25977.9	-4597.92	-788.71	-784.49	-4134.44	-7739.43	-7267.75	-3393.26	-48.28	1686.14	1103.76	-122.75	-849.16	-492.65	-433.40	196.75	1597.94
	-25858.9	-3848.80	-1379.08	-1517.75	-3823.84	-7536.56	-7039.43	-3671.58	215.38	2396.58	1979.71	-419.35	-1263.71	-170.43	-264.59	-29.10	1113.77
Female	-14263.7	-3916.81	191.31	-626.71	-1489.78	794.30	-2457.58	-5386.56	-1913.40	689.99	-521.07	-1847.22	-1345.27	-577.01	-112.18	1197.69	3060.55
	-13964.4	-3932.27	249.05	-608.72	-1801.80	-418.74	-3036.74	-4359.83	-1039.89	960.78	-209.83	-1687.79	-1442.78	-682.74	-243.80	1167.15	3123.54
	-13080.2	-3993.50	380.56	-543.94	-2458.89	-3045.32	-4407.05	-2372.43	755.87	1582.29	495.84	-1241.14	-1567.52	-657.40	-401.38	1229.89	3360.89
1901-1911																	
Male	-57626.9	-6650.61	-2553.98	-1803.22	-5354.59	-10745.1	-12732.7	-9118.56	-3756.24	-510.13	-954.03	-1675.50	-1925.51	-1727.40	-483.96	565.16	1692.49
	-57773.6	-6144.27	-2873.46	-2140.99	-5102.06	-10489.9	-13034.4	-9311.11	-3649.41	-117.33	-449.60	-1924.37	-2329.43	-1525.05	-370.09	361.67	1326.19
	-57694.5	-4928.09	-3634.50	-3239.70	-4651.63	-10005.3	-13639.4	-9701.52	-3449.62	712.37	597.15	-2309.29	-2982.78	-1130.75	-121.81	9.93	580.47
Female	-39144.0	-6147.34	-1740.81	-2131.25	-3872.15	-1850.67	-5767.73	-9295.64	-4522.97	-965.38	-2412.71	-3628.56	-2398.44	-820.27	720.40	2002.37	3687.19
	-38829.9	-6126.88	-1867.55	-2158.95	-4215.79	-3304.38	-6538.20	-7825.63	-3344.73	-803.61	-2012.37	-3375.19	-2621.06	-1061.67	525.97	1955.67	3744.50
	-37768.0	-6137.65	-1513.64	-2160.20	-4949.40	-6502.89	-8338.00	-4932.49	-915.63	-382.56	-1082.91	-2686.33	-2986.09	-1512.29	272.14	2023.33	3998.60

CENTRAL LOWLANDS   Age–Band in Years

	Total	<5	<10	<15	<20	<25	<30	<35	<40	<45	<50	<55	<60	<65	<70	<75	75+
1861-1871																	
Male	-53562.5	-20827.6	-3814.76	3483.60	4537.71	-12661.8	-8516.72	-2262.00	-1130.17	-750.09	-1778.37	-2766.25	-1892.59	-109.91	775.07	1151.89	2075.10
	-53266.7	-20284.6	-3083.59	2812.57	-663.70	-8089.94	-2947.44	-1675.56	-783.17	-1999.53	-2845.02	-1727.77	-14.19	1061.93	1402.06	2182.94
	-52757.7	-18195.0	-3999.19	1465.59	-4952.92	-10186.0	-7237.48	-4179.22	-2683.63	-872.00	-2438.36	-3016.33	-1448.03	150.75	1604.75	1870.07	2359.22
Female	-40338.0	-19602.5	-3424.34	4382.20	-1501.22	-10617.5	-9285.56	-2510.57	-3.46	297.67	-772.74	-1850.25	-487.72	1533.07	266.95	293.03	2924.87
	-40658.6	-19359.3	-3362.12	4000.39	-575.41	-8512.03	-9705.77	-4495.42	-816.08	-7.83	-984.18	-1956.30	-598.95	1566.93	567.61	534.46	3056.21
	-41371.4	-18869.4	-3223.11	3244.91	1245.76	-4326.08	-10560.9	-8423.21	-2426.06	-621.84	-1476.56	-2250.44	-849.51	1658.44	1167.19	1003.48	3334.90
1871-1881																	
Male	-60375.2	-24422.9	-6779.87	2955.40	-5132.47	-14583.9	-9535.17	-3088.94	-1128.12	272.91	-669.21	-2196.26	-1402.05	881.30	1126.20	1074.06	2213.27
	-60011.6	-24217.9	-6690.62	2517.76	-5452.48	-14007.5	-8994.59	-3555.62	-1687.49	47.77	-1054.63	-1851.18	-902.12	824.63	1291.10	1392.37	2436.91
	-59337.1	-23796.8	-6496.78	1620.44	-6136.53	-12930.9	-7922.28	-4433.24	-2731.33	-392.31	-1800.24	-1521.35	13.91	710.18	1601.82	2002.57	2875.70
Female	-45681.3	-23361.0	-6371.94	2950.32	-2454.06	-12514.1	-8598.47	323.29	1729.98	577.13	-361.66	-1068.80	-214.05	1529.11	-17.29	-99.58	2289.80
	-45931.1	-23212.3	-6314.99	2694.31	-1546.20	-10061.5	-6605.38	-2143.65	333.33	158.87	-666.57	-1091.27	-109.06	1665.68	404.25	211.23	2383.18
	-46460.5	-22891.1	-6166.07	2122.98	192.92	-5161.65	-8567.74	-7031.01	-2436.62	-671.60	-1320.24	-1211.04	80.43	1961.62	1252.78	823.82	2562.09
1881-1891																	
Male	-83238.7	-22376.0	-10617.8	-1921.07	-9611.44	-21337.7	-14663.2	-3770.54	-1785.85	-911.14	-702.91	-1978.44	-684.51	2223.39	1803.16	1053.44	2241.91
	-82754.0	-22597.4	-10338.9	-2011.25	-10166.5	-21222.2	-14192.4	-3814.33	-2313.83	-1383.79	-1270.57	-1334.74	217.48	1966.73	1791.51	1442.37	2575.90
	-81832.9	-23027.1	-9732.07	1835.46	-11324.0	-20974.9	-12865.5	-4188.11	-3310.98	-2281.64	-2359.58	-168.70	1900.04	1487.80	1788.05	2199.25	3252.18
Female	-59052.3	-20114.2	-10093.7	-2775.66	-6946.81	-15641.9	-10285.7	1098.44	2413.13	194.43	132.02	-398.16	-327.91	1272.46	-173.43	-156.35	2751.11
	-59197.1	-20060.8	-10046.6	-2906.22	-5181.73	-13004.2	-9841.92	-1900.61	359.82	-263.18	-175.46	-258.73	100.83	1576.81	394.15	228.43	2782.23
	-59508.5	-19921.9	-9912.94	3219.70	-4753.68	-7706.53	-8807.21	-7864.55	-3706.70	-1162.19	-653.55	-65.09	941.05	2216.82	1550.91	992.66	2846.11
1891-1901																	
Male	-54025.3	-17432.4	-5602.94	840.65	-8314.58	-17889.4	-9896.19	955.12	451.00	-2018.48	-951.86	-1810.43	-545.72	3478.37	1839.48	532.68	2439.40
	-53343.7	-18128.5	-5068.36	1194.81	-9204.85	-18370.4	-9041.36	1296.31	-10.79	-2883.77	-1860.33	-633.32	783.63	2941.29	1623.12	1034.72	2992.11
	-52012.8	-19510.2	-3941.40	1835.46	-10999.9	-19259.8	-7374.79	1932.30	-900.96	-4509.79	-3589.61	1516.62	3474.47	1956.30	1216.27	2025.00	4117.13
Female	-32343.2	-15547.3	-5407.63	-619.61	-4596.78	-11648.0	-5050.16	6062.76	3698.79	-1148.19	70.43	330.17	-497.28	950.35	-977.86	-797.73	2834.74
	-32375.9	-15569.6	-5371.29	-616.86	-3943.72	-8579.12	-3829.63	2541.45	811.33	-1811.18	-427.74	527.64	232.01	1406.08	-238.85	-317.22	2811.03
	-32453.9	-15590.4	-5270.39	-657.31	-2731.83	-2404.97	-1344.67	-1486.08	-4881.46	-3099.43	-1516.03	811.32	1570.92	2362.98	1282.60	643.91	2757.03
1901-1911																	
Male	-98601.3	-21764.8	-10433.8	-3775.59	-20628.6	-35343.1	-20424.9	-2061.12	-212.62	-1606.82	263.22	56.43	1378.18	6141.23	4732.79	1683.02	3295.19
	-97645.4	-22786.9	-9674.91	-3040.63	-21713.3	-36424.5	-19365.4	-1147.09	-622.21	-2820.16	-854.74	1777.02	3356.53	5240.43	4145.07	2268.62	4015.83
	-95710.5	-24823.7	-8094.22	-1609.66	-24070.6	-34057.3	-17320.3	530.66	-1433.89	5088.99	2977.17	4930.86	7104.41	3606.07	3047.48	3440.81	5504.98
Female	-75417.8	-19513.2	-10491.7	-5331.68	-12719.7	-23142.5	-12731.1	2926.61	1046.09	-3957.19	-504.28	2218.41	129.19	566.79	825.80	1026.62	4232.08
	-75207.6	-19559.2	-10446.1	-5248.29	-12337.9	-19974.8	-10857.8	-1290.64	-2762.98	-4605.41	-953.32	2650.05	1330.23	1261.05	1740.19	1604.73	4132.55
	-74790.9	-19653.0	-10344.7	-5088.67	-11600.5	-13291.4	-7116.07	-9739.49	-10232.0	-5836.75	-1992.81	3356.77	3707.48	2720.15	3645.07	2761.17	3907.75

Appendix 13

Emigrants by Age-Band of Departure, County-of-Birth, Decade and Gender

Estimates shown with two standard errors added or deducted.*

Key

* See Appendix 1 for further information on the calculation of standard errors.

Three estimates are provided for each calculation.

The top estimate has been calculated with two standard errors added to every age-band in the migrant age-structure according to population category.

The middle estimate is the original measurement with the correct application of the migrant age-structure.

The bottom estimate has been calculated with two standard errors deducted from every age-band in the migrant age-structure according to population category.

Age-Band in Years

ABERDEEN

	TOTAL	<5	<10	<15	<20	<25	<30	<35	<40	<45	<50	<55	<60	<65	<70	<75	75+
1861-1871																	
MALE	-7423.21	-1195.31	-119.86	-39.46	-1527.36	-2749.99	-1986.89	-647.95	-41.35	55.28	39.05	6.09	-18.09	-20.12	-52.88	204.48	671.14
	-7376.06	-1192.95	-125.31	-35.50	-1526.02	-2764.03	-2015.05	-658.32	-19.75	83.08	48.86	-3.51	-14.83	-2.87	-45.25	209.92	685.49
	-7259.84	-1184.61	-136.16	-29.47	-1523.98	-2790.09	-2080.02	-693.06	23.69	148.50	69.70	-25.86	-4.31	39.52	-22.01	226.7	721.55
FEMALE	-3579.09	-776.03	-86.70	-86.06	-256.84	-534.49	-1005.06	-771.08	-653.81	-166.90	-58.22	2.28	-11.13	-1.00	-40.65	168.69	799.91
	-3553.78	-785.55	-89.10	-74.17	-269.54	-577.15	-1016.01	-968.32	-425.13	-124.26	-62.27	-14.45	-103.02	14.38	-37.08	170.08	806.79
	-3497.38	-804.84	-89.28	-51.58	-294.36	-662.37	-1045.05	-968.05	-365.13	-33.11	-73.37	-51.78	-85.42	50.67	-24.67	176.81	824.16
1871-1881																	
MALE	-8154.94	-1077.62	-530.16	-454.56	-1352.03	-2494.76	-2016.28	-803.68	-144.15	46.83	14.62	55.52	-8.71	3.83	-64.93	100.97	570.16
	-8121.94	-1044.72	-540.16	-459.11	-1348.99	-2507.18	-2044.75	-808.66	-120.71	76.70	34.04	44.60	-14.17	18.70	-60.24	99.48	572.21
	-8036.74	-1030.47	-561.46	-471.33	-1348.23	-2531.93	-2107.43	-829.61	-73.89	145.41	74.69	22.56	-13.43	53.88	-44.46	102.59	581.37
FEMALE	-5813.74	-711.52	-471.29	-596.59	-501.97	-529.71	-1181.85	-1291.88	-669.11	-297.46	-98.99	-94.23	-105.83	-58.91	-117.80	196.60	716.79
	-5788.56	-720.09	-470.14	-586.88	-525.89	-604.21	-1204.40	-1252.95	-622.49	-257.59	-90.33	-100.24	-101.83	-50.62	-120.50	195.45	724.15
	-5727.58	-738.43	-465.11	-568.27	-575.20	-756.69	-1259.86	-1184.83	-525.59	-170.96	-74.11	-113.41	-91.70	-28.84	-118.69	199.43	744.69
1881-1891																	
MALE	-13594.9	-1581.61	-888.94	-527.24	-1946.33	-3724.93	-3297.88	-1716.48	-496.57	-31.31	-11.39	-27.10	-62.76	-97.07	-23.39	221.39	636.75
	-13581.2	-1556.53	-905.43	-542.59	-1935.92	-3726.91	-3326.90	-1722.05	-473.85	3.16	20.03	-45.86	-103.06	-80.92	-18.18	211.93	621.87
	-13535.3	-1493.99	-942.14	-584.26	-1923.58	-3732.27	-3386.91	-1740.62	-429.23	79.74	84.51	-80.28	-132.85	-45.14	-2.31	199.73	594.30
FEMALE	-8266.24	-1850.22	-970.24	-591.84	-417.87	-762.92	-1538.08	-1617.80	-849.99	-261.68	-137.83	-246.04	-151.57	-26.10	-4.73	284.47	916.20
	-8241.61	-1854.75	-945.78	-586.26	-450.96	-869.20	-1576.11	-1534.84	-774.58	-225.10	-120.41	-246.87	-157.21	-27.21	-14.69	279.55	922.81
	-8173.78	-1865.78	-953.89	-574.84	-520.72	-1089.37	-1665.46	-1579.33	-618.56	-143.04	-85.36	-247.00	-204.62	-23.75	-24.56	278.72	943.80
1891-1901																	
MALE	-7654.91	-1261.40	-206.15	-138.39	-1375.15	-2795.53	-2272.67	-750.46	4.97	217.19	168.13	51.96	-63.99	-34.59	-26.28	165.36	642.08
	-7661.43	-1216.93	-232.37	-172.61	-1352.64	-2778.32	-2308.11	-768.46	22.37	262.46	218.07	20.06	-84.52	-11.74	-15.40	147.53	609.16
	-7651.77	-1110.41	-292.59	-258.26	-1318.74	-2748.09	-2379.32	-909.90	53.80	399.22	318.75	-36.04	-148.09	36.29	12.77	122.20	546.66
FEMALE	-4050.82	-1075.14	39.24	116.67	-219.93	-381.02	-1297.87	-1488.81	-449.87	127.87	-2.08	-185.04	-194.52	-58.72	-46.60	249.10	813.84
	-4026.79	-1074.46	47.21	115.91	-204.48	-537.31	-1372.94	-1335.	-330.61	168.15	33.72	-171.46	-209.95	-69.45	-64.59	240.32	818.37
	-3949.51	-1076.09	65.85	116.66	-359.08	-846.44	-1542.91	-1102.53	-84.18	259.81	108.01	-141.40	-232.95	-83.51	-85.52	236.91	837.86
1901-1911																	
MALE	-18608.5	-1668.15	-867.13	-818.22	-2588.72	-4591.18	-4325.72	-2394.69	-914.08	-187.88	-131.65	-267.8°	-349.56	-268.67	-59.00	197.32	646.66
	-18638.2	-1605.76	-900.55	-872.77	-2558.78	-4554.64	-4367.2	-2428.77	-902.45	-131.91	-64.06	-311.39	-420.81	-233.33	-36.64	169.92	593.01
	-18665.1	-1453.20	-980.15	-1007.32	-2512.06	-4489.18	-4448.53	-2497.41	-883.62	-14.14	73.88	-385.44	-528.99	-167.50	12.90	127.07	488.64
FEMALE	-12797.2	-1536.00	-808.60	-747.65	-1178.16	-1519.68	-2389.06	-2429.68	-1261.57	-472.65	-530.67	-662.10	-488.9	-188.20	99.29	413.72	922.81
	-12769.3	-1552.00	-798.24	-754.26	-1227.46	-1712.14	-2494.79	-2234.87	-1092.30	-444.81	-488.96	-644.23	-522.20	-212.71	75.91	404.78	929.02
	-12663.3	-1550.39	-776.58	-761.87	-1333.47	-2125.54	-2733.83	-1860.80	-746.96	-374.94	-399.12	-593.88	-574.31	-250.32	51.83	409.32	957.52

Age-Band in Years

ARGYLL

	TOTAL	<5	<10	<15	<20	<25	<30	<35	<40	<45	<50	<55	<60	<65	<70	<75	75+
1861-1871																	
MALE	-3143.12	143.18	28.98	-497.22	-632.82	-343.41	-556.06	-565.26	-537.27	-252.24	-68.96	-38.65	-107.66	-140.62	-246.95	.41	471.60
	-3168.56	95.77	43.42	-443.20	-623.17	-392.03	-574.93	-525.06	-314.47	-261.23	-56.69	-26.18	-121.04	-151.23	-262.09	-16.57	460.12
	-3225.14	-3.14	67.08	-332.48	-596.50	-483.97	-608.67	-445.98	-271.84	-281.86	-32.85	-.45	-148.80	-172.87	-293.13	-52.66	433.00
FEMALE	-2152.72	147.12	66.48	-424.09	-88.15	730.49	-16.63	-433.93	-730.09	-542.01	-357.36	-148.23	-155.48	-139.41	-250.31	20.06	669.04
	-2131.16	141.38	66.81	-414.42	-181.87	565.92	42.79	-664.39	-545.06	-545.06	-339.70	-129.50	-149.01	-146.07	-278.39	-7.56	644.99
	-2097.99	129.15	60.22	-392.5	-338.56	242.84	162.17	-345.82	-539.36	-552.22	-301.21	-93.72	-138.46	-162.28	-340.11	-65.93	597.85
1871-1881																	
MALE	-2171.32	109.02	-1.57	-464.93	-369.19	192.70	-149.77	-543.37	-267.70	-203.06	-206.87	-96.55	-129.81	-188.47	-241.38	-15.99	405.62
	-2200.39	69.69	-1.25	-417.46	-336.74	166.67	-173.42	-517.40	-246.04	-203.87	-190.51	-102.34	-160.81	-191.03	-249.89	-36.38	390.39
	-2267.69	-23.38	-10.29	-393.73	-250.23	118.13	-221.16	-463.96	-203.92	-211.45	-157.25	-108.08	-225.46	-199.22	-271.21	-84.18	332.68
FEMALE	-1360.76	98.55	38.55	-393.80	179.47	1067.54	156.50	-727.09	-702.37	-435.51	-356.95	-181.65	-176.39	-165.17	-156.80	82.61	511.77
	-1348.87	96.03	29.65	-387.28	113.81	909.28	185.75	-605.37	-605.37	-433.86	-333.96	-174.75	-189.51	-182.62	-195.48	49.78	491.77
	-1344.79	88.10	-3.39	-365.63	5.63	593.74	242.67	-290.56	-420.63	-438.96	-294.12	-154.77	-218.63	-224.99	-285.19	-24.63	446.57
1881-1891																	
MALE	-3017.43	-44.41	-60.35	-366.23	-338.55	50.88	-419.39	-852.15	-453.78	-225.63	-183.20	-126.88	-106.68	-133.92	-140.82	38.44	347.24
	-3056.67	-68.11	-71.27	-324.50	-289.11	35.91	-457.28	-842.71	-632.59	-214.74	-160.76	-147.65	-153.22	-129.27	-144.52	13.91	328.23
	-3155.86	-137.52	-100.67	-215.49	-155.88	4.11	-541.79	-820.27	-389.08	-202.95	-115.86	-178.35	-248.12	-127.35	-159.20	-46.93	279.48
FEMALE	-1680.99	-138.07	-26.38	-202.09	391.94	1178.05	62.73	-1060.07	-743.03	-443.69	-372.44	-310.12	-214.31	-114.62	-102.67	69.22	344.56
	-1688.82	-144.56	-45.73	-190.21	364.05	1032.02	60.77	-845.44	-620.93	-438.53	-354.47	-314.47	-248.73	-146.34	-155.32	29.48	329.19
	-1735.76	-161.25	-101.08	-154.32	339.47	736.36	54.99	-377.91	-591.66	-447.53	-299.95	-305.95	-321.87	-225.07	-283.18	-65.70	288.88
1891-1901																	
MALE	-1169.22	-52.55	77.11	-339.84	-277.59	216.52	-97.29	-466.12	-99.14	59.75	-92.12	-77.77	-70.38	-136.70	-129.69	40.26	276.32
	-1223.61	-61.93	51.69	-310.10	-209.34	220.12	-141.84	-467.59	-74.91	83.59	-61.49	-117.06	-132.13	-125.33	-132.33	7.70	247.36
	-1365.85	-109.25	-3.54	-217.75	-38.53	224.76	-240.22	-462.22	-19.98	118.25	.11	-179.32	-265.15	-115.16	-151.34	-77.83	171.30
FEMALE	-1291.15	-57.47	33.60	-219.89	318.54	1088.55	-24.09	-1126.89	-658.55	-276.33	-311.54	-309.01	-233.08	-47.32	32.52	124.08	375.71
	-1329.50	-69.29	7.91	-198.57	325.48	948.71	-61.80	-914.9	-516.64	-264.08	-287.28	-321.21	-286.07	-93.07	-35.32	75.86	361.87
	-1455.81	-95.25	-55.82	-146.20	349.02	666.40	-130.16	-458.67	-255.88	-271.69	-210.23	-314.89	-398.90	-210.92	-207.88	-47.81	313.27
1901-1911																	
MALE	-3577.28	-267.11	-239.05	-471.74	-120.04	253.35	-364.30	-898.78	-378.99	-217.33	-403.22	-357.86	-267.88	-264.97	-105.47	118.63	317.51
	-3654.73	-275.41	-282.23	-442.34	-27.38	289.72	-419.79	-818.90	-347.27	-181.65	-367.25	-414.03	-346.78	-245.70	-105.84	74.12	274.17
	-3878.96	-334.64	-369.92	-537.05	200.59	300.12	-542.46	-825.12	-268.43	-127.73	-293.91	-502.54	-522.07	-228.61	-130.76	-50.44	153.98
FEMALE	-2716.22	-240.53	-143.61	-355.05	108.89	774.58	-363.77	-1375.67	-729.88	-249.18	-337.47	-333.10	-248.07	-54.00	209.92	264.19	356.52
	-2792.70	-264.49	-179.88	-317.60	154.77	642.95	-433.09	-1148.07	-573.05	-234.33	-310.74	-355.43	-321.47	-115.45	125.66	208.72	347.79
	-3025.65	-311.22	-259.34	-239.10	271.70	381.99	-553.17	-707.91	-294.94	-253.78	-216.19	-354.66	-481.14	-280.02	-93.30	60.38	305.04

Age-Band in Years

AYR

	TOTAL	5	10	15	20	25	30	35	40	45	50	55	60	65	70	75	75+
1861-1871																	
MALE	-8746.05	-1391.22	-715.15	-506.01	-1540.87	-2248.47	-1589.38	-889.92	-487.62	-285.90	-118.58	138.99	92.96	63.93	37.22	153.68	540.30
	-8606.35	-1424.60	-729.83	-446.41	-1531.31	-2316.88	-1648.6	-902.53	-413.64	-209.70	-86.89	114.67	93.92	109.49	56.43	166.56	583.05
	-8238.69	-1480.14	-763.25	-333.21	-1512.41	-2444.79	-1847.47	-965.24	-262.50	-22.59	53.51	104.06	224.07	118.73	215.5		707.78
FEMALE	-6317.11	-787.56	-697.54	-925.63	-518.03	-258.19	-1016.74	-1367.16	-905.68	-307.23	-70.03	-59.47	-150.36	-204.04	-56.59	268.45	738.71
	-6241.88	-834.04	-697.62	-875.72	-584.69	-455.36	-1040.85	-1275.33	-790.15	-181.40	-81.00	-109.17	-124.05	-153.21	-55.21	260.39	755.32
	-6092.32	-928.35	-695.27	-779.86	-706.96	-841.24	-1116.56	-1128.42	-557.40	88.31	-117.46	-237.13	-72.71	-27.61	-33.95	255.97	808.33
1871-1881																	
MALE	-5948.68	-1339.22	-387.95	-436.29	-1154.14	-1409.09	-882.58	-457.63	-161.48	54.56	-42.50	-13.75	-97.67	-140.70	-88.80	118.46	490.11
	-5869.18	-1324.74	-416.98	-407.17	-1126.01	-1465.73	-974.68	-461.47	-90.03	132.74	13.88	-46.15	-125.98	-102.51	-76.62	109.59	492.69
	-5660.62	-1275.08	-483.33	-562.09	-1075.84	-1576.31	-1175.03	-497.74	54.00	310.63	132.03	109.78	-168.38	-12.17	-33.77	104.96	509.31
FEMALE	-3988.88	-494.74	-359.73	-1044.46	-809.16	216.39	-148.54	-809.99	-578.71	-59.99	-96.38	-203.53	-197.44	-169.03	-27.32	257.77	633.98
	-3917.88	-327.30	-358.47	-1003.06	-888.33	-223.31	-52.49	-678.75	-410.36	49.28	-74.33	-227.04	-194.36	-150.08	-50.16	240.75	650.13
	-3757.54	-596.60	-354.38	-720.11	-1038.12	-598.91	-366.97	-343.30	-68.66	284.83	-30.15	-280.73	-185.80	-78.24	-81.45	221.80	699.25
1881-1891																	
MALE	-10332.5	-1263.87	-775.76	-811.10	-1106.02	-1573.59	-1825.02	-1500.00	-729.64	-232.34	-189.31	-153.63	-219.85	-217.72	-111.69	43.88	333.13
	-10306.3	-1198.39	-837.57	-831.81	-1050.73	-1590.00	-1918.03	-1511.96	-664.89	-143.92	-103.37	-200.14	-280.32	-177.73	-100.63	11.85	291.30
	-10219.3	-1037.96	-778.36	-895.96	-947.68	-1623.88	-2114.46	-1554.66	-534.45	49.77	76.77	-278.36	-379.38	-90.83	-67.88	-44.89	202.93
FEMALE	-6574.98	-720.89	-665.98	-1101.83	-629.46	620.39	-430.63	-1655.72	-779.68	-258.26	-342.57	-544.91	-377.63	-199.18	-13.55	277.87	647.06
	-6509.53	-941.38	-660.18	-1075.16		293.06	-532.05	-1368.39	-747.59	-166.87	-294.53	-547.20	-801.19	-211.06	-55.71	254.38	660.87
	-6342.80	-989.13	-647.69	-1017.00	-887.08	-391.07	-779.94	-814.57	-278.65	28.92	-185.25	-534.98	-637.66	-224.21	-122.19	227.16	710.53
1891-1901																	
MALE	-4022.64	-1020.08	-119.54	-177.94	65.78	64.61	-831.93	-1043.34	-270.86	228.37	-51.76	-178.87	-315.48	-358.37	-236.48	-7.52	230.75
	-4037.91	-896.18	-213.28	-255.42	152.51	90.43	-941.77	-1079.59	-221.39	337.47	80.96	-238.58	-809.40	-306.88	-219.13	-62.74	145.08
	-4038.16	-605.31	-429.55	-45.57	319.59	134.20	-1173.14	-1164.31	-124.02	567.70	358.23	-323.63	-564.62	-203.98	-177.13	-167.29	-37.32
FEMALE	-3400.23	-652.81	57.41	-518.42	-276.01	1222.94	88.10	-1464.06	-777.48	-90.49	-436.09	-698.96	-494.14	-253.65	27.89	304.91	560.63
	-3330.04	-664.03	66.19	-503.30	-370.56	804.62	-96.81	-1079.59	-488.32	-10.83	-340.43	-658.10	-539.62	-296.64	-31.51	282.40	576.49
	-3125.24	-698.91	83.20	-461.18	-560.21	-92.75	-528.63	-327.62	151.23	156.91	-116.74	-526.64	-608.62	-575.82	-126.69	269.31	637.93
1901-1911																	
MALE	-13505.1	-2047.49	-950.25	-361.33	-114.90	-746.83	-2571.74	-2984.35	-1449.64	-271.19	-441.13	-594.40	-604.51	-588.42	-119.63	125.42	215.25
	-13559.4	-1881.62	-1076.56	-495.50	.34	-671.49	-2687.07	-3037.98	-1406.29	-141.20	-265.39	-670.83	-741.57	-527.29	-93.80	47.34	89.49
	-13636.8	-1501.62	-1370.77	-811.45	233.03	-530.88	-2929.00	-3146.28	-1318.21	129.38	102.64	-776.34	-975.63	-415.64	-42.35	-104.51	-179.19
FEMALE	-8523.60	-1804.42	-516.09	-525.85	-557.26	942.22	-587.33	-2578.51	-1394.28	-344.29	-807.00	-1147.93	-642.94	-198.67	255.28	564.90	818.59
	-8444.15	-1808.15	-503.89	-519.17	447.89	-843.38	-2064.21	-991.79	-294.89	-674.12	-1048.12	-725.54	-289.52	172.43	537.23	831.59	
	-8171.30	-1833.42	-479.82	-485.10	-841.47	-634.54	-1434.81	-1038.24	-180.74	-187.52	-351.68	-822.85	-859.69	-473.80	32.56	522.81	897.01

Age-Band in Years

BANFF

	TOTAL	<5	<10	<15	<20	<25	<30	<35	<40	<45	<50	<55	<60	<65	<70	<75	75+
1861-1871																	
MALE	-1874.21	-195.25	-56.72	-219.85	-657.12	-694.12	-440.57	-178.45	3.52	85.10	74.58	53.36	43.72	20.02	-6.41	65.26	228.71
	-1880.22	-194.19	-59.93	-221.74	-659.75	-698.51	-436.43	-166.34	11.28	85.19	75.35	52.50	41.71	18.08	-11.49	60.65	223.38
	-1894.63	-191.44	-66.19	-225.98	-666.21	-707.33	-436.94	-141.61	27.07	85.60	76.48	50.51	37.83	14.09	-21.59	50.78	210.32
FEMALE	-736.53	-140.44	-30.00	-99.27	-183.86	-160.23	-203.68	-276.81	-135.03	-12.28	-18.18	-4.27	2.62	23.43	-34.58	42.41	283.64
	-940.63	-142.18	-29.67	-86.37	-187.73	-171.63	-200.88	-263.93	-133.79	-12.17	-14.93	-4.29	1.64	20.96	-39.47	39.72	284.09
	-949.56	-145.47	-28.12	-81.13	-195.74	-193.09	-194.54	-237.30	-130.87	-12.35	-9.24	-5.37	-.99	15.96	-49.37	33.69	284.39
1871-1881																	
MALE	-1957.48	-60.48	-80.84	-330.68	-701.55	-705.96	-479.94	-152.09	55.44	89.28	82.43	49.10	29.42	-3.55	-32.40	59.42	244.92
	-1971.42	-57.99	-81.96	-352.27	-704.00	-710.03	-474.26	-139.68	61.18	87.44	82.73	45.28	23.65	-6.28	-37.20	54.85	239.12
	-2002.05	-51.24	-83.42	-337.09	-712.04	-718.32	-466.20	-114.00	71.73	82.72	81.11	36.55	12.77	-12.39	-46.46	46.87	227.37
FEMALE	-1154.07	38.09	12.68	-319.88	-497.67	-324.17	-234.31	-185.33	-27.38	25.50	-6.54	-15.76	40.64	53.81	-29.32	61.50	254.08
	-1162.71	36.83	13.15	-317.73	-506.48	-341.50	-229.58	-163.00	-18.96	26.79	-3.21	-17.18	37.84	50.37	-34.43	55.39	250.98
	-1182.62	34.59	15.39	-314.30	-525.24	-371.85	-216.58	-118.02	-1.77	29.09	.60	-23.62	30.86	43.55	-50.52	41.98	243.21
1881-1891																	
MALE	-3469.17	-371.16	-193.68	-365.60	-736.41	-833.99	-581.63	-266.31	-55.62	22.86	-.54	-49.36	-70.71	-77.88	-87.31	14.27	183.90
	-3482.53	-363.31	-196.92	-371.01	-735.49	-831.56	-579.27	-259.98	-53.20	21.47	-.05	-59.52	-81.28	-76.67	-88.57	11.30	181.52
	-3507.94	-343.18	-203.88	-385.71	-737.99	-826.32	-570.55	-246.84	-50.54	17.17	-2.25	-61.08	-99.98	-73.97	-90.21	8.09	179.30
FEMALE	-2799.41	-281.83	-122.07	-408.44	-509.05	-214.64	-271.59	-389.98	-242.95	-87.65	-90.34	-148.20	-138.72	-58.34	-57.64	18.94	203.09
	-2811.58	-282.51	-120.60	-520.48	-237.58	-271.92	-362.16	-225.37	-85.01	-90.36	-154.60	-144.07	-59.66	-63.39	13.13	200.74	
	-2840.61	-284.11	-116.42	-407.08	-545.03	-277.35	-288.20	-310.10	-191.39	-80.11	-75.81	-173.12	-155.10	-59.81	-72.70	1.43	194.30
1891-1901																	
MALE	-1903.80	-247.12	30.93	-168.64	-643.91	-657.28	-436.08	-114.50	47.72	30.34	38.38	6.83	-35.06	-39.95	-40.74	61.49	263.80
	-1915.64	-237.48	29.30	-176.76	-638.37	-644.64	-436.38	-119.17	46.47	33.33	39.91	-14.23	-53.37	-32.61	-36.16	60.50	264.02
	-1935.03	-213.34	26.59	-197.96	-633.81	-619.81	-432.22	-129.10	39.78	37.10	37.08	-58.60	-85.22	-16.99	-24.11	64.80	270.77
FEMALE	-1175.65	-127.05	-17.89	-231.93	-294.84	29.12	-106.54	-333.10	-207.96	-9.69	13.43	-92.35	-82.06	12.14	-.14	48.46	214.76
	-1186.17	-125.23	-14.60	-234.87	-300.44	-.21	-115.94	-298.23	-171.86	1.53	10.05	-106.68	-91.00	13.50	-5.26	40.94	212.13
	-1212.09	-121.41	-6.74	-241.77	-334.15	-48.14	-126.70	-233.41	-101.44	24.37	-6.64	-145.79	-108.95	20.94	-11.39	26.21	204.91
1901-1911																	
MALE	-3535.99	-96.25	21.53	-213.90	-655.21	-706.82	-546.96	-331.83	-173.84	-186.83	-189.34	-177.83	-210.78	-177.66	-88.17	25.36	171.55
	-3563.67	-82.87	17.12	-227.29	-645.77	-684.45	-551.06	-349.86	-178.29	-177.30	-183.09	-204.54	-233.15	-161.89	-76.31	23.66	171.40
	-3547.46	-48.77	6.23	-281.90	-633.00	-638.78	-552.44	-385.42	-191.63	-159.40	-176.54	-259.67	-270.34	-128.10	-50.98	25.65	176.62
FEMALE	-2128.64	-21.28	-.28	-276.45	-315.42	14.36	-231.54	-499.73	-362.03	-148.68	-82.86	-184.83	-184.13	-62.59	-14.43	47.12	184.13
	-2141.80	-18.13	4.44	-282.14	-331.94	-16.98	-240.23	-457.03	-305.19	-133.61	-205.83	-209.84	-198.84	-58.87	-16.84	38.96	180.27
	-2175.19	-12.46	14.61	-295.59	-347.96	-67.01	-268.57	-383.91	-194.17	-101.58	-136.08	-274.01	-226.44	-42.97	-14.36	24.03	169.29

Age-Band in Years

BERWICK

	TOTAL	<5	<10	<15	<20	<25	<30	<35	<40	<45	<50	<55	<60	<65	<70	<75	75+
1861-1871																	
MALE	-1775.60	-178.88	-152.80	-220.00	-234.60	-235.98	-344.95	-235.20	-67.44	-37.19	-48.35	-87.12	-54.61	-10.03	-24.83	20.70	135.67
	-1793.74	-188.37	-152.65	-210.29	-216.43	-247.01	-362.92	-232.21	-70.56	-39.57	-38.35	-71.68	-48.05	-15.78	-40.00	9.64	129.57
	-1837.01	-210.04	-153.25	-189.22	-265.56	-285.56	-399.23	-234.50	-86.87	-44.55	-12.23	-28.46	-23.12	-30.63	-79.01	-18.74	113.08
FEMALE	-1756.64	-193.21	-151.86	-157.20	-46.40	114.89	-192.35	-29.29	-308.17	-173.96	-113.42	-139.72	-94.68	-14.72	-25.92	18.85	150.54
	-1732.05	-194.44	-159.26	-146.85	-66.23	64.06	-177.74	-378.75	-297.61	-181.42	-92.99	-101.06	-83.70	-32.29	-30.42	18.15	128.50
	-1655.15	-197.97	-174.90	-124.57	-118.32	-54.06	-137.25	-257.98	-273.21	-203.52	-30.09	27.95	-65.22	-89.06	-48.36	12.81	58.60
1871-1881																	
MALE	-1578.51	-53.91	-135.15	-268.04	-233.36	-228.93	-311.55	-228.45	-67.67	-13.98	-18.77	-52.51	-45.76	-9.31	-39.17	6.02	122.03
	-1588.92	-54.42	-134.98	-265.81	-224.01	-235.44	-326.78	-228.11	-64.47	-8.20	-7.61	-48.98	-48.05	-11.28	-48.06	-1.92	119.18
	-1613.74	-59.23	-134.73	-259.00	-200.89	-247.85	-357.98	-231.44	-64.14	3.59	18.37	-34.46	-47.29	-18.81	-71.82	-21.15	112.10
FEMALE	-1338.04	-72.50	-163.23	-189.70	.65	136.66	-121.88	-364.09	-253.61	-115.57	-96.31	-121.20	-76.89	-11.41	-43.44	15.82	138.66
	-1319.45	-70.35	-167.77	-184.61	-17.23	89.56	-116.89	-310.98	-229.10	-115.18	-79.90	-98.37	-75.56	-27.24	-51.11	13.25	124.04
	-1267.52	-67.92	-177.14	-177.51	-57.50	-11.15	-97.55	-192.45	-176.21	-115.76	-34.81	-25.71	-66.22	-75.27	-74.37	5.08	76.97
1881-1891																	
MALE	-2132.08	-153.96	-173.69	-289.30	-246.06	-238.69	-382.77	-329.20	-127.33	-46.81	-38.57	-43.34	-46.99	-54.36	-37.41	9.56	66.85
	-2134.77	-144.50	-173.59	-296.52	-242.85	-237.21	-397.25	-333.35	-118.52	-33.43	-27.08	-54.08	-60.39	-69.80	-37.89	4.93	66.74
	-2142.45	-128.75	-171.82	-307.03	-234.90	-235.99	-426.11	-341.11	-103.50	-7.69	-4.06	-72.37	-84.77	-43.69	-11.73	-5.26	66.33
FEMALE	-1703.64	-152.65	-121.04	-127.28	-20.32	45.73	-237.33	-472.76	-293.68	-119.94	-111.90	-115.69	-63.15	-18.35	-39.06	12.79	130.99
	-1691.00	-147.83	-123.44	-130.87	-32.17	6.68	-240.40	-414.93	-254.87	-115.47	-103.84	-112.90	-74.42	-31.97	-50.20	7.90	127.75
	-1663.45	-139.00	-127.63	-135.94	-55.65	-70.17	-239.21	-294.24	-174.06	-103.69	-84.38	-101.69	-77.69	-68.04	-79.19	-5.39	112.51
1891-1901																	
MALE	-1127.63	-45.90	-60.98	-125.97	-48.53	-10.33	-215.59	-255.28	-122.72	-64.60	-59.99	-10.31	-21.71	-107.81	-78.61	15.36	85.33
	-1127.32	-28.03	-62.19	-141.95	-50.06	.56	-232.13	-269.27	-109.22	-41.48	-46.84	-37.69	-48.13	-65.42	-68.06	14.99	87.64
	-1128.16	6.34	-61.55	-171.01	-56.51	19.05	-262.07	-291.53	-81.94	2.33	-23.58	-92.38	-101.04	-73.98	-47.90	14.90	92.70
FEMALE	-982.86	-73.15	-70.06	-109.89	40.86	197.14	-77.76	-382.87	-253.62	-68.56	-88.55	-101.72	-52.91	-43.45	-32.95	28.96	125.68
	-975.35	-63.79	-70.78	-120.68	33.85	159.49	-117.55	-321.44	-197.27	-55.81	-84.17	-117.09	-76.14	-54.50	-47.11	22.77	134.87
	-963.32	-65.73	-70.93	-143.39	22.61	93.45	-149.09	-199.16	-62.15	-23.46	-79.41	-159.52	-128.27	-79.19	-80.41	7.78	151.54
1901-1911																	
MALE	-1390.61	-37.27	-108.64	-179.26	-51.19	38.50	-198.16	-334.38	-181.40	-85.14	-89.91	-14.15	-20.10	-138.20	-96.13	20.13	84.68
	-1383.05	-10.12	-109.07	-204.75	-59.75	58.08	-215.29	-357.07	-161.01	-51.06	-77.57	-57.99	-58.72	-116.10	-73.36	22.84	87.89
	-1370.47	47.14	-104.80	-255.47	-87.86	93.35	-242.44	-397.12	-140.40	12.02	-58.75	-148.13	-137.76	-75.52	-27.24	30.38	95.13
FEMALE	-1168.12	-113.08	-127.57	-74.02	143.28	332.23	-101.25	-500.28	-222.60	-120.60	-139.50	-155.86	-85.28	-68.20	-11.48	63.75	110.20
	-1166.18	-99.27	-127.92	-92.72	146.03	307.75	-131.04	-433.08	-247.06	-165.54	-147.20	-193.39	-125.26	-78.36	-27.95	56.06	130.77
	-1175.04	-65.08	-127.40	-137.60	154.99	275.88	-180.36	-304.33	-94.72	-64.21	-173.06	-299.57	-215.03	-95.88	-64.37	39.13	176.58

Age-Band in Years

BUTE

	TOTAL	<5	<10	<15	<20	<25	<30	<35	<40	<45	<50	<55	<60	<65	<70	<75	75+
1861–1871																	
MALE	-204.44	-79.67	35.05	40.02	-105.05	-155.94	-86.40	-30.78	.12	-2.99	11.33	37.24	22.37	21.77	7.48	17.56	63.43
	-195.08	-77.27	31.68	41.41	-105.08	-159.63	-72.59	-34.11	4.00	2.33	13.34	34.88	22.89	25.98	9.79	19.45	67.81
	-171.46	-70.43	24.34	43.16	-105.40	-166.08	-106.92	-44.76	11.15	14.95	17.53	29.48	25.04	36.44	16.46	24.87	78.72
FEMALE	-197.44	-9.72	-10.24	-11.30	54.01	64.98	-65.72	-172.86	-101.80	-25.84	24.09	19.32	-17.57	-30.31	-16.18	36.59	95.10
	-187.44	-14.48	-10.09	-7.16	49.60	47.41	-101.01	-168.54	-90.50	-11.98	22.63	14.59	-14.50	-24.56	-14.21	37.49	97.86
	-165.22	-24.57	-9.36	.87	41.51	11.89	-114.79	-163.39	-67.39	17.55	19.23	4.73	-7.54	-11.28	-8.48	40.90	104.92
1871–1881																	
MALE	-317.58	-115.41	43.17	38.43	-85.61	-108.10	-78.78	-53.20	-32.89	-11.94	-1.07	9.11	-1.27	-9.74	9.98	24.65	55.06
	-307.86	-109.09	38.04	36.50	-84.30	-110.49	-86.14	-56.56	-27.83	-4.36	3.52	6.84	-1.91	-5.55	12.17	24.96	56.34
	-282.98	-92.84	26.31	30.23	-82.63	-114.81	-102.59	-66.60	-17.85	13.21	13.63	2.69	-1.39	4.36	18.17	26.96	60.26
FEMALE	-123.61	-60.22	-36.50	-33.00	41.67	119.31	-29.07	-148.05	-83.63	-10.57	3.39	5.12	-13.01	-17.23	.75	30.16	87.29
	-111.88	-43.86	-35.69	-29.46	36.09	93.85	-37.74	-135.52	-67.71	1.98	4.71	3.00	-11.56	-14.11	1.13	30.95	90.05
	-84.45	-52.06	-33.38	-22.04	25.15	46.02	-60.25	-113.80	-34.85	29.39	8.17	.02	-7.41	-6.38	4.11	33.01	97.84
1881–1891																	
MALE	-506.80	-106.47	5.81	2.90	-122.61	-149.21	-137.02	-111.36	-39.87	.80	20.03	30.76	12.17	4.01	8.28	20.15	54.83
	-500.74	-96.74	-2.00	-3.25	-119.33	-149.27	-144.61	-114.67	-35.16	9.40	27.60	28.77	10.04	7.79	9.91	18.59	52.16
	-484.36	-72.29	-20.40	-19.52	-113.78	-149.12	-160.96	-123.49	-25.67	28.91	44.15	26.12	8.02	14.38	14.38	16.36	46.65
FEMALE	-170.48	-71.05	-15.26	-12.32	4.66	60.36	-60.24	-166.23	-59.97	10.81	7.45	-28.43	-7.54	13.48	10.12	46.67	97.01
	-158.61	-73.70	-14.30	-9.39	-2.20	28.33	-74.77	-144.74	-39.15	21.50	13.80	-25.72	-7.63	13.49	8.46	47.34	100.04
	-128.02	-80.53	-12.00	-2.38	-15.90	-41.89	-111.26	-104.53	3.98	45.61	29.35	-16.51	-5.80	14.69	7.76	52.16	109.23
1891–1901																	
MALE	-316.78	-72.58	-6.54	-13.22	-90.04	-71.49	-57.75	-86.74	-23.05	27.23	12.66	3.41	-7.87	-7.79	16.97	23.34	36.68
	-313.82	-59.67	-16.19	-23.38	-84.88	-69.76	-66.56	-90.21	-18.96	36.99	23.93	1.97	-11.83	-4.02	19.04	20.06	29.66
	-303.42	-27.93	-39.33	-49.06	-75.23	-66.45	-85.52	-98.54	-10.72	58.60	48.28	1.54	-16.70	4.07	24.40	14.48	14.71
FEMALE	-268.81	-72.24	19.06	-5.75	-33.97	50.96	-40.18	-154.24	-70.19	-7.34	-25.54	-41.51	-21.19	2.56	6.31	31.52	92.92
	-254.18	-72.37	20.67	-5.83	-42.07	9.84	-60.79	-126.69	-43.72	-.33	-13.42	-32.54	-23.41	-1.95	2.33	32.52	96.59
	-213.10	-77.32	24.34	1.88	-58.65	-83.36	-112.90	-55.46	11.55	16.99	16.20	-7.43	-25.03	-10.46	-2.33	39.74	109.14
1901–1911																	
MALE	-776.01	-104.59	-24.54	-28.04	-106.80	-171.53	-202.75	-192.22	-81.12	19.89	8.50	8.87	14.00	2.79	21.61	28.99	30.93
	-777.89	-89.36	-35.33	-41.92	-100.77	-167.40	-211.23	-194.60	-76.53	30.74	23.19	6.88	6.73	5.64	22.62	23.41	20.07
	-777.33	-52.55	-61.60	-76.19	-88.97	-159.49	-229.23	-199.30	-66.78	54.46	54.77	6.17	-4.53	10.85	24.98	13.07	-2.99
FEMALE	-486.15	-107.10	14.95	-.39	-127.56	-88.66	-100.62	-148.46	-24.99	21.95	32.46	-57.98	-22.37	-12.18	29.21	67.12	123.38
	-471.34	-107.08	16.45	.36	-136.61	-139.36	-126.57	-100.63	7.81	24.54	-33.41	-42.09	-28.15	-22.97	22.13	67.29	125.96
	-425.10	-108.94	19.61	4.20	-155.60	-252.77	-191.45	-4.17	77.43	34.02	13.08	.18	-36.66	-65.47	11.48	73.46	136.50

Age-Band in Years

CAITHNESS

	TOTAL	<5	<10	<15	<20	<25	<30	<35	<40	<45	<50	<55	<60	<65	<70	<75	75+
1861–1871																	
MALE	-1536.89	-88.22	29.86	-75.21	-283.05	-474.94	-487.89	-250.84	-66.03	17.74	47.76	18.57	-19.02	-28.19	-59.80	9.02	173.33
	-1543.19	-96.56	32.30	-66.20	-281.76	-463.44	-490.85	-244.17	-62.90	16.32	51.40	22.23	-21.05	-30.19	-62.78	5.13	169.33
	-1557.94	-113.89	36.54	-47.84	-278.21	-499.46	-495.37	-230.10	-57.03	12.33	58.14	29.50	-25.72	-34.68	-69.10	-3.24	160.16
FEMALE	-1021.96	-43.10	39.47	-41.53	-112.73	-185.51	-365.28	-319.49	-153.68	-47.24	21.29	2.81	-7.11	3.78	-38.68	24.83	200.20
	-1020.72	-44.70	39.18	-40.23	-128.68	-211.70	-357.21	-289.60	-142.39	-46.85	26.03	8.16	-5.14	2.74	-43.78	19.14	194.34
	-1019.98	-47.90	37.72	-37.32	-158.80	-262.57	-340.78	-230.31	-121.17	-46.38	33.59	17.37	-2.23	.39	-54.85	7.43	183.84
1871–1881																	
MALE	-1267.26	30.46	15.82	-147.72	-309.93	-417.76	-410.15	-188.78	-1.65	38.54	22.12	-7.65	-13.58	-18.95	-58.61	23.82	174.76
	-1276.21	24.69	16.28	-140.03	-305.34	-424.34	-414.84	-179.57	3.50	38.73	26.45	-9.18	-20.53	-19.78	-61.25	18.76	170.24
	-1296.39	11.40	16.37	-123.00	-293.97	-436.95	-423.57	-154.78	13.16	37.44	34.27	-11.46	-34.78	-22.26	-66.92	8.12	160.56
FEMALE	-631.95	54.59	13.72	-105.06	-146.54	-95.39	-159.33	-202.41	-73.53	-19.58	-10.70	-49.77	-54.12	16.87	-38.99	24.39	213.89
	-633.35	53.66	12.35	-102.90	-162.42	-132.35	-157.19	-162.33	-53.09	-15.62	-4.18	-47.27	-55.80	13.93	-47.52	17.16	210.23
	-638.85	51.52	7.69	-97.59	-191.01	-204.69	-152.51	-81.81	-13.78	-9.23	9.12	-42.76	-60.16	7.27	-65.88	1.82	203.13
1881–1891																	
MALE	-1920.36	-81.14	-26.61	-122.70	-320.33	-464.87	-492.10	-306.69	-58.90	2.69	-13.68	-57.09	-73.10	-60.42	-43.43	19.70	158.36
	-1931.23	-63.79	-28.33	-117.19	-311.64	-466.54	-498.83	-303.08	-53.59	5.40	-8.32	-44.99	-85.58	-58.55	-44.10	14.09	153.82
	-1955.15	-92.04	-32.46	-103.10	-291.16	-470.10	-512.20	-295.37	-43.67	8.60	1.11	-59.21	-110.36	-55.98	-46.01	2.34	144.45
FEMALE	-1232.45	-48.88	-6.42	-107.43	-71.83	-.70	-257.60	-336.80	-179.39	-91.60	-93.94	-111.01	-104.13	-15.59	-25.97	22.22	216.62
	-1236.27	-49.59	-8.57	-105.63	-83.52	-39.80	-260.46	-306.31	-147.76	-87.20	-90.28	-114.66	-112.35	-21.33	-36.98	13.73	214.45
	-1247.19	-51.27	-14.73	-100.75	-103.23	-116.38	-265.67	-204.85	-86.66	-80.88	-82.68	-121.78	-129.55	-33.82	-60.48	-4.38	209.87
1891–1901																	
MALE	-960.77	1.62	-53.42	-176.57	-260.28	-245.70	-253.78	-140.51	41.67	52.62	19.72	.52	-19.24	-36.68	-34.16	31.05	112.37
	-974.34	3.63	-56.89	-174.58	-246.64	-240.02	-263.87	-143.84	46.28	60.80	28.82	-16.41	-39.42	-30.42	-32.11	24.30	106.02
	-1004.28	4.64	-63.47	-166.87	-217.30	-230.16	-284.14	-149.60	54.88	74.23	44.65	-47.85	-78.81	-19.67	-28.68	10.48	93.36
FEMALE	-611.36	30.97	-32.11	-172.31	-116.43	133.98	-101.11	-334.01	-137.50	-18.39	-25.57	-55.77	-24.81	5.85	-5.70	58.69	182.82
	-617.99	30.46	-34.54	-170.89	-126.64	83.16	-121.12	-276.59	-98.88	-6.20	-18.68	-61.88	-37.38	-.62	-18.63	48.72	181.75
	-635.56	29.42	-40.69	-167.25	-144.50	-15.58	-159.36	-162.54	5.37	15.14	-5.84	-74.51	-63.26	-14.38	-45.30	28.10	179.63
1901–1911																	
MALE	-2230.20	-63.76	-23.28	-131.79	-243.07	-317.67	-439.57	-356.89	-157.36	-103.85	-151.26	-116.02	-107.48	-112.39	-48.55	28.42	134.12
	-2247.58	-62.13	-28.89	-131.48	-225.86	-305.24	-451.75	-369.27	-154.53	-92.98	-142.93	-139.39	-132.87	-100.63	-39.96	22.13	128.19
	-2285.29	-82.94	-39.81	-126.57	-189.99	-282.54	-475.93	-393.01	-150.10	-74.47	-129.25	-183.33	-181.50	-79.32	-23.56	10.04	116.98
FEMALE	-1089.25	-20.19	-26.92	-113.07	23.82	237.40	-129.67	-448.83	-277.63	-107.08	-123.05	-171.55	-146.57	-77.78	20.12	97.65	174.10
	-1098.83	-21.72	-29.75	-111.11	19.52	186.63	-158.12	-279.59	-211.20	-95.91	-123.40	-186.36	-167.74	-86.68	6.40	86.53	173.66
	-1121.39	-24.48	-36.06	-107.16	11.92	89.02	-211.16	-243.02	-82.59	-76.34	-125.49	-216.27	-209.30	-104.20	-21.56	63.46	171.78

Age–Band in Years

CLACKMANNAN

	TOTAL	<5	<10	<15	<20	<25	<30	<35	<40	<45	<50	<55	<60	<65	<70	<75	75+
1861–1871																	
MALE	-1019.44	-211.06	-45.10	-23.77	-168.58	-247.43	-153.81	-49.66	-26.40	-23.93	-2.08	-1.06	-13.85	-19.60	-31.89	-16.60	15.38
	-1002.00	-207.57	-48.33	-18.51	-169.06	-257.10	-165.84	-52.64	-16.76	-13.59	1.75	-4.66	-13.21	-13.30	-29.51	-15.00	21.12
	-945.65	-196.77	-55.55	-9.57	-170.62	-275.07	-193.20	-65.00	2.22	11.05	10.00	-12.96	-10.01	2.59	-21.69	-6.29	45.21
FEMALE	-525.04	-22.56	-33.06	-146.24	-32.22	57.00	-102.20	-114.21	-62.88	-22.12	-9.26	-4.52	-16.41	-51.06	-42.22	12.39	64.52
	-512.34	-30.16	-33.00	-137.38	-38.85	27.48	-108.87	-104.35	-65.83	-1.98	-11.72	-12.37	-12.51	-43.63	-40.89	12.98	68.72
	-484.80	-46.06	-32.67	-120.26	-51.19	-31.68	-126.70	-89.82	-10.88	40.99	-17.67	-29.16	-3.69	-26.07	-35.54	16.29	78.90
1871–1881																	
MALE	-455.95	-276.74	17.15	87.15	-115.78	-213.45	-131.14	-54.89	-.87	15.37	37.72	39.14	-18.25	-35.73	-39.46	-10.09	43.93
	-642.09	-267.48	8.95	84.99	-113.23	-218.36	-142.69	-57.31	9.54	28.47	46.63	34.76	-21.16	-29.56	-37.80	-11.62	43.77
	-604.04	-245.18	-9.43	76.71	-110.13	-227.22	-167.72	-66.85	30.41	58.41	65.62	26.45	-24.31	-15.15	-32.25	-12.19	46.78
FEMALE	-601.97	-193.54	-17.32	-46.66	-37.19	91.54	-40.27	-175.98	-73.99	3.24	-.89	-25.50	-46.95	-67.40	-42.27	11.40	59.80
	-588.93	-199.51	-16.48	-40.27	-46.55	53.31	-52.12	-153.25	-69.28	21.67	1.67	-29.01	-45.53	-63.75	-43.59	10.92	62.84
	-557.47	-212.80	-13.84	-27.15	-64.87	-26.46	-82.55	-112.44	1.61	61.81	7.60	-34.90	-41.15	-54.32	-43.23	13.18	72.01
1881–1891																	
MALE	-1127.75	-265.80	-21.00	9.45	-128.81	-197.84	-157.07	-105.97	-65.28	-14.80	-3.81	-2.52	-55.48	-79.48	-49.37	-18.27	6.28
	-1122.44	-246.54	-33.83	-.43	-122.37	-198.43	-171.05	-110.33	-36.55	-.53	9.63	-8.27	-62.66	-72.40	-46.37	-22.56	.24
	-1105.78	-203.40	-63.64	-27.05	-112.02	-199.05	-200.34	-122.69	-19.50	31.13	38.26	-17.23	-72.88	-57.02	-38.63	-29.62	-12.10
FEMALE	-862.50	-141.92	24.74	-36.69	-45.47	57.58	-83.59	-219.10	-97.81	4.86	-25.12	-110.89	-122.48	-83.83	-40.37	17.76	39.83
	-988.56	-145.70	26.67	-32.13	-56.15	10.98	-101.81	-182.56	-65.44	18.98	-18.04	-109.77	-124.75	-85.05	-44.02	17.28	42.95
	-812.15	-155.22	31.45	-21.64	-77.75	-89.60	-147.68	-113.54	1.34	51.01	-.82	-103.37	-126.77	-85.73	-47.63	20.74	53.05
1891–1901																	
MALE	716.84	-249.61	27.85	252.69	235.79	98.26	-40.84	-95.60	60.30	174.26	135.92	82.73	12.61	-26.77	-1.99	22.67	28.59
	721.54	-224.20	6.89	231.35	250.69	107.63	-56.18	-101.05	70.90	195.47	158.78	73.07	-1.91	-19.47	-.11	14.78	14.92
	738.09	-164.12	-42.67	178.55	280.45	127.92	-87.67	-113.30	93.17	241.30	206.78	57.98	-26.14	-5.27	4.65	.49	-14.03
FEMALE	956.88	-236.32	59.14	160.41	159.26	325.37	140.98	-66.82	76.63	129.03	52.66	-24.80	-39.29	9.33	43.75	64.10	102.44
	977.89	-237.09	62.29	163.19	145.62	261.12	108.14	-13.37	122.48	145.49	72.72	-13.60	-43.47	1.29	33.50	62.00	105.58
	1036.96	-240.82	69.61	171.88	118.24	120.06	30.14	93.64	218.99	183.46	119.50	17.05	-51.52	-15.60	22.29	62.77	117.23
1901–1911																	
MALE	-1531.35	-233.51	-9.98	30.40	-26.81	-142.55	-319.98	-320.06	-85.38	47.94	-29.44	-71.59	-90.98	-101.19	-31.35	13.66	39.45
	-1337.31	-199.14	-32.32	1.09	-9.87	-125.97	-337.31	-330.17	-77.55	71.00	-1.31	-87.90	-115.99	-90.66	-25.79	2.81	21.70
	-1343.00	-119.30	-84.14	-68.32	22.25	-93.78	-372.24	-349.75	-61.67	119.12	56.73	-114.19	-159.34	-71.50	-14.65	-16.96	-15.25
FEMALE	-938.74	-195.91	8.55	56.89	-45.53	-5.74	-180.31	-340.14	-119.73	11.55	-105.53	-150.06	-80.13	-35.28	43.80	81.11	115.76
	-923.68	-194.22	11.99	56.89	-61.73	-82.30	-222.36	-262.22	-57.50	21.51	-81.83	-136.53	-93.59	-50.24	31.13	77.67	119.65
	-872.23	-193.36	19.28	55.76	-95.45	-250.04	-319.05	-106.57	70.69	46.05	-26.23	-98.52	-116.93	-80.77	10.28	77.73	134.90

Age-Band in Years

DUMFRIES

	TOTAL	<5	<10	<15	<20	<25	<30	<35	<40	<45	<50	<55	<60	<65	<70	<75	75+
1861-1871																	
MALE	-4210.48	-430.95	-215.93	-506.91	-1007.32	-1032.54	-774.31	-573.49	-68.52	5.17	-32.96	-112.27	-52.89	40.76	-31.31	57.94	325.07
	-4235.90	-443.63	-218.42	-494.90	-984.16	-1047.58	-794.91	-369.17	-73.84	1.25	-19.05	-89.99	-40.69	33.55	-52.41	42.33	315.70
	-4294.89	-473.11	-223.19	-468.50	-930.33	-1072.67	-833.67	-372.00	-99.24	-7.46	17.27	-27.55	-2.30	15.16	-106.62	2.38	290.97
FEMALE	-3116.08	-391.32	-210.63	-333.94	-352.17	-127.21	-359.23	-602.47	-332.67	-151.90	-231.87	-219.03	-105.75	-24.76	-94.92	38.03	383.76
	-3095.41	-392.73	-219.77	-320.47	-377.22	-191.12	-545.43	-544.43	-321.73	-161.73	-209.81	-176.40	-91.55	-60.88	-77.75	37.19	338.43
	-3028.98	-397.17	-239.03	-291.39	-441.77	-338.34	-308.81	-410.21	-299.18	-192.64	-144.39	-35.30	-42.62	-91.24	-108.35	31.99	279.45
1871-1881																	
MALE	-2321.31	-223.02	-135.09	-391.06	-711.55	-573.51	-376.12	-171.77	41.24	9.55	3.42	-21.75	-58.09	-29.08	-53.78	64.32	304.99
	-2332.90	-221.55	-135.89	-390.99	-697.49	-581.13	-398.85	-174.45	43.25	15.77	18.00	-15.76	-58.18	-29.12	-64.35	55.02	302.82
	-2361.90	-225.36	-138.30	-385.19	-661.44	-594.99	-444.35	-185.49	37.47	27.00	51.33	7.51	-49.20	-32.91	-93.53	31.12	294.64
FEMALE	-2452.24	-189.39	-209.68	-448.10	-311.51	61.06	-239.08	-493.59	-291.03	-129.45	-147.01	-190.23	-104.54	-27.56	-90.04	30.43	327.46
	-2428.26	-184.22	-216.35	-446.66	-334.40	-.09	-235.00	-427.65	-262.92	-132.71	-128.37	-162.55	-101.61	-44.44	-96.98	29.45	314.23
	-2362.11	-177.16	-230.00	-332.98	-386.91	-132.06	-217.56	-283.14	-204.19	-143.66	-77.82	-73.79	-84.46	-93.37	-117.86	24.29	268.56
1881-1891																	
MALE	-3827.55	-521.54	-277.46	-409.49	-735.43	-754.41	-605.83	-414.28	-150.12	-48.44	-55.25	-6.41	-9.72	-63.27	-61.50	48.06	237.56
	-3824.11	-500.99	-276.88	-626.56	-734.24	-751.05	-631.92	-427.61	-138.08	-25.13	-36.26	-22.01	-27.23	-54.38	-59.72	45.01	242.93
	-3821.45	-466.27	-273.60	-653.28	-728.13	-747.40	-683.91	-452.54	-118.50	19.68	2.03	-47.90	-38.40	-41.44	-61.09	36.69	252.62
FEMALE	-3700.30	-517.16	-406.48	-417.80	-193.06	96.59	-324.72	-463.20	-514.93	-233.96	-228.04	-221.31	-144.17	-67.64	-64.81	61.92	280.56
	-3480.75	-503.28	-411.12	-426.31	-208.48	45.17	-332.80	-710.0	-464.93	-216.55	-216.55	-217.01	-159.82	-106.29	-76.71	59.38	280.23
	-3637.15	-478.19	-419.18	-444.89	-239.13	-56.05	-337.82	-532.46	-360.30	-218.52	-189.90	-201.11	-191.39	-135.08	-109.05	49.62	266.31
1891-1901																	
MALE	-2061.68	-281.68	-85.74	-239.59	-495.08	-417.13	-318.70	-274.11	-137.04	-18.78	18.46	68.44	37.68	-75.77	-76.50	34.16	199.69
	-2043.59	-237.82	-86.35	-278.15	-508.63	-398.44	-348.58	-302.11	-111.48	26.12	41.82	22.20	-4.51	-54.57	-56.92	39.65	214.19
	-2012.06	-152.08	-81.47	-349.39	-542.45	-367.62	-403.03	-345.95	-58.70	112.02	83.77	-71.41	71.02	-18.90	-19.88	51.02	243.02
FEMALE	-1385.73	-327.79	-210.18	-133.66	33.39	378.36	80.89	-643.20	-390.64	-84.24	-68.48	-90.59	-46.59	-23.93	-16.45	80.88	238.28
	-1366.25	-308.07	-212.76	-158.10	28.20	334.79	-110.83	-557.25	-307.58	-64.49	-61.51	-115.99	-84.65	-42.19	-38.04	74.25	257.99
	-1332.36	-286.01	-215.01	-208.65	23.38	264.10	-155.79	-385.30	-135.32	-10.33	-54.82	-190.11	-172.67	-84.41	-91.77	55.70	294.66
1901-1911																	
MALE	-2983.31	-264.54	-156.98	-221.45	-306.41	-263.37	-382.12	-465.59	-304.32	-106.28	-78.13	45.36	-10.15	-208.06	-126.69	49.39	216.16
	-2541.37	-193.24	-156.19	-286.70	-341.63	-228.05	-418.35	-511.73	-259.06	-53.90	-52.57	-38.43	-81.33	-169.23	-81.12	67.00	243.16
	-2464.34	-41.01	-142.77	-418.06	-438.11	-165.86	-347.42	-578.58	-160.81	102.84	-11.69	-213.71	-232.65	-101.18	10.24	104.85	297.59
FEMALE	-2618.75	-314.14	-235.59	-105.35	28.78	181.06	-347.70	-886.74	-565.64	-206.30	-164.64	-155.72	-151.03	-122.89	40.53	162.69	216.93
	-2616.43	-284.99	-239.87	-143.72	42.67	158.00	-397.21	-787.17	-446.30	-176.58	-175.48	-229.42	-223.98	-142.12	8.31	150.57	270.84
	-2630.59	-213.00	-239.09	-535.98	79.39	146.41	-475.59	-596.65	-201.38	-90.48	-216.84	-434.28	-393.46	-178.54	-67.16	120.80	365.26

Age-Band in Years

DUNBARTON

		TOTAL	<5	<10	<15	<20	<25	<30	<35	<40	<45	<50	<55	<60	<65	<70	<75	75+
1861-1871																		
MALE		-1823.91	-667.90	-62.80	130.52	-318.58	-569.44	-417.36	-175.98	-47.42	14.64	13.41	-12.73	6.66	44.77	51.83	71.46	115.01
		-1815.30	-653.53	-67.84	108.10	-322.13	-544.30	-406.59	-198.41	-63.69	16.21	9.80	-13.66	14.11	49.73	60.70	79.20	117.02
		-1800.70	-624.70	-77.36	63.01	-330.23	-495.93	-385.13	-239.52	-94.02	18.70	2.69	-15.72	27.66	58.67	77.48	93.75	119.96
FEMALE		-1212.95	-471.08	-37.56	70.05	-180.96	-340.98	-327.20	-180.94	-39.82	12.93	-30.31	-57.16	23.59	94.29	38.41	46.13	167.68
		-1215.43	-464.94	-36.73	58.10	-157.73	-294.90	-340.95	-236.68	-60.48	7.39	-34.37	-57.93	22.67	97.33	48.63	53.59	171.57
		-1220.35	-452.59	-34.45	34.54	-112.42	-173.99	-367.60	-346.41	-101.17	-3.81	-43.10	-60.52	20.36	103.61	68.99	68.34	179.88
1871-1881																		
MALE		-1792.89	-642.57	-126.89	79.30	-255.14	-537.29	-316.49	-49.93	-10.84	11.97	-16.46	-75.52	-45.63	34.36	31.74	29.03	97.49
		-1775.73	-632.86	-123.11	61.51	-288.36	-518.39	-297.92	-64.56	-28.13	2.84	-32.14	-67.51	-28.43	31.55	38.64	42.45	108.67
		-1743.23	-612.83	-114.58	25.09	-296.03	-481.88	-261.66	-91.57	-60.47	-14.43	-61.90	-53.26	3.62	26.53	52.08	68.10	129.77
FEMALE		-1250.33	-518.37	-217.52	-6.59	-36.43	-340.11	-337.21	-34.92	47.96	65.92	24.34	-44.58	-19.25	42.96	-10.24	6.86	126.86
		-1252.35	-511.12	-214.77	-16.62	-5.15	-256.39	-331.01	-108.31	2.63	47.65	9.42	-48.86	-18.07	46.33	3.99	17.82	130.12
		-1256.07	-496.05	-208.13	-37.47	54.64	-89.92	-317.21	-253.48	-86.91	11.61	-21.21	-58.75	-15.98	53.51	32.61	39.67	137.00
1881-1891																		
MALE		-3383.11	-1087.35	-343.15	55.69	-319.11	-754.62	-667.60	-263.36	-76.06	-35.67	-26.17	-83.13	-50.08	75.86	70.75	41.67	79.23
		-3357.62	-1101.39	-326.09	50.93	-347.66	-748.61	-637.21	-269.30	-97.30	-57.97	-54.55	-52.87	-9.14	62.85	71.48	61.03	98.19
		-3307.58	-1128.55	-290.72	39.94	-405.29	-736.02	-578.15	-280.25	-137.24	-99.56	-108.08	2.47	67.49	39.22	73.42	98.38	135.35
FEMALE		-2376.24	-785.90	-274.01	-23.21	-61.05	-406.84	-542.91	-124.89	73.09	-42.89	-55.10	-72.66	-92.83	17.11	-28.51	-25.90	90.25
		-2377.57	-783.39	-272.51	-29.86	-22.55	-277.93	-509.19	-244.86	-17.08	-74.43	-79.83	-93.34	-80.02	25.97	-3.32	-7.63	92.39
		-2379.52	-777.44	-268.20	-44.62	50.72	-21.13	-440.44	-482.94	-195.06	-136.16	-130.54	-96.85	-54.85	44.53	47.62	28.90	96.96
1891-1901																		
MALE		-1176.86	-661.46	-80.48	254.99	-207.04	-528.77	-343.19	-24.47	109.38	-17.91	-33.95	-71.73	.71	176.61	100.00	31.20	119.24
		-1142.65	-677.71	-49.55	273.88	-256.91	-554.31	-299.94	-8.31	86.75	-57.52	-74.36	-10.15	73.46	146.72	85.94	55.60	145.76
		-1077.09	-749.44	13.83	310.01	-355.70	-601.97	-216.63	21.75	43.57	-131.26	-150.43	103.09	209.88	91.07	58.94	102.90	192.90
FEMALE		-520.77	-561.96	-160.92	-75.15	-197.80	-373.20	-156.00	345.38	350.92	-14.47	6.72	74.84	44.83	73.29	-6.84	-5.85	135.43
		-517.65	-563.65	-160.98	-73.95	-162.70	-221.47	-100.15	161.93	202.72	-44.33	-11.22	91.76	85.00	96.55	30.28	18.80	133.77
		-511.97	-566.38	-160.19	-72.81	-95.63	81.19	11.87	-202.60	-89.17	-101.95	-49.46	121.95	163.91	143.88	105.30	67.82	130.27
1901-1911																		
MALE		-4329.24	-926.29	-242.53	-225.63	-1113.81	-1587.80	-824.08	39.50	86.73	-50.79	-48.65	-99.74	-12.01	242.80	223.95	78.65	131.46
		-4278.85	-1008.55	-191.54	-171.51	-1181.95	-1656.97	-770.20	90.56	70.21	-120.25	-115.63	3.88	101.06	192.14	195.44	111.15	173.31
		-4180.99	-1171.97	-87.96	-65.13	-1314.34	-1787.91	-668.02	186.98	38.18	-249.47	-241.28	194.91	314.19	98.69	141.17	174.61	258.36
FEMALE		-3592.58	-642.79	-234.64	-427.05	-1048.29	-1374.03	-542.80	547.57	354.91	-139.30	-70.75	99.57	1.28	-20.73	9.79	45.56	189.09
		-3572.00	-651.06	-356.92	-414.91	-1014.30	-1175.40	-422.01	324.16	140.31	-192.20	-128.10	117.74	60.05	11.57	61.46	80.47	189.14
		-3531.21	-668.45	-361.58	-589.74	-953.10	-777.79	-184.67	-120.70	-280.13	-293.82	-206.27	148.24	174.93	77.54	166.64	150.53	189.19

Age-Band in Years

EDINBURGH (MIDLOTHIAN)

	TOTAL	<5	<10	<15	<20	<25	<30	<35	<40	<45	<50	<55	<60	<65	<70	<75	75+
1861-1871																	
MALE	-10589.1	-4181.19	-777.96	672.54	-934.49	-2421.41	-1606.31	-56.84	-214.98	-189.97	-358.05	-551.09	-384.81	-4.60	186.45	235.41	398.21
	-10524.0	-4055.56	-790.75	523.14	-971.43	-2243.63	-1511.52	-594.57	-327.26	-202.32	-410.45	-572.01	-354.66	14.05	249.84	293.25	429.92
	-10411.9	-3803.18	-811.91	223.07	-1053.98	-1904.28	-1321.69	-638.92	-532.47	-232.03	-516.02	-619.67	-306.73	47.21	372.73	402.90	483.03
FEMALE	-8604.39	-4407.34	-965.83	1256.91	394.92	-2257.44	-2428.82	-767.74	-198.87	-146.72	-310.10	-475.25	-191.66	195.40	20.81	92.02	585.31
	-8694.34	-4343.92	-947.13	1161.30	631.85	-1729.53	-2532.51	-1250.15	-403.40	-232.46	-376.94	-515.17	-226.58	203.26	93.33	150.67	623.01
	-8892.61	-4216.35	-907.18	972.06	1101.65	-676.48	-2736.82	-2208.68	-810.08	-403.40	-524.85	-625.93	-306.24	229.98	239.70	266.98	713.02
1871-1881																	
MALE	-12068.5	-4329.04	-1224.99	445.21	-809.30	-2636.89	-1923.76	-638.43	-586.11	-264.16	-284.97	-492.51	-303.48	170.65	299.10	277.43	432.73
	-11978.6	-4283.71	-1209.16	340.85	-803.15	-2505.72	-1797.47	-942.21	-707.38	-318.24	-375.04	-440.29	-195.48	157.36	338.70	332.13	490.21
	-11807.9	-4191.08	-1170.31	127.98	-1038.81	-2251.14	-1547.25	-1128.32	-932.43	-424.13	-549.52	-530.05	1.05	132.08	415.34	495.97	602.68
FEMALE	-10049.9	-4450.97	-1388.95	1019.25	431.36	-2679.47	-2461.84	-372.70	-10.77	-268.15	-236.62	-271.68	-96.30	276.56	-3.49	-5.78	469.63
	-10119.0	-4412.88	-1376.19	946.52	680.18	-2018.75	-2460.91	-1023.15	-381.13	-386.12	-327.79	-287.10	-73.00	314.53	110.31	77.75	498.92
	-10268.9	-4331.52	-1345.03	795.36	1163.17	-700.59	-2448.72	-2313.47	-1117.22	-620.54	-521.69	-340.15	-32.33	398.30	339.14	242.72	563.69
1881-1891																	
MALE	-13588.6	-4739.96	-1902.94	138.82	-1735.60	-3317.80	-3020.35	-944.51	-496.76	-288.72	-112.10	-275.22	35.14	626.58	571.31	347.41	526.14
	-15475.3	-4790.76	-1847.62	120.48	-1853.72	-4290.47	-2872.47	-976.73	-613.17	-390.91	-232.76	-133.63	231.95	569.76	566.31	433.30	605.11
	-15258.3	-4892.03	-1728.24	78.66	-2094.73	-4232.23	-2581.46	-1033.58	-632.08	-585.58	-463.74	123.87	598.11	464.43	557.04	599.44	763.81
FEMALE	-6638.64	-4799.20	-2068.04	334.49	-31.46	-3080.24	-2195.69	740.82	917.40	350.64	546.83	474.29	389.81	594.98	180.84	127.04	786.83
	-6676.56	-4789.15	-2061.01	323.06	164.33	-2352.29	-2115.28	-59.33	386.51	254.22	491.48	530.31	515.39	682.01	327.18	226.44	799.57
	-6762.48	-4762.42	-2040.83	250.01	536.75	-1038.98	-1941.53	-1648.70	-667.26	62.63	367.33	623.33	761.84	863.12	623.56	422.83	825.84
1891-1901																	
MALE	-12006.2	-3491.53	-929.43	266.51	-2760.40	-5612.74	-3065.97	132.76	308.27	-73.97	282.66	147.33	292.65	1004.09	612.26	263.91	617.42
	-11856.3	-3612.30	-855.78	331.77	-2929.17	-5709.45	-2894.84	203.16	211.17	-245.78	108.09	385.39	582.15	892.13	559.83	364.91	733.46
	-11559.5	-3854.33	-638.02	457.64	-3265.77	-5888.83	-2563.79	332.82	24.74	-569.32	-223.41	822.29	1127.07	687.44	458.24	563.29	970.43
FEMALE	-10845.2	-3796.06	-1240.77	993.51	-107.37	-3880.61	-2919.65	447.27	218.92	-717.57	-117.89	46.02	-171.12	124.84	-293.52	-161.91	730.76
	-10842.6	-3803.64	-1236.08	998.24	75.80	-3084.06	-2599.20	-449.50	-529.08	-902.81	-253.36	99.05	236.38	236.38	-104.24	-35.87	730.96
	-10844.4	-3814.60	-1222.58	999.63	424.78	-1491.01	-1954.45	-2234.11	-2006.53	-1267.59	-536.09	186.93	379.24	467.16	281.28	214.69	728.90
1901-1911																	
MALE	-15854.8	-3382.05	-1709.67	-572.21	-404.27	-8101.05	-4389.86	202.39	648.06	212.66	547.81	522.86	666.35	1474.19	1120.43	488.51	821.02
	-15652.4	-3534.82	-1589.81	-653.13	-4592.17	-8274.24	-4196.89	336.63	564.98	1.44	363.85	821.14	1016.19	1306.71	997.91	595.03	956.73
	-15235.4	-3841.71	-1538.70	-219.44	-4944.78	-8605.26	-3826.01	666.69	400.70	-394.69	13.88	1368.63	1680.48	1005.22	769.97	808.78	1240.80
FEMALE	-10949.2	-3259.83	-1819.15	408.47	-1286.43	-6269.38	-4194.77	763.24	632.05	-471.51	509.01	1134.32	530.42	504.13	359.60	333.96	1176.62
	-10888.2	-3272.30	-1812.56	429.73	-1182.85	-5490.61	-3767.63	-314.19	-332.93	-605.43	447.66	1284.02	852.42	677.99	578.25	474.37	1145.90
	-10775.5	-3298.94	-1798.43	472.65	-984.80	-3931.52	-2920.62	-2462.20	-2228.94	-864.77	390.74	1559.21	1489.13	1035.12	1029.12	753.62	1076.11

Age-Band in Years

ELGIN (MORAY)

	TOTAL	<5	<10	<15	<20	<25	<30	<35	<40	<45	<50	<55	<60	<65	<70	<75	75+
1861-1871																	
MALE	-2152.63	-313.23	-94.18	-88.16	-457.84	-651.22	-444.44	-210.26	-51.32	-7.50	1.52	-1.21	-7.46	13.92	-8.58	33.31	136.02
	-2134.36	-304.52	-100.18	-94.32	-460.34	-653.23	-452.33	-211.97	-41.84	3.04	4.55	-5.62	-6.22	19.89	-7.01	34.78	140.97
	-2088.13	-284.31	-111.64	-108.29	-467.09	-656.62	-466.97	-220.52	-22.69	27.90	10.96	-15.55	-2.03	34.68	-.99	40.31	154.70
FEMALE	-1812.63	-282.42	-128.54	-117.01	-206.17	-272.62	-342.34	-289.66	-133.89	-93.44	-38.51	3.49	-16.56	-12.17	-63.65	6.89	173.98
	-1805.55	-287.74	-128.70	-112.14	-208.18	-286.08	-350.46	-293.34	-124.13	-74.85	-40.23	-4.87	-13.77	-5.65	-61.88	8.38	178.90
	-1788.28	-298.58	-126.94	-103.39	-212.87	-315.59	-370.38	-304.63	-103.04	-35.40	-45.30	-22.97	-7.37	10.06	-55.53	13.33	190.34
1871-1881																	
MALE	-1310.46	-8.61	13.32	-113.57	-385.01	-616.21	-447.03	-125.00	37.47	70.46	32.58	29.79	23.51	8.42	-18.72	32.41	155.74
	-1300.21	.50	7.74	-121.05	-386.47	-617.79	-453.31	-129.11	45.89	80.23	38.55	25.07	21.64	13.33	-17.74	31.94	156.37
	-1272.79	23.57	-3.16	-140.38	-394.00	-620.42	-466.42	-129.21	62.42	103.03	50.87	15.26	20.67	25.18	-13.40	33.56	159.71
FEMALE	-958.89	61.29	-2.80	-170.97	-341.60	-306.21	-240.23	-160.74	-27.31	23.12	26.88	5.34	-10.11	.87	-29.19	32.81	179.96
	-948.06	57.83	-.75	-166.70	-350.68	-334.85	-250.68	-148.10	-9.30	40.61	29.67	1.40	-8.54	4.46	-29.92	33.12	184.38
	-920.09	50.66	6.32	-159.50	-371.88	-393.01	-275.29	-127.28	29.08	79.20	34.03	-7.57	-4.37	14.22	-27.76	36.87	186.19
1881-1891																	
MALE	-2579.97	-238.46	-78.58	-149.10	-533.81	-802.86	-420.78	-282.10	-57.76	26.92	10.41	13.13	-9.16	-26.23	-34.60	26.66	156.34
	-2575.69	-226.20	-84.20	-159.53	-534.18	-801.35	-427.96	-281.99	-30.74	37.92	19.90	6.23	-15.34	-20.72	-32.66	24.42	152.74
	-2560.03	-194.44	-96.32	-187.45	-541.42	-798.17	-441.43	-290.73	-17.62	62.88	39.01	-7.14	-23.24	-8.12	-26.35	23.28	147.24
FEMALE	-1417.66	-111.59	-53.31	-198.15	-315.36	-229.56	-224.16	-249.45	-131.76	-18.70	-16.82	-43.04	-34.94	-44.42	-12.45	67.23	176.78
	-1408.01	-112.58	-29.61	-197.07	-329.77	-267.34	-237.17	-220.24	-104.11	-4.73	-12.00	-45.24	-37.18	-44.18	-14.97	68.34	179.93
	-1379.70	-114.88	-19.44	-196.03	-362.83	-344.97	-267.59	-167.35	-45.97	28.00	-3.93	-50.45	-39.82	-40.44	-14.75	70.92	189.80
1891-1901																	
MALE	-999.70	-51.67	44.60	-62.98	-351.02	-469.32	-294.70	-69.11	31.18	46.69	40.29	61.38	12.20	-51.22	-36.48	29.94	120.52
	-1000.42	-36.12	39.07	-77.64	-349.82	-462.98	-303.60	-75.72	35.50	60.51	54.87	51.83	1.24	-43.69	-31.87	26.10	111.91
	-992.20	4.70	25.91	-116.80	-355.29	-451.23	-320.05	-91.43	62.14	91.03	84.12	34.28	-13.73	-27.03	-19.47	23.55	97.12
FEMALE	-608.12	42.46	66.05	-196.79	-286.34	-13.67	-44.95	-205.23	-98.50	32.75	-11.75	-67.29	-19.45	-26.75	-40.21	66.10	195.45
	-596.56	43.81	71.75	-199.35	-306.33	-66.86	-69.93	-161.09	-57.33	46.14	-1.68	-64.54	-23.81	-28.26	-63.34	65.68	198.68
	-559.51	45.58	85.41	-204.78	-331.38	-178.70	-127.33	-80.84	28.01	79.93	17.13	-58.69	-28.73	-26.11	-41.10	72.38	210.73
1901-1911																	
MALE	-2062.28	-213.55	-117.43	-86.70	-248.40	-502.95	-521.51	-294.87	-72.61	11.02	-15.52	-44.15	-56.15	-73.27	-21.83	63.83	131.80
	-2066.78	-195.69	-122.92	-105.97	-246.28	-489.84	-530.02	-305.97	-70.36	27.72	3.84	-57.33	-73.04	-63.60	-14.51	58.53	118.69
	-2061.90	-148.48	-137.81	-157.17	-250.18	-464.41	-544.01	-328.79	-68.15	44.21	43.11	-81.37	-42.93	-63.93	3.03	54.09	94.98
FEMALE	-1562.33	-115.67	-67.31	-214.22	-280.67	-72.75	-217.10	-374.48	-194.34	-9.63	-54.05	-165.33	-108.74	-13.73	18.75	95.09	231.84
	-1547.70	-111.51	-59.95	-220.67	-304.21	-66.86	-154.06	-310.87	-136.29	.09	-63.69	-161.77	-118.99	-19.46	14.64	93.94	234.44
	-1495.51	-104.97	-63.98	-232.34	-356.57	-285.11	-323.00	-192.26	-14.76	28.62	-24.64	-154.21	-133.90	-24.17	17.82	101.39	246.55

FIFE

Age-Band in Years

	TOTAL	C5	C10	C15	C20	C25	C30	C35	C40	C45	C50	C55	C60	C65	C70	C75	75+
1861-1871																	
MALE	-3862.32	-606.29	96.18	-264.10	-1564.32	-1943.86	-1038.87	-77.54	254.50	298.10	199.94	10.36	9.96	.74	-57.41	180.77	639.55
	-3894.51	-595.83	90.56	-290.02	-1575.13	-1939.68	-1020.66	-49.94	261.14	289.38	199.11	9.69	6.25	-7.47	-68.21	173.28	623.03
	-3977.47	-575.81	82.91	-341.85	-1600.96	-1933.52	-979.83	12.05	274.62	267.05	193.67	6.84	-5.74	-27.58	-90.65	156.64	582.64
FEMALE	-2093.70	-509.37	-11.90	-206.62	-463.33	-301.26	-502.32	-525.04	-116.40	-14.58	-104.40	-183.34	-72.81	47.20	-72.98	167.00	794.44
	-2115.94	-503.24	-12.94	-212.80	-464.36	-288.96	-495.37	-527.70	-132.75	-24.44	-94.57	-181.29	-149.28	39.28	-81.53	163.43	800.38
	-2163.07	-489.57	-12.53	-226.29	-468.14	-260.63	-477.75	-529.16	-164.22	-46.55	-79.12	-184.11	-116.65	23.87	-98.42	155.25	810.94
1871-1881																	
MALE	-3988.48	-549.08	-95.90	-496.99	-1437.27	-1568.14	-876.50	-131.00	161.12	202.05	143.29	-18.43	-80.90	4.14	-45.69	156.46	644.35
	-4017.67	-541.61	-88.09	-515.40	-1454.54	-1566.57	-857.60	-102.77	167.24	189.97	137.24	-25.31	-89.26	-4.67	-55.20	152.43	636.47
	-4063.77	-525.59	-66.59	-555.09	-1498.87	-1564.63	-812.87	-42.36	177.58	162.00	119.37	-42.86	-105.86	-23.61	-73.07	147.35	621.33
FEMALE	-2742.95	-529.77	-149.28	-395.58	-555.28	-26.54	-491.52	-676.56	-298.94	-147.70	-127.96	-142.09	-144.95	.28	-49.01	134.53	657.43
	-2761.09	-522.44	-146.21	-403.72	-365.12	-15.33	-475.40	-673.19	-310.52	-156.87	-127.60	-147.49	-53.66	-2.51	-53.66	130.68	658.12
	-2802.41	-505.05	-135.44	-424.13	-391.43	16.77	-435.00	-668.09	-333.24	-175.98	-135.99	-169.83	-162.73	-4.78	-59.81	122.89	659.72
1881-1891																	
MALE	-5881.95	-648.34	-213.33	-611.09	-1314.95	-1323.47	-980.51	-533.38	-206.19	-112.96	-134.95	-184.49	-194.03	-132.01	-100.67	158.14	650.30
	-5899.59	-660.95	-190.33	-619.00	-1338.28	-1312.76	-954.59	-517.46	-208.64	-130.38	-152.24	-194.69	-199.57	-137.98	-103.58	162.94	657.92
	-5931.55	-683.43	-137.52	-640.38	-1398.35	-1291.05	-893.53	-483.86	-217.41	-167.40	-193.23	-221.34	-208.06	-147.55	-106.01	178.76	678.82
FEMALE	-4826.80	-618.81	-264.61	-546.34	-431.85	-4.63	-607.32	-1064.03	-601.84	-307.43	-233.72	-265.53	-289.41	-146.21	-140.12	99.50	595.36
	-4841.45	-613.23	-258.85	-555.72	-636.64	41.00	-572.78	-1077.65	-622.75	-325.81	-257.09	-285.90	-263.94	-141.66	-133.38	100.13	592.81
	-4875.11	-598.56	-242.13	-580.66	-456.76	146.81	-491.96	-1112.79	-664.15	-360.70	-318.31	-343.20	-303.68	-125.07	-112.98	102.50	586.52
1891-1901																	
MALE	-1741.61	-421.93	-145.11	-284.50	-761.29	-492.99	-234.19	-15.44	76.56	-37.07	-13.90	-119.32	-138.85	71.82	31.26	145.36	597.98
	-1741.24	-479.86	-72.84	-259.07	-799.52	-493.60	-201.89	-10.92	61.20	-63.77	-45.53	-113.29	-120.38	62.22	30.34	163.36	622.71
	-1730.68	-592.11	18.72	-215.14	-891.41	-493.02	-128.52	-3.87	24.46	-116.58	-114.49	-111.76	-81.20	49.96	33.94	207.94	680.38
FEMALE	492.51	-298.11	-122.77	-387.82	150.94	819.15	179.74	246.52	-62.78	21.27	21.77	-92.10	-108.14	14.68	-128.18	61.92	689.26
	490.00	-297.54	-116.74	-391.85	151.60	911.74	232.67	-324.43	-141.51	1.15	17.79	-113.92	-94.07	36.46	-101.05	72.43	682.86
	482.15	-293.50	-100.60	-405.70	141.30	1115.30	352.52	-493.64	-256.83	-34.18	-118.37	-179.97	-64.96	91.92	-35.72	96.16	668.03
1901-1911																	
MALE	-6678.48	-775.21	-226.44	-538.02	-1273.45	-1048.06	-673.17	-294.07	-333.25	-649.84	-532.68	-565.70	-450.06	-38.39	17.39	133.84	568.23
	-6651.76	-925.72	-121.86	-438.25	-1356.42	-1112.98	-621.97	-267.21	-355.63	-721.22	-616.59	-489.39	-357.44	-73.09	10.59	175.11	628.48
	-6579.16	-1254.23	93.62	-245.37	-1531.57	-1234.19	-513.44	-222.44	-405.40	-854.60	-781.53	-357.77	-176.36	-127.32	8.32	265.83	755.29
FEMALE	-5142.84	-525.63	-215.14	-904.44	-619.10	123.68	-374.77	-412.99	-564.72	-638.63	-381.48	-279.61	-348.27	-229.52	-199.79	28.14	619.43
	-5140.07	-536.33	-214.25	-891.17	-604.90	319.66	-238.99	-779.73	-714.79	-699.77	-474.69	-314.35	-331.42	-187.64	-137.48	57.71	608.08
	-5128.89	-557.78	-211.51	-865.78	-585.32	732.21	44.33	-1133.09	-1008.02	-811.41	-687.86	-412.42	-254.03	-65.36	3.51	121.85	581.79

FORFAR (ANGUS)

Age–Band in Years

	TOTAL	<5	<10	<15	<20	<25	<30	<35	<40	<45	<50	<55	<60	<65	<70	<75	75+
1861–1871																	
MALE	-6358.67	-2311.12	29.55	456.04	-1571.57	-2523.15	-1099.62	-11.60	140.81	96.42	61.78	139.86	-17.60	-63.78	-89.59	58.25	366.65
	-6205.73	-2274.14	8.42	445.40	-1569.81	-2528.76	-1164.96	-74.69	172.32	166.03	80.07	114.27	-2.86	-34.17	-55.68	88.22	424.61
	-5804.64	-2185.55	-35.08	416.95	-1568.15	-2534.33	-1320.18	-239.05	234.95	330.16	121.31	56.57	37.60	85.62	31.89	172.90	589.75
FEMALE	-5326.78	-2005.79	-176.13	898.83	1210.06	216.90	-1168.59	-1314.17	-503.74	115.67	123.57	11.71	-283.17	-470.75	-293.75	-3.17	315.76
	-3232.75	-2033.89	-175.96	918.25	1214.93	166.01	-1250.02	-1410.58	-429.87	258.47	86.81	-52.78	-255.32	-402.97	-247.91	26.40	354.68
	-3016.66	-2094.37	-171.12	955.07	1228.73	54.76	-1446.41	-1640.60	-271.42	565.72	7.77	-186.04	-189.52	-247.37	-133.50	104.86	450.77
1871–1881																	
MALE	-7944.26	-2331.28	-322.45	224.90	-1663.28	-2778.71	-1309.53	-244.19	51.63	240.72	93.52	63.78	-11.02	-95.01	-181.04	-4.11	339.81
	-7821.39	-2275.92	-354.81	196.29	-1660.31	-2804.46	-1377.08	-296.71	88.21	318.45	134.59	48.49	-1.80	-51.82	-153.32	8.76	360.05
	-7513.28	-2136.40	-424.81	119.02	-1667.18	-2818.48	-1532.19	-453.38	162.60	500.51	227.18	19.65	32.84	50.25	-81.44	49.90	418.64
FEMALE	-5627.95	-2126.54	-531.28	525.24	561.95	-407.80	-1382.33	-1309.23	-501.09	97.85	32.83	-254.05	-352.93	-440.57	-253.07	136.30	376.80
	-5709.14	-2150.90	-523.34	544.00	548.28	-522.86	-1488.62	-1340.30	-407.12	226.72	35.11	-273.65	-324.23	-393.47	-218.26	167.34	412.18
	-5414.52	-2205.91	-498.51	581.45	515.30	-788.54	-1755.43	-1436.26	-204.43	512.88	49.66	-298.50	-251.50	-281.48	-123.05	258.61	511.22
1881–1891																	
MALE	-12191.9	-2063.21	-911.44	-253.07	-2054.53	-3677.34	-2361.78	-932.05	-388.61	92.54	78.23	-25.67	-50.00	-32.44	-47.07	68.88	365.65
	-12106.4	-1990.05	-953.97	-304.29	-2048.05	-3678.23	-2423.65	-846.93	-347.00	175.14	144.67	-34.20	-54.90	1.46	-28.81	61.58	342.83
	-11885.1	-1803.54	-1050.77	-447.56	-2055.37	-3677.58	-2358.36	-1057.00	-259.81	366.62	292.27	-41.97	-43.98	79.27	19.79	57.57	297.29
FEMALE	-6793.71	-2062.45	-1066.79	-77.75	-475.97	-1312.80	-1710.82	-1464.24	-461.33	107.60	-107.13	-390.66	-350.23	-262.73	-64.77	276.16	650.20
	-8658.26	-2076.45	-1052.18	-84.28	-513.73	-1498.57	-1831.67	-1398.03	-345.92	205.48	-57.95	-339.17	-330.75	-250.51	-50.91	301.90	679.79
	-8298.02	-2112.15	-1013.54	-54.59	-601.50	-1924.67	-2143.20	-1286.59	-63.08	436.56	67.04	-259.45	-273.54	-215.07	4.78	388.17	772.22
1891–1901																	
MALE	-8722.25	-1720.76	-249.86	64.41	1912.75	-3826.70	-2481.15	-563.33	105.87	597.99	531.42	186.40	17.06	65.74	7.49	87.61	368.33
	-8679.36	-1623.43	-301.46	-17.35	1898.53	-3809.60	-2539.25	-589.95	142.68	684.22	626.17	170.58	-15.67	95.62	20.89	63.37	312.34
	-8543.49	-1381.19	-422.96	-227.58	1894.64	-3777.65	-2859.54	-654.47	218.20	878.10	829.07	155.02	-53.65	160.74	59.14	28.93	198.98
FEMALE	-3779.98	-1693.46	-184.59	429.78	-326.75	-1149.07	-1268.74	-959.66	3.45	606.54	98.92	-321.72	-159.04	-65.23	15.58	391.77	822.25
	-3633.63	-1693.04	-164.27	429.03	-394.03	-1414.40	-1419.11	-781.78	159.93	672.78	202.36	-235.43	-154.91	-109.72	5.32	411.11	852.52
	-3210.12	-1700.32	-115.99	433.32	-544.52	-2026.29	-1801.58	-435.50	508.45	845.00	448.40	-12.83	-125.46	-152.59	18.24	493.67	957.85
1901–1911																	
MALE	-13328.1	-1605.91	-481.19	-307.38	-1794.78	-3888.90	-3424.62	-1553.25	-494.65	220.69	96.67	-212.57	-281.78	-183.56	-4.76	91.16	296.71
	-13531.6	-1482.09	-541.83	-421.88	-1774.69	-3846.09	-3481.43	-1594.54	-465.90	311.43	216.90	-241.26	-347.43	-147.80	16.98	51.01	208.06
	-13478.1	-1175.36	-489.99	-715.11	-1760.82	-3746.83	-3594.46	-1649.53	-409.90	510.75	471.15	-275.58	-442.21	-74.23	70.92	-10.48	30.55
FEMALE	-9472.77	-1758.74	-441.11	-153.68	-1071.02	-1926.91	-2126.91	-1853.50	-640.77	149.02	-256.08	-488.65	-630.32	-67.27	307.18	565.19	960.26
	-9326.57	-1746.79	-416.59	-170.37	-1157.49	-2153.25	-2302.90	-1572.48	-428.17	173.26	-222.02	-569.52	-655.31	-129.29	276.19	577.77	990.38
	-8859.61	-1734.38	-363.99	-192.85	-1347.69	-2907.24	-2746.77	-911.58	41.53	267.38	93.23	-269.44	-479.40	-247.56	256.72	656.96	1105.65

Age-Band in Years

HADDINGTON (EAST LOTHIAN)

	TOTAL	<5	<10	<15	<20	<25	<30	<35	<40	<45	<50	<55	<60	<65	<70	<75	75+
1861-1871																	
MALE	-1571.79	-210.78	-84.43	-64.32	-187.41	-201.21	-206.38	-214.49	-81.59	-9.27	-59.29	-44.32	-27.17	-39.70	-63.02	3.69	117.91
	-1344.26	-215.60	-87.74	-52.36	-190.52	-220.27	-218.24	-203.81	-59.15	2.74	-55.09	-52.34	-32.61	-33.02	-60.84	5.87	128.73
	-1261.79	-222.00	-95.26	-30.22	-198.11	-256.86	-244.99	-188.23	-12.33	31.19	-48.60	-73.81	-43.91	-14.39	-49.49	19.01	166.21
FEMALE	-1231.64	-87.78	-96.05	-241.26	-66.34	273.57	-61.46	-21.80	-258.59	-94.08	-48.46	-46.85	-76.50	-119.70	-82.82	33.22	163.27
	-1218.67	-98.66	-94.49	-230.63	-87.22	219.96	-60.89	-384.93	-226.12	-62.25	-54.91	-67.48	-75.37	-106.33	-85.81	28.19	168.26
	-1202.52	-120.69	-90.62	-210.50	-123.57	117.78	-89.33	-330.49	-161.40	7.12	-75.25	-124.66	-70.40	-70.20	-86.40	20.75	185.34
1871-1881																	
MALE	-1079.65	-100.01	-49.08	-115.13	-65.78	-42.06	-171.43	-206.78	-80.39	-18.40	-34.82	-11.44	-52.43	-86.33	-104.11	-37.36	95.90
	-1067.40	-95.56	-57.18	-109.61	-60.42	-55.20	-188.15	-200.02	-61.43	-4.50	-23.89	-21.68	-63.74	-78.68	-102.23	-40.88	95.78
	-1031.82	-81.11	-75.80	-102.35	-51.84	-80.46	-223.59	-191.64	-22.97	26.63	-2.65	-43.23	-65.93	-60.06	-93.88	-43.97	99.04
FEMALE	-948.90	20.48	-60.16	-246.30	-42.49	293.68	5.02	-336.18	-206.42	-59.24	-49.14	-89.86	-100.97	-131.65	-75.58	36.45	113.45
	-932.73	12.21	-58.93	-238.61	-65.87	220.90	-7.09	-279.77	-159.44	-30.26	-65.87	-100.75	-101.78	-125.69	-82.88	30.60	118.53
	-900.07	-5.42	-56.05	-217.28	-109.52	74.03	-42.21	-176.48	-65.07	32.08	-61.41	-128.49	-103.52	-107.25	-72.18	22.94	135.74
1881-1891																	
MALE	-1573.47	-186.41	-89.11	-79.15	-35.23	-40.05	-283.01	-370.32	-148.62	-8.66	-38.10	-57.53	-68.88	-106.67	-90.20	-17.56	46.01
	-1572.65	-171.48	-104.68	-84.08	-20.24	-42.57	-303.30	-369.69	-132.65	10.14	-18.03	-72.26	-88.28	-96.94	-87.82	-26.47	35.69
	-1564.08	-134.80	-140.32	-99.69	7.93	-47.14	-344.80	-372.15	-160.80	50.32	22.57	-98.58	-122.02	-76.29	-80.74	-42.18	14.58
FEMALE	-2102.63	-174.59	-125.26	-199.68	-25.55	251.60	-175.66	-537.91	-323.24	-134.80	-154.12	-232.06	-193.51	-141.84	-77.40	27.10	114.28
	-2087.27	-179.32	-123.49	-193.02	-48.33	167.39	-198.91	-658.51	-261.59	-113.22	-144.89	-236.06	-201.60	-145.39	-88.77	20.51	117.94
	-2047.61	-190.58	-119.70	-178.34	-92.84	-8.97	-258.19	-505.87	-137.36	-66.96	-123.49	-240.46	-215.02	-148.77	-106.12	12.91	132.13
1891-1901																	
MALE	-1245.91	-183.86	-10.17	-90.64	33.44	158.99	-185.53	-532.63	-132.63	-14.14	-68.44	-88.23	-121.29	-120.53	-86.53	-37.34	33.73
	-1260.45	-153.52	-34.24	-109.46	57.70	168.42	-211.44	-341.31	-121.19	10.80	-37.65	-108.78	-150.89	-107.00	-81.73	-52.55	12.41
	-1285.34	-81.69	-89.88	-156.09	104.71	185.93	-264.70	-361.19	-99.08	62.19	25.26	-142.32	-202.13	-80.87	-71.33	-81.59	-32.58
FEMALE	-338.69	-27.07	62.74	-92.45	51.71	446.33	100.02	-344.39	-160.21	15.98	-88.68	-195.25	-149.44	-63.15	-36.23	22.85	98.55
	-342.25	-29.85	64.97	-88.76	26.21	336.78	52.31	-242.82	-77.97	38.34	-43.37	-165.41	-161.76	-74.83	-55.02	15.44	101.49
	-292.73	-38.41	69.38	-78.34	-25.10	102.61	-58.31	-43.43	87.12	85.20	-4.56	-153.02	-190.96	-96.95	-81.13	8.21	114.98
1901-1911																	
MALE	-1439.65	-321.71	5.12	71.40	264.81	388.30	-162.48	-516.12	-235.84	-52.09	-132.16	-170.95	-197.69	-228.78	-140.57	-22.54	11.66
	-1462.22	-281.11	-28.24	37.55	297.29	408.77	-193.40	-532.86	-227.74	-20.72	-89.11	-192.59	-234.07	-209.73	-130.93	-43.82	-21.51
	-1504.37	-184.06	-107.83	-44.62	363.59	447.68	-258.03	-567.39	-212.68	43.53	.20	-223.70	-296.20	-175.19	-112.45	-85.32	-91.90
FEMALE	-1492.93	-310.30	73.48	-125.58	-108.31	431.81	46.98	-511.62	-236.79	-12.63	-202.74	-323.71	-217.20	-135.71	-30.60	61.94	108.05
	-1473.90	-312.63	76.34	-122.08	-132.72	302.71	-18.69	-375.52	-130.97	-.84	-169.99	-304.92	-239.62	-159.52	-52.53	55.14	112.03
	-1408.62	-322.75	81.72	-109.09	-182.86	19.70	-170.16	-104.41	81.46	24.59	-69.83	-244.92	-276.30	-207.97	-89.90	52.77	131.32

Age-Band in Years

INVERNESS

	TOTAL	<5	<10	<15	<20	<25	<30	<35	<40	<45	<50	<55	<60	<65	<70	<75	75+
1861-1871																	
MALE	-2718.02	-101.81	155.49	-157.65	-552.06	-752.63	-880.13	-554.24	-178.72	-19.25	33.48	48.41	-7.80	-62.44	-173.38	7.51	472.20
	-2747.90	-134.10	166.55	-122.47	-545.12	-773.37	-882.88	-533.76	-176.91	-32.32	39.27	59.90	-14.96	-72.01	-182.31	-2.98	459.58
	-2820.89	-203.28	185.51	-59.24	-526.13	-812.72	-882.55	-486.83	-174.22	-64.53	48.82	83.17	-32.40	-94.26	-202.81	-27.41	427.98
FEMALE	-1187.31	-70.39	280.95	105.45	53.56	51.91	-470.93	-695.61	-458.79	-279.39	-186.41	-32.61	39.92	65.86	-233.95	-41.04	694.16
	-1189.98	-68.97	281.06	103.80	16.34	-1.45	-445.00	-617.3	-441.57	-297.91	-173.61	-12.70	41.73	58.33	-247.10	-54.87	669.24
	-1203.46	-66.22	276.25	102.57	-51.88	-103.63	-388.52	-457.77	-411.81	-337.72	-146.21	24.44	41.80	40.09	-278.94	-85.99	640.07
1871-1881																	
MALE	-2665.29	-198.33	-136.23	-247.62	-107.94	-131.56	-561.01	-497.27	-156.06	-158.08	-203.09	-150.31	-142.49	-144.95	-230.40	-21.76	421.82
	-2696.32	-229.91	-132.57	-213.27	-86.39	-145.86	-569.38	-480.41	-150.81	-167.68	-197.12	-150.18	-160.46	-150.40	-257.46	-34.71	410.28
	-2769.48	-305.88	-131.73	-132.65	-26.39	-172.35	-584.77	-441.53	-140.67	-194.12	-185.74	-146.53	-200.82	-164.98	-256.24	-66.98	381.71
FEMALE	-2030.59	-52.05	38.27	-140.53	-63.53	172.45	-335.49	-751.14	-480.47	-393.42	-261.33	-62.82	-25.82	38.81	-235.54	-48.20	610.23
	-2042.45	-51.68	32.21	-139.71	-91.08	111.36	-339.95	-663.81	-448.49	-403.33	-248.75	-31.24	28.65	28.65	-255.43	-66.18	597.07
	-2080.56	-52.05	10.75	-133.12	-132.21	-6.58	-304.29	-682.06	-391.37	-430.90	-219.84	-49.63	-45.71	2.86	-304.37	-109.10	567.06
1881-1891																	
MALE	-2908.51	-201.97	-58.19	-65.29	-30.46	-373.49	-1052.88	-877.83	-200.23	-66.86	-137.24	-36.96	-9.44	-61.74	-143.44	15.23	392.29
	-2941.44	-224.00	-62.04	-31.78	4.93	-383.83	-1074.81	-869.94	-191.01	-65.38	-124.48	-48.38	-38.31	-61.28	-148.45	-1.84	379.16
	-3026.02	-286.49	-73.98	56.31	100.36	-405.68	-1124.55	-849.25	-171.36	-72.36	-100.00	-63.80	-102.84	-66.49	-165.02	-46.15	345.28
FEMALE	-1774.84	-156.07	-49.21	-112.30	116.77	310.80	-354.79	-840.05	-471.83	-259.09	-200.12	-101.78	-71.57	-4.91	-157.73	18.98	558.06
	-1795.63	-158.92	-61.57	-106.38	105.05	244.04	-353.06	-742.56	-420.03	-259.90	-189.11	-102.19	-87.54	-20.00	-185.47	-3.63	547.65
	-1860.45	-166.25	-96.67	-87.85	99.97	114.42	-350.99	-536.90	-326.90	-275.69	-160.88	-97.43	-123.71	-58.56	-254.00	-59.20	520.17
1891-1901																	
MALE	-2354.31	68.51	34.71	-293.12	-481.99	-518.39	-732.59	-494.26	61.61	52.26	-120.86	-58.33	-10.28	-92.04	-123.70	50.02	304.16
	-2399.80	43.14	14.84	-255.34	-421.71	-517.95	-764.21	-493.52	77.16	64.13	-103.05	-86.36	-55.76	-85.78	-127.13	25.99	285.76
	-2520.78	-41.85	-29.66	-144.01	-266.07	-519.34	-836.05	-485.07	113.49	75.01	-68.44	-129.89	-157.18	-83.79	-145.40	-39.15	236.64
FEMALE	-472.96	72.86	95.81	-153.63	55.93	493.43	-111.17	-651.98	-304.14	-100.80	-92.07	-78.90	-90.58	31.39	-61.06	26.26	395.71
	-504.90	61.40	70.29	-134.89	69.83	412.50	-137.06	-539.52	-225.89	-87.71	-74.20	-86.14	-118.44	7.75	-103.42	-5.43	385.98
	-601.61	36.84	7.62	-89.96	121.07	255.47	-178.18	-293.65	-85.81	-84.21	-24.42	-85.50	-179.06	-55.37	-212.87	-87.51	333.93
1901-1911																	
MALE	-3507.25	189.97	-67.49	-350.87	-304.94	-434.78	-845.76	-767.29	-272.69	-187.51	-412.01	-289.22	-158.33	-172.24	21.94	188.53	355.44
	-3565.95	162.52	-100.43	-303.84	-218.44	-430.72	-894.33	-775.74	-251.55	-165.45	-391.08	-334.05	-219.08	-158.60	22.48	159.02	333.34
	-3727.81	60.00	-165.52	-156.92	-2.74	-431.17	-1007.09	-783.11	-198.71	-136.78	-350.96	-406.80	-335.62	-147.60	6.46	75.96	272.79
FEMALE	-1058.33	142.98	52.86	-263.63	29.64	482.36	-277.48	-891.14	-519.34	-230.31	-263.58	-207.28	-229.21	-43.70	336.05	366.90	456.55
	-1112.42	118.28	15.66	-224.83	77.98	392.57	-334.51	-766.01	-414.25	-214.98	-252.74	-231.20	-276.96	-76.49	287.12	332.95	454.99
	-1272.72	70.72	-65.67	-144.39	194.72	221.23	-435.12	-693.83	-229.00	-217.64	-213.41	-258.49	-382.31	-165.63	159.10	244.74	442.26

Age-Band in Years

KINCARDINE

	TOTAL	<5	<10	<15	<20	<25	<30	<35	<40	<45	<50	<55	<60	<65	<70	<75	75+
1861-1871																	
MALE	-1344.29	-75.52	-66.54	-190.20	-409.19	-433.69	-270.05	-104.93	15.68	51.13	15.30	-23.64	4.90	-8.98	-43.02	33.64	160.83
	-1355.12	-78.17	-66.72	-188.58	-410.76	-439.19	-267.49	-95.93	20.05	48.45	15.89	-22.71	2.53	-12.49	-47.90	31.59	156.32
	-1384.33	-63.75	-66.95	-185.30	-450.29	-260.82	-72.45	28.69	42.08	16.40	-2.70	-20.40	-58.18	21.95	142.83		
FEMALE	-653.53	10.29	-26.21	-197.21	-204.14	-53.22	-106.91	-139.80	-51.95	-47.46	-76.43	-78.15	-53.44	4.65	-27.92	7.52	166.86
	-862.41	10.14	-26.50	-195.40	-209.66	-43.52	-98.66	-120.41	-53.55	-55.68	-71.58	-74.11	-55.90	-1.21	-34.67	3.38	164.91
	-883.45	10.20	-26.82	-192.04	-220.78	-62.59	-80.11	-79.61	-57.29	-73.82	-62.25	-66.67	-61.99	-13.91	-49.21	-6.27	159.72
1871-1881																	
MALE	-1222.48	-11.11	-91.60	-183.02	-240.11	-282.45	-276.70	-168.97	-39.12	24.33	-10.80	-31.72	-11.92	-28.03	-40.41	27.99	141.17
	-1255.28	-11.94	-91.73	-182.17	-240.68	-285.43	-273.76	-159.08	-35.59	21.08	-11.22	-34.14	-17.08	-30.65	-44.09	24.22	136.99
	-1265.25	-13.51	-91.61	-180.80	-242.98	-291.32	-265.80	-138.02	-29.16	13.13	-13.53	-39.50	-27.49	-36.63	-51.77	16.51	127.23
FEMALE	-991.89	84.52	-73.51	-297.31	-208.13	40.58	-65.18	-190.59	-120.34	-67.81	-92.14	-69.80	-17.73	.24	-31.10	16.23	120.18
	-1001.47	84.60	-73.42	-296.23	-214.13	31.18	-57.07	-170.68	-117.46	-93.25	-90.58	-70.51	-21.49	-4.26	-37.44	11.34	117.91
	-1025.28	85.28	-72.60	-294.68	-226.70	16.31	-36.91	-129.91	-112.47	-105.66	-89.61	-74.63	-30.38	-13.74	-50.87	-.16	111.44
1881-1891																	
MALE	-1408.16	-84.46	-15.65	-108.27	-249.01	-391.50	-377.47	-159.88	-12.94	-1.12	-27.76	-44.80	-11.55	-20.16	-46.41	15.79	129.02
	-1417.53	-81.24	-17.37	-110.02	-247.41	-390.40	-376.32	-155.46	-11.70	-2.89	-27.70	-51.31	-19.20	-19.76	-47.62	13.25	127.63
	-1441.78	-73.17	-21.03	-114.94	-246.00	-387.97	-371.74	-146.12	-10.65	-8.16	-29.78	-64.92	-33.62	-19.23	-49.92	9.29	126.18
FEMALE	-866.09	-31.95	-2.64	-181.45	-185.39	28.90	-47.01	-171.03	-104.75	-60.93	-75.06	-78.87	-49.91	-6.40	-30.25	7.01	123.66
	-877.58	-31.85	-2.29	-181.35	-191.77	19.07	-42.99	-153.32	-96.11	-62.44	-75.80	-84.24	-54.54	-8.11	-34.89	2.23	121.82
	-906.87	-31.48	-1.17	-181.73	-205.23	5.27	-29.90	-119.52	-80.46	-66.88	-84.49	-99.63	-64.79	-10.57	-43.85	-8.56	116.14
1891-1901																	
MALE	-1219.50	-70.51	-49.93	-222.43	-290.74	-225.14	-184.07	-65.11	35.65	-9.37	-31.49	-55.16	-51.34	-32.08	-65.98	-7.67	83.88
	-1230.54	-56.90	-57.41	-231.39	-285.38	-219.67	-187.82	-46.91	34.60	-6.71	-27.46	-64.54	-60.97	-27.04	-62.89	-10.45	80.39
	-1252.13	-21.42	-76.12	-254.87	-276.75	-208.97	-193.90	-55.31	30.09	-2.73	-21.43	-82.80	-77.34	-16.50	-55.56	-13.89	75.39
FEMALE	-831.18	14.41	51.84	-312.40	-250.45	223.50	112.67	-78.12	-102.30	-115.43	-88.02	-119.87	-104.16	-62.69	-57.88	-12.28	70.00
	-842.39	13.15	52.57	-311.57	-257.58	204.74	105.50	-61.47	-86.39	-112.13	-89.60	-125.76	-107.65	-60.65	-59.80	-14.75	66.99
	-872.46	8.99	54.02	-309.00	-271.97	170.53	92.85	-34.57	-58.08	-106.75	-97.57	-141.69	-113.55	-52.80	-60.58	-18.29	66.00
1901-1911																	
MALE	-1616.32	-231.45	-119.62	1.17	-51.01	-195.85	-351.40	-278.36	-131.79	-123.82	-88.42	-60.46	-56.41	-49.73	-29.10	27.84	122.10
	-1627.46	-221.17	-128.40	-11.56	-39.25	-181.12	-357.85	-287.60	-132.24	-115.80	-80.80	-74.47	-70.79	-42.17	-23.91	24.01	115.65
	-1647.19	-195.54	-151.00	-44.39	-15.29	-149.42	-369.06	-306.29	-135.12	-100.18	-67.25	-101.61	-55.52	-27.07	-12.81	18.94	104.42
FEMALE	-755.67	-168.91	-23.06	-103.92	69.78	324.07	113.90	-283.18	-222.15	-177.96	-105.60	-74.23	-100.60	-44.25	9.86	47.88	122.25
	-763.30	-168.10	-21.24	-103.79	77.47	298.59	99.42	-257.04	-192.32	-81.49	-107.14	-81.49	-108.25	-45.03	7.18	43.90	120.18
	-783.45	-167.27	-17.03	-101.85	-63.67	248.88	70.69	-210.58	-133.61	-154.81	-114.78	-100.06	-122.40	-43.25	5.49	36.99	113.84

Age-Band in Years

KINROSS

	TOTAL	<5	<10	<15	<20	<25	<30	<35	<40	<45	<50	<55	<60	<65	<70	<75	75+
1861-1871																	
MALE	-290.38	9.96	-20.51	-60.05	-89.06	-74.63	-62.68	-29.47	-1.95	6.04	17.46	3.02	-1.04	-1.34	-18.66	-1.23	33.75
	-293.52	1.11	-17.31	-49.24	-86.91	-82.78	-66.52	-25.47	.30	5.23	19.56	5.30	-2.49	-2.65	-20.44	-3.49	32.28
	-300.97	-17.39	-11.88	-27.11	-81.30	-78.35	-73.56	-17.35	4.54	3.19	23.64	9.89	-5.67	-5.40	-24.20	-8.47	28.45
FEMALE	-277.53	7.42	-62.00	-75.37	15.10	33.13	-43.81	-80.01	-42.07	-14.15	-22.65	-15.22	-5.04	-5.38	-13.73	1.95	42.31
	-274.15	6.50	-61.88	-73.93	4.99	17.06	-37.72	-57.78	-33.71	-15.34	-20.82	-11.54	-3.60	-5.92	-16.58	-1.64	37.77
	-268.94	4.53	-62.90	-70.60	-13.48	-18.16	-25.21	-13.56	-18.11	-17.64	-16.45	-4.62	-1.23	-7.62	-23.47	-9.37	28.95
1871-1881																	
MALE	-44.22	24.85	-22.38	-38.78	-4.12	11.14	-21.41	-29.78	-10.52	7.24	5.98	3.64	1.22	-4.71	-10.20	5.17	38.43
	-48.81	18.24	-21.87	-29.96	1.04	5.64	-25.81	-25.99	-7.45	7.49	8.80	2.92	-3.16	-5.03	-11.63	2.00	35.94
	-59.71	2.77	-22.25	-10.07	14.64	-5.14	-34.87	-18.17	-1.56	7.02	14.24	2.17	-12.30	-6.22	-14.98	-5.11	30.11
FEMALE	39.15	3.09	-16.30	-18.73	56.38	121.48	10.24	-84.93	-37.17	-11.11	-13.87	-18.76	-11.67	-2.71	.23	18.45	44.32
	39.73	2.51	-17.62	-17.37	49.38	102.61	12.84	-60.69	-25.62	-11.09	-11.15	-16.68	-12.81	-4.93	-4.65	14.03	40.98
	37.53	.97	-22.52	-13.38	38.50	64.95	17.78	-11.07	-4.06	-12.49	-4.31	-11.71	-15.76	-10.62	-16.35	3.85	33.77
1881-1891																	
MALE	-244.63	5.91	-18.60	-46.58	1.56	51.27	-22.95	-71.27	-34.62	-19.38	-15.99	-20.23	-20.92	-24.90	-26.17	-3.23	21.48
	-251.07	1.38	-21.21	-38.95	10.83	48.65	-28.85	-69.33	-31.25	-17.71	-12.50	-24.19	-28.47	-23.83	-26.62	-7.26	18.25
	-266.38	-12.06	-28.03	-18.98	34.81	42.93	-41.84	-64.89	-24.45	-15.90	-5.72	-30.65	-44.20	-22.81	-28.63	-16.71	10.76
FEMALE	-72.85	28.52	-19.28	-14.72	75.55	136.12	5.37	-126.98	-87.87	-27.07	-26.63	-31.26	-21.87	-1.89	11.49	11.47	16.21
	-75.48	27.47	-22.45	-12.61	72.67	116.44	4.04	-99.92	-72.42	-26.06	-23.33	-31.13	-26.19	-6.23	4.21	5.98	14.04
	-85.17	24.79	-31.51	-6.52	71.65	76.74	1.45	-42.91	-43.76	-27.00	-14.19	-28.44	-35.68	-17.30	-13.76	-7.33	8.59
1891-1901																	
MALE	-22.28	36.95	-16.90	-30.94	43.50	117.31	27.01	-44.53	-27.33	-20.98	-26.23	-18.82	-4.78	-20.12	-30.98	-5.77	20.36
	-30.92	33.76	-22.56	-43.25	58.13	116.79	18.35	-44.59	-23.44	-17.39	-21.49	-25.60	-15.27	-17.66	-31.02	-11.34	15.71
	-55.43	20.44	-34.89	-19.77	95.34	114.30	-1.75	-33.30	-14.56	-12.56	-11.99	-36.49	-38.02	-15.17	-33.69	-25.65	4.32
FEMALE	-28.93	20.59	-27.96	-31.89	86.52	181.19	11.22	-128.97	-78.50	-26.28	-10.20	-13.96	-20.13	-10.21	5.27	8.19	6.16
	-34.64	17.55	-34.33	-26.72	91.21	162.14	5.74	-99.75	-59.30	-26.22	-15.45	-28.05	-28.05	-17.31	-5.03	1.16	4.75
	-55.14	10.87	-50.05	-14.15	106.77	123.04	-4.92	-35.98	-25.39	-27.50	6.34	-13.66	-45.48	-36.15	-31.68	-16.93	-.27
1901-1911																	
MALE	-395.59	-16.19	-29.02	-57.19	20.38	102.03	-2.06	-113.20	-64.65	-44.87	-68.93	-39.14	-18.09	-33.02	-36.96	-7.59	14.92
	-406.68	-18.24	-38.53	-50.02	39.34	103.16	-13.00	-114.52	-59.31	-39.39	-63.40	-48.34	-31.22	-29.75	-37.01	-15.03	8.56
	-443.44	-31.94	-57.69	-24.83	86.58	103.78	-38.16	-114.66	-45.92	-31.38	-51.95	-62.76	-60.83	-27.53	-41.98	-35.69	-8.48
FEMALE	-255.70	-11.99	-39.06	-33.14	89.36	175.12	-18.67	-187.76	-81.67	-26.68	-56.56	-53.30	-36.11	-5.57	17.67	10.71	.95
	-253.33	-17.69	-46.78	-23.88	102.61	163.67	-21.91	-157.88	-60.67	-60.67	-52.23	-56.41	-47.29	-15.83	3.61	1.91	.43
	-277.52	-28.78	-63.87	-4.45	134.87	131.86	-34.12	-89.29	-24.69	-29.81	-35.70	-54.31	-71.87	-43.93	-34.65	-22.41	-4.35

Age-Band in Years

KIRKCUDBRIGHT

	TOTAL	<5	<10	<15	<20	<25	<30	<35	<40	<45	<50	<55	<60	<65	<70	<75	75+
1861-1871																	
MALE	-1277.91	-207.94	35.77	-26.05	-468.25	-695.28	-683.19	-64.87	133.61	96.93	54.90	6.73	31.15	77.92	26.03	40.55	164.08
	-1289.30	-212.02	37.94	-22.26	-456.44	-698.07	-498.14	-70.70	125.81	99.47	67.30	23.09	40.03	70.65	11.46	31.26	161.29
	-1316.94	-221.04	42.48	-14.10	-479.86	-701.15	-529.70	-90.47	101.32	107.74	66.06	69.51	66.06	50.13	-28.94	5.56	153.68
FEMALE	-1453.21	-202.29	-50.43	-32.34	-207.76	-281.39	-296.89	-279.71	-106.66	-6.90	-41.76	-103.18	-51.15	16.58	-33.07	29.60	196.14
	-1430.95	-202.34	-54.79	-26.81	-215.40	-306.08	-288.31	-253.81	-100.71	-10.97	-25.91	-71.60	-42.93	.04	-38.52	30.33	176.87
	-1359.27	-202.66	-63.87	-15.10	-239.94	-367.84	-259.01	-182.65	-83.43	-22.25	25.13	34.27	-14.80	-58.57	-55.94	29.45	115.95
1871-1881																	
MALE	-3323.78	-195.59	-232.93	-450.57	-679.73	-757.17	-510.16	-208.86	-48.57	-56.81	-91.06	-86.49	-69.91	-33.73	-52.57	10.05	140.31
	-3328.10	-193.19	-233.89	-452.20	-676.65	-755.03	-518.04	-216.76	-51.86	-53.90	-84.18	-80.58	-65.55	-33.08	-57.05	7.07	140.79
	-3339.06	-192.03	-236.79	-453.04	-666.87	-761.09	-532.26	-235.80	-64.16	-49.04	-67.82	-61.95	-51.51	-34.09	-71.22	-1.88	140.49
FEMALE	-3122.33	-163.04	-251.15	-427.38	-539.89	-422.35	-535.08	-302.31	-185.79	-114.23	-130.32	-154.39	-115.03	-51.76	-76.08	-8.50	173.57
	-3109.16	-159.42	-253.99	-427.56	-589.42	-444.02	-553.23	-280.87	-176.14	-118.88	-120.02	-134.95	-112.05	-61.02	-75.06	-5.53	165.02
	-3073.01	-154.33	-259.87	-425.67	-573.99	-494.28	-550.20	-239.03	-159.70	-131.61	-90.24	-73.02	-97.54	-89.74	-76.55	-1.21	134.97
1881-1891																	
MALE	-2252.40	-256.79	-191.68	-263.56	-436.17	-564.01	-475.52	-244.21	-47.54	19.95	13.68	33.33	57.52	-1.60	-31.95	27.56	108.61
	-2247.56	-248.91	-190.93	-271.86	-436.80	-561.46	-487.14	-255.23	-42.41	33.62	23.40	28.98	52.55	1.02	-32.67	26.35	111.94
	-2241.17	-235.71	-188.08	-284.77	-436.14	-558.03	-510.94	-270.60	-54.59	60.79	44.36	23.42	44.12	2.73	-38.01	22.16	118.31
FEMALE	-1788.39	-273.03	-180.93	-216.09	-280.91	-237.13	-228.13	-271.27	-59.12	33.78	-47.07	-40.39	-26.67	7.91	-8.19	28.94	147.89
	-1771.04	-267.50	-183.52	-221.06	-284.78	-230.80	-230.80	-244.06	-109.80	-31.57	-38.98	-33.12	-31.97	-2.20	-13.52	28.80	146.35
	-1730.06	-257.47	-188.07	-228.52	-292.44	-285.76	-229.10	-183.45	-66.43	-24.03	-18.72	-12.14	-42.77	-31.27	-31.10	25.57	133.65
1891-1901																	
MALE	-1776.83	-237.55	-79.71	-167.07	-414.40	-513.49	-334.29	-131.67	-27.66	19.97	-7.88	30.08	28.65	-30.82	-48.97	9.23	108.75
	-1786.69	-219.73	-78.91	-182.98	-422.93	-507.47	-348.19	-145.32	-14.77	41.82	1.46	10.81	12.42	-21.54	-39.50	12.78	115.38
	-1768.45	-185.08	-74.60	-212.36	-442.85	-498.15	-373.26	-166.19	12.14	83.80	18.22	-29.03	-22.06	-6.26	-21.62	19.99	128.85
FEMALE	-1659.23	-216.77	-130.51	-139.28	-277.77	-222.12	-225.79	-266.89	-121.69	-47.12	-35.16	-42.89	-47.05	-37.71	-33.52	35.52	149.51
	-1649.05	-205.27	-131.60	-151.57	-277.36	-253.86	-237.25	-236.06	-90.63	-39.51	-32.54	-54.61	-44.12	-46.06	-42.22	33.93	159.68
	-1631.20	-180.82	-132.27	-177.37	-273.52	-249.11	-252.73	-173.56	-24.76	-16.53	-30.58	-89.85	-104.73	-66.19	-65.55	27.79	178.59
1901-1911																	
MALE	-1809.19	-169.02	-117.28	-159.35	-364.96	-509.18	-371.44	-170.85	-61.85	-15.31	-9.28	69.05	55.12	-74.65	-48.04	42.41	95.44
	-1789.90	-143.40	-116.79	-184.56	-379.96	-495.33	-385.29	-189.26	-39.71	17.27	-.30	52.90	26.03	-57.38	-27.60	49.81	103.67
	-1754.63	-88.50	-111.19	-235.19	-620.40	-471.34	-406.27	-214.66	7.74	77.97	12.37	-43.93	-34.68	-26.00	14.50	66.22	120.72
FEMALE	-1473.18	-141.24	-149.38	-105.06	-125.71	-86.41	-208.71	-317.15	-183.07	-100.76	-100.31	-48.15	-71.24	-47.25	25.48	61.88	123.91
	-1488.77	-124.24	-150.88	-127.06		-116.35	-229.67	-281.13	-135.93	-67.40	-105.41	-103.42	-104.34	-54.75	12.01	58.25	149.92
	-1488.81	-81.95	-151.88	-180.31	-63.24	-68.70	-258.40	-212.77	-37.79	-46.66	-125.54	-203.97	-182.96	-68.60	-20.57	48.32	196.20

Age-Band in Years

LANARK & RENFREW

	TOTAL	<5	<10	<15	<20	<25	<30	<35	<40	<45	<50	<55	<60	<65	<70	<75	75+
1861-1871																	
MALE	-32720.8	-13900.2	-2799.91	2930.02	-1016.27	-6542.65	-4449.54	-1080.18	-1004.31	-882.43	-1550.82	-2097.57	-1527.62	-235.26	498.38	469.68	467.92
	-32478.4	-13541.2	-2832.13	2515.36	-1072.68	-5951.42	-4183.62	-1615.91	-1410.75	-893.52	-1705.22	-2145.86	-1400.76	-159.63	710.37	649.62	558.93
	-32023.7	-12821.1	-2885.92	1683.72	-1203.67	-3689.60	-2601.00	-2169.17	-924.37	-2001.91	-2242.93	-1174.56	-24.90	1107.60	986.53	726.06	
FEMALE	-24466.2	-13327.6	-2132.87	3648.05	-504.09	-7431.06	-5750.48	-721.83	452.05	531.67	-192.27	-981.03	-174.18	1124.72	325.91	-118.04	764.91
	-24651.9	-13170.7	-2091.72	3423.33	143.89	-5992.58	-4080.83	-2117.39	-91.97	337.72	-344.17	-1033.38	-234.14	1151.98	567.48	58.02	842.56
	-25032.2	-12856.9	-2003.18	2941.74	1415.05	-3145.03	-6720.68	-4849.50	-1168.02	-51.15	-657.78	-1160.45	-360.59	1210.92	984.38	404.14	1004.78
1871-1881																	
MALE	-38322.7	-17925.6	-5013.26	3148.39	-1708.46	-8651.59	-5725.04	-1878.79	-774.76	263.34	-386.33	-1378.56	-810.48	635.87	782.77	476.21	625.53
	-38055.1	-17799.0	-4963.06	2982.85	-1900.20	-8276.75	-5384.39	-2266.05	-1180.57	128.90	-638.74	-1193.77	-447.34	609.80	904.38	691.67	772.23
	-37547.3	-17525.7	-4841.77	2341.14	-2301.13	-7351.14	-4717.98	-2978.81	-1939.09	-128.16	-1117.69	-658.52	221.74	554.39	1128.17	1100.23	1066.82
FEMALE	-28930.3	-17157.9	-4350.91	3067.06	-1448.60	-9157.86	-5382.81	1390.68	1894.86	923.12	159.40	-403.74	152.03	1182.27	44.95	-357.82	535.00
	-29080.0	-17067.2	-4316.59	2904.59	-848.57	-7534.25	-5421.91	-288.01	967.14	661.07	-30.13	-393.23	235.03	1271.94	331.81	-143.75	592.13
	-29382.8	-16873.5	-4228.83	2565.63	344.74	-4304.47	-5467.78	-3605.79	-871.47	141.00	-422.75	-397.73	393.12	1456.29	902.23	277.31	709.23
1881-1891																	
MALE	-50504.2	-14280.0	-7199.24	-626.51	-5049.18	-13426.2	-9125.46	-1587.70	-758.40	-355.98	-290.45	-1245.46	-380.81	1557.00	1198.95	413.13	622.16
	-50166.9	-14402.9	-7039.79	-681.38	-5400.10	-13363.6	-8702.32	-1679.78	-1120.22	-656.35	-657.57	-793.09	242.91	1394.14	1199.23	667.15	826.74
	-49533.3	-14842.3	-6693.38	-809.51	-6116.43	-13228.1	-7876.16	-1901.99	-1799.73	-1222.18	-1352.59	36.01	1404.61	1084.67	1190.78	1154.27	1238.66
FEMALE	-38302.1	-12565.6	-6632.14	-1086.51	-4868.35	-11615.1	-6667.34	2277.74	441.01	85.46	-311.82	-196.40	778.68	-185.80	-461.82	812.74	
	-38390.6	-12531.7	-6605.86	-1163.26	-4349.20	-9902.62	-6402.61	-81.38	933.85	148.88	-200.09	85.87	948.19	181.91	-207.12	832.10	
	-38572.2	-12447.9	-6551.28	-1344.80	-3369.36	-6479.51	-5837.02	-3994.92	-1725.95	-425.16	-487.59	-12.83	639.17	1356.23	921.22	296.33	871.21
1891-1901																	
MALE	-34225.0	-11506.7	-3633.89	889.19	-4050.84	-10256.5	-5509.05	1022.60	43.77	-1676.03	-1014.23	-1499.88	-650.81	2007.55	946.45	-35.52	698.90
	-33776.2	-11925.5	-3326.27	1087.62	-4633.79	-10590.2	-4950.22	1256.31	-254.00	-2253.25	-1626.49	-684.95	323.79	1653.04	815.33	291.87	1046.55
	-32896.6	-12759.2	-2678.44	1464.34	-5794.38	-11207.1	-3870.85	1691.50	-818.96	-3333.71	-2781.53	812.15	2152.43	984.11	557.27	927.90	1747.90
FEMALE	-18399.5	-10105.6	-3510.61	-274.78	-3149.57	-7788.96	-2370.88	3229.45	-317.47	181.55	-121.64	396.13	331.98	687.99	-565.94	-797.63	831.65
	-18399.7	-10116.8	-3491.36	-274.71	-2717.22	-5844.71	-1619.84	3061.17	1377.74	-732.52	-106.55	543.16	338.98	962.62	-108.39	-492.65	821.34
	-18400.6	-10125.3	-3436.35	-296.04	-1903.62	-1946.89	-77.52	-1427.25	-2269.81	-1538.46	-723.20	781.09	1242.28	1527.11	820.97	112.93	799.42
1901-1911																	
MALE	-63329.6	-15394.3	-7510.62	-1980.92	-12423.7	-22489.3	-12918.4	-1454.07	-248.97	-691.74	579.46	507.69	1315.56	4152.42	3081.06	816.32	1349.95
	-62704.1	-15911.2	-7105.85	-1598.86	-13190.8	-23188.3	-12222.9	-834.30	-527.73	-1465.11	-124.37	1644.77	2613.14	3562.76	2689.59	1180.96	1778.02
	-61468.6	-16940.4	-6257.44	-855.57	-14710.1	-24503.7	-10889.5	312.76	-1028.14	-2922.11	-1453.97	3734.03	5061.42	2476.95	1940.96	1902.17	2663.95
FEMALE	-49077.4	-14480.8	-7666.05	-2737.34	-7721.23	-14640.4	-7430.59	2272.09	907.45	-2226.99	-287.72	1451.72	242.06	392.02	601.80	475.18	1771.44
	-48973.2	-14490.2	-7633.75	-2704.53	-7475.20	-12668.8	-6327.97	-343.54	-1452.31	-2595.63	-500.40	1749.96	979.30	803.82	1137.45	824.72	1725.87
	-48771.7	-14506.5	-7561.99	-2652.86	-7010.83	-8705.57	-4131.12	-5562.13	-6078.05	-3294.86	-996.43	2239.45	2428.61	1655.48	2239.44	1521.68	1623.90

Age-Band in Years

LINLITHGOW (WEST LOTHIAN)

	TOTAL	<5	<10	<15	<20	<25	<30	<35	<40	<45	<50	<55	<60	<65	<70	<75	75+
1861-1871																	
MALE	-1576.61	-493.43	-165.80	102.59	-58.90	-189.40	-247.85	-249.45	-130.43	-51.29	-92.50	-49.79	28.95	29.09	26.15	50.49	114.94
	-1571.02	-492.82	-171.99	89.40	-57.80	-170.65	-238.84	-259.92	-137.92	-49.77	-92.81	-50.06	32.33	31.70	30.20	53.78	114.11
	-1562.22	-491.74	-184.06	62.98	-56.07	-153.97	-220.41	-278.35	-151.55	-47.50	-93.95	-51.15	38.08	36.33	38.02	59.81	111.31
FEMALE	-993.73	-433.37	-159.38	-88.62	-199.57	42.66	87.01	-119.92	-106.76	-73.66	-66.73	-50.80	7.76	31.90	-24.77	17.57	142.95
	-993.38	-434.94	-161.13	-73.09	-198.03	54.88	88.30	-127.45	-109.89	-74.09	-65.98	-50.73	7.32	32.66	-23.67	18.18	144.29
	-993.79	-437.82	-164.29	-101.89	-194.70	79.66	90.86	-142.46	-116.10	-74.94	-65.48	-52.83	5.45	34.77	-21.36	19.34	148.01
1871-1881																	
MALE	-1222.73	96.48	-108.05	-181.96	-335.06	-447.40	-235.85	-13.83	34.32	11.26	-54.53	-76.12	-40.24	10.80	4.43	20.55	92.45
	-1218.99	93.50	-109.13	-180.55	-334.97	-445.54	-232.66	-18.05	28.99	9.72	-56.90	-73.36	-34.86	9.79	5.36	24.56	95.10
	-1213.36	87.35	-110.64	-177.82	-335.50	-442.27	-226.07	-25.18	19.16	6.34	-61.95	-68.85	-25.15	7.95	7.42	32.22	99.62
FEMALE	-960.68	197.50	-22.11	-394.70	-605.49	-290.86	30.00	41.96	31.26	-12.65	-48.16	-29.78	-28.17	.78	9.89	40.48	119.36
	-960.14	195.42	-22.71	-391.80	-607.82	-298.37	24.72	39.42	32.59	-8.00	-43.42	-26.95	-25.54	3.11	10.12	39.87	119.22
	-960.35	191.71	-23.38	-386.67	-613.02	-312.12	14.70	33.84	35.11	1.14	-35.31	-23.29	-20.87	8.51	11.15	38.74	119.40
1881-1891																	
MALE	-1662.39	-304.81	-117.06	-215.53	-249.21	-288.70	-213.01	-63.61	-26.72	-11.14	-31.01	-42.66	-21.29	21.75	21.16	16.43	63.01
	-1655.30	-507.86	-113.60	-213.08	-252.41	-290.45	-208.39	-63.78	-31.99	-16.63	-37.30	-36.80	-12.02	17.93	19.59	21.82	69.28
	-1641.37	-514.22	-105.94	-208.31	-259.47	-293.88	-199.02	-63.72	-40.89	-27.33	-49.78	-26.58	5.24	11.30	17.25	32.44	81.56
FEMALE	-1686.54	-431.45	-73.20	-671.73	-596.14	-213.29	38.98	19.49	-28.03	-28.17	-66.88	-31.71	.17	5.76	11.38	33.54	134.75
	-1696.70	-431.20	-72.14	-470.56	-599.12	-219.42	40.18	27.75	-23.61	-27.79	-67.84	-34.40	-1.25	5.75	10.43	32.38	134.14
	-1697.64	-430.18	-69.47	-469.09	-606.22	-229.95	43.58	43.15	-14.83	-26.93	-71.38	-41.62	-.09	6.74	9.47	30.27	132.91
1891-1901																	
MALE	-1141.71	-343.76	-299.15	-17.77	179.91	36.33	-117.12	-164.65	-103.99	-114.35	-125.47	-130.82	-92.71	15.81	31.82	27.80	76.43
	-1131.50	-339.90	-288.11	-9.29	169.22	30.18	-106.38	-160.16	-109.77	-126.51	-138.55	-115.77	-73.97	6.81	27.25	35.90	87.53
	-1111.43	-392.38	-265.11	7.57	147.74	18.66	-85.35	-151.88	-121.17	-149.53	-163.80	-88.58	-38.85	-8.97	19.81	51.66	108.75
FEMALE	-162.85	-1.70	39.02	-271.69	-395.31	105.47	293.83	94.41	7.64	-36.32	-202.58	-40.45	-38.83	-18.46	-5.57	42.62	100.92
	-158.99	-1.36	39.93	-272.54	-398.11	106.39	297.98	99.04	11.04	-38.95	-226.13	-44.08	-39.15	-16.79	-4.27	42.33	99.57
	-151.88	-.23	42.15	-275.05	-405.21	110.43	307.64	106.42	17.84	-39.77	-270.85	-53.63	-39.41	-11.98	-.13	42.20	96.59
1901-1911																	
MALE	-2578.83	-465.27	-281.31	-120.41	-121.87	-336.40	-403.57	-209.57	-190.53	-202.63	-202.58	-174.51	-88.79	62.11	75.56	23.61	77.34
	-2563.75	-498.52	-258.92	-96.56	-145.14	-379.95	-385.85	-193.69	-196.73	-226.25	-226.13	-141.95	-50.84	45.33	64.89	34.84	91.70
	-2553.33	-565.78	-213.06	-48.75	-190.51	-424.58	-351.82	-164.71	-209.36	-270.51	-270.85	-82.22	20.87	16.11	46.36	56.54	118.94
FEMALE	-1864.64	-152.66	-69.14	-578.30	-857.58	-191.20	192.98	71.30	-90.88	-96.88	53.37	-86.55	-65.73	-29.27	1.84	32.43	108.37
	-1863.31	-153.73	-68.40	-577.67	-858.47	-175.89	205.95	64.32	-55.36	-46.61	-94.60	-72.56	-82.26	-26.33	7.08	34.70	106.57
	-1859.94	-155.90	-66.77	-576.60	-861.65	-142.58	233.55	47.99	-67.77	-107.33	-120.29	-107.39	-78.29	-18.22	19.69	39.60	102.12

Age-Band in Years

NAIRN

	TOTAL	<5	<10	<15	<20	<25	<30	<35	<40	<45	<50	<55	<60	<65	<70	<75	75+
1861-1871																	
MALE	-295.24	-57.08	-13.66	48.14	3.73	-99.66	-119.85	-71.47	-2.11	3.64	-1.68	1.36	-21.40	-11.42	-.75	11.20	35.76
	-288.50	-53.44	-16.04	45.21	2.67	-99.43	-121.00	-72.48	.21	6.51	-1.29	-.23	-20.80	-9.54	.18	12.49	38.49
	-270.50	-45.21	-20.67	38.76	-.07	-98.81	-124.19	-76.14	4.77	13.28	-.51	-3.80	-18.99	-4.86	3.04	16.44	46.47
FEMALE	-167.99	-1.34	16.54	20.00	7.92	-38.24	-65.03	-51.81	-29.75	-16.65	-18.53	-19.01	-6.48	.88	-7.72	4.55	36.69
	-165.54	-2.96	16.48	21.71	8.67	-40.84	-67.86	-54.90	-27.89	-11.07	-19.42	-22.18	-6.01	2.58	-7.08	5.68	39.55
	-158.99	-6.26	17.24	24.71	9.61	-46.28	-74.75	-62.28	-23.56	.71	-21.75	-28.74	-4.68	6.87	-4.71	8.80	46.08
1871-1881																	
MALE	-399.62	-86.26	-26.07	26.62	-8.86	-114.24	-133.44	-61.99	-9.71	17.15	-1.83	-8.83	-6.46	-15.50	-6.63	9.45	26.97
	-395.12	-81.45	-28.01	22.81	-10.26	-113.94	-135.06	-63.05	-7.61	20.29	-.48	-10.12	-6.23	-13.83	-5.80	10.01	27.62
	-383.39	-69.58	-31.83	13.43	-14.86	-113.27	-138.72	-66.56	-3.47	27.87	2.49	-12.83	-4.79	-9.74	-3.29	12.04	29.71
FEMALE	-447.38	-27.72	-18.94	-52.65	-28.36	-37.04	-102.07	-65.59	-37.19	-18.60	-13.62	-24.68	-4.56	-8.56	-27.37	5.29	34.27
	-443.64	-28.85	-18.14	-51.43	-29.77	-43.19	-105.96	-85.50	-33.43	-13.48	-13.45	-26.30	-3.95	-6.99	-26.54	6.54	36.81
	-433.13	-31.28	-15.29	-49.57	-34.08	-56.10	-115.16	-87.06	-25.03	-1.93	-13.55	-29.70	-2.11	-2.76	-23.32	10.51	43.30
1881-1891																	
MALE	-469.45	-70.29	-14.53	22.02	-35.25	-132.84	-163.62	-97.99	-24.21	-.80	9.99	-5.56	-14.40	.21	-4.48	10.88	51.41
	-465.75	-65.24	-16.54	16.98	-36.71	-131.61	-164.77	-99.06	-22.39	2.57	12.42	-6.67	-14.80	1.73	-3.77	10.91	51.19
	-455.56	-51.90	-20.92	3.70	-62.22	-128.84	-166.71	-102.20	-18.86	10.61	17.55	-8.90	-14.23	5.42	-1.51	12.09	51.35
FEMALE	-104.47	-25.08	-5.57	6.63	-5.02	-21.72	-51.86	-49.44	-3.54	13.88	9.56	-10.14	-16.55	-3.39	-6.91	11.37	53.30
	-99.37	-25.31	-3.66	6.71	-8.94	-30.75	-56.59	-45.06	2.83	18.38	10.73	-10.45	-16.37	-2.58	-6.20	12.56	55.35
	-84.77	-25.86	1.61	6.29	-18.91	-49.99	-68.09	-38.58	17.01	29.52	12.49	-11.39	-15.22	.40	-2.45	17.07	61.34
1891-1901																	
MALE	-260.47	-49.60	1.84	17.59	-22.88	-107.14	-104.89	-38.86	3.14	31.26	22.44	.35	-20.68	-8.59	-3.50	.42	18.63
	-259.22	-43.62	.06	11.25	-24.63	-105.19	-106.01	-40.48	3.92	34.61	26.02	-.64	-21.76	-6.97	-2.32	-.04	16.58
	-253.36	-27.11	-4.62	-6.08	-31.24	-100.95	-107.47	-44.55	4.96	42.54	33.47	-2.44	-21.88	-2.98	1.17	-.63	13.18
FEMALE	-306.31	12.30	21.56	-53.20	-71.64	-46.09	-66.04	-66.76	-23.07	-1.06	2.93	-30.08	-41.04	-15.11	-11.12	8.25	53.87
	-300.67	13.01	24.25	-34.62	-77.95	-57.73	-71.79	-58.04	-14.56	2.01	4.93	-28.88	-41.22	-14.75	-10.04	9.84	55.49
	-282.92	14.11	30.78	-37.81	-93.16	-63.24	-86.20	-45.61	4.43	11.32	8.20	-26.80	-40.15	-11.86	-4.28	16.22	61.14
1901-1911																	
MALE	-424.11	-36.67	23.89	16.61	-43.92	-118.48	-129.34	-72.67	-29.35	9.52	11.62	-22.35	-30.17	-15.82	-2.85	3.04	12.83
	-422.92	-28.97	22.66	8.11	-46.74	-115.78	-130.41	-74.74	-29.18	13.27	16.75	-22.80	-31.62	-13.84	-1.12	2.15	9.35
	-415.57	-7.03	18.27	-15.51	-55.77	-109.98	-131.62	-79.49	-29.66	22.16	27.53	-23.26	-31.77	-8.99	3.73	2.53	3.29
FEMALE	-300.08	-13.74	10.03	-27.89	-63.82	-40.22	-34.94	-38.67	-8.02	-10.51	-31.29	-57.01	-41.76	-19.38	1.76	31.51	55.86
	-292.70	-12.06	13.31	-30.55	-72.25	-45.48	-42.69	-26.35	2.65	-9.15	-59.55	-52.89	-41.80	-19.67	3.34	33.66	56.80
	-268.49	-9.67	20.40	-33.27	-91.39	-90.38	-63.03	-5.49	26.77	-2.20	-32.72	-44.46	-39.55	-17.16	11.71	42.44	61.50

Age-Band in Years

ORKNEY

	TOTAL	<5	<10	<15	<20	<25	<30	<35	<40	<45	<50	<55	<60	<65	<70	<75	75+
1861–1871																	
MALE	-1417.10	-53.71	-57.76	-113.89	-401.12	-589.37	-399.76	-131.63	14.97	35.27	33.75	30.16	17.70	23.54	-16.26	12.33	128.69
	-1416.13	-38.95	-55.84	-107.98	-399.79	-563.26	-402.50	-131.39	15.24	35.94	36.82	33.32	17.76	23.28	-16.71	10.70	127.18
	-1414.84	-49.94	-52.55	-95.93	-396.30	-570.40	-407.34	-130.54	15.75	37.00	42.88	39.67	17.55	22.59	-17.93	6.99	123.66
FEMALE	-717.05	-50.96	-13.08	-40.02	-106.50	-135.91	-215.65	-185.61	-71.44	-30.11	-1.14	-25.06	-7.95	11.88	-28.61	34.39	148.71
	-714.28	-51.72	-13.11	-39.85	-116.60	-151.48	-211.28	-168.13	-63.91	-29.57	1.59	-21.17	-6.11	11.80	-30.93	31.30	144.90
	-709.80	-53.26	-13.76	-39.27	-135.63	-181.84	-202.35	-133.45	-49.77	-28.55	7.37	-14.05	-2.97	11.33	-36.32	24.83	137.89
1871–1881																	
MALE	-946.77	.55	-40.49	-106.96	-301.82	-404.49	-237.31	-24.73	61.21	42.99	25.06	1.23	-16.93	-8.74	-38.89	1.21	101.35
	-949.94	-3.32	-39.91	-101.86	-298.38	-407.26	-240.19	-22.63	62.96	43.03	27.47	1.27	-20.12	-8.94	-39.85	-1.32	99.10
	-957.61	-12.47	-39.47	-90.30	-289.33	-412.21	-245.80	-17.93	66.49	42.15	32.38	2.12	-27.14	-9.87	-42.47	-7.46	93.71
FEMALE	-608.98	-19.59	-.56	-78.51	-108.78	-84.06	-140.85	-162.27	-54.38	11.19	-14.29	-33.05	-25.82	-11.44	-41.50	11.87	143.04
	-609.08	-19.92	-1.35	-77.55	-117.16	-103.86	-138.94	-139.00	-42.87	12.48	-11.12	-31.39	-26.80	-13.23	-46.18	7.66	140.15
	-611.11	-20.79	-4.15	-74.97	-131.79	-142.89	-134.90	-91.74	-20.92	14.01	-3.97	-27.72	-29.32	-17.68	-56.91	-1.62	134.27
1881–1891																	
MALE	-1763.81	-44.99	-90.15	-172.71	-363.40	-512.98	-398.81	-182.67	-30.08	24.56	-9.71	-36.96	-10.77	1.69	-21.33	4.63	79.90
	-1768.87	-47.60	-91.23	-168.41	-357.74	-514.06	-402.99	-181.60	-27.58	26.07	-6.48	-39.61	-16.67	2.32	-21.86	1.33	77.22
	-1781.55	-55.32	-94.07	-157.12	-343.21	-516.06	-411.87	-178.92	-22.42	27.56	-.23	-43.54	-29.45	2.50	-23.74	-6.63	70.97
FEMALE	-937.41	-2.85	-52.14	-103.57	-73.16	-84.23	-193.32	-252.06	-121.13	-22.81	-17.20	-54.43	-56.19	-26.14	-19.12	35.34	125.60
	-939.58	-3.30	-53.55	-102.63	-99.47	-106.24	-195.33	-223.96	-103.62	-20.14	-13.88	-55.08	-60.43	-29.75	-25.92	30.03	123.70
	-946.90	-4.40	-57.56	-99.90	-109.59	-149.64	-198.94	-166.37	-70.18	-16.87	-6.09	-55.33	-69.67	-38.40	-41.46	18.04	119.46
1891–1901																	
MALE	-903.41	-25.63	-51.25	-137.12	-294.38	-312.94	-180.93	-16.76	65.27	45.29	5.25	-20.57	-3.72	-20.19	-54.46	3.80	84.94
	-910.94	-28.18	-54.96	-132.43	-273.40	-310.85	-186.91	-16.42	69.70	50.08	11.60	-27.68	-14.74	-18.17	-55.84	-2.39	79.74
	-929.38	-38.52	-62.99	-117.89	-245.98	-305.92	-199.07	-13.39	80.36	57.40	24.78	-38.96	-38.78	-16.26	-61.73	-18.99	66.50
FEMALE	-494.49	-9.78	-25.97	-106.42	-73.03	18.16	-97.63	-203.52	-92.46	16.22	-9.00	-32.46	-33.58	-15.13	-21.62	36.69	145.03
	-499.41	-10.36	-27.87	-105.23	-77.83	-10.38	-108.36	-195.97	-65.42	22.72	-3.87	-34.93	-31.07	-20.06	-30.63	29.96	143.89
	-513.66	-11.57	-32.62	-102.25	-85.30	-66.11	-128.28	-101.26	-13.78	32.60	7.49	-38.43	-46.91	-31.83	-51.04	14.81	140.82
1901–1911																	
MALE	-1504.60	15.13	-20.79	-133.05	-304.10	-380.01	-322.02	-202.21	-94.55	45.30	-85.87	-31.23	-6.89	-21.01	5.58	36.18	105.35
	-1519.82	14.82	-24.22	-129.18	-291.12	-375.97	-331.69	-207.31	-91.65	58.68	-85.32	-44.15	-24.35	-16.44	9.01	31.83	101.59
	-1561.39	10.16	-30.08	-115.52	-281.59	-370.27	-353.84	-217.63	-85.96	53.39	-77.90	-67.42	-57.61	-10.76	15.21	21.87	93.32
FEMALE	-812.96	16.50	-22.08	-99.47	-17.77	69.68	-133.06	-281.68	-172.18	49.95	-66.51	-103.90	-72.71	-37.77	-13.80	40.85	130.89
	-820.97	14.54	-25.21	-96.90	-17.70	41.44	-148.67	-285.75	-171.09	-44.34	-65.59	-111.80	-85.75	-44.58	-23.60	33.56	130.89
	-842.22	10.85	-32.06	-91.72	-16.13	-12.88	-177.09	-160.43	-135.57	-36.87	-62.62	-125.83	-112.45	-60.27	-45.90	17.09	129.97

Age-Band in Years

PEEBLES

	TOTAL	<5	<10	<15	<20	<25	<30	<35	<40	<45	<50	<55	<60	<65	<70	<75	75+
1861–1871																	
MALE	-305.24	-105.12	-58.55	20.21	43.74	21.82	-64.39	-93.59	-38.53	-33.88	-3.74	20.02	-.37	-19.30	-30.43	-1.22	38.12
	-294.91	-106.80	-60.74	25.70	43.02	13.05	-71.03	-89.52	-28.43	-28.15	-1.67	16.62	-2.38	-16.12	-29.55	-.69	41.79
	-265.56	-108.41	-65.77	33.72	41.15	-3.60	-65.98	-84.79	-7.78	-14.43	1.91	7.88	-6.02	-7.32	-24.90	1.25	53.54
FEMALE	-339.94	-30.51	-73.13	-45.87	175.06	297.91	9.69	-212.17	-156.25	-87.91	-57.46	-39.95	-52.21	-67.18	-41.93	2.99	38.97
	-334.49	-36.01	-72.89	-40.51	165.89	272.94	11.98	-193.41	-142.23	-75.85	-47.60	-59.83	-50.99	-62.32	-43.47	.38	39.43
	-331.41	-47.41	-72.17	-30.14	149.62	223.61	11.59	-161.30	-114.51	-49.82	-66.96	-67.79	-49.27	-48.94	-44.15	-4.44	40.66
1871–1881																	
MALE	-499.93	-79.99	-25.74	12.47	62.44	40.03	-62.84	-143.73	-106.78	-43.76	-33.11	-19.64	-31.29	-44.99	-35.76	-10.89	23.65
	-492.70	-77.05	-30.66	14.33	65.36	34.62	-71.63	-142.97	-98.70	-36.57	-27.94	-23.87	-35.27	-40.80	-34.24	-11.88	24.58
	-473.07	-68.15	-42.02	16.00	70.43	24.31	-90.73	-144.58	-82.55	-20.17	-17.32	-32.33	-41.72	-30.81	-29.20	-12.15	27.98
FEMALE	-422.15	-33.04	-54.87	-34.57	162.24	248.37	-35.66	-226.15	-154.29	-61.57	-43.55	-58.07	-65.04	-59.14	-35.09	4.67	33.59
	-413.21	-37.34	-37.34	-29.71	153.73	217.50	-41.30	-212.03	-134.28	-52.72	-62.31	-62.72	-65.44	-56.81	-37.04	1.32	35.36
	-395.48	-46.74	-52.46	-19.70	138.08	153.67	-58.34	-167.99	-94.09	-25.03	-41.12	-71.55	-65.63	-49.69	-38.53	2.65	41.00
1881–1891																	
MALE	-566.33	-99.73	-48.53	-3.21	35.63	-28.55	-132.35	-165.24	-88.80	-5.31	4.21	-10.92	-12.42	-22.34	-20.15	3.96	27.58
	-563.80	-91.82	-56.67	-6.37	42.00	-30.09	-142.44	-166.59	-81.50	4.42	13.50	-15.78	-18.77	-18.02	-18.66	.36	22.63
	-555.71	-72.01	-75.63	-15.97	54.03	-33.02	-163.85	-171.50	-66.70	25.93	33.13	-23.85	-29.12	-8.34	-14.65	-6.14	12.00
FEMALE	-523.86	-76.90	-33.46	12.16	102.12	153.47	-75.99	-240.67	-118.64	-35.41	-65.39	-80.03	-57.75	-61.64	-13.97	14.80	33.10
	-515.44	-79.71	-32.48	17.19	93.68	116.76	-88.62	-209.63	-93.16	-25.52	-60.27	-60.27	-60.06	-43.02	-17.83	13.39	33.51
	-494.00	-86.47	-30.39	25.57	77.48	37.65	-121.48	-150.46	-41.54	-3.86	-47.45	-75.68	-63.01	-44.59	-23.27	13.72	39.80
1891–1901																	
MALE	-338.94	-62.20	1.62	45.38	29.66	-18.14	-98.76	-136.64	-48.35	25.56	15.97	-8.32	-31.33	-34.73	-25.69	-3.84	10.87
	-340.62	-49.88	-9.08	36.93	38.92	-15.75	-110.64	-140.41	-43.19	37.01	30.15	-13.50	-40.07	-29.05	-23.72	-9.82	1.48
	-342.16	-21.15	-33.84	15.98	57.12	-11.46	-135.90	-149.47	-32.95	61.52	60.11	-20.32	-54.21	-17.92	-19.13	-21.42	-19.11
FEMALE	-440.76	-103.88	16.75	57.35	49.19	85.99	-75.03	-227.38	-103.89	1.84	-36.85	-72.37	-41.94	-33.73	-13.53	22.90	35.85
	-429.62	-105.16	18.01	59.47	39.88	40.67	-95.40	-186.33	-72.11	9.64	-25.10	-65.38	-45.98	-41.28	-19.40	21.65	37.21
	-399.54	-108.90	20.68	65.19	21.08	-59.59	-145.48	-105.11	-7.21	27.04	3.90	-43.90	-51.61	-52.63	-28.90	22.77	43.10
1901–1911																	
MALE	-799.44	-91.33	-34.36	2.76	11.06	-68.30	-176.23	-180.12	-87.95	2.62	-44.16	-62.18	-44.48	-43.10	-8.30	11.07	13.54
	-806.14	-76.48	-47.07	-9.84	22.46	-61.91	-187.32	-184.02	-82.88	15.37	-26.52	-68.14	-57.68	-38.33	-6.68	2.65	.27
	-817.72	-42.18	-76.71	-39.72	45.59	-50.22	-210.81	-191.90	-72.22	42.49	10.92	-75.29	-80.25	-30.45	-4.13	-14.14	-28.71
FEMALE	-685.88	-95.29	8.64	-14.51	-54.60	10.29	-70.79	-197.67	-58.30	28.43	-72.44	-116.70	-81.32	-43.00	.31	26.81	44.25
	-675.53	-96.22	9.83	-13.16	-63.97	-41.01	-96.17	-144.39	-20.65	30.98	-55.84	-103.76	-88.77	-54.37	-7.63	25.33	44.18
	-647.17	-100.09	12.13	-8.17	-83.27	-156.88	-157.85	-36.49	56.72	37.84	-14.13	-66.15	-100.50	-78.83	-21.49	25.43	44.53

Age-Band in Years

PERTH

	TOTAL	<5	<10	<15	<20	<25	<30	<35	<40	<45	<50	<55	<60	<65	<70	<75	75+
1861-1871																	
MALE	-4671.74	-533.57	-315.04	-256.26	-342.49	-732.25	-1309.33	-1060.01	-388.64	-56.58	-35.30	-167.72	-84.77	-89.05	-271.60	63.93	706.95
	-4724.59	-429.66	-283.17	-157.82	-319.09	-795.44	-1324.78	-1010.39	-378.52	-84.87	-18.92	-137.96	-105.15	-111.54	-292.47	39.72	686.48
	-4862.98	-633.65	-229.39	46.18	-257.08	-914.59	-1342.28	-898.93	-359.25	-152.65	11.86	-77.07	-153.18	-162.36	-341.27	-23.53	624.24
FEMALE	-3277.97	-366.74	-288.95	-112.09	442.87	566.15	-721.62	-1387.43	-776.25	-653.87	-410.43	-310.10	-222.23	-97.27	-216.19	123.15	973.03
	-3251.08	-365.82	-288.99	-111.44	342.09	411.87	-647.05	-1158.43	-734.48	-500.16	-387.26	-260.78	-212.48	-111.13	-244.85	88.43	927.40
	-3222.37	-364.56	-297.28	-104.38	158.87	114.60	-487.48	-495.32	-625.23	-597.25	-333.39	-167.91	-200.79	-147.59	-319.18	8.18	836.34
1871-1881																	
MALE	-3516.59	48.45	-249.57	-484.76	-92.12	-65.62	-793.89	-868.60	-369.51	-184.74	-193.07	-255.04	-124.80	-144.72	-328.51	15.06	574.81
	-3387.88	-36.55	-239.44	-388.97	-34.23	-108.12	-822.34	-829.26	-354.22	-203.90	-174.06	-252.49	-170.33	-157.41	-345.25	-18.71	547.40
	-3767.88	-239.41	-223.17	-166.99	125.16	-187.97	-877.35	-738.04	-323.86	-260.35	-137.33	-238.13	-273.57	-192.72	-390.67	-104.49	473.03
FEMALES	-2488.55	35.36	-204.32	-328.83	552.18	983.13	-440.40	-1247.16	-678.93	-456.29	-515.24	-380.62	-237.73	-111.43	-190.58	63.09	669.23
	-2501.58	36.73	-223.01	-323.93	492.64	835.76	-392.21	-1011.65	-594.68	-491.48	-488.77	-349.99	-251.52	-139.85	-241.18	14.71	626.85
	-2572.60	35.41	-290.95	-297.98	416.81	548.49	-283.84	-515.08	-446.77	-584.62	-418.28	-278.76	-288.53	-216.04	-374.46	-106.21	528.22
1881-1891																	
MALE	-5541.15	-324.54	-333.37	-530.24	-293.42	-282.15	-1194.70	-1338.33	-476.21	-138.12	-250.77	-281.84	-105.33	-188.02	-290.62	22.59	423.97
	-5630.16	-390.32	-348.06	-437.06	-197.27	-308.08	-1246.49	-1315.87	-653.60	-140.10	-224.93	-308.98	-177.02	-158.53	-293.65	-21.04	391.65
	-5862.95	-576.47	-391.04	-192.66	62.97	-363.47	-1363.41	-1257.13	-404.33	-169.42	-174.51	-344.74	-339.80	-176.40	-539.15	-137.23	303.84
FEMALES	-4055.07	-355.77	-394.89	-243.85	685.13	951.39	-712.08	-1632.53	-871.51	-523.74	-562.69	-477.09	-262.90	-102.68	-68.13	68.63	397.62
	-4107.72	-364.56	-435.51	-224.41	683.37	819.42	-694.69	-1395.89	-764.90	-546.49	-535.84	-418.49	-303.95	-150.30	-145.45	6.24	363.72
	-4285.07	-387.56	-551.02	-162.82	741.80	558.32	-646.60	-874.61	-584.86	-638.85	-449.37	-370.69	-399.18	-280.16	-353.38	-157.99	271.90
1891-1901																	
MALE	-4465.41	137.13	-116.38	-992.32	-538.06	-123.13	-833.01	-979.11	-270.80	-134.06	-425.64	-354.50	-195.17	-232.77	-301.22	-50.76	344.39
	-4584.30	91.57	-159.71	-510.32	-203.73	-126.00	-905.46	-973.01	-235.76	-114.10	-391.88	-415.91	-286.82	-220.79	-311.78	-108.92	298.31
	-4909.81	-71.73	-252.35	-266.08	143.70	-134.93	-1071.57	-942.82	-152.42	-105.07	-325.09	-510.06	-528.13	-224.68	-365.14	-270.89	169.44
FEMALES	-3611.63	-141.87	-183.82	-250.07	648.21	1092.78	-617.84	-1645.92	-656.84	-465.00	-566.57	-456.53	-325.89	-101.32	-9.13	35.06	211.11
	-3716.88	-167.16	-242.26	-205.91	727.01	948.72	-637.95	-1407.42	-725.45	-468.14	-533.63	-469.86	-363.05	-171.86	-120.07	-47.00	180.10
	-4047.90	-221.06	-386.46	-99.07	908.18	727.11	-647.92	-856.55	-513.43	-548.32	-412.83	-439.79	-535.19	-570.01	-427.19	-275.43	72.06
1901-1911																	
MALE	-5698.33	-.01	-307.36	-801.22	-379.99	-120.26	-1055.15	-1272.57	-304.05	-52.73	-528.04	-453.38	-221.16	-338.45	-215.40	72.99	278.46
	-5849.56	-46.77	-382.11	-712.55	-200.72	-108.43	-1151.27	-1282.32	-255.35	-14.49	-492.83	-545.36	-348.26	-313.19	-220.56	2.36	222.27
	-6289.07	-239.26	-529.05	-626.12	249.89	-95.20	-1375.18	-1279.87	-131.43	24.23	-425.65	-590.87	-644.20	-305.14	-277.11	-203.63	59.51
FEMALE	-3951.99	-206.80	-354.49	-281.40	673.47	1182.88	-733.84	-1997.68	-756.24	-377.08	-565.89	-387.10	-299.25	-103.23	209.07	187.07	101.67
	-4127.44	-259.57	-434.45	-281.40	807.44	1070.32	-791.74	-1786.54	-812.01	-365.90	-521.05	-418.03	-363.05	-207.45	54.05	82.80	79.14
	-4662.71	-360.83	-609.44	-109.11	1135.43	863.35	-949.38	-1191.04	-603.27	-457.44	-340.73	-384.45	-403.59	-512.25	-390.04	-221.39	-28.47

ROSS & CROMARTY

Age-Band in Years

	TOTAL	<5	<10	<15	<20	<25	<30	<35	<40	<45	<50	<55	<60	<65	<70	<75	75+
1861-1871																	
MALE	-2995.77	-102.53	127.94	-189.27	-603.68	-772.83	-767.33	-454.49	-154.74	-135.83	-42.56	11.13	-102.13	-58.75	-166.81	-12.19	428.32
	-3020.75	-112.52	131.52	-179.14	-604.91	-786.27	-765.34	-435.32	-149.73	-144.02	-41.74	14.28	-107.19	-66.22	-174.54	-18.91	419.30
	-3079.01	-133.66	138.10	-158.20	-606.85	-812.78	-758.07	-393.91	-140.75	-164.01	-42.14	20.19	-118.69	-83.11	-190.66	-32.99	398.52
FEMALE	-1961.86	-111.59	108.55	-37.09	-144.27	-124.73	-418.49	-564.53	-390.57	-305.27	-195.96	-90.62	17.05	99.22	-256.82	-103.55	556.81
	-1949.22	-112.24	108.12	-36.13	-161.63	-152.02	-405.90	-528.21	-383.59	-310.65	-188.56	-84.12	16.17	93.72	-266.02	-110.58	552.43
	-1988.66	-113.52	105.79	-33.66	-194.36	-204.40	-379.26	-454.62	-370.80	-322.98	-174.24	-72.91	12.74	82.04	-285.33	-125.44	544.30
1871-1881																	
MALE	-2802.87	78.29	105.77	-343.39	-754.42	-706.83	-459.74	-364.62	-70.91	-50.12	-30.61	-9.47	-84.14	-107.96	-180.26	-22.51	398.02
	-2822.74	71.26	107.32	-334.67	-751.68	-716.72	-460.90	-349.20	-64.58	-54.40	-29.20	-13.26	-93.55	-111.61	-185.46	-28.41	392.32
	-2866.70	54.92	110.00	-315.16	-744.88	-737.06	-461.54	-317.30	-53.80	-65.84	-29.21	-21.25	-112.11	-120.08	-195.52	-39.09	381.23
FEMALE	-1875.21	48.92	72.89	-169.57	-182.33	-46.93	-401.96	-602.31	-376.08	-277.07	-151.01	-60.92	-40.07	63.24	-234.19	-74.37	556.62
	-1884.45	48.57	70.84	-168.14	-200.78	-85.80	-396.64	-557.10	-356.33	-275.29	-143.66	-59.47	-43.71	58.41	-245.17	-83.11	552.94
	-1906.92	47.57	63.80	-163.73	-253.31	-160.14	-384.58	-467.10	-318.36	-273.62	-130.89	-59.29	-52.54	48.58	-267.32	-101.28	545.30
1881-1891																	
MALE	-3213.51	-108.91	32.74	-327.61	-801.76	-749.99	-558.19	-406.06	-146.38	-81.84	-34.47	-34.40	-119.88	-120.47	-170.87	17.48	397.11
	-3228.89	-117.83	28.50	-317.24	-786.20	-752.03	-562.76	-398.88	-141.46	-81.55	-31.21	-47.19	-135.51	-118.05	-171.57	12.47	393.63
	-3258.41	-143.55	17.43	-289.81	-755.98	-757.71	-570.54	-384.01	-133.96	-83.47	-28.20	-73.00	-164.49	-113.37	-172.03	4.94	389.30
FEMALE	-2246.85	-158.18	29.16	-146.18	-112.43	70.17	-422.13	-741.39	-365.49	-185.13	-109.69	-160.66	-169.87	-4.34	-215.96	-59.38	504.64
	-2256.34	-159.50	23.98	-143.36	-124.97	25.37	-425.03	-684.39	-329.54	-179.63	-106.71	-167.58	-179.58	-9.65	-228.17	-69.44	501.86
	-2278.94	-162.87	9.32	-135.13	-143.75	-60.07	-429.01	-572.05	-259.77	-170.30	-103.70	-184.69	-199.59	-19.47	-252.48	-90.44	495.07
1891-1901																	
MALE	-2511.68	-66.37	51.01	-334.46	-808.85	-600.61	-291.93	-191.90	-94.76	-39.38	-10.90	-45.67	-132.22	-122.36	-136.00	2.56	310.16
	-2526.22	-71.80	45.06	-322.73	-783.96	-596.42	-306.15	-175.64	-90.68	-31.13	-2.32	-68.27	-156.78	-113.50	-132.42	-4.35	304.86
	-2551.67	-92.64	32.69	-287.63	-726.23	-593.22	-336.31	-201.23	-84.05	-17.32	11.62	-112.10	-202.67	-96.02	-125.57	-17.02	296.00
FEMALE	-783.30	-60.01	73.40	-144.19	-75.70	292.57	-101.31	-501.68	-254.89	-61.25	-54.47	-97.53	-126.21	26.79	-116.34	-32.04	449.54
	-795.15	-63.17	65.90	-138.42	-81.73	234.60	-124.47	-434.81	-196.66	-46.70	-50.45	-109.18	-141.46	21.06	-130.39	-44.32	447.06
	-817.90	-69.85	47.30	-124.34	-87.39	124.15	-167.95	-305.95	-83.82	-20.19	-46.66	-136.37	-172.21	10.67	-158.04	-69.74	440.49
1901-1911																	
MALE	-3672.02	-197.14	-167.19	-257.11	-106.02	45.14	-210.88	-410.33	-332.24	-416.32	-508.84	-456.34	-438.39	-341.54	-139.67	34.58	210.30
	-3708.87	-213.09	-186.11	-237.27	-63.34	55.21	-230.58	-415.14	-318.00	-396.32	-489.80	-481.84	-472.18	-329.55	-140.22	14.04	195.32
	-3739.55	-270.13	-226.11	-174.96	43.10	77.76	-267.73	-412.08	-279.78	-359.22	-445.84	-522.91	-543.42	-310.19	-156.46	-44.70	153.11
FEMALE	-3326.40	-59.73	5.83	-238.14	-197.01	96.93	-403.66	-888.57	-634.16	-366.36	-361.00	-411.87	-384.69	-141.86	120.33	196.83	338.73
	-3339.91	-69.01	-8.06	-225.06	-184.27	38.79	-435.77	-803.65	-554.73	-349.75	-361.04	-431.17	-409.90	-153.81	97.98	179.08	333.46
	-3373.15	-86.78	-38.34	-198.34	-158.80	-70.71	-489.95	-634.37	-463.47	-321.56	-359.94	-467.58	-457.90	-178.94	45.73	133.14	314.65

Age-Band in Years

ROXBURGH

	TOTAL	<5	<10	<15	<20	<25	<30	<35	<40	<45	<50	<55	<60	<65	<70	<75	75+
1861-1871																	
MALE	-2977.97	-626.14	-241.28	-176.48	-388.19	-654.57	-693.24	-367.45	-65.74	-57.72	-50.03	-79.51	-4.28	126.57	81.14	61.55	157.39
	-2999.92	-446.88	-242.23	-157.10	-668.48	-729.89	-739.10	-380.10	-80.01	-47.77	-18.43	-42.50	15.67	110.79	48.42	40.92	150.86
	-3050.00	-692.33	-245.71	-115.86	-274.04	-690.45	-807.71	-626.08	-128.98	-18.29	68.39	62.56	74.80	66.58	-41.62	-15.72	134.46
FEMALE	-2354.58	-503.56	-340.98	-199.28	-70.46	12.49	-231.74	-831.63	-275.81	-95.10	-89.33	-167.24	-102.71	.12	-50.66	14.45	176.86
	-2275.99	-508.25	-353.81	-179.47	-96.15	-63.49	-213.76	-361.96	-254.99	-98.25	-52.18	-98.14	-81.76	-29.16	-54.97	20.31	150.05
	-2029.56	-519.52	-380.82	-137.15	-167.60	-242.77	-153.29	-182.37	-202.73	-112.42	63.90	132.89	-10.94	-130.39	-77.41	33.95	57.12
1871-1881																	
MALE	-2454.23	-81.62	-148.93	-324.51	-410.18	-509.89	-480.37	-249.19	-69.07	-51.94	-63.08	-70.08	-71.27	-21.72	-50.07	-1.34	149.03
	-2460.25	-80.91	-148.92	-317.95	-394.27	-521.99	-510.06	-240.90	-49.87	-41.78	-45.60	-60.73	-66.94	-20.47	-60.05	-9.18	149.38
	-2475.84	-85.81	-149.93	-299.37	-354.19	-544.36	-570.29	-272.13	-82.65	-21.46	-4.14	-27.97	-47.40	-22.18	-89.61	-30.96	146.60
FEMALE	-2265.06	-80.34	-202.06	-271.78	-103.35	75.38	-175.57	-462.43	-305.41	-159.59	-178.69	-194.57	-154.08	-84.81	-87.99	-7.47	127.71
	-2212.68	-75.71	-209.67	-264.44	-125.72	5.19	-175.01	-391.52	-275.11	-165.75	-156.19	-155.55	-148.44	-104.91	-89.52	-.60	120.27
	-2070.34	-70.58	-225.54	-243.97	-180.88	-151.25	-163.05	-222.28	-211.04	-184.19	-91.09	-28.23	-120.52	-164.74	-99.15	12.03	84.18
1881-1891																	
MALE	-1221.69	45.66	90.67	11.29	-176.75	-454.90	-506.72	-303.82	-87.79	16.64	46.46	45.91	1.02	-45.69	-31.13	21.22	106.26
	-1210.70	67.34	86.51	-3.77	-172.30	-453.14	-534.54	-319.31	-74.09	45.26	68.14	33.42	-13.57	-37.85	-31.17	17.36	111.01
	-1193.44	105.74	80.08	-27.44	-159.79	-452.68	-591.19	-349.64	-51.40	102.09	114.00	15.15	-38.77	-28.16	-57.51	6.69	119.38
FEMALE	-901.70	-84.97	2.71	162.84	257.48	250.61	-177.50	-561.99	-331.28	-75.83	-94.00	-156.55	-135.29	-82.28	-49.74	32.36	141.74
	-855.00	-72.62	-2.48	153.79	244.74	194.56	-189.28	-480.56	-274.67	-69.90	-75.85	-144.18	-151.11	-105.85	-62.70	34.04	147.07
	-740.72	-50.84	-11.73	141.02	219.98	81.87	-199.14	-305.49	-153.44	-51.01	-30.68	-105.46	-182.22	-170.31	-101.85	33.17	145.41
1891-1901																	
MALE	-3841.28	-148.87	-199.05	-654.31	-693.12	-777.48	-661.13	-395.58	-214.34	-142.20	-86.05	17.04	4.60	-116.37	-84.45	16.08	93.97
	-3822.33	-115.37	-206.00	-685.41	-696.34	-760.92	-684.49	-417.32	-189.33	-101.67	-66.17	-21.07	-30.72	-68.75	18.36	103.08	
	-3787.99	-49.52	-215.80	-543.30	-707.35	-733.26	-733.58	-651.66	-138.81	-24.29	-29.87	-97.35	-102.43	-67.14	-38.68	23.56	121.49
FEMALE	-3148.84	-195.80	-254.60	-206.25	-189.75	-167.71	-471.22	-742.83	-445.56	-179.70	-159.03	-114.66	-96.18	-84.39	-17.46	58.54	117.76
	-3123.96	-179.65	-257.07	-227.02	-189.35	-205.82	-499.22	-654.24	-362.34	-165.20	-154.26	-140.34	-137.74	-105.82	-38.47	54.01	138.60
	-3076.21	-165.51	-259.59	-269.27	-181.48	-267.18	-541.61	-673.53	-188.68	-119.88	-149.97	-214.52	-233.76	-156.01	-72.77	39.93	179.61
1901-1911																	
MALE	-2229.67	-124.63	-123.54	-186.28	-245.14	-204.41	-364.27	-328.19	-179.97	-76.65	-114.48	-18.56	-7.59	-179.49	-107.59	38.28	92.85
	-2201.55	-79.44	-128.25	-229.72	-260.74	-277.80	-393.84	-362.40	-144.85	-20.82	-93.65	-82.90	-63.30	-148.71	-72.93	48.86	108.94
	-2150.82	16.57	-131.08	-317.05	-307.80	-230.89	-442.16	-412.00	-69.04	84.41	-59.69	-216.63	-180.73	-94.65	-4.07	72.12	141.86
FEMALE	-2015.77	-189.89	-117.44	30.26	73.04	107.41	-282.41	-719.35	-440.37	-166.07	-174.70	-129.41	-128.61	-113.46	18.33	93.96	122.87
	-2018.05	-170.08	-118.64	1.91	92.02	87.21	-331.39	-628.39	-531.79	-140.60	-183.49	-198.81	-198.97	-132.12	-12.14	82.92	164.33
	-2040.49	-121.43	-118.77	-65.39	141.32	77.66	-412.31	-454.04	-108.20	-63.02	-218.79	-393.88	-363.19	-167.67	-84.64	56.04	255.75

Age-Band in Years

SELKIRK

	TOTAL	<5	<10	<15	<20	<25	<30	<35	<40	<45	<50	<55	<60	<65	<70	<75	75+
1861-1871																	
MALE	-12.97	115.27	.48	-28.36	-36.92	-54.73	-22.81	-6.44	-30.08	-8.83	3.04	2.74	-8.56	-2.25	11.71	20.83	31.94
	-10.34	132.68	1.22	-44.22	-49.24	-43.57	-10.17	-9.01	-33.00	-11.73	-4.82	-3.24	-10.60	-1.19	18.24	25.29	33.04
	-6.79	168.40	3.30	-76.55	-76.18	-23.13	15.61	-10.06	-35.30	-18.32	-22.76	-19.25	-17.86	1.81	33.47	35.27	34.75
FEMALE	181.14	74.98	29.74	39.59	84.22	19.34	-60.67	-6.46	5.64	-3.46	-1.42	-5.72	-3.89	-1.94	-3.11	-.83	15.14
	163.73	82.87	34.59	28.01	99.02	60.25	-61.50	-33.55	-8.82	-11.68	-13.68	-20.81	-10.60	1.17	.33	.33	17.80
	89.00	98.94	44.59	4.52	131.21	145.76	-67.16	-63.92	-39.49	-27.50	-45.54	-66.04	-28.15	13.57	8.76	-2.96	12.41
1871-1881																	
MALE	-75.58	-385.27	-101.86	113.64	96.18	55.73	7.49	-33.43	-10.47	19.84	24.91	4.08	14.53	27.66	23.05	26.70	41.64
	-69.39	-380.62	-101.39	99.95	86.20	70.02	23.08	-38.18	-18.08	14.54	16.70	6.56	21.33	27.10	27.02	32.11	44.28
	-58.36	-370.27	-99.99	71.42	64.52	98.09	54.68	-45.21	-30.91	3.69	-.58	8.65	32.36	26.82	35.81	42.98	49.57
FEMALE	28.94	-351.79	-122.51	133.30	197.51	89.35	-26.14	17.60	17.60	26.47	28.03	26.38	24.78	9.63	-6.00	2.76	14.57
	17.79	-348.51	-120.42	123.63	215.20	146.15	-22.34	-84.87	-11.45	16.86	17.46	19.64	25.41	14.80	2.42	7.51	16.30
	-12.48	-341.08	-115.95	103.19	250.79	261.01	-16.16	-186.68	-70.18	-2.09	-7.08	-.86	25.13	28.70	20.77	16.95	21.06
1881-1891																	
MALE	-2251.15	-525.01	-335.22	-214.94	-341.68	-442.43	-295.65	-126.35	-63.24	-13.73	-3.30	-36.38	-5.21	30.03	27.37	18.25	56.34
	-2243.67	-535.17	-328.65	-224.00	-351.70	-439.25	-280.57	-126.35	-72.34	-23.70	-13.59	-25.18	9.66	44.72	26.69	24.64	60.90
	-2229.97	-554.66	-315.30	-213.44	-372.47	-432.18	-250.44	-125.88	-89.13	-43.04	-33.86	-5.29	37.08	35.39	26.07	37.18	70.00
FEMALE	-1891.27	-441.61	-351.78	-247.98	-160.85	-252.93	-266.34	-93.54	-14.67	-17.16	6.78	-4.93	-25.42	-14.24	-20.46	-9.83	23.69
	-1895.51	-442.81	-350.75	-249.62	-192.48	-255.02	-161.33	-61.68	-27.70	6.78	-1.54	-2.86	-14.80	-5.56	-7.56	-2.14	23.89
	-1907.21	-444.26	-348.65	-254.27	-110.13	-71.73	-233.10	-297.17	-155.95	-49.45	-19.74	-1.11	6.21	13.81	19.64	13.46	25.21
1891-1901																	
MALE	434.13	-131.79	-47.71	99.03	-203.93	-412.36	-109.92	156.26	176.38	150.69	173.27	121.91	103.92	142.39	96.64	46.92	74.46
	446.69	-140.66	-42.36	108.38	-209.68	-417.85	-97.27	161.92	166.91	140.08	167.30	136.04	120.65	135.31	90.24	50.83	76.83
	465.21	-158.73	-31.67	126.24	-220.72	-427.45	-72.50	171.45	148.07	119.43	155.33	162.43	152.94	121.92	77.40	58.71	82.35
FEMALE	366.41	-191.80	-95.89	61.48	-39.87	-233.67	-90.04	160.32	186.33	109.01	108.52	94.89	71.56	77.69	47.37	28.13	71.36
	366.87	-195.44	-95.27	65.28	-32.27	-196.70	-82.82	88.47	134.05	109.00	115.06	111.19	94.69	90.39	59.17	34.38	67.69
	365.95	-202.79	-94.40	72.56	-20.68	-125.69	-68.80	-54.44	29.42	108.77	127.42	145.16	141.92	116.82	84.36	46.77	59.54
1901-1911																	
MALE	-604.06	21.95	-30.99	-104.62	-354.34	-535.99	-244.09	104.60	103.98	77.57	84.02	26.97	21.95	68.39	46.35	31.67	78.52
	-604.42	5.20	-25.49	-90.53	-352.33	-542.97	-235.14	112.70	95.06	62.23	74.39	42.99	38.37	59.21	38.02	33.33	80.56
	-603.87	-30.31	-14.74	-61.87	-345.67	-555.16	-218.85	124.93	75.71	33.89	56.03	74.00	71.53	43.42	22.45	36.78	84.98
FEMALE	-402.64	34.31	-11.06	-107.06	-208.12	-397.57	-218.75	145.51	111.18	-7.12	40.15	79.15	23.58	25.32	25.26	14.79	47.81
	-394.48	29.20	-100.08	-206.71	-206.71	-365.17	-195.99	91.66	61.16	-14.34	38.68	93.73	46.13	35.78	38.01	21.73	42.35
	-378.10	17.19	-10.22	-84.07	-205.64	-303.27	-151.93	-15.13	-38.88	-32.45	36.21	128.51	94.02	57.34	65.67	35.53	29.02

Age-Band in Years

SHETLAND

	TOTAL	<5	<10	<15	<20	<25	<30	<35	<40	<45	<50	<55	<60	<65	<70	<75	75+
1861-1871																	
MALE	-1468.93	-19.74	19.04	-159.21	-600.17	-641.90	-229.99	39.37	40.93	3.36	19.03	9.93	-6.78	-13.05	-29.00	16.32	82.92
	-1470.82	-23.20	19.86	-185.57	-599.38	-644.74	-230.98	41.48	41.98	2.92	19.95	10.73	-7.39	-13.54	-29.97	15.22	81.80
	-1475.03	-30.31	21.30	-148.20	-597.50	-650.10	-232.58	45.85	43.95	1.75	21.68	12.36	-8.74	-14.65	-32.03	12.88	79.32
FEMALE	-630.71	-80.37	-7.96	11.96	41.98	40.96	-189.86	-278.73	-154.81	-53.20	.54	-33.98	-44.69	-21.00	-41.38	19.45	160.37
	-631.29	-81.10	-8.14	12.70	34.65	28.60	-188.83	-266.66	-150.63	-52.11	2.90	-32.68	-44.15	-21.41	-43.72	17.58	159.71
	-632.86	-82.57	-8.81	14.28	20.55	4.44	-180.79	-242.70	-142.51	-50.16	7.46	-30.47	-43.35	-22.19	-48.42	13.76	158.61
1871-1881																	
MALE	-2119.80	-72.62	-124.41	-276.37	-597.85	-647.24	-272.56	-14.18	15.15	3.89	-22.64	-26.42	-31.32	-37.86	-49.51	-14.66	48.80
	-2122.54	-75.99	-124.55	-272.34	-594.71	-648.97	-274.19	-12.26	16.50	3.54	-21.10	-26.75	-33.86	-37.94	-50.48	-16.56	47.14
	-2128.54	-83.81	-125.48	-263.33	-586.86	-651.79	-277.03	-7.86	19.33	2.22	-17.81	-26.76	-39.39	-38.45	-53.16	-21.37	43.07
FEMALE	-1777.83	-85.90	-120.81	-131.62	-77.07	-121.49	-258.39	-313.24	-191.17	-142.11	-108.91	-108.47	-101.18	-42.34	-49.59	5.80	88.65
	-1778.26	-86.33	-121.47	-130.63	-104.12	-138.08	-257.14	-295.06	-182.08	-140.20	-106.39	-108.15	-102.17	-43.61	-53.28	2.90	87.56
	-1779.59	-87.36	-123.77	-128.17	-116.80	-170.60	-254.42	-258.61	-164.33	-136.73	-101.27	-107.64	-104.37	-46.37	-61.11	-3.28	85.24
1881-1891																	
MALE	-1303.27	-92.83	-16.87	-121.86	-411.14	-490.49	-262.02	-61.87	13.66	18.53	-2.45	2.41	19.13	2.92	.52	27.06	72.05
	-1306.95	-94.90	-18.09	-118.08	-406.01	-491.49	-265.61	-61.07	15.68	19.91	.44	.50	14.46	3.40	-.05	24.25	69.72
	-1316.27	-101.20	-21.15	-108.30	-392.98	-493.14	-273.13	-58.94	19.98	21.38	6.19	-2.06	4.20	3.43	-2.07	17.27	64.22
FEMALE	-644.17	-75.84	-11.61	-15.89	62.88	86.94	-121.22	-223.05	-119.88	-48.77	-57.12	-84.26	-87.73	-18.44	-22.15	5.82	106.14
	-645.55	-76.18	-12.80	-15.00	57.83	69.00	-122.80	-200.24	-105.53	-66.54	-55.18	-85.71	-91.31	-21.03	-27.18	1.99	105.13
	-649.36	-77.02	-16.26	-12.50	49.73	33.66	-125.80	-154.20	-77.75	-63.04	-50.96	-88.27	-89.66	-26.71	-38.12	-6.32	102.86
1891-1901																	
MALE	-635.42	49.56	-8.18	-107.47	-253.33	-299.19	-151.37	-4.74	55.73	46.06	-9.45	-22.62	29.09	-6.32	-33.03	18.55	70.31
	-641.61	48.62	-10.97	-104.38	-245.47	-298.03	-156.23	-4.83	58.75	49.05	-5.55	-27.73	12.07	-4.84	-33.36	14.43	66.85
	-657.31	43.33	-16.79	-94.53	-226.02	-295.56	-186.56	-3.81	65.72	53.25	2.21	-35.88	-5.37	-3.49	-35.78	3.71	58.27
FEMALE	-538.87	-9.13	-13.21	-27.20	50.96	120.19	-93.04	-225.80	-129.65	-64.56	-65.02	-77.72	-68.01	-40.94	-27.86	22.64	109.46
	-541.71	-9.93	-15.29	-25.83	48.78	100.96	-99.30	-200.28	-109.85	-61.04	-62.92	-80.65	-74.12	-44.75	-34.25	17.93	108.82
	-549.45	-11.59	-20.45	-22.51	46.39	63.34	-110.80	-148.16	-71.84	-55.75	-57.89	-85.55	-86.64	-53.49	-48.74	7.28	106.94
1901-1911																	
MALE	-1352.52	-7.26	-30.57	-171.06	-334.21	-351.22	-228.80	-80.21	-1.23	-17.06	-64.93	-58.53	-27.34	-25.82	-37.59	4.14	79.21
	-1361.44	-10.60	-34.01	-166.19	-322.10	-348.70	-235.08	-80.78	3.72	-12.47	-60.47	-65.86	-38.17	-23.56	-37.98	-1.89	74.64
	-1384.94	-23.74	-47.12	-150.02	-291.78	-342.92	-248.25	-79.27	16.38	-5.43	-50.92	-77.19	-62.75	-22.02	-42.77	-19.17	62.04
FEMALE	-603.44	-41.02	-7.42	-21.83	21.27	97.95	-74.85	-228.33	-145.75	-71.37	-68.64	-96.19	-88.49	-42.88	-12.23	44.65	131.71
	-608.41	-43.33	-10.98	-18.60	24.11	80.72	-84.06	-201.33	-121.94	-68.14	-68.28	-101.76	-97.73	-48.28	-19.84	39.23	131.82
	-621.52	-47.78	-18.75	-12.02	31.59	47.78	-100.04	-145.07	-76.90	-64.49	-65.83	-111.03	-116.72	-61.17	-38.28	26.10	131.05

Age-Band in Years

STIRLING

	TOTAL	<5	<10	<15	<20	<25	<30	<35	<40	<45	<50	<55	<60	<65	<70	<75	75+
1861–1871																	
MALE	-2976.88	-894.09	-104.95	-59.60	-668.24	-940.26	-733.97	-215.63	42.57	69.68	6.62	-68.16	-17.18	57.60	57.95	123.25	307.54
	-2973.17	-878.34	-112.67	-89.20	-615.28	-918.46	-718.53	-219.68	35.93	68.58	4.87	-69.88	-14.46	58.63	60.79	127.64	306.89
	-2974.95	-846.84	-126.16	-148.82	-631.83	-876.68	-688.44	-223.42	24.25	64.48	-.08	-74.46	-10.89	59.21	66.10	135.15	301.47
FEMALE	-2148.22	-528.66	-146.55	-357.16	-632.43	-348.74	-283.07	-189.66	.70	-8.51	-67.50	-96.94	-56.53	41.51	-17.33	89.18	452.44
	-2151.32	-524.40	-147.06	-364.46	-630.05	-331.20	-282.91	-203.50	-8.78	-10.27	-64.48	-97.00	-58.33	41.26	-16.78	90.23	456.40
	-2158.38	-515.10	-146.06	-379.78	-626.90	-295.36	-281.80	-232.07	-27.00	-14.47	-60.70	-100.55	-63.69	41.70	-14.84	92.39	465.85
1871–1881																	
MALE	-2904.80	-687.86	-108.92	-152.18	-683.43	-778.29	-465.03	-123.53	58.62	28.60	-95.11	-159.20	-135.85	-2.18	30.80	87.68	281.08
	-2896.11	-678.56	-104.67	-171.46	-697.47	-764.52	-447.63	-123.80	50.42	20.04	-105.74	-157.50	-128.08	-6.30	32.20	97.02	289.94
	-2883.11	-658.60	-92.90	-212.29	-730.71	-737.92	-411.13	-121.98	34.84	2.33	-127.99	-156.46	-113.85	-13.98	35.87	115.72	305.90
FEMALE	-1776.09	-549.70	-120.66	-472.43	-617.06	-108.61	71.04	9.81	48.01	-9.87	-160.69	-203.31	-102.20	16.62	-3.39	79.39	346.95
	-1776.30	-545.56	-118.11	-478.28	-614.92	-84.31	80.47	-5.54	34.08	-15.72	-164.51	-207.28	-103.06	17.47	-.73	81.34	348.36
	-1777.48	-533.61	-109.31	-492.94	-615.96	-32.34	102.44	-37.34	7.29	-26.74	-176.22	-220.43	-105.91	21.10	6.69	85.83	351.99
1881–1891																	
MALE	-3967.35	-590.44	-506.88	-447.51	-601.71	-784.51	-560.63	-281.62	-158.48	-92.95	-104.93	-111.10	-68.22	24.19	14.29	58.41	244.73
	-3955.34	-598.39	-492.62	-455.20	-624.65	-777.06	-536.86	-280.94	-170.58	-107.85	-122.56	-98.47	-46.31	15.30	11.80	71.51	257.76
	-3930.76	-611.94	-460.96	-474.57	-677.31	-761.41	-486.73	-278.82	-194.49	-136.55	-158.31	-77.84	-4.43	.36	9.50	98.78	283.98
FEMALE	-3320.70	-472.25	-429.95	-754.39	-797.10	-140.89	-45.08	-271.98	-210.56	-201.58	-151.33	-165.98	-113.84	36.41	9.23	81.13	307.49
	-3318.77	-469.25	-425.44	-760.27	-795.01	-100.51	-27.23	-303.81	-235.43	-210.55	-163.12	-172.44	-110.41	42.11	18.88	86.38	307.32
	-3314.36	-461.15	-412.38	-776.28	-798.69	-14.02	13.27	-371.17	-283.51	-226.42	-193.32	-192.81	-103.55	57.47	42.38	98.38	307.47
1891–1901																	
MALE	-4170.08	-875.23	-467.17	-364.81	-511.00	-622.35	-516.76	-151.93	-159.37	-249.85	-220.23	-257.93	-160.60	60.11	21.05	53.01	254.97
	-4148.54	-912.49	-433.46	-348.47	-544.59	-635.23	-490.84	-143.69	-173.04	-277.04	-250.79	-230.59	-122.07	45.07	15.19	72.25	281.25
	-4102.75	-983.96	-360.72	-315.20	-619.67	-660.03	-437.16	-129.46	-202.10	-328.81	-311.29	-183.00	-47.79	20.75	8.68	112.61	334.42
FEMALE	-3313.88	-592.07	-315.69	-633.17	-858.80	-297.15	12.84	-56.88	-211.69	-189.53	-94.12	-149.16	-173.93	-7.68	-25.18	34.99	275.33
	-3313.77	-591.15	-310.79	-667.32	-860.80	-250.31	41.54	-95.23	-243.62	-202.73	-114.92	-159.51	-167.24	-.47	-10.36	43.36	274.85
	-3313.14	-587.65	-298.43	-679.90	-872.77	-148.69	104.08	-180.46	-306.41	-226.24	-166.61	-190.22	-152.07	28.07	26.54	63.33	274.29
1901–1911																	
MALE	-5226.34	-843.63	-432.27	-233.78	-837.59	-1224.42	-971.74	-448.91	-258.63	-302.05	-164.16	-161.13	-74.81	179.73	168.06	110.42	268.66
	-5190.10	-903.30	-381.44	-191.78	-894.47	-1267.04	-932.46	-421.78	-274.17	-347.00	-210.27	-103.63	-3.95	147.36	148.63	138.17	307.02
	-5109.07	-1019.35	-275.94	-113.53	-1013.62	-1346.52	-852.58	-373.54	-307.59	-430.51	-299.45	-.72	132.27	93.01	118.25	196.09	384.67
FEMALE	-4388.46	-485.81	-356.55	-785.96	-978.94	-393.60	-162.36	-258.11	-345.89	-382.75	-210.12	-180.20	-216.16	-75.16	27.29	96.56	319.32
	-4376.41	-484.90	-349.57	-787.65	-983.45	-318.59	-111.19	-333.29	-409.08	-401.44	-241.86	-188.50	-193.98	-54.09	55.42	111.02	314.65
	-4345.57	-482.63	-334.18	-792.27	-999.12	-160.90	-5.61	-494.21	-530.21	-452.12	-318.90	-218.84	-146.90	-1.75	122.09	144.39	305.61

Age-Band in Years

SUTHERLAND

	TOTAL	<5	<10	<15	<20	<25	<30	<35	<40	<45	<50	<55	<60	<65	<70	<75	75+
1861-1871																	
MALE	-827.17	27.91	60.94	-25.80	-167.71	-212.92	-204.31	-139.50	-56.12	-24.59	-5.33	-28.18	-22.72	-85.34	-56.50	-4.46	117.49
	-834.04	24.48	61.59	-22.86	-167.62	-217.01	-203.68	-132.29	-53.04	-27.11	-5.61	-28.37	-64.88	-47.33	-59.19	-6.43	115.32
	-849.36	17.25	62.60	-16.72	-167.15	-224.96	-201.74	-117.57	-47.25	-32.85	-6.66	-28.92	-69.41	-51.67	-64.48	-10.32	110.52
FEMALE	-625.43	-2.98	12.33	-23.68	-25.49	-26.67	-153.79	-207.80	-113.21	-80.17	-76.05	-27.63	-6.82	5.68	-63.16	-11.99	176.01
	-628.76	-3.26	12.29	-23.51	-32.05	-36.23	-150.73	-198.84	-111.02	-78.70	-73.49	-27.56	-7.28	4.40	-66.22	-13.53	176.97
	-635.35	-3.83	11.79	-23.02	-44.69	-54.81	-144.59	-180.92	-106.37	-76.03	-66.93	-27.90	-8.51	2.00	-71.97	-16.52	178.94
1871-1881																	
MALE	-941.93	-11.95	-14.95	-116.22	-176.98	-174.74	-207.06	-129.66	-39.65	-35.42	-14.41	-20.70	-50.90	-42.35	-46.04	10.68	128.42
	-947.16	-15.65	-14.70	-112.02	-174.62	-177.95	-208.37	-125.00	-36.96	-36.23	-13.54	-22.17	-54.34	-43.12	-47.57	8.57	126.51
	-958.19	-24.53	-15.01	-102.32	-168.37	-184.38	-210.69	-115.50	-31.96	-38.48	-12.32	-25.03	-61.10	-44.92	-50.70	4.45	122.67
FEMALE	-836.50	-27.44	-7.09	-55.58	-49.62	-32.81	-131.31	-210.17	-132.08	-102.97	-76.31	-50.28	-32.72	-10.45	-81.80	-6.21	170.33
	-839.64	-27.51	-7.73	-55.12	-56.11	-46.69	-129.89	-195.26	-124.93	-100.89	-74.43	-51.46	-34.08	-11.48	-85.02	-8.40	170.38
	-842.62	-27.80	-10.07	-53.71	-67.77	-73.60	-126.99	-166.02	-110.54	-96.58	-71.50	-54.74	-36.86	-13.09	-91.04	-12.73	170.42
1881-1891																	
MALE	-1004.06	-20.56	-21.49	-87.84	-136.56	-124.98	-172.39	-204.57	-114.99	-53.43	-28.04	-42.97	-40.96	-35.36	-46.33	8.14	98.29
	-1008.50	-21.59	-21.21	-84.85	-133.24	-126.57	-175.41	-202.63	-112.86	-32.73	-26.45	-46.65	-46.12	-34.55	-46.54	6.10	96.80
	-1017.24	-24.61	-20.52	-77.25	-125.28	-130.54	-182.00	-198.62	-109.09	-32.12	-24.04	-53.71	-56.07	-33.16	-46.89	2.34	94.36
FEMALE	-491.49	17.48	36.32	-19.05	-35.17	11.09	-87.30	-149.57	-123.33	-42.32	-27.21	-53.07	-33.88	-10.91	-73.60	-28.19	147.21
	-492.96	17.21	35.24	-18.47	-40.42	-5.22	-89.16	-150.24	-110.10	-39.33	-26.21	-55.66	-37.03	-12.37	-77.26	-31.03	147.09
	-495.59	16.56	32.13	-16.68	-49.39	-36.78	-93.05	-112.93	-65.87	-33.23	-25.58	-62.24	-43.35	-14.59	-83.70	-36.23	147.33
1891-1901																	
MALE	-381.09	-6.18	42.89	-43.82	-112.93	-78.01	-55.03	-49.83	-14.62	8.13	5.09	-35.00	-54.72	-24.75	-44.07	-11.27	93.01
	-385.68	-6.58	41.67	-42.36	-107.54	-75.64	-58.22	-50.44	-12.54	11.03	8.47	-41.43	-62.63	-22.34	-45.59	-14.27	90.75
	-394.05	-9.06	39.21	-37.76	-90.86	-63.98	-63.98	-50.69	-8.21	15.79	14.80	-53.30	-78.28	-17.98	-43.52	-21.00	86.23
FEMALE	-337.74	2.55	11.90	-52.06	-52.41	66.44	-12.40	-126.09	-83.47	-49.19	-46.98	-67.52	-52.39	-21.19	-31.89	28.71	148.26
	-339.33	1.81	10.10	-50.84	-55.59	47.14	-19.16	-102.78	-63.65	-44.36	-45.72	-71.24	-57.33	-23.17	-34.64	24.70	147.41
	-342.16	.23	5.64	-47.94	-66.64	9.89	-31.70	-57.05	-24.79	-34.66	-44.14	-79.53	-66.60	-26.35	-46.00	16.40	145.08
1901-1911																	
MALE	-1099.49	1.04	-10.29	-99.37	-178.51	-137.05	-182.61	-199.97	-96.92	-76.18	-86.72	-63.44	-64.56	-54.99	-1.20	48.57	102.71
	-1106.98	-1.71	-14.72	-95.58	-168.27	-132.73	-187.62	-203.55	-94.82	-71.82	-65.02	-72.33	-75.05	-51.04	.92	44.88	99.74
	-1124.44	-12.48	-14.84	-84.27	-144.27	-124.15	-197.45	-209.56	-90.05	-64.79	-76.25	-88.28	-86.44	-44.60	3.66	35.82	92.73
FEMALE	-596.87	-15.93	-.63	-69.87	-41.95	48.32	-111.97	-232.14	-132.63	-49.17	-46.61	-74.66	-63.68	-60.17	17.80	93.84	161.97
	-600.47	-18.85	-4.22	-66.08	-39.92	28.68	-122.88	-205.43	-106.99	-44.44	-46.71	-80.46	-91.75	-63.71	11.88	88.96	161.45
	-608.62	-24.56	-13.37	-58.31	-34.63	-8.93	-142.67	-151.98	-57.43	-36.22	-47.09	-91.79	-107.46	-70.92	-.97	78.19	159.53

Age-Band in Years

WIGTOWN

	TOTAL	C5	C10	C15	C20	C25	C30	C35	C40	C45	C50	C55	C60	C65	C70	C75	75+
1861-1871																	
MALE	-2238.06	-199.32	-105.66	-283.20	-679.95	-826.93	-581.19	-141.97	115.21	72.19	-.67	-23.69	-1.07	95.70	72.68	62.83	186.98
	-2257.02	-208.20	-106.37	-275.23	-662.47	-835.02	-597.61	-145.40	105.41	72.95	16.46	.29	11.39	85.74	51.24	48.43	181.38
	-2301.08	-228.86	-108.80	-257.54	-622.00	-847.40	-431.18	-163.49	72.52	77.56	63.52	67.76	48.76	58.84	-6.67	9.42	166.47
FEMALE	-1592.15	-159.74	-49.82	-177.85	-367.71	-364.92	-376.96	-283.65	-75.32	9.19	-62.69	-85.64	-17.13	65.45	39.73	69.19	245.75
	-1589.81	-160.22	-57.11	-168.08	-387.30	-414.26	-357.55	-227.69	-60.95	4.47	-54.73	-36.64	-6.06	38.95	29.48	64.91	212.97
	-1458.76	-162.18	-72.57	-146.90	-439.01	-529.48	-298.26	-84.52	-22.68	-8.17	51.33	124.75	31.90	-50.57	-9.65	48.56	108.51
1871-1881																	
MALE	-1244.57	-119.88	-14.38	-183.05	-412.15	-456.83	-303.82	-81.27	70.07	90.53	23.06	-21.80	-1.47	-3.49	-18.82	45.88	142.84
	-1254.61	-119.83	-13.68	-182.24	-404.14	-461.50	-317.25	-82.93	70.53	95.32	33.40	-16.34	-1.49	-6.43	-28.13	38.85	141.25
	-1290.00	-123.25	-12.10	-177.43	-383.87	-470.23	-344.58	-90.02	64.88	104.98	58.26	2.63	3.84	-16.48	-53.93	20.62	136.68
FEMALE	-1735.27	-125.08	-69.87	-172.70	-216.25	-139.34	-262.07	-352.95	-171.93	-61.84	-104.15	-131.25	-109.46	-40.37	-27.14	42.93	206.22
	-1735.39	-122.54	-63.82	-170.31	-231.28	-178.90	-254.46	-302.92	-151.47	-65.12	-104.02	-109.81	-109.09	-56.34	-34.68	41.01	194.36
	-1680.86	-118.93	-101.94	-162.93	-265.86	-264.21	-229.47	-190.32	-106.92	-73.35	-50.07	-40.98	-101.93	-104.09	-58.27	33.77	154.67
1881-1891																	
MALE	-1901.42	-108.65	-127.27	-192.82	-383.33	-527.49	-456.56	-235.85	-61.57	22.81	6.31	-16.48	-8.50	-2.06	-2.16	41.17	131.02
	-1901.83	-101.57	-127.00	-199.26	-381.29	-525.12	-466.78	-239.44	-34.41	34.26	15.31	-24.77	-18.89	.70	-3.42	37.77	132.09
	-1905.27	-90.50	-124.86	-208.62	-375.85	-521.69	-486.76	-245.90	-22.87	55.91	33.51	-38.49	-37.81	3.24	-8.92	29.94	134.40
FEMALE	-1589.57	-159.12	-132.45	-148.16	-147.90	-44.70	-206.34	-404.07	-227.38	-49.55	-65.94	-134.11	-81.93	11.64	9.07	42.53	149.84
	-1576.72	-154.36	-135.55	-151.97	-158.26	-76.22	-207.84	-355.45	-194.89	-46.32	-58.80	-130.89	-91.02	.07	-.30	38.52	146.55
	-1546.72	-145.55	-139.27	-157.85	-178.94	-137.29	-203.02	-253.19	-127.09	-37.61	-41.90	-119.63	-109.54	-30.82	-24.81	27.68	132.01
1891-1901																	
MALE	-1307.86	-115.64	-57.71	-211.19	-375.41	-424.82	-300.90	-90.03	12.39	31.10	14.84	34.22	36.03	-21.25	-14.71	48.22	127.02
	-1305.97	-100.93	-58.26	-223.99	-375.75	-413.88	-309.23	-78.44	22.44	47.79	23.39	12.03	14.64	-12.52	-8.53	46.95	128.33
	-1304.42	-73.11	-56.52	-246.86	-379.32	-394.27	-323.18	-111.57	41.68	78.05	37.24	-32.40	-27.73	2.69	3.26	45.36	132.26
FEMALE	-1010.16	-86.50	-83.11	-126.18	-131.31	10.31	-108.56	-340.60	-211.26	-13.20	-12.04	-76.72	-69.13	3.21	27.19	56.46	151.27
	-1005.55	-79.35	-83.71	-135.11	-139.85	-20.45	-123.57	-291.12	-184.83	-2.88	-9.54	-89.70	-86.31	-4.16	16.45	50.48	156.11
	-1000.05	-63.87	-83.91	-153.87	-152.50	-74.08	-146.68	-193.44	-71.21	21.71	-8.76	-121.83	-124.33	-19.96	-7.92	36.47	164.17
1901-1911																	
MALE	-1255.37	-65.66	-40.35	-131.49	-165.85	-168.17	-240.46	-189.31	-93.27	-73.38	-68.87	-42.86	-30.91	-78.23	-31.10	49.85	114.71
	-1255.83	-45.24	-41.01	-150.91	-168.70	-148.12	-250.22	-207.39	-82.64	-51.34	-60.50	-77.50	-61.70	-61.93	-15.71	50.45	116.63
	-1258.53	-2.49	-38.21	-189.24	-182.87	-110.57	-243.91	-237.32	-61.21	-11.51	-48.81	-147.96	-123.32	-31.70	15.23	53.40	121.95
FEMALE	-1197.71	-43.66	-62.48	-82.60	32.64	143.00	-180.35	-449.83	-291.65	-128.65	-127.97	-126.00	-85.92	-52.70	55.83	108.94	115.70
	-1202.58	-33.18	-62.45	-96.97	30.63	118.65	-204.28	-376.13	-230.51	-115.75	-134.28	-154.63	-113.81	-58.70	43.61	100.93	126.25
	-1220.55	-7.23	-61.18	-131.45	-152.87	83.02	-243.91	-294.09	-169.07	-115.35	-157.35	-229.93	-174.85	-67.69	17.58	85.18	148.46

Appendix 14

Current Immigrants into Scotland 1861–1911

Birthplace	Decade	Males	Females
England and Wales	1861–1871	12,416	11,687
	1871–1881	16,976	16,734
	1881–1891	16,324	16,963
	1891–1901	19,440	20,957
	1901–1911	28,240	22,887
Ireland	1861–1871	26,626	18,614
	1871–1881	32,656	22,223
	1881–1891	11,337	6,685
	1891–1901	33,811	13,678
	1901–1911	1,722	3,652
British Subject	1861–1871	2,243	2,492
	1871–1881	3,705	3,526
	1881–1891	2,412	1,961
	1891–1901	4,705	5,192
	1901–1911	2,255	2,083
Foreign Born*	1861–1871	1,024	526
	1871–1881	1,759	844
	1881–1891	2,192	1,082
	1891–1901	7,117	3,477
	1901–1911	5,593	4,314

* It is not clear whether foreign seamen and immigrants passing through Scotland on their way to other destintions were defined as foreign. Whether they were or not may have varied according to census.

Bibliography

1. Manuscript Sources

The Enumeration books are preserved in the General Register Office for Scotland, New Register House, Edinburgh.

The following enumeration books were consulted many in all the four enumerations 1861–1891, (title includes the parish name and registration district number): Aberdeen (Rd. 168), Abernethy (Rd. 326), Alva (Rd. 470), Alyth (Rd. 328), Anstruther-Easter (Rd. 402), Anwoth (Rd. 855), Arbuthnott (Rd. 250), Ardclash (Rd. 120), Ardesier (Rd. 98), Ardnamurchan (Rd. 505), Ardrossan (Rd. 576), Arisaig (Rd. 505), Arngask (Rd. 404), Ashkirk (Rd. 781), Auldearn (Rd. 121), Ballachulish (Rd. 506), Banchory-Devenick (Rd. 251), Banchory-Ternan (Rd. 252), Bathgate (Rd. 662), Beath (Rd. 410), Beith (Rd. 581), Bellie (Rd. 126), Boharm (Rd. 128a), Bonhill (Rd. 493), Bothwell (Rd. 625), Cabrach (Rd. 177), Caddonfoot (Rd. 774a), Cairney (Rd. 178), Cambusnethan (Rd. 628), Cameron (Rd. 412), Caputh (Rd. 337), Cawdor (Rd. 122), Ceres (Rd. 415), Cleish (Rd. 460), Cockburnspath (Rd. 731), Coupar-Angus (Rd. 279), Cramond (Rd. 679), Crieff (Rd. 342), Cromdale (Rd. 128b), Croy and Dalcross (Rd. 94), Culross (Rd. 343), Cutler (Rd. 637), Dalry (Rd. 587), Dalserf (Rd. 638), Dalziel (Rd. 639), Dalmeny (Rd. 665), Daviot and Dunlichty (Rd. 95), Dingwall (Rd. 62), Dollar (Rd. 467), Drumoak (Rd. 189), Dryfesdale (Rd. 820), Dunbarton (Rd. 496), Dumfries (Rd. 821), Dunbar (Rd. 706), Dundee (Rd. 282), Dunfermline (Rd. 424), Dunse (Rd. 735), Duthill (Rd. 96b), Dyke and Moy (Rd. 133), Dysert (Rd. 426), Earlston (Rd. 736), Edinburgh (Rd. 685), Edrom (Rd. 738), Edzell (Rd. 285), Elie (Rd. 427), Ellon (Rd. 192), Errol (Rd. 351), Eyemouth (Rd. 739), Fala and Soutra (Rd. 686), Falkirk (Rd. 479), Fenwick (Rd. 592), Forgandenny (Rd. 353), Fossoway and Tulliebole (Rd. 461), Fowlis-Easter (Rd. 356), Fraserburgh (Rd. 196), Galashiels (Rd. 775), Gartly (Rd. 198), Girthon (Rd. 866), Glasgow (Rd. 644), Glass (Rd. 199), Govan (Rd. 646), Greenock (Rd. 564), Hamilton (Rd. 647), Hawick (Rd. 789), Innerleithen (Rd. 762), Inverarary (Rd. 513), Inverness (Rd. 98), Inveravon (Rd. 157), Keith (Rd. 159), Kelso (Rd. 793), Kettins (Rd. 294), Kildonan (Rd. 52), Kilmalie (Rd. 520), Kilmorack (Rd. 100), Kilmore and Kilbride (Rd. 523), Kincardine O'Neil (Rd. 209), King Edward (Rd. 210), Kinross (Rd. 462), Kinnettles (Rd. 297), Kippen (Rd. 484), Kirkliston (Rd. 667), Kirkpatrick-Juxta (Rd. 838), Kirkwall and St Ola (Rd. 21), Lecropt (Rd. 371), Leith (Rd. 692), Lerwick (Rd. 5), Liff, Benvie and Invergowrie (Rd. 301), Linlithgow (Rd. 668),

Lismore (Rd. 525), Logie (Rd. 374), Maybole (Rd. 605), Melrose (Rd. 799), Moffat (Rd. 842), Monifieth (Rd. 310), Moy and Dalarossie (Rd. 105), Muthill (Rd. 386a), Nairn (Rd. 123), New Cumnock (Rd. 608), New Kilpatrick (Rd. 500), New Machar (Rd. 227), North Berwick (Rd. 713), Old Deer (Rd. 228), Oldhamstocks (Rd. 714), Old Kilpatrick (Rd. 501), Old Monkland (Rd. 652), Orwell (Rd. 463), Oyne (Rd. 230), Peebles (Rd. 768), Penninghame (Rd. 895), Persie (Rd. 386b), Peterculter (Rd. 231), Petty (Rd. 106), Portmoak (Rd. 464), Portree (Rd. 114), Prestonpans (Rd. 718), Raey (Rd. 40), Roberton (Rd. 777), Rothes (Rd. 141), Rothesay (Rd. 558), Row (Rd. 503), St. Fergus (Rd. 166), Scone (Rd. 394a), Selkirk (Rd. 778), Small Isles (Rd. 116), Sorn (Rd. 613), Stanley (Rd. 393b), Stirling (Rd. 490), Stornoway (Rd. 88), Stow (Rd. 699), Stranraer (Rd. 899), Terregles (Rd. 880), Tobermory (Rd. 549), Torphichan (Rd. 671), Traquair (Rd. 771), Tulliallan (Rd. 397), Urquhart and Logie-Wester (Rd. 84), Urray (Rd. 85), Wick (Rd. 43), Yarrow (Rd. 779).

2. Contemporary Published Sources

Burns, J. *Three Years amoung the Working Classes in the United States during the War,* (Smith, Elder and Co. 1865).

Doyle, A.C. 'The man with the twisted lip' *The Adventures of Sherlock Holmes* (London, 1892).

Duncan, S.J. *The Simple Adventures of a Memsahib,* (Thomas Nelson, not dated).

McKerlie, W. *An Account of the Scottish Regiments, with statistics of each, from 1801 to March 1861,* (Edinburgh, 1862).

Sinclair, Sir J. (ed) *The Statistical Account of Scotland, 1791–99 (Edinburgh, 1791–9), 21 vols.* New edition by Grant, I & Withrington (Wakefield 1975–9).

Shennan, H. *Boundaries of the Counties and Parishes in Scotland. As settled by the Boundary Commissioners under the Local Government (Scotland) Act, 1889,* (William Green & Sons, Edinburgh).

Stevenson, R.L. *The Amateur Emigrant. Part I: From the Clyde to Sandy Hook,* (Hogarth, published 1895, reprinted 1984).

The Times, August 24th. 1816.

3. Parliamentary Papers

(7th–56th) Detailed Annual Reports. (Edinburgh, 1865–1912).

Census of England and Wales 1861–1911.

Census of Ireland 1861–1911.

Census of Scotland 1851–1951.

Civil Registration Act, 1854, 17 & 18 Vic, c 80.

Tenth Decennial Census of the Population of Scotland taken 5th April 1891. Supplement to Volume I, Showing the effect of the Orders of the Boundary Commissioners appointed under the provisions of the Local Government

(Scotland) Act 1889 (52 and 53 Vict. c. 50, sections 44–50, as regards to the Population & co., of the Counties and Parishes of Scotland. With Report, (Edinburgh, HMSO. 1893), [c.6936].

Report from the Select Committee on Emigration from the United Kingdom, [Commanded by the Commons to the Lords]. Ordered to be printed 8 December 1826.

4. Unpublished Theses and Articles

Brock, J.M. 'Scottish Migration and Emigration 1861–1911' (2 vols) (unpublished Ph.D. thesis, University of Strathclyde, 1990).

Fallon, J.A. 'Scottish Mercenaries in the service of Denmark and Sweden 1626–1632' (unpublished Ph.D. thesis, University of Glasgow, 1972).

Fewster, M.I. 'The Yarmouth Fishing Industry 1880–1960' (unpublished M.Phil. thesis, University of East Anglia, Norwich, 1985).

Findlay, A.M. and Garrick, L. 'A Migration Channels Approach to the Study of Skilled International Migration: the case of Scottish emigration in the 1980s', unpublished 'ARPU Discussion Paper 89/1', University of Glasgow, Department of Geography, 1989.

Hildebrandt, R.N. 'Migration and Economic Change in the Northern Highlands during the Nineteenth Century, with particular reference to the period 1851–1891' (unpublished Ph.D. thesis, University of Glasgow, 1980).

Lamont, D.W. 'Population Migration and social area change in Central Glasgow 1871–1891 and a study in Applied Factorial Ecology' (unpublished Ph.D. thesis, University of Glasgow, 1976).

Lobban, R.D. 'The Migration of Highlanders to Lowland Scotland 1750–1890' (unpublished Ph.D. thesis, University of Edinburgh, 1969).

Tagg, S.K. and Brock, J.M. 'The Scottish Census 1861–1911', in Assess SPSS European Users' Group, 2nd User Group Conference, Glasgow, 1990, Proceedings.

5. Books and Book Chapters

Alberg, A. 'Scottish Soldiers in the Swedish Armies in the Sixteenth and Seventeenth Centuries' in G.G. Simpson (ed), *Scotland and Scandinavia*, (Edinburgh, 1990).

Anderson, M. and Morse, D.J. 'The People' in Fraser, W.H. and Morris, R.J. (eds.) *People and Society in Scotland, Vol. II, 1830–1914,* (Edinburgh, 1990).

Bailyn, B. assisted by DeWolfe, B. *Voyagers to the West. Emigration from Britain to America on the Eve of the Revolution,* (1986).

Baines, D.E. 'The Labour Supply and the Labour Market 1860–1914' in Floud, R. and McCloskey, D. eds. *The Economic History of Britain since 1700, Vol. 2: 1860 to the 1970s.* (Cambridge, 1981.

Baines, D. *Migration in a Mature Economy. Emigration and Internal Migration in England and Wales, 1861–1900,* (Cambridge, 1985).

Baines, D. *Emigration from Europe 1815–1930* (1991)

Barker, T. and Drake, M. (eds.), *Population and Society in Britain 1850–1980,* (1982)

Barnes, R.M, *The Uniforms and History of the Scottish Regiments: Britain-Canada-Australia-New Zealand-South Africa,* (no date).

Barnett, V. *Elements of Sampling Theory,* (1974).

Beckett, J.D. *A Dictionary of Scottish Emigrants into England and Wales,* (Manchester, 1984).

Berthoff, B.T. *British Immigrants in Industrial America,* (Cambridge. USA, 1953).

Bieganska, A. 'A note on Scots in Poland, 1550–1800' ' in Smout, T.C. (ed.) *Scotland and Europe 1200–1850,* (Edinburgh, 1986).

Boswell, J. *Life of Johnson* (1791) Chapman (ed), corrected Freeman (1976).

Brander, M. *The Emigrant Scots,* (1982).

Brock, J.M. 'The Importance of Emigration in Scottish Regional Population Movement, 1861–1911' in Devine, T.M. (ed), *Scottish Emigration and Scottish Society,* (Edinburgh, 1992).

Bumstead, J.M. *The People's Clearance; Highland Emigration to British North America 1770–1815,* (Edinburgh, 1982).

Cage, R.A. 'The Scots in England' in Cage, R.A. (ed). *The Scots Abroad: Labour, Capital, Enterprise, 1750–1914,* (1985).

Cain, A.M. *The Cornchest for Scotland: Scots in India,* (Edinburgh, 1986).

Campbell, A.B. *The Lanarkshire Miners. A Social History of their Trades Unions. 1775–1974.* (Edinburgh, 1979).

Campbell, R.H. *The Rise and Fall of Scottish Industry 1707–1939,* (Edinburgh, 1980).

Campbell, R.H. 'Agricultural Labour in the South–West', in Devine, T.M. (ed.) *Farm Servants and Labour in Lowland Scotland 1770–1914,* (Edinburgh, 1984).

Campbell, R.H. 'Scotland'. in Cage, R.A. *The Scots Abroad. Labour, Capital, Enterprise, 1750–1914,* (1985).

Campbell, R.H. and Devine, T.M. 'The Rural Experience' in Fraser, W.H. and Morris, R.J. (eds.) *People and Society in Scotland, Vol. II, 1830–1914,* (Edinburgh, 1990).

Carrier, N.H. and Jeffery, J.R. 'External Migration', *Studies on Medical and Population Subjects, no. 6,* General Register Office (HMSO 1953).

Carrothers, W.A. *Emigration from the British Isles* (D.S.King, 1929).

Carter, I. *Farm Life in Northeast Scotland. The Poor Man's Country,* (Edinburgh, 1979).

Collins, B. 'The Origins of the Irish Immigration to Scotland in the Nineteenth and Twentieth Centuries' in T.M.Devine (ed) *Irish Immigrants and Scottish Society in the Nineteenth and Twentieth Centuries,* (Edinburgh, 1991).

Contamine, P. 'Scottish Soldiers in France in the Second Half of the Fifteenth Century: Mercenaries, Immigrants or Frenchmen in the Making?' in Simpson, G.G. (ed) *The Scottish Soldier Abroad 1247–1967*, (Edinburgh, 1992).

Coull, J.R. *The Sea Fisheries of Scotland*, (Edinburgh, 1996),

Curtin, P.D. *Death by Migration: Europe's Encounter with the Tropical World in the Nineteenth Century*, (Cambridge, 1989).

Crowther, M.A. 'Poverty, Health and Welfare', in Fraser, W.H. and Morris, R.J. (eds.) *People and Society in Scotland, Vol. II, 1830–1914*, (Edinburgh, 1990).

Cullen, L.M. *An Ecomonic History of Ireland since 1660*, (2nd edtn. 1987).

De Vries, *European Urbanization 1500–1800*, (London 1984).

Devine, T.M. 'Woman Workers, 1850–1914', in Devine, T.M. (ed.) *Farm Servants and Labour in Lowland Scotland 1770–1914*, (Edinburgh, 1984).

Devine, T.M. 'Scottish Farm Labour in the era of Agricultural Depression, 1875–1900' in Devine, T.M. (ed.) *Farm Servants and Labour in Lowland Scotland 1770–1914*, (Edinburgh, 1984).

Devine, T.M. assisted by Orr, W. *The Great Highland Famine. Hunger, Emigration and the Scottish Highlands in the Nineteenth Century*, (Edinburgh, 1988).

Devine, T.M. 'Introduction'. in Devine, T.M. and Mitchison, R. (eds.) *People and Society in Scotland, Vol. I, 1760–1830* (Edinburgh, 1988).

Devine, T.M. 'Urbanisation'. in Devine, T.M. and Mitchison, R. (eds.) *People and Society in Scotland, Vol. I, 1760–1830* (Edinburgh, 1988).

Devine, T.M. 'Social Responses to Agrarian 'Improvement': The Highland and Lowland Clearances in Scotland' in Houston, R.A. and Whyte, I.D. (eds) *Scottish Society 1500–1800* (Cambridge, 1989).

Devine, T.M. 'Landlordism and Highland Emigration' in T.M.Devine (ed), *Scottish Emigration and Scottish Society*, (Edinburgh, 1992).

Devine, T.M. *Clanship to Crofters' War*, (Manchester, 1994).

Devine, T.M. *The Transformation of Rural Scotland*, (Edinburgh, 1994).

Devine, T.M. & Jackson, G. *Glasgow. volume 1: beginnings to 1830*, (Manchester, 1995).

Dingwall, H. *Late Seventeenth Century Edinburgh: a demographic study*, (Aldershot, 1994).

Dodgshon, R.A. "Pretense of Blude' and 'Place of thair Duelling': The Nature of Scottish Clans, 1500–1745' in in Houston, R.A. and Whyte, I.D. (eds) *Scottish Society 1500–1800* (Cambridge, 1989).

Dobson, D. *Scottish Emigration to Colonial America, 1607–1785* (Athens, USA 1994).

Donaldson, G. *The Scots Overseas*, (1966).

Erickson, C.J. 'Who were the English and Scots emigrants in the late nineteenth century?' in Glass, D.V. and Revelle, R. (eds.), *Population and Social Change*, (1972).

Erickson, C.J. 'The Uses of Passenger Lists for the Study of British and Irish Emigration', in Glazier, I.A. and de Rosa, L. (eds) *Migration across time and nations: Population, Mobility in the Historical Contexts*, (New York, 1986).

Ferenczi, I and Willcox, W.F. *International Migrations: Vol. I. Statistics* and *Vol. II. Interpretations*, (National Bureau of Economic and Social Research, New York, 1929–31).

Flinn, M. et al. *Scottish Population History from the Seventeenth Century to the 1930s*, (Cambridge, 1977).

Floud, R, Wachter, K. Gregory, A. *Height, Health and History* (Cambridge, 1990).

Fontaine, L. *History of Pedlars in Europe* (Cambridge, 1996).

Gibson, A.J. & Smout, T.C. *Prices, Food and Wages in Scotland, 1550–1780*, (1995).

Glass, D.V. and Taylor, P.A.M. *Population and Emigration*, (Dublin, 1976).

Guide for searchers: No. 1, Civil Parish Map Index, (General Register Office for Scotland, Edinburgh). [no date or author].

Gray, M. *The Highland Economy 1750–1850*, (Greenwood, Connecticut, 1957 reprinted 1976).

Gray, M. 'Farm Workers in Northeast Scotland'. in Devine, T.M. (ed.) *Farm Servants and Labour in Lowland Scotland 1770–1914*, (Edinburgh, 1984).

Gray, M. *Scots on the Move*, (Dundee, 1990).

Hammond, R. and McCullagh, P.S. *Quantitative Techniques in Geography*, 2nd. edn. (Oxford, 1982).

Handley, J.E. *The Irish in Modern Scotland*, (Cork, 1947).

Handley, J.E. *The Irish in Scotland*, (Cork, 1945).

Hanham, M.H.J. 'Religion and Nationality in the Mid-Victorian Army' in Foot, M.R.D. (ed) *War and Society: Historical essays in honour and memory of J.R. Western 1828–1971* (1973).

Harper, M. *Emigration from North-East Scotland, Vol. I, Willing Exiles*, and *Vol. II, Beyond the Broad Atlantic*, (Aberdeen, 1988).

Hayward, J.B. (ed) *Casualty Roll for the Crimea: The Casualty Rolls for the Seige of Sabastopol and other Major Actions during the Crimean War 1854–1856*, (Hayward, London, 1976).

Henderson, D.M. *Highland Soldier 1820–1920*, (Edinburgh, 1989).

Hill, D. *Great Emigrations. The Scots to Canada*, (1972).

Hobsbawn, E.J. *Industry and Empire*, (1968, reprinted 1980).

Hoerder, D. (ed), *Labour Migrations in the Atlantic Economies. The European and North American Working Class during the period of Industrialisation* (Westport, Conn, 1985).

Hollingsworth, T.H. *Migration. A study based on the Scottish Experience between 1939 and 1964*, (Edinburgh, 1970).

Hollingsworth, T.H. *Historical Demography*, (1969).

Houston, R.A. and Whyte, I.D. 'Introduction Scottish Society in Perspective' in Houston, R.A. and Whyte, I.D. (eds) *Scottish Society 1500–1800* (Cambridge, 1989).

Hunt, E.H. *Regional Wage Variations in Britain 1850–1914*, (Oxford, 1973).

Hunt, E.H. 'Wages' in Langton, J. and Morris, R.J. eds. *Atlas of Industrializing Britain 1780–1914*, (1986).

Hunt, J. *The Making of the Crofting Community,* (Edinburgh, 1976).

Hyde, F.E. *Cunard and the North Atlantic, 1840–1973, A history of shipping and financial management.* (1975).

Jackson, G. *The British Whaling Trade,* (1978).

Jerome, H. *Migration and Business Cycles,* (New York, National Bureau Economic Research, 1926).

Jones, H.R. *A Population Geography,* (1981).

Jones, M.A. 'Ulster Emigration, 1783–1815' in E.R.R.Green, (ed) *Essays in Scotch-Irish History,* (London 1969).

Laslett, J.H.M. *Nature's Noblemen: The Fortunes of the Independent Collier in Scotland and the American Midwest, 1855–1889.* (Institute of Industrial Relations Publications, no.34, Los Angeles, 1983).

Lawton, R. 'Population' in Langton, J. and Morris, R.J. eds. *Atlas of Industrializing Britain 1780–1914,* (1986).

Lee, C.H. *The British Economy since 1700,* (Cambridge, 1986).

Lenman, B. *An Economic History of Modern Scotland 1660–1976,* (1977).

Levitt, I. and Smout, C. *The State of the Scottish Working Class in 1843. A statistical and spatial enquiry based on the data from the Poor Law Commission Report of 1844.* (Edinburgh, 1979).

Lindsay, I. 'Migration and Motivation: A Twentieth Century Perspective' in Devine, T.M. (ed), *Scottish Emigration and Scottish Society,* (Edinburgh, 1992).

Lochart, D.G. 'The Planned Villages' in Parry, M.L. & Slater, T.R. (eds) *The Making of the Scottish Countryside* (1980).

Lydon, J. 'The Scottish Soldier in Medieval Ireland: The Bruce Invasion and Gallowglass' in Simpson, G.G. (ed) *The Scottish Soldier Abroad 1247–1967,* (Edinburgh, 1992).

Lythe, S.G.E. and Butt, J. *An Economic History of Scotland 1100–1939,* (Glasgow, 1975).

MacArthur, E.M. *Iona: the living memory of a crofting community 1750–1914,* (Edinburgh, 1990).

Macdonald, D.F. *Scotland's Shifting Population 1770–1850,* (Glasgow, 1937).

MacPhail, I.M.M., *The Crofters' War,* (1989).

Mitchell, B.R and Deane, P. *Abstract of British Historical Statistics,* (Cambridge, 1962).

B.R.Mitchell, *European Historical Statistics: 1750–1970,* (1975).

Mitchison, R. *A History of Scotland,* (1984, 2nd edition).

Morris. R.J. 'Introduction: Scotland, 1830–1914. The Making of a Nation within a Nation'. in Fraser, W.H. and Morris, R.J. (eds.) *People and Society in Scotland, Vol. II, 1830–1914,* (Edinburgh, 1990).

Murray, N. *The Scottish Hand Loom Weavers 1790–1850. A Social History,* (Edinburgh, 1990).

Orr, W. *Deer Forests, Landlords and Crofters. The Western Highlands in the Victorian and Edwardian Times.* (Edinburgh, 1982).

Patterson, A. 'The Poor Law in Nineteenth Century Scotland'. in Fraser, D. (ed.) *The New Poor Law in the Nineteenth Century,* (1976).

Pressat, R. (Wilson, C. ed.), *The Dictionary of Demography.* (Oxford, 1988).

Redford, A. *Labour Migration in England, 1800–1850,* (Manchester, 1926).

Richards, E. *A History of the Highland Clearances. Vol. I: Agrarian Transformation and the Evictions 1746–1886,* (1982).

Richards, E. *A History of the Highland Clearances. Volume II: Emigration, Protest, Reasons.* (1985).

Richards, E. 'Australia and the Scottish Connection, 1788–1914' in Cage, R.A. (ed.) *The Scots Abroad: Labour, Capital, Enterprise, 1750–1914,* (1985).

Riis, T. 'Scottish-Danish Relations in the Sixteenth Century' in Smout, T.C. (ed.) *Scotland and Europe 1200–1850,* (Edinburgh, 1986).

Robson, M. 'The Border Farm Worker' in Devine, T.M. (ed.) *Farm Servants and Labour in Lowland Scotland 1770–1914,* (Edinburgh, 1984).

Rodgers, R. 'The Labour Force' in Fraser, W.H. & Maver, I. *Glasgow, Vol. II 1830–1912* (Manchester, 1996).

Shepperson, W. 'British Backtrailers'. in Ander, O.F. (ed.) *On the Track of Migrants,* (Rock Island, Ill. 1964).

Shepperson, W. *Emigration and Disenchantment,* (Oklahoma, 1966).

Simpson, G.G. 'Introduction' in Simpson, G.G. (ed) *The Scottish Soldier Abroad 1247–1967,* (Edinburgh, 1992).

Skelly, A.R. *The Victorian Army at Home: The Recruitment and Terms and Conditions of the British Regular, 1859–1899,* (1977).

Smith, H.D. *Shetland Life and Trade 1550–1914,* (Edinburgh, 1984).

Smith, J.S. 'Aberdeen Harbour — the Taming of the Dee' in Smith, J.S. and Stevenson, D. (eds) *Aberdeen in the Nineteenth Century: The Making of the Modern City,* (Aberdeen, 1988).

Smout, T.C., Landsman, N.C. and Devine, T.M 'Scottish Emigration in the Seventeenth and Eighteenth Centuries' in Canny, N. (ed) *Europeans on the Move: Studies on European Emigration, 1500–1800,* (Oxford, 1994) pp76–112.

Smout, T.C. (ed), *Scotland and Europe 1200–1850,* (Edinburgh, 1986).

Smout, T.C. *A History of the Scottish People 1560–1830,* (1969).

Thomas, B. *Migration and Economic Growth; A Study of Great Britain and the Atlantic Economy,* (Cambridge, 2nd. edt. 1973).

Tranter, N.L. *Population and Society 1750–1940. Contrasts in Population Growth,* (1985).

Treble, J.H. 'The Occupied Male Labour Force'. in Fraser, W.H. and Morris, R.J. (eds.) *People and Society in Scotland, Vol. II, 1830–1914,* (Edinburgh, 1990).

Tyson, R.E. 'The Economy of Aberdeen' in Smith, J.S. and Stevenson, D. (eds) *Aberdeen in the Nineteenth Century: The Making of the Modern City,* (Aberdeen, 1988).

Walker, W.M. *Juteopolis Dundee and its textile workers 1885–1923,* (Edinburgh, 1979).

Withers, C.W.J. *Highland Communities in Dundee and Perth, 1787–1891: a study in the social history of migrant Highlanders,* (Dundee, 1986).

Withers, C.W.J. *Gaelic Scotland: The Transformation of a Culture Region,* (1988).

Withers, C.W.J. 'The Demographic History of the City', in Fraser, W.H. & Maver, I. *Glasgow, Vol. II 1830–1912* (Manchester, 1996).

Whyte, I.D. *Agriculture and Society in Seventeenth Century Scotland,* (Edinburgh, 1979).

Whyte, I.D. 'Migration in early-modern Scotland and England: a comparative approach' in Pooley, C.G. & Whyte, I.D. *Migrants, Emigrants and Immigrants: A social history of migration,* (1991).

6. Journals

Anderson, M and Morse, D.J. 'High Fertility, High Emigration, Low Nuptiality: Adjustment Processes in Scotland's Demographic Experience, 1861–1914', 2 parts, *Population Studies, 47* (1993) pp 5–25 & 319–43.

Anderson, O. 'Emigration and marriage breakup in mid-Victorian England' *Economic History Review, L.* (1997) pp. 104–9.

Baines, D. 'European Emigration, 1815–1930: looking at the emigration decision again' ' *Economic History Review, XLVII.* (1994) pp. 525–44.

Blair, A.J.W. 'Structural Changes in Aberdeen and the Northeast 1851–1911', *Northern Scotland, 5, 1,* (1982).

Bisset-Smith, G.T. 'A Statistical Note on Birth Registration in Scotland Previous to 1855; Suggested by Inquiries as to Verification of Birth for Old Age Pensions', *JRSS.* 72 (1909).

Boyce, A.J. 'Endogamy and Exogamy in the Orkney Islands', *Northern Scotland, 6, 1,* (1984).

Brock, J.M. 'Spurious Migration in the Scottish Census', *Scottish Economic and Social History, 9,* (1989), pp.80–7.

Brock, J.M. and Tagg, S.K. 'Using SPSS-X to Create a Suitable Database for Estimating Scottish Population Movement, 1861–1911', *History and Computing, 2 (1),* (1990), pp. 17–23.

Brock, J.M. 'The militia: an aspect of Highland Temporary Migration 1871–1907' *North Scotland 17* (1997) pp.135–51.

Brock, J.M. 'Emigration by Default: Scottish Military Deaths Overseas 1883–90' *Dispatch,* 145 (1997) pp.17–22.

Burton, V.C. 'A Floating Population in Vessel Enumeration Returns in the Censuses 1851–1921', *Local Population Studies, 38,* (1987).

Campbell, R.H. 'Inter-county Migration in Scotland and the Experience of the Southwest in the Nineteenth Century'. *Scottish Economic and Social History, 4,* (1984).

Carter, I. 'Dorset, Kincardine and Peasant Crisis: A comment on David Craig'. *Journal of Peasant Studies,* (1975).

B.Collins, 'Proto-industrialisation and pre-Famine Emigration', *Social History,* Vol. 7.2. (1982), pp. 127–46.

Collins, E.J.T. 'Migrant Labour in British Agriculture in the Nineteenth Century', *Economic History Review,* (1976).

Cramond, R.D. and Marshall, J.L. 'Housing and Mobility', *Scottish Journal of Political Economy,* XI, 1.

Cousens, S.N. 'The Regional Pattern of Emigration during the Great Irish Famine', *Transactions of the Institute of British Geographers,* 28, (1960).

Cullen, L.M. 'Population Trends in Seventeenth-Century Ireland', *Economic History Review,* VI, (1975) pp. 146–65.

Curti, M. and Birr, K. 'The Immigrant and the American image in Europe, 1860–1914', *Mississippi Valley Historical Review, 37,* (1950).

De Vries, J. 'Population and Economy of Preindustrial Netherlands' *Journal of Interdisciplinary History,* XV (1985).

Devine, T.M. 'Temporary Migration and the Scottish Highlands in the Nineteenth Century' *Economic History Review,* 32 (3), (1979).

Devine, T.M. 'The Highland Clearances', *Refresh,* Spring (1987), pp. 1–4.

Erickson, C.J. 'The Encouragement of Emigration by British Trades Unions 1850–1900', *Population Studies,* 3, (1949–50).

Fewster, J.M. 'The Keelmen of Tyneside' *Durham University Journal,* 50, (1957).

Findlay, A.M. and Garrick, L. 'Scottish Emigration in the 1980s: a migration channels approach to the study of skilled international migration' *Transactions of the Institute of British Geographers,* (1990) pp. 177–92.

Friedlander, D. and Roshier, R.J. ' A Study of Internal Migration in England and Wales: Part I', *Population Studies,* XIX, (1966), pp. 239–79.

Galloway, J.A. and Murray, I. 'Scottish Migration to England 1400–1560' *Scottish Geographical Magazine,* 112 (1996) pp. 29–38.

Gould, J.D. 'European Inter-Continental Emigration 1815–1914: Patterns and Causes'. *Journal of European Economic History,* 8, (1979), pp. 593–675.

Gray, M. 'Scottish Emigration: the Social Impact of Agrarian Change in the Rural Lowlands, 1775–1875'. *Perspectives in American History,* 7, (1973). pp. 95–174.

Gray, M. 'Famine and Emigration'. *Scottish Economic and Social History,* 10, (1990) pp. 70–3.

Jackson, R.V 'The heights of rural-born English female convicts transported to New South Wales' *Economic History Review* XLIX, (1996) pp. 584–90.

Jones, M.A. 'Background to Emigration from Great Britain in the nineteenth century', *Perspectives in American History,* 7, (1973).

Landers, J. 'Mortality and Metropolis: the Case of London 1675–1825', *Population Studies,* 41, (1987), pp. 59–76.

Lee, C.H. 'Regional Growth and Structural Change in Victorian Britain' *Economic History Review,* XXXIV, (1981). p. 448.

Lee, C.H. 'Modern Economic Growth and Structural Change in Scotland. The Service sector Reconsidered' *Scottish Economic and Social History,* 3. (1983), pp. 5–35.

Lovett, A.A. Whyte, I.D. and White, K.A. 'Poisson Regression analysis and migration fields: the example of apprenticeship records of Edinburgh in the seventeenth and eighteenth centuries', *Transactions of the Institute of British Geographers,* 10 (1985) pp. 317–33.

McKay, J.B. 'The National Character of Scottish Regiments, parts 1–4' *Dispatch,* 132–35, (not dated). I am very grateful to Mrs E.Philip (the Archivist, Scottish United Services Museum) who said that the library received volumes 132 and 133 in 1993 and volumes 134 and 135 in 1994.

Nicholas, S. and Oxley, D. 'The living standards of women during the industrial revolution, 1795–1820' *Economic History Review,* XLVI, (1993) pp. 723–49.

Nicholas, S. and Oxley, D. 'The living standards of women during the industrial revolution, 1795–1815: new evidence from Newgate prison records' *Economic History Review* XLIX, (1996) pp. 591–99.

Shannon, H.A. 'Migration and the Growth of London 1841–1891', *Economic History Review,* V, (1935).

Storrie, M. 'They go much from home: nineteenth-century islanders of Gigha, Scotland' *Scottish Economic and Social History,* 16. (1996), pp. 92–115

Voth, H-J, and Leunig, T. 'Did smallpox reduce height? Stature and the standard of living debate in London, 1770–1873' *Economic History Review,* XLIX, (1996), pp. 541–60.

Watson, A. and Allan, E. 'Depopulation by clearances and non-enforced emigration in the north East'. *Northern Scotland,* Vol. 10, (1990), pp. 31–46.

Withers, C.W.J. 'Highland Migration to Dundee, Perth and Stirling, 1753–1891', *Journal of Historical Geography,* 11, (1985), pp. 395–418.

Withers, C.W.J. 'Highland-Lowland Migration and the Making of the Crofting Community, 1755–1891', *Scottish Geographical Magazine,* 103, (1987).

Withers, C.W.J. and Watson, A.J. 'Stepwise mobility and Highland migration to Glasgow 1852–1898' *Journal of Historical Geography* 17 (1991) pp. 35–56.

Whyte, I.D. and White, K.A. 'Continuity and change in a seventeenth century Scottish farming community' *Agricultural History Review,* 32 (1984) pp. 159–69.

Whyte, I.D. and White, K.A. 'Patterns of Migration of Apprentices into Aberdeen and Inverness during the Eighteenth and Early Nineteenth Centuries' *Scottish Geographical Magazine,* 102, (1986) pp. 81–92.

Whyte, I.D. 'Urbanization in early-modern Scotland: a preliminary analysis' *Scottish Economic and Social History,* 9. (1989) pp. 21–35.

Young, C. 'Rural Independent Artisan Production in the East-Central Lowlands of Scotland, c.1600–1850' *Scottish Economic and Social History,* 16. (1996) pp. 17–37.

Index

385